Mastering
Windows Server® 2016

Mastering
Windows Server® 2016

Brian Svidergol

Vladimir Meloski

Byron Wright

Santos Martinez

Doug Bassett

Senior Acquisitions Editor: Kenyon Brown
Development Editor: Kim Wimpsett
Technical Editor: Rodney R. Fournier
Production Editor: Barath Kumar Rajasekaran
Copy Editor: Kathy Carlyle
Editorial Manager: Pete Gaughan
Production Manager: Kathleen Wisor
Proofreader: Nancy Bell
Indexer: Johnna VanHoose Dinse
Project Coordinator, Cover: Brent Savage
Cover Designer: Wiley
Cover Image: © Thomas Northcut/Getty Images, Inc.

Acknowledgments

Many talented and hardworking people gave their best efforts to produce *Mastering Windows Server 2016*. We offer our sincerest gratitude to those individuals who helped bring this book to you.

Many thanks go out to the editorial and production teams at Wiley for their efforts. Kenyon Brown managed the project (which took much more effort than he signed up for!) and helped recruit the right resources to make this project happen. Kim Wimpsett, the developmental editor, did a great job turning around the chapters, communicating with the team, and tracking down late chapters. Thanks! We also want to thank the technical editor, Rodney Fournier, for his work reviewing all of the work and ensuring that we have things right. Finally, we want to thank the production editor, Barath Kumar Rajasekaran; the copy editor, Kathy Carlyle; and the proofreader, Nancy Bell. All of them contributed to making this book a high-quality production.

I'd like to thank my wife, Lindsay; my son, Jack; and my daughter, Leah, for their continued support and for the joy they bring me regularly.

—*Brian Svidergol*

To my loving family who always supports me.

—*Vladimir Meloski*

I'd like to thank Tracey, Sammi, and Michelle for consistently being the best part of my day.

—*Byron Wright*

I want to dedicate this book to the following: my wife, Karla; you are my soulmate, and I want to grow old with you. To my kids, Bryan and Naomy, I hope this gives you some inspiration one day of what you can possibly achieve; and finally thank you to all my family and friends for their support in my craziness. Also to my martial arts students, peers, and masters, thank you for allowing me to be who I am as a professional and a martial arts master.

I want to thank my colleagues across Microsoft for their support on this book. Thank you to the contributing authors for their great work and especially to Jose Rodas for his commitment and dedication to the OMS and Operations Manager Technology and for his contributions to making the content of this book better.

To my peer author, Brian Svidergol, thanks for the opportunity and making this happen for us. To my friend Elias Mereb, as he continues to evolve and assist us in many ways, thanks

Brother for all your feedback and commitment to Windows technology. Finally, I want to thank all the Configuration Manager and the Enterprise Mobility + Security community, who have always been so passionate about the technology and willing to help us improve our writing. Let's keep it up as we evolve together.

–Santos Martinez

I dedicate this book to my grandmother, Helen Wells, who bought me my first computer, and to my grandfather, Lyle Wells, for not killing her.

–Doug Bassett

About the Authors

Brian Svidergol designs and builds infrastructure, cloud, and hybrid solutions. He holds many industry certifications including the Microsoft Certified Trainer (MCT) and Microsoft Certified Solutions Expert (MCSE) – Cloud Platform and Infrastructure. Brian is the author of several books covering everything from on-premises infrastructure technologies to hybrid cloud environments. He has worked with startup organizations and large Fortune 500 companies on design, implementation, and migration projects.

Vladimir Meloski is a Microsoft Most Valuable Professional on Office Server and Services, Microsoft Certified Trainer and consultant, providing unified communications and infrastructure solutions based on Microsoft Exchange Server, Skype for Business, Office 365, and Windows Server. With a bachelor's degree in computer sciences, Vladimir has devoted more than 20 years of professional experience in information technology. Vladimir has been involved in Microsoft conferences in Europe and in the United States as a speaker, moderator, proctor for hands-on labs, and technical expert. He has been also involved as an author and technical reviewer for Microsoft official courses, including Exchange Server 2016, 2013, 2010, 2007, Office 365, and Windows Server 2016, 2012; and he is one of the book authors of *Mastering Microsoft Exchange Server 2016*. As a skilled IT professional and trainer, Vladimir shares his best practices, real-world experiences, and knowledge with his students and colleagues, and he is devoted to IT community development by collaborating with IT Pro and developer user groups worldwide. He enjoys his spare time in country with his son and wife.

Byron Wright is the owner of BTW Technology Solutions where he designs and implements solutions using Microsoft technologies. He has been a consultant, author, and instructor for 20 years, specializing in Windows Server, Active Directory, Office 365, and Exchange Server. Byron was a Microsoft MVP for Exchange Server/Office 365 from 2012–2015.

Santos Martinez was born in Caguas, Puerto Rico, in 1982, and grew up in Caguas. Santos has more than 18 years of experience in the IT industry. He has worked on major implementations and in support of Configuration Manager and Enteprise Mobility + Security for many customers in the United States and Puerto Rico. Santos was a Configuration Manager engineer for a Fortune 500 financial institution and an IT consultant before joining Microsoft. For the Fortune 500 companies, he helped with the implementation and support of more than 200+ Configuration Manager Site Server and support of more than 300,000 Configuration Manager and Intune clients worldwide.

Santos was a SQL Server MVP from 2006 to 2009 and then a ConfigMgr MVP from 2009 to 2011. He is well known in the Microsoft communities as a mentor for other MVPs, Microsoft FTEs, and for helping other IT community members. He has also participated in Microsoft TechEd, MMS, and Ignite as a technical expert for Configuration Manager, Database, and Microsoft Intune. Santos is also a former Puerto Rican martial arts champion and currently holds a Six Degree black belt in TaiFu-Shoi Karate-Do where he earned the title of Shihan Sensei.

Santos and Karla, a pastry chef, have been married for 16 years and have two kids, Bryan Emir and Naomy Arwen. Santos currently is a senior program manager for Microsoft in the Enterprise Management and Mobility Product Group. You can follow him on Twitter (@ConfigNinja) or at his blog (http://aka.ms/ConfigNinja).

Doug Bassett has been involved in the computer industry since the early 1980s when he taught a high school computer science class, while still a high school student. Doug has many certifications from Microsoft, Cisco, CompTIA, and others, and has been MCSE certified since the old Windows NT days. Doug has also been a Microsoft Certified Trainer (MCT) for over 20 years. He was one of the first 100 people in the world to certify on Windows 2008. Doug has lectured at both Apple and Microsoft corporate headquarters and was invited by Microsoft to present at the Microsoft world conference in Barcelona, Spain, on virtual classroom and online learning. Doug is currently teaching live classes over the Internet and enjoys not having to shovel snow while living in Arizona.

About the Contributing Author

Jose Rodas is an IT professional certified as A +, CCEA, MCSA + M, MCSE, MCTS, MCITP EA, and MCT, and he has more than 20 years of industry experience. He started working at Microsoft in the System Center Team in October 2007 supporting System Center Operations Manager and System Center Service Manager. Currently, he is a Microsoft Premier Field Engineer dedicated to customers while traveling to customer sites to provide proactive/reactive assistance in System Center and Azure Log Analytics projects.

Contents at a Glance

Introduction . . . .*xxiii*

Chapter 1 • Windows Server 2016 Installation and Management. 1

Chapter 2 • PowerShell 35

Chapter 3 • Compute 115

Chapter 4 • Storage 157

Chapter 5 • Networking 179

Chapter 6 • File Services. 227

Chapter 7 • Windows Server Containers. 259

Chapter 8 • Security Mechanisms 285

Chapter 9 • Active Directory Domain Services. 339

Chapter 10 • Active Directory Certificate Services 385

Chapter 11 • Active Directory Federation Services 423

Chapter 12 • Management with System Center 457

Chapter 13 • Management with OMS 541

Index. *559*

Contents

Introduction . . . .*xxiii*

Chapter 1 • Windows Server 2016 Installation and Management **1**
Windows Server 2016 Editions and Licensing. 1
    Processor Core-Based Licensing 3
    Client Access Licenses 3
    Licensing Programs 3
    Other Editions of Windows Server 2016 4
Installing Windows Server 2016 4
    Installation Steps. 5
    Post-Installation Configuration 9
    Activation. 10
Automating the Installation of Windows Server 2016 11
    Sysprep and Imaging. 12
    Windows System Image Manager 14
    Windows Deployment Services 16
    Microsoft Deployment Toolkit 19
    Deployment Solutions for Virtualization 19
Common Management Tools 20
    Overview of Server Manager 21
    Computer Management. 24
    Device Manager 24
    Task Scheduler 25
Monitoring and Troubleshooting Tools 27
    Event Viewer 28
    Task Manager 29
    Resource Monitor 30
    Performance Monitor 32
The Bottom Line. 33

Chapter 2 • PowerShell. **35**
What Is PowerShell? 35
    Forward Compatible. 36
    PowerShell Versions 36
Running and Customizing PowerShell 37
    Customizing the PowerShell Console 37
    Cutting and Pasting in PowerShell 37
    Using PowerShell Integrated Scripting Environment (ISE). 38
    Exploring the Command Add-On Pane 38

Setting Up PowerShell ISE Profiles 41
    Editing Profiles 42
Setting Up Execution Policies. 43
    Recording PowerShell Sessions 44
Using Aliases and Getting Help 44
    Using *CMD.EXE*-Like Commands in PowerShell. 44
    Exploring a *Get-Help* Example 46
    Getting *Get-Help* Updates 47
    Updating Help for Servers Without Internet Access. 48
    Accessing Online Help Files 48
Understanding Cmdlet Syntax 49
    Interpreting the Syntax 49
    Using Spaces in Cmdlets 51
    Passing Multiple Values to a Parameter 51
    Using *Show-Command*. 52
    Using *-WhatIf*. 53
    Using *-Confirm*. 54
    All About "About" Files. 55
Understanding Shortened Command Syntax 56
Exploring PowerShell Command Concepts. 58
    Implementing Pipelines. 59
    Exploring Objects and Members 59
    Exploring Properties, Events, and Methods. 60
    Performing Object Sorting 61
    Measuring Objects 62
    Using *Select-Object* to Select a Subset of Objects in a Pipeline. 63
Using File Input and Output Operations 65
    Converting Objects to Different Formats 66
    Using *ConvertTo-CSV* 66
    Using *Export-Csv*. 67
    Using *ConvertTo-Html*. 68
    Using *ConvertTo-Xml*. 69
    Using *Export-Clixml* 71
    Encrypting an Exported Credential Object with *Export-Clixml* 71
    Saving the Credentials to an XML File 73
    Importing Data into PowerShell. 74
Processing Pipeline Data. 74
    Using Comparison Operators. 75
    Using Wildcards and the *-like* Operator 76
    Exploring Common Data Types. 77
    Determining Data Type with *-is*. 79
    Finding Portions of Strings with *-match* 80
    Using the Containment Operators *-contains* and *-notcontains* 81
    Using the *-in* and *-notin* Operators. 81
    Using the *-replace* Operator 82

Using Variables. 83
   Exploring Types of PowerShell Variables 83
   Clearing and Removing Variables 84
   Using the Variable Drive 84
   Using Environmental Variables 84
Using Functions 85
   Seeing Them in Action. 85
   Splatting 86
   Creating Functions 86
   Using Parameters 88
   Sending Pipeline Objects to a Function with *Begin, Process,* and *End* 93
   Viewing All Functions in a Session 94
Formatting Output. 94
   Using *Format-Wide* 94
   Using *Format-List*. 95
   Using *Format-Table*. 96
Using Loops 96
   Using the *For* Loop 96
   Using the *Foreach* Loop. 97
   Using the *If* Statement 99
   Using the *Switch* Statement 100
   Using the *While* Loop 102
   Using the *Where-Object* Method 104
Managing Remote Systems via PowerShell. 109
   Using *Enable-PSRemoting* 109
   Remoting to Workgroup Servers 110
   Running PowerShell Commands on Remote Systems 110
   Running Remote Scripts on Remote Computers 111
   Establishing Persistent Remote Connections 111
   Using PowerShell Direct 112
The Bottom Line. 112

Chapter 3 • Compute. **115**
Overview of Hyper-V 115
What's New in Windows Server 2016 Hyper-V 116
Installing Hyper-V. 118
Nested Virtualization 119
Storage Options in Hyper-V. 120
   Virtual Hard Disk Types 120
   Virtual Hard Disk Recommendations. 121
Configuring Hyper-V 121
   Hyper-V Networking 121
   Hyper-V Virtual Machine Configurations 122
   Shielded Virtual Machines 123
   Virtual Machine Settings. 124
   Virtual Machine State 124

Virtual Machine Checkpoints................................... 125
Importing and Exporting Virtual Machines 125
Live Migration 126
PowerShell Direct.. 126
Virtual Machine Migration...................................... 126
Overview of Live Migration 127
Live Migration Requirements................................ 128
Hyper-V Replica.. 129
Planning for Hyper-V Replica 130
Implementing Hyper-V Replica 130
Failover Options in Hyper-V Replica 131
High Availability with Failover Clustering in Windows Server 2016 132
Host Clustering.. 132
Guest Clustering 132
Network Load Balancing.................................... 133
What Is Failover Clustering?................................. 134
High Availability with Failover Clustering 135
Clustering Terminology..................................... 136
Clustering Categories and Types 137
Failover-Clustering Components.............................. 137
Hardware Requirements for a Failover-Cluster Implementation...... 139
Dynamic Quorum.. 140
Planning for Migrating and Upgrading Failover Clusters 141
The Validation Wizard and the Cluster Support Policy Requirements ... 142
Configuring Roles.. 143
Managing Failover Clusters 144
Configuring Cluster Properties 145
Managing Cluster Nodes.................................... 145
Configuring Quorum Properties.............................. 147
What Is Cluster-Aware Updating?............................ 148
What Is a Stretch Cluster? 149
Failover Clustering with Hyper-V............................... 151
Implementing Hyper-V Failover Clustering 152
Implementing CSVs 154
The Bottom Line... 155

Chapter 4 • Storage 157
Overview of Storage in Windows Server 2016.................... 157
File Systems... 158
NTFS... 158
ReFS.. 159
Comparing NTFS and ReFS 159
Data Deduplication 161
How Data Is Optimized..................................... 162
How Optimized Data Is Read................................ 163
How Data Deduplication Works in the Background............... 164

How to Enable Data Deduplication 164
Data Deduplication Advanced Settings 165
Storage Spaces. 166
Storage Spaces Configuration Options 167
Storage Spaces Direct 168
Storage Replica 170
Types of Replication 171
Deploying Storage Replica 174
Storage Quality of Service 176
Working with Storage QoS 176
The Bottom Line. 177

Chapter 5 • Networking. **179**
Windows Server 2016 Network Configuration 179
IP Configuration 180
Network Adapter Teaming 182
Windows Firewall. 185
DNS 188
DNS Zones 189
Name Resolution Processing 192
Removing Stale DNS Records. 197
Securing DNS 198
Monitoring and Troubleshooting DNS 199
DHCP. 202
DHCP Scopes. 204
DHCP Options. 206
DHCP Policies and Filters 207
High Availability 208
DHCP Database. 209
Remote Access 210
VPN. 211
WAP 218
Network Load Balancing 219
Software Defined Networking. 220
Network Controller 221
Hyper-V Network Virtualization. 221
RAS Gateway 221
Datacenter Firewall. 222
Software Load Balancing. 222
Switch Embedded Teaming 223
Internal DNS Service 224
The Bottom Line. 224

Chapter 6 • File Services **227**
File Services Overview 227
File Server 229
Installing the File Server 230

Creating a File Share 230
Assigning Permissions 231
BranchCache for Network Files 232
BranchCache Modes of Operation 233
DFS Namespaces and DFS Replication 237
Accessing Shared Folders in DFS 238
Configuring DFS Replication 241
DFS Monitoring and Troubleshooting 243
File Server Resource Manager 245
FSRM Features Deployment 246
Configuring General FSRM Options 247
Classification Management 248
File Management Tasks 249
Quota Management 250
Templates for Monitoring Disk Usage 251
File Screening Management 251
Work Folders 252
The Bottom Line 257

Chapter 7 • Windows Server Containers **259**
Containers Overview 259
Container Limitations 261
Container Terminology 261
Hyper-V Containers 262
Creating and Maintaining Containers 263
Hardware and Software Requirements 263
Installing Docker 264
Retrieving Container Images from Docker Hub 266
Creating and Running a Container 267
Manually Customizing an Image 270
Automating Image Creation 271
Managing Container Images 274
Configuring Containers 275
Storage 275
Networking 276
Resource Constraints 279
Authentication to AD 280
Application Development and Deployment 281
The Bottom Line 282

Chapter 8 • Security Mechanisms **285**
Security Overview 285
Where to Begin? 285
What Are the Risks? 286
Thinking Like an Attacker 287
Ethical Hacking 288

Protecting Accounts. 288
  Privileged Access 289
  Securing User Accounts. 292
  Configuring Account Policy Settings 293
  Protected Users, Authentication Policies, and Authentication Policy Silos. 294
  Delegating Privileges. 295
  Credential Guard 296
Protecting Data at Rest 297
  Encrypting File System 297
  BitLocker 298
Protecting Data in Transit. 300
  Windows Firewall with Advanced Security 300
  IPsec 304
Protecting Administrative Access. 312
  Privileged Access Workstations. 312
  Local Administrator 313
  Just Enough Administration. 315
  Role-Capability Files 316
  Session-Configuration Files 317
Protecting Active Directory Infrastructure. 318
  Enhanced Security Administrative Environment. 318
  Privileged Access Management 319
Malware Protection 322
  Software Restriction Policies. 323
  AppLocker 323
  Device Guard. 324
Hardening Operating Systems Security with Additional Microsoft Products 327
  Advanced Threat Analytics 327
Evidence of the Attack. 328
  Auditing. 329
The Bottom Line. 336

Chapter 9 • Active Directory Domain Services **339**
Overview of Features 339
  What Changed in AD DS for Windows Server 2016 339
  Features from Windows Server 2012 R2 340
  Features from Windows Server 2012 340
Revisiting Privileged Access Management 340
Design Considerations 342
  Forests and Domains 342
  Active Directory Trusts 344
  Active Directory Sites. 345
  Active Directory Replication. 348
  Flexible Single Master Operation Roles. 350
  Designing the Organizational Unit Structure 351
  Domain Controllers 353

Computer, User, and Group Management 363
  Computer Management 363
  User Management 366
  Group Management 370
Group Policy 373
  Group Policy Inheritance and Enforcement 374
  Group Policy Day-to-Day Tasks 376
The Bottom Line 383

Chapter 10 • Active Directory Certificate Services **385**
What's New in AD CS Windows Server 2016 385
  Windows Server 2012 R2 386
  Windows Server 2012 386
Introduction to a Public Key Infrastructure and AD CS 387
Planning and Design Considerations 389
Implementing a Two-Tier Hierarchy 393
Working with Certificate Templates 406
Auto-Enrollment 417
The Bottom Line 419

Chapter 11 • Active Directory Federation Services **423**
Overview of AD FS 423
  AD FS Terminology 425
  How AD FS Works 426
Planning and Design Considerations 429
  Where Should You Place the AD FS Components? 429
  Should You Use SQL Server for the AD FS Database? 431
  What Are Your Certificate Options for Your AD FS Environment? 432
  Should You Use a Group-Managed Service
    Account for Your AD FS Environment? 432
Deploying an AD FS Environment 433
  Installing the AD FS Server Role 433
  Configuring Internal DNS Name Resolution 439
  Configuring a Sample Federated Application 441
  Configuring an AD FS Relying Party 445
  Testing Application Access from an Internal Client 445
  Installing Web Application Proxy Server Role Service 447
  Publishing the Sample Federated Application 450
  Testing Application Access from an External Client 452
The Bottom Line 454

Chapter 12 • Management with System Center **457**
Overview of System Center 2016 457
  Understanding the Upgrade Sequence 457
  Understanding the Install Sequence 459
  Installing an Instance in a Cluster 461

Using System Center Virtual Machine Manager 465
  Installing and Configuring VMM 466
  Managing the VMM Compute Fabric 470
  Managing the VMM Library.. 470
  Managing the VMM Host Groups.................................... 470
  Managing Hyper-V Hosts and Clusters 470
  Managing VMware Servers 470
  Managing Infrastructure Servers.................................. 470
  Managing the VMM Networking Fabric 472
  Creating a Logical Network 473
  Creating a VM Network 475
  Managing the Storage Fabric 476
  Creating Virtual Machines 478
Managing Windows Server 2016 with System Center Operations Manager 482
  The Operations Manager Infrastructure 482
  Installing the Prerequisites....................................... 484
Managing Windows Server 2016 with System Center Configuration Manager 499
  Three Branches 499
  What You Should Know About Site Server Differences...................... 501
  ConfigMgr Prerequisites 503
  Installing a Primary Site Server 505
  Configuring System Center Configuration Manager 517
  Boundaries and Boundary Groups 526
  Installing Clients.. 530
  Using Client Settings 532
  Using Collections 535
The Bottom Line.. 539

Chapter 13 • Management with OMS **541**
What Is Operations Management Suite? 541
  A Brief History 542
  OMS Services.. 542
OMS Pricing 543
  SLA Details 543
System Requirements 544
Log Analytics 546
  Performance Queries 552
  Event Queries 554
The Bottom Line.. 555

Index *559*

Introduction

Welcome to *Mastering Windows Server 2016*. This book covers Windows Server 2016 and the core technologies built into the operating system. It has a mix of content ranging from networking, identity and access, storage, and much more. We don't cover every single feature or option but focus on providing a deep understanding of the key topics that we cover throughout the chapters. This book is best read from front to back and can later used as a reference.

Major Changes in Windows Server 2016

Most of the major components of Windows Server 2016 have new features, enhancements, and changes for Windows Server 2016. With that said, most of the changes involve improvements to existing services and the introduction of new features. Throughout the chapters, we will look at some of these new features in detail. The following major changes represent the changes that we feel stand out from the rest:

Nested Virtualization   With nested virtualization, a brand new feature for Windows Server 2016, you can deploy a Hyper-V host inside of a VM. This simplifies the process for testing failover clustering and for testing a variety of virtualization-related features and configurations. Note that nested virtualization is best suited for nonproduction environments, such as a lab environment. See Chapter 3 for more information.

Shielded Virtual Machines   This new feature enhances the security of Hyper-V hosts and VMs. It protects against scenarios such as malicious administrators trying to view the console or trying to view the data on the virtual hard disks. See Chapter 3 for more information.

Device Guard and Credential Guard   These new features protect Generation 2 VMs against exploits. See Chapter 8 for more information.

Privileged Access Management (PAM)   PAM enhances the security of Active Directory Domain Services environments by completely changing the way many administrators manage their environments. See Chapter 9 for more information.

Storage Spaces Direct   This new feature provides a highly available and highly scalable storage solution using local server storage. See Chapter 4 for more information.

Software Defined Networking (SDN)   There are many new enhancements to networking in Windows Server 2016. SDN enables you to configure your on-premises environment like Azure and manage it using System Center Virtual Machine Manager. See Chapter 5 for more information.

Containers   Containers are a feature that offers a way for app teams to have a prepackaged way to deploy app environments quickly (for example, IIS with ASP.NET). The container contains everything an app team needs—and the container is portable; it can run on-premises or in the public cloud. See Chapter 7 for more details.

Nano Server   When Microsoft introduced the Server Core installation of Windows Server, it was lauded for the small size, small requirements, high performance, and enhanced security. Nano Server went a step further (albeit with more limitations). Initially, it was just a smaller footprint deployment, without a GUI, that could run some core roles such as Hyper-V and Scale-Out File Server. However, recently Microsoft announced some big changes for Windows Server 2016 (release 1709). With 1709, Nano Server will no longer support the core roles such as Hyper-V. Instead, it will be dedicated for containers and be geared for the cloud. Nano Server is introduced in Chapter 1.

The Mastering Series

The *Mastering* series from Sybex provides outstanding instruction for readers with intermediate and advanced skills in the form of top-notch training and development for those already working in their field, and clear, serious education for those aspiring to become pros. Every *Mastering* book includes the following:

◆ Skill-based instruction with chapters organized around real tasks rather than abstract concepts or subjects

◆ End of chapter "Master It" scenarios to test your knowledge of the information in the chapter

How to Use This Book

How you use this book will depend on your goals and your level of experience across the Windows Server technologies. For example, if you have limited experience with Windows Server, then reading the book from front to back might provide the best experience. If you are an experienced server administrator but want to learn more about the networking components of Windows Server 2016, then you might want to go straight to the networking-related chapters. If you are studying for a certification exam, you might want to read specific topics from various chapters to strengthen your knowledge in very specific areas. While the book is ordered so that it is easiest to read it front to back, take the path that best suits your experience and goals.

In several parts of the book, we will perform step-by-step installations and configurations. We highly recommend that you perform those same steps in your lab or nonproduction environment (whether at home or at work). Reading about a technology is good for learning. Deploying, troubleshooting, and maintaining a technology is good for learning. Doing both is great for learning!

Windows Server is a huge product. There is a plethora of technologies in it—and the technologies are complex, much more so than in previous versions (especially older and legacy versions) of Windows Server. Therefore, as authors, we must pick and choose exactly what we cover while still trying to keep the book manageable in size. In general, for this book, we have opted to cover the most used parts of Windows Server, and we try to go into detail in specific parts of every chapter. Lastly, we avoid the introductory information unless it is imperative to the topic. Our readers have historically been experienced administrators who are looking to enhance their knowledge of the newest version of Windows Server. Therefore, we try to avoid material that is "too basic" for our typical reader.

How This Book Is Organized

Each *Mastering Windows Server 2016* chapter represents a milestone in your progress toward becoming an expert Windows Server 2016 user. We start off by walking you through the installation, Server Manager, and PowerShell. It is a good way to start and enables you to have a Windows Server 2016 computer to reference while working through the step-by-step sections of chapters. It is also good to know the tools that we are going to reference throughout the book (especially PowerShell) before we dive into them!

- Chapter 1, "Windows Server 2016 Installation and Management," shows you how to install Windows Server 2016 and how to work with Server Manager for server administration.

- Chapter 2, "PowerShell," details how to work with PowerShell. It covers a huge amount of information in a single chapter and will be especially beneficial to readers who aren't well-versed in PowerShell yet.

After you have an installation and know your way around the management of Windows Server, you are ready to dive deeper into the foundational technologies.

- Chapter 3, "Compute," is all about the compute portions of Windows Server, such as Hyper-V and failover clustering.

- Chapter 4, "Storage," details file systems, data deduplication, Storage Spaces, Storage Replica, and Storage Quality of Service.

- Chapter 5, "Networking," dives into remote access, DNS, DHCP, and a host of new networking technologies in Windows Server 2016.

At this point, you'll have a pretty good grasp of the basics of Windows Server 2016 and understand some of the new technologies. The next chapters are designed to help you branch out into smaller (but still important) technologies in Windows Server.

- Chapter 6, "File Services," tells you how to implement and manage file services—not just shared folders but the advanced aspects of managing file services.

- Chapter 7, "Windows Server Containers," explains what containers are, how they work, and how to create and manage them. This technology is new and rapidly evolving.

- Chapter 8, "Security Mechanisms," is where you'll learn about Just Enough Administration (JEA), Just In Time (JIT) administration, Credential Guard, and other new security features in Windows Server 2016.

Several Active Directory technologies are built into Windows Server 2016. In this book, we cover the three most deployed. We exclude AD LDS and AD RMS.

♦ Chapter 9, "Active Directory Domain Services," covers AD DS, including information about design and architecture, deployment, and day-to-day administration.

♦ Chapter 10, "Active Directory Certificate Services," covers AD CS and public key infrastructure technologies. It also walks through a step-by-step two-tier hierarchy.

♦ Chapter 11, "Active Directory Federation Services," takes you through AD FS and design considerations. Then, it walks you through a step-by-step implementation of AD FS and Web Application Proxy.

Earlier in the book, we cover managing servers one at a time with Server Manager and PowerShell. In this part of the book, we look at managing servers at the enterprise level where automation and self-service are keys to successful management.

♦ Chapter 12, "Management with System Center," introduces you to the entire suite of Microsoft System Center. It walks through deployment and configuration, as well as introduces the concepts around enterprise management.

♦ Chapter 13, "Management with OMS," shows you how to use Microsoft Operations Management Suite OMS), an Azure service, to manage your on-premises and cloud-based Windows servers.

Getting More Information

In each chapter, you will see links to external sources for additional information. Whenever you have an interest in a particular topic and we link to an external resource, you should opt to spend a few minutes exploring that content. We specifically tried to link to value-adding material that complements and sometimes expands upon the information in the book.

Errata

We hope that *Mastering Windows Server 2016* will be of benefit to you and that, after you've read the book, you'll continue to use the book as a reference. Please note that while we have made every effort toward accuracy, sometimes software updates will cause a screenshot to look slightly different than the interface you see on your screen. You should still be able to follow along with the instructions given. However, if you find errors, please let our publisher know by emailing to errata@wiley.com.

Thanks for choosing *Mastering Windows Server 2016*!

Chapter 1

Windows Server 2016 Installation and Management

Windows Server 2016 builds on the installation and management processes of earlier Windows Server versions. To install Windows Server 2016, you need to understand the editions of Windows Server 2016 and how they are licensed. This will enable you to select the edition of Windows Server 2016 that best meets your needs. You also need to select an appropriate installation method such as automation with Windows Deployment Services.

After installing Windows Server 2016, Server Manager is the main interface that you'll use for management. From Server Manager, you can launch tools that you can use to manage and monitor Windows Server 2016.

IN THIS CHAPTER, YOU WILL LEARN TO:

- ◆ Define a deployment process
- ◆ Select an edition of Windows Server 2016
- ◆ Select an activation method
- ◆ Monitor Windows Server 2016

Windows Server 2016 Editions and Licensing

Microsoft has had various editions of Windows Server with each generation. Depending on the generation of Windows Server, varying editions came with different features or different licensing. You can obtain Windows Server 2016 Standard or Windows Server 2016 Datacenter. The vast majority of features are the same between the two editions, but there are some significant differences worth noting and they are listed in Table 1.1.

TABLE 1.1:   Windows Server 2016 Edition Differences

FEATURE	DESCRIPTION
Virtualization Licensing	One Windows Server 2016 Standard license can be used for two virtual machines on a single virtualization host.
	One Windows Server 2016 Datacenter license can be used for an unlimited number of virtual machines on a single virtualization host.

TABLE 1.1:　Windows Server 2016 Edition Differences　(CONTINUED)

FEATURE	DESCRIPTION
Software Defined Networking	This feature that applies policies to control network configuration and security is not included in Standard edition.
Shielded Virtual Machines	To configure Shielded virtual machines, the Hyper-V host must be running Windows Server 2016 Datacenter edition.
Hyper-V Containers	Windows Server 2016 Standard has a limit of two Hyper-V Containers per Hyper-V host. Windows Server 2016 can have an unlimited number of Hyper-V Containers.
	Both editions of Windows Server 2016 can have an unlimited number of standard containers.
Storage Replica	This feature that synchronizes data between two servers is available only in Windows Server 2016 Datacenter edition.
Storage Spaces Direct	This feature that provides high availability for file shares is available only in Windows Server 2016 Datacenter edition.

As you can see from Table 1.1, there are only a few feature differences between Windows Server 2016 Standard and Windows Server 2016 Datacenter. If those features are not required, then the primary driver for selecting an edition of Windows Server 2016 is usually virtualization licensing.

Most organizations deploy new servers as virtual machines. With a single Windows Server 2016 Standard license, you can install Windows Server 2016 Standard with Hyper-V for a virtualization host and configure two virtual machines with Windows Server 2016 Standard. By purchasing a second Windows Server 2016 Standard license, you can add two more virtual machines running Windows Server 2016 Standard. In smaller organizations with only a few virtual machines per virtualization host, it is often cost-effective to use Windows Server 2016 Standard.

In larger organizations with many virtual machines, it is often more cost-effective and easier to manage if you use Windows Server 2016 Datacenter. With a single Windows Server 2016 Datacenter license, you can install Windows Server 2016 Datacenter with Hyper-V for a virtualization host and configure an unlimited number of virtual machines on that host.

> **VIRTUALIZATION LICENSING WITHOUT HYPER-V**
>
> Hyper-V is an excellent hypervisor that is widely used to implement server and desktop virtualization. However, there are other hypervisors such as VMware, XenServer, and others. When you use a hypervisor other than Hyper-V, the licensing for the virtual servers works exactly the same as if you were using Hyper-V. A Windows Server 2016 Standard license allows you to implement two virtual machines running Windows Server 2016 Standard on any hypervisor. A Windows Server 2016 Datacenter license allows you to implement an unlimited number of virtual machines running Windows Server 2016 Datacenter on any hypervisor.

Processor Core-Based Licensing

At one time, before virtualization became common, Windows Server was licensed based on a ratio of one-to-one with physical machines. Older editions of Windows Server were limited based on the number of physical processors and the amount of memory they could address. When virtualization became common, a number of virtual machines were included per license. Now, physical hardware has become so powerful that limitations have been introduced based on the number of processor cores in the physical server.

Windows Server 2016 Standard and Windows Server 2016 Datacenter use the same core-based licensing structure. The base operating system license provides licensing for two eight-core processors (a total of 16 cores). If there are more than eight physical cores per processor (hyperthreading does not count as additional cores), then you need to purchase additional core licenses in minimum increments of two cores.

Each processor in a server must be licensed for a minimum of eight cores. So, if you have four processors in a server, then you need to be licensed for a minimum of 32 cores. You can meet this requirement by purchasing two Windows Server licenses. In the case of Windows Server 2016 Standard, this would give you rights to install two virtual machines. To allow four virtual machines, you would need to fully license all processors in the server again.

Client Access Licenses

On a Windows-based network, you need to license your clients in addition to the servers. A Client Access License (CAL) provides users or devices with rights to access services that are running on the servers. For example, if a computer is joined to the domain and a user signs in to the network, then a CAL is required. That CAL can be a user CAL for the person who is connecting to the network. The CAL can also be a device CAL for the computer that is being used to connect to the network. Only one CAL is required, either a user CAL or a device CAL.

When you purchase CALs, you need to determine whether user or device CALs are most cost-effective for your organization. If a single user has multiple devices that access network services, such as a desktop computer and laptop computer, then a user CAL is most cost-effective. If a single device is used by multiple users, such as a call center with multiple shifts, then a device CAL is most cost-effective. You can combine user and device CALs as you deem appropriate.

CALs are paper-based licensing. This means that you need to track your users and devices accurately, but Windows Server 2016 does not monitor licenses in use. You also do not need to specifically assign your licenses to user accounts or computers.

Licensing Programs

Microsoft has a variety of different licensing programs with different benefits, restrictions, and costs. You can obtain Windows Server 2016 licenses and CALs through a number of these programs. As these programs change over time, you'll need to talk with an expert about how you should purchase your licenses. However, here is a high-level overview of a few licensing methods:

◆ Original Equipment Manufacturer (OEM). This type of licensing can be purchased when you buy a new physical server. It is generally the least expensive option but cannot be moved to other hardware.

◆ Volume license. This type of license is more flexible than OEM licensing because it is not restricted to a specific physical server. The frequency that you can move this license between servers is restricted. This is an important consideration for high-availability scenarios where virtual machines can move between virtualization hosts.

◆ **Software assurance.** This type of license is added on to volume licensing to include software upgrades. Software assurance also offers additional benefits such as the ability to move licenses between physical servers as often as you like.

◆ **Enterprise agreement.** This type of licensing is user-based rather than server-based. For a set fee per user in the organization, you can run the number of server instances necessary to meet your needs. This type of license also includes CALs and may include other products such as SQL Server and Exchange Server.

Other Editions of Windows Server 2016

Windows Server 2016 Essentials is an edition of Windows Server 2016 that is targeted at small businesses. Licensing for this edition of Windows Server 2016 is simpler than Standard or Datacenter editions because it does not require CALs. Instead, Windows Server 2016 Essentials has a limit of 25 users and 50 devices. There are also no virtualization rights for multiple instances, a 64 GB limit on memory, and a limit of two physical CPUs. To simplify deployment some server roles and features are automatically installed and configured.

Windows Storage Server 2016 is available only through hardware vendors for storage appliances. There are a limited number of server roles because this edition is designed to be a general-purpose operating system. For example, you can't configure Windows Storage Server 2016 as a domain controller.

For more information about Windows Server 2016 licensing, see Windows Server 2016 Licensing & Pricing at https://www.microsoft.com/en-us/cloud-platform/windows-server-pricing.

Installing Windows Server 2016

Physical servers are specialized hardware that often require drivers that are not included as part of Windows Server 2016. Before you begin installing, you should obtain all the necessary drivers for your server. Some manufacturers have a specialized process for installing Windows Server 2016 that injects the drivers during the installation process.

The firmware for a modern server is Unified Extensible Firmware Interface (UEFI) rather than the older Basic Input Output System (BIOS). Although you can set UEFI firmware to legacy mode to emulate BIOS, there is no need to do that. Windows Server 2016 can be booted using UEFI firmware. Additionally, using UEFI provides advantages such as booting from larger disks and a more secure boot process.

Real World Scenario

INSTALLING IN VIRTUAL MACHINES

It's likely that you'll be deploying most servers as virtual machines. Virtual machines provide a lot of flexibility for deployment and management. To work properly in a virtual environment, Windows Server 2016 needs to have the correct drivers for that virtual environment, just as Windows Server 2016 needs to have the correct drivers to work properly on physical hardware.

When you install Windows Server 2016 in a virtual machine on a Hyper-V host, the installation files include all the necessary drivers. If you create a Generation 1 virtual machine, it emulates BIOS firmware. If you create a Generation 2 virtual machine, it uses UEFI firmware. Windows Server 2016 works properly with either type of firmware.

If you install Windows Server 2016 in a virtual machine using another type of hypervisor, such as VMware, then you generally need to install additional drivers. For example, you would install VMware Tools for virtual machines running on VMware.

Before installing, you should also plan the disk partitioning for your server. A key consideration is the size of the C: drive that is used for the operating system. The C: drive needs to be large enough to support not only the initial installation of Window Server 2016, but also any updates that are installed over time. Additionally, most organizations keep applications and data on separate partitions from the operating system whenever possible. Separating applications and data from the operating system helps to prevent the operating system drive from running out of space and can simplify backup and restore.

Installation Steps

To begin installing Windows Server 2016, ensure that your server is configured to boot from DVD. This will be a configuration option in the firmware. Place the installation DVD in the DVD drive and complete the following process.

1. Start the server and press a key, when prompted, to start installing from DVD.

2. Select a language, time and currency format, and a keyboard layout that are appropriate for your location, as shown in Figure 1.1, and click Next.

3. Click Install Now.

4. In the Activate Windows window, enter your product key and click Next. If you select I Don't Have a Product Key, you can enter the product key later.

5. In the Select the Operating System You Want to Install window, select the operating system version you want to install, as shown in Figure 1.2, and then click Next.

FIGURE 1.1
Select localization
settings

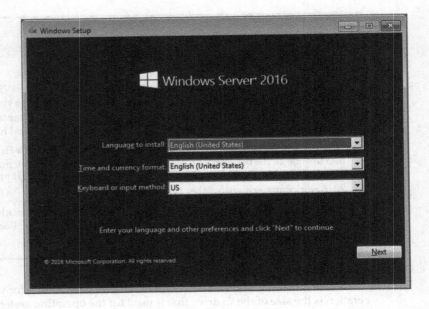

FIGURE 1.2
Select an operat-
ing system.

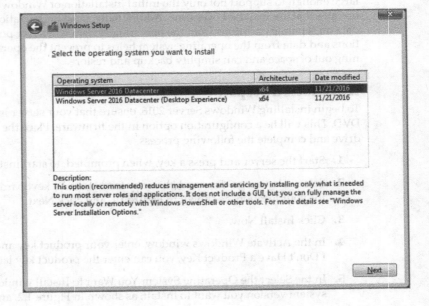

6. In the Applicable Notices and License Terms Window, select the I Accept the License
Terms check box and click Next.

SERVER CORE AND DESKTOP EXPERIENCE

When you install Windows Server 2016 Standard or Datacenter edition, you have the option of installing Server Core or Desktop Experience. The Desktop Experience is the full server installation that includes the graphical interface. This installation type can run all the management tools at the server console. In Windows Server 2012 R2, you could add or remove the graphical interface. This is not possible in Windows Server 2016.

Server Core is a stripped-down version of Windows Server 2016 that does not include the graphical interface. To manage Server Core, you can use a command prompt or Windows PowerShell locally. To use graphical tools, you can use the Remote Server Administration Tools (RSAT) in Windows 10.

A subset of server roles is available in Server Core. These roles include most of the network services such as DNS, DHCP, Active Directory Domain Services (AD DS), Active Directory Certificate Services, File Services, and Windows Server Update Services. If you are running applications on the server, you need to verify that the applications are compatible with Server Core.

The limited functionality in Server Core, reduces the attack surface of the operating system. It also reduces the need to update and consequently increases uptime. Disk utilization is also reduced, which allows more efficient disk utilization in large-scale virtualization.

7. In the Which Type of Installation Do You Want window, shown in Figure 1.3, click Custom: Install Windows Only (Advanced). Performing an in-place upgrade from one server operating system version to another is rare. It is more common to install a new server and migrate services and applications to the new server.

FIGURE 1.3
Select an installation type.

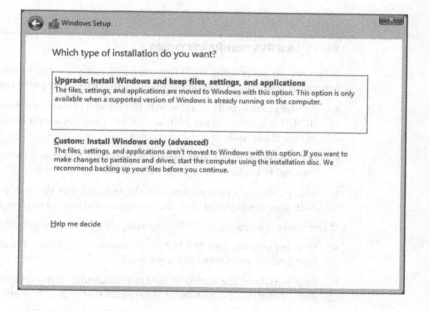

8. In the Where Do You Want to Install Windows window, shown in Figure 1.4, select the correct drive for the operating system installation and click Next. If your disk is not displaying in this window, then you can use the Load Driver option to install the missing storage driver. You also have the option manually create and delete partitions.

FIGURE 1.4
Select the installation location.

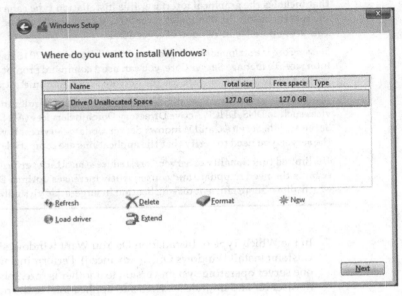

BOOT AND SYSTEM PARTITIONS

When the server is using UEFI firmware and you allow the Windows Server 2016 installation process to create partitions on the disk, it will create three partitions:

◆ Recovery partition. This partition is 450 MB and contains the recovery tools for Windows Server 2016. If Windows Server 2016 can't start, then the server boots from this partition and you can use these tools to attempt recovery.

◆ EFI system partition. This partition is 100 MB and stores the operating system files that are required to begin the Windows Server 2016 boot process.

◆ Boot partition. This partition uses the remainder of the disk and stores the Windows Server 2016 operating system files. This partition is also used to store the paging file.

If the server is using legacy BIOS firmware, only two partitions are created:

◆ System partition. This 500 MB partition contains files used to start the Windows Server 2016 boot process and files used for recovery.

◆ Boot partition. The partition uses the remainder of the disk and stores the Windows Server 2016 operating system files. This partition is also used to store the paging file.

9. Wait while files are copied and the installation finishes. This can take up to 30 minutes if your server or disks are slow.

10. After the server reboots, on the Customize Settings screen, in the Password and Reenter Password boxes, type a password for the local Administrator account and click Finish.

Post-Installation Configuration

To simplify the installation process for Windows Server 2016, many settings have a default value. However, you'll probably want to change these four items right away:

- Computer name. During installation, a computer name is generated automatically in the format of WIN-*RandomString*. You'll want to change that computer name to match the naming standard used by your organization.

- Workgroup. Each computer is automatically a member of a workgroup named WORKGROUP. In most cases, you'll want to join the domain.

- IPv4 address. IPv4 is configured to obtain an IP address automatically from DHCP after installation. Most organizations set a static IPv4 address rather than using DHCP.

- Time zone. The default time zone (UTC-08:00) Pacific Time (US & Canada). Change the time zone to match where the server is located.

If the Desktop Experience is installed, you can use Server Manager, shown in Figure 1.5, to configure these items. You can also use Server Manager to review and configure other common settings.

FIGURE 1.5
Server Manager

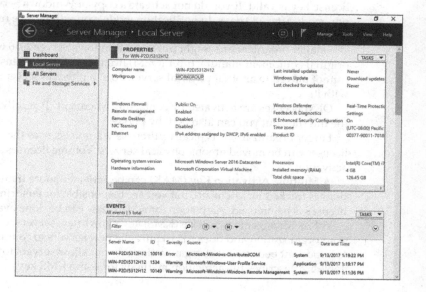

If Server Core is installed, you need to use either command-line tools or Windows PowerShell to configure these items. To simplify configuration of Server Core, you can use sconfig.cmd, shown in Figure 1.6. This script is included with Server Core and provides a menu-driven interface for configuring common items.

FIGURE 1.6
Sconfig.cmd

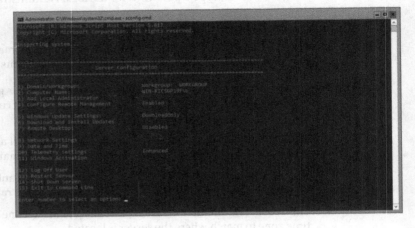

Activation

All editions of Windows Server 2016 need to be activated. Activation is what proves that your license key is valid. If you do not activate a copy of Windows Server 2016, it will enter notification mode after 180 days. In notification mode, you will receive reminders to activate and some features such as personalization will be disabled.

Smaller organizations might purchase Windows Server 2016 with the physical servers. The original equipment manufacturer (OEM) licenses are less expensive than volume licensing but cannot moved to another physical server. So, if a physical server is retired, the license is retired with it.

OEM licenses are activated by contacting Microsoft. Typically, you activate the server over the Internet, but you can also do it by phone.

Larger organizations typically purchase volume licenses that are more flexible. Volume licenses can be moved among physical servers. Volume licenses also have more options for activation.

A Multiple Activation Key (MAK) can be activated more than once. The number of activations is tracked by Microsoft, but you are responsible for ensuring that the correct number of licenses is being used. Activation for a MAK key can be done over the Internet or by phone.

A Key Management Service (KMS) key allows new servers to activate automatically within your organization and does not require the new servers to communicate over the Internet. This is important because most organizations do not allow servers to communicate with the Internet. Table 1.2 describes the activation methods for using KMS keys.

TABLE 1.2:   Activation Methods for Using KMS Keys

METHOD	DESCRIPTION
KMS host	You can configure Windows Server 2016 to be a KMS host. Then you can add the KMS key to the KMS host. When you add the KMS key to the KMS host, it is activated with Microsoft. However, new servers activate by contacting the KMS host.
	A KMS host has minimum activation thresholds. For server operating systems, the activation threshold is five. If you have fewer than five servers using a KMS host for activation, then activation never occurs. This makes a KMS host difficult to use for smaller organizations or remote sites.
Active Directory-Based Activation	When you implement Active Directory-Based Activation, the activation information is stored in Active Directory instead of on a KMS host. Because the new server communicates with Active Directory, there is no single point of failure for activation. Also, there are no minimum activation thresholds for Active Directory-Based Activation. This is the preferred activation method for software that supports it.

To configure a KMS host or Active Directory-Based Activation, install the Volume Activation Services server role in Windows Server 2016. After installing this server role, you run Volume Activation Tools, which allows you to select to enable either KMS or Active Directory-Based Activation and manage keys.

GENERIC VOLUME LICENSE KEYS

When you use KMS or Active Directory-Based Activation, you do not manually install a license key in Windows Server 2016. By default, Windows Server 2016 includes a generic volume license key (GVLK) that activates against KMS or Active Directory-Based Activation.

In rare cases, volume activation fails because someone accidentally changes the key. You can change the key back to the correct GVLK.

For a list of GVLKs, see Appendix A: KMS Client Setup Keys at `https://technet.microsoft .com/en-us/library/jj612867(v=ws.11).aspx`.

For detailed information about volume activation, see Planning for Volume Activation at `https://technet.microsoft.com/en-us/library/dd996589.aspx`.

Automating the Installation of Windows Server 2016

To simplify the installation of Windows Server 2016 in larger organizations, you should automate the process. An automated deployment process reduces the administrative effort required to deploy new servers. So, instead of taking 30 to 60 minutes to perform an installation, you can start the automated process and walk away until it's done.

Automated deployment also provides consistent results. You can define specific sets of features to be installed. For example, you can automatically enable BitLocker to encrypt the local hard disk. With a manual installation, you would need to enable BitLocker as a separate process after the server is deployed.

Windows Server 2016 deployment can be automated a few different ways. Some options have no additional cost, while others use tools you'll need to buy. If your environment is virtualized, you'll have additional options.

Sysprep and Imaging

Imaging is the process of taking a prepared computer and copying its configuration. The image that you take of the prepared computer is stored in a file, and that image can be applied to other physical computers or virtual machines.

When you install Windows Server 2016, it configures system-specific information such as the computer name, hardware information, and a local machine internal security identifier (SID). Those system-specific configuration items need to be removed as part of the imaging process. When those items are removed, the image can be applied to a computer running different hardware.

The Sysprep (System Preparation) utility is included in Windows Server 2016 to prepare the operating system for imaging. Sysprep removes the computer name, hardware information, and SID. Then when the image is applied to a new computer, those items are re-created.

SYSPREP OPTIONS

Sysprep.exe is stored in C:\Windows\System32\Sysprep. When you run Sysprep with the graphical interface, you need to select a system cleanup action, as shown in Figure 1.7. The system cleanup action controls what happens after Sysprep runs and the operating system is restarted.

FIGURE 1.7
Sysprep graphical
interface

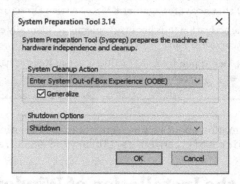

The two system cleanup actions are

♦ Enter System Out-of-Box Experience (OOBE). This option causes Windows to run the OOBE process that occurs during the installation of Windows. During the OOBE process, a new computer name is generated and you are prompted for a new administrator password.

◆ Enter System Audit Mode. This option is used for maintenance of the image. Instead of running OOBE, the operating system starts and you can perform tasks such as adding drivers and updates. After modifying the image, you can put it into audit mode again or OOBE to ready it for deployment.

When preparing an image for deployment, you should select the Generalize option. This option removes computer-specific information such as the computer name, SID, and hardware drivers.

The three shutdown options are

◆ Quit. Sysprep will quit and the operating system will remain running. You will need to shut down the operating system to capture the image.

◆ Reboot. The computer will restart and enter the mode defined by the system cleanup action. This is not appropriate if you want to capture the image.

◆ Shutdown. The computer will shut down after Sysprep completes. This is the option you should use before capturing the image.

 Real World Scenario

RUNNING SYSPREP FOR VIRTUALIZATION

You are creating a new Windows Server 2016 image for deployment. One of the complaints you had in previous deployments after using Sysprep was that it took a long time for new images to detect the hardware. When many servers were being deployed, it significantly slowed down the deployment process.

To speed up the initial configuration of each VM, you can use the /mode:vm option when you run Sysprep. This will prevent generalization from removing the hardware drivers. Leaving the hardware drivers in place significantly speeds up the deployment process for new virtual machines.

When you use /mode:vm, the image will be specific to a hypervisor. So, an image you create from a Hyper-V virtual machine would not be appropriate to use on VMware hypervisor.

DISM

Many tools are available to perform imaging. Some of those tools allow you to capture all the partitions on a disk, and some only do one partition at a time. The Deployment Image Servicing and Management (DISM) tool included with Windows Server 2016 images the contents of one partition at a time and stores the image in a .wim file. It is a file-based imaging tool.

The .wim format used by DISM can store multiple images in a single file. When multiple images are stored in the .wim file, deduplication is used. If there are multiple copies of the same file, only one copy is stored in the .wim, but that copy is available to each image contained in the file.

When multiple images are stored in a single .wim file, you need to reference either the index number or name of the image inside the file. The index number is based on the order in which the images were added to the file. The names are assigned as each image is added to the file.

To use DISM to capture an operating system image, the operating system must be shut down to ensure that there are no open files. To run DISM, you need to boot the computer using an alternative operating system. Microsoft provides Windows PE as part of the Windows Assessment and Deployment Kit (ADK). You can configure Windows PE to boot from a USB drive or other boot media.

For more information about Windows ADK and creating Windows PE boot media, see Download WinPE (Windows PE) at https://docs.microsoft.com/en-us/windows-hardware/manufacture/desktop/download-winpe--windows-pe.

When you boot from the Windows PE media, you can run DISM to capture or apply images. Typically, the images are stored on network drives, but they can also be stored on local media such as a USB drive.

If you were capturing the local C: drive to a .wim file on a network drive Z:, you would use the following syntax:

```
Dism /Capture-Image /ImageFile:Z:\Win2016.wim /CaptureDir:C: /Name:Win2016Image
```

To apply an image to the local C: drive, you would use the following syntax:

```
Dism /Apply-Image /ImageFile:Z:\Win2016.wim /Name:Win2016Image /ApplyDir:C:\
```

In addition to capturing and deploying images, DISM can also be used to mount and modify images stored in .wim files. You can make simple modifications such as adding, removing, or editing files. You can also apply Windows Updates or install new drivers to the image.

Windows System Image Manager

One way to automate the installation of Windows Server 2016 is by using answer files. An answer file provides information to the Windows Server 2016 setup process that modifies the default installation options. For example, you could create an answer file that defines the disk partitions to be created during installation, the install language, and the local Administrator password to avoid the need to interact with Setup during deployment.

The tool that you use to create answer files is Windows System Image Manager (SIM), which is included as part of Windows ADT.

Beyond creating a simple answer file, Windows SIM also creates a distribution share that you can use for deployment (Figure 1.8). In the distribution share, you can store the .wim file being used for installation (copied from installation media or customized), drivers to be added during deployment, and updates to be added during deployment. Note that adding drivers and updates during deployment avoids the need to update the image in the .wim file.

The installation process for Windows Server 2016 has multiple configuration phases. Settings for unattended installations are applied during specific stages of the installation process. When you add a setting, you might be offered multiple configuration-phase options to which you can add it. You need to ensure that you add the setting to a configuration pass that is being used in your scenario. The configuration passes are listed in Table 1.3.

FIGURE 1.8
Windows SIM

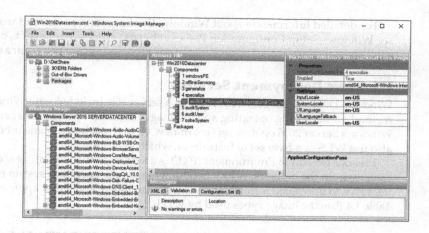

TABLE 1.3:   Configuration Passes

CONFIGURATION PASS	DESCRIPTION
windowsPE	These settings are implemented when you run setup.exe and before the Windows operating is installed. You can include settings required by setup.exe, such as the language and keyboard settings. You can also include disk-partitioning information. These settings are not used after an image has been prepared with Sysprep.
offlineServicing	This configuration pass copies and applies drivers and Windows updates. Adding drivers may be required for specialized hardware such as storage drivers that are not included with Windows Server 2016. These settings are not used after an image has been prepared with Sysprep.
Generalize	These settings are applied when you select the Generalize option in Sysprep. These settings are not used when you run setup.exe.
Specialize	These settings are applied after Windows detects new hardware and generates the SID.
AuditSystem	These settings are applied only when you enter audit mode after running Sysprep.
AuditUser	These settings are applied only when you enter audit mode after running Sysprep.
oobeSystem	This is the final configuration pass before the user is prompted to sign in.

For detailed information about Windows Configuration passes and using answer files, see Windows Setup Configuration Passes at https://docs.microsoft.com/en-us/windows-hardware/manufacture/desktop/windows-setup-configuration-passes.

Windows Deployment Services

Windows Deployment Services (WDS) is a server role included with Windows Server 2016 as a method for deploying operating system images over the network. You can use WDS to install Windows Server 2016 on new servers or new virtual machines. Some other deployment methods also use WDS as a base set of features on which to build.

Preboot Execution Environment (PXE) is a system that allows all new computers to boot directly from the network. A PXE boot downloads the operating system over the network. WDS uses PXE to download a small operating-system image and either apply or capture images. Table 1.4 lists the image types used by WDS.

TABLE 1.4:   WDS Image Types

IMAGE TYPE	DESCRIPTION
Boot	A boot image is based on Windows PE and is delivered to computers via PXE boot to apply an image containing the desired operating system. The boot.wim file included on the Windows Server 2016 installation media displays a menu that allows you to select which image you want to install from the WDS server. If necessary, you can customize the boot.wim file with network or storage drivers required for your hardware.
Capture	A capture image is based on Windows PE and is delivered to computers via PXE boot to capture an image containing the operating system of the computer. You need to run Sysprep before the image is captured.
Install	An install image contains the operating system that you want to deploy. A boot image is used to deploy an install image. A capture image is used to collect an install image and store it on the WDS server.
Discover	A discover image is a bootable ISO that contains Windows PE. This ISO can be used with removable media on computers that do not support PXE boot. It is very uncommon to require discover images because almost all computers support using PXE to boot.

INSTALLING WDS

A typical deployment of WDS requires Active Directory, DNS, and DHCP. Active Directory is used for authentication, and the WDS server is a domain member. Client computers to which you are deploying use DNS and DHCP during the deployment process.

When you install the Windows Deployment Services server role, you are prompted to select the Deployment Server and Transport Server role services. You should select both role services to have a fully functional WDS server. The Transport Server role service can be used alone in a lab environment for multicasting images, but this is not typical.

After installation is complete, you must configure WDS. To configure WDS:

1. Open the Windows Deployment Services tool in Server Manager.

2. In Windows Deployment Services, click Servers, right-click the server to be configured, and click Configure Server.

3. In the Windows Deployment Services Configuration Wizard, on the Before You Begin page, click Next.

4. On the Install Options page, click Integrated with Active Directory and click Next.

5. On the Remote Installation Folder Location page, enter a path to store all the images and click Next. Because this directory can become very large, it should not be stored on the C: drive.

6. On the PXE Server Initial Settings page, shown in Figure 1.9, select the option for computers that the server will respond to and click Next. As a best practice, you should select Do Not Respond to Any Client Computers. After you have configured images, you can configure the server to Respond Only to Known Client Computers or Respond to All Client Computers (Known and Unknown). When you respond to unknown devices, you have the option to require administrator approval.

FIGURE 1.9
PXE Server Initial
Settings page

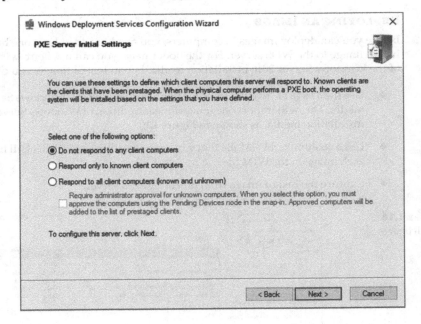

7. On the Operation Complete page, click Finish.

The Configuration Wizard configures some of the basic options for the server, but you can view the properties of the server to access additional configuration options such as:

- PXE Response settings. These settings define how PXE responds to clients. If you selected to not respond to any clients during initial configuration, then you need to allow responses here before deploying images.

- AD DS settings. These settings define the format for computer names and which organizational unit in AD DS should store the computer objects.

- Boot settings. These settings define options for the PXE boot process, such as whether pressing F12 is required to boot from PXE.

- Client settings. These settings allow you to provide an answer file that clients will use and whether the client should be joined to the domain.

- DHCP settings. If WDS is deployed on the same server as DHCP, these options need to be enabled to avoid conflicts.

- Multicast settings. These settings define which multicast addresses should be used and whether clients should be split into separate groups based on speed.

DEPLOYING AN IMAGE

Before you can deploy images to computers, you need to add at least one boot image and one install image to the WDS server. For the boot image, you can use boot.wim from Sources folder of the Windows Server 2016 installation media. For an install image, you can:

- Use the install.wim file from the Sources folder on the Windows Server 2016 installation media. This will import one image for each edition of Windows Server 2016 that is on the installation media, as shown in Figure 1.10.

- Use a customized WIM file that you have already created. This will import one image for each image in the WIM file.

- Capture the install image from preconfigured server.

FIGURE 1.10
Install images.

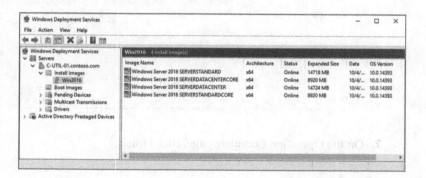

When you deploy the image, you can deploy by using unicast or multicast. *Unicast* is typical for servers and allows you to deploy to one server at a time. *Multicast* is more useful for client computers because it allows a single image to be sent to multiple computers at the same time.

The process for deploying an image is as follows:

1. Perform a PXE boot on the computer.

2. PXE downloads the boot image to the computer.

3. The boot image starts on the computer and presents a menu.

4. From the menu, you select the install image that you want to deploy.

5. The install image you select is copied to the computer.

6. The computer restarts and you complete the configuration.

Microsoft Deployment Toolkit

To help automate the deployment of Windows Server 2016, you can use the Microsoft Deployment Toolkit (MDT). MDT is primarily a tool for automating the deployment of desktop operating systems, such as Windows 10, but it also works for Windows Server 2016.

One of the difficult parts of automating the installation of Windows Server 2016 is building an answer file. There are many settings that need to be configured to completely automate an installation and require no user input. MDT creates the answer file for you. You can also use MDT to inject drivers as part of the deployment process.

MDT uses task sequences to define operations that need to be performed. Within the task sequence, you can configure detailed information such as how disks should be partitioned. The task sequence also defines where addition drivers are located. You can also define how the computer name is generated. For example, you could configure the computer name based on the computer serial number.

You have the option to create a Lite Touch ISO for the task sequence. If you add this ISO to WDS as a boot image, you can automate the deployment of the operating system to a new computer or virtual machine. The Lite Touch ISO automatically deploys the image defined in the task sequence.

If you have System Center Configuration Manager in your organization, you can implement Zero Touch deployment. A Zero Touch deployment can be pushed out from Configuration Manager and won't require you to be at the console of the server or virtual machine to which it is being deployed.

For detailed information about MDT, see the Microsoft Deployment Toolkit at https://technet.microsoft.com/en-us/windows/dn475741.aspx.

Deployment Solutions for Virtualization

Most data centers are now virtualized, and this provides you with additional options for automatically creating and configuring virtual machines. Rather than having to go through an imaging process, a virtual hard disk with a prepared operating system can be copied instead. The operating system must be prepared by using Sysprep, just as when imaging is performed.

You can copy the virtual hard disks of a virtual machine after running Sysprep instead of performing an imaging process. Then you can create a new virtual machine using the copied virtual hard disk. You can do more advanced deployment of virtual machines that includes virtual hardware configuration by using more advanced tools.

If you are using Hyper-V, System Center Virtual Machine Manager (VMM) can be used to manage the Hyper-V hosts and virtual machines. In VMM, you can create virtual machine templates and store them in a library. Then when you need to deploy a new server, you can use the virtual machine template.

For more information about VMM, see the Virtual Machine Manager Documentation at https://docs.microsoft.com/en-us/system-center/vmm/.

 Real World Scenario

ACTIVATION FOR HYPER-V VIRTUAL MACHINES

You are creating a new image for Windows Server 2016 virtual machines and want activation for the new image to be as easy as possible. You don't ever want to manually enter a product key during deployment. You also want to ensure that activation can occur without other infrastructure in test environments where network connectivity is limited.

If you are using Windows Server 2016 Datacenter for your hypervisor, you have the option to use Automatic Virtual Machine Activation (AVMA) to activate virtual machines running Windows Server 2016 or Windows Server 2012 R2. Effectively, the activation of the Hyper-V host is being used to allow the activation of the virtual machines.

When a virtual machine uses an AVMA key, it activates directly with the Hyper-V host. This works even if the virtual machine has no network connectivity. You need to enter the AVMA key in the virtual machine. There are no minimum activation thresholds for AVMA.

To obtain a list of AVMA keys, see Automatic Virtual Machine Activation at https://technet.microsoft.com/en-us/library/dn303421(v=ws.11).aspx.

If you are using VMware ESXi as your virtualization host, you can use VMware vSphere client and vCenter Server to manage the deployment of new servers by using templates. The vSphere client is used to initiate and manage the process, but the vCenter Server stores the template.

For more information about vSphere client and vCenter Server, see the VMware website at http://www.vmware.com.

Common Management Tools

You can use Windows PowerShell to manage almost any aspect of Windows Server 2016, but there are still graphical tools that many administrators prefer to use. Server Manager is the main graphical administration tool that you can use to configure Windows Server 2016 and start other administration tools. Computer Management, Device Manager, and Task Scheduler are also commonly used graphical tools for server administration.

Overview of Server Manager

Server Manager is the starting point for graphical administration tools in Windows Server 2016. It provides an interface to perform some of the common post-installation tasks and links to start other graphical administration tools. You can also use Server Manager to add or remove server roles and features.

A single Server Manager console can be used to manage multiple computers running Windows Server 2016. This allows you to configure a single central instance of Server Manager for centralized administration of multiple servers. For example, you could install the Remote Server Administration Tools on a computer running Windows 10 and centrally manage all your computers running Windows Server 2016.

On a Server Core installation of Windows Server 2016, there is no graphical interface for administration. However, you can use Server Manager to remotely manage Server Core.

To manage a server remotely by using Server Manager, Windows PowerShell remoting needs to be enabled on the remote server. This is enabled by default on Windows Server 2016.

To add a server to Server Manager, follow these steps:

1. In Server Manager, click Manage and click Add Servers.

2. In the Add Servers window, on the Active Directory tab, type the name of the server and click Find Now.

3. Double-click the server name and click OK.

4. Verify that the server is listed in the All Servers view.

ROLE AND FEATURES

The functionality of Windows Server 2016 is divided into roles and features. *Roles* perform a specific service for clients such as Active Directory Domain Service, DNS server, DHCP server, or web server. *Features* are generally software that support those roles but don't provide services to clients. When you install a server role, you are often prompted to install additional features that are required. Some examples of features are .NET Framework 4.6 Features, BitLocker Drive Encryption, Failover Clustering, and Windows Server Backup.

To install roles and features, follow these steps:

1. In Server Manager, click Manage and click Add Roles and Features.

2. In the Add Roles and Features Wizard, on the Before You Begin Page, click Next.

3. On the Select Installation Type page, select Role-Based or Feature-Based Installation and click Next. The Remote Desktop Services Installation option is used to configure one or more servers to provide access to session-based desktops or virtual desktops.

4. On the Select Destination Server page, select the server you want to install roles and features on and click Next.

5. On the Select Server Roles page, shown in Figure 1.11, select any server roles you want to install and click Next. If prompted to add required features, click Add Features.

FIGURE 1.11
Server roles

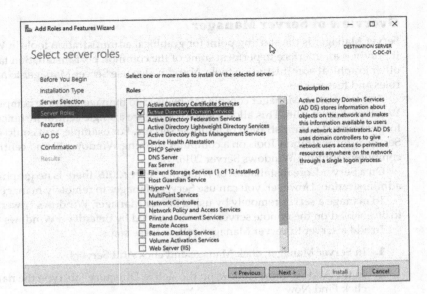

6. On the Select Features page, shown in Figure 1.12, select any features you want to install and click Next.

FIGURE 1.12
Features

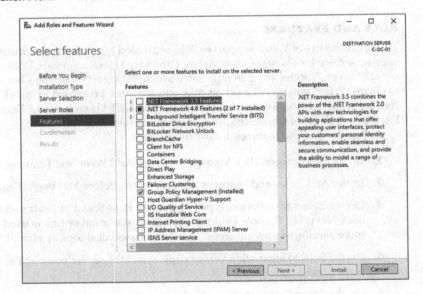

7. Complete any additional pages required by the server roles you are adding. Some server roles add pages to the wizard to gather additional configuration information.

8. On the Confirmation page, click Install.

9. On the Installation Progress page, click Close. If you close the wizard before installation is complete, the installation continues in the background.

After the server roles and features are installed, you might be prompted to restart the server. Some server roles required additional configuration after installation. In most cases, if a server role requires additional configuration, you will be notified in Server Manager and provided with a link to begin that additional configuration.

For some server roles, administrative and monitoring functionality is added to Server Manager. This is accessible in the far-left navigation menu.

MONITORING

Server Manager provides high-level monitoring functionality that you can use to quickly identify if there are problems that need to be addressed. The Dashboard view, shown in Figure 1.13, provides an overview of servers and server roles. If there are problems that need to be investigated, the role or server appears in red. You can drill down into the identified areas by clicking on them.

FIGURE 1.13
Dashboard view

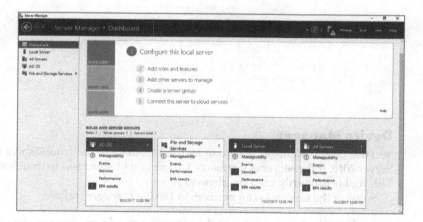

The Local Server view provides an overview of server configuration and some monitoring information. The monitoring information available includes:

◆ Events. This section lists warning and error events from the event logs.

◆ Services. This area shows the status of services and allows you to stop and start services.

◆ Best Practices Analyzer (BPA). This area shows the results of BPA scans. Unlike most other monitoring, this shows potential configuration problems rather than just functional problems such as a failing service. You need to trigger a BPA scan to collect results.

◆ Performance. This area shows performance alerts for CPU usage and memory based on thresholds that you can configure. The functionality is not enabled by default.

◆ Role and Features. This area shows the server roles and features that are installed on the server.

The All Servers view displays the same information types as the Local Server view, but aggregates the information for all servers being monitored by this instance of Server Manager.

Computer Management

Computer Management, shown in Figure 1.14, contains many useful tools for managing and monitoring Windows Server 2016. These tools include: Task Scheduler, Event Viewer, Shared Folders, Performance, Device Manager, Disk Management, and Services. Each of these tools can be run separately from the Tools menu in Server Manager or by adding a snap-in to a Microsoft Management Console (MMC), but Computer Management provides one central place to access them.

FIGURE 1.14
Computer
Management

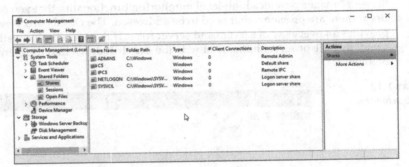

Device Manager

You use Device Manager, shown in Figure 1.15, to view and troubleshoot hardware in Windows Server 2016. If the server is virtualized, there is seldom a need to troubleshoot hardware drivers. This tool is primarily used for physical servers.

Some of the tasks you can perform in Device Manager include:

◆ View device properties. In the properties of a device, you can view the driver that is loaded and view many device properties such as the hardware IDs that are used by plug-and-play to identify the device and load an appropriate driver.

◆ Identify unknown devices. If Windows Server 2016 cannot locate a driver for hardware, it will appear as an unknown device. This is common for specialized hardware such as storage controllers. After identifying the unknown device, you can load the driver for it. The necessary driver is typically obtained from the manufacturer.

◆ Update drivers. If the hardware vendor doesn't distribute device driver updates as an executable file that automatically installs them, you can update drivers from within Device Manager. The device driver installation is based on an .inf file that defines the other files that need to be loaded.

- ◆ Roll-back drivers. If hardware is not performing properly after a driver update, you can roll back the device driver to the previous version.

- ◆ Disable hardware. In rare cases, if hardware is malfunctioning, disabling it in Device Manager can prevent it from interfering with server operation. It can be enabled again for troubleshooting.

FIGURE 1.15
Device Manager

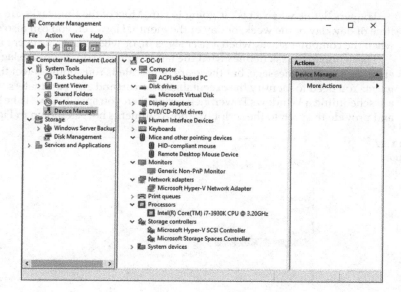

Task Scheduler

Task Scheduler, shown in Figure 1.16, is used by Windows Server 2016 to perform many background maintenance tasks. In most cases, you do not need to interact with scheduled tasks created by the operating system. If you use Task Scheduler, it is more likely that you will use it to run your own scripts for scheduled maintenance. For example, you can create a scheduled task to delete log files from Internet Information Services when they are more than 30 days old.

FIGURE 1.16
Task Scheduler

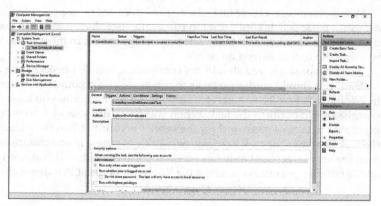

When you create a new task, the critical items to consider are

- Triggers
- Action
- Security

Triggers define when a task is going to run. Most of the time tasks are scheduled based on time of day, day of the week, or day of the month. However, you can also schedule a task to run when the computer starts, when a user signs in, or when a specific event is logged.

The action for a task defines what the task is going to do. There are legacy options to send an email or display a message, but those are deprecated. You should select the option to start a program. You need to identify the executable to be run and any parameters that it required. If you are scheduling a Windows PowerShell script, then you specify powershell.exe as the program and provide the path to the script in Add Arguments box, as shown in Figure 1.17.

FIGURE 1.17
Task action

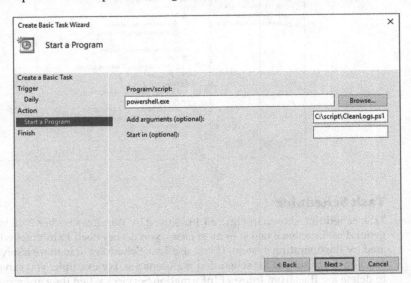

When you create a basic task, the wizard does not prompt you for security information. By default, a basic task is configured to run as the user that created the task and run only when the user is logged on. You saw these settings in Figure 1.16. In most cases, you want the task to run whether the user is logged on or not.

As a best practice, you should not configure scheduled tasks to run as normal user accounts. Instead, you should configure tasks to run as service accounts or as special accounts defined in Windows Server 2016. A service account is a user account you have created with the correct permissions to perform the task. When you configure a service account for a task, you will be prompted to enter a password for the service account. When the password is saved as part of the task, it allows the task to access network resources. If you choose not to store the password, then the service account only has access to local resources. If you need the account to run with administrative permissions, select the Run with Highest Privileges check box.

The special accounts in Windows Server 2016 do not require you to enter a password. The special accounts are listed here:

- ◆ SYSTEM. This account has full access to all local resources and the permissions of the computer account on the network. If the server running the task is a domain controller, then SYSTEM has access to modify Active Directory objects.

- ◆ SERVICE. This account has limited permissions on the local computer and anonymous permissions on the network.

- ◆ NETWORK SERVICE. This account has limited permissions on the local computer and the permissions of the computer account on the network.

For detailed information about the permissions for the special accounts, see Service User Accounts at https://msdn.microsoft.com/en-us/library/windows/desktop/ms686005(v=vs.85).aspx.

Monitoring and Troubleshooting Tools

When a server or application is not performing properly, you need to troubleshoot to identify the source of the problem and then resolve it. Application problems can be identified by error messages or just generally slow performance.

If there is an error message, that is your starting point for troubleshooting. Often, you can enter the error message into a search engine to identify possible resolutions. This works well for commonly used software when many people have posted information on the Internet.

The better you understand the process you are trying to troubleshoot, the better you will be at interpreting which web pages have relevant information for you. For example, if you understand that the application server is running on Windows Server 2016 with Internet Information Services (IIS) and the backend is a Microsoft SQL Server database, that will help you identify places where you should look for error messages to aid in your troubleshooting. If you are limited only to error messages directly within the application user interface, you have much less data with which to work.

For more specialized software, you are unlikely to find much troubleshooting information on the Internet. In this case, you should contact the vendor for support. Many vendors include support as part of the product purchase. Even if there is a cost for opening a support case, the cost of the support case is often less than the cost of downtime for the applications.

Some of the most difficult problems to troubleshoot are performance issues because there is often no error, just an application running slower than users expect. Performance problems are typically caused by bottlenecks in CPU utilization, memory capacity, network utilization, and disk utilization.

Microsoft has System Center Operations Manager as a full-featured system for monitoring errors and performance. Operations Manager can generate alerts and send notification to specific groups of administrators when errors occur or when system utilization is high. However, Operating Manager is an extra cost that not all organizations choose to implement. There are tools included with Windows Server 2016 that can be used to troubleshoot and monitor performance.

Event Viewer

Most components of Windows Server 2016 record information to the event logs, which are viewed by using Event Viewer, shown in Figure 1.18. The logs are broadly grouped in the Windows Logs and Applications and Services Logs. The Windows Logs are a general set of event logs that have remained the same for many versions of Windows and are probably familiar to you. The Applications and Services Logs are much more detailed about the type of information they contain. Each log contains events for a specific Windows component, such as the DNS server.

FIGURE 1.18
Event Viewer

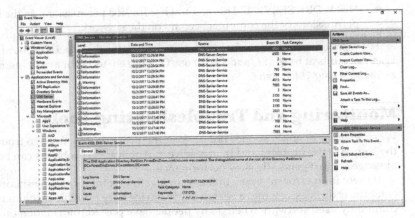

These Windows Logs are commonly used for troubleshooting:

◆ **Application.** This log contains events from Windows services and applications. Applications installed on a server often also write events in this log. For example, Microsoft SQL Server and Microsoft Exchange Server both write events to this log. Errors and warnings in this log should be investigated.

◆ **Security.** This log contains events related to auditing resource access and authentication. Some basic auditing is in place by default, but you can configure additional auditing. For example, you can configure auditing of file system access to identify which users are accessing or modifying files.

◆ **System.** This log contains operating-system-level events. Information about drivers loading or services starting and stopping are located here.

You should scan the Application and System logs occasionally to identify any errors or warnings. These are items that may indicate a problem. Most of the time, it is not worthwhile to read all of the information events. However, when you review the entire process performed by a piece of software, it can be useful to review the information events from that software along with the error and warning events.

To simplify reading events in a log, you can filter the log to show specific event types and events from specific sources. You can also create custom views that search across multiple event logs and display events matching the criteria that you specify. An Administrative Events custom view exists by default that shows the warnings and errors from all event logs. Some server roles also create a custom view to display events related to that server role.

Each event log has a maximum log size. Most logs have a maximum log size of 20 megabytes (MB) or larger, but this varies among logs. You can modify the maximum log size to a level that you determine is appropriate. Generally, you want the logs to contain enough information to be useful for troubleshooting. So, there should be enough room in the logs to contain at least a few weeks of information. The amount of data collected in logs varies widely, depending on how busy a server is and whether it is experiencing errors. For example, the default size of 128 MB for a security log may contain months of events for a small organization but only an hour of events for a large organization.

By default, when an event log is full, it begins to overwrite older events to maintain the maximum number of events in the log but not skip any newer events. You also have the option to archive event logs that hit the maximum size. However, you will need to monitor the size of the archived event logs over time because they are never removed automatically and could fill up the C: drive on your server. Finally, you have the option to stop collecting events when the event log is full. This option is seldom used because in most scenarios the most recent events are the most important.

If there are events you are watching for across multiple servers, you can configure event log subscriptions. Event log subscriptions allow you to collect specific events from multiple servers into a single log on one server. Centralizing the events on a single server will make it easier to review.

For detailed information about forwarding event logs, see Windows Event Collector at https://msdn.microsoft.com/en-us/library/bb427443(v=vs.85).aspx.

Task Manager

In Windows Server 2016, the default view for Task Manager shows only the name of the applications running on the system. It does not show any details about resource utilization or services. Fortunately, if you click More Details, it shows a view with much more information, as shown in Figure 1.19.

The tabs in Task Manager display the following:

◆ Processes. The list of processes running on the server are displayed along with the CPU and memory utilization for each. The processes are grouped as apps, background processes, and Windows processes.

◆ Performance. Information about CPU utilization, memory utilization, and network utilization are displayed. That information can be useful to identify if a specific resource is a bottleneck for performance.

◆ **Users.** All users signed in to the server at the console or via Remote Desktop are displayed along with the CPU and memory utilization for processes started by that user. If you expand the user, you can view individual processes.

◆ **Details.** For each process, the executable name, process ID, status, user name, CPU utilization, memory utilization, and description are displayed. You can sort the data based on those columns.

◆ **Services.** For each service, the service name, process ID, description, and status are displayed. This is a fast way to get a quick overview of service information.

Depending on the tab you are reviewing, you can perform various actions on the items displayed. You can stop, start, and restart services. You can also end specific tasks that are not responding properly. You can also open the file location for a process to identify the location of the executable.

FIGURE 1.19
Task Manager

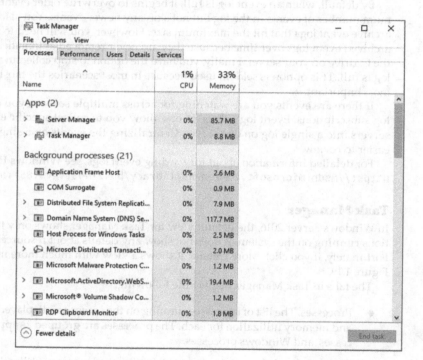

Resource Monitor

Resource Monitor, shown in Figure 1.20, shows more detailed performance information than what is available in Task Manager. Information is grouped into the four resources that are most likely to be bottlenecks: CPU, memory, disk, and network.

FIGURE 1.20
Resource Monitor

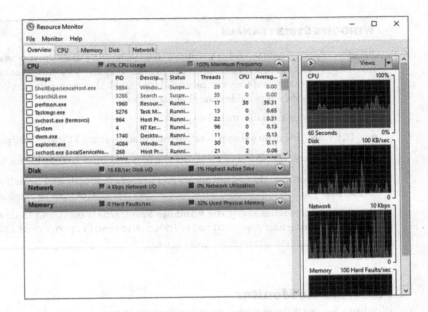

A useful feature in Resource Monitor is the ability to filter the view based on processes. If you select the check boxes for specific processes, the view is filtered to show only information for those processes and that filtering is applied to all the tabs.

The Overview tab shows a summary of the most commonly used information for CPU, memory, disk, and network. You can expand each section to view detailed information for each process.

On the CPU tab, you can see the CPU utilization for each process or service. If you select a specific process, you can also see all of the resources it is accessing in the Associated Handles section. The Associated Modules section shows the Dynamic Link Library (DLL) files that the process uses. This tab also shows the utilization of each CPU core so that you can identify if a process is saturating one core.

The Memory tab identifies the memory used by each process and how it is allocated overall to the operating system. It shows how much memory is in use, how much is being used for cache, and how much is free.

The Disk tab shows how much disk activity is being generated by each process. It also shows how much disk activity is being performed for each file. This can help identify problematic processes when disk utilization is high. The storage section shows the level of activity for each drive, including the disk queue length, which is an indicator of disk utilization. If the disk queue length is above one for extended periods of time, then the disk system is a bottleneck.

The Network tab displays network utilization for each process. It shows overall utilization for the process and breaks it down into individual conversations with other hosts. You can also see a list of all TCP connections and listening ports.

WINDOWS SYSINTERNALS

Windows Sysinternals is a set of advanced troubleshooting tools that are available for download at no charge from Microsoft. These tools can provide very low-level information about how Windows is performing tasks, and they can be useful for troubleshooting difficult problems when standard Windows tools do not provide enough information.

Some of the tools available include:

◆ TCPView. This utility shows detailed information about TCP and UDP ports on your computer.

◆ Process Explorer. This tool identifies the files and DLLs that a process has open.

◆ Process Monitor. This utility allows you to capture the file and Registry activity for a process so that you can understand what it does over a period of time or when an error occurs.

For more information about the Windows Sysinternals tools and to download them, see the Windows Sysinternals page at https://docs.microsoft.com/en-us/sysinternals/.

Performance Monitor

Windows Server 2016 includes an extensive set of performance counters that allow you to monitor many detailed aspects of system performance. The data provided by the performance counters is much more detailed than what is available in Task Manager or Resource Monitor but can be harder to interpret. You can use Performance Monitor, shown in Figure 1.21, to record and view these performance counters.

FIGURE 1.21
Performance
Monitor

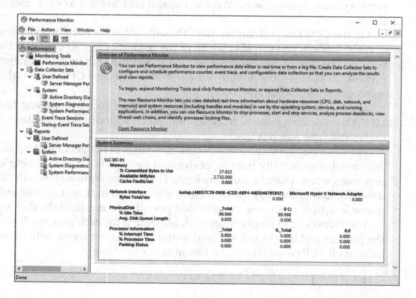

The Performance node provides an overview of commonly monitored performance counters. The data displayed here is similar to what is available on the Performance tab in Task Manager.

When you want to monitor performance counters in real time, you use the Performance Monitor node. In this node, you can add and remove various performance counters and choose how they are displayed. Performance counters can be displayed as a line graph, a histogram bar chart, or a report displaying numerical values.

To log system activity for later analysis, you need to create a data collector set. The data collector set defines which performance counters to record, when to start, and when to stop. Create your data collector sets in the User Defined node.

The System node in Data Collector Sets contains data collector sets included with Windows Server 2016. When you add server roles, they sometimes include a data collector set for troubleshooting that server role. For example, when you install the AD DS server role an Active Directory Diagnostics data collector set is added.

After a data collector set runs, a report is generated and stored in the Reports node. The report provides a summary of the data that was collected. For performance counters, it displays mean, minimum, and maximum values.

If you are trying to troubleshoot a performance problem that happened at a specific point in time, you need to review the value of performance counters over time. To view the value of performance counters at various points in time, use the Performance Monitor node to open the log files from the data collector set. The line graph view in the Performance Monitor node will allow you to select a specific point in time when viewing performance counter values.

The Bottom Line

Define a deployment process.   You can deploy Windows Server 2016 by running setup.exe or by using various imaging processes. In general, you should try to automate deployment as much as possible, but you need to define a consistent deployment process that works for your organization. A well-defined deployment process helps to ensure consistency in your server configuration for easier troubleshooting.

Master It   Your organization has completely virtualized its infrastructure for deploying servers. To create new servers, your team copies a virtual hard drive with an operating system that has been prepared by using Sysprep. How can you improve this process?

Solution   If your organization is large enough to justify the cost, you should implement software that manages the deployment of virtual machines. You can use VMM for Hyper-V hosts or vCenter for VMware hosts. By using more advanced deployment software, you can automate processes better.

Select an edition of Windows Server 2016.   Windows Server 2016 can be purchased as Standard edition or Datacenter edition. The basic functionality of both editions is the same, but some advanced features are available only in the Datacenter edition. If you need those advanced features, such as Storage Replica or shielded virtual machines, then you should purchase the Datacenter edition.

Master It   You are planning the standardized images that you will be using to deploy Windows Server 2016. For previous versions of Windows Server, you have always used the graphical interface on each server. What would be the benefits of introducing Server Core in a highly virtualized environment?

Solution   The basic benefits of Server Core are a reduced attack surface and a reduced requirement for updates. In a highly virtualized environment, you also get increased server density. Server Core uses less disk space and less memory, which allows you to have more virtual machines running on each virtualization host.

Select an activation method.   When you use volume licensing, Windows Server 2016 can be activated by using a MAK key, KMS, or Active Directory–Based Activation. A MAK key is entered on each server. A KMS key is entered in a KMS host or Active Directory.

Master It   In the past, your organization has used OEM licensing for servers. As part of your migration to Windows Server 2016, you have purchased volume licenses to allow greater flexibility to move virtualized servers between hosts. The deployment will be small at first with only two or three servers in the first year. What is the preferred activation method?

Solution   In this scenario, you can't use a KMS host because this deployment will not meet the minimum activation threshold for over a year. As a best practice, you should not require your servers to access the Internet for activation. This leaves Active Directory–Based Activation as the best solution.

Monitor Windows Server 2016.   Windows Server 2016 includes a number of tools for monitoring and troubleshooting. Task Manager and Resource Monitor are good tools for getting a quick overview of current system performance. Performance Monitor can provide detailed information about current system performance or log performance for later analysis. Event Viewer allows you to review logs to look for errors related to performance issues.

Master It   You work for a large organization with several hundred servers. Your server monitoring is reactive rather than proactive. You don't know that there is a performance problem until users begin calling the help desk. How can monitoring be managed better?

Solution   In a large organization, it's not possible to manually scan event logs and performance statistics to be proactive. Instead, you need centralized monitoring software like System Center Operations Manager. When you implement Operations Manager, performance information is constantly collected over time and event logs are monitored for errors. When a problem occurs, the administration team can be notified by email.

Chapter 2

PowerShell

The need for basic PowerShell skills is sprouting up everywhere in operating systems, such as Windows Server 2016, and in customized line-of-business applications. In fact, many configuration changes can be accomplished only via PowerShell. Throughout this book, you will be shown various scripts and commands. This chapter is not going to teach you everything there is to know about PowerShell; its goal is to provide you with enough background information to enable you to understand what is going on in the various commands and scripts you will see throughout this book and online. Being able to find commands and understand documentation will enable you to develop your own scripts and functions to automate your day-to-day responsibilities in a consistent and methodical way. This chapter will also prepare you with an excellent base of knowledge if you decide to dive into the exciting and complex world of programming with Windows PowerShell.

IN THIS CHAPTER, YOU WILL LEARN TO:

◆ Customize the PowerShell and PowerShell ISE environments

◆ Perform command discovery and interpret PowerShell syntax notation and concept documentation

◆ Write and analyze code that supports functions, loops, comparisons, pipeline processing, variables, and scripts

◆ Manage remote servers with PowerShell

What Is PowerShell?

PowerShell was introduced in 2006. It reminded many people of the old DOS prompt because of its command-line interface (CLI), but PowerShell isn't really a CLI. It is an object-oriented administrative automation engine (see Figure 2.1). PowerShell has a CLI, but PowerShell can also be the backend to a graphical user interface (GUI).

FIGURE 2.1
The Windows PowerShell console on Windows Server 2016

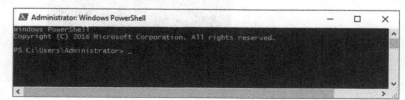

A great example of the flexibility and utility of PowerShell is how PowerShell can be hosted by other applications. Many line-of-business (LOB) applications are written specifically to act as wrappers around PowerShell. These applications require specific classes, modules, properties, and settings. If PowerShell gets updated to a version that is incompatible with the LOB application, that application may fail. You always want to check the manufacturer of any LOB software to ensure compatibility prior to upgrading.

Typically, a GUI doesn't offer every possible configuration setting. Many of the more advanced features, or the ones that Microsoft wanted tucked away, can be configured only by using the CLI. As operating systems and enterprise applications evolve, we are seeing an increased turn toward automation and configuration standards. This provides reproducibility; in other words, having configuration done via a script makes it easier to ensure uniform configurations throughout all of your systems. They also provide excellent and detailed documentation of what configurations have been applied to systems and help ensure that if a system needs to be brought online quickly, you can use these scripts to automate much of this process.

Forward Compatible

PowerShell is *forward compatible*, which means that any script you may have created in an older version of PowerShell should run in a newer version. However, even though the modules and classes of PowerShell 1.0 are still included in PowerShell 5.0, newer operating systems may not use these old modules or classes. Older scripts may seem to run, but you may not have the pieces in the OS needed to provide a result. That means your scripts might not behave as expected or might simply refuse to run.

PowerShell Versions

PowerShell has 32-bit and 64-bit versions. The modern Microsoft operating systems are typically 64-bit. The 32-bit version is used for compatibility when the shell is hosted in a 32-bit application. PowerShell version 1 was only 32-bit. The rest will have a designation of (x86) for the 32-bit version. This will appear with the application name of Windows PowerShell (x86) or Windows PowerShell ISE (x86). When you run the PowerShell application, the title bar at the top of the screen will display the same names. Figure 2.2 shows the differences in the name.

FIGURE 2.2
The 32-bit and
64-bit versions of
PowerShell

If you are using a 32-bit operating system, you can run only 32-bit applications. That means you will only be able to run the 32-bit version of PowerShell. On a 64-bit operating system, such as Windows Server 2016, you can use either one, but we strongly encourage you to use the 64-bit version whenever possible.

Running and Customizing PowerShell

If you have an operating system that uses User Account Control (UAC), such as Windows Server 2016, PowerShell will not open as an administrator. To run PowerShell with full administrative credentials, right-click the icon and select Run As Administrator from the shortcut menu. This change will be displayed in the title bar and the PowerShell CLI, as illustrated in Figure 2.3.

FIGURE 2.3
PowerShell's Run As Administrator

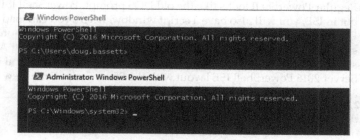

Customizing the PowerShell Console

Few things are worse than spending countless hours debugging a script only to find out the problem was something silly like a single quotation mark being replaced by a grave accent or mistaking a curly brace for an open parenthesis. Each of these characters is used in different situations, and if you swap one for the other, you may get unexpected results. This is typically displayed as a bunch of error messages that can be difficult to understand. You need to change the font and the font size to make it easier to recognize the different characters.

To change the font, right-click the PowerShell window and select Properties. Then select the Font tab. Raster fonts seem to be particularly prone to confusion, so you may want to select a TrueType font.

You can also control the size of the shell window. Most people like to have big windows to work in, but they don't like horizontal scroll bars. You can go into the Layout tab and adjust the window size. You may notice there is a buffer size as well. You typically want to have the Width value for both Buffer Size and Window Size to be the same. The values will differ, depending on the resolution. Most administrators like to fill the width without a scroll bar being present. The values for Buffer Size and Window Size don't need to be the same. In fact, a large height buffer size will give you the vertical scroll bar. This means you will be able to scroll up and down more without the shell deleting previous lines so quickly.

Cutting and Pasting in PowerShell

You can also perform cut and paste operations in PowerShell, but they work a bit differently from what you might expect.

Note that when you copy, whatever is highlighted goes into the Clipboard. That means that if you drag your mouse across and get just the middle of several lines of text, that is the only text that will actually be copied. Be sure to select exactly what you want when you highlight, or you could get some unexpected results.

If you want to enable a more traditional method of selection, where you can grab entire lines and not just stacked sections of lines, go into the properties of your PowerShell console window and on the Options tab, select Enable Line Wrapping Selection. If copy and paste does not work at all, go into the properties of your PowerShell window and make sure that QuickEdit mode is enabled.

Using PowerShell Integrated Scripting Environment (ISE)

Regular PowerShell looks like the old DOS prompt. PowerShell ISE also has a console window; but in ISE, you will also have a script window, where you can load and edit scripts and text files. Depending on the OS and the screen resolution, additional add-ons may be visible. You can select View to see what you can make visible. You can also select Add-ons and make different selections, depending on your needs. Refer to Figure 2.4 to look at the default Windows Server 2016 PowerShell ISE layout with the Show Script Pane view option selected.

FIGURE 2.4
PowerShell ISE on Windows Server 2016

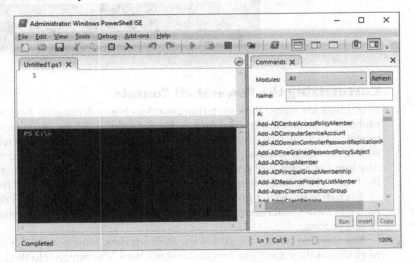

Exploring the Command Add-On Pane

One of the most popular add-ons usually included with the ISE is the Command add-on. This gives you an alphabetized reference for commands. These commands are typically called *cmdlets* in PowerShell. These cmdlets are included with the various modules you may have loaded on your local system.

Windows Server 2016 has several modules installed by default. You will also typically get additional modules when you install different roles or install additional applications and services. You can also get modules provided by third parties who have written their own. Figure 2.5 shows just the Command add-on pane in PowerShell ISE with "All" selected.

FIGURE 2.5
Command pane
with "All" selected

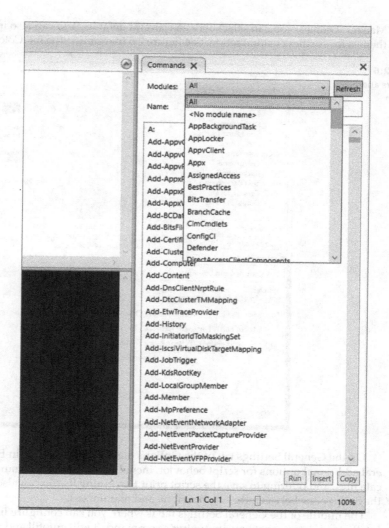

When you select a module, only the cmdlets for that module will be shown in the command pane.

Another handy add-on is the Script pane. This lets you have scripts loaded, and you can edit and run entire scripts without the need to cut and paste. You can also highlight particular lines of the script and execute just the lines that are highlighted.

To run the entire contents of the Script pane, you can click the green Play button on the top of the screen or you can simply press F5. If you want to execute just the lines you have highlighted, you can press the Play button with the small text document behind it or press F8. If your script needs to be stopped, you can press the red square or you can press Ctrl+Break.

Other options are available for ISE. If you select Tools and then Options, you can do tons of customization of the fonts and have extensive control over the colors of text. When you select

Manage Themes, you can select between several defaults. You can also import and export themes for further customization. See Figure 2.6 to examine the ISE Colors and Fonts tab.

FIGURE 2.6
ISE Colors and
Fonts tab

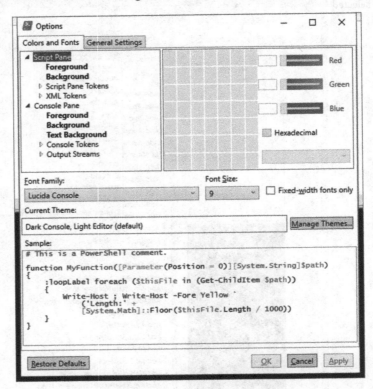

On the General Settings tab of the Options dialog box, as shown in Figure 2.7, you have several additional options for script behavior, including outlining, line numbers, detecting duplicate files, and offering to save the script prior to running it. You can also modify the location of the Script pane between the top, the right, and maximized.

The middle of the General Settings tab is where you can configure Intellisense. When Intellisense detects that you are typing a command, it will autofill and allow you to quickly select between the different commands available that match what you have typed. You can adjust the Intellisense timeout, which mandates how long the Intellisense suggestion is displayed. The default is just 3 seconds. The range in the dialog box is between 1 and 5 seconds. You can set the timeout to other values using the following command:

```
$host.PrivateData.IntellisenseTimeoutInSeconds = X
```

where X is replaced with the number of seconds to display the Intellisense suggestion.

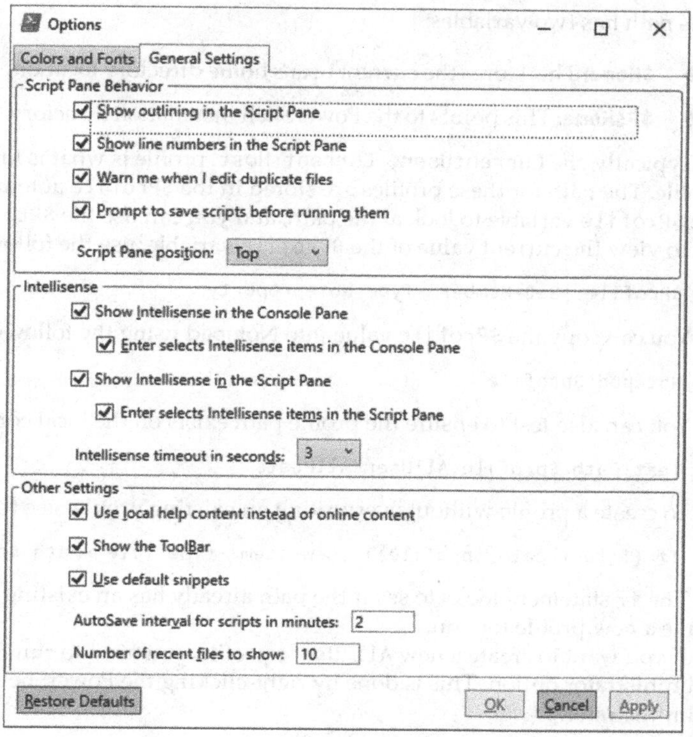

FIGURE 2.7
ISE General
Settings

Setting Up PowerShell ISE Profiles

Re-creating your favorite scripting environment every time you launch PowerShell or PowerShell ISE can be difficult. A way to retain these settings, session by session, is to use PowerShell profiles.

A PowerShell profile is a script that executes every time PowerShell starts. You can have tons of commands, functions, variables, snap-ins, aliases, modules, and drives. You can also add additional session-specific elements that load each and every session using PowerShell profiles.

These PowerShell Profiles are stored as files. You can have several profile files, and you can even have profiles that are specific to a particular host. There are several that can be associated with your session, and they are listed in precedence order. The first profile listed has the highest precedence. These profiles are stored in various locations. Here are the basic profile file paths:

```
Current User, Current Host $Home[My ]Documents\WindowsPowerShell\Profile.ps1 Current
User, All Hosts $Home[My ]Documents\Profile.ps1 All Users, Current Host $PsHome\
Microsoft.PowerShell_profile.ps1 All Users, All Hosts $PsHome\Profile.ps1
```

This path has two variables:

- **$Home:** This stores the current user's home directory location.
- **$PsHome:** This points to the PowerShell installation directory.

Typically, the CurrentUser, Current Host profile is what is known as your PowerShell profile. The path for these profiles are stored in the $Profile automatic variable. You can use the $Profile variable to look at the path, and you can use the $Profile variable in a command.

To view the current value of the $Profile variable, use the following command:

```
$Profile |Get-Member -Type Noteproperty
```

You can copy the $Profile value into Notepad using the following command:

```
Notepad $profile
```

You can also test to ensure the profile path exists on the local computer by entering this:

```
Test-Path $profile.AllUsersAllHosts
```

To create a profile without overwriting an existing profile, use the following:

```
if (!(test-path $profile)) {new-item -type file -path $profile -force}
```

The if statement looks to see if the path already has an existing profile. If it doesn't, it will make a new profile for you.

If you want to create a new All Users profile, you need to run PowerShell using the Run As Administrator option. This is done by right-clicking the PowerShell icon and selecting Run As Administrator.

Editing Profiles

Profiles are just text files. You can edit them in any text editor that doesn't embed extra information. Notepad is a perfectly good editor for PowerShell profiles. To open the current user's profile in something like Notepad, enter the following:

```
Notepad $Profile
```

If you want to edit other profiles, you just specify the profile name. For example, to open the profile that is used for all of the users on all of the host applications, you can enter the following:

```
Notepad $profile.AllUsersAllHosts
```

Initially, the profile will be blank.

Maybe you want a customized prompt that will tell you the current computer name and the current path. You can use this command:

```
function awesome-prompt { $env:computername + "\" + (get-location) + "> " }
```

If you want to open PowerShell using Run As Administrator automatically, you can use the following:

```
Function Open-AsAdmin {Start-Process PowerShell -Verb RunAs}
```

Once you have made the appropriate changes, you simply save the profile file and then restart PowerShell.

Setting Up Execution Policies

You don't want to allow just anyone to execute scripts or run scripts from unknown or untrusted sources. Execution policies specify if a user can load configuration files, such as profiles. They also determine whether you are even allowed to run scripts, which scripts you can run, and whether the scripts have to be digitally signed with a digital certificate before they are allowed to run. Policies are configured with the Set-ExecutionPolicy command.

The execution policy can be set for a particular PowerShell session, for the current user, or for the local machine. The execution policy does *not* need to be set in the PowerShell profile because its setting is stored in the Registry. However, session execution policies are exceptions; they exist only during the session and are not stored in the Registry. When you exit the session, the execution policy associated with the session is deleted.

Remember that the execution policy sets the behavior for processing scripts. If you have a determined user or you are the determined user, you can enter all of the commands into the console. Execution policies help make users aware of the security context of their scripts and help them avoid running inappropriate scripts accidentally.

The Restricted execution does not let you run scripts, but you can run individual commands. You are blocked from all script files.

```
Set-ExecutionPolicy Restricted
```

With AllSigned, you can run scripts. All of these scripts and configuration files will need to be signed by a trusted publisher. This includes scripts that you have written and have on the local computer.

```
Set-ExecutionPolicy AllSigned
```

This is the default policy for Windows Server 2012 R2 and Windows Server 2016:

```
Set-ExecutionPolicy RemoteSigned
```

This policy mandates that any script or configuration has to be signed by a trusted publisher. If you want to run an unsigned script, you can unblock that script using the Unblock-File cmdlet. Any scripts that you have created on the local system will run without signing.

The following will let the user run anything. It will notify the users if they try to run scripts or configuration files that were downloaded, but it will not block their execution.

```
Set-ExecutionPolicy Unestricted
```

This is the most dangerous policy. It will run anything and everything without any prompts.

```
Set-ExecutionPolicy Bypass
```

Undefined execution policies are typically ignored. If all of the applied policies are set to undefined, your system will use the default execution policy which, in Windows Server 2016, is RemoteSigned.

```
Set-ExecutionPolicy Undefined
```

Recording PowerShell Sessions

You may find it necessary to record PowerShell sessions. The transcription operations will capture all input and any output that displayed on the console and store it to a file. To enable transcripts, you can enter the following:

```
Start-Transcript c:\mystranscript.txt
```

You can use the Help Start-Transcript command to view the various options. This example will create a transcription file and store it at C:\mytranscript.txt. PowerShell will overwrite any file that already exists. To avoid overwriting the file, you can use the -NoClobber parameter. If the specified file already exists, the -NoClobber will cause the command to fail. If you want to specify only a directory and have PowerShell automatically name the files, you can use the -OutputDirectory parameter. If you want to just append to the existing file, instead of creating a new file, you can use the -Append parameter.

To stop recording the transcript, you can simply close your console session, or you can use the Stop-Transcript cmdlet. Note that this will stop all transcriptions from all sessions. There are other options, so you are encouraged to look around in the Help About_Start-Transcript files.

Using Aliases and Getting Help

PowerShell offers plenty of ways to make using commands easier.

Using *CMD.EXE*-Like Commands in PowerShell

When you run PowerShell for the first time, it may remind you of the old DOS command prompt. In fact, many of the same commands seem to be supported. Here are some of the commands that you may remember that still seem to operate:

```
MKDIR
DIR
CD
PING
IPCONFIG
```

In many cases, these commands are the actual commands and haven't changed. That is because they are external commands that PowerShell sends to external apps to process. Some examples would be IPCONFIG and PING.

But not all of the older commands will work the way you may anticipate. For example, the DIR command is used to display the contents of the current directory. You can also use several options to do sorting, show file ownership, display the folder listing in a wide format, or display only files that have certain attributes, such as hidden files.

A great example is the DIR /S Importantfile.txt command. This command is used to find every occurrence of that particular filename within a particular directory, as well as all the subdirectories underneath the current directory. This is known as a *recursive search*.

Here is what happens when you run the command from within cmd.exe instead of PowerShell:

```
Dir /s Importantfile.txt

Volume in drive C is OSDisk
Volume Serial Number is 8636-D98D

Directory of C:\templates\HR
03/05/2017  11:56 AM              480 importantfile.txt
               1 File(s)          480 bytes
Directory of C:\templates\sales
03/05/2017  11:56 AM              480 importantfile.txt
               1 File(s)          480 bytes
Total Files Listed:
               2 File(s)          960 bytes
        0 Dir(s)  377,296,039,936 bytes free
```

This is a pretty useful result. This could prove vital in a script where you may want to try to consolidate a bunch of files into a single location. In Figure 2.8, you can see the result of performing the same command in PowerShell.

FIGURE 2.8
Dir /S in
PowerShell

As you can see, Dir /S is completely misunderstood by PowerShell. It thinks you are trying to get a listing of the contents of the C:\S folder. It tells you that it can't find the path because it doesn't exist.

Dir /S fails because many of the "old" commands use an alias to redirect them to new PowerShell cmdlets. The aliases are used because the old "tried and true" commands don't always follow the PowerShell verb-noun format. Any options that the user sends to these aliases are processed by that underlying PowerShell cmdlet. If you want to find help on DIR in PowerShell, you can simply enter the following:

```
Help DIR
```

Here is a partial list of the output:

```
NAME
    Get-ChildItem
```

```
SYNOPSIS
Gets the files and folders in a file system drive.

SYNTAX
Get-ChildItem [[-Filter] <String>] [-Attributes {ReadOnly | Hidden | System |
Directory | Archive | Device | Normal |
```

This will give you the default help information for a Get-ChildItem PowerShell cmdlet. When you use DIR, PowerShell gets the information you provided and sends it to the Get-ChildItem cmdlet. Get-Childitem does not support the /s switch. That is why you get the error and your script fails.

You need to remember that "tried and true" commands are typically either a call to an external application or an alias to an internal PowerShell command.

If you want to find out what aliases are available and which PowerShell cmdlet they really call, simply enter the following to see all the aliases in all the modules that are available in the current session:

```
Get-Alias
```

Exploring a *Get-Help* Example

You can request help by prefacing any command with Get-Help, Help, or Man. The output is *mostly* the same because if you use Get-Help, all of the help output is dumped right to your console and will likely scroll off the screen. You can then scroll up and down to look at the particular area of information you need. If you use Help or Man, one screen of information will display at a time and you can press almost any key to get the next screen. If you press CTRL-C, the output will stop and you will go back to the command prompt.

A way to display the help file in a separate window that you can keep up on the screen, or even move to a different monitor, is to use the –ShowWindow parameter. Figure 2.9 shows the output from Get-Help Get-ChildItem –ShowWindow.

FIGURE 2.9
–ShowWindow
parameter

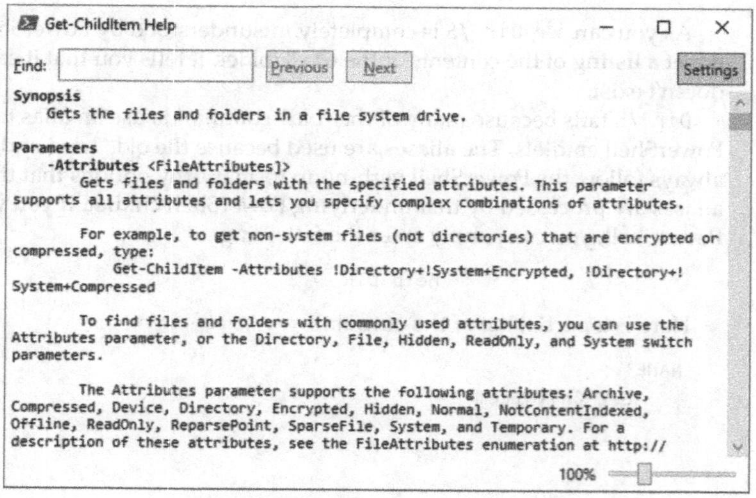

You can take this window and use it as a constant reference when you are creating your scripts or typing directly into your console. It is searchable so you can use it to quickly pinpoint exactly what you are looking to accomplish.

PowerShell help will show examples. The problem is you will need to scroll around past all the syntax and stuff to find just the examples. If you want to jump right to the example code, simply change your help request to something similar to the following:

```
Get-Help Dir -Example
```

Here is a relevant portion of the output:

```
Example 2: Get all files with the specified file extension in the current directory
and subdirectories
        PS C:\>Get-ChildItem -Path "*.txt" -Recurse -Force
```

This command gets all of the .txt files in the current directory and its subdirectories. The Recurse parameter directs Windows PowerShell to get objects recursively, and it indicates that the subject of the command is the specified directory and its contents. The Force parameter adds hidden files to the display.

Now you are getting somewhere. You can try the following:

```
Get-ChildItem -Recurse
```

And that provides the same output as DIR /S, if it were run from cmd.exe.

Because you know that DIR is an alias for Get-ChildItem, let's see what happens if you try this command:

```
DIR -Recurse
```

If you try it, you will find that it is the same result.

Getting *Get-Help* Updates

PowerShell help files haven't been included with the operating system since PowerShell 3.0. If you run PowerShell as an administrator, you may notice that the system attempts to download the help files from an online service owned by Microsoft. If you have PowerShell modules provided by a third-party vendor, they can also be updated with downloadable help. You do have to run this with credentials that are part of the local administrators group because the PowerShell core command help is stored in your %systemdir%. If PowerShell is unable to download the updated help files, it will create a default help display for the commands in the module that lacks updates.

Not all modules will support updating its help files. You can get a list of modules that have pointers to updatable information by entering the following:

```
Get-Module -ListAvailable |Where HelpInfoURI
```

If you want to update your help files immediately, you can perform the following command:

```
Update-Help
```

The Update-Help command will look for all of your installed modules in the default module path on your system. This path is stored in the environmental variable $env:PSModulePath. To view this path, use the following:

```
$env:PSModulePath
```

Here is a typical output:

```
C:\Users\Administrator\Documents\WindowsPowerShell\Modules;C:\Program Files\
WindowsPowerShell\Modules;C:\Windows\system32\WindowsPowerShell\v1.0\Modules
```

If you want to add an additional, temporary path that exists only during this session, modify this environmental variable as follows:

```
$env:PSModulePath = $env:PSModulePath + ";f:\OurAddedPath"
```

If you want to make the change permanent, you will need to add this command to the profile.

If you want to update a module that isn't in your module path, you can import the module into the current session and then use the Update-Help command. You can import the module with the following command:

```
Import-Module "D:\LOBModuleswebought\LOBModule"
```

If you run Update-Help more than once in a 24-hour period, nothing will actually be updated. There is also a 1 GB of uncompressed content limit. If you don't want to wait the 24 hours or you want to bypass the 1 GB limit, you can use the following command:

```
Update-Help -Force
```

This Update-Help -Force command can be added to your PowerShell profile to ensure that your help is always updated.

Updating Help for Servers Without Internet Access

Many times, you are going to have servers that are for internal use only and these systems don't have direct Internet access. The good news is that Microsoft has addressed this concern with the Save-Help cmdlet. You will download the help file to a file share on an Internet-connected machine. You can then copy the files to a system that is reachable by the internal machines. Here is an example:

```
Save-Help -DestinationPath \\SMBFileServer01\Sharename\PSHelpFolder -Credential
Domainname\Username
```

This will download the help files to a file share on SMBFileServer01. You also need to ensure that the credentials used are members of the administrator's group on each machine or are domain administrators where all of the computers are members. Also know that Update-Help and Save-Help will update files only for modules that are installed on the local system.

Accessing Online Help Files

If you don't want to download updates, but want access to the latest version of the help file, you can add the -Online parameter. Here is an example:

```
Get-Help Get-ChildItem -Online
```

SHOULD YOU REALLY BOTHER WITH UPDATES?

It is a good idea to have the latest help files as you are creating scripts or looking to perform a specific task. However, remember that these help files are written by people and may contain mistakes and omissions. As Microsoft updates modules, needed parameters may be added or removed. By keeping your system updated, you can be sure to have the latest information to help you with your PowerShell administration.

Understanding Cmdlet Syntax

PowerShell cmdlets are typically set in a Verb-Noun format and can include a number of mandatory and optional parameters. `Update-Help` follows that context. You may also notice that not all verbs are actually verbs. `New-VM` is a valid cmdlet, but New is not an English language verb.

Be aware that cmdlets are generally not case-sensitive. There are some rare exceptions, but the following examples are functionally identical:

```
Get-Vm
get-vm
GeT-vM
```

As you can tell, having odd casing in your cmdlets can make it very difficult to read and troubleshoot. Traditionally, you will capitalize the first letter of each word that is crammed together to make a cmdlet or parameter. There are also various conventions for variables and functions and modules. Traditionally, the first character of a variable is not capitalized, but subsequent words are capitalized. The variable `$computerList` is the traditional practice. It is still easy to read because additional words are capitalized, but it is a bit more obvious that this is a variable because the first word is not capitalized.

STANDARDS ARE GOOD

We recommend that you go with a standard that makes it easy for others to read and understand your scripts. When maintaining scripts, don't make life difficult by getting too creative with your capitalization.

Interpreting the Syntax

You will need to know which parameters are mandatory, which are optional, and which parameters won't work together with other parameters.

Let's examine a sample of syntax that is generated by the `Help Get-Eventlog` cmdlet.

```
NAME
    Get-EventLog
SYNOPSIS
```

Gets the events in an event log, or a list of the event logs, on the local or remote computers.

```
SYNTAX
Get-EventLog [-LogName] <String> [[-InstanceId] <Int64[]>] [-After <DateTime>]
[-AsBaseObject] [-Before <DateTime>]   [-ComputerName <String[]>] [-EntryType
{Error | Information | FailureAudit | SuccessAudit | Warning}] [-Index <Int32[]>]
[-Message <String>] [-Newest <Int32>] [-Source <String[]>] [-UserName <String[]>]
[<CommonParameters>] Get-EventLog [-AsString] [-ComputerName <String[]>] [-List]
[<CommonParameters>]
```

You can identify parameters because they are prefaced with a hyphen. Look at the following example:

```
Get-Eventlog -LogName Security
```

The Get-Eventlog cmdlet has a single parameter, -LogName. The string Security tells PowerShell which event log it is supposed to "get." This command will get the security event log and dump its contents on your console screen. Many people who are new to PowerShell get confused with parameters. Look at this broken cmdlet:

```
Get-Eventlog -Security
```

You have swapped the parameter value for the name of the parameter. The PowerShell module that hosts this cmdlet has no idea what -Security means, because that isn't one of the accepted parameters and Security is tagged as a parameter because it has the hyphen in the front of it.

You also need to determine which parameters are mandatory and which are optional. Anything surrounded *entirely* by square brackets is optional. Anything not entirely surrounded by square brackets is mandatory.

```
[-optionalstuffhere]
[-Optionalstuff] mandatorystuff
```

Let's examine the very first parameter associated with the Get-EventLog cmdlet:

```
Get-EventLog [-LogName] <string>
```

This syntax block says that the word -LogName is optional, but the <string> portion isn't surrounded by square brackets. You *always* have to have a <string> for this cmdlet. That means that any time you use the Get-Evenlog cmdlet you *must* include a string that has the name of the log. Even though the string value is required, you don't need to include, in this instance, the parameter name of -LogName. That is shown by the fact that LogName is completely surrounded by square brackets.

The rest of the parameters are completely surrounded by square brackets. That means all of the other parameters are optional. Note that some of these optional parameters, when used, have mandatory values.

Let's look at an optional parameter with a mandatory value block from the same Get-EventLog cmdlet:

```
[-After <DateTime>]
```

Notice how the entire parameter of -After and the <DateTime> value are completely surrounded by square brackets. That tells you that this entire parameter is optional. But note that <DateTime> doesn't have additional square brackets. That means that any time you use the –After parameter, it is mandatory that you include a value for the <DateTIme>. If it were optional, the syntax block would look like this:

```
[-After [<DateTime>]]
```

Because the –LogName parameter is listed as the first parameter, this is also known as a positional parameter. You don't have to identify that the first parameter value you are sending, in this case Security, is the value associated with –LogName because -LogName is the first parameter expected in this command.

In certain cmdlets, if you are careful, you can pass a ton of parameters without labeling them if you do it in a very specific order. However, doing so makes the script almost illegible. Do yourself a favor and always include the parameter name in written scripts so they become self-documenting. Including parameter names also means you can put the parameters in a different order, but PowerShell knows which parameter value goes to which parameter because you so helpfully identified it

Using Spaces in Cmdlets

PowerShell uses spacing to separate cmdlets from parameters and parameters from values. You do need to be cautious where you place spaces, but you can put as many as you like, where spaces are allowed. Here is an example:

```
Get-EventLog                          -LogName                       Security
```

This is perfectly acceptable to PowerShell because the spaces, or blocks of spaces, are located where PowerShell expects a single space. You have to ensure that the space is in the correct location. Consider the following cmdlet examples:

```
Get-Eventlog - LogName Security
Get-Event Log -LogName Security
Get- EventLog -Logname Security
Get-EventLog -Log Name Security
```

These are all invalid and will produce errors because spaces have been placed where PowerShell isn't expecting spaces. If you get too creative, it gets hard to read, and PowerShell may think you are passing additional values or putting in some other piece.

You also want to avoid mixing spaces and tabs to make your code line up. Use one or the other. This is particularly important when you are copying code from one script to another. Mixing tabs and spaces frequently leads to failures.

Passing Multiple Values to a Parameter

There are many instances where you will want to provide multiple values to a parameter. Part of your Get-Eventlog syntax includes the following notation:

```
[-ComputerName <String[]>]
```

Notice that this entire parameter, including the string, is optional, because the entire thing is surrounded by brackets. Also notice that the `<String[]>` has little square brackets inside of it. When you see the two square brackets displayed in this manner, it means that you can pass multiple values using a comma-separated list. Examine the following code:

```
Get-EventLog Security –ComputerName Server01, Server02, Server03
```

This tells the `Get-EventLog` cmdlet to get the security logs from three different servers. Also notice that the syntax for the –LogName parameter is listed as `[-LogName]` `<String>`. The lack of the small square brackets here means you can have only a single value for the `–LogName` parameter. Functionally, that means you can get only one named event log, such as Security or Application, but not both. `-Computername` `<String[]>` tells us that you can get the single log from multiple computers.

Another way to get multiple values loaded into a parameter is to read a comma-separated list of values from a file. Here is an example:

```
Get-EventLog Security –ComputerName (Get-Content c:\computerlist.txt)
```

This is known as a *parenthetical* command. You have a command inside of parentheses to provide values to a different parameter. The `Get-Content` will read the file, one line at a time, and place each line as a separate value to the `–ComputerName` parameter. Parenthetical commands work just like the math rules you learned in school. You will do what is in the parentheses first, and that result will become the value that is handed to the parameter.

You can also place values into variables, and then the variable can pass the values to the parameter. Look at the following commands:

```
$computers = Get-Content c:\Computerlist.txt
Get-EventLog –LogName Security –ComputerName $computers
```

You will be talking more about variables a bit later, but you are using the first line to load up the variable called `$computers` with comma-separated values of text. You then take this variable and use it as the value for the `–ComputerName` parameter.

Using *Show-Command*

PowerShell can automatically take a cmdlet and display it in a dialog box with areas for each of the parameters. Look at the following command:

```
Show-Command Get-EventLog
```

When this command is executed, you will get a dialog box as shown in Figure 2.10. We have added values in the `ComputerName` and `LogName` block to illustrate how those are populated. By default, all the parameters will have blank values.

This shows you all of the parameters that are specific for this command, and it will let you fill out each of these parameters. Note that LogName has an asterisk. That means that that parameter is mandatory.

The List tab will show you which parameter will take a list of values. You can enter them separated by a comma in the `ComputerName` field.

FIGURE 2.10
Show-Command
Get-EventLog

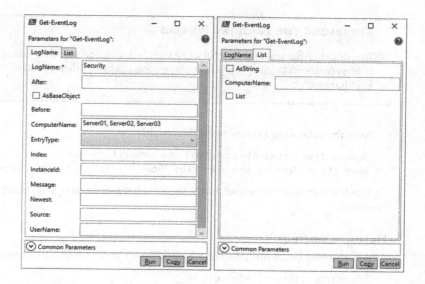

When you select Copy, PowerShell will copy the resultant command in your Clipboard. If you select Run, it will put the resultant command in the PowerShell console that was used to launch the Show-Command. This is how the result will appear:

```
Get-EventLog -LogName security -ComputerName Server01, Server02, Server04^M
```

The ^M at the end represents the Enter character. If you then press Enter on your keyboard, the command will execute.

Using -WhatIf

-WhatIf is a handy parameter. It lets you see the result of a cmdlet without the cmdlet making any changes to your system. Note that the colon is mandatory if you pass $true or $false. If you don't pass any parameters, it will default to $true. This helps you to verify that the command you used gave you the desired output and results. Nothing is changed and no actions are performed when you use a cmdlet with the -WhatIf parameter.

You will see whatever output would be generated *if* the cmdlet executed. This can be a big help when you are unsure of the exact format. This can also help you out a lot if you decide to do cmdlets without labeling the parameters and instead rely on parameter positions. Putting the parameter in the wrong order is very common, and -WhatIf can help prevent you from making a serious configuration error. Of course, Microsoft recommends that you always put parameter labels on any written script or reference file. Doing so makes it much easier to read and troubleshoot. Then you can use -Whatif as a failsafe to ensure you get the expected output.

Note the following example and the result:

```
Remove-Item C:\nano\nano-srv02.vhd -WhatIf
What if: Performing the operation "Remove File" on target "C:\nano\nano-srv02.vhd".
```

The file was never removed, but it shows what would have happened if the cmdlet had been executed.

Using -*Confirm*

This parameter helps mitigate risks by asking for confirmation prior to running a command:

```
-Confirm[:{$true | $false}]
```

It will temporarily override the $ConfirmPreference variable. The $ConfirmPreference variable has a default value of High. This is compared to the estimated risk potential of a cmdlet. If the risk potential is equal or greater that the $ConfirmPreference setting, the cmdlets will always ask for confirmation unless you add a -Confirm: $False. Other, less risky cmdlets will typically suppress confirmation.

The -Confirm parameter is also useful if you are doing mass changes, possibly as part of a loop. It will ask you to confirm for each operation. This can help prevent applying incorrect configurations to items that may not be readily obvious, like contents read from a file or items that are identified by calculation or other less visible means.

When you use -Confirm in ISE, you will get a dialog box as displayed in Figure 2.11.

FIGURE 2.11
-Confirm parameter in ISE

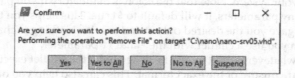

When you use the -Confirm parameter in a regular PowerShell console, you will see the following:

```
Remove-Item C:\nano\nano-srv05.vhd -Confirm
Are you sure you want to perform this action?
Performing the operation "Remove File" on target "C:\nano\nano-srv05.vhd".
[Y] Yes  [A] Yes to All  [N] No  [L] No to All  [S] Suspend  [?] Help (default is
"Y"):
```

It doesn't matter if you get the dialog box or the text on the console; the options presented are identical and have identical results.

If you select Yes, the operation will be performed. If the operation is part of a loop, you will receive additional confirmation prompts. If you select Yes To All, the operation will be performed, including any looping, and further confirmation prompts will be suppressed for this cmdlet's operation. If you select No, the operation will not be performed, but you may be further prompted if the cmdlet is performing multiple iterations of the cmdlet, possibly in a loop. If you select No To All, all operations will cease for this cmdlet and you will not see any subsequent prompts.

The Suspend option is going to put the current cmdlet on hold and start a nested PowerShell session. This nested session will be indicated by adding two additional caret symbols (>>) in the command prompt. In this nested session, you can run additional cmdlets and scripts. When you are done with the nested session, you can leave it by entering **Exit**. This will return you back to the -Confirm prompt. You will then need to decide your confirmation options, as previously discussed. This can give you an opportunity to load up some variables or do other tasks you need to ensure the cmdlet will work when you return.

The ? option for this -Confirm prompt will display help for the confirm choices.

The default action is Y, or Yes. This will be sent to the console if you are just holding down the Enter key. Be cautious! If you are holding down the Enter key, it will automatically confirm to Yes and the cmdlet will execute.

All About "About" Files

Get-Help is very useful to find specific information on particular cmdlets. Microsoft has also included "About" files that help explain PowerShell concepts covering items such as scripting techniques, scripting languages, operators, and others. The About help files do not support -Full or -Example, because they cover only concepts and topics. They will support -Online and -ShowWindow.

To see a listing of all of the locally available About files, simply enter the following:

```
Get-Help About
```

Get-Help About can be used when you want to see the About file for a particular topic. You simply would add the topic name. For example:

```
Get-Help About_Aliases
```

This help topic will have a short description and a long description. Here is a sample portion of the output:

```
PS C:\Users\Administrator> Get-Help about_Aliases

TOPIC
    about_aliases

SHORT DESCRIPTION
    Describes how to use alternate names for cmdlets and commands in Windows
    PowerShell.
```

```
LONG DESCRIPTION
     An alias is an alternate name or nickname for a cmdlet or for a command
element, such as a function, script, file, or executable file. You can use the
alias instead of the command name in any Windows PowerShell commands.
     To create an alias, use the New-Alias cmdlet. For example, the following
command creates the "gas" alias for the Get-AuthenticodeSignature cmdlet:
     New-Alias -Name gas -Value Get-AuthenticodeSignature

     After you create the alias for the cmdlet name, you can use the alias instead
of the cmdlet name. For example, to get the Authenticode signature for the
SqlScript.ps1 file, type:
     Get-AuthenticodeSignature SqlScript.ps1
Or, type:
     gas SqlScript.ps1
```

Looking at this small portion of the About_Alias, you can start to see how you can make your own alias. You can create an alias for cmdlets, scripts, functions, or even executables. Reading further in the About file should tell you what you need to do to create an alias.

ALIASES CAN MAKE LIFE EASY, OR HARD

Administrators will sometimes make aliases to replace long commands with something that is easier to type—and remember. Dir is an alias for Get-ChildItem. Just remember that unless you declare aliases in the code or load them in your profile, your aliases won't survive between sessions. If you build a library of aliases, you will also make it very difficult for anyone not familiar with your "home-brew" replacement commands to maintain your code. Customization is awesome, but you need to balance convenience with long-term usability.

Understanding Shortened Command Syntax

PowerShell tries to be very accommodating. Microsoft knows there are hundreds of cmdlets. Microsoft has also spent a great deal of effort trying to make these cmdlets fairly intuitive. When you are using the same commands over and over, typing the entire command becomes tedious, especially since some of these commands are quite long. You also run into the issue of not being entirely certain of the exact cmdlet syntax you should use. Microsoft has included a shortened syntax, as well as aliases and tab-completion to make your jobs a bit easier.

Shortened command syntax with tab completion means you can type part of a command and then press the Tab key to ask PowerShell to look at all of the session-loaded modules to try to figure out which command you are trying to use. If there are several choices, you can keep pressing the Tab key to cycle through the commands until you find the one you want. You can also do this with parameters.

Figuring out the exact command or parameter name with tab completion provides two advantages: you can get the correct cmdlet or parameter and the complete cmdlet and parameter name will be displayed so the text is easier to read, understand, maintain, and troubleshoot. Here is an example:

```
Get-Service MpsSVC -ComputerName Boston-Srv01
```

If you just typed **G** and then pressed the Tab key, you would have to cycle through all of the cmdlets, verbs, and aliases that start with the letter *G*. The list is quite long. The problem is you are too ambiguous. You need to disambiguate, or type enough letters so PowerShell has a better idea as to which command you are looking to use. Get- is pretty easy to understand and remember because it is used all the time. You will just type **Get-S**. There are a lot of Get commands where the "noun" starts with the letter S. If you kept pressing the Tab key over and over, you would eventually get there; but to save time, let's disambiguate even more by adding a few more characters. Be aware that PowerShell will be sifting through all the modules you have loaded for this particular session. Depending on the profile, defaults, and the modules located and loaded in the $env:PSModulePath variable, the number of letters you need to type to thin down the list may vary by system, session, and profile.

The next thing you would like in your command is the name of the service. If you read the Get-Help Get-Service information, you will see that you can simply press the Enter key and the Get-Service command will give you a list of services that are running on the local machine. If you just press the Tab key instead, the services will be listed automatically until you see the one you want.

Remember that PowerShell doesn't possess magic powers that automatically reach out to remote machines to guess what you mean to type. You can write scripts and functions that help automate the process, but you may need to start a session on the remote machine to load all the modules or import the modules to your local console. Of course, you can simply just type the command as well. The end result is the same. Our tab completion exercise on your cmdlet now looks like this:

```
Get-Ser MP TAB TAB
```

This turns into Get-Service MpsSvc.

The next bit is a parameter. You type and find that it becomes unique when you merely type -C TAB. Pressing the spacebar and then pressing the Tab key again won't give you a list of computers you can use. Here you will simply have to know the needed value.

So, what will happen if you just type enough characters to disambiguate the sections but you don't press the Tab key? This is how it would appear:

```
Get-ser mp -c boston-srv01
```

That's not very easy to read. If you press the Enter key, here is the result:

```
get-ser : The term 'get-ser' is not recognized as the name of a cmdlet, function,
script file, or operable program. Check the spelling of the name, or if a path was
included, verify that the path is correct and try again.
At line:1 char:1
+ get-ser mp -c boston-srv01
+ ~~~~~~
    + CategoryInfo          : ObjectNotFound: (get-ser:String) [],
CommandNotFoundException
    + FullyQualifiedErrorId : CommandNotFoundException
```

The little squiggle underneath + `get-ser` tells you that PowerShell has no cmdlet called `get-ser` in any of the loaded modules. This is an important concept. Typing sufficient characters to disambiguate cmdlets for tab completion does not resolve to shortcuts for commands. Disambiguation of parameters works, but commands need to be complete or an alias needs to be used.

MAKING YOUR LIFE EASIER

You should always try to use tab completion and full parameter names to make your code easier to read, understand, troubleshoot, and maintain. Shortened commands are nice for quick and dirty operations, but tab completion gives you additional assurances because it makes it more obvious that what you are asking PowerShell to accomplish is what you actually intend. In written code, as with your scripts, always use complete commands and parameters. Always.

Exploring PowerShell Command Concepts

Using the alias `Help`, instead of `Get-Help`, tells PowerShell to display only one screen full of information at a time. You can use `Get-Help` or `Help` to discover more commands. Remember that asking for help doesn't make any changes to your system. You can guess all you want to try to discover exactly what it is you are trying to accomplish.

Let's say that you want to change the MAC address of a network adapter. You can start off pretty basic with the following command:

```
Get-Command *adapter
```

The * is a wildcard character that says to get any command that ends with adapter. Removing the Hyper-V specific stuff at the bottom, here is the output:

```
CommandType     Name                            Version    Source
-----------     ----                            -------    ------
Function        Add-NetEventNetworkAdapter      1.0.0.0    NetEventPacketCapture
Function        Add-NetEventVmNetworkAdapter    1.0.0.0    NetEventPacketCapture
Function        Disable-NetAdapter              2.0.0.0    NetAdapter
Function        Enable-NetAdapter               2.0.0.0    NetAdapter
Function        Get-NetAdapter                  2.0.0.0    NetAdapter
Function        Get-NetEventNetworkAdapter      1.0.0.0    NetEventPacketCapture
Function        Get-NetEventVmNetworkAdapter    1.0.0.0    NetEventPacketCapture
Function        Remove-NetEventNetworkAdapter   1.0.0.0    NetEventPacketCapture
Function        Remove-NetEventVmNetworkAdapter 1.0.0.0    NetEventPacketCapture
Function        Rename-NetAdapter               2.0.0.0    NetAdapter
Function        Restart-NetAdapter              2.0.0.0    NetAdapter
Function        Set-NetAdapter                  2.0.0.0    NetAdapter
```

`Set-NetAdapter` looks promising. Let's do a `Help Set-Netadapter` command. Here seems to be the relevant output:

```
Set-NetAdapter [-Name] <String[]> [-AsJob] [-CimSession <CimSession[]>]
[-IncludeHidden] [-MacAddress <String>] [-NoRestart] [-PassThru] [-ThrottleLimit
<Int32>] [-VlanID <UInt16>] [-Confirm] [-WhatIf] [<CommonParameters>]
```

The -MacAddress stuff is highlighted. Remember, PowerShell doesn't yet have mind-reading powers. Give Cortana a bit of time.

If you do the same command but add the -Examples parameter and scroll a bit, you discover the following:

```
Example 2: Set the MAC address of the specified network adapter

    Set-NetAdapter -Name "Ethernet 1" -MacAddress "00-10-18-57-1B-0D"
    This command sets the MAC address of the network adapter named Ethernet 1.
```

So, now you know that you can change the MAC address with a simple command. You can use the same technique to discover all sorts of additional commands. The idea is that if you want to accomplish a specific task, you can usually find a command that does the job.

Implementing Pipelines

You frequently want to chain commands together with the output of one command becoming the input to the next command. Microsoft PowerShell makes it easy by using the vertical pipe (|) character. On many keyboards, this character is on the same key as the backslash character (\) only shifted.

You can use the pipe character to connect several commands together. These will be evaluated from the left to the right. The output of the left command will be added to the pipeline and will be sent as an input to the following command, to the right. If you have multiple pipeline characters, they are always evaluated from the left to the right.

Each time you press the Enter key, you will run the entire pipeline and any final output of the last command will be displayed. Not all commands will have a displayable output. Look at the following example:

```
Get-EventLog Security | Out-File c:\SecurityEvents.txt
```

This will get the contents of the local Security event logs and put them in the pipeline. This data is then fed to the Out-File command, which takes the contents of the pipeline and uses that as the input source. The end result is that the contents of the Security event log will be sent to a text file because of the nature of the Out-File cmdlet. Most PowerShell commands do not produce text files. PowerShell commands will typically produce objects.

Exploring Objects and Members

Objects have something called a *member*. Members are just the various components that make up an object. The members for an object may include properties, events, and methods. You can use the pipeline to get information about the members of a particular object by getting the object and then piping the results into the Get-Member cmdlet, as illustrated:

```
Get-Service | Get-Member
```

Be aware that the first command, Get-Service, *will* run. In this example, it isn't too dangerous; but if you were looking at the members of a destructive command, such as Remove-Item, you will actually remove the specific item. The -WhatIf parameter won't work because it only provides a text output to the console and doesn't produce any actual output to the Get-Member cmdlet.

You also need to ensure that the output of the first command will match the expected input of the next command in the pipeline. Examine the following code:

```
Get-Service | Set-ACL
```

The Get-Service command's output doesn't match the input requirements of the Set-ACL command. This will just produce an error for each of the objects the Get-Service command places into the pipeline. When you are using pipelines, you always need to match the output of the previous command to the expected input of the next command.

As you move back to your original command, Get-Service | Get-Member, you will see that the members of the objects that Get-Service places in the pipeline have properties, events, and methods.

Exploring Properties, Events, and Methods

Properties describe the various attributes of an object. Using Get and Set commands will typically work with properties. Some of the properties of the Service object are MachineName, StartType, and CanShutdown. These properties can be used to instruct PowerShell what to display or manipulate.

Events can be triggered as an operation does something to an object. Opening a file or running a process may trigger an event. The only event listed as a member from Get-Service is the Disposed event. Disposed tells you that the script has been instructed to free up external resources such as file handles, database connections, or TCP ports. When you get deeper into PowerShell programming, the event of Disposed can help you ensure these resources are released.

This can be particularly important if you get a bit too creative in copying snippets of scripts for reuse. Frequently, administrators will grab promising sections but forget to grab the garbage cleanup sections. This results in resource consumption, without resource release. This can make systems unstable or actually cause the exhaustion of resources, leading to a possible crash. As you get more advanced into PowerShell scripting, you'll want to ensure you always clean up your mess, and the Disposed event lets you know that cleanup has occurred.

Methods are used when you want to tell an object to perform some type of action. Close, Pause, Start, and Stop are all examples of methods associated with the Service object. This will help us, obviously, close, pause, start, and stop service. Pretty handy. Maybe you should add that to your library of cool cmdlets.

Properties, events, and methods are very specific to each type of object. Remember that it is the command that produces the objects. Some commands will produce multiple types of objects. If you use a Get-Member command on a pipeline with multiple types of objects, you will get separate member lists for each type of object. If you didn't send this to a text file, you can pull in so many objects and members that it will overwhelm the console buffer and will produce unusable output. It looks pretty cool, but it's ultimately pointless.

Performing Object Sorting

Visualizing objects as a table in a spreadsheet can be useful. Each column will have a different property, and each row identifies the particular object. Running a command that returns several objects will be like adding rows to the table.

For example, Get-Service, if dumped into a spreadsheet, would create a table as illustrated in Table 2.1.

TABLE 2.1:   Get-Service Objects

STATUS	NAME	DISPLAYNAME
Stopped	AJRouter	AllJoyn Router Service
Stopped	ALG	Application Layer Gateway Service
Stopped	ApplDsvc	Application Identity
Running	Appinfo	Application Information
Stopped	AppMgmt	Application Management
Stopped	AppReadiness	App Readiness

Only some of the objects were included because there are more than 200. Each row in the table is an object. Each column is a property of that object. Not all properties are displayed by default, but they are still included in the objects that are put into the pipeline. This group of objects is called a *collection*, or an *array*, of objects.

You can use PowerShell to pull a list of objects into a pipeline and then sort the objects according to whatever criteria you need. Frequently, cmdlets will automatically sort objects in the pipeline alphabetically by the name of the object. That is what the default is on the Get-Service cmdlet in Table 2.1.

You can instruct PowerShell to sort on different properties or even a combination of properties if you know the particular name of the desired property of an object. By default, string properties aren't case-sensitive and are sorted in ascending order. The objects sorted are based on the default properties of an object type.

You have the ability to change the defaults to meet your particular needs. You will use the Sort-Object cmdlet. This cmdlet has an alias of simply Sort. Here are some examples of the Sort-Object cmdlet:

```
Get-Service | Sort-Object -Property Name -Descending
Get-Service | Sort-Object Name -Descending
Get-Service | Sort-Object -Descending
```

All three examples do the same thing because the name is the default sorting key. If you look at Help Sort-Object, you will get the following syntax:

```
Sort-Object [[-Property] <Object[]>] [-CaseSensitive] [-Culture <String>]
[-Descending] [-InputObject <PSObject>] [-Unique] [<CommonParameters>]
```

You can explore the deeper syntax by searching for About_Sort-Object, but some parameters are immediately useful.

◆ [[-Property] <Object[]>] tells you that you can specify one or more properties. This is an optional parameter, but you can pass multiple parameters in a comma-separated list. If you pass multiple properties, they will be sorted by the first listed property. If more than one object has the same first property, then the objects will be sorted by the second listed property. If the first two properties have more than one result, it will be sorted by the third property, etc.

◆ [-Unique] is an optional parameter that looks through the pipeline and identifies only unique members of the pipeline collection. Any duplicates will simply be discarded. This parameter is not case-sensitive.

So, if you wanted to sort the services based on status and then by name, you would use the following command:

```
Get-Services | Sort-object -Property Status, Name
```

Status	Name	DisplayName
Stopped	AJRouter	AllJoyn Router Service
Stopped	ALG	Application Layer Gateway Service
Stopped	AppIDSvc	Application Identity
Stopped	AppMgmt	Application Management
Stopped	AppReadiness	App Readiness
Stopped	AppVClient	Microsoft App-V Client
Stopped	AppXSvc	AppX Deployment Service (AppXSV)
Stopped	AudioEndpointBu...	Windows Audio Endpoint Builder
Stopped	Audiosrv	Windows Audio
Stopped	AxInstSV	ActiveX Installer (AxInstSV

If you examined the pipeline, you would see the objects and their properties sorted by the Status property, followed by the Name property.

Measuring Objects

You may find it useful in your scripts to measure the various objects. This can include the number of objects in a pipeline. You will use the Measure-Object cmdlet. Here is the syntax:

```
Measure-Object [[-Property] <String[]>] [-Average] [-InputObject <PSObject>]
[-Maximum] [-Minimum] [-Sum] [<CommonParameters>]
```

The Measure-Object cmdlet, by default, will count just the number of objects in a collection. You can also perform four other types of measurements: the average, the sum, the maximum, and the minimum. Note the output of the following command:

```
Get-Process | Measure-Object -Property WorkingSet -Minimum -Maximum -Average -Sum

Count    : 70
Average  : 40100776.2285714
Sum      : 2807054336
Maximum  : 684228608
Minimum  : 4096
Property : WorkingSet
```

The working set is the amount of RAM associated with a particular process. This command will gather all of the running processes in a system. You have 70. These objects, with all their properties, will then be handed over as a collection in the pipeline to the Measure-Object cmdlet.

You also provided instructions to measure the objects based on the object's WorkingSet property. The Measure-Object cmdlet will then show you the average amount of memory consumed by all 70 processes. It also shows you the largest amount of RAM assigned to a process, the Maximum. It shows the least amount of RAM assigned to a process working set, the Minimum. Potentially, the most useful would be the Sum. This is the total amount of RAM that is assigned to all the processes on this system. You can use this information to determine the minimum amount of RAM needed to support the running processes without the need to start sending RAM to the page file.

WHAT IS RUNNING NOW MAY NOT BE WHAT IS RUNNING LATER

Remember that things can change. You shouldn't rely on one measurement of the current sum of the working set to spec out your servers. You need to measure these things over time. If you were going to use your little snippet of code, you might want to add additional bits and lump the entire thing into a script that runs as a scheduled job. This shows how you can take the things you have learned earlier in the chapter, and in the book, and use them with things you are learning now and in the future.

Using *Select-Object* to Select a Subset of Objects in a Pipeline

You may not want to look at all the objects in a pipeline collection. This is particularly true if you only want to look at the top or bottom number of objects in a collection. To do that, you use the Select-Object cmdlet. Here is the syntax:

```
Select-Object [[-Property] <Object[]>] [-ExcludeProperty <String[]>]
    [-ExpandProperty <String>] [-First <Int32>] [-InputObject <PSObject>] [-Last
    <Int32>] [-Skip <Int32>] [-Unique] [-Wait] [<CommonParameters>]
```

Select-Object will go into the pipeline collection and allow you to select the first, or last, of however many objects. These correspond to the rows in your collection. You can also select specific properties to include and exclude. For example, if you want to look at the top five processes consuming RAM on your system, you use the following command:

```
Get-Process|Sort-Object -Property WorkingSet -Descending | Select-Object -Property
Workingset, ProcessName -First 5
```

```
WorkingSet        ProcessName
----------        -----------
 635871232          powershell
 177840128                vmms
 147591168       powershell_ise
 143896576              LobAPP
 112848896       ServerManager
```

You can select specified properties of an object. You can specify -First and -Last to display a certain number from the top or the bottom of the collection. Note that if you don't sort the collection before you select the objects, they will be in random order. You can skip a particular number of objects with the -Skip parameter. You can also select only unique values with the -Unique parameter.

Select-Object will remove all nonspecified properties when you use the -Properties parameter. If you want to view all of the properties, but selectively remove specific properties, use the -Exclude parameter.

POWERSHELL GETS IT WRONG SOMETIMES

Be aware that PowerShell doesn't always display the correct property names for an object. If you just ran a Get-Process command, you would see the default displayed properties. The property titles listed at the top of the column might not be the actual name of the property. For example, WS (k) refers to the property WorkingSet. There is an alias for WorkingSet, WS. You could use -Parameter WorkingSet or -Parameter WS. If you tried -Parameter WS (k), the command would fail because the object does not contain a WS (k) property, and any script that tries to use that false name will fail. To determine the actual property name, use the Get-Member cmdlet.

When you use pipelines, especially pipes that go to other pipes that go to other pipes, you have to be careful about the type and format of data. It is typically easier to troubleshoot one command at a time. You should take the first cmdlet and run it alone and see its outcome. Once that cmdlet works properly, you add the next command and work with that until it provides the outcome you need. You should continue this process as you build your ultimate command.

You can also type each command on a separate line so you can keep the various cmdlets straight in your head. If you end a command line with a pipe character, or you don't put in all of the mandatory parameters, or if you don't close all the quotation marks or bracket or braces, etc., you will go into the extended prompt mode. This is illustrated here:

```
PS C:\Users\Administrator> get-process|get-member |
>> sort-object '
>> name
>> '
```

In the first line, you pressed the Enter key after the pipe character. That told PowerShell there was more to come. You ended the second line with a single quote and you didn't close that quote until the fourth line. PowerShell understands that there is more to come, so you continue to get prompted. When you finally press the Enter key on the fourth line, PowerShell isn't expecting any other parameters or characters and finally executes the commands. You will see similar behavior any time you enter a command where you don't include mandatory parameters or you fail to include characters, such as closing quotes. If you find yourself stuck in extended prompt jail, with no idea what is to come next, you can always leave the extended prompt mode by pressing Ctrl+C. None of the commands you were carefully building will execute, and you will return to the normal command prompt.

Using File Input and Output Operations

Sometimes you want to save the results of a command or script to a file. You can use the redirection operator, or greater-than sign (>). Here is an example:

```
Get-Process|Sort-Object -Property WorkingSet -Descending | Select-Object -Property
Workingset, ProcessName -First 5 > "c:\Top 5 Processes Consuming RAM.txt"
```

This is a quick way to take whatever would have been displayed on the console and dump it directly into a file. The only issue is you are just blindly dumping the information. If you want more control, you should use the Out-File command. Here is the syntax:

```
Out-File [-FilePath] <String> [[-Encoding] {unknown | string | unicode |
bigendianunicode | utf8 | utf7 | utf32 | ascii | default | oem}] [-Append] [-Confirm]
[-Force] [-InputObject <PSObject>] [-NoClobber] [-NoNewline] [-WhatIf] [-Width
<Int32>]  [<CommonParameters>]
```

Here is an example of using the parameters of the Out-File command where you want to ensure you don't overwrite an existing file:

```
Get-Process|Sort-Object -Property WorkingSet -Descending | Select-Object -Property
Workingset, ProcessName -First 5 |Out-File "c:\Top 5 Processes Consuming RAM.txt"
-NoClobber
```

By default, Out-File will use Unicode format for the text file. This can be a problem for some search programs. You can add the -Encoding ASCII parameter. You may also want to avoid having a newline character. This will put everything in one big line. This is used if you don't want a line-separated list of values. Putting in a new line can be suppressed with the -NoNewline parameter.

You also need to pay attention to the width of the output. By default, the output is truncated based on the characteristics of the host. The default for the PowerShell console is 80 characters.

Note that any characters in a line beyond that are truncated and not word-wrapped. If you have more than 80 characters per line, you will need to use the -Width parameter, or you will lose any characters after the first 80 per line.

Converting Objects to Different Formats

PowerShell pipeline objects can be in several different formats. If you are trying to save these objects to a file, you may need to convert from the object's native format. PowerShell uses two verbs for object conversion, ConvertTo and Export. If you execute a Get-Command ConvertTo-*, you will find six cmdlets and one function. The command and output are shown here:

```
PS C:\Users\Administrator> Get-Command ConvertTo-*

CommandType          Name                    Version          Source
-----------          ----                    -------          ------

Function       ConvertTo-HgsKeyProtector   1.0.0.0                        HgsClient
Cmdlet                    ConvertTo-Csv     3.1.0.0    Microsoft.PowerShell.Utility
Cmdlet                   ConvertTo-Html     3.1.0.0    Microsoft.PowerShell.Utility
Cmdlet                   ConvertTo-Json     3.1.0.0    Microsoft.PowerShell.Utility
Cmdlet           ConvertTo-SecureString     3.0.0.0   Microsoft.PowerShell.Security
Cmdlet           ConvertTo-TpmOwnerAuth     2.0.0.0           TrustedPlatformModule
Cmdlet                    ConvertTo-Xml     3.1.0.0    Microsoft.PowerShell.Utility
```

Our primary focus resolves around converting pipeline contents to CSV, HTML, or XML.

Using *ConvertTo-CSV*

The ConvertTo-Csv cmdlet is pretty basic. Here is the syntax:

```
ConvertTo-Csv [-InputObject] <psobject> [[-Delimiter] <char>] [-NoTypeInformation]
[<CommonParameters>]
```

The value for the parameter -InputObject is the contents of the PowerShell pipeline. It is referenced as the <psobject> in the syntax. This piped-in object can be identified with a legacy $_ or the more recent $PSItem.

Many administrators still use the older $_ to use the object in the pipeline, but $PSItem is the current identifier. Either reference works in your expressions, but you may see one or the other in scripts, help files, and About_ documents so you have to be familiar with both. We recommend that you transition to $PSItem, but there aren't any advertised plans to retire $_.

The -Delimiter parameter lets you change the character that identifies the various values. If you don't want commas to separate your values, but want a semicolon instead, you can use the -Delimiter ";" parameter.

The ConvertTo-Csv command will take the objects and convert them into comma-separated values. Each object will be converted into a string, and these strings will replace the contents of the pipeline. This ConvertTo-Csv command will not provide any output to the console. You are converting the contents of the pipeline to CSV format and replacing the current contents of the pipeline with resultant CSV strings. You will have a single string for each object.

The very first thing placed in the pipeline is the type information. You may not want this information in either the pipeline or in an output text file. You can suppress it with the

-NoTypeInformation parameter. The following is an example of the output with the type information:

```
Get-EventLog System | Select-Object EventId, EntryType -First 3 |ConvertTo-Csv
|Out-File "C:\Events.txt"
```

This command provides the following output in your text file:

```
#TYPE Selected.System.Diagnostics.EventLogEntry
"EventID","EntryType"
"7040","Information"
"7040","Information"
"7040","Information"
```

If you want to import this CSV into something like Excel, you will need to clean it. Notice the difference when you remove the type information:

```
Get-EventLog System | Select-Object EventId, EntryType -First 3 |ConvertTo-Csv -
NoTypeInformation |Out-File "C:\Events.txt"

"EventID","EntryType"
"7040","Information"
"7040","Information"
"7040","Information"
```

This result is much easier to manipulate and import. Remember that ConvertTo-Csv changes the contents of the pipeline collection of objects into a collection of strings. All methods and actions are discarded. The first object in the pipeline will have its properties used to define the field headers, with the values following. If subsequent objects in the pipeline don't have a property that was defined with the first object, or has no value for the defined property, the place where the value would be stored will be filled with a null value that is represented by two commas. If you have mixed objects in the pipeline and subsequent objects have additional properties that weren't included in the first object, those additional properties are simply discarded.

Using *Export-Csv*

Export-Csv creates a CSV file of the objects in the pipeline. Here is the syntax:

```
Export-Csv -InputObject <PSObject> [[-Path] <String>] [-LiteralPath <String>]
[-Force] [-NoClobber] [-Encoding <String>] [-Append] [-UseCulture]
[-NoTypeInformation] [-WhatIf] [-Confirm] [<CommonParameters>]
```

These parameters are similar to what you have previously seen in the Out-File cmdlet. An important point is that you don't want to format the output prior to conversion. If you do, the Export-Csv cmdlet will convert the formatting properties to a csv file and not the object properties. You can select the properties of the object by using the Select-Object cmdlet because when you Select-Object specific properties, all of the other properties are removed.

Using *ConvertTo-Html*

The ConvertTo-Html cmdlet converts PowerShell objects in the pipeline to either an HTML page or an HTML fragment. Here is the syntax:

```
ConvertTo-Html [-InputObject <PSObject>] [[-Property] <Object[]>] [[-Body]
<String[]>] [[-Head] <String[]>] [[-Title] <String>] [-As <String>] [-CssUri
<Uri>] [-PostContent <String[]>] [-PreContent <String[]>] [<CommonParameters>]

Get-EventLog System | Select-Object EventId, EntryType -First 3 |ConvertTo-Html
|Out-File "C:\Events.htm"
```

This produces the following output:

```
<!DOCTYPE html PUBLIC "-//W3C//DTD XHTML 1.0 Strict//EN"
"http://www.w3.org/TR/xhtml1/DTD/xhtml1-strict.dtd">
<html xmlns="http://www.w3.org/1999/xhtml">
<head>
<title>HTML TABLE</title>
</head><body>
<table>
<colgroup><col/><col/></colgroup>
<tr><th>EventID</th><th>EntryType</th></tr>
<tr><td>7040</td><td>Information</td></tr>
<tr><td>7040</td><td>Information</td></tr>
<tr><td>7040</td><td>Information</td></tr>
</table>
</body></html>
```

This is displayed in a browser as illustrated in Figure 2.12.

FIGURE 2.12
ConvertTo-
Html output in
the default table
format

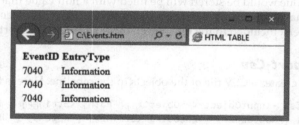

Note that you can use the –Head, -Body, and –Title parameters to replace any of these default entries with a custom value of choice. The –As parameter lets you choose between a table and a list. Table is the default and will be used if you omit the -As parameter. Figure 2.13 shows the same output with an –As List parameter added.

FIGURE 2.13
ConvertTo-Htm
with -As List

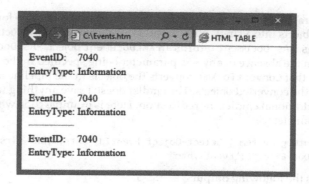

You can also use a -Fragment parameter, which only produces an HTML table. All of the other HTML elements, such as <Head>, <Body>, etc., are discarded.

There is no equivalent cmdlet to export to an HTML formatted file. You can perform a redirect, as illustrated here:

```
Get-EventLog System | Select-Object EventId, EntryType -First 3 |ConvertTo-Html >
c:\TopSystemLogs.html
```

Using *ConvertTo-Xml*

ConvertTo-XML will take objects in the PowerShell pipeline and convert them to an XML representation of the objects. When there are several objects in the pipeline, ConvertTo-Xml will create a single XML document that includes all of the objects. This cmdlet takes the created XML and replaces the content currently in the pipeline. Here is the syntax:

```
ConvertTo-Xml [-Depth <Int32>] [-InputObject] <PSObject> [-NoTypeInformation] [-As
<String>]
  [<CommonParameters>]
```

-Depth controls the level of conversion when an object's properties contain other objects. The lower object, in turn, may have properties that contain even more objects. You need to ensure that when you have objects that contain other objects, you let PowerShell know the depth of conversion you want; otherwise, you will lose the XML representation of these contained objects. This setting can be overridden for the object types in the Types.ps1xml files.

Types.ps1xml files allow you to add additional members to object types in PowerShell. This allows the addition of extended type data consisting of additional properties and methods to objects. The Types.ps1xml file is located in the PowerShell installation directory and is loaded any time a PowerShell session is stated. You will also load a Types.ps1xml file when you import a module into a session. You can also temporarily add extended type data using the Update-TypeData cmdlet. This is not saved to a file and is discarded when a session closes.

-NoTypeInformation removes the type attribute from the object nodes. You have seen the results of this parameter in the ConvertTo-Csv cmdlet.

The `-As` parameter instructs PowerShell to convert to one of three formats. `-As String` converts the objects into a single string. `-As Stream` converts the objects in the pipeline into an array of strings. `-As Document` returns an XMLDocument object. `-As Document` is the default and will be used in the absence of any `-As` parameter being specified in the cmdlet.

Remember that `ConvertTo-Xml` converts the objects in the pipeline and then replaces the pipeline with the converted objects. The cmdlet doesn't save anything to a file. Saving the results will require additional cmdlets or redirection. Here is example code where you specified the `-As Document` parameter.

```
Get-EventLog System | Select-Object EventId, EntryType -First 3 |ConvertTo-Xml -As
Document|Out-File "C:\Events.htm"
```

This produces the following output:

```
xml                               Objects
---                               -------
version="1.0" encoding="utf-8" Objects
```

The input objects, in this case, don't seem to convert well into a standard XML document. The following is the output with the `-As String` parameter that loads the entire pipeline into a single string:

```
<?xml version="1.0" encoding="utf-8"?>
<Objects>
  <Object Type="System.Management.Automation.PSCustomObject">
    <Property Name="EventID" Type="System.Int32">7036</Property>
    <Property Name="EntryType" Type="System.Diagnostics.
EventLogEntryType">Information</Property>
  </Object>
  <Object Type="System.Management.Automation.PSCustomObject">
    <Property Name="EventID" Type="System.Int32">7036</Property>
    <Property Name="EntryType" Type="System.Diagnostics.
EventLogEntryType">Information</Property>
  </Object>
  <Object Type="System.Management.Automation.PSCustomObject">
    <Property Name="EventID" Type="System.Int32">7036</Property>
    <Property Name="EntryType" Type="System.Diagnostics.
EventLogEntryType">Information</Property>
  </Object>
</Objects>
```

Here is the output with the `-As Stream` parameter, which loads each object as a separate string that is stored as an array:

```
<?xml version="1.0" encoding="utf-8"?>
<Objects>
<Object Type="System.Management.Automation.PSCustomObject">
  <Property Name="EventID" Type="System.Int32">7036</Property>
```

```
      <Property Name="EntryType" Type="System.Diagnostics.
EventLogEntryType">Information</Property>
    </Object>
    <Object Type="System.Management.Automation.PSCustomObject">
      <Property Name="EventID" Type="System.Int32">7036</Property>
      <Property Name="EntryType" Type="System.Diagnostics.
EventLogEntryType">Information</Property>
    </Object>
    <Object Type="System.Management.Automation.PSCustomObject">
      <Property Name="EventID" Type="System.Int32">7036</Property>
      <Property Name="EntryType" Type="System.Diagnostics.
EventLogEntryType">Information</Property>
    </Object>
  </Objects>
```

Using *Export-Clixml*

Export-Clixml is quite similar to ConvertTo-Xml; but just as with Export-Csv, the output will be saved to a file and won't just replace the contents of the pipeline. Here is the syntax:

```
Export-Clixml [-Depth <Int32>] [-Path] <String> -InputObject <PSObject> [-Force]
[-NoClobber] [-Encoding <String>] [-WhatIf] [-Confirm] [<CommonParameters>]
```

Encrypting an Exported Credential Object with *Export-Clixml*

One frequent use of Export-Clixml is to export credentials in an encrypted format. This allows you to store credentials you would use in a script without exposing the credentials in cleartext inside the body of a script or in the pipeline itself.

To get the credential, you can use the Get-Credential cmdlet to pop up a dialog box and put the username and password into a variable. Get-Credential can use a generic credential dialog box, a custom dialog box with a message, or it can prompt the user via the command line. The command-line prompting requires a Registry entry.

Here is the required code to allow command-line prompting for credentials:

```
Set-ItemProperty "HKLM:\SOFTWARE\Microsoft\PowerShell\1\ShellIds" -Name
"ConsolePrompting" -Value $True
```

Here is the syntax:

```
Get-Credential [-Credential] <PSCredential> [<CommonParameters>]
```

The simplest form is getting the credential and storing it into a variable as follows:

```
$CredentialStorageVariable = Get-Credential -Credential "Contoso\ServiceAcct01"
```

This prompts the user for a username and password and then creates a PSCredential object. Since you used the -Credential parameter, the user name field will already be populated, but it is still editable. If you leave off the -Credential parameter, all of the fields will be blank. Refer to Figure 2.14 to see the Get-Credential dialog box.

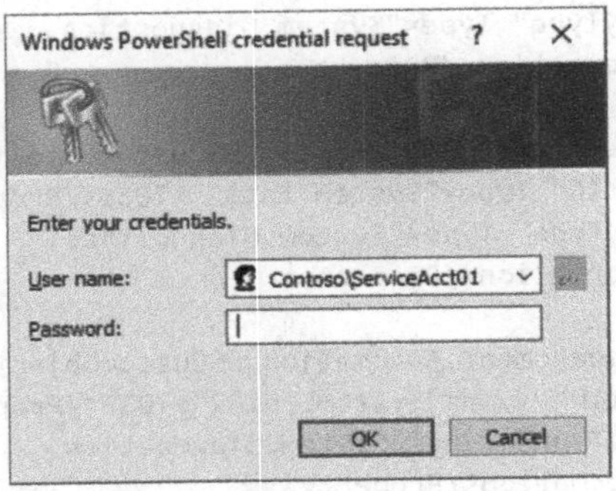

FIGURE 2.14
Get-Credential
dialog box

You can also create the dialog box with a custom message. This is called a `MessageSet`. This is accomplished using the following code:

```
$credentialStorageVariable = Get-Credential -Message "We need your credentials to
connect to the remote server"
```

The custom message is displayed, as illustrated in Figure 2.15.

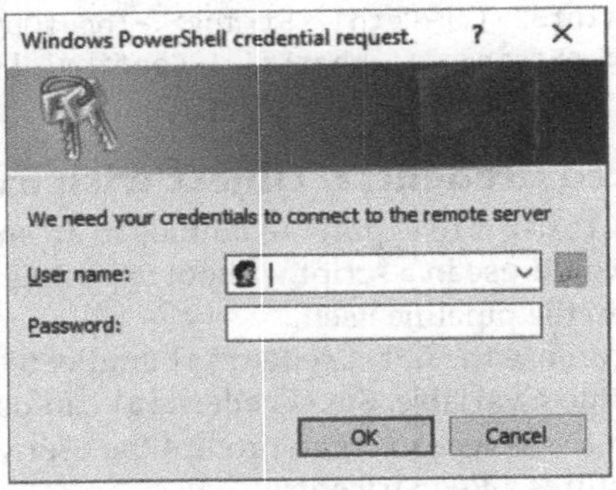

FIGURE 2.15
Get-Credential
MessageSet
dialog box

The `PSCredential` object is then stored in the identified variable. In this case, you store the results in the `$credentialStorageVariable`. This is just a variable name you created. You can call the variable whatever you like.

The members of the `PSCredential` object include only two properties, `Password` and `Username`. You can view the contents of both by simply typing the variable in its own line:

```
$credentialStorageVariable
UserName                        Password
--------                        --------
Contoso\ServiceAcct01    System.Security.SecureString
```

Note that the username is stored in cleartext in the variable, but the password is stored as a secure string. You can access these values individually by specifying the variable and then appending the name of the member you want, prefaced with a period. If you want to look at the value of the Username property of the variable, you can state the variable and append the property. Here is how you can view just the contents of the UserName and the Password property of your credential variable:

```
$credentialStorageVariable.UserName

Contoso\ServiceAcct01

$credentialStorageVariable.Password

System.Security.SecureString
```

Saving the Credentials to an XML File

Once you have the credential stored in a variable, you can then export the credentials into an XML file. Here is the code showing these two operations:

```
$credentialStorageVariable = Get-Credential
$credentialStorageVariable | Export-Clixml c:\OurCredentialFile
```

Note that you can replace the path with another variable to make this more modular. This command encrypts the object using the Windows Data Protection API.

If you load the resultant file into a text editor, this is what you will see:

```
<Objs Version="1.1.0.1" xmlns="http://schemas.microsoft.com/powershell/2004/04">
  <Obj RefId="0">
    <TN RefId="0">
      <T>System.Management.Automation.PSCredential</T>
      <T>System.Object</T>
    </TN>
    <ToString>System.Management.Automation.PSCredential</ToString>
    <Props>
      <S N="UserName">Contoso\ServiceAcct01</S>
      <SS N="Password">01000000d08c9ddf0115d1118c7a00c04fc297eb010000000cf4a23d
fab49a4c85b4026968824dc30000000002000000000010660000000100002000000285a7b2ff
b2022b66f3a89d321fcc13535f7fa75abff48479265484b9aae9b34000000000e80000000020000
20000000e802cd61458770bd5213de0bdc0944722abf28a6c86d7d81c8bb9ba96112860630000000
594c5e154bdec29b151d55c654de32ddfc222a3cd0a20fbedb6485e440bd516c3cdc225b722636
f1d02edb4fe027227f4000000025b101384a5ead762f526d315f71b1291c54368f6ffffaee4a6027
aa17e9529bdf8bb26d498a715aec9e56bdb5c7ff497e3ca27383d0894169220c5c8e8cb55a</SS>
    </Props>
  </Obj>
</Objs>
```

The username is still in cleartext, but the password is encrypted.

To import the credential into the script, simply load a variable with the object using the Import-Clixml command, as shown here:

```
$newCredentialVariable = Import-Clixml c:\OurCredentialFile
```

The `Password` property is still encrypted, but the credentials can now be used throughout your script.

Importing Data into PowerShell

When you import data from a file, or other external storage, you will be converting this formatted data back into objects. These objects can then be loaded into the pipeline and passed to other commands. PowerShell understands a number of formats, but not all formats are equally import friendly.

WHY NOT JUST USE CSV FILES?

Many administrators love CSV files. They are easy to create, and the first line will tell you what the property names are and then the rest is just blocks of data that are separated by commas or some other delimiter. One problem with using CSVs for storage is that you lose the hierarchical relationships. As such, storing and retrieving complex data structures is not supported when you use them.

There is a difference between importing data and reading data. Importing data is like reading a csv file into a spreadsheet, such as Microsoft Excel. With Excel, you will have column headings, typically the first line of the file. This prepares PowerShell with the Property to Value information. The header will list all of the properties these objects will use. As the rest of the file is imported, the CSV values will be added into the appropriate property. This makes it easy to pass the objects, with their intact parameters, to other commands for further processing.

If you use the `Get-Content` cmdlet, you aren't importing the file, you are merely reading it. No properties are defined, and the values are all loaded together. This is similar to simply reading the file with a basic text editor, such as Notepad. No intelligence is attached to match properties and values. The data that is read in may not have the expected structure, and you will need to ensure that your script gets the type of information it accepts.

Here is the syntax for the `Import-CSV` command:

```
Import-Csv [[-Path] <String[]>] [[-Delimiter] <Char>] [-Encoding {Unicode | UTF7 |
UTF8 | ASCII | UTF32 | BigEndianUnicode | Default | OEM}] [-Header <String[]>]
[-LiteralPath <String[]>] [<CommonParameters>]
```

When `Import-Csv` is used, it will first try to read the header of the input file to determine the properties of the objects it is importing. If there is no header, or it is empty, `Import-Csv` will insert a default header row name and will display a message. Before PowerShell version 3, the script would simply fail.

Processing Pipeline Data

The PowerShell pipeline can hold many objects with a variety of members. You may not want all of the objects that are loaded into the pipeline. This is particularly true if you have some complex sorting or processing further down in the script. You need to eliminate those objects that are unneeded. This process of selectively removing objects is called *filtering*.

SORTING ALL OF THE OBJECTS

Sorting all of the objects may not be efficient, particularly if you are just going to discard a bunch of them. It is like sorting candy by color and then eating them all in a mixed-up handful. It doesn't really accomplish anything. Having your script sort things you are just going to discard wastes resources, adds complexity, and is not a best practice.

When you want to remove an object, you typically compare it to some criteria. If the object matches the criteria, it will be evaluated as $True. Objects that come out as $True will be allowed to remain in the pipeline. If the object doesn't match your criteria, the object will be evaluated as $False and it will be removed.

Using Comparison Operators

Comparison operators come in many forms. They can be case-sensitive or case-insensitive. Some comparison operators allow wild cards. Some comparison operators will look for more than just string values stored in the properties of an object. Some will use regular expressions. It is useful to test comparison operators while writing scripts to ensure you are getting the value you expect. If you use a scalar value, in other words a single value, these comparison operators will return a $True or $False value. $True or $False are known as Boolean values. Look at the following code:

```
10 -eq 10
```

The -eq means equals. This will evaluate as $True. One to one comparisons will return only Boolean values. The two values you are comparing have names. In this case, the one on the right is the testing value. That is the data you are testing. The left value is the reference value. Both of these values are also known as *operands*.

If you have multiple values to compare, PowerShell will return any values that match, instead of returning $True or $False. Look at the following code and its result:

```
10,8,35,17,99,8,17,888,786 -eq 8

8
8
```

This is comparing a collection of numbers to the number 8. Note that none of the values are enclosed in quotation marks. If the values were surrounded by quotes, they wouldn't be numbers, they would be a *strings*. We will discuss data types a bit later.

Because you have to match the value exactly, you return two results. If you don't match any values, this operation will not return anything. Let's see what happens when you wrap it all up in quotation marks and evaluate this as a bunch of characters, also known as a string:

```
" 8","8 ", " 8 ", "888" -eq "8"
```

This returns nothing because none of the values *exactly* match. Enclosing the values in quotations makes them strings of text. A space is a character, just like an 8. When you compare

SPACE8 and 8SPACE to 8, they obviously don't match. You will see a comparison operator that can use wildcards a bit later.

This type of comparison, taking an expected value and comparing it to the actual contents of a variable or specific text, is a very useful troubleshooting technique. PowerShell will let you enter most comparisons directly into the console to test your logic. This is useful when building scripts to ensure you are evaluating the correct values and are getting the expected results.

Here are some basic comparison operators you can use to get started:

- **-eq:** This means equals. `10 -eq 10` comes out as true.
- **-ne:** This means not equal. `11 -ne 10` comes out as true.
- **-gt:** This means greater than. `11 -gt 10` comes out as true.
- **-lt:** This is a lowercase L, but you can put it in uppercase. This means less than. `11 -lt 10` is false.
- **-le:** This means less than or equal to. `10 -le 10` is true, but so is `2 -le 10`.
- **-ge:** This means greater than or equal to. `11 -ge 10` is true, but so is `200 -ge 10`.

All of these operators are case-insensitive. `"A" -eq "a"` is true. If you want your comparisons to be case-sensitive, you should precede the operator with a c. In other words, `-eq` becomes `-ceq`. If you want to make case-insensitivity explicit, precede the operator with an i. In other words, `-eq` becomes `-ieq`.

It is important to understand that these comparisons all require exact values. None of these comparison operators allow for any wildcards.

Using Wildcards and the *like* Operator

Sometimes you will allow a variety of values to match. This is where you can use wildcards. Wildcards can be used only with the `-like` or `-clike` operators. These are similar to the `-eq` operator, but you can use wildcards. The wildcard character of * means any number of characters, where ? means just this one character.

`"AAA" -like "*"` is True.

`"AAA" -like "*a"` is True.

`"aAA" -like "A?A"` is True.

`"ABA" -like "A?A"` is also True.

Consider the following:

`"Wyoming" -like "W*om?ng"`

The long form of what you are saying with this comparison is "Does the first value have a W in the first position, with any number of any characters between the W and the o? Is o directly followed by m? The next character after the m doesn't matter, but there has to be a character, and the string's next two characters have to be n and g. Also, there can't be anything after the g in the first value." The comparison will evaluate as True. The operator `-clike` does the same thing but is case-sensitive.

`"Wadfakdsfbasd123sdfasjomXng" -clike "W*om?ng"`

This comparison will also be evaluated as True.

COMPARING STRINGS TO FIND OUT WHICH IS GREATER

Question 3 brings up an interesting scenario. When evaluating two strings with -gt and -lt, the values are processed in alphabetical order. This means "a" is less that "b." Evaluating a string with -clt means that lowercase letters are "less" than uppercase letters. For example, "a" is less than "A."

Note that if you try 1 -gt "a", you will get an error because the 1 without quotes around it is interpreted as type System.Int32 value, where "a" is a type string. Because you are comparing literal values, the type of the first value will determine the expected type of the second value, and some types are not compatible with others.

If you try "1" -gt "a", you are comparing the character "1", the character "a". The character "1" is less than "a" in PowerShell. If you try "a" -gt 1, you will get a True because the "a" value is a string type so PowerShell will assume 1 is also a string.

If you try 1 -gt "a", you will get an error. That is because the 1 is an integer, and not a string. Since the first item being compared determins the type of the following items, PowerShell will try to convert "a" to an integer, and it will fail.

Type mismatch is a common mistake in PowerShell. If the values are in a variable, PowerShell may be able to convert. Obviously, the value of "ABCE" will never automatically convert to a 32-bit integer. It is good practice to test comparisons against known values to ensure you have the correct type and that your operators are acting as expected.

FORCING THE TYPE

You can force the type by prefixing the value or variable with the type enclosed in square brackets. This is known as *casting* the data type. This technique is useful to ensure that user-entered data will match your needed type, even if the user gets overly creative. For example, if you want to treat all input that is loaded into a variable by the user as text, use the following:

```
[String] $somethingTheUserInput
```

That way if the user types **12345**, it will be converted to the string "12345" and not the value of twelve thousand, three hundred, and forty-five.

Exploring Common Data Types

There are many data types in PowerShell. Some of which are really obscure. You can also create your own data types. Here are the most common you will use:

♦ [string]: Fixed-length string of Unicode characters

♦ [char]: Unicode 16-bit character

- ◆ [byte]: 8-bit unsigned character
- ◆ [int]: 32-bit signed integer
- ◆ [long]: 64-bit signed integer
- ◆ [decimal]: 128-bit decimal value
- ◆ [single]: Single-precision 32-bit floating-point number
- ◆ [double]: Double-precision 64-bit floating-point number
- ◆ [DateTime]: Holds the date and the time. Be careful of the format.
- ◆ [xml]: XML object
- ◆ [array]: Array of values, like rows and columns of a spreadsheet
- ◆ [hashtable]: Hash table object
- ◆ [void]: Discards the value

Consider the following:

```
[string] $myStringVar = "123.456"
```

This will load the variable $myStringVar with the characters 123.456. Remember this is just a bunch of characters. It is not a number. What do you expect will happen with the following commands?

```
[string]$MyStringVar = "123.456"
213.45 -gt $MyStringVar
```

PowerShell will look at the first value 213.45 and decide that this is a [single] data type because it isn't surrounded by quotations and has a decimal point. When PowerShell gets to the second value, it sees that that data type has been cast as a [string]; but when looking at the value, PowerShell realizes that it can be converted to a [single] because it doesn't contain anything but numbers and a decimal point. Because 213.45 is larger than 123.456, the comparison evaluates as True. Note that the $myStringVar remains a data type of [string]. The conversion is only for this comparison.

You need to be cautious when you convert an [int] data type from a value that is fractional, such as a [single] or a [string], to a value that contains only numeric characters and a decimal point. PowerShell will perform a Round() operation. This will round the value up or down. The value 123.1 will convert to 123. The value 123.5 will convert to 124. This can give you unexpected results that can be tricky to troubleshoot.

If you just want to truncate the decimals to the right of the decimal point, you will need to do a separate operation and call the system math function. Examine the following code:

```
[long] $myVar= 1234.5
[int]$myVar
```

This will give the result of 1235 as PowerShell, in the background, performs a Round() function. PowerShell doesn't have separate math functions, so you will need to call for [System .Math] or simply [Math]. Because you are doing a static method, you will need to separate it with double colons (::) before you call the actual function. Static simply means the function, [System.Math], already exists and you will be using its Truncate method.

Here is the code example:

```
[long] $myVar = 1234.5
[Math]::Truncate($myVar)
```

This will return the value of 1234. It simply sliced off everything to the right of the decimal point. Note that this is also a temporary operation. $myVar still actually equals 1234.5. The result of the Truncate method is only for the single call. The value of the variable doesn't actually change. If you wanted to make it permanent, you would need to assign the value directly to the variable, either by typing the characters or loading up $myVar from another variable with the [int] data type. You could also simply use this operation to load a different variable:

```
$myTruncatedValueVar = [Math]::Truncate($myVar)
```

If you want to get a list of other static methods inside of [System.Math], you can use the following code:

```
[System.Math] | Get-Member -Static
```

This will give you a list of many mathematic methods.

Determining Data Type with *-is*

If you want to determine the data type, you can use the type operator -is. You can use the following code to verify the data type of your two values, as shown here:

```
[string] $myStringVar = "123.456"
$myStringVar -is [String]
```

This will evaluate as True.

```
$mymysteryVar = "1234.5678"
$myMysteryVar -is [String]
```

This will also evaluate as True because you placed the characters inside of quotation marks. You can permanently convert the data type to an [int] by doing the following operation:

```
$myMysteryVar = "12345.2343"
$myMysteryVar = 12345
$myMysteryVar -is [string]
$myMysteryVar -is [int]
```

The first -is comparison will evaluate as False, and the second will evaluate as True. $myMysteryVar was a string; but when you assigned 12345 without quotes or a decimal point, it became an integer. What will be the outcome following the execution of the following lines of code?

```
$myStringVar = "12345"
$myIntVar = 98765
$myStringVar = $MyIntVar
$myStringVar -is [string]
```

This will evaluate as False. You replaced the value in $myStringVar with the contents of $myIntVar. PowerShell knows that the content of $myIntVar is [int] data type. Even though $myStringVar started off as a [string], PowerShell converted it to an [int] and replaced the value. This automatic conversion can be very handy when it is done intentionally. If you don't pay attention to data type, you can end up with scripts that sometimes work and sometimes don't. You should test with known values and be particularly careful when handling input data, especially data manually entered by people.

You can also invert this type operator by using -isnot. Note that the type operators, -is and -isnot, will return only True or False.

Finding Portions of Strings with *-match*

Sometimes you need to find if certain text is contained within a string or collection of strings. The operand -match can't search against anything except strings. Examine the following code:

```
"January" -match "Jan"
```

This will evaluate as True. This is a scalar input, which means it is a single value and not part of an array or collection of data. A single reference value is the important part. When you run this code, it will evaluate as True. Because the input is scalar, this operation will also populate the $Matches automatic variable. You can view the value of $Matches here:

```
$Matches
```

Name	Value
0	Jan

That shows that Jan did match something in the string. But what if you wanted to see what exactly you matched? Examine the following code:

```
"Srv-Den01", "DenaliRRAS04", "DC-Hedenar-05", "Lon-Win16-CA-05" -match "dEn"
```

This provides the following result:

```
Srv-Den01
DenaliRRAS04
DC-Hedenar-05
```

Because you are comparing your test value to multiple reference values, an array, you will not get a True or False. Instead, you will get a list of all of the matches. This will *not* populate the $Matches automatic variable; so if you run $Matches again to view the variable's value, it will still say Jan.

You can invert the selection to find which strings do *not* match with the following code:

```
"Srv-Den01", "DenaliRRAS04", "DC-Hedenar-05", "Lon-Win16-CA-05" -notmatch "dEn"
```

with the output of:

```
Lon-Win16-CA-05
```

This shows you the reference values you didn't match. Because the reference values are in an array, you will not get a True or False. You will get a list of all the reference values you matched, even if you match only one. You can use the -match operator to quickly locate strings for further manipulation.

Using the Containment Operators -*contains* and -*notcontains*

Containment operators return only Boolean results, True or False. Many people get this confused with your earlier operator -like. When you use -contains with a single value, you have to match the reference values, the left operand, exactly to the right operand, or testing value. Here's an example:

```
"Mark" -contains "M"
```

This will evaluate as False because it isn't the exact match. What about the following?

```
"M","Mark" -contains "m"
```

This evaluates as True because one of the reference values exactly matches the test value. So, this is pretty much like -eq, except "M","Mark" -eq "m" will return M and Mark because when you compare an array, or collection, of reference values, it will return all the reference values that match.

The advantage of -contains is that it returns only a Boolean value of True or False. You won't have to do additional processing if you have more than one match. Remember that if the -like operator matches more than one reference value, it will not return True or False. When you match more than one reference, -like will return all the matching values.

What happens if you compare an array to an array? Consider the following code:

```
"M", "Mark" -contains "m", "mar", "M", "Mark"
```

This always returns False because when the *test values*, the values on the right of the comparison, are an array, PowerShell shifts to what is called *reference equality*. What this means is that all of the attributes and properties of the *reference value*, the operands on the left, have to match all of the properties of the operands on the right. Look at the following code example:

```
"M","Mark" -contains "M","Mark"
```

Oddly enough, this also evaluates as False. Reference equality means that all attributes and properties of the reference value must match the test values' attributes and properties exactly. It looks like they match, but due to the strangeness that is reference equality, they are not exactly the same.

This is noteworthy because many administrators use the -contains or -notcontains operator to try to compare an array to an array, and they run into the wall of reference equality and can't figure out why their code fails. Digging into all the nuances of reference equality is a bit beyond the scope of this chapter. Most administrators will just use -like; just remember -like doesn't always return a Boolean True or False. You may need to code additional steps to provide a Boolean return.

Using the -*in* and -*notin* Operators

These operators will always return a Boolean True or False value. The test value is on the *left* this time, and the reference value is on the *right*. This is exactly the opposite of how -contains is set up. Also, the `-in` operator will use reference equality if your test value is an array. Just remember, the test value in this command is on the *left*. Consider the following code:

```
"J" -in "Jan", "January", "J"
```

This evaluates as True because your test value, "J", exactly matches at least one of your reference values. Consider the following code:

```
"J" -in "Jan", "January"
```

This will evaluate as False because your test value, "J", doesn't exactly match any of the reference values. It is similar to `-like`, except you can't use wildcards and you will return only a Boolean True or False.

If you switch the reference and the test values, things go off into reference equality land as now the test values are an array.

```
"Jan", "January", "Janus", "Bob" -in "Jan"
"Jan", "January", "Janus", "Bob" -in "Jan", "January", "Janus", "Bob"
```

Both of these will return False. The primary point is you need to know that the reference and test values are on opposite ends with the `-in` and `-notin` operators. Unless you understand how reference equality works, you need to ensure you have a single test value for both `-in` and `-contains`. This will give you a nice, clean Boolean True or False. If you try to get too clever and start using arrays as your test value, the results may be unexpected.

Using the *-replace* Operator

You may get data that requires you to change the input values to something else. For example, you may need to change a server's name value from "PHX-SER-01" to "SEASRV-01". This is what you can do:

```
"Phx-Ser-01" -replace "PHX-SER","SEASRV"

SEASRV-01
```

The format is INPUTSTRING -replace "MATCHME" , "Replacement".

Another interesting thing is the replacement doesn't have to be the same size. Here's an example:

```
"ABCDEFG" -replace "de","ILOVECOOKIES"
```

This will return ABCILOVECOOKIESFG.

You can also use `-replace` to delete by leaving off the replacement value: Look at the following code and result:

```
"ABCDEFG" -replace "de"
ABCFG
```

The `-replace` operator gives you a lot of power to manipulate items.

Using Variables

Variables are areas of memory that contain something. They can contain different types of data, as previously discussed. You will use variables to hold items that are used with commands, and you typically use variables to store the results of commands and provide input into other commands.

Variables are identified as a text string that starts with a $. The name $myVariable is one example. Note the variable itself is a text string, but that doesn't necessarily mean that the variable contains a text string. Think of a variable as a pointer to an area in memory that has some value, even if the value is NULL.

Because a variable is a text string and is not case-sensitive, you can include all sorts of characters in the variable's name. Variable names can include spaces and special characters. Placing spaces and special characters in the name of a variable can cause mass confusion as your code becomes difficult to read and difficult to use. PowerShell will refuse any variable name that contains spaces or special characters, with the exception of the underscore (_) character. If you insist on using characters, such as a hyphen or a space, you will need to enclose the command in a brace, as illustrated:

```
${my poorly-chosen variable name} = "This is a really bad idea."
```

Sometimes, you have to reference a variable that may have special characters. A good example is the environmental variable ${ENV:ProgramFiles(x86)}. If you needed to get a list, using your old friend Get-ChildItem, you would need to do the following:

```
Get-ChildItem ${ENV:ProgramFiles(x86)}
```

It is also a great idea to have some naming standard for variables. You should try for something that makes the purpose of a variable more obvious. $v is much harder to understand than $listOfServers. If there are several administrators, or coders, you want to have an approved naming standard that is intuitive, standardized, and rigorously enforced.

Exploring Types of PowerShell Variables

There are three types of variables: preference, automatic, and user-created. You already explored preference variables when you set up your custom PowerShell console. These variables are automatically created and populated with default values when your PowerShell session starts. You can change these values inside of your session, but the changes are lost when you close your session. If you want these preference variables to keep your changes between sessions, you will need to add the changes to your profiles.

Automatic variables are created by PowerShell and are automatically updated when PowerShell needs to keep track of something. $Matches is an example of an automatic variable. Users can't directly change these variables, but actions you do with cmdlets and operators, such as -match, will cause PowerShell to automatically change the values.

User-created variables are created from the console and from within scripts and functions. These variables exist only during the session and will be forgotten unless you save them in your profile.

Clearing and Removing Variables

To delete the value of a variable, you can simply set its value to $null or you can use a Clear-Variable cmdlet, as illustrated here:

```
$removeMyValue = $NULL
Clear-Variable -Name removeMyValueToo
```

Notice that these variables still exist. Their value has just been assigned to $Null. They are still taking up space.

If you want to actually remove a variable, you can use:

```
Remove-Variable $myUnneededVar
```

This will clear the value and remove the variable from memory. You still need to be aware of scoping because if you remove a variable that is locally scoped, only the locally scoped variable will be cleared. If there is a parent variable of the same name, you will now see that variable in the local scope.

Using the Variable Drive

PowerShell will create a pretend drive that will act like a drive that has a file system. This is used to hold all the variables and their assigned values that exist in your current session. You can change to the Variable: drive by treating it like file system drive, as follows:

```
Cd Variable:
```

This will, of course, call an alias. If you want to do this without the alias, you can do the following:

```
Set-Location Variable:
```

You can see the contents of this Variable: drive by changing your location and running the Dir or ls alias, or by using your friend Get-ChildItem, as illustrated here:

```
Set-location Variable:
Dir
Get-ChildItem Variable:
```

Using Environmental Variables

PowerShell will store environmental variables in another PowerShell drive called Env:. This is used to store information such as the Windows installation directory, the user directory, and the location of temp directory. To view the contents of this directory, you can do the same operations, as shown here:

```
Set-location env:
Dir
Get-ChildItem env:
Get-Item env:
```

These objects in the Env: drive won't have child items, so Get-Item and Get-ChildItem will return the same information.

Environmental variables are shared by parent and child sessions. This allows you to share values between parent and child sessions. You can view and manipulate environmental variables by prefacing the variable name with $env:, as shown here:

```
$env:Tmp
$windowsdirectory = $env:windir
$env:myNewEnvironmentalVariable = "Data that is available to the parent and child"
```

Using Functions

So far, you have executed cmdlets pretty much one at a time. Functions let you collect any number of PowerShell statements, give this series of statements a name, and execute them, one after the other. You can pass parameters to a function. You can make your own parameters for your function. You can take the output of a function and put it in a variable, or load up a pipeline, or even send the output to other cmdlets or functions.

Seeing Them in Action

Simply enter **Get-Help About_Functions** to see that a function is a block of code that is given a name. You also discover the basic format of a function. Here would be the code you use to create your function:

```
Function Snag-SecurityLog {Get-EventLog Security}
```

This command will create a function called Snag-SecurityLog. You can then create an alias to call your function:

```
New-Alias -Name View-SecurityLog -Value Snag-SecurityLog
```

So now you can enter **View-SecurityLog** to call the Snag-SecurityLog function that runs the Get-EventLog cmdlet. This isn't the most efficient way to get the logs, and it seems rather redundant. If you dig a bit deeper into the About_Functions file, you will find the following section:

```
Using Splatting to Represent Command Parameters
    You can use splatting to represent the parameters of a command.
    This feature is introduced in Windows PowerShell 3.0.
    Use this technique in functions that call commands in the session. You do not
need to declare or enumerate the command parameters, or change the function when
command parameters change.

    The following sample function calls the Get-Command cmdlet. The command uses
@Args to represent the parameters of Get-Command.
        function Get-MyCommand { Get-Command @Args }
```

Splatting

Splatting sounds strange, but by looking at the sample, and maybe digging a bit further, you will find that you can modify your alias to allow you to pass a parameter to the function and you won't have to declare the parameter, or even the number of parameters. So now your function and alias can be changed as follows:

```
Function View-ALog {Get-EventLog @Args}
New-Alias -Name Grab-Log -Value View-ALog
```

You have now modified your function and alias to give you the opportunity to use a single alias and pass a parameter to the function. This new alias can let you tell the function which log you are looking to retrieve. Here are some examples of what your newly discovered alias and function skills have provided:

```
Grab-Log Security
Grab-Log Application
Grab-Log System
```

This is not designed for efficiency but is designed to show you the breadth of information that is available in the About files and how to use these files to discover new ways of performing needed operations.

Creating Functions

Functions can be rather simple. If you want to find out how much RAM is being consumed by PowerShell, via a function, it could look like this:

```
PS C:\> Function Pull-ShellRam {Get-Process PowerShell}
PS C:\> Pull-ShellRam
Handles    NMP(K)    PM(K)    WS(K)    VM(M)    CPU(s)    ID    ProcessName
-------    ------    -----    -----    -----    ------    --    -----------
    657        22    50836     2967      571      0.72   312    powershell
```

You can name your function whatever you like. It is best practice to follow the standard verb-noun convention currently used by PowerShell. The verb should state what action your function is performing. The noun should identify the item that you are doing the action against.

NAMING FUNCTIONS AFTER EXISTING CMDLETS

You should avoid cmdlets that already exist. If you use a name that is already in use, your name will mask the original cmdlet and your function will be called in its place.

Here is the syntax for a function:

```
function [<scope:>]<name> [([type]$parameter1[,[type]$parameter2])]
{
  param([type]$parameter1 [,[type]$parameter2])
  dynamicparam {<statement list>}
  begin {<statement list>}
```

```
process {<statement list>}
end {<statement list>}
}
```

This function can hold parameters. You can type a single parameter. You can add several parameters by separating them with commas. These are all at the very first where you declared your function. If you declare your parameters when you declare your function, you can't declare any additional parameters in the body of the function.

You open the body of the function with a brace ({) and start adding statements. You will return to the different kinds of parameters and parameter declarations in a moment.

The Begin, Process, and end are used in pipelines, which will be discussed in a moment.

After the brace ({), you will add any number of statements. You will need to add a semicolon (;) between statements if the statements are on the same line. You can also place each statement on a separate line and then you won't have to use the semicolon. This can enhance readability. It is also a good idea to indent the various sections to make them easier to read. When you indent, use either all spaces or all tabs. If you combine the two, the spaces could be interpreted oddly if you cut and paste between scripts. It could lead the script to think the space was identifying a parameter. If you use either all spaces or all tabs for your indentation, you won't have that problem.

To aid in readability, you can add comments to document your script. These comments are prefaced by a pound sign (#). Anything to the right of the pound sign is ignored on that line. If you want your comment to cover multiple lines, you need to use the # before each line. You can make a block of comments by starting the block with a less than sign and a pound sign (<#). You would then put in any number of comments on as many lines as desired. You will then close with another pound sign and a greater than sign (#>).

You have the basics of a function. You have the name and you have comments. You also have code pieces on one line and on separate lines. This process is illustrated here in pseudocode:

```
Function Dostuff-OurCoolThing
{
    #Here is a comment on a single line. Our function is designed to process your
     # cool thing. Broken line so you have to have another comment mark
    <# This is a comment block that you started.
Our comments can be endless and your spacing and tab location doesn't matter as
The comment block ends when you end it #>
Put-codeline1 ; Put-Codeline2
Put-codleine3nosemi
Put-Codeline4nosemi
}
```

WHAT IN THE WORLD IS PSEUDOCODE?

Pseudocode is merely text you use to start to develop your code. It lets you figure out the general format without the need to dig too deeply or worry about the fine details of syntax. This is a bit lower level than flowcharting. You are sort of using standard commands, but you aren't getting all hung up on the exact coding. Pseudocode is typically used while you are designing code to speed development and enhance readability during the early stages.

You need to keep in the habit of commenting everything about your functions and scripts. You need to establish standards for spacing, variable names, function name, and basically everything. This will make your code much easier to create, use, troubleshoot, and maintain.

Using Parameters

It is a best practice to send data to a function only via parameters. This makes it easy to document and makes the function self-contained. It also mimics how the rest of PowerShell operates, preserving the familiar environment.

You can have parameters assigned to functions. These parameters can be named, like most cmdlet parameters. You can also make them positional. This is useful when you are always feeding a function with the same expected parameters in the same order. It can make it difficult to read, but it can reduce the amount of data you need to send.

NAMED PARAMETERS

Named parameters are like the parameters you used earlier in the chapter. They will have a name and can have a value, or an array of values, assigned. You can name them inside or outside of the braces that start your code area. Here is an example of declaring the parameters when you declare a function:

```
Function Display-Values ($Parameter1, $Parameter2)
    {
    $var1 = $Parameter1
    Write-Host ("This is from var1 "+$var1)
    Write-Host ("This is from Parameter2 "+$Parameter2)
    Write-Host($Parameter1,$Parameter2)
    }
```

POWERSHELL COPIES EVERYTHING

You can assign the value of a parameter to a variable, or you can reference the parameter directly. This is because PowerShell does something sneaky. When you create or reference a parameter, PowerShell secretly makes a copy of the parameter into a variable by the same name.

For the function to work, you have to load the code into your session. In ISE, you can just type the code in, select it, and press F8. If it is the only thing in your script window, you can press F5, which will run everything in the script window.

In the regular console, you can enter only one line of code at a time. Unless you can get lucky with line breaks, you can't enter everything on a single line. This mega-line would also be very difficult to read and could require extensive scrolling to ensure you typed everything correctly.

Normally, you would save your function code as a .ps1 file, also known as a script. You would then load and run the script. This will load the function into your session by placing the function into Function: drive for your scope. You can view this just as you did earlier for the Variable: drive.

You would call this function and pass the parameters as follows:

```
PS C:\Windows\system32> Display-Values -Parameter1 Hello -Parameter2 World

This is from var1 Hello
This is from Parameter2 World
Hello World
```

Notice that parameters are passed with a space in between each parameter. You can also leave out the parameter names and rely on the position in the order they were defined. This is what it looks like when you leave off the names of the parameters:

```
PS C:\Windows\system32> Display-Values Learning PowerShell

This is from var1 Learning
This is from Parameter2 PowerShell
Learning PowerShell
```

Again, it is important that you notice the parameters are passed to the function separated with a space. If you pass the parameter values with a comma, all of the values will be added to the first parameter as an array.

If you decide to declare parameters inside your function body, you can't declare them when the function itself is declared. PowerShell will throw an error telling you exactly that. Below you will define the parameters in the function body. Note the parameter names are just names. The position of the parameter is defined by when they are declared. The first parameter that is passed is actually in position 0.

In this example, the order of the output is varied to illustrate that you can use the parameters in any order. A default value is even assigned to one of the parameters when it is declared. Pay attention to the commas between the parameters during declaration:

```
Function Display-Values
{
    Param(
            $Parameter1, $Parameter2,
            $Parameter3,
            [String]$Parameter4 = "Nano",
            $Parameter5
          )
    Write-Host($Parameter3,$Parameter4,$Parameter1,$Parameter2,$Parameter5)
}

PS C:\Windows\system32> Display-Values Server 2016 Windows

Windows Nano Server 2016
```

Running the function is identical. Any parameters you define that aren't sent a parameter value, or assigned a default value, are assigned $NULL, unless you pass a value to the parameter when you call the function.

It is also important to realize that if you do pass a parameter that has a default value, the passed value will overwrite the default value. Using the same function, let's add a fourth passed parameter:

```
PS C:\Windows\system32> Display-Values Server 2016 Windows Installation
Windows Installation Server 2016
```

That output may have been unexpected because you might have thought the fourth parameter would be somehow overwritten by being defined with a default value. You would have been wrong. With the strange order, you would need to pass the parameters in the following way to get it to make your cool sentence and not overwrite the default value:

```
PS C:\Windows\system32> Display-Values Server 2016 Windows -Parameter5 Installation

Windows Nano Server 2016 Installation
```

This illustrates why naming the parameters while you pass them make it so much easier to read. You can also pass named parameters in any order, as long as you specify the parameter's name. This also lets you define exactly just the parameters you have passed.

MANDATORY PARAMETERS

Many times, your functions will be worthless if they don't get the parameters they need. You can define, in [Parameters], the properties associated with a parameter. One property is Position, another is Mandatory. You will set a parameter as mandatory in your code block, as follows:

```
Function Show-OurValues
{
    Param ($Param1,
            [Parameter(Mandatory = $True)][string]$StringParam
        )
    Write-Host ($Param1,$StringParam)
}


Show-OurValues PassingJustTheFirstParam
```

Because you passed only the first parameter, position 0, and the second parameter, position 1, is mandatory, the console will ask you for the second value. In ISE, you will get a dialog box, as shown in Figure 2.16.

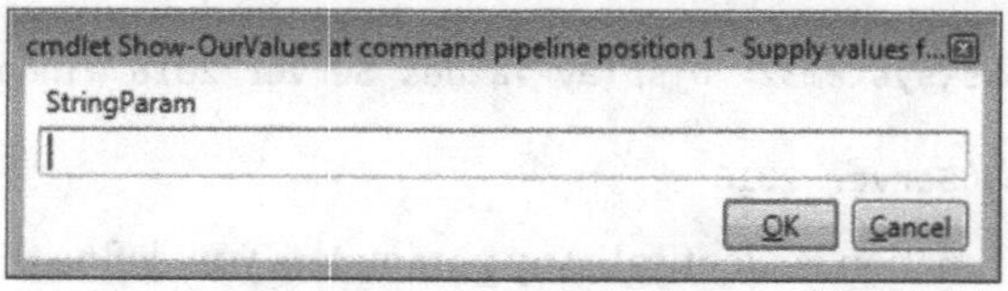

FIGURE 2.16
You forgot the
mandatory
parameter.

```
cmdlet Show-OurValues at command pipeline position 1 - Supply values f... 
StringParam
[                                                                    ]
                                              OK    Cancel
```

Notice that ISE is nice enough to tell you which parameter you forgot. This illustrates why it is important to have meaningful parameter names. You will also get a similar output on the console. You can also provide a help message that will be displayed only when you forget a parameter, as shown here:

```
Param
(
[Parameter(Mandatory=$True, HelpMessage="Enter one or more AD site names, separated
by a comma.")] [String[]] $townName
)
```

You have to use `[Parameter(Mandatory = $True)] $myParameterName` to modify the parameter's properties. You can also set other properties, like its position:

```
Param (
[Parameter(Mandatory = $True,Position1)] $myParameter
)
```

This block shows that you can set multiple parameter properties in the Parameter section. This example will set $myParameter as the second parameter. Remember that positions start with 0. The parameter will also be mandatory. Of course, if you reference the named parameter by name, PowerShell will ignore the position of that named parameter and go with the direct value assignment.

POSITIONAL PARAMETERS

The parameters that you create are assigned a position based on the order in which they are defined, or by *hard-coding* the position, as shown earlier. All parameters are positional, by default, but you can store them another way. With this method, you don't give them a name, but you do have them automatically stored in an array. You saw an example of this before with splatting, but instead of passing arguments with the @, you will put them into the $args array.

Whatever you pass to the function will be stored in the $args array. The first one will be in the first position, starting at 0. The $args array looks a bit like a spreadsheet where you will have other properties, not just the value, but the position is the row. You need to remember that the first parameter is stored in $Args[0]. To add to the fun, if you use the Get-Help cmdlet, it will display the Position attribute, but this value is incremented by 1. Therefore, the first positional parameter, Position 0, will have the parameter attribute of "Position? 1". This can be rather confusing and if you forget, it can lead to some interesting troubleshooting.

Here is an example function:

```
Function Add-Domain
{
$FQDN = $args[0]+".Contoso.com"
$FQDN
}

PS C:\Windows\system32> Add-Domain Server15

Server15.Contoso.com
```

If you fail to pass the parameter value, the $args[0] will be $NULL and the output will reflect it:

```
PS C:\Windows\system32> Add-Domain

Contoso.com
```

SWITCH PARAMETERS

Switch parameters act like a light switch. The idea is that if a value for the switch parameter is passed, the parameter will become $True, regardless of the actual value passed, unless you pass $False. When the switch parameter is defined as a switch parameter, the parameter will be default to $False.

If you don't send the switch parameter when you call the function, it will remain $False. If you do pass the parameter to your function, even with no value, PowerShell will evaluate the parameter as being set to $True. Again, you can pass the parameter as being $False, and it will remain $False.

This gives you the ability to write code that *mostly* ignores the value of your switch parameter and performs operation only if the switch parameter is passed. You can also have code that operates only in your function if the switch parameter's value remains $False. Passing the switch parameter "switches" the value. Here is how you set up a switch parameter and run some sample values to see if you are passing the -DomainParam to the function:

```
Function Check-Domain
{
param (
        [switch]$DomainParam #This sets -DomainParam to $False
    )
If ($DomainParam -eq $True) {"There is a domain."}
else {"No Domain Found."}
}
PS C:\Windows\system32> Check-Domain

No Domain Found.

PS C:\Windows\system32> Check-Domain Value1 Value2 Value3

No Domain Found.

PS C:\Windows\system32> Check-Domain -DomainParam

There is a domain.
```

You can pass a Boolean value to a parameter by adding it after the parameter name, as shown here:

```
PS C:\Windows\system32> Check-Domain -DomainParam:$False

No Domain Found.
```

```
PS C:\Windows\system32> Check-Domain -DomainParam:$True

There is a domain.

PS C:\Windows\system32> Check-Domain -DomainParam:$Grapefruit

There is a domain.
```

Remember, passing the switch parameter with any value besides $False will always revaluate as True. If statements will be discussed a bit later in the chapter.

Sending Pipeline Objects to a Function with *Begin*, *Process*, and *End*

You can pipeline objects to a function. You will execute the Begin statement only at the beginning of the function. You haven't pulled anything from the pipeline yet. Once the Begin statement is done, the Process statements will run once for each object in the pipeline. As objects are assigned to the pipeline, they are referenced by the $PSItem automatic variable and the older $_ automatic variable. Both automatic variables refer to the current object in the PowerShell pipeline. Just remember that $PSItem is supported only in PowerShell 3.0 and later.

Once all of the items are processed, the End statement runs once. If you don't include Begin, Process, or End keywords, every statement will be treated as an End statement list. Here is some sample code:

```
Function Examine-Pipeline
{
    Begin {$myVar = "Nothing first pulled from the pipeline --->$PSItem<---"
           $myVar
          }
    Process {
            $myVar = "Value from the pipeline $PSItem"
             $myVar
            }
    End
           {
           $mYVar = "This only executes at the end"
           $myvar
           }
}
PS C:\Windows\system32> 2,4,8 | Examine-Pipeline

Nothing first pulled from the pipeline ---><---
Value from the pipeline 2
Value from the pipeline 4
Value from the pipeline 8
This only executes at the end
```

Viewing All Functions in a Session

Functions are stored in the Function: drive. This is just like the Variables: drive you saw earlier. You can view all the functions that are loaded in a session by changing to the drive and using the alias Dir, or you can simply use the following command:

```
Get-ChildItem -Path Function:
```

This command will also work for the other drives because, as you learned earlier, Dir is an alias.

Formatting Output

PowerShell has many different ways to present output to the console. Table 2.2 lists these format cmdlets with their aliases.

TABLE 2.2:   Output Formats

CMDLET	ALIAS
Format-Wide	FW
Format-List	FL
Format-Table	FT

These format cmdlets will have their own parameter, called a *property*. This property will hold the list of properties you are trying to display. You can modify this property by passing the various attributes you want displayed. Each format type will display specific default properties. Format-Wide has only a single property. Format-List and Format-Table can hold several.

Using *Format-Wide*

Format-Wide is the default output format to the console. Here is an example of the Format-Wide cmdlet:

```
PS C:\Users\Administrator> Get-ChildItem |Format-Wide

    Directory: C:\Users\Administrator

Documents                                                    Desktop
Dropbox                                                      Downloads
Links                                                        Favorites
Pictures                                                     Music
Searches                                                     Videos
```

Format-Wide tries to fill up the entire screen of the console. That is why it is called wide. It can lead to some interesting looking output.

Using *Format-List*

Format-List shows many properties of an object. Each property will be labeled and on a separate line. If you want to limit what is shown, you can specify the individual properties by passing values to the -Property parameter. Let's compare the default properties as shown here:

```
PS C:\Users\Administrator> Get-ChildItem |Format-List


    Directory: C:\Users\Administrator


Name          Contacts
CreationTime  : 2/24/2017 2:03
LastWriteTime : 3/17/2017 7:53
LastAccessTime : 2/24/2017 2:03
Mode          : d-r---
LinkType      :
Target        : {}
```

This displays only the properties of the Contacts folder. Now you will tell Format-List to show all of the properties of the same file object:

```
Get-ChildItem | Format-List -Property *


PSPath         : Microsoft.PowerShell.Core\FileSystem::C:\Users\Administrator\Contacts
PSParentPath   : Microsoft.PowerShell.Core\FileSystem::C:\Users\Administrator
PSChildName    : Contacts
PSDrive        : C
PSProvider     : Microsoft.PowerShell.Core\FileSystem
PSIsContainer  : TRUE
Mode           : d-r---
BaseName       : Contacts
Target         : {}
LinkType       :
Name           : Contacts
Parent         : Administrator
Exists         : TRUE
Root           : C:\
FullName       : C:\Users\Administrator\Contacts
Extension      :
CreationTime   : 2/24/2017 2:03
CreationTimeUtc: 2/24/2017 9:03
LastAccessTime : 2/24/2017 2:03
```

```
LastAccessTimeUtc : 2/24/2017 9:03
LastWriteTime     : 3/17/2017 7:35
LastWriteTimeUtc  : 3/17/2017 14:35
Attributes        : ReadOnly, Directory
```

You can selectively filter to whatever properties you want to view by simply adding a comma-separated list of values to the -Properties parameter with full wildcard support.

Using *Format-Table*

Format-Table is used for tabular output. Remember that each format has its own defaults. Here is the same directory listing displayed by a Format-Table:

```
Get-ChildItem | Format-Table

Mode            LastWriteTime    Length    Name
------          -------------    ------    ----
d-r---    3/17/2017    7:35 AM              Contacts
d-r---    3/17/2017    7:35 AM              Desktop
d-r---    3/17/2017    7:35 AM              Documents
d-r---    3/17/2017    7:35 AM              Downloads
d-r---    3/20/2017   11:55 AM              Dropbox
d-r---    3/19/2017    7:35 AM              Favorites
d-r---    3/11/2017    7:35 AM              Links
d-r---    2/19/2017    7:35 AM              Music
d-r---    2/14/2017    7:35 AM              Pictures
d-r---    2/19/2017    7:35 AM              Saved Games
d-r---    2/19/2017    7:35 AM              Searches
d-r---    2/19/2017    7:35 AM              Videos
```

There are other options for setting up output formatting. The appropriate type depends on the user's need and the type of data. You can filter by passing the -Property parameter, which helps reduce the clutter of your output.

Using Loops

Sometimes when scripting, you may need to do the same operation over and over, but with different objects. You may have a pipeline filled with objects that need to be manipulated. You may need to refill the pipeline over and over. You can accomplish this by creating a variety of loops and conditional loops. This is where individual command and variable elements really come together.

Using the *For* Loop

The for loop will run a block of code a specific number of times. This is useful for running the same code over and over, or for processing members of an array that match a particular characteristic. If you want to do the same thing for all members of an array, you will probably be better off using the foreach loop that is discussed next.

Here is the syntax for the for loop:

```
for (<init>; <condition>; <repeat>)
        {<statement list>}
```

The for loop will start with an initiation section that has one or more commands. If you use multiple commands, you will need to separate the commands by a comma. This section is used to initialize a variable with the starting value that is used to keep track of how many times you step through the loop.

The condition section has some type of Boolean comparison or condition. This is typically to see if you have executed the loop enough times. If this comparison is True, the section in the command block runs once and then the commands in the repeat section run.

The repeat section is used to typically increment the variable that was set in the init section. Then the condition section is performed again. If the condition is still true, the statements in the statement list, known as the command block, will run again and the repeat section will run again. This repeats until the condition evaluates to $False, in which case the for loop ends.

The statement list section will contain code that is executed each time the loop condition evaluates to True. You can also change the variable being tested in the condition section inside the statement list section.

The init, condition, and repeat sections are separated by a semicolon, but you can also separate them with carriage returns. At a minimum, you have to have these three sections, surrounded by parentheses, and you must have a command in the statement list section. Here is an example:

```
PS C:\Users\Administrator> For ($i=1 ; $i -lt 3; $I++) {"The counter is at $i"}

The counter is at 1
The counter is at 2
```

The first time through, $i was set to 1. When you did the comparison, $i is less than 3, so you run the command block for your output. Then you go to the repeat section where $i is incremented by 1. This makes $i now equal to 2. If you want to increment more than one, you can do $i+=5. That will increment the value of $i by 5. Here, you will just increment by 1.

PowerShell will then test the condition again. This time $i = 2, so the comparison is still True, the code block runs again, and $i gets incremented to 3.

When PowerShell does the comparison, it finds that $i, with a value of 3, is no longer less than 3, so the for loop ends.

Using the *Foreach* Loop

The foreach loop is used to run through all the members of an array. This loop will run commands against each item. The items will be identified by a variable that doesn't need to be declared. This variable will represent each item, one at a time, in the array. Unlike the for loop, foreach doesn't need to know the number of times it needs to run though the loop and doesn't need any initialization of counting variables. Here is the syntax:

```
foreach ($<item> in $<collection>){<statement list>}
```

You can set up an array and run through the processing. Note that in this example, you will use a variable that is created just for the foreach loop:

```
$ourCityArray = "Paris","Perth","Atlanta","Phoenix"
Foreach ($magicCreatedVariable in $ourCityArray)
{"The City here is $magicCreatedVariable."}
"There are no more cities."

The city here is Paris.
The city here is Perth.
The city here is Atlanta.
The city here is Phoenix.
There are no more cities.
```

If you run this from the command line, the entire Foreach statement, including the command statement list section, has to appear in a single line. If you want these to be in separate lines, you will need to run these commands in a .ps1 script. Of course, you can run this for testing inside of PowerShell ISE.

You can also use a cmdlet instead of an array. You will use a Get-ChildItem to view all of the functions in your scope that start with the letter *G*, as illustrated here:

```
Foreach ($Functions in Get-ChildItem -Path Function: -Name -Include G*) {$Functions}

Get-Verb
G:
Get-IseSnippet
Get-FileHash
```

You aren't limited to having just a single statement in the statement list. You can also include foreach inside the command pipeline. When you do this, foreach doesn't need the variable or the array identified. It will simply pull each item from the pipeline values provided by the previous command and run the statement items against each item as illustrated here:

```
Get-ChildItem -Path ENV: -include "*Win*" -name| foreach {"[ENV]:$PSItem"}

[ENV]:windir
```

This will go through the environmental variables and display any that have "Win" somewhere in their name.

You can also use -Begin, -Process, and -End command blocks. This is similar to the Begin, Process, and End portions of the function block you saw earlier. The -Begin section is processed just once, prior to pulling objects from the pipeline. The –Process block is executed once per item. The -End block is performed only once, after all of the objects in the pipeline have been processed. You can view the code here:

```
$citiesVisited = "Paris","Perth","Atlanta","Phoenix"
$citiesVisited | ForEach-Object -Begin {Write-Host("AD Site Cities")} -Process
{Write-Host($PSItem)} -End {Get-Date}

AD Site Cities
Paris
Perth
Atlanta
Phoenix
Tuesday, March 23, 2022 6:48:07 PM
```

Using the *If* Statement

The If statement is used to run code blocks based on the results of a Boolean conditional test. The If statement gives you multiple combinations of three options that also enable multiple levels of nesting:

- Run a code block if the condition test result evaluates to $True

- Run a code block if the condition test result evaluates to $True and all the previous conditions evaluated to $False

- Run a code block if all of the previous conditions test result evaluated to $False

Here is the syntax:

```
if (<test1>) {<statement list 1>} [elseif (<test2>) {<statement list 2>}] [else
{<statement list 3>}]
```

These If statements can be pretty simple, as illustrated here:

```
If ($a -eq 3) {Write-Host "$A equals 3." }
```

The code block will be executed only if the evaluation results in True. You can also use an If statement where you have one block run if the condition is True, and a different code block if the condition evaluates as False.

```
If ($a -gt 3)
  {
  Write-Host "Variable a is greater than 3."
  }
Else
  {
  Write-Host "Variable a is less than 3 or Variable a is empty."
  }
```

The Else portion of this code will run only if the prior If statement is $False. This could be because the $a variable is 3 or less. It could also be due to the fact that $a is $Null.

If you want the Else statement to test another condition prior to running the code block, you could put in another If statement, but PowerShell has Elseif. With Elseif, the second condition will occur only if the first condition evaluates as $False.

```
If ($a -Lt 10)
  {
    Write-Host "Site Link cost is less than 10."
  }
Elseif ($a -Eq $Null)
  {
    Write-Host "Site Link cost is Null."
  }
Elseif ($a -Lt 21)
  {
    Write-Host "Site Link cost is between 10 and 20."
  }
Else
  {
    Write-Host "Site Link a is greater than 20"
  }
```

Any time your condition is evaluated as True, the associated code block will run and none of the remaining Else or ElseIf statements will be evaluated. You can place an Else statement at the end that will only be executed if all the previous conditional statements evaluated as $False.

If you find that you are using a lot of Elseif statements in your code, you should probably use a Switch statement instead.

Using the *Switch* Statement

The switch statement is not like a switch parameter. The switch statement will specify a test value and will then contain multiple conditions. If the test value matches the conditions, the associated action will execute. Unlike the Elseif statements, all switch conditions are typically tested. Here is the basic syntax:

```
Switch (<test-value>)
  {
      <reference-value> {<action>}
      <reference-value> {<action>}
  }
```

The actual switch syntax is a bit more involved, and you will examine it in a moment.

You need to understand the test value is checked against each reference value, even if the test value matched a previous reference value in the same switch block. If the test value matches the reference value, the action code block is performed. If the test value doesn't match any of the switch reference values, none of the blocks are performed for that test value. See the following code:

```
Switch (7)
{
  2 {"This matches the reference value two"}
```

```
    94{"This matches ninety-four"}
    7{"This is matching seven"}
    4{"This matches four"}
    7{"This matched seven again"}
}
```

```
This is matching seven
This matched seven again
```

Here is an example of code processing an array of location codes and showing what happens if the test value doesn't match any reference values:

```
Switch ("Perth","Phoenix","Dallas")
  {
    Wyoming {"This matches Wyoming"}
    Perth {"This matches Perth"}
    Phoenix {"This matches Phoenix"}
    Perth {"This matches Perth again"}
}
```

```
This matches Perth
This matches Perth again
This matches Phoenix
```

The switch values can be in any order, but each test value is tested by every reference value, even when the test value matches other reference values in the same switch block.

If you want to prevent matching on multiple reference values, you can add a Break to the switch, as illustrated here:

```
Switch ("Perth","Phoenix","Dallas")
  {
    Wyoming {"This matches Wyoming"}
    Perth {"This matches Perth";Break}
    Phoenix {"This matches Phoenix"}
    Perth {"This matches Perth again"}
}
```

```
This matches Perth
```

When PowerShell is executing a switch block and it hits a Break in the switch reference values, the Switch block will stop evaluating that test value and will exit, even if the test value will match later reference values in the same switch block or there are more test values to check.

If you want to stop further processing just that particular test value, but want to move to process any additional test values, you would use a Continue as illustrated here:

```
Switch ("Perth","Phoenix","Dallas")
  {
    Wyoming {"This matches Wyoming"}
    Perth {"This matches Perth";Continue}
    Phoenix {"This matches Phoenix"}
```

```
      Perth {"This matches Perth again"}
}
```

```
This matches Perth
This matches Phoenix
```

You can also identify a default switch that will be used if the test value doesn't match any other conditions, as illustrated here:

```
Switch ("Perth","Phoenix","Dallas")
  {
    Wyoming {"This matches Wyoming"}
    Perth {"This matches Perth"}
    Phoenix {"This matches Phoenix"}
    Perth {"This matches Perth again"}
    Default {"We don't match anything"}
}
```

```
This matches Perth
This matches Phoenix
We don't match anything
```

There can be only a single default statement in each switch statement, and each switch statement must include at least one condition statement.

The actual Switch syntax will take parameters that identify regular expressions, a wildcard, or an exact value. Only one parameter is used. If more than one is specified, the last one specified will be the only one that is used. You can also make the test value case-sensitive.

```
switch [-regex|-wildcard|-exact][-casesensitive] (<value>)
```

You can also use a file instead of just a value.

```
switch [-regex|-wildcard|-exact][-casesensitive] -file filename
```

In either case, the switch statement is followed by the code block:

```
{
"string"|number|variable|{ expression } { statementlist }
default { statementlist }
}
```

If you use switch after a pipeline, the values will be passed to the switch and processed in order. If you hit a Break, you will stop processing the switch block, even if additional objects are in the pipeline. Because the pipeline isn't empty, this can lead to unexpected results to cmdlets that are next in line to extract objects from the pipeline.

Using the *While* Loop

Using While loops is an easy alternative to using for loops. Here is the syntax:

```
While (<Condition>) {<statement list>}
```

As long as the condition is True, PowerShell will endlessly loop through the statement lists. At the end of the block, the condition is again evaluated. If the condition is no longer True, the loop ends. Note that the condition is evaluated only at the beginning of each loop. If you have multiple statements that would temporarily make the condition False and it becomes True before you are finished with the loop, you will continue the loop. The evaluation only means that the condition is True at the time it was checked. Here is some code:

```
While ($count -ne 5)
{
$count++
Write-Host "The count is "$count
}


The count is 1
The count is 2
The count is 3
The count is 4
The count is 5
```

Notice that the first time you run the code, the variable $count is $Null. Also, you need to notice that when the count becomes 5, the loop stops only after the condition is checked. When $count equals 5, you still finish the statement list even though you no longer match the condition. If you had placed the $count++ statement after the Write-Host statement, you would have a different output:

```
While ($Count -ne 5)
{
Write-Host "The count is "$Count
$Count++
}


The count is
The count is 1
The count is 2
The count is 3
The count is 4
```

KILLING YOUR SERVER WITH A SINGLE *WHILE* BLOCK OF CODE

It is important to know that if your statement list has an error that makes your condition always be true, your loop will loop forever. You will need to use Ctrl+C to stop processing. This could become a big issue if this loop is used to write text files with incrementing names and doesn't produce any output visible to the console. You could fill up your server's disk drive with one single line of code.

If you want to write the While loop in a single line, you should separate the different statement lines with a semicolon, as illustrated here:

```
While($Count -ne 5) {$Count++ ; Write-Host "The count is "$Count}
```

It is critical to understand that as long as your condition is True, the loop will run forever.

Using the *Where-Object* Method

If statements are quite powerful, but they can require quite a bit of coding. Where statements are used when you want to select objects in a collection based on a property value. Where has several syntax options, based on what you are using as your conditional statement. Here is an example of two:

```
Where-Object [-Property] <String> [[-Value] <Object>] -comparisonoperand
[-InputObject <PSObject>] [<CommonParameters>]
```

The comparison is what is typically different between the various syntax versions of the Where method, so it is italicized in the example.

To view the entire syntax list, enter **Help Where-Object**.

PowerShell provides two ways to use Where. The first is to use a script block. A script block allows you to specify the name of the property, a comparison operator, and the reference value. Here is an example with a script block:

```
Get-Service | Where-Object {$PSItem.Status -eq "Stopped"}
```

The other format is the comparison statement format. Here is the same command:

```
Get-Process | Where Status -eq "Stopped"
```

Both methods work, and there is no difference in the output.

 Real World Scenario

FINDING ALL THE RUNNING PROCESSES THROUGHOUT YOUR DOMAIN

Typically, parameters expect a particular type of data. When you are dealing with objects in a pipeline, you may not have the exact value type the next cmdlet's parameters require. You will frequently have objects but need something else. Let's examine a need and how you can fulfill that need.

Let's say you need to get a listing of all of the running processes of the computers in your domain. You want to have a text file named after each computer. Inside each file, you want a list of all of the running processes on that particular host. If a host isn't available, you need a separate file that lists all of the unresponsive systems.

Your first step is to get a list of all of the running computers. You can do this with the following code:

```
Get-ADComputer -Filter *
```

The -Filter parameter lets you select individual machines. You want all of them, so you use the only allowed wildcard, the asterisk (*).

This command provides a list of all of the computers, with all the associated properties, in your domain. For this part of the discussion, you will trim the output to a single computer. The output is an object that contains a list of properties with the associated values, as shown here:

```
DistinguishedName : CN=DEN-DC07,OU=Domain Controllers,DC=Contoso,DC=com
DNSHostName       : DEN-DC07.contoso.com
Enabled           : True
Name              : DEN-DC07
ObjectClass       : computer
ObjectGUID        : d9fca1f2-68d7-48ab-984d-9f81c7e5dab9
SamAccountName    : DEN-DC07$
SID               : S-1-5-21-1070347451-1483549047-3396811997-1001
UserPrincipalName :
```

You want to use the fully qualified domain name of the computer, so you want the contents of the DNSHostName property. You also want to use the output of the Get-ADComputer command as a parameter value for another command. You can do this by setting the Get-ADComputer inside parentheses. You can try the following code:

```
Get-Process -ComputerName (Get-ADComputer -Filter *)

get-process : Couldn't connect to remote machine.
At line:1 char:1
+ get-process -ComputerName( Get-ADComputer -Filter *)
+ ~~~~~~~~~~~~~~~~~~~~~~~~~~~~~~~~~~~~~~~~~~~~~~~~~~~~~~~
    + CategoryInfo      : NotSpecified: (:) [Get-Process], InvalidOperationException
    + FullyQualifiedErrorId : System.InvalidOperationException,Microsoft.PowerShell.
Commands.GetProcessCommand
```

The issue is that the Get-Process command's parameter, -ComputerName, is looking for a string with a computer's name. Get-ADComputer returns much more information. Let's try thinning that information down with a Select-Object command to just pull the DNSHostname, as shown here:

```
Get-Process -ComputerName (Get-ADComputer -Filter * | Select-Object -Property
DNSHostName)

Get-Process : Couldn't connect to remote machine.
At line:1 char:1
+ Get-Process -ComputerName (Get-ADComputer -Filter * | Select-Object -Property
DN ...
+ ~~~~~~~~~~~~~~~~~~~~~~~~~~~~~~~~~~~~~~~~~~~~~~~~~~~~~~~~~~~~~~~~~~~~~~~~~~~~~~~~~~~~
    + CategoryInfo          : NotSpecified: (:) [Get-Process],
InvalidOperationException
    + FullyQualifiedErrorId : System.InvalidOperationException,Microsoft.
PowerShell.Commands.GetProcessCommand
```

continued

Again, there is another failure. Maybe you need to see what the output is from the `Get-ADComputer` command when the filter is applied. Let's assign it to a variable and examine the value. For now, let's just limit it to a single computer, as shown here:

```
$hosts = (Get-ADComputer -filter * |Select-Object -Property DNSHostName)
Write-Host $hosts

@{DNSHostName=DEN-DC07.Contoso.com} @{DNSHostName=DEN-Win16-01.Contoso.com} @
{DNSHostName=DEN-Win16-02.Contoso.com} @{DNSHostName=DEN-Win16-03.Contoso.com}
```

Here is the problem. The `-Computername` property wants a string. The `Get-ADComputer` command returns objects that have several properties. When the output is filtered down to just the `DNSHostName`, the object contains the string you need, but it isn't in the form of a string. It is still an object with a single property. What if you wrote it to a file and then read the file back, a little CSV action? Here is the code and the output:

```
Get-ADComputer -Filter *|Select-Object -Property DNSHostname|ConvertTo-Csv
-NoTypeInformation |Out-File c:\computers.txt
```

When you open this in Notepad, here is what you'll find inside:

```
"DNSHostname"
```

```
"DEN-DC07.Contoso.com"
```

```
"DEN-Win16-01.Contoso.com"
```

```
"DEN-Win16-02.Contoso.com"
```

```
"DEN-Win16-03.Contoso.com"
```

Even though you stripped out the type information, you still have text `"DNSHostname"`, which is a header that identifies the single property. How do you extract the strings without the header?

EXPANDING A PROPERTY

You could write rather convoluted code that searches and extracts just the `DNSHostname`, but it would have to be purpose-built and would not be very flexible. Fortunately, PowerShell has an alternative. You can expand the property from the object. Expanding the property will take just a single property and extract just the value.

Let's try the same parenthetical command but expand the property for the `DNSHostname`. Remember, you can expand only a single property from the object in the pipeline. Here is the code and the output:

```
$hosts = (Get-ADComputer -filter * |Select-Object -ExpandProperty DNSHostName)
Write-Host $hosts

DEN-DC07.Contoso.com
DEN-Win16-01.Contoso.com
DEN-Win16-02.Contoso.com
DEN-Win16-03.Contoso.com
```

That is exactly what you are looking to use. This has loaded the $hosts variable as an array, with each expanded property being stored as the needed string. You just need to process each of the members of the array.

Then take each object from the array and use that as the input to the Get-Process -ComputerName parameter. You won't know how many computers are in your array so you can use a Foreach statement.

Load a variable that just has a single value and pass that variable to the Get-Process cmdlet. Because one of your original requirements is to create a text file for each individual server, you need to pipe the output to an Out-File cmdlet. For testing, you will also need to list, on the console, each computer from which you are attempting to extract this information. So you'll know where it fails, you need to print the name of the system before trying to extract the list of processes. Here is your code with the output:

```
$hosts = (Get-ADComputer -Filter *| Select-Object -ExpandProperty DNSHostName)
ForEach ($hostname in $hosts)
    {
      Write-Host $hostname

      Get-Process -ComputerName $hostname |Out-File c:\$hostname" Processes.txt"
    }


DEN-DC07.Contoso.com
DEN-Win16-01.Contoso.com
DEN-Win16-02.Contoso.com
Get-Process : Couldn't connect to remote machine.
At line:7 char:8
+        Get-Process -ComputerName $Hostname |Out-File c:\$Hostname" Processes.
txt ...
+        ~~~~~~~~~~~~~~~~~~~~~~~~~~~~~~~~~~~~
    + CategoryInfo          : NotSpecified: (:) [Get-Process],
InvalidOperationException
    + FullyQualifiedErrorId : System.InvalidOperationException,Microsoft.
PowerShell.Commands.GetProcessCommand

DEN-Win16-03.contoso.com
```

It looks like DEN-Win16-02.contoso.com isn't responding. You can perform a test against each machine to give you a simple Boolean value that indicates whether or not you can connect to the machine. After a bit of searching, you should have a Test-Connection cmdlet with a -Quiet parameter. This returns a simple $True or $False.

This will give you the opportunity to do an If statement to produce your required list of the unresponsive systems in a separate text file. You will want to append to the unresponsive list so you don't have a list that contains only the last unresponsive system. Here is the code:

```
$hosts = (Get-ADComputer -Filter *| Select-Object -ExpandProperty DNSHostName)
ForEach ($hostname in $hosts)
```

continued

```
        {
            Write-host $hostname
            If(Test-Connection $hostname -Quiet)
              {
                Get-Process -ComputerName $hostname |out-file c:\$hostname"
Processes.txt"
              }
            Else {
                    $hostname+" doesn't respond" |Out-File c:\Unresponsive.txt
-append
                }
          }
DEN-DC07.contoso.com
DEN-Win16-01.contoso.com
DEN-Win16-02.contoso.com
DEN-Win16-03.contoso.com
```

This is excellent. You have the list of servers, as they are being tried. You know DEN-Win16-02 .contoso.com is down, and you didn't throw an error.

Now you can look in your folder to see whether the files worked. You should be greeted by this list:

```
PS C:\> dir *.txt


    Directory: C:\


Mode                LastWriteTime      Length Name
----                -------------      ------ ----
-a---      2/15/2017  11:38 AM          12164 DEN-DC07.Contoso.com Processes.txt
-a---      2/15/2017  11:38 AM          29984 DEN-Win16-01.Contoso.com
Processes.txt
-a---      2/15/2017  11:38 AM          27824 DEN-Win16-03.contoso.com
Processes.txt
-a---      2/15/2017  11:38 AM             98 Unresponsive.txt
```

When you open an individual system's text file to see the contents, you'll see exactly what you are looking for, truncated here for brevity:

```
Handles  NPM(K)    PM(K)      WS(K) VM(M)   CPU(s)     Id ProcessName
-------  ------    -----      ----- -----   ------     -- -----------
     61       7     2440      11324    74            4016 conhost
    187      11     1560       3720    46             360 csrss
    176      12     1676      32048    97             424 csrss
```

When you open up the Unresponsive.txt, here is what you'll find:

```
DEN-Win16-02.contoso.com doesn't respond
```

This exactly meets your requirements.

Managing Remote Systems via PowerShell

PowerShell provides a means of managing thousands of systems to do thousands of different things. So far, you have pretty much stayed on the local system. Typically, you will want to connect to remote systems.

By default, your systems are locked down from remote PowerShell access. The way access is enabled will depend on whether your target systems are part of an Active Directory domain or are just in a workgroup. Let's explore domain-joined systems first.

Using *Enable-PSRemoting*

You will need to run PowerShell as an administrator. PowerShell relies on the WinRM service. It is important to ensure that the services is set to start automatically. You will also need to create firewall rules that allow PowerShell to connect to the system. Fortunately, Microsoft has made it easy to do both operations with a single command:

```
Enable-PSRemoting –Force
```

This command runs the `Set-WSManQuickConfig` cmdlet. That cmdlet is responsible for starting the service, changing the startup to automatic, and enabling a firewall exception. Here is a list of the other things it does:

1. Creates a listener that accepts requests from any IP address.

2. Registers Microsoft.PowerShell and Microsft.PowerShell.WorkFlow session configuration.

3. Registers Microsoft.PowerShell32 session configuration on 64-bit computers.

4. Enables all session configurations.

5. Changes security descriptor on all session configurations to permit remote access.

6. Finally, restarts the WinRM service so all the configuration changes will take effect.

`Enable-PSRemoting` has several options. Because `Enable-PSRemoting` starts listening services, you typically don't want to run `Enable-PSRemoting` on systems that are used only to send commands. You don't want to have services listening when you are not the ones receiving the remote PowerShell connection.

If you want to disable PSRemoting, you should use the following command:

```
Disable-PSRemoting –Force
```

DON'T LET POWERSHELL 2.0 RUIN YOUR DAY

If PowerShell 2.0 is installed on your systems, do not run `Enable-PSRemoting` inside of PowerShell 2.0 because it will not work and will be difficult to repair. It will appear to properly configure, but you won't be able to connect, and it is very challenging to remove and correct the configuration.

Remoting to Workgroup Servers

If the target server is not domain-joined, you will need to run `Enable-PSRemoting` on both the target system and the system you will use to run your console. You will also need to configure the TrustedHosts setting for WsMan. To do this, use the following command:

```
Set-Item WsMan:\localhost\client\trustedhosts *
```

This will allow any system to connect. The user will still need to have local administrator credentials on the managed machine. If you want to restrict management computers, you can replace the * with a comma-separated list of IP addresses or host names of systems you trust to manage this remote machine.

Once the configuration is changed, you will need to restart the WinRM service. This can be accomplished by using the following:

```
Restart-Service WinRM
```

You will need to run this command on both the local and the remote system. You can test to see if you have communication by using this command:

```
Test-WsMan Server06.contoso.com
```

Of course, you will need to replace the computer name used in the example with the actual name. This command tests whether the WinRM service is running, and then it will display the MS-Management identity schema, the protocol version, the product vendor, and the product version.

Running PowerShell Commands on Remote Systems

If you want to start an interactive session on the remote computer, use the following:

```
Enter-PSSession Server15.contoso.com
```

You can use the computer name or the IP address. This cmdlet will change your prompt to reflect the remote system, as illustrated here:

```
PS C:\Users\Administrator> Enter-PSSession 10.102.50.50
[10.102.50.50]: PS C:\Users\Administrator\Documents>
```

Any commands you use will be executed on the remote system. Any output displayed to the console, including errors, will be displayed locally. To exit the session, use the following command:

```
Exit-PSSession
```

Not all cmdlets need to have a remote session. To find a list of cmdlets that do not require a session, you can use the following:

```
Get-Command | where {$PSItem.Parameters.Keys -contains "ComputerName" -and
$PSItem.Parameters.Keys -NotContains "Session"}
```

This will give you a list of commands that do have the –ComputerName parameter but do not have a –Session parameter. These commands will not need to have the WinRM service running. They will not need to be configured for PowerShell remoting and will not have to match remoting system requirements.

If you need to run single commands that require the ability to remote, you can use the Invoke-Command cmdlet, as shown here:

```
Invoke-Command -Computername Server12.contoso.com -ScriptBlock {Get-ChildItem C:\}
```

A *script block* is just a list of statements, very similar to a function. It can receive parameters. Unlike a function, the parameters have to be included inside the braces. Script blocks also support Begin, Process, and End keywords.

These Invoke-Command cmdlets are designed to send a single cmdlet to one or more computers. If you want to send the command to several, just place the computer names or IP addresses, separated by a comma, in place of the single computer name. The connection only lasts long enough to send the command and receive whatever output is returned.

Running Remote Scripts on Remote Computers

If you want to run a script that resides on all of the remote computers in the session, use the -FilePath parameter. Here is an example:

```
Invoke-Command -ComputerName Server01, Server02, LocalHost -FilePath
C:\scriptstorage\myscript.ps1
```

The scripts need to be in the same location and have the same name on every machine. You can be clever and store script paths and names in a variable. You can then pass the file path using the variable instead of the literal path.

To interrupt a remote command, press Ctrl+C. The interrupt will be sent to the remote computer.

Establishing Persistent Remote Connections

If you want to run a series of commands, and you want to share data between these commands, you need to establish a persistent session. This is done by using the -Session parameter of the invoke command, as illustrated here:

```
$mySession = New-PSSession -ComputerName Server01, Server02, Server03
```

This command creates a persistent remote connection to three servers and saves the PSSession to a variable $mySession. You can use this variable to send identical commands to all of the systems at the same time. If you use variables, these variables will be the same on all the sessions. This makes it easy to pass and use variables without wondering if the variables exist in the remote session. Here is an example:

```
Invoke-Command -Session $MySesssion -ScriptBlock {$services = Get-Services}
```

This code uses the $mySession variable, created earlier, to send the contents of the script block to each machine. This will generate a list of all the services on each computer. Each system's services will be stored in a variable called $services on that machine. If you want to perform additional manipulation using the list of these services (maybe using a While, Switch, If, or ElseIf statement), you can target individual sessions to individual servers or do the same command on all the servers at once using this variable. You can have other variables that identify other servers to allow selective invocation of commands, without getting bogged down keeping track of the various sessions or having to deal with different variables not matching the expected names on these remote machines.

Because this is a persistent connection, you can run additional commands against these systems, and any variables or data created for each session will be available until you disconnect the session. If you want to include the local system, you can use either a dot (.) or the term `LocalHost` in the `-Session` parameter.

Using PowerShell Direct

PowerShell Direct is used to manage Hyper-V virtual machines from the host system. The Hyper-V host and guest machines need to be running Windows 10 or Windows Server 2016. The operating systems of the host and guest do not need to have network connectivity, configuration, or even a network adapter. You do have to be logged on the Hyper-V host as an administrator and have user credentials on the virtual machine. The virtual machine will need to be local to the Hyper-V server, and it will need to be booted. Here is the command:

```
Enter-PSSession -VMName Server01.contos.com
```

This is a direct interactive session with the virtual machine. You can also use the GUID by replacing `-VMName` with `-VMGUID` and then entering the virtual machine's GUID instead of the computer name.

You will then have an interactive session with the virtual machine. To exit the session, do the following:

```
Exit-PSSession
```

You can run script blocks and scripts on the virtual machines pretty much the same way you do with regular `PSSessions`. You just replace the `-ComputerName` parameter with the `-VMName` parameter, as shown here:

```
Invoke-Command -VMName Server01 -FilePath C:\scriptstorage\myscript.ps1
Invoke-Command -VMName Server12 -ScriptBlock {Get-ChildItem C:\}
```

The Bottom Line

Customize the PowerShell and PowerShell ISE environments.   Microsoft PowerShell and PowerShell ISE are great environments for creating and managing Windows Server 2016 systems. Having the appropriate modules, functions, variables, and configuration settings preloaded into profiles can speed the development process. You'll want to have everything set up properly to help maximize your workflow.

Master It   You have just set up your Windows Server 2016 system and need to customize Windows PowerShell so it will automatically be in Run As Administrator mode. You also need to determine which modules can have their help files automatically update online. Finally, you need to start a transcript of your current PowerShell session in a text file called C:\PowerShellTranscript.txt that will close when you exit your session.

Solution   Run PowerShell as an administrator. You can accomplish this by right-clicking the PowerShell icon and selecting Run As Administrator. Then modify your profile to include `Function Open-AsAdmin {Start-Process PowerShell -Verb RunAs}`.

Identify the modules that have the ability to update online by using `Get-Module -ListAvailable |Where HelpInfoURI`.

Start the transcripts by using `Start-Transcript C:\PowerShellTranscript.txt`. The transcript will end when you close out of your session.

Perform command discovery and interpret PowerShell syntax notation and concept documentation. Frequently, you will be tasked with creating PowerShell configuration with limited documentation. You need to master the skill of command discovery when how-to documents are difficult to find.

Master It Find the PowerShell commands that will create a formatted list that contains only the network interface aliases and the IP addresses for all the network adapters on the local server. The command should save the list to `c:\Networkadapters.txt`.

Solution Use `Get-Command -Noun *IpAddress*` to find the commands that contain IP addressing. Use `Get-NetIpaddress |FL` to find all the parameters and assemble them into `Get-NetIpaddress| fl InterfaceAlias, IpAddress > c:\Networkadapters.txt` to create the text file that lists all of the interface names and assigned IP addresses.

Write and analyze code that supports functions, loops, comparisons, pipeline processing, variables, and scripts. There are many building blocks to creating useful scripts. You will frequently need to assemble scripts using a variety of components to produce useful output. Developing the skills to create new basic scripts is critical. You will also frequently need to read and understand external scripts before you run them in your production environment.

Master It Locate all the systems in the domain and create a web page that lists all of the installed hotfixes on each running machine. Have a separate web page for each machine. Display the Hotfix ID and when each hotfix was installed. Create a single, separate web page that lists all the machines that do not respond to the probe.

Solution

```
$hosts = (Get-ADComputer -Filter *| Select-Object -ExpandProperty DNSHostName)
foreach ($hostname in $Hosts)
    {
        If(Test-Connection $hostname -Quiet)
          {
          Get-Hotfix -ComputerName $hostname |Select-Object
Hotfixid,installedon|convertto-html -Fragment|out-file c:\$hostname" Hotfixes.
html"
          }
        Else {
                $hostname+" doesn't respond" |Out-File c:\Unresponsive.html
 -append
              }

    }
```

Manage remote servers with PowerShell. You will frequently need to send the same command to multiple machines. Many of these commands will require an interactive session and the use of credentials.

Master It You need to disable the use of SMB version 1 on all of your running servers, throughout your domain. Use a script to locate all of the hosts in your domain that are running the WinRM service. Open an interactive session with all of them and disable SMB1 protocol without the need for confirmation.

Solution

```
$hosts = (Get-ADComputer -Filter *| Select-Object -ExpandProperty DNSHostName)
foreach ($hostname in $Hosts)
    {
        If(Test-Connection $hostname -Quiet)
            {
                If((Get-Service -computername $hostname "winrm"|Select-Object
-expandproperty Status) -eq "Running")
                    {
                        Invoke-Command -ComputerName $hostname -ScriptBlock {Set-
SmbserverConfiguration -EnableSMB1Protocol $False -Force}
                    }
            }
    }
```

Chapter 3

Compute

Windows Server's computing capabilities have rapidly changed with each new version, and the latest version has introduced dramatically higher performance, support for more CPUs and memory capacity, a larger number of virtual machines if used as Hyper-V virtualization hosts, and improved energy efficiency.

Beginning from Windows Server 2012, it is also named a cloud operating system, meaning that the Windows Server computing capabilities allow organizations to deploy different scenarios on cloud solutions including private, hybrid, and public clouds. Windows Server 2016 is designed to be extensible and powerful so that it can fit any organization and any scenario, supporting a wide variety of solutions. It could be a host for virtualization, a clustering solution that supports different high-availability requirements, an operating system for different Microsoft or third-party applications, and supporting both scaling-up and scaling-out configurations for increased application performance. Later in this book, in Chapter 7, you will also learn about Windows Server containers, a new virtualization technology.

IN THIS CHAPTER, YOU WILL LEARN HOW TO:

- ◆ Use Windows Server as a Hyper-V virtualization host
- ◆ Implement virtualization solutions
- ◆ Tailor your Hyper-V solution to the specific product that will run in a VM environment
- ◆ Deploy high-availability scenarios with Windows Failover Clustering features

Overview of Hyper-V

Hyper-V is the hypervisor virtualization technology available as a server role in Windows Server 2016 (see Figure 3.1). Hardware virtualization allows organizations to dedicate the hardware capacity of a single physical computer to multiple virtual machines running different operating systems and applications. The operating system in each virtual machine runs in a virtually isolated environment independent from other virtual machines and from the operating system running on the physical computer, also known as Hyper-V *host computer*.

The operating systems running in the virtual machines are referred to as the *guest operating systems.*

FIGURE 3.1
Hyper-V
architecture

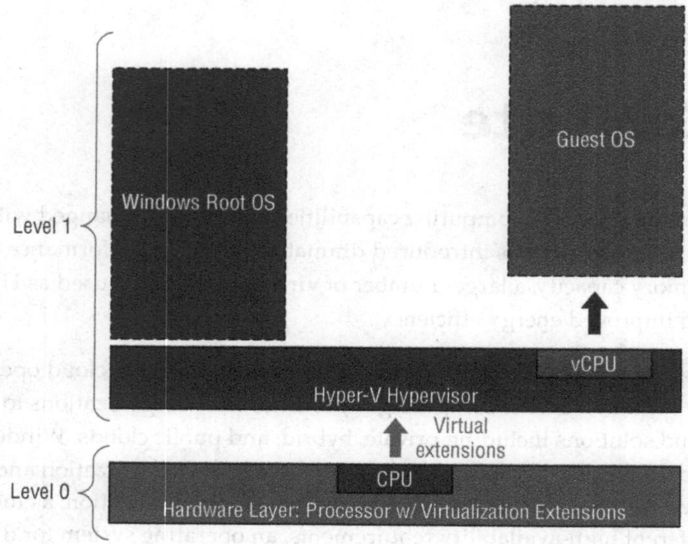

What's New in Windows Server 2016 Hyper-V

Hyper-V was introduced in Windows Server 2008 and has been improved with multiple new technologies in each subsequent operating system edition, including the R2 releases. Table 3.1 describes the new functionalities of the Hyper-V role in Windows Server 2016.

TABLE 3.1: What's New in Windows Server 2016 Hyper-V

FUNCTIONALITY	DESCRIPTION
Nested virtualization	This functionality allows you to enable the Hyper-V server role in a virtual machine running Windows Server 2016.
Rolling Hyper-V cluster upgrade	If your organization runs Windows Server 2012 R2 Hyper-V cluster, you can now upgrade it to Windows Server 2016 by adding nodes to an existing cluster and then moving virtual machines between nodes running Windows Server 2012 R2 and Windows Server 2016 during coexistence.
PowerShell Direct	This functionality provides you with the capability to run Windows PowerShell cmdlets on a virtual machine from the Hyper-V host without configuring network connectivity to the virtual machine from the host.

TABLE 3.1: What's New in Windows Server 2016 Hyper-V *(CONTINUED)*

FUNCTIONALITY	DESCRIPTION
Shielded virtual machines	This functionality encrypts the entire virtual machine.
Start order priority	This functionality determines a specific startup order for virtual machines after restarting the host computer.
Storage Quality of Service (QoS)	This functionality provides you with capability to configure storage QoS policies on a Scale-Out File Server (SOFS), thereby guaranteeing an amount of storage throughput.
Host resource protection	This functionality prevents a virtual machine from utilizing all of the resources on a Hyper-V host, so that other virtual machines have enough resources for themselves.
Hyper-V Manager functionalities	Hyper-V Manager allows alternative credentials when connecting to a Hyper-V host. Furthermore, it uses HTTP-based Web Services-Management (WS-MAN) for management.

In addition to the improvements at the host level, Hyper-V has new features for virtual machines that include the functionalities shown in Table 3.2.

TABLE 3.2: Hyper-V's New Features for Virtual Machines

FUNCTIONALITY	DESCRIPTION
Hot add or remove for network adapters and memory	Network adapters and virtual memory can be added to a running virtual machine.
Memory and processor capacity improvements	Virtual machine now supports up to 12 terabytes (TB) of memory and 240 virtual processors.
Integration services delivered through Windows Update	Deployment of the most recent version of integration services through a Windows update that simplifies management.
Key storage drive	Enables Generation 1 virtual machines to store BitLocker Drive Encryption keys.
Linux Secure Boot	Verifies digital signatures on files during the boot process to prevent malware on Linux virtual machines.
Production checkpoints	Provides supported applications with a consistent state when the checkpoint is created.
Virtual machine configuration file format	Virtual machine configuration file is written in a binary format instead of the previous XML format.

TABLE 3.2: Hyper-V's New Features for Virtual Machines *(CONTINUED)*

FUNCTIONALITY	DESCRIPTION
Discrete device assignment	Provides virtual machines with direct access to peripheral component interconnect express (PCIe) devices in the Hyper-V host.
Virtual machine configuration version	Virtual machines that are migrated from Windows Server 2012 R2 (such as during a rolling cluster upgrade) are provided with backward compatibility by retaining version 5 instead of upgrading to version 8.

Installing Hyper-V

Installing the Hyper-V server role can be performed in Server Manager or with Windows PowerShell. Before the installation can begin, several hardware prerequisites must be met for the host computer. These prerequisites include the following:

◆ A 64-bit processor with second-level address translation (SLAT)

◆ A processor with VM Monitor Mode extensions

◆ A minimum of 4 gigabytes (GB) of memory

◆ Intel Virtualization Technology (Intel VT) or AMD Virtualization (AMD-V) enabled

◆ Hardware-enforced Data Execution Prevention (DEP) enabled (Intel XD bit, AMD NX bit)

Of course, you should also ensure that the Hyper-V host has sufficient hardware resources for the virtual machines, including enough physical processor cores, physical memory (RAM), storage, and network throughput. The design process for estimating hardware resources before purchasing the Hyper-V host is critical for a successful deployment of the virtualization solution, so that all of the virtual machines have sufficient resources. Furthermore, you should plan for extra resources in case some virtual machines need more virtual processor cores, memory, or storage due to increased usage or scaling the solution.

Because Hyper-V is a server role, you will add it by starting the Add Roles and Features Wizard, choosing the Hyper-V server role (Figure 3.2), and by installing features needed to manage the Hyper-V role.

Next, you will be guided to the Create Virtual Switches page, where you will be able to select at least one physical network adapter from the host server. Then you will need to choose whether you will allow live migrations to be sent and received. This option can be configured later; if the host is a cluster member, this option should be selected after the cluster creation. At the end of the wizard, you should choose a default location for storing virtual hard disk files and virtual machine configuration files, which can be edited later. After completing the wizard, the physical host should be restarted.

In order to install Hyper-V with Windows PowerShell, run the following command:

```
Install-WindowsFeature -Name Hyper-V -ComputerName <computer_name> -
IncludeManagementTools -Restart
```

FIGURE 3.2
Installing
Hyper-V

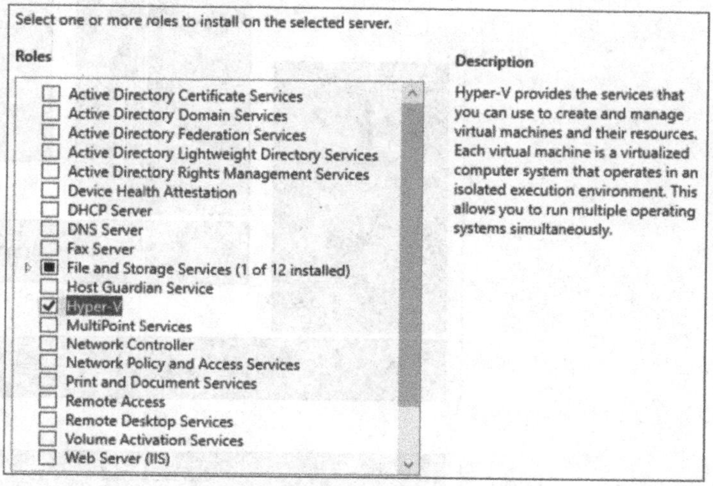

Select one or more roles to install on the selected server.

Roles

- [ ] Active Directory Certificate Services
- [ ] Active Directory Domain Services
- [ ] Active Directory Federation Services
- [ ] Active Directory Lightweight Directory Services
- [ ] Active Directory Rights Management Services
- [ ] Device Health Attestation
- [ ] DHCP Server
- [ ] DNS Server
- [ ] Fax Server
- [▪] File and Storage Services (1 of 12 installed)
- [ ] Host Guardian Service
- [✓] Hyper-V
- [ ] MultiPoint Services
- [ ] Network Controller
- [ ] Network Policy and Access Services
- [ ] Print and Document Services
- [ ] Remote Access
- [ ] Remote Desktop Services
- [ ] Volume Activation Services
- [ ] Web Server (IIS)

Description

Hyper-V provides the services that you can use to create and manage virtual machines and their resources. Each virtual machine is a virtualized computer system that operates in an isolated execution environment. This allows you to run multiple operating systems simultaneously.

Nested Virtualization

Windows Server 2016 introduces the capability to deploy Hyper-V into virtual machines, enabling you to host virtual machines inside of a Hyper-V virtual machine; this technique is called *nested virtualization* (Figure 3.3). Nested virtualization is used for evaluation, for testing, for development, as a lab environment, and for providing proof of concept. It should not be used for production. Before configuring nested virtualization for a virtual machine, you should enable virtualization extensions for the virtual machine processor. As an example, in the virtual machine that will act as a virtualization host named VirtualHost, you could run the following command:

```
Set-VMProcessor -VMName VirtualHost -ExposeVirtualizationExtensions $true
```

Another requirement for nested, guest virtual machines is that you enable MAC address spoofing on the virtual machine that you configured as a Hyper-V host, so that the nested virtual machine can communicate on the external network. Furthermore, nested virtualization requires the configuration version of the virtual machine to be 8.0. (Note: Configuration version 8.0 is supported in operating systems Windows Server 2016 and Windows 10 Anniversary Update or newer updates.)

Once the prerequisites are met, you can install Hyper-V on a virtual machine in the same way you would a Hyper-V host. However, some of the Hyper-V features will not work in nested virtualization, including virtualization-based security, Device Guard, dynamic memory, hot-add static memory, checkpoints, live migration, and Save or Restore state.

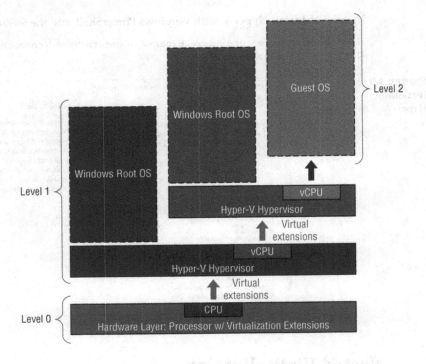

FIGURE 3.3
Nested virtualiza-
tion architecture

Storage Options in Hyper-V

Virtual machines use virtual hard disks for their storage. You can configure the virtual disk with partitions and store files and folders. Virtual hard disks can be created with the Hyper-V Manager console or with the New-VHD PowerShell cmdlet.

Hyper-V was introduced in Windows Server 2008, and at that time the file format for virtual disks was VHD format. However, this virtual hard disk was limited to 2 TB in size. Windows Server 2012 introduced the new VHDX format for virtual hard disks, and it offered many improvements, including bigger size (64 TB), a robust file structure resistant to corruptions, and larger block sizes for dynamically expanding and differencing disks for better performance. Windows Server 2016 introduced the VHDS format, used for virtual hard disks where multiple virtual machines can access simultaneously for high availability with clustering.

Note: At the time of this writing, Microsoft Azure doesn't support the VHDX format for virtual hard disks.

Virtual Hard Disk Types

When creating virtual hard disks, you can choose between different types and formats. The type of hard disk you select will vary depending on your requirements and on supportability. The virtual hard disk types include the following:

Fixed Size   The virtual hard disk allocates all the specified space immediately.

Dynamically Expanding   The virtual hard disk allocates space as required. Disks that have the VHDX format can also dynamically shrink; however, the shrinking occurs when the virtual machine is shut down.

Pass-Through   Direct access to a physical disk is provided.

Differencing   The virtual hard disk can be configured to store data in two files: the parent disk and the *differencing* disks. When data has changed when compared to a parent disk, it is stored in the differencing disks. These types of disks are used to reduce the amount of physical storage used in testing and evaluation purposes.

Virtual Hard Disk Recommendations

When deciding what type of virtual disk to use, you should first read the recommendations of the specific product you want to deploy in your virtual machine, such as Exchange Server, Skype for Business Server, or a domain controller. Some types of virtual hard disks are not supported in specific products—for example, differencing disks for Exchange Server.

If virtual disks must be compatible with older virtualization technologies running on Windows Server 2008 or Windows Server 2008 R2, you should use the VHD format; otherwise, you should use the VHDX format.

If you link multiple differencing disks, you should expect decreased performance. Be careful not to modify the parent virtual hard disk; if you do, the differencing disk will no longer be valid.

You can now add up to four Hyper-V virtual Fibre Channel virtual hardware components to a virtual machine, which will enable a virtual machine to access Fibre Channel storage on storage area networks (SANs).

Virtual hard disks should be located on high-performance storage. Furthermore, the storage should be redundant so that the storage solution will not become a single point of failure. Virtual machines should continue to work even if some of the physical hard disks fail or are replaced.

Hyper-V supports storing virtual machine data SMB 3.0 file shares. Although convenient for some organization, this functionality is limited to Windows Server 2012 or newer operating systems.

Configuring Hyper-V

Once the Hyper-V server role is installed, multiple settings will need to be configured on both the Hyper-V host and Hyper-V guest servers. For example, you will need to configure the type of disk storage and the path where virtual disk files will be located, the amount of memory allocated to each virtual machine, the number of processors, and the networking parameters that allow virtual machines to communicate with each other and with servers on the physical network. Each setting should be carefully configured to provide optimal performance for the solution that runs on the virtual machine. Therefore, each product (such as the domain controller, Exchange Server, Skype for Business Server) has its own recommendations and supported scenarios regarding how to be configured when running on a virtual machine.

Hyper-V Networking

Like physical machines, virtual machines use network resources to communicate with other computers, devices, internal organization networks, and the Internet. Network settings in virtual machines are configured with virtual switches. *Virtual switches* control how network traffic flows between virtual machines that are hosted on a Hyper-V server and the rest of the organizational network. You will use Virtual Switch Manager to create three types of virtual switches: external, internal, and private.

An *external* virtual switch maps a network to a specific network adapter on the Hyper-V host that provides virtual machines access to a network to which the host is connected.

An *internal* virtual switch is used for communication between the virtual machines on a Hyper-V host and between the virtual machines and the Hyper-V host itself.

A *private* virtual switch is used only for communication between virtual machines on a Hyper-V host.

When configuring an external or internal virtual network, you can also configure additional networking features, including the following:

◆ You can configure a VLAN ID to partition network traffic.

◆ Virtual networks should be provisioned with adequate bandwidth to ensure the best performance for virtual machines. Therefore, you might consider deploying physical network interface card teaming.

◆ You might configure bandwidth allocation to guarantee that each virtual machine has enough bandwidth allocated.

◆ Network adapters that support virtual machine queue (VMQ) use hardware packet filtering to deliver network traffic directly to a virtual machine, which improves performance.

◆ You might use QoS to guarantee minimum bandwidth for virtual machines.

◆ Remote Direct Memory Access (RDMA), which is also known as SMB Direct, is a feature that requires hardware support in the network adapter. A network adapter with RDMA functions at full speed with low resource utilization on network adapters that are attached to a Hyper-V switch.

◆ Windows Server 2016 includes a new NAT virtual switch type, which avoids the need to create a virtual machine that performs NAT.

Hyper-V Virtual Machine Configurations

Each operating system version supports specific virtual machine configuration versions. Table 3.3 shows the virtual machine configuration versions that can run on various versions of Windows operating systems.

TABLE 3.3:   Hyper-V Virtual Machine Configurations

WINDOWS VERSION OF THE HYPER-V HOST	CONFIGURATION VERSIONS
Windows Server 2016	8.0, 7.1 ,7.0 ,6.2, 5.0
Windows 10 Anniversary Update	8.0, 7.1 ,7.0 ,6.2, 5.0
Windows 10 build 10565 or later	7.0 ,6.2, 5.0
Windows 10 builds earlier than 10565	6.2, 5.0
Windows Server 2012 R2	5.0
Windows 8.1	5.0

To check a virtual machine's configuration version, use the following Windows PowerShell command prompt:

```
Get-VM * | Format-Table Name, Version
```

If you decide to update the configuration version of a virtual machine, it will be updated to the highest configuration level supported by the Hyper-V host on which it is running.

To update the version of a single virtual machine, use the following Windows PowerShell command:

```
Update-VMVersion <vmname>
```

Each version of the virtual machine configuration has different features, so you will not be able to use the new Hyper-V features until you upgrade the configuration version for Windows Server 2016.

Windows Server 2012 R2 introduced a new type of virtual machine called a Generation 2 virtual machine. All virtual machines that were created on platforms such as Windows Server 2012 and Windows Server 2008 R2 Hyper-V are considered to be Generation 1 virtual machines. You will select the virtual machine generation when you create the virtual machine. Because the guest operating systems must support booting from UEFI instead of BIOS, only x64 editions of Windows 8 and newer and Windows Server 2012 and newer guest operating systems are supported for Generation 2 virtual machines.

Hyper-V includes a dynamic memory feature that allows you to allocate a variable amount of memory where you can choose from minimum to maximum value. However, some applications (such as Microsoft SQL Server or Microsoft Exchange Server) do not support dynamic memory because of the way they utilize available memory for caching to optimize performance.

Shielded Virtual Machines

Windows Server 2016 introduces shielded virtual machines that are BitLocker-encrypted to protect the data in case the virtual hard drive is accessed directly (Figure 3.4). For example, if someone copies a virtual hard disk and takes it offsite, it cannot be accessed. The keys for decrypting the virtual hard drive are controlled by a Host Guardian Service (HGS).

FIGURE 3.4
Shielded virtual machine architecture

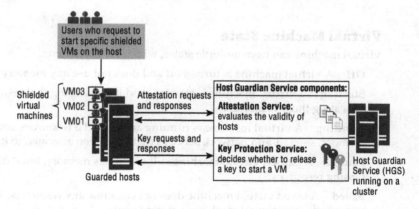

A shielded virtual machine must be a Generation 2 virtual machine that includes a virtual TPM, which means it does not require a hardware TPM to be present in the server. To implement shielded virtual machines, you implement a guarded fabric, which requires a Host Guardian Service. A shielded virtual machine can be started only on authorized hosts.

Host Guardian Service authorizes the hosts by using two methods:

◆ Active Directory (AD) trusted.

    ◆ Computer accounts for trusted Hyper-V hosts are placed in an Active Directory Domain Services security group, which is simpler to configure but has a lower level of security.

◆ TPM-trusted attestation.

    ◆ Trusted Hyper-V hosts are approved based on their TPM identity, which provides a higher level of security but is more complex to configure. Hosts must have a TPM 2.0 and UEIF 2.3.1 with secure boot enabled.

Virtual Machine Settings

Hyper-V administrators must be skilled at configuring virtual machines in case their company decides to virtualize the complete infrastructure. If it does, almost all of their servers will need to be virtualized, which will require careful planning, deployment, and management. Setting up a virtual machine includes the following components:

◆ *Integration services* provide the guest operating system with Hyper-V-specific device drivers. This allows the guest operating system to use the virtual hardware provided by Hyper-V.

◆ *Smart paging* is a feature that uses disk paging for additional temporary memory when virtual machines are starting and need more memory than the host can allocate.

◆ *Resource metering* measures CPU and memory usage, disk allocation, and network traffic.

◆ Assigning discrete devices allows guest virtual machines to communicate directly with PCI Express (PCIe) devices.

◆ A secure boot is needed for Linux and FreeBSD virtual machines.

Virtual Machine State

Virtual machine can have multiple states, which are listed here:

Off   A virtual machine is turned off and does not use any memory or processing resources.

Starting   A virtual machine is starting, and it is verifying that resources are available before allocating those resources.

Running   A virtual machine is running and uses the resources, such as virtual processors, memory, storage, and network services that have been allocated to it.

Paused   A paused virtual machine still consumes memory, but it does not consume any processing resources.

Saved   A saved virtual machine does not consume any resources. The resources are consumed once the virtual machine is started again.

Virtual Machine Checkpoints

Checkpoints enable administrators to make point-in-time snapshots of a virtual machine. However, these checkpoints might affect the virtual machine's performance and might not be supported for some applications, such as Exchange Server, SQL Server, and Skype for Business. Therefore, you should use checkpoints only with those server applications that support their use.

You can create a checkpoint in the Actions pane of the Virtual Machine Connection window or in the Hyper-V Manager console. Each virtual machine can have a maximum of 50 checkpoints.

You cannot use checkpoints as replacements for backups. Because checkpoint data is stored on the same volume as the virtual hard disk, your physical disk would be a single point of failure if you did not have a backup.

When you create a standard checkpoint, Hyper-V creates a VHD file (differencing disk) that stores the data that differentiates the checkpoint from the previous checkpoint or the parent virtual hard disk. When you delete standard checkpoints, this data is either discarded or merged into the previous checkpoint or parent virtual hard disk.

After applying a checkpoint, the virtual machine reverts to the state that existed at the time the checkpoint was created. However, as mentioned, you need to ensure that reverting the virtual machine is supported, depending on what application is deployed on the virtual machine. Also, be aware that the more checkpoints you create, the more performance will be impacted on that virtual machine due to the multiple VHD files that will create the chain of the virtual disk.

Importing and Exporting Virtual Machines

You can use Hyper-V import and export functionalities to transfer virtual machines between Hyper-V hosts, if the application that runs on the virtual machines supports that procedure.

During the import process, Hyper-V in Windows Server 2016 performs verification on the configuration in order to identify any issues, such as missing components.

In Windows Server 2016, you can import virtual machines from already-exported virtual machines and from copies of virtual machine configurations, checkpoints, and virtual hard disk files

During the virtual-machine import process, you can choose between the following options:

- ◆ Register the virtual machine in-place (use the existing unique ID) to create a virtual machine by using the files in the existing location.

- ◆ Restore the virtual machine (use the existing unique ID) to copy the virtual machine files back to the location from which they were exported and then create a virtual machine by using the copied files.

- ◆ Copy the virtual machine (create a new unique ID) to copy the virtual machine files to a new location that you specify, and then create a new virtual machine by using the copied files.

You can export virtual machines when the machine is running or turned off. During the virtual-machine export process, you can choose between following options:

◆ Export a Checkpoint creates an exported virtual machine because it existed when the checkpoint was created. The exported virtual machine will have no checkpoints.

◆ Export Virtual Machine with Checkpoints exports the virtual machine and all of the checkpoints that are associated with the virtual machine.

Live Migration

If the virtual machine is in production, you should choose live migration instead of an export and import process. *Live migration* is the process of moving the virtual machine from one Hyper-V host to another while the virtual machine is still running. However, users will not be impacted because the state of the virtual machine is maintained during a live migration and the network connections to virtual machines will be maintained.

If the virtual machine is stored locally on a Hyper-V host, all of the virtual machine data will be copied to the new Hyper-V host. However, if the virtual machine is stored on an SMB share, only the virtual machine configuration data will be moved. You will learn more about live migration in the section "Virtual Machine Migration."

PowerShell Direct

Windows Server 2016 introduces new functionality with PowerShell Direct. This functionality enables you to connect to virtual machines and run Windows PowerShell cmdlets without connecting over the network from the host computer to the guest virtual machine. It also provides a way to easily run automation scripts to multiple virtual machines running on a Hyper-V host.

To enable PowerShell Direct, the following requirements should be met:

◆ The host operating system must be either Windows Server 2016 or Windows 10.

◆ The guest operating system must be either Windows Server 2016 or Windows 10.

◆ You must be running an elevated Windows PowerShell console.

◆ You must use credentials to authenticate to the virtual machine.

◆ The virtual machine configuration version must be updated.

To enter a session on a virtual machine, use the following command:

```
Enter-PSSession -VMName <VM1>
```

To invoke a command on a virtual machine, use the following command:

```
Invoke-Command -VMName <VM1> -ScriptBlock {<Windows PowerShell commands>}
```

Virtual Machine Migration

One of the biggest benefits of virtualization is flexibility of the virtual machines so that their resources can be edited at any time and they can be easily moved or migrated to a different host. There are several scenarios in which you would want to migrate a virtual machine from one location to another. For example, you might want to move a virtual machine's virtual hard disk from one physical drive to another on the same host. In another example, you might move a virtual machine from one host to another.

The following options are available for migrating virtual machines in Windows Server 2016:

Virtual Machine and Storage Migration Running virtual machine is moved from one location to another or from one host to another by using the Move Virtual Machine Wizard in Hyper-V Manager. Virtual Machine and Storage Migration does not require failover clustering or any other high-availability technology.

Live Migration Enables you to migrate a virtual machine from one host to another without experiencing downtime. In Windows Server, you also can perform Shared Nothing Live Migration, which does not require failover clustering. In addition, hosts do not have to share any storage for this type of migration to be performed.

Quick Migration This method also is available in older operating system versions, such as Windows Server 2008. It requires that you install and configure failover clustering. During the migration process, a virtual machine is placed in a saved state. This causes downtime until it copies the memory content to another node and restores the machine from the saved state.

Exporting and Importing Virtual Machines The process consists of exporting a virtual machine on one host and then performing an import operation on another host. It requires that you turn off a virtual machine during export and import. In Windows Server 2016, you can import a virtual machine to a Hyper-V host without exporting it before import.

Figure 3.5 shows a virtual machine migration.

FIGURE 3.5
Virtual machine migration

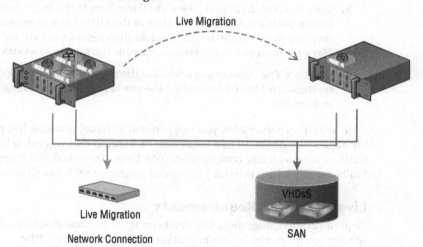

Live Migration

Live Migration
Network Connection

VHDsS

SAN

Overview of Live Migration

Windows Server 2016 Hyper-V allows you to move virtual machines between physical Hyper-V nodes without the need to shut down the virtual machines. This process is called live migration, and you can perform it in a cluster or noncluster environment. When used within a failover cluster, live migration enables you to move running virtual machines from one failover cluster node to another node. If used without a cluster, it is called *shared-nothing live migration*. Live migration can be performed from the Failover Cluster Management console, System Center Virtual Machine Manager (VMM) Administrator console, or Windows PowerShell.

The Live Migration process consists of four steps:

1. Migration setup. When the administrator starts the failover of the virtual machine, the source node creates a TCP connection with the target physical host. This connection transfers the virtual machine configuration data to the target physical host. Live migration creates a temporary virtual machine on the target physical host and allocates memory to the destination virtual machine. The migration preparation also checks to determine whether you can migrate a virtual machine.

2. Guest-memory transfer. The guest memory is transferred iteratively to the target host while the virtual machine is still running on the source host. Hyper-V on the source physical host monitors the pages in the working set. As the system modifies memory pages, it tracks and marks them as being modified. During this phase, the migrating virtual machine continues to run. Hyper-V iterates the memory-copy process several times, and every time it copies a smaller number of modified pages to the destination physical computer. A final memory-copy process copies the remaining modified memory pages to the destination physical host. Copying stops as soon as the number of dirty pages drops below a threshold or after 10 iterations are complete.

3. State transfer. To migrate the virtual machine to the target host, Hyper-V stops the source partition, transfers the state of the virtual machine, including the remaining dirty memory pages, to the target host and then restores the virtual machine on the target host. Hyper-V must pause the virtual machine during the final state transfer.

4. Cleanup. The cleanup stage finishes the migration by tearing down the virtual machine on the source host, terminating the worker threads, and signaling the completion of the migration.

In Windows Server 2016, you can perform a virtual-machine live migration by using Server Message Block (SMB) 3.0 as a transport. This means that you can take advantage of key SMB features, such as traffic compression, SMB Direct (remote direct memory access), and SMB Multichannel, which provide high-speed migration with low CPU utilization.

Live Migration Requirements

To perform a live migration, you must configure the host machines. Moreover, you must meet specific requirements for live migration in Windows Server 2016:

◆ The live migration should be enabled; it is not enabled by default.

◆ The host computers should have identical processor architecture.

◆ User accounts must be members of the local Hyper-V Administrators group, or the Administrators group on both hosts of the virtual machines.

◆ Both source and destination hosts must have the Hyper-V role installed.

◆ Both source and destination hosts must be members of the same domain, or members of different domains that trust each other.

◆ Hyper-V management tools should be installed on both source and destination hosts if you run the tools from source or destination hosts. Otherwise, you should install management tools on a computer running Windows Server 2016 or Windows 10.

◆ You should configure the authentication protocol for live-migration traffic. You can choose from following authentication protocols:

  ◆ Kerberos requires you to configure a constrained delegation. When Kerberos is enabled, there is no need to sign in to the server.

  ◆ Credential Security Support Provider (CredSSP) does not require you to configure a constrained delegation, but it requires the administrator to sign in to the server.

◆ You might choose to configure the performance options for live migration to reduce network and CPU utilization; doing so might increase the speed of the live migration.

◆ You should perform live migration on a separate network, and you might use an encryption such as Internet Protocol security (IPsec) to protect the traffic between hosts in live migration.

◆ You can configure bandwidth limits for live migration to optimize network bandwidth during the live migration process by using the Windows PowerShell cmdlet `Set-SMBbandwidthlimit`.

Hyper-V Replica

Hyper-V Replica, which was introduced in Windows Server 2012, enables virtual machines running at a primary site to be replicated to a secondary site. Hyper-V Replica is used for disaster-recovery scenarios where you to have two instances of a single virtual machine residing on different hosts, one as the primary, or live, copy and the other as a replica, or offline copy. These copies synchronize at regular intervals, which you can configure in Windows Server 2016. You also can fail over at any time.

In the event of a failure at a primary site, an administrator can use Hyper-V Manager to execute a failover of production workloads to replica servers at a secondary location within minutes, thus incurring minimal downtime. Later, when failure in the primary site is fixed, Hyper-V Replica enables an administrator to fail back virtualized workloads.

Hyper-V Replica technology consists of several components (Figure 3.6), which are listed here:

◆ The replication engine manages the replication configuration details and handles the initial replication, delta replication, failover, and test-failover operations. The replication engine also monitors virtual machine and storage-mobility events, and performs appropriate actions.

◆ Change Tracking tracks changes that are performed on the primary copy of the virtual machine.

◆ The network module provides the transfer of virtual machine replicas between the primary host and the replica host. It also enables data compression by default; it also enables HTTPS and certification-based authentication to secure the replication traffic.

◆ The Hyper-V Replica Broker role enables you to have Hyper-V Replica functionality even when the virtual machine you are replicating is highly available and can move from one cluster node to another.

FIGURE 3.6
Hyper-V Replica
architecture

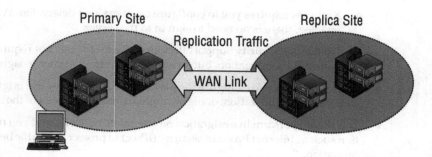

Hyper-V Replica does not have to use the same server or storage hardware. However, the physical host in the disaster recovery location should have sufficient resources to run the replica if failover is performed.

It is important to know that Hyper-V replica is not a high-availability technology but a disaster-recovery technology. It does not provide automatic failover.

Planning for Hyper-V Replica

Hyper-V Replica in Windows Server 2016 has following features:

◆ You can change the replication frequency. In Windows Server 2016, you can set the replication interval to 30 seconds, 5 minutes, or 15 minutes.

◆ You can replicate a single virtual machine to two independent servers, where the server that is running an active copy of the virtual machine replicates to the replica server, and the replica server then replicates to the extended replica server.

◆ Hyper-V Replica can leverage a Microsoft Azure instance as a replica repository, which is more convenient than building a disaster-recovery site.

Implementing Hyper-V Replica

Before you implement Hyper-V Replica technology, ensure that you meet these prerequisites:

◆ Sufficient storage exists on both the primary and replica servers to host the files that are used by the replicated virtual machines.

◆ Network connectivity exists between the locations that host the primary and replica servers. This can be a WAN or LAN link.

◆ Firewall rules are correctly configured to enable replication between the primary and replica sites (default traffic is going over TCP port 80 or port 443).

◆ An X.509v3 certificate exists to support Mutual Authentication with certificates if desired.

To enable Hyper-V Replica technology, complete the following steps:

1. In the Replication Configuration group of options, enable the Hyper-V server as a replica server.

2. Configure the Hyper-V server settings. Select the authentication and port options and configure the authorization options.

3. Configure the location for replica files. You should configure these settings on each server that serves as a replica server.

4. Specify both the replica server name and the connection options.

5. Select which virtual hard disk drives you want to replicate; configure the replication interval to 30 seconds, 5 minutes (this is a default in Windows Server 2016), or 15 minutes.

6. After you make the initial replica in Windows Server 2016, you also can make an extended replica to a third physical or cloud-based instance running Hyper-V.

Failover Options in Hyper-V Replica

You can use Hyper-V Replica to perform three types of failovers: test failover, planned failover, and failover.

Test Failover   This type of failover performs a nondisruptive task that enables you to test a virtual machine on the replica server while the primary virtual machine is running, and it does so without interrupting the replication. The test virtual machine is not started. It is disconnected by default to avoid potential conflicts with the running primary virtual machine.

Planned Failover   This type of failover moves the primary virtual machine to a replica site—for example, before site maintenance is performed. A planned failover confirms that the primary virtual machine is turned off before the failover executes. During the failover, the primary virtual machine sends all the data that it has not yet replicated to the replica server. The planned failover process then fails over the virtual machine to the replica server and starts the virtual machine on the replica server. After the planned failover, the virtual machine runs on the replica server and does not replicate its changes. If you want to establish replication again, you should reverse the replication.

Failover   Failover is performed at the replicated virtual machine only if the primary virtual machine is either unavailable or turned off. A failover is an unplanned event that can result in data loss because changes at the primary virtual machine might not have replicated before the disaster happened. During a failover, the virtual machine runs on a replica server. After you recover the primary site, you can reverse the replication direction to reestablish replication.

High Availability with Failover Clustering in Windows Server 2016

Virtualization brings many benefits to an organization's IT solutions and computing capabilities. However, it does not provide high availability out of the box. Therefore, you should provide a high-availability solution for virtual machines. Most organizations have applications that are business critical and must be highly available. To make an application highly available, you must deploy it in an environment that provides redundancy for all of the components the application requires.

The high-availability solution will depend on the type of application that is running on the virtual machine. You should carefully read about the best practices for a given application's high-availability solution. Depending on which application you run, the high-availability solution will be completely different. For example, the high-availability solutions for Exchange Server, Skype for Business Server, and File Server running in virtual environment are completely different.

Let's assume that an application that runs in a virtual machine supports a solution where high availability will be deployed at the virtual-machine level. In that case, you should implement failover clustering on the Hyper-V host computers, which means the application running on the virtual machine itself is not aware of the failover clustering that runs on the Hyper-V host machines.

For virtual machines to be highly available, you can choose from several options. You can implement virtual machines as a clustered role, which is called *host clustering*, or you can implement clustering inside the virtual machines, which is called *guest clustering*.

Host Clustering

Host clustering is deployed by installing the Failover Clustering feature on the Hyper-V host servers. In this scenario, the virtual machine will be configured as a highly available resource. This means that the guest operating system and applications that are running within the virtual machine do not need to be cluster-aware. However, the virtual machine is still highly available.

If the host node that controls the virtual machine unexpectedly becomes unavailable, the secondary host node takes control and restarts, or resumes, the virtual machine as quickly as possible. You can also move the virtual machine from one node in the cluster to another in a controlled manner. For example, you could move the virtual machine from one node to another while installing the updates on the host operating system.

The applications or services that are running in the clustered virtual machines do not have to be compatible with failover clustering, and they do not have to be aware that the virtual machine is clustered. The failover is at the virtual-machine level within the hosted cluster; therefore, there are no dependencies on software that you have installed in the virtual machine.

Guest Clustering

Guest failover clustering is configured on virtual machines. In this scenario, you create two or more virtual machines and enable failover clustering within the guest operating system. You, then, enable the application or service for high availability between the virtual machines.

Furthermore, virtual machines that are members of the cluster should be located on different Hyper-V host computers, since placing them on the same host computer will represent a single point of failure. When you implement failover clustering at both the host and virtual-machine levels, the resource can restart regardless of whether the node that fails is a virtual machine or a host. This configuration is also known as a *Guest Cluster Across Hosts*. It is considered an optimal high-availability configuration for virtual machines running mission-critical applications in a production environment.

You should consider several factors when you implement guest clustering:

◆ The application or service must be failover-cluster-aware. This includes any of the Windows Server 2016 services that are cluster-aware and any applications, such as clustered Microsoft SQL Server and Microsoft Exchange Server.

◆ You should deploy multiple network adapters on the host computers and the virtual machines. Ideally, you should dedicate a network connection to the iSCSI connection if you use this method to connect to storage. You should also dedicate a private network between the hosts and a network connection that the client computers use.

Network Load Balancing

Network Load Balancing (NLB) has been a Windows Server feature since the earliest versions (Figure 3.7). It distributes IP traffic to multiple instances of a TCP/IP host—for example, web servers that are running on hosts where NLB is installed. NLB transparently distributes client requests among the hosts, and it enables the clients to access the cluster by using a virtual host name or a virtual IP (VIP) address. From the client computer's perspective, the cluster appears to be a single server that answers these client requests. As enterprise traffic increases, you can add another server to the cluster.

FIGURE 3.7
Windows Network
Load Balancing
architecture

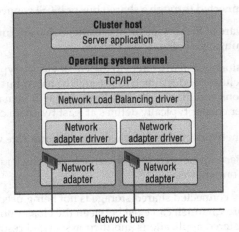

Therefore, NLB is an appropriate solution for resources that do not have to accommodate exclusive read or write requests and do not host databases. Examples of NLB-appropriate applications include web-based frontend applications and services.

When you configure an NLB cluster, you must install and configure the application on all the virtual machines that will participate in the NLB cluster. Older versions of Windows Server also support NLB; however, you should use the same operating system versions within one NLB cluster. Similar to a Guest Cluster Across Hosts, the NLB resource typically benefits from overall increased I/O performance when you locate the virtual machine nodes on different Hyper-V hosts. As with older versions of Windows Server, you should not implement Windows Server 2016 NLB and failover clustering within the same operating system because the two technologies conflict with each other.

What Is Failover Clustering?

High availability represents a set of technologies that work together in order to provide continuous functionality and access of services and data, even in a case of unpredicted failures of some computer or network components. Failover clusters in Windows Server 2016 provide a high-availability solution for many server roles and applications. By implementing failover clusters, you can maintain application or service availability if one or more computers in the failover cluster fail.

A *failover cluster* is a group of independent computers that work together to increase the availability of applications and services. Physical cables and software connect the clustered servers, known as *nodes*. If one of the cluster nodes fails, another node begins to provide service. This process is known as *failover*. With failover, you can minimize service disruptions.

In a failover cluster, each node in the cluster has following properties:

◆ Has full connectivity and communication with the other nodes in the cluster

◆ Is aware when another node joins or leaves the cluster

◆ Is connected to a network through which client computers can access the cluster

◆ Is connected through a shared bus or iSCSI connection to shared storage

◆ Is aware of the services or applications that are running locally and the resources that are running on all other cluster nodes

Cluster storage usually refers to logical devices—typically drives or logical units (LUNs)—that all the cluster nodes attach to through a shared bus. The shared disks store resources such as applications and file shares that the cluster will manage.

A failover cluster typically defines at least two data communications networks:

◆ One network enables the cluster to communicate with clients.

◆ The second, isolated network, enables the cluster node members to communicate directly with one another.

If directly connected shared storage is not being used, then a third network segment (for iSCSI or Fibre Channel) can exist between the cluster nodes and a data storage network.

Most clustered applications and their associated resources are assigned to one cluster node at a time. The node that provides access to those cluster resources is the active node. If the nodes detect the failure of the active node for a clustered application, or if the active node is offline for maintenance, the clustered application starts on another cluster node.

Figure 3.8 shows a typical clustering architecture.

FIGURE 3.8
Clustering
architecture

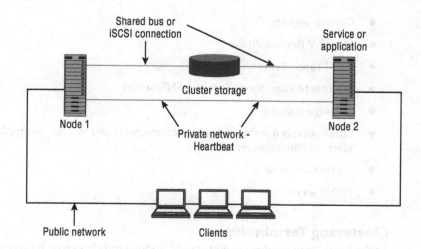

High Availability with Failover Clustering

Failover clustering addresses an organization's business needs for high availability by providing that data, application, and services are available in different failure scenarios. However, a specific hardware configuration should be installed to meet the prerequisites for failover clustering. Furthermore, you should install specific operating system features and application components as prerequisites for deploying failover clustering.

Before you deploy a failover cluster for a specific technology, read the failover-clustering planning and deployment guides and best practices documents for that specific technology. High-availability deployments for different applications can vary. For example, Microsoft Exchange Server uses the Failover Clustering feature in the Windows Server operating system; however, you use Exchange Server management tools to perform the process of high-availability deployment and failover-clustering installation. You must install the Failover Clustering feature from the Server Manager console or Windows PowerShell in the Windows Server operating system to deploy high availability for Hyper-V.

An application must be cluster-aware to user failover clustering. Failover clustering in the Windows Server operating system provides high availability for the following applications and features:

- DFS namespace server
- DHCP server
- Distributed Transaction Coordinator (DTC)
- File Server
- Generic application
- Generic script

- ◆ Generic service
- ◆ Hyper-V Replica Broker
- ◆ iSCSI Target Server
- ◆ Internet Storage Name Service (iSNS) server
- ◆ Message queuing
- ◆ Other servers (creates only client access point and storage. An application will be added after the cluster is created.)
- ◆ Virtual machine
- ◆ WINS server

Clustering Terminology

To deploy failover clustering, you should understand clustering terminology. The terminology for failover clustering is similar in both Windows Server and third-party failover-clustering products.

Table 3.4 defines failover-clustering terminology.

TABLE 3.4: Failover-Clustering Terminology

TERM	DESCRIPTION
Node	A Windows Server 2016 computer that is part of a failover cluster and has the Failover Clustering feature installed.
Service or application	A service that can be moved between cluster nodes (for example, a clustered file server can run on either node).
Shared storage	External storage that is accessible to all cluster nodes.
Quorum	The number of elements that must be online for a cluster to continue to run. The quorum is determined when cluster nodes vote.
Witness	A server that is participating in cluster voting when the number of nodes is even.
Failover	The process of moving cluster resources from the first node to the second node, as a result of node failure or an administrator's action.
Failback	The process of moving cluster resources back from the second node to the first node, as a result of the first node going online again or an administrator's action. If the service or application fails over from Node1 to Node2, when Node1 is again available, the service or application will fail back to Node1.
Clients	Computers that connect to the failover cluster and are not aware which node the service is running on.

Clustering Categories and Types

Clustering technology includes different types of clusters, depending on the type of the application you need to configure for high availability. Cluster deployment might differ depending on the location of the cluster nodes. Moreover, cluster functionality can differ according to the activity performed on each cluster member node.

Consider deploying different categories and types of clustering depending on your organization's specific business requirements. Clustering categories and types include:

◆ Type of the clusters. For example, you achieve Hyper-V high availability by deploying failover clustering, whereas you achieve high availability for web servers with NLB clustering.

◆ Failover clusters are deployed for stateful applications, such as SQL Server and Exchange Server. Stateful applications have long-running in-memory states or have large, frequently updated data states. Other types of failover cluster applications include Hyper-V, file servers, and print servers.

◆ NLB is deployed for stateless applications, such as web servers. Stateless applications do not have long-running in-memory states and work with data that is read-only or that does not change frequently. Stateless applications treat each client request as an independent operation, and they can load-balance each request independently. Stateless applications include web servers, virtual private networks (VPNs), File Transfer Protocol (FTP) servers, and firewall and proxy servers. NLB clusters support different TCP- or UDP-based services and applications.

◆ Single-site clusters and multisite clusters. Cluster deployments could include a scenario where all nodes are located in a single data center. However, some companies want to extend their application availability in case the main data center becomes unavailable. Therefore, organizations deploy *stretch clusters*, where they deploy nodes in multiple data centers. Multiple-site clusters can also include scenarios where organizations locate some of the cluster nodes, or the witness server, in the cloud environment, such as Azure.

◆ Active-Active and Active-Passive clusters. In Active-Active cluster configurations, such as Scale-Out File Server Cluster, multiple nodes run cluster application resources and accept client connections. In Active-Passive cluster configurations, one node runs cluster applications, while other nodes are passive and do not accept client connections. If an active node fails for any reason, some of the remaining passive nodes become active and run the application, accepting client connections.

Failover-Clustering Components

A failover-clustering solution consists of several components, which are listed in Table 3.5.

TABLE 3.5:   Failover-Clustering Components

COMPONENT	DESCRIPTION
Nodes	Computers that are members of a failover cluster. These computers run the cluster service, and any resources and applications associated to the cluster.
Network	A network across which cluster nodes can communicate with one another and with clients.
Resource	A node hosts a resource. The cluster service manages the resource and can start, stop, and move it to another node.
Cluster storage	A storage system that cluster nodes share. In some scenarios, such as clusters of servers that run Exchange Server, you do not require shared storage.
Quorum	The number of elements that must be online for a cluster to continue to run. The quorum is determined when cluster nodes vote.
Witness	A witness can be a file share or disk, which you use to maintain quorum. Ideally, the witness should be located on a network that is both logically and physically separate from those used by the failover cluster. However, the witness must remain accessible by all cluster node members.
Service or application	A software entity that Microsoft presents to clients and that clients use.
Clients	Computers (or users) that use the cluster service.

Organizations deploy different technologies for data protection, high availability, site resilience, and disaster recovery. However, none of the technologies can cover every failure or data-loss scenario. Therefore, organizations should know what combination of technologies can protect them from different failure scenarios.

For example, failover clustering protects organizations from server hardware failure, but it does not protect organizations from data loss caused by data deletion or data corruption. Windows Server Backup protects organizations from data loss caused by data deletion or data corruption, but it does not protect organizations from server hardware failure. As a result, organizations should use failover clustering to protect their applications from server hardware failures and also use Windows Server Backup to protect data from data deletion and corruption.

Table 3.6 lists multiple Windows Server technologies and how they respond to different failure scenarios:

TABLE 3.6:   Failover-Clustering Scenarios

	ZERO DOWNTIME	HARDWARE FAILURES	SITE FAILURES	DATA DELETION OR CORRUPTION	AUTOMATIC FAILOVER
Live Migration	Yes	No	No	No	No
Clustering	Depends on application	Yes	Depends on application	No	Yes
Hyper-V Replica	No	Yes	Yes	Depends on application	No
Windows Server Backup	No	Yes	Depends on scenario	Yes	No

Hardware Requirements for a Failover-Cluster Implementation

When you select hardware for cluster nodes, you must understand the hardware requirements. To meet availability and support requirements, your failover clusters must satisfy the following hardware criteria.

◆ You should use hardware that is certified for Windows Server.

◆ You should install the same or similar hardware on each failover cluster node. For example, if you choose a specific model of network adapter, you should install this adapter on each of the cluster nodes. This helps you avoid compatibility and capacity issues.

◆ You should ensure that if you use iSCSI storage connections, each clustered server has one or more network adapters or host bus adapters that are dedicated to the cluster storage. You should not use the network that you use for iSCSI storage connections for nonstorage network communication. In all clustered servers, the network adapters that you use to connect to the iSCSI storage target should be identical, and we recommend that you use Gigabit Ethernet or faster adapters.

◆ You should ensure that after you configure the servers with hardware, the servers pass all the tests in the Validate a Configuration Wizard before you consider the cluster a configuration that Microsoft supports.

When you select the infrastructure for cluster nodes, you must ensure that your failover clusters satisfy the following hardware criteria so that they meet availability and support requirements, including the following:

◆ You should run the supported version of Active Directory domain controllers, and they should use Windows Server 2008 or newer.

◆ Domain-functional level and forest-functional level should use Windows Server 2008 or newer.

◆ You should run the supported version of Domain Name System (DNS) servers, and they should use Windows Server 2008 or newer.

◆ The application that you configure for high availability should support the Windows Server 2016 operating system.

Windows Server 2016 includes the same quorum modes from Windows Server 2008 and newer operating systems, but there are changes to the process and recommendations for configuring quorum. However, a majority of votes still determines whether a cluster achieves quorum. Nodes can vote, as can a disk witness (disk in cluster storage), a file share witness (a file share), or an Azure Cloud Witness, where appropriate.

Before Windows Server 2012, there were only four quorum modes:

Node Majority Each node that is available and is in communication can vote. The cluster functions only with a majority, or more than half of votes. This model is preferred when the cluster consists of an odd number of server nodes and requires no witness to maintain or achieve quorum.

Node and Disk Majority Each node can vote, as can a designated disk in the cluster storage (the disk witness) when they are available and in communication. The cluster functions only with a majority (more than half) of votes. The basis for this model is that an even number of server nodes can communicate with each other and the disk witness.

Node and File Share Majority Each node can vote, as can a designated file share (file share witness) that an administrator creates, as long as they are available and in communication. The cluster functions only with a majority of votes. The basis for this model is that an even number of the cluster's server nodes can communicate with each other and the file share witness.

No Majority: Disk Only The cluster has quorum if one node is available and in communication with a specific disk in the cluster storage. Only the nodes that are in communication with that disk can join the cluster.

Dynamic Quorum

In Windows Server 2012, a new mode was introduced called *dynamic quorum*, which refers to the dynamic adjustment of quorum votes on the basis of how many servers are online. For example, if you have a five-node cluster, and you place two of the nodes in a paused state, and one of the remaining nodes crashes, your cluster would fail to achieve quorum and go offline in any legacy configuration. However, dynamic quorum would adjust the cluster's voting when the first two servers go offline, thereby making the cluster's quorum require two rather than three votes. The benefit is that a cluster with dynamic quorum stays online.

Windows Server 2012 R2 introduced *dynamic witness,* which builds on the dynamic quorum mode. A dynamic witness is a witness that dynamically has a vote, depending on the cluster's number of nodes. If there is an even number of nodes, the witness has a vote. If there are an odd number of nodes, the witness does not have a vote. The recommended configuration for a cluster was to create a witness only when you had an even number of nodes. However, with a dynamic witness's ability to remove voting, so that the cluster always has an odd number of votes, you should configure a witness for all clusters. This now is the default mode of configuration and is a best practice in most Windows Server 2016 and Windows Server 2012 R2 scenarios. In Windows Server 2016, the only suggested quorum mode is dynamic quorum, which is the default configuration.

In Windows Server 2016, you can choose whether to use file share witness, disk witness, or Azure Cloud Witness, as follows:

Disk Witness   Disk witness is the primary witness you would use for most scenarios, especially for local clustered scenarios. In this configuration, all nodes have access to a shared disk. One of the biggest benefits of this configuration is that the cluster stores a copy of the cluster database on the disk witness.

File Share Witness   File share witness is ideal when shared storage is not available or when the cluster spans geographical locations. This option does not store a copy of the cluster database.

Azure Cloud Witness   Azure Cloud Witness is new in Windows Server 2016, and it is the ideal option when you run Internet-connected stretched clusters. This technology does not require that you configure a file share witness at a third data-center location or a cloud VM. Instead, this option is built into a failover cluster and does not store a copy of the cluster database. Cloud Witness uses Microsoft Azure as the arbitration point. You can use the Configure a Cluster Quorum Wizard to configure a cloud witness as a quorum witness. Cloud Witness uses the publicly available Microsoft Azure Blob Storage to read/write a blob file, which is then used as an arbitration point in case of split-brain resolution for eliminating the extra maintenance overhead of VMs hosted in a public cloud. You can use the same Microsoft Azure Storage Account for multiple clusters where one blob file is used per cluster and a blob file name is equal to the cluster unique ID. Because Failover Cluster writes very small data per blob file during the cluster nodes' stat changes, Azure Cloud Witness does not create high cost for the Storage Account.

You also should consider the capacity of your cluster's nodes and factor their ability to support the services and applications that might fail over to that node. For example, a cluster that has four nodes and a disk witness still has quorum after two nodes fail. However, if you deploy several applications or services on the cluster, each remaining cluster node might not have the capacity to provide services.

Planning for Migrating and Upgrading Failover Clusters

Windows Server 2016 has a new process for upgrading a failover cluster named Cluster Operating System Rolling Upgrade. If you are performing cluster operating-system upgrades, you first upgrade the cluster operating system (OS) before you upgrade the cluster's functional level. For example, if you take a two-node cluster with Windows Server 2012 R2, you can upgrade it to Windows Server 2016 by draining the roles from one node, taking the node offline, and then removing it from the cluster. You then can upgrade that node to Windows Server 2016 and add the node back to the cluster. The cluster will continue to run on the Windows functional level of Windows Server 2012 R2. You can then drain the roles back to the Windows Server 2016 node. Then remove the Windows Server 2012 R2 node from the cluster, upgrade it, and add it back to the cluster. Finally, now that both nodes are running Windows Server 2016, you can upgrade the functional level by running the following Windows PowerShell command:

```
Update-ClusterFunctionalLevel
```

For example, let's assume that you need to upgrade a Hyper-V failover cluster. This task can be performed in Windows Server 2016 without downtime.

The upgrade steps for each node in the cluster include:

1. Move all the virtual machines that run on the cluster node and then pause the cluster node.

2. Perform a clean installation to replace the cluster node operating system with Windows Server 2016.

3. Add the node now running the Windows Server 2016 operating system back to the cluster.

4. Next, upgrade all nodes to Windows Server 2016.

5. Finally, use the Windows PowerShell cmdlet `Update-ClusterFunctionalLevel` to upgrade the cluster functional level to Windows Server 2016.

The Validation Wizard and the Cluster Support Policy Requirements

The Validation Wizard performs multiple tests for different failover-cluster hardware configurations and settings. You can run the wizard before and after you configure the failover cluster, and it verifies whether every component of the failover cluster node meets the hardware, network, infrastructure, and software requirements. The wizard must certify each of the cluster node components for Windows Server 2016 failover clustering.

The Validation Wizard helps you perform multiple types of tests, such as:

◆ Cluster

◆ Inventory

◆ Network

◆ Storage

◆ System

Additionally, it helps you:

◆ Detect any issues with hardware or configuration settings

◆ Validate changes to a cluster's hardware or configuration settings

◆ Perform diagnostic tests on a cluster

You also can run validation tests by using the `Test-Cluster` cmdlet. Some of the tests require you to perform administrative action before the tests start. For example, before you run storage tests on the disks or storage pools that a clustered role uses, you have to run the `Stop-ClusterGroup` cmdlet to stop the clustered role. After the tests are complete, you can restart clustered roles.

If there are any issues and errors during the validation, use the report that the Cluster Validation Wizard generates to analyze and perform troubleshooting. You also can send the report to the product support team.

You must install the Failover Clustering feature before you configure any failover cluster role. To implement clustering for a server role, perform the following procedure:

1. Install the Failover Clustering feature. Use Server Manager or Windows PowerShell to install the Failover Clustering feature on all computers that will be cluster members.

2. Verify the configuration and create a cluster with the appropriate nodes. Use the Failover Cluster Management snap-in to validate the configuration, and then use it to create a cluster with the selected nodes.

3. Install the role on all cluster nodes. Use Server Manager to install the server role that you want to use in the cluster.

4. Create a clustered role by using the Failover Clustering Management snap-in.

5. Configure the cluster role. Configure options on the application that the cluster uses.

6. Use the Failover Cluster Management snap-in to test failover by intentionally moving the service from one node to another.

Configuring Roles

Failover clustering supports clustering several Windows Server roles such as File Services, DHCP, and Hyper-V. After you install the Failover Clustering feature on the servers that you plan to configure as failover cluster nodes, you should install a clustered role by using Cluster Manager or Windows PowerShell.

Table 3.7 lists the clustered roles that you can configure on failover cluster nodes and the components that each role requires that you install.

TABLE 3.7: Clustered Roles

CLUSTERED ROLE	ROLE OR FEATURE PREREQUISITE
DFS Namespace Server	DFS Namespaces (part of File Server role)
DHCP Server	DHCP Server role
Distributed Transaction Coordinator (DTC)	None

TABLE 3.7: Clustered Roles *(CONTINUED)*

CLUSTERED ROLE	ROLE OR FEATURE PREREQUISITE
File Server	File Server role
Generic Application	Not applicable
Generic Script	Not applicable
Generic Service	Not applicable
Hyper-V Replica Broker	Hyper-V role
iSCSI Target Server	iSCSI Target Server (part of File Server role)
iSNS Server	iSNS Server Service feature
Message Queuing	Message Queuing Services feature
Other Server (creates only client access point and storage)	None
Virtual Machine	Hyper-V role
WINS Server	WINS Server feature

To configure a cluster node in Cluster Manager, you should expand the cluster name, right-click Roles, click Configure Role, and then follow the steps in the wizard. After you complete the installation, you should ensure that the role has a Running status on all nodes in the Failover Clustering console.

Managing Failover Clusters

You can perform several failover-cluster management tasks, ranging from adding and removing cluster nodes to modifying quorum settings. Some of the most frequently used configuration tasks include:

Managing Cluster Nodes For each node in a cluster, you can stop the cluster service temporarily, pause it, initiate a remote desktop session to the node, or evict the node from the cluster. You also can choose to drain the nodes in the cluster, such as if you want to perform maintenance or install updates. This functionality is part of the infrastructure that enables Cluster-Aware Updating (CAU) for patching a cluster's nodes.

Managing Cluster Networks You can add or remove cluster networks, and you can configure networks that you will dedicate solely to intercluster communication.

Managing Permissions If you manage permissions, you delegate rights to administer a cluster.

Configuring Cluster Quorum Settings If you configure quorum settings, you determine how quorum is achieved and who can vote in a cluster.

Migrating Services and Applications to a Cluster You can implement existing services to a cluster and make them highly available.

Configuring New Services and Applications to Work in a Cluster You can implement new services in a cluster.

Removing a Cluster You might remove a cluster if you are removing or moving a service to a different cluster. However, you first must remove the service that you are clustering.

You can perform these administrative tasks by using the Failover Cluster Management console or Windows PowerShell.

Configuring Cluster Properties

Cluster nodes are mandatory for each cluster. After you create a cluster and move it into production, you might need to configure cluster properties, which you can do by using the Failover Cluster Manager console.

You can configure cluster properties by right-clicking the cluster object in Failover Cluster Manager and then clicking Properties. The tabs available in the properties window include:

General Displays the name of the cluster and manages cluster group properties. In Cluster Group properties, you can select preferred owners for the core cluster resource group and configure failover and failback settings.

Resource Types Allows you to manage current cluster resource types and add new cluster resource types.

Balancer Allows you configure virtual machine balancing

Cluster Permissions Allows you configure cluster security permissions.

Managing Cluster Nodes

There are three aspects to managing cluster nodes:

Add a Node You can add a node to an established failover cluster by selecting Add Node in the Actions pane of the Failover Cluster Management console. The Add Node Wizard prompts you for information about the additional node.

Pause a Node You can pause a node to prevent resources from failing over or moving to that node. You typically pause a node when it is undergoing maintenance or troubleshooting.

Evict a Node You can evict a node, which is an irreversible process for a cluster node. After you evict the node, you must add it back to the cluster. You evict nodes when a node is damaged beyond repair or is no longer needed in the cluster. If you evict a damaged node, you can repair or rebuild it, and then add it back to the cluster by using the Add Node Wizard.

Each of these configuration actions is available in the Actions pane of the Failover Cluster Management console and in Windows PowerShell (Figure 3.9).

FIGURE 3.9
Managing cluster nodes

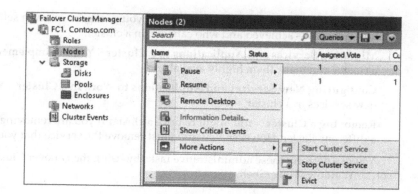

Failover transfers responsibility for providing access to a cluster's resources from one node to another. Failover can occur when one node experiences unplanned downtime because of hardware failure, or service failure on an active node can initiate failover to another node. A failover also can occur when an administrator intentionally moves resources to another node for maintenance.

A failover attempt consists of the following steps:

1. The cluster service takes all of the instance's resources offline in the order determined by the instance's dependency hierarchy. The dependent resources go offline first, and then the resources on which they depend go offline. For example, if an application depends on a physical disk resource, the cluster service takes the application offline first, which enables the application to write changes to the disk before the disk goes offline.

2. The cluster service attempts to transfer the instance to the node that is next on the instance's list of preferred owners. This occurs after all resources are offline.

3. If the cluster service moves the instance to another node successfully, it attempts to bring all resources online. It begins in reverse order of the dependency hierarchy. In this example, the cluster service attempts to bring the disk back online first and then the application. Failover is complete when all resources are online on the new node.

There are exceptions to this rule. One exception is that when failing over Hyper-V servers that are running Windows Server 2012 R2 or newer, the role does not go offline. Instead, it writes to the source location and the resource owner's destination until the failover is complete. It then moves the I/O to the new failover cluster node.

You can preconfigure the cluster service to fail back instances, which were hosted originally on an offline node, after that offline node becomes active again. When the cluster service fails back an instance, it uses the same procedures that it performs during failover, which means that the cluster service takes all of the instance's resources offline, moves the instance, and then brings all the resources in the instance back online.

PLANNED VERSUS UNPLANNED FAILOVER

The steps discussed previously occur when a failover cluster completes in a planned failover. For an unplanned failover, the failback steps are the same as for a planned failover. However, an unplanned failover usually occurs when one node goes offline without any planning. Therefore, the services abruptly shut down on the node that owns them. This causes the Failover Cluster Manager to skip to step 3, and then nodes attempt to bring the offline services back online as quickly as possible.

CONFIGURING CLUSTER NETWORKING

Networking and network adapters are important parts of every cluster implementation. You cannot configure a cluster without configuring the networks that the cluster will use. A network can perform one of three roles in a cluster, including:

Private Network   A private network carries internal cluster communication. When you use this type of network, cluster nodes exchange heartbeats and check for other nodes. The failover cluster authenticates all internal communication. However, administrators who are concerned about security might want to restrict internal communication to networks that are secure physically.

Public Network   A public network provides client computers with access to cluster-application services. The failover-clustering application creates IP address resources on the network that provides clients with access to the cluster service.

Public-and-Private Network   A public-and-private network, or mixed network, carries internal cluster communication and connects clients to cluster application services.

Configuring Quorum Properties

Cluster quorum is a critical resource in a failover cluster, because if the quorum is lost, the cluster nodes will not respond to client requests. Therefore, you must configure cluster quorum correctly. Proper cluster configuration ensures that cluster resources will be online during the cluster membership changes, such as planned or unplanned node shutdown, network issues, or any other failure scenarios.

To modify the quorum configuration in a Windows Server 2016 failover cluster, you can use the Configure Cluster Quorum Wizard or Windows PowerShell cmdlets. Three quorum configuration options are available:

Use Typical Settings   When you use this option, the failover cluster automatically assigns a vote to each node and dynamically manages the node votes. If hardware configuration includes cluster shared storage, the cluster will select a disk witness. In this scenario, the failover cluster software will automatically choose a quorum and witness configuration that provides the highest availability for the specific cluster configuration.

Add or Change the Quorum Witness   When you use this option, you can add, change, or remove a witness resource. A witness resource can be a file share or a disk. In this scenario, the failover cluster software will automatically assign a vote to each node and dynamically manage the node votes.

Advanced Quorum Configuration and Witness Selection   This option is needed only when there are specific requirements by the application or by the site location for quorum configuration. In this scenario, you will manually modify the quorum witness and add or remove node votes. You might also choose that that cluster dynamically manages node votes. By default, the votes are assigned to all nodes, and the node votes are managed dynamically.

What Is Cluster-Aware Updating?

You must be careful when applying operating-system updates to a cluster's nodes. In earlier Windows Server versions, you can provide zero downtime for a clustered role, but you must update cluster nodes manually and one at a time. Additionally, you must move resources manually from the node that you are updating to another node. This procedure can be very time-consuming. In Windows Server 2012, Microsoft implemented Cluster-Aware Updating (CAU), a feature for automatic updating of cluster nodes.

CAU is a feature that allows administrators to update cluster nodes automatically with little or no loss of availability during the update process. During an update procedure, CAU transparently takes each cluster node offline, installs the updates and any dependent updates, performs a restart if necessary, brings the node back online, and then moves to update the next node in a cluster.

For many clustered roles, this automatic update process triggers a planned failover, and it can cause a transient service interruption for connected clients. However, for continuously available workloads in Windows Server 2016, such as Hyper-V with live migration or file server with SMB Transparent Failover, CAU can orchestrate cluster updates with no effect on the service availability.

CAU orchestrates complete cluster updating in one of the following two modes:

Remote Updating Mode   In this mode, you configure a computer that runs Windows Server 2012 R2, Windows 8.1 or newer as a CAU orchestrator. To configure a computer as a CAU orchestrator, you must install the failover-clustering administrative tools. The orchestrator computer should not be a member of the cluster that you are updating. From the orchestrator computer, the administrator triggers on-demand updating by using a default or custom Updating Run profile. Remote-updating mode is useful for monitoring real-time progress during the Updating Run and for clusters that run on Server Core installations of Windows Server 2016.

Self-Updating Mode   In this mode, you configure the CAU clustered role as a workload on the failover cluster that you are updating, and then you define an associated update schedule. In this scenario, CAU does not have a dedicated orchestrator computer. The cluster updates itself at scheduled times by using a default or custom Updating Run profile. During the Updating Run, the CAU orchestrator process starts on the node that currently owns the CAU clustered role, and the process performs updates sequentially on each cluster node.

In the self-updating mode, CAU can update the failover cluster by using a fully automated, end-to-end updating process. An administrator also can trigger updates on-demand in this mode or use remote updating. In the self-updating mode, an administrator can access summary information about an Updating Run in progress by connecting to the cluster and then running the Windows PowerShell Get-CauRun cmdlet.

To use CAU, you must install the Failover Clustering feature in Windows Server 2016, and then create a failover cluster. The components that support CAU functionality then install automatically on each cluster node.

You also must install the CAU tools, which the Failover Clustering Tools include. These tools also are part of the Remote Server Administration Tools (RSAT). The CAU tools consist of the CAU GUI tools and the Windows PowerShell cmdlets. When you install the Failover Clustering feature, the Failover Clustering Tools install by default on each cluster node. You also can install these tools on a local or a remote computer that runs Windows Server 2016 or Windows 10, and that has network connectivity to the failover cluster.

In organizations that have clusters with large number of nodes, or that have many different types of clusters, administration becomes more challenging. Therefore, it is more efficient for administrators to use Windows PowerShell to automate the creation, management, and trouble-shooting of clusters.

Some of the more common cmdlets for managing and troubleshooting failover clustering include the following:

Get-Cluster   Returns information about one or more failover clusters in a given domain.

Get-ClusterAccess   Returns information about permissions that control access to a failover cluster.

Get-ClusterDiagnostics   Returns diagnostics for a cluster that contains virtual machines.

Get-ClusterGroup   Returns information about one or more clustered roles (resource groups) in a failover cluster.

Get-ClusterLog   Creates a log file for all nodes, or a specific a node, in a failover cluster.

Get-ClusterNetwork   Returns information about one or more networks in a failover cluster.

Get-ClusterResourceDependencyReport   Generates a report that lists the dependencies between resources in a failover cluster.

Get-ClusterVMMonitoredItem   Returns the list of services and events being monitored in the virtual machine.

Test-Cluster   Runs validation tests for failover-cluster hardware and settings.

Test-ClusterResourceFailure   Simulates a failure of a cluster resource.

What Is a Stretch Cluster?

A *stretch cluster* provides highly available services in more than one location. Although stretch clusters can solve several specific problems, they also present specific challenges.

Stretch-cluster storage replication allows each site to be independent, and it provides fast access to the local disk. With separate storage systems, you cannot share a disk between sites (Figure 3.10).

FIGURE 3.10
Stretch-cluster architecture

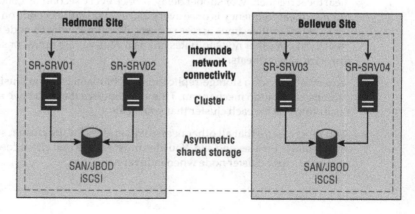

When compared to a remote server, a stretch cluster has three main advantages in a failover site. These advantages include the following scenarios:

◆ When a site fails, a stretch cluster can fail over the clustered service or application automatically to another site.

◆ Because the cluster configuration automatically replicates to each cluster node in a stretch cluster, there is less administrative overhead than if you were to use a standby server, which requires you to replicate changes manually.

◆ The automated processes in a stretch cluster reduce the possibility of human error, which is inherent in manual processes.

However, because of the increased cost and complexity of a stretch-failover cluster, it might not be an ideal solution for every application or business. When you are considering whether to deploy a stretch cluster, you should evaluate the importance of applications to your business, the type of applications you are using, and any alternative solutions. Some applications can provide stretch redundancy easily by using log shipping or other processes, and you can achieve sufficient availability with only a modest increase in cost and complexity.

The complexity of a stretch cluster requires more detailed architectural and hardware planning than is required for a single-site cluster. It also requires that you to develop business processes that test cluster functionality regularly.

There are different prerequisites for implementing a stretch cluster than for implementing a single-site cluster. It is important that you understand these differences and how to prepare properly for implementing a multisite cluster.

Before you implement a multisite failover cluster, you must ensure the following:

◆ You must have enough nodes and votes on each site so the cluster can be online even if one site is down. This setup requires additional hardware and can increase costs significantly.

◆ All nodes must have the same operating-system and service-pack version.

◆ You must provide at least one low-latency and reliable network connection between sites. This is important for cluster heartbeats. By default, regardless of subnet configuration, heartbeat frequency, or subnet delay, is once every second or 1,000 milliseconds. The range for heartbeat frequency is once every 250 to 2,000 milliseconds on a common subnet and 250 to 4,000 milliseconds across subnets. By default, when a node misses a series of five heartbeats, another node initiates failover. This value's range, or subnet threshold, is three through 10 heartbeats.

◆ You must provide a storage-replication mechanism. Failover clustering does not provide a storage-replication mechanism. This also requires that you have multiple storage solutions, including one for each cluster that you create.

◆ You must ensure that all other necessary services for the cluster, such as AD DS and DNS, are available on a second site. You also must ensure that client connections can be redirected to a new cluster node when failover happens.

Failover Clustering with Hyper-V

When you implement failover clustering and configure VMs as highly available resources, the failover cluster treats the VMs like any other application or service. For example, if host failure occurs, failover clustering acts to restore access to the VM as quickly as possible on another host in the cluster. Only one node at a time runs the VM. However, you also can move the VM to any other node in the same cluster as part of a planned migration.

The failover process transfers the responsibility of providing access to resources in a cluster from one node to another. Planned failover (also known as *switchover*) can occur when an administrator intentionally moves resources to another node for maintenance or other reasons, or when unplanned downtime of one node occurs because of hardware failure or other reasons. The failover process consists of the following steps:

1. The node where the VM is running owns the clustered instance of the VM, controls access to the shared bus or iSCSI connection to the cluster storage, and has ownership of any disks or logical unit numbers (LUNs) that you assign to the VM. All the nodes in the cluster use a private network to send regular signals, known as heartbeat signals, to one another. The heartbeat indicates that a node is functioning and communicating on the network. The default heartbeat configuration specifies that each node sends a heartbeat over TCP/UDP port 3343 each second (or 1000 milliseconds [ms]).

2. Failover initiates when the node that is hosting the VM does not send regular heartbeat signals over the network to the other nodes. By default, this is five consecutively missed heartbeats (or 5000 ms elapsed). Failover might occur because of a node failure or network failure. When heartbeat signals stop arriving from the failed node, one of the other nodes in the cluster begins taking over the resources that the VMs use.

You define the one or more nodes that could take over by configuring the Preferred Owner and the Possible Owners properties. The Preferred Owner property specifies the hierarchy of ownership if there is more than one possible failover node for a resource. By default, all nodes are members of Possible Owners. Therefore, removing a node as a Possible Owner excludes it from taking over the resource in a failure situation.

For example, suppose that you implement a failover cluster by using four nodes. However, you configure only two nodes as Possible Owners. In a failover event, the resource might still be taken over by the third node if neither of the Preferred Owners is online. Although you did not configure the fourth node as a Preferred Owner, if it remains a member of Possible Owners, the failover cluster uses it to restore access to the resource if necessary.

Resources are brought online in order of dependency. For example, if the VM references an iSCSI LUN, it stores access to the appropriate host bus adapters (HBAs), network (or networks), and LUNs in that order. Failover is complete when all the resources are online on the new node. For clients interacting with the resource, there is a short service interruption, which most users might not notice.

3. You also can configure the cluster service to fail back to the offline node after it becomes active again. When the cluster service fails back, it uses the same procedures that it performs during failover. This means that the cluster service takes all the resources associated with that instance offline, moves the instance, and then brings all the resources in the instance back online.

There are many improvements to the functionality of Hyper-V with failover clustering since the introduction of Hyper-V in Windows Server 2008. Windows Server 2016 continues to build on Hyper-V with failover clustering with some updated features and improvements in the following areas:

◆ Maximum node and VM supported. Failover clustering supports up to 64 nodes and 8000 VMs per cluster (and 1024 VMs per node).

◆ File share storage. Windows Server 2012 introduced the possibility of storing VMs on Server Message Block (SMB) file shares in a file server cluster. This is a way to provide shared storage that is accessible by multiple clusters, by providing the ability to move VMs between clusters without moving the storage. To enable this feature, deploy a file server cluster role and select Scale-Out File Server for application data.

◆ Shared virtual disk. Windows Server 2012 R2 introduced the ability to use a .vhdx as a shared virtual disk for guest clusters. Windows Server 2016 introduced improved features to the shared disks and introduced a new disk format, .vhds (VHD Set).

◆ Rolling Hyper-V cluster upgrades. In Windows Server 2016, you can upgrade the nodes one at a time when upgrading from Windows Server 2012 R2. After upgrading all nodes in a Hyper-V cluster, you can upgrade the functional level of the entire cluster.

◆ VM configuration version. Windows Server 2016 builds on the rolling upgrades by not updating the VM's configuration version automatically. You can now manually update the VM configuration version. This allows a VM to migrate back and forth from both Windows Server 2016 and Windows Server 2012 R2 until you have completed the rolling upgrades, and you are ready to upgrade to the version for Windows Server 2016 and take advantage of the new features for Windows Server 2016 Hyper-V.

Implementing Hyper-V Failover Clustering

To implement failover clustering for Hyper-V, you must complete the following high-level steps:

1. Install and configure the required versions of Windows Server 2016. After you complete the installation, configure the network settings, join the computers to an Active Directory domain, and then configure the connection to the shared storage.

2. Configure the shared storage. You must use Disk Manager to create disk partitions on the shared storage.

3. Install the Hyper-V and Failover Clustering features on the host servers. You can use Server Manager in the Microsoft Management Console (MMC) or Windows PowerShell to do this.

4. Validate the cluster configuration. The Validate This Cluster Wizard checks all the pre-requisite components that are required to create a cluster and provides warnings or errors if any components do not meet the cluster requirements. Before you continue, resolve any issues that the Validate This Cluster Wizard identifies.

   We strongly recommend that you run the Validate This Cluster Wizard and resolve all issues before creating a cluster and putting it into production.

5. Create the cluster. When the components pass the validation by the Validate This Cluster Wizard, you can create a cluster. When you configure the cluster, assign a cluster name and an IP address. You create a computer object also referred to as the cluster name object (CNO) by using the cluster name in AD DS and registering the IP address in DNS. In Windows Server 2012 R2 and later, you can create an Active Directory–detached cluster, which allows you to create the cluster name object in DNS; however, it does not require you to have the cluster name object in AD DS.

   You can enable Clustered Shared Storage for the cluster only after you create the cluster and add eligible storage to it. If you want to use CSV, you should configure CSV before you move to the next step.

6. Create a VM on one of the cluster nodes. When you create the VM, ensure that all files associated with the VM—including both the virtual hard disk and VM configuration files—are stored on the shared storage. You can create and manage VMs in either Hyper-V Manager or Failover Cluster Manager. We recommend that you use the Failover Cluster Manager console to create VMs. When you create a VM by using Failover Cluster Manager, the VM is automatically highly available.

7. Make the VM highly available only for existing VMs. If you created a VM before implementing failover clustering, you need to make it highly available manually. To make the VM highly available, in the Failover Cluster Manager, select a new service or application to make it highly available. Failover Cluster Manager will present a list of services and applications that can be made highly available. When you select the option to make VMs highly available, you can select the VM that you created on shared storage.

   When you make a VM highly available, you see a list of all the VMs that are hosted on all cluster nodes, including VMs that are not stored on the shared storage. If you make a VM that is not located on shared storage highly available, you receive a warning, but Hyper-V adds the VM to the services and applications list. However, when you try to migrate the VM to a different host, the migration will fail.

8. Test VM failover. After you make the VM highly available, you can migrate the computer to another node in the cluster. You can select to perform a Quick Migration or a Live Migration. In most cases, you should perform a live migration to reduce downtime. We will discuss these differences later.

CSVs in a Windows Server 2016 failover cluster allow multiple nodes in the cluster to have read-write access simultaneously to the same disk that you provision as an NTFS volume, and Windows Server 2016 failover cluster adds them as storage to the cluster. When you use CSVs, clustered roles can fail over from one node to another more quickly, and without requiring a change in drive ownership or dismounting and remounting a volume. CSVs also help simplify the management of a potentially large number of LUNs in a failover cluster.

CSVs provide a general-purpose, clustered file system, which you layer on NTFS. Windows Server 2016 does not restrict CSVs to specific clustered workloads; it only supports them for Hyper-V clusters and Scale-Out File Server clusters.

Although CSVs provide additional flexibility and reduce downtime, you do not need to configure and use CSVs when you implement high availability for VMs in Hyper-V. You also can create clusters on Hyper-V by using the regular approach (with disks that you do not assign as CSVs). However, we recommend that you use CSVs because they provide the following advantages:

Reduced LUNs for the Disks   You can use CSVs to reduce the number of LUNs that your VMs require. When you configure a CSV, you can store multiple VMs on a single LUN, and multiple host computers can access the same LUN concurrently.

Improved Use of Disk Space   Instead of placing each .vhd file on a separate disk with empty space so that the .vhd file can expand, you can oversubscribe disk space by storing multiple .vhd files on the same LUN.

Single Location for VM Files   You can track the paths of .vhd files and other files that VMs use. Instead of using drive letters or GUIDs to identify disks, you can specify the path names.

When you implement a CSV, all added storage displays in the \ClusterStorage folder. The \ClusterStorage folder is created on the cluster node's system folder, and you cannot move it. This means that all Hyper-V hosts that are members of the cluster must use the same drive letter as their system drive, or VM failovers fail.

No Specific Hardware Requirements   There are no specific hardware requirements to implement CSVs. You can implement CSVs on any supported disk configuration, and on either Fibre Channel or iSCSI SANs.

Increased Resiliency   CSVs increases resiliency because the cluster can respond correctly even if connectivity between one node and the SAN is interrupted, or if part of a network is down. The cluster reroutes the CSV traffic through an intact part of the SAN or network.

Implementing CSVs

After you create the failover cluster, you can enable a CSV for the cluster and then add storage to the CSV.

In Windows Server 2012 R2 and later versions, when a shutdown is initiated on a Hyper-V host machine, the action that is taken by that VM depends on the settings set for each VM. These options are found in the VM settings by selecting the Automatic Stop Action tab.

The options for what a VM does on the shutdown of a host are as follows:

Save the Virtual Machine State   This option is the first and default option. In Windows Server 2012 R2 and later this option creates a .bin file reserving space for the memory to be saved when placing the VM in a saved state. If the host begins a shutdown, Hyper-V Virtual Machine Management Service (VMMS) will begin saving the VM's memory to the hard drive and placing the VM in a saved state.

Turn Off the Virtual Machine   This second option will allow VMMS to turn off the VM in a graceful manner for Hyper-V and enter an off state. However, the VM operating system views this as no different from removing power on a physical machine.

Shut Down the Guest Operating System   Unlike the other two options, this third and final option requires that integrated services is working properly on the VM and that, specifically, you have selected and installed Operating System Shutdown on the guest VM. However, unlike the Turn Off The Virtual Machine option, this option allows a graceful shutdown of the VM—including the guest—from the host's perspective. By utilizing the integrated services, VMMS will trigger a shutdown on the guest machine. Once initiated, the VM will shut down the guest operating system and enter an off state.

If the Hyper-V host goes offline unexpectedly, the VMMS process will not have received any information about the shutdown; therefore, none of these actions will occur. This is useful only when a shutdown is initiated on a Hyper-V host.

The Bottom Line

Focus on designing the solution.   In this chapter, you learned about the compute functionalities in Windows Server 2016. However, to make the most of the new technology, you should spend enough time on design so that your solution meets the business requirements and provides return on investment for your organization. When designing Hyper-V solutions, always start from the question "What applications will be hosted on the virtual machines?" Once you answer that question, you should continue with "What are the best practices and preferred deployment strategies recommended by the application vendor?" For example, you might find that the recommendations for running web server in a virtual environment are completely different from the recommendations for running Exchange Server in a virtual environment. The same questions go for the high-availability solutions, where every application has its own preferred and optimized deployment model.

Once you complete the design process, provide an estimate for performance and scalability in the near future.

Master It   What is the primary goal when designing a virtualization solution for your organization, and what is your approach to the design process? Do you have a long-term plan regarding solution support, scalability, and high availability?

Solution   Virtualization solution design includes the following components:

◆ *Number of users*: You should estimate the right performance for your virtualized servers. This will help you estimate the hardware for the host computers.

◆ *High availability*: You need to provide continuous access to virtual machines for your organization. This will help you design the high availability for virtual machines.

◆ *Server placement and a disaster-recovery solution*: You need to optimize WAN links between data centers and branch offices. This will help you design Hyper-V Replica as a disaster-recovery solution.

Tailor your Hyper-V solution to the specific product that will run in the VM environment. During the design and deployment phase of virtual machines, you will meet different questions that are related to networking, security, databases, or any other application that will be hosted in Hyper-V. Invite product-specific experts to join and give their own vision of the new virtualization solution. Together you will come up with an optimal design for the best performance, high availability, and security of the solution.

Master It You need to design an Exchange Server in Hyper-V for your organization. What parameters you will take into consideration for choosing the topology that will best suit your organization most?

Solution Invite Exchange admins, network admins, and security experts to discuss the project of Exchange virtualization. Together you will design the optimal virtualization solution for Exchange Server. Some of the outcomes of your work might include the following:

- Capacity of the virtual machines such as virtual CPU, RAM, networking, and storage that need to be configured for Exchange Server virtual machines.

- Supported scenarios for Exchange Server virtualization must be considered. For example, dynamic memory, differential hard disks, and checkpoints are not supported for Exchange Server virtual machines.

- High availability and disaster-recovery solution for Exchange Server virtual machines.

- Security for data on Exchange databases, virtual hard drives, and data in transit.

Automate the configuration processes in your virtualization environment. You have been tasked to migrate your physical infrastructure to the Hyper-V virtualization solution. However, your organization consists of hundreds of servers. You need to create the same number of virtual machines optimized for their purpose. Furthermore, you need to create a number of virtual machines on a regular basis for testing and development.

Master It You will need to work on creating Windows PowerShell scripts that will allow you to provision and manage a large number of virtual machines at the same time.

Solution Start with a single script that will provision one virtual machine. Save the script and create a copy that will be specific for different types of virtual machines. Then create a library for different types of management activities, such as provisioning virtual machines, managing virtual machine properties, deleting virtual machines that are not needed, and collecting logs for monitoring the performance of the virtual machines. After some amount of time, you will be able to efficiently respond to any requests, such as:

- The need for a new virtual machine: You will be able to provision it in minutes, instead of hours.

- The need to perform test failovers for Hyper-V Replica for selected virtual machines: You will be able to run any task within a short amount of time.

- The need to change the virtual machine parameters of each member of the application server farms. With Windows PowerShell this can be done in minutes, instead of hours.

Chapter 4

Storage

Over the last couple of releases, Microsoft has invested heavily in expanding the storage functionality built into Windows Server. It has always had core-storage technologies to enable it to connect to storage area networks (SANs) or to serve as a file server. But today, with Windows Server 2016, Windows Server has enterprise-class foundational storage technologies, enabling many companies to bypass or complement traditional, dedicated storage solutions. We will focus on some of the newer storage technologies.

IN THIS CHAPTER, YOU WILL LEARN TO:

- ◆ Understand the what/why/how of new storage technologies in Windows Server 2016
- ◆ Learn about deployment considerations for Windows Server storage technologies
- ◆ Maintain and support a Windows Server storage environment

Overview of Storage in Windows Server 2016

For administrators who haven't spent much time with storage technologies in the last couple of versions of Windows Server, it is important to understand the capabilities. So, before we get into the details of any of these technologies, we will first introduce the technologies and key terminology.

File Systems When we talk about file systems for Windows Server, we are talking about New Technology File System (NTFS) and Resilient File System (ReFS).

Data Deduplication Data deduplication is a new data-compression technology introduced in Windows Server 2012. Not unlike technology such as NTFS compression or the technology built into WinZip, data deduplication eliminates unneeded duplicate copies of data. Prior to the introduction of the term "data deduplication," the term "single-instance storage" was sometimes used. In fact, Single Instance Store (SIS) was Microsoft's implementation of single-instance storage in Windows Storage Server 2008 R2. Prior to that, it was available as a feature in Microsoft Exchange Server.

Storage Spaces Storage Spaces is a storage virtualization technology that enables you to create virtual disks from a storage pool. You can customize the storage resilience and availability, based on requirements.

Storage Replica Storage Replica is a storage replication technology that enables you to replicate data from one server to another server, from one server to itself (using other volumes), and from one failover cluster to another failover cluster.

Storage Quality of Service Like network-based Quality of Service (QoS), Storage QoS enables you to provide customized storage performance based on need. The technology is supported with Hyper-V.

Now let's elaborate on each of these. Distributed File System (DFS) and Work Folders, while closely tied to storage, are covered in Chapter 6.

File Systems

The two primary file systems for use in Windows Server 2016 are NTFS and ReFS. You're probably already familiar with NTFS, but you may not have deployed ReFS. In this section, we will provide a brief overview of both file systems along with typical use cases. You will also look at some of the advanced concepts of the file systems.

NTFS

First introduced in Windows NT 3.1 in 1993, NTFS has been around a long time. In other words, the file system is mature. It has gone through minor and major improvements all the way through Windows Server 2016. For a long time, NTFS was the only choice for organizations that needed a file system on Windows that offered security, supported large volumes, and provided built-in encryption support. Today, there are two such file systems: NTFS and ReFS. We will look at ReFS in the next section.

NTFS offers a plethora of features. While we won't describe the common features you are probably already familiar with, let's review some of the more advanced features in this section:

Reparse Points These are used to extend the I/O functionality. Think of a reparse point as a file system object that has user-defined data. Applications can use reparse points to extend the functionality of the file system. For example, a technology that moves unused files to lower-cost storage (such as storage tiering) can use reparse points to identify the new location of the data. When you use mount points (whereby you attach storage to a folder on an existing volume), reparse points are used, too. Developers can take advantage of reparse points to provide additional functionality to their applications and how they work with data. You can check for reparse points on files by using the `fsutil` command with the `reparsepoint` parameter.

Change Journal The change journal is used to keep track of files that are added, deleted, and modified on an NTFS volume. This feature was introduced with NTFS 5.0 (with Windows 2000).

Sparse File Support This feature saves disk space by consuming disk space only as it is needed. For example, if you have a large file (say a 100 GB file) and the file contains 80 GB of actual data (with the rest being taken up by zeros in the data), then NTFS can store the file by using 80 GB of space. However, you must enable sparse file support to take advantage of it. Once you do, sparse operations happen transparently in the background. Applications don't need to be aware of it. You can mark a single file as sparse by using the `fsutil` command-line tool. For example, to mark `D:\Data\HugeFile.csv` as sparse, run the `fsutil sparse setflag D:\Data\HugeFile.csv` command.

To look at more detail about NTFS, visit `https://msdn.microsoft.com/en-us/library/cc781134(v=ws.10).aspx`. Although the material was produced a long time ago, it has a good overview of how NTFS works and it looks at the NTFS architecture in detail.

ReFS

When Resilient File System (ReFS) was first introduced in Windows Server 2012, many administrators were thinking that it would replace NTFS as the default file system. Instead, it complemented it. Due to some initial limitations, ReFS was rarely used or sometimes used in very niche use cases. One of the biggest limitations, which still exists, is that ReFS cannot be used for the system volume (that's because ReFS isn't a bootable file system, at least yet). It can only be used with data volumes. However, ReFS in Windows Server 2016 is now version 2 of ReFS—and it has been improved, and many limitations and issues have been removed or fixed. ReFS provides outstanding data integrity, scalability (support for huge volumes), and performance (especially when working with huge volumes). The primary use cases for ReFS are Storage Spaces Direct (where it is required), Storage Spaces, very large volumes (larger than 256 TB), virtualization scenarios with Hyper-V, and some backup scenarios.

A couple of features stand out as key features for ReFS:

Block Cloning   Block cloning is a method used to copy data without the overhead of reading and writing normally associated with a copy. With a standard NTFS file copy, the file system reads the data and then writes it to a new location. The larger the file, the longer the copy takes. With ReFS block cloning, copying is a high-performance operation that only remaps a file to a new location.

Integrity Streams   ReFS integrity streams is an optional feature that you can enable on individual files, folders, and volumes. Integrity streams help to maintain the integrity of your data by using checksums. This is different from the default ReFS checksums for metadata (because this just involves metadata, not the actual data). From a performance perspective, there is an impact. Thus, for performance-sensitive systems or systems that have low-latency performance requirements, you should perform adequate testing prior to enabling integrity streams.

Comparing NTFS and ReFS

Now that you've looked at the file systems and some of their advanced features, let's look at the details. You can use the `fsutil` tool to look at the supported file-system feature. For example, to look at the file-system features of the F: volume, run the `fsutil fsinfo volumeinfo f:` command. Table 4.1 reviews file-system features and shows some differences between the file systems.

TABLE 4.1:   Comparison of File-System Features

FILE-SYSTEM FEATURE	FEATURE IN NTFS?	FEATURE IN ReFS?
Case-sensitive filenames	Yes	Yes
Preserves case of filenames	Yes	Yes
Preserves and enforces ACLs	Yes	Yes
File-based compression	Yes	No

TABLE 4.1: Comparison of File-System Features *(CONTINUED)*

FILE-SYSTEM FEATURE	FEATURE IN NTFS?	FEATURE IN REFS?
Disk quotas	Yes	No
Sparse files	Yes	Yes
Reparse points	Yes	Yes
Object identifiers	Yes	No
Encrypted File System	Yes	No
Named streams	Yes	Yes
Transactions	Yes	No
Hard links	Yes	No
Extended attributes	Yes	No
Open file FileID	Yes	Yes
USN journal	Yes	Yes
Integrity streams	No	Yes
Block cloning	No	Yes
Sparse VDL	No	Yes
File ghosting	No	Yes

For many administrators, there are a few key differences that prevent widespread deployment of ReFS:

◆ ReFS is not bootable. This is the number one reason why more administrators aren't using ReFS. Because it can only be used on data volumes, you must deploy a mix of file systems on each server if you want to use ReFS. If you are deploying high-performance virtualization or backup solutions, you can overlook this to take advantage of the ReFS performance and scalability.

◆ Compression isn't available. Compression is not always used, but it is popular on Windows-based file servers. Even when not actively used, it can be helpful when you are running low on space on a volume.

◆ Quotas aren't available. Quotas are typically used on Windows-based file servers, such as with user home folders. But without quotas, administrators will be hard-pressed to deploy ReFS on servers for user home folders because quotas are almost universally used for such scenarios.

For a complete list of ReFS features and additional information, see "Resilient File System (ReFS) Overview" at https://docs.microsoft.com/en-us/windows-server/storage/refs/refs-overview.

Data Deduplication

Data deduplication in Windows Server 2016 optimizes volumes for space savings. It supports the NTFS and ReFS file systems. The results of data deduplication are like those of other compression technologies, although the methods used to achieve the space savings are often different. Table 4.2 compares common space-saving technologies.

TABLE 4.2: Comparison of Space-Saving Technologies

SPACE-SAVING TECHNOLOGY	SPACE-SAVING METHOD	SPACE SAVINGS POTENTIAL
Single Instance Storage (SIS)	Stores exact file duplicates once. In Exchange Server, limited to email messages and attachments.	Limited, except for niche uses. Microsoft Exchange removed the technology in Exchange Server 2010.
NTFS data compression	Compresses every file individually.	Limited, except for niche uses. Excellent for text-based files.
File compression tools such as WinZip	Copies files and then compresses them into an archive file. You must remove the compression to work with the files.	Moderate, based on file types (with text-based files being excellent). Not transparent space savings as with other technologies.
Data deduplication	Background and transparent space savings. Identifies repeated patterns and eliminates duplicate patterns.	Potentially excellent, depending on the data type (VDI files, software installation files being excellent).

Data deduplication, like other space saving technologies, has specific data types that it optimizes greatly and other data types that it doesn't. The following points summarize the data types and typical savings rates.

Virtualization Files Specifically, it can optimize virtual hard disks that are used for VDI (virtual desktop infrastructure). This is an excellent data type for data deduplication. You can routinely achieve about 80 percent space savings. Imagine having 25 virtual hard disks for VMs (virtual machines) on a volume. They all run Windows 10. There is a large amount of duplication in the data. That enables data deduplication to achieve great space savings. Officially, outside of VDI, Microsoft doesn't support data deduplication for VMs on Hyper-V. However, you can achieve excellent space savings in such a scenario. But because it isn't supported, you should restrict such uses in nonproduction or lab environments.

Shared Folders When dealing with home folders for users, you typically achieve between 25 and 50 percent space savings. Users often store data that isn't friendly to space-saving technologies (such as videos and music files).

Software Installation Data When dealing with install files, ISO files (especially of operating systems), and other software installation files, you can often achieve 50 to 75 percent space savings.

You can estimate the total space savings for a volume by using the ddpeval.exe tool. This tool is added to a server once the Data Deduplication role service is installed. To estimate the space savings for the G:\ volume, run the ddpeval.exe G: command.

There are many times when you should avoid the use of data deduplication. For example, avoid data deduplication for Exchange Server and SQL Server. Check with your software vendor to ensure that an application supports (and works well with) data deduplication before you deploy it.

How Data Is Optimized

The data deduplication optimization process is interesting, and understanding how it works will help you troubleshoot it if it doesn't do what you expect it to do. Figure 4.1 shows the high-level steps in the optimization process.

FIGURE 4.1
How data is optimized

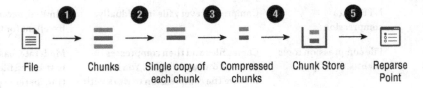

File Chunks Single copy of Compressed Chunk Store Reparse
      each chunk chunks   Point

The following steps describe the details of the data deduplication process shown in Figure 4.1.

1. When data deduplication is optimizing data, it first breaks the data into smaller chunks. These chunks, which are variably sized, are typically 32 KB to 128 KB.

2. Once data is broken into smaller chunks, data deduplication looks for duplicate chunks. In Figure 4.1, you can see that two of the chunks are identical (as depicted by two being green or darker and the other chunk being red or lighter). Duplicate chunks are replaced with a pointer to the single copy of the chunk that remains.

3. The remaining chunks (all unique chunks) are compressed. The compression task is optional, although it is enabled by default. In some cases, such as if you are deduplicating file types that aren't compression friendly (e.g., multimedia data), you can disable compression. In Figure 4.1, you can see the chunks are smaller in size, like what you would expect with compression.

4. The chunks are sent to a chunk store. Chunk stores are special container files stored under a folder named Dedup in the System Volume Information folder of the optimized volume. There are multiple data deduplication folders. However, they are meant to be used by the system for data deduplication, so you should be careful when you're working with the data.

5. The optimized file is replaced with a reparse point. The reparse point is a pointer that tells the file system how to find the data. For data deduplication, the reparse point directs the file system to the chunk store (where the data is stored after optimization).

After data is optimized, the way in which it is read is different than the way unoptimized data is read. We will look at how optimized data is read next.

How Optimized Data Is Read

Once data is optimized, there is a unique way of handling access to the data. The process is completely transparent to the user. Figure 4.2 shows the process of reading an optimized file.

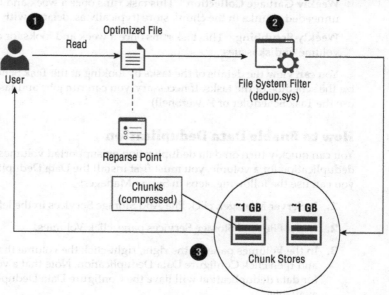

FIGURE 4.2
How optimized data is read

The following steps describe the process shown in Figure 4.2 in more detail:

1. In this scenario, a user is attempting to open an optimized file. When the user opens the file, a reparse point intercepts the read request and sends the request to the data deduplication file system filter (dedup.sys).

2. The file system filter, dedup.sys, redirects the read request to the chunk store that contains the optimized data.

3. The file system completes the read operation by providing the data to the user. If the user changes any of the data and saves it, the file system will save that data like a standard save (unoptimized). Later, during the next scheduled deduplication job, the data will be optimized based on the configuration.

How Data Deduplication Works in the Background

Like other Windows services, data deduplication runs transparently in the background. It uses scheduled tasks to perform data deduplication jobs. The following points describe the data deduplication jobs:

Background Optimization This is the primary job for data deduplication. This job runs every hour, by default, and performs the core functions of data deduplication (breaking data down into chunks, checking for duplicate chunks, compressing chunks, and moving data to the chunk store).

Weekly Garbage Collection This task runs once a week and reclaims disk space if it finds unneeded chunks in the chunk store (typically associated with data deletion).

Weekly Scrubbing This task runs once a week and looks for chunk store corruption due to volume or disk issues.

You can view the details of the tasks by looking at the Task Scheduler. You can also customize the schedule of the tasks. If necessary, you can run jobs and tasks manually (whether you use the Task Scheduler or PowerShell).

How to Enable Data Deduplication

You can quickly turn on data deduplication on supported volumes. Before you turn on data deduplication for a volume, you must first install the Data Deduplication role service. Thereafter, you can use the following steps in Server Manager:

1. In Server Manager, click File And Storage Services in the left pane.

2. In the File And Storage Services pane, click Volumes.

3. In the Volumes pane on the right, right-click the volume that you want to deduplicate and then click Configure Data Deduplication. Note that a volume that is not supported for data deduplication will have the Configure Data Deduplication item grayed out (not available).

4. Choose the server usage of General Purpose File Server, Virtual Desktop Infrastructure (VDI) server, or Virtualized Backup Server. If none of these are a match for the server type, choose the General Purpose File Server option and customize the settings (if needed).

5. Configure other settings or accept the defaults. Click OK when you're ready to turn on data deduplication.

You can also use PowerShell to enable data deduplication. For example, to enable deduplication on F:\, run the `Enable-DedupVolume 'F:'` command. Note that this will use default settings from the General Purpose File Server mode.

Once you have data deduplication enabled for some volumes, it will mostly be a "set it and forget it" technology. But before it gets to that point, you will need to ensure that it is functional and performing its job (saving you space). The following commands are helpful when you're examining an existing data-deduplication configuration and when you're determining if everything works as expected.

Get the F: volume and report the saved space:

```
Get-DedupVolume F:
```

Get all of the volumes configured for data deduplication and report detailed information, along with the space savings percentage:

```
Get-DedupStatus | FL
```

Show the deduplication schedule (this is especially useful if you customized the schedule):

```
Get-DedupSchedule
```

Next, we will look at some of the advanced settings. They are optional but can be useful in specific scenarios.

Data Deduplication Advanced Settings

Many implementations of data deduplication use the default settings. When you are using data deduplication for typical workloads (for example, VDI files or a general-purpose file server), the default settings are effective. However, in some scenarios, configuring advanced settings or changing the default settings will help your implementation achieve better results. In this section, we will review some of the advanced settings. We won't cover all the available settings, but we will link to additional information at the end of the section.

Scheduling You can use PowerShell to review and change the existing schedule. Not only can you change the schedule, but you can also change the parameters of the scheduled tasks. For example, if you want to change the ThroughputOptimization scheduled task to use up to 75 percent of the memory (instead of the default 50 percent), you should run the `Set-DedupSchedule 'ThroughputOptimization' -Memory 75` command.

Exclude Files from Deduplication You can manually choose to exclude specified file types from deduplication. Data deduplication doesn't work with .edb or .jrs files. But if you have other file types that would not benefit from data deduplication, you can exclude those, too. To exclude a file type with an extension of .IGES on the F:\ volume, run the Set-DedupVolume F: -ExcludeFileType IGES command.

Change the Minimum File Size   You can configure data deduplication so that it skips files if they are not a minimum size. This is useful if you have many small files that would not save much space if deduplicated. To set data deduplication to work with files that are a minimum of 64 KB on the F:\ volume, run the Set-DedupVolume F: -MinimumFileSize 65536 command.

There are many settings that you can modify to suit your organization's specific needs. To see additional settings, see https://docs.microsoft.com/en-us/windows-server/storage/data-deduplication/advanced-settings.

Storage Spaces

Storage Spaces is the virtualized storage solution built into Windows Server. It was originally introduced in Windows Server 2012. Subsequently, it was improved in Windows Server 2012 R2 and further improved in Windows Server 2016. It is an enterprise-ready storage solution for a variety of demanding workloads. Microsoft even markets it to cloud-hosting companies. Unlike software-based disk resiliency solutions in older versions of Windows Server that were relegated to occasional use by small businesses, Storage Spaces is a fully featured storage solution that includes different levels of resiliency, storage tiering, and many high-availability features. It integrates with failover clustering and Cluster Shared Volumes (CSVs) for scale-out file server implementations.

Figure 4.3 shows a high-level view of Storage Spaces.

FIGURE 4.3
Storage Spaces
overview

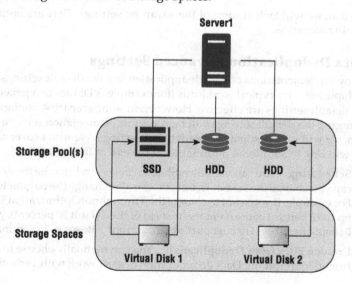

Figure 4.3 shows a high-level overview of Storage Spaces. The following points describe the components in the diagram.

Server1   In the diagram, a single physical server is shown. The server has multiple hard drives; some of the hard drives are solid state drives (SSDs) and some of them are standard hard disk drives (HDDs).

Storage Pools   In the diagram, a representation of the hard drives is shown. Storage pools are created from the hard drives. Storage pools represent a virtualized view of the available storage. Instead of having to target individual disk drives or volumes, you can use storage pools to target a specific set of hard drives (even mixing hard drive types).

Storage Spaces   The term "Storage Spaces" refers to the virtual disks created from the storage pools. At the Storage Spaces level, you can specify attributes of the virtual disks, such as whether the disks have resiliency and storage tiering.

In the next section, we will look at some of the configuration options for your virtualized storage.

Storage Spaces Configuration Options

When you deploy Storage Spaces, you must make specific choices during the deployment, and those choices have a big impact on the performance and resiliency of the storage. Before you start configuring, it is important for you to understand your organization's (or your project's) requirements and the use cases. For example, you might choose different configuration options to provide storage for a small team in a single location than you would to provide storage for your entire company.

One of the primary configuration options is the type of resilience to use. *Resilience* refers to the capability of the storage to continue being available in the event a disk becomes unavailable. Three settings are available:

Simple   With simple resiliency, there is no resilience! This configuration is like a RAID 0 array, which stripes data across all the available disks. There are no extra copies of the data, and there is no parity information that could be used to rebuild data in the event of a failed drive. On the plus side, simple resiliency provides excellent performance. So, if you need the highest performance and don't require any resiliency, this configuration option might be your best choice.

Parity   Parity is sometimes referred to as "erasure encoding." With parity, data is striped across all the available disks. In addition to the data, parity information is also written to disk. You can choose to write parity information to one disk or two disks, if you have enough disks. With parity information written to two disks, you are protected against simultaneous failure of two disks. The downside of parity is that write performance is impacted due to the parity information being written to disk(s). If your workload requires outstanding write performance, avoid this option. However, for heavy read operations, this option might be optimal. This configuration is like RAID 5.

Mirror   In this configuration, data is striped across multiple disks. Additionally, an extra copy or two extra copies of the data is also written to disk. Mirroring can support one or two simultaneous disk failures based on how many extra copies of the data is written to disk. Mirror is like RAID 1. Mirroring is the most widely deployed resiliency option because it provides good all-purpose performance and supports disk failure(s).

Besides resilience, there are other configuration options, too. The following points describe some of the other options. This isn't an exhaustive list of options, but instead some of the most widely used options.

Storage Tiering   When talking about storage options, it has been common to assign a tier to specific levels of performance. For example, Tier 0 storage represents the "best of the best" (such as when SSDs were first introduced to the enterprise). Tier 5, the lowest tier, typically represented the slowest storage available (often S-ATA storage with minimal performance but massive amounts of free space). Organizations manually placed data in the various tiers based on the requirements. For example, critical applications might use Tier 1 or Tier 2 storage. Archive data from mailboxes might be stored in Tier 4 or Tier 5 storage. Manually managing that data is an enormous task. With Storage Spaces, tiering is automated. Storage Spaces combines SSD (high performance) with HDD (low or lower performance) and automatically relocates frequently used data ("hot data") to SSD while relocating infrequently accessed data ("cold data") to HDD. Storage tiering improves storage performance.

Continuous Availability   Storage Spaces uses failover clustering to deliver high-availability storage. You can create a pool and make it available across multiple nodes.

Write-Back Cache   Write-back cache is used to improve the performance of your storage by writing random writes to a special place on your SSD storage. Later, that storage is transparently relocated to HDD. Without write-back cache, all data is written to HDD from the beginning. That reduces performance.

Storage Spaces Direct

Two new storage-related features were released with Windows Server 2016: Storage Spaces Direct, which we will talk about now, and Work Folders, which is covered in Chapter 6. While Storage Spaces enables a single server to provide virtualized storage, Storage Spaces Direct enables multiple servers (with their local storage) to combine to provide virtualized storage. Instead of requiring specialized networking to connect the servers (common with Storage Area Networks), Storage Spaces Direct takes advantage of the existing network. Microsoft has identified two specific use cases for Storage Spaces Direct: combining storage and compute (such as with a Hyper-V server or a SQL server) and separating storage and compute. When you separate storage and compute, you use Scale-out File Servers to provide file shares to remote servers (such as Hyper-V servers). The following diagram, Figure 4.4, shows an overview of Storage Spaces Direct.

FIGURE 4.4
Storage Spaces
Direct overview

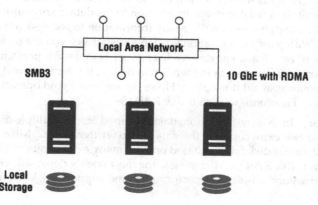

Figure 4.4 illustrates a small Storage Spaces Directory environment, and here we walk through the components:

Servers   Three servers are participating. Storage Spaces Direct supports up to 16 servers.

Local Storage   In the diagram, each server is shown with local storage. It can be a mix of drive types (such as SSD and HDD). Storage Spaces Direct supports up to 400 drives and up to 1 Petabyte (PB) of storage.

SMB   The servers communicate by using SMB3. SMB3 was first introduced in Windows Server 2012, and it offers higher performance and better security. Storage Spaces Direct takes advantage of SMB Direct and SMB Multichannel, both introduced with SMB3.

Local Area Network   Storage Spaces Direct uses the existing network. That means you need to evaluate your network to see if it makes sense to introduce Storage Spaces Direct. The minimum recommended NICs are 10 Gbps for cluster communications. Many organizations do not deploy 10 Gbps NICs yet, or the network itself doesn't support that speed. But this is quickly changing as companies acquire new hardware or public cloud resources.

Now you have an idea of the high-level components involved in Storage Spaces Direct. Figure 4.5 shows the converged deployment option, sometimes referred to as a disaggregated deployment.

FIGURE 4.5
Storage Spaces
Direct converged

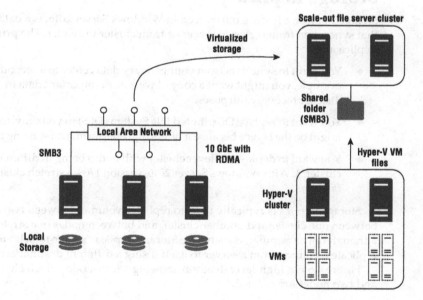

In Figure 4.5, we take Figure 4.4 and layer in the converged components:

Scale-out File Servers   In Figure 4.5, two servers are acting as a cluster.

Share Folder(s)   In Figure 4.5, a single shared folder is accessed through SMB3.

Hyper-V Hosts   In Figure 4.5, two Hyper-V hosts each have VMs. The Hyper-V VM files are stored on the SMB file share.

The primary difference between the converged deployment, shown in Figure 4.5, and the hyper-converged deployment is that the hyper-converged deployment combines everything. In some ways, this simplifies things. It is simpler to deploy and manage. However, the scale-out options are more limited, and overall performance is reduced. Hyper-converged deployments are typically used for smaller organizations and organizations that are deploying to a secondary data center or branch office.

Interested in trying Storage Spaces Direct using Windows Server 2016 VMs? Look at this step-by-step guide from the Failover Clustering and Network Load Balancing team blog at Microsoft: `https://blogs.msdn.microsoft.com/clustering/2015/05/27/testing-storage-spaces-direct-using-windows-server-2016-virtual-machines/`.

Storage Replica

Storage Replica, a feature introduced in Windows Server 2016, is a data replication technology that syncs data from server to server or from cluster to cluster. The primary use cases for Storage Replica are:

◆ You want to sync data from your primary data center to a secondary data center. For example, you might want a copy of your most important data in a secondary data center for disaster recovery purposes.

◆ You want to replace Distributed File System (DFS) in your environment. Storage Replica might be the choice because it offers high-performance syncing compared with DFS.

◆ You want to deploy a failover cluster with nodes being in different data centers (a "stretch cluster"). With Windows Server 2016, version 1709, a stretch cluster now offers automatic failovers.

Storage Replica is typically used to replicate volumes between two standalone servers, between one cluster and another cluster, and between nodes of a stretch cluster. Another use, although not as popular, is using the Storage Replica "server-to-self" mode. In this mode, you replicate a volume from a server to itself (using a different destination volume).

Figure 4.6 is a high-level diagram showing a four-node stretch cluster. Two nodes are in Site1 and two nodes are in Site2.

FIGURE 4.6
Storage Spaces
stretch cluster

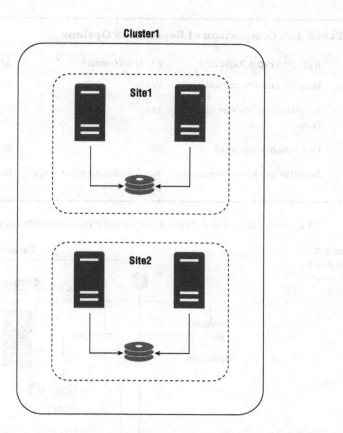

In the stretch cluster shown in Figure 4.6, each site has its own local shared storage. When you have storage that isn't shared across all cluster nodes, as in the figure, it is known as *asymmetric storage.* Conversely, if every node in a cluster can access the storage (and take ownership of it), the storage is known as *symmetric storage.* The two nodes in each site read and write data from the local shared storage. The shared storage is kept in sync by using Storage Replica.

Types of Replication

Storage Replica offers two forms of replication, based on your network topology. The first form, synchronous replication, is ideal for local area networks or campus environments (high performance, low latency). Synchronous replication is the default replication when you configure Storage Replica. The second form of replication, asynchronous replication, doesn't have latency requirements and is suitable for wide area networks (WANs) or networks with high latency. Table 4.3 compares the two forms of replication.

TABLE 4.3: Comparison of Replication Options

REPLICATION FEATURE	SYNCHRONOUS	ASYNCHRONOUS
Ideal for mission-critical data	Yes	No
Zero data loss in event of a failure	Yes	No, near zero data loss
Performance overhead	Yes	No
Requires low-latency network	Yes, 5 ms round-trip time, or better	No, latency agnostic

Figure 4.7 shows the steps of the synchronous replication process.

FIGURE 4.7
Storage Replica
synchronous
replication

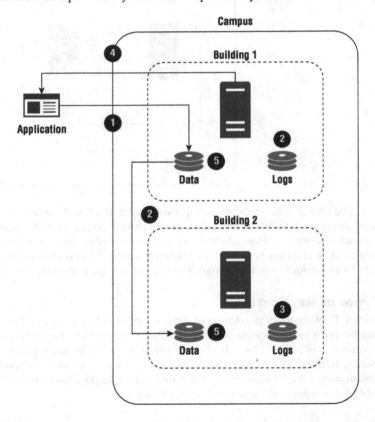

The following steps describe the numbered steps in Figure 4.7. Thus, number 1 in the list corresponds to the number 1 in the diagram.

1. Data is written to a replicated volume by an application (could be an application, service, script, user, or other process).

2. Log data is written to the source site and data is replicated to the remote location. This happens simultaneously.

3. Log data is written to the remote site. Note that logs are always written to before the data is written to the data volumes.

4. The application is notified that the data was written successfully. By this time, the data exists in two distinct locations. This makes synchronous replication suitable for your most important workloads.

5. The data is written to the data volumes at the source and remote location (from the logs).

Because of the slower write times with synchronous replication, you need to use a high-performing network (low latency, high bandwidth) along with high-performing storage subsystems (such as SSD). This will help minimize performance impacts from synchronous replication. Next, let's look at the process for asynchronous replication. Figure 4.8 shows the asynchronous replication steps.

FIGURE 4.8
Storage Replica asynchronous replication

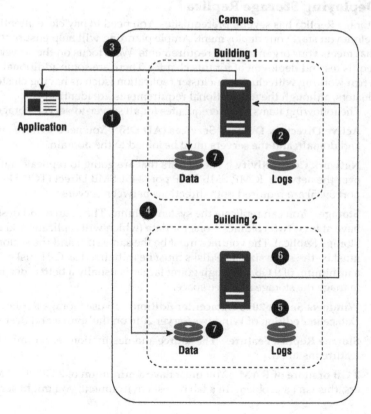

In the following list, the numbers in the steps correspond to the numbers in Figure 4.8.

1. Data is written to a replicated volume by an application (could be an application, service, script, user, or other process).

2. Log data is written to the source site.

3. The application is notified that the data was written successfully. The order of the application being notified differs from synchronous replication. With asynchronous replication, the application is notified before there is confirmation that the data was transmitted to the remote location. At the time of notification, there is only a single copy of the data. This makes asynchronous replication less suitable for your most important workloads.

4. Data is replicated to the remote location.

5. Log data is written to the remote location.

6. The remote location confirms the transmittal of data.

7. The data is written to the volumes at the source and remote location (from the logs).

Deploying Storage Replica

Storage Replica has several prerequisites. You need to pay close attention to the prerequisites before you start your deployment. Ample planning will help ensure that you have a deployment that meets your organization's requirements. We'll focus on the server-to-server replication prerequisites and deployment for this chapter. There are some additional requirements and steps when working with cluster-to-cluster replication (such as having clustered disks) or stretched clusters, although the foundational requirements are identical.

The following items are prerequisites for all server-to-server storage replication:

Active Directory Domain Services (AD DS)   You need to have an existing AD DS forest and domain and the servers must be joined to the domain.

Network Connectivity   The servers that are going to replicate must be able to communicate over the network. ICMP, SMB (TCP port 445), SMB Direct (TCP 5445), and WS-MAN (TCP port 5985) are required both directions between servers.

Storage   You can replicate the system volume. The source and destination server need to have at least two volumes—one for data (which will replicate) and one for logs (used for Storage Replica). The volumes must be the same size, and the sector size on all the data disks must be the same size. The disks must be initialized as GPT disks. The log volume must be a minimum of 9 GB, although going larger is usually a better idea to avoid having to micromanage the storage and free space.

Windows Server 2016 Datacenter Edition   To use Storage Replica, you must have the Datacenter edition of Windows Server 2016 on the source and destination server.

Storage Replica Feature   The source and destination server must have the Storage Replica feature installed.

2 GB or more of RAM   You must have a minimum of 2 GB of RAM. For most modern servers, this isn't a problem. In a lab or test environment, you might sometimes use less RAM.

If you use VMs with dynamic memory, you might need to adjust the startup RAM (shown as just "RAM" in Windows Server 2016 Hyper-V). While 2 GB is the absolute minimum, 4 GB or more is recommend for optimum performance.

Beyond the core requirements in the previous list, there are some "nice-to-haves" that are important for the performance of the replication:

High-Speed Network Although a typical Ethernet network will suffice, especially for small volumes with low usage, you should try to use RDMA (remote direct memory access) for high performance needs. You should also consider having a dedicated network for replication, like how you might approach deploying iSCSI in your environment.

Low-Latency Network If you want to use synchronous replication, you need to have low latency. You need a round-trip time of 5 ms or lower. If latency is higher, you must use asynchronous replication.

High-Speed Log Volumes To enhance performance, you should use SSD storage for the log volumes. At a minimum, you should use your fastest storage for the log volumes.

After you configure your environment and check it for prerequisites, you are ready to validate the environment with the Test-SRTopology cmdlet. In the following example, we run a 30-minute test between Server1 (the source) and Server2 (the destination) with a data volume named J: and K: being the log volume. We save the results to D:\Temp. We run the command from the source server using an administrative PowerShell prompt (required).

```
Test-SRTopology -SourceComputerName Server1 -SourceVolumeName J:
-SourceLogVolumeName K: -DestinationComputerName Server2 -DestinationVolumeName
J: -DestinationLogVolumeName K: -DurationinMinutes 30 -ResultPath D:\Temp
```

If the prerequisites have been met, the command will complete the test and save the results to the specified result path. Because we used a 30-minute duration, the command tests performance. Optionally, you can use the -IgnorePerfTests parameter to avoid performance testing (mostly useful if you have already tested performance). There are 20 tests. Many of the tests are simple, such as checking to ensure the volumes exist and checking to see if the partitions are using GPT. The results file is an .HTML file, and you should save that file with any related project files in case you need to refer to it in the future.

If your tests are successful, you are now ready to establish storage replication. In the following example, we use the same source and destination servers and the same volumes. The only part of the command that you might not recognize is the -SourceRGName parameter. In this case, RG stands for Replication Group. When you establish storage replication, you name the replication group. In this case, we are naming our replication group RGJ (for Replication Group J, since we are replicating the J: volume).

```
New-SRPartnership -SourceComputerName Server1 -SourceRGName RGJ -SourceVolumeName
J: -SourceLogVolumeName K: -DestinationComputerName Server2 -DestinationRGName
RGJ -DestinationVolumeName J: -DestinationLogVolumeName K:
```

After you have Storage Replica up and running, you can use the Get-SRPartnership and Get-SRGroup cmdlets for basic management. Additionally, you can look at the dedicated Storage Replica logs in Event Viewer. Open Event Viewer, expand Applications and Services Logs, expand Microsoft, expand Windows, and then expand StorageReplica. You'll see an Admin log and an Operational log. The Operational log has key details about the ongoing replication, while the Admin log has key details about the initial setup and configuration changes.

If you are interested in setting up cluster-to-cluster replication, see https://docs.microsoft .com/en-us/windows-server/storage/storage-replica/cluster-to-cluster-storage-replication for step-by-step instructions. If you are interested in setting up a stretch cluster, see https://docs.microsoft.com/en-us/windows-server/storage/storage-replica/ stretch-cluster-replication-using-shared-storage.

Storage Quality of Service

Imagine that you have a Hyper-V environment and one VM is paralyzing the performance of your storage. It is impacting other VMs on the same host. Or, imagine that you have an application team that requires a minimum amount of storage I/O at all times. In both scenarios, you can use Storage Quality of Service (Storage QoS). Storage QoS minimizes the chances of a single VM consuming all the available storage I/O. It can also be used to help ensure that a specified application has a specified minimum amount of I/O. This is like how network-based QoS functions (whereby traffic such as voice traffic is given priority/higher performance over data traffic, for example). Storage QoS is part of Microsoft's software-defined storage solutions.

Two use cases are supported for Storage QoS. Both involve Hyper-V. One use case is having Hyper-V in a failover cluster with a scale-out file server cluster for the storage. The other use case is having Hyper-V in a failover cluster using Cluster Shared Volumes (CSVs) for storage.

The requirements for Storage QoS are minimal. All servers participating must be running Windows Server 2016. Beyond that, you just need to have Hyper-V, the failover cluster, and the storage previously described. You don't have to install a role. You don't have to install a feature. In fact, you don't even need to enable Storage QoS! By default, it will be enabled once you build an environment that has the required components.

Working with Storage QoS

If you decide to use Storage QoS in your environment, you'll need to create Storage QoS policies. Policies are assigned to virtual disks (VHD or VHDX). This means that you can have a different policy for multiple disks on the same VM. There are two types of policies:

Dedicated   A dedicated policy takes the minimum and maximum values you assign for the storage I/O operations per second (iOPS) and applies them to assigned virtual disks. For example, if you set a minimum of 500 IOPS and a maximum of 1000 iOPS to Server1 and Server2, each server will have a minimum of 500 iOPS and a maximum of 1000 IOPS. Dedicated policies are simple to manage and are typically the right choice for your high-performance workloads.

Aggregated   An aggregated policy takes the minimum and maximum values you assign for storage iOPS and applies them to a group of virtual disks. The group of virtual disks then have a pool of iOPS that they share. For example, if you set a minimum of 500 IOPS and a maximum of 1000 iOPS to the virtual disks on Server1, Server2, Server3, and Server4, then all the servers together can use up to 1000 iOPS (and will have access between them of a minimum of 500 iOPS). If all the VMs have similar performance needs at the same time, they are going to have a similar amount of iOPS. In this scenario, the disks would have a minimum of

125 iOPS each (500 / 4 virtual disks). Aggregated policies are the right choice for nonproduction workloads, lab environments, or VMs that do not require high-performance storage.

After you create policies, you can associate them with virtual disks. You do this by using the `Set-VMHardDiskDrive` cmdlet. Use the `Get-StorageQosFlow` cmdlet to ensure that your policies are applied. You can look at all your Storage QoS policies by using the `Get-StorageQosPolicy` cmdlet (without any parameters).

The Bottom Line

Understand the what/why/how of new storage technologies in Windows Server 2016. Storage is changing at a rapid pace in Windows Server. To take advantage of the latest features, you need to understand the capabilities, prerequisites, and deployment considerations. Beyond just reading about them, implement them in your lab environment to take them for a test drive.

Master It You are deploying a new file server on Windows Server 2016. The data will consist solely of unstructured data. Some of the data will be used routinely, such as Word and Excel files that are still being created and edited by users. Other data will be stored for historical purposes and rarely read or edited. You need to choose a storage technology to maximize the performance of the data that will be used routinely.

Solution In this scenario, storage tiering will provide the best performance for the routinely used data. This is because such data will be stored on the fastest drives, while the rarely used data will be stored on the lowest performing drives. In this scenario, using Storage Spaces with a mix of SSD and HDD, enabled with storage tiering, you can provide a solution to meet the requirements.

Learn about deployment considerations for Windows Server storage technologies. Sometimes, a technology will have some cool new feature. Or, it will provide out-of-this-world performance. But those reasons alone are not enough to help you make a deployment decision. You also need to understand other deployment considerations. For example, if you deploy a new storage technology, will you no longer be able to do something else? Or, will it be compatible with everything else on the server? Is the technology designed for your use case? These are the questions you need to be able to answer before you choose a deployment strategy.

Master It You are planning to deploy Storage Replica to replicate data between servers in different data centers. The servers are connected over a WAN. Latency is not low, although it isn't high either. Which type of replication should you use in this scenario?

Solution There are two choices for the replication: synchronous and asynchronous. Synchronous replication has low-latency requirements and is typically deployed in a LAN or a MAN (metropolitan area network). In this scenario, with a WAN and medium latency, you need to use asynchronous replication (which doesn't have latency requirements).

Maintain and support a Windows Server storage environment. After you deploy new storage technologies, you need to keep them running. Maintaining the storage technologies is much different than planning them or deploying them. It requires totally different skills and knowledge. Be sure that your team is ready to support new technologies as you prepare to deploy them. It is a good practice to deploy the new technologies into a lab or nonproduction environment and enable the support teams to gain some experience with them prior to going live in your production environment.

Master It   You have Windows Server 2012 R2 and Windows Server 2016 in your environment. You want to compare the features of NTFS and ReFS in Windows Server 2012 R2 and Windows Server 2016. How can you do this from the servers?

Solution   We know some of you are thinking, "Oh, just open a browser from the servers and go find a comparison chart on the Internet." Good thinking! But, we are really looking for a way to do that with the built-in tools. In this scenario, you can use the `fsutil` tool to look at the features of NTFS and ReFS on existing volumes on the servers. Run `fsutil fsinfo volumeinfo D:` to look at the features of the D: volume, for example. Then, compare the supported features between Windows Server 2012 R2 and Windows Server 2016. Also compare the features between NTFS and ReFS.

Chapter 5

Networking

Most of the core networking functionality in Windows Server 2016 is the same as in previous versions of Windows Server. However, even though there have been few changes, networking is still a critical functionality. Windows Server 2016 is used to provide network services to clients on the network. Domain Name Service (DNS) is almost always installed and configured on domain controllers to support the use of Active Directory. Frequently, Dynamic Host Configuration Protocol (DHCP) is configured on Windows Server 2016 to provide desktop computers and other devices with IP address configurations.

It is possible to configure Windows Server 2016 as a remote access server that allows clients to connect to your internal network from the Internet. You may also choose to use Network Load Balancing (NLB) to provide high availability for some applications. Finally, Software Defined Networking (SDN) can be used to enhance flexibility in virtual environments that use Hyper-V.

IN THIS CHAPTER, YOU WILL LEARN TO:

- ◆ Configure networking in Windows Server 2016
- ◆ Make DNS highly available
- ◆ Configure DHCP for a new subnet
- ◆ Configure a VPN server
- ◆ Identify a load-balancing solution

Windows Server 2016 Network Configuration

There are some network configuration settings that you need to consider for all computers running Windows Server 2016. Regardless of the role of the server, you need to consider common settings such as Internet Protocol (IP) addresses and Windows Firewall.

DOMAIN JOIN

When you first install Windows Server 2016, it is part of a workgroup named WORKGROUP. When multiple computers are members of the same workgroup, there is no security integration. A user account on one workgroup member does not have permissions to use resources on other workgroup members. Each server has a local Security Accounts Management (SAM) database with independent users and groups.

continued

To integrate security with other servers and user accounts in Active Directory Domain Services (AD DS), you join Windows Server 2016 to a domain. After joining the domain, the Domain Admins group becomes a member of the local Administrators group and the Domain Users group becomes a member of the local Users group.

After the server is joined to the domain, you can modify the security settings and provide permissions for any groups you want. For example, application administrators are typically given access to the servers that are part of their application. To give access to the application administrators, you can make them members of the local Administrators group on the server. Preferably, you should only grant application administrators access to specific servers that are part of their application, rather than making them members of Domain Admins.

IP Configuration

To configure IPv4 and IPv6 settings for servers, use the same process that you would use to configure desktop computers. The main difference is that servers generally have a static IP address, while desktop computers usually have dynamic IP addresses. Figure 5.1 shows the IPv4 configuration for a network adapter.

FIGURE 5.1
IPv4
configuration

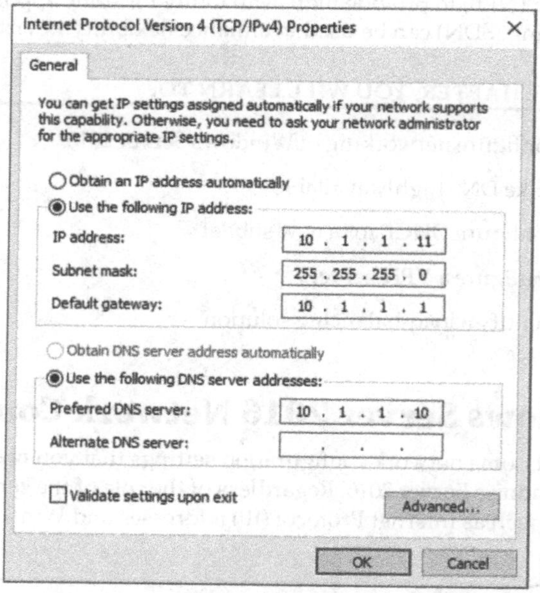

At bare minimum, a server should be configured with:

♦ IPv4 address

♦ Subnet mask

♦ Default gateway

◆ DNS server

◆ IPv6 enabled

Although it is technically possible to use a dynamic IPv4 address on a server, it is typical to assign a static IPv4 address. This is done because it allows administrators to retain complete control over the allocation of IPv4 addresses and access servers if DNS resolution fails.

For better long-term manageability of IPv4 addresses, some organizations use DHCP reservations. A DHCP reservation is defined based on the MAC address of the server. Then the DHCP server hands out the same IPv4 configuration to the server at each renewal. If IPv4 configuration information is changed in the future, such as the IPv4 address range or DNS servers, the information can be updated in DHCP without needing to change the configuration directly on each server.

Member servers should use only internal DNS servers with the resource records necessary for AD DS connectivity. In smaller organizations, a common mistake is to configure one internal DNS server as primary and an external DNS server, such as an Internet Service Provider (ISP), as secondary. However, the ISP DNS server doesn't have the records needed to find the domain controllers for authentication. If there is a short network outage and the primary DNS server is unavailable, the server will begin using the secondary DNS server, and authentication errors will begin to occur when users access resources on the server. When Windows Server 2016 begins using the secondary DNS server, there is no automated mechanism to begin using the primary DNS server again, and you may need to disable and then reenable the network card, or restart the server to resolve the issue.

Another common mistake made in both large and small organizations is disabling IPv6. This is done primarily because many administrators don't understand IPv6 and think they're being safe by disabling it. However, in reality, they are introducing risk.

Microsoft does not test applications or updates with IPv6 disabled. So, there is a risk that applications or updates will not perform correctly when IPv6 is disabled. There are instances of applications, such as Exchange Server, experiencing errors when IPv6 is disabled.

Also, when you uncheck the box for IPv6 in the network configuration, it does not fully disable IPv6. Instead, you've partially turned it off. If you really want to disable IPv6, you need to make additional Registry modifications. However, this is not recommended.

When IPv6 is enabled but not configured, the only IPv6 connectivity is performed through a locally generated link-local address. A link-local address is similar to an Automatic Private IP Addressing (APIPA) address for IPv4. The link-local address is not routable, but it can be used for communication on the local network.

USING PING WITH SPECIFIC IP VERSIONS

The Ping utility is used to confirm connectivity to a remote host. The lack of a response to a ping does not guarantee that a remote host is not reachable, because a firewall may be blocking ping requests. However, a response to a ping does confirm that a host is reachable.

When you use Ping it will use either IPv4 or IPv6, depending on the how your DNS is configured. If it contains both IPv4 and IPv6 addresses for a name, then IPv6 is preferred. To confirm connectivity using a specific IP protocol, you can specify it as part of running the Ping utility.

To ping a host by using IPv4, use: `ping -4 hostname`.

To ping a host by using IPv6, use: `ping -6 hostname`.

You can use Windows PowerShell to manage networking in Windows Server 2016. Table 5.1 lists some of the cmdlets you can use to manage your network configuration.

TABLE 5.1: Windows PowerShell Cmdlets for Network Configuration

CMDLET	DESCRIPTION
New-NetIPAddress	Configures a new IP address, subnet mask, and default gateway on an interface. This does not remove an existing IP address.
Set-NetIPAddress	Modifies an IP address and subnet mask assigned to an interface.
Remove-NetIPAddress	Removes an IP address and subnet mask assigned to an interface.
Get-NetRoute	Views the local routing table, including 0.0.0.0, which is the default gateway.
New-NetRoute	Creates a new route in the routing table.
Remove-NetRoute	Removes a route in the routing table.
Set-DnsClientServerAddress	Modifies the DNS servers used by a computer.

When you use Windows PowerShell cmdlets for networking, you might notice references to the Active policy store and Persistent policy store. The Active policy store is where you find the settings that the operating system is currently using. The Persistent policy store is where the settings that will be applied when the operating system is restarted are stored. Most cmdlets modify the Active and Persistent policy stores, but you can specify to modify only one or the other.

For detailed information about using Windows PowerShell cmdlets for network configuration, see "Windows PowerShell Cmdlets for Networking" at https://technet.microsoft.com/en-us/library/jj717268(v=ws.11).aspx.

Network Adapter Teaming

Network adapter teaming is the ability to join the capacity of multiple network adapters to function as a single unit. When you configure a team of two adapters, they can be used at the same time for higher throughput. A network team is also fault tolerant because remaining adapters continue to function if one team member fails.

🌐 Real World Scenario

NETWORK ADAPTER TEAMING FOR VIRTUALIZATION HOSTS

In general, network adapter teaming is useful for any scenario where you want to reduce downtime due to network failure or need to increase network throughput. Computers running Hyper-V are virtualization hosts that can take advantage of both benefits.

A network failure on a virtualization host results in a service outage for all of the virtual machines running on that host. Even when virtual machines are configured to be highly available, an unexpected failure results in some downtime. When a single virtualization host could be hosting 10 to 20 virtual machines, the result is a large impact to users. Having teamed network adapters that are connected to separate switches provides fault tolerance for a switch failure.

Virtualization hosts can also take advantage of the increased network throughput available when network adapters are teamed. With many virtual machines, a single 1 Gbps network adapter might cause a network performance bottleneck. When you team two 1 Gbps network adapters, the overall throughput for the team will be 2 Gbps, thereby reducing the risk that network throughput will be a performance bottleneck.

You can configure network adapter teaming by using software provided by a network adapter manufacturer or by using the NIC Teaming function in Windows Server 2016. If you choose to use software from the network adapter manufacturer, you must have either multi-port network adapters or network adapters of the same type. NIC Teaming in Windows Server 2016 can be performed with network adapters of different types, but they should be the same speed. You can put up to 32 network adapters in a single NIC team.

To configure NIC Teaming, follow these steps:

1. In Server Manager, in the Navigation pane, click Local Server.

2. In the Properties area, next to NIC Teaming, click Disabled.

3. In the NIC Teaming window, in the Teams area, click Tasks and click New Team.

4. In the NIC Teaming dialog box, shown in Figure 5.2, in the Team name box, enter a name for the new team.

5. Select the network adapters you want to include in the team and click OK.

After you create a NIC team, the network configuration for the individual network adapters is removed. The only protocol that remains bound to each NIC team network adapter is the Microsoft Network Adapter Multiplexor protocol. A new network adapter is created that represents the NIC team with the typical network protocols bound to it. You can configure IP addresses and other network configurations in the properties of the network adapter for the team.

FIGURE 5.2
Creating a new
team

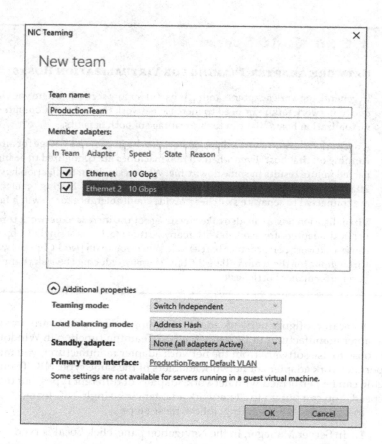

The NIC Teaming window, shown in Figure 5.3, shows the status of the NIC team and each network adapter. From here you can view and modify the properties for both the NIC team and the network adapters.

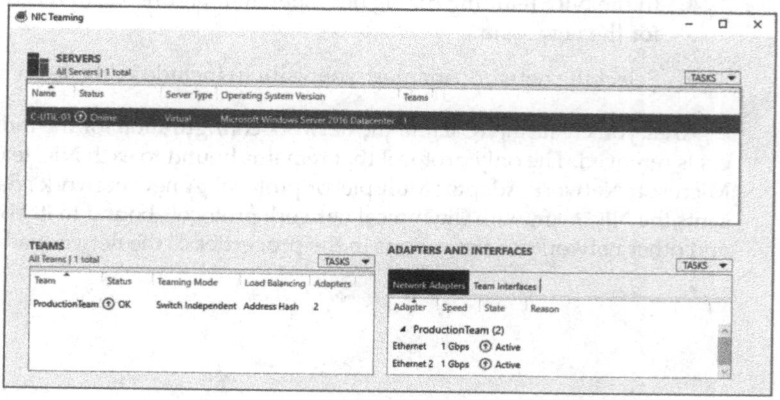

FIGURE 5.3
NIC Teaming
window

In most cases, the default configuration for a NIC team is preferable. It will provide the best performance and experience the fewest faults. However, you can adjust the teaming mode, load-balancing mode, standby adapter, and primary team interface if applicable to your scenario.

The teaming mode can be Switch Independent, Static Teaming, or Link Aggregation Control Protocol (LACP). When you use Switch Independent mode, Windows Server is in control of the load-balancing process and the network adapters can be attached to separate switches. Static Teaming and LACP are both switch-dependent modes in which the switch makes load-balancing decisions and all network adapters in the NIC team must be attached to the same switch (or stack). Static Teaming requires you to statically configure switch ports. LACP is a switch protocol that automates the configuration.

Load balancing of data transfer among network adapters in a team is controlled by the load-balancing mode you select. Table 5.2 describes the load-balancing modes.

TABLE 5.2:   NIC Teaming Load-Balancing Modes

MODE	DESCRIPTION
Address Hash	Source and destination TCP ports and IP addresses are used to create a unique identifier for each network connection, which is then assigned to a specific network adapter in the team.
Hyper-V Port	Designed for Hyper-V hosts with virtual machines where each virtual machine has a unique MAC address for network communication. Network connections are identified based on the MAC address of the virtual machine, and each virtual machine is assigned to a network adapter.
Dynamic	A combination of Address Hash and Hyper-V Port load-balancing modes. Outbound communication uses Address Hash mode. Inbound communication uses Hyper-V Port mode. This is the recommended load-balancing mode for all teaming modes.

A standby adapter in a NIC Team is not used unless a network adapter in the team has failed. Most NIC Teams are configured to use a standby adapter of None. This configuration uses all available member adapters.

The primary team interface is relevant only when VLANs are used on your network. This configures the VLAN used for incoming packets that are not tagged with a VLAN. You can configure a specific VLAN if required.

For a more detailed description of the NIC Teaming options, see "Create a New NIC Team on a Host Computer of VM" at https://docs.microsoft.com/en-us/windows-server/networking/technologies/nic-teaming/create-a-new-nic-team-on-a-host-computer-or-vm.

Windows Firewall

Network security is a multilayered process rather than a specific product or feature. Security is the combination of tactics you use for security. More layers equals better security. However, you need to balance the need for security with usability. The best security is pointless if it makes resource access so awkward that users or administrators avoid it.

Everyone knows that you need to have a network firewall between your corporate network and the Internet to control access. Some larger networks have network firewalls in the internal network to control communication between different areas. Unfortunately, many organizations disable the host-based firewall included in Windows. This is an important security layer that should not be disabled.

Windows Firewall is enabled by default in Windows Server 2016. The default configuration allows all outbound communication but limits inbound communication based on rules. Inbound communication requires a specific rule to be allowed. You can manage Windows Firewall by using the simplified interface in Control Panel, shown in Figure 5.4, or the Windows Firewall with Advanced Security tool. Windows Firewall with Advanced Security provides more advanced options for configuring rules.

FIGURE 5.4
Windows Firewall

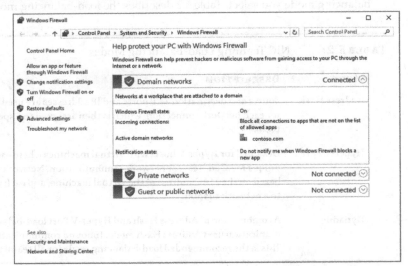

PROFILES

Profiles in Windows Firewall are used to adjust settings based on the location of the computer. Each profile has a different configuration for Windows Firewall. Windows Firewall can be enabled or disabled independently for each profile and can have different rules enabled for each profile.

The Domain profile is automatically used when a domain-joined computer can communicate with a domain controller. This is the most commonly used profile for domain-joined servers.

If a computer is connected to a network that is not a domain network, it is classified as either public or private. Public networks are more restricted than private networks. You will be prompted to classify a new network when you connect to it, and it is important that you select the profile that is appropriate for your scenario.

A server with multiple network interfaces can use different profiles for each network adapter. For example, a server configured as a VPN server could have one network adapter connected to the internal network and one network adapter connected to a DMZ. The network adapter on the internal network would use the Domain profile, and the network adapter connected to the DMZ network would use the Private profile.

PUBLIC PROFILE IN USE ON DOMAIN NETWORK

When troubleshooting an error, you will sometimes find a network connection for a server classified as a Public network instead of a Domain network. Using the wrong profile will cause a different set of firewall rules to be used and probably block communication that is necessary for users or applications.

A server that can't communicate with a domain controller will prevent the internal network from properly identifying a Domain network. Sometimes it is a transient error that occurred during the most recent startup of the server that can be resolved by restarting the server. In other cases, it may be due to firewall changes or DNS lookup errors. You will need to investigate and resolve the communication error.

FIREWALL RULES

Windows Firewall is preconfigured with rules that are applicable to most Windows services. For example, there are rules for file and printer sharing, iSCSI, network discovery, Remote Desktop, and Windows Remote Management. These rules are enabled or disabled for different profiles. You have the option to enable and disable the rules in each profile. Figure 5.5 shows the inbound rules in Windows Firewall with Advanced Security.

FIGURE 5.5
Inbound rules

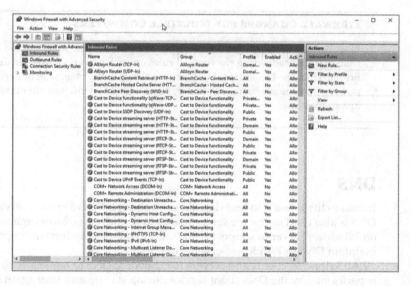

When Windows Firewall was first introduced many versions ago, enabling it prevented many applications from working. Then it was necessary to modify the firewall rules to get the applications working again. Most modern applications expect Windows Firewall to be in place and add the rules required for that application during installation. For example, when you install Exchange Server on Windows Server 2016, all the necessary rules for client access and mail delivery are created during installation. However, you should check with the vendor of your application to see if any rule modifications are necessary.

Enabling the File and Printer Sharing (Echo Request - ICMPv4-In) rule is one common firewall change that is made for member servers. This rule allows the server to receive ping requests from the network. Many administrators use Ping to verify network connectivity; if you don't enable this rule, the member servers don't respond to ping requests because the Windows Firewall blocks the incoming requests by default. This rule is enabled on domain controllers and when some server roles are installed on member servers.

You can also create your own firewall rules by using Windows Firewall with Advanced Security. The application vendor will provide the configuration information necessary for the firewall rule. Some of the criteria that can be included in the rules are listed here:

◆ TCP or UDP port

◆ Program (executable communicating on the network)

◆ Protocol type

◆ Source and destination IP addresses

◆ Allow or deny

◆ Profile

FIREWALL CHANGES FOR MULTIPLE COMPUTERS

Most firewall rule changes are made for groups of servers rather than for a single server. Rather than manually adjusting the firewall rules on each server, you should use Group Policy to deploy firewall changes. The settings you place in a Group Policy object can be deployed to groups of servers, making implementation much faster. As an added benefit, you can make any future modification in a single place.

DNS

Because clients use it to find domain controllers, DNS is a critical service for Windows networks. DNS is also used to resolve server names to IP addresses. Most organizations use DNS running on Windows Server to support AD DS. Consequently, understanding how to implement and maintain DNS in Windows Server is important.

All Windows clients and servers use dynamic DNS to register their DNS names. Registration is performed by the DNS client service during startup and later again if the IP address is changed. The name for the computer is registered in the domain in which the computer is a member. For example, if C-UTIL-01 is a member of the contoso.com domain, it will register C-UTIL-01.contoso.com with its IP address.

Domain controllers register additional DNS records that allow Windows clients to locate domain controllers, shown in Figure 5.6. Service Location (SRV) records for services such as Kerberos and LDAP are registered. The SRV records are in subdomains such as _msdcs, _sites, _tcp, and _udp. These additional DNS records are registered by the netlogon service and contain the name of a server that provides the service. Clients resolve that name to an IP address to access the service.

FIGURE 5.6
SRV records for a
domain controller

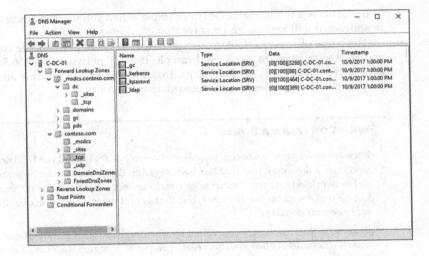

FIGURE 5.6
SRV records for a
domain controller

DNS Zones

The DNS zone used for AD DS is a forward lookup zone. A forward lookup zone can have multiple record types, but it is most commonly used to convert host names to IP addresses. If you have an AD DS domain named contoso.com, you need to have a DNS zone named contoso.com to support the domain. Table 5.3 lists some of the DNS record types that can be created in a forward lookup zone.

TABLE 5.3:   DNS Record Types

RECORD TYPE	DESCRIPTION
A (host)	Resolves a name to an IPv4 address.
AAAA (host)	Resolves a name to an IPv6 address.
CNAME (alias)	Resolves a name to another name.
MX (mail exchanger)	Identifies the host that receives email for that domain.
NS (name server)	Identifies a server that is authoritative for that domain.
SRV (service location)	Identifies where a service can be contacted.
TXT (text)	Provides a text string that can be used by applications.

As a best practice, you should also implement reverse lookup zones on your network. A reverse lookup zone resolves IP addresses to names. Various utilities and applications use this information when it is available. For example, when you use the Tracert utility with an IP address, it will look up and resolve that IP address to a name.

The name of a reverse lookup zone is based on the IP network the computers are located on and ends with in-addr.arpa. For example, if the IP network is 172.16.5.0/24, the reverse lookup zone will be 5.16.172.in-addr.arpa. Inside a reverse lookup zone are PTR (pointer) records that resolve IP addresses on that network to host names.

WHO CONTROLS A ZONE?

Forward lookup zones are controlled by whoever has registered the DNS domain name. You should never use a domain name that has been registered on the Internet by someone else on your internal network. At one time, some organizations used .local domain names internally that could not be registered on the Internet, but that is no longer a best practice. Instead, ensure that you register your domain.

Reverse lookup zones are controlled by whoever has routing control over the network. For your internal network, this is you. So, create reverse lookup zones for your internal network as needed. Typically, for publicly accessible IP addresses, your ISP creates and manages the reverse lookup zone. However, for some large organizations, the ISP might delegate resolution to your organization.

Because DNS is a critical service on your network, it shouldn't have a single point of failure. Traditionally, to make DNS highly available, you used primary and secondary zones. All updates are made to the primary DNS zone, and changes are replicated periodically to the secondary zone. This system is still used when integrating with Linux-based DNS or DNS appliances.

You can use primary and secondary zones with the DNS server in Windows Server 2016, but there is a problem. Windows clients and servers use dynamic DNS, and changes can be made only in the primary zone. This means that only one DNS server can perform updates. To work around this problem, Windows-based DNS servers have a unique capability to store a DNS zones in AD DS (Active Directory–integrated).

Because it is stored in AD DS instead of a local zone file, an Active Directory–integrated DNS zone can be updated by multiple DNS servers. Effectively, this means that each DNS server behaves as though it has a primary DNS zone. AD DS is responsible for replicating the changes to all domain controllers where the data is available to all DNS servers that need it. A typical deployment of DNS on a Windows-based network uses Active Directory integrated zones for all forward lookup zones.

Only domain controllers that are also DNS servers can access and update Active Directory integrated zones. So, it is typical for domain controllers to also be DNS servers.

DNS is installed as a server role, named DNS Server, in Windows Server 2016. After DNS is installed, you can use the following steps to create an Active Directory–integrated zone:

1. In Server Manager, click Tools and click DNS.

2. In DNS Manager, expand the server if necessary, right-click Forward Lookup Zones, and click New Zone.

3. In the New Zone Wizard, click Next.

4. On the Zone Type page, shown in Figure 5.7, click Primary Zone.

FIGURE 5.7
Zone Type
selection

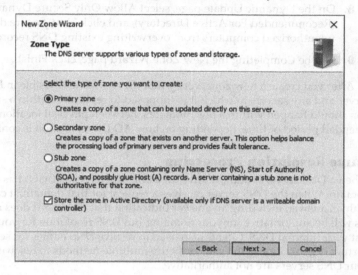

5. Select the Store The Zone In Active Directory (Available Only If DNS Server Is A Writable Domain Controller) check box and click Next.

6. On the Active Directory Zone Replication Scope page, shown in Figure 5.8, select the replication option appropriate for your network and click Next.

FIGURE 5.8
Active Directory
Zone Replication
Scope selection

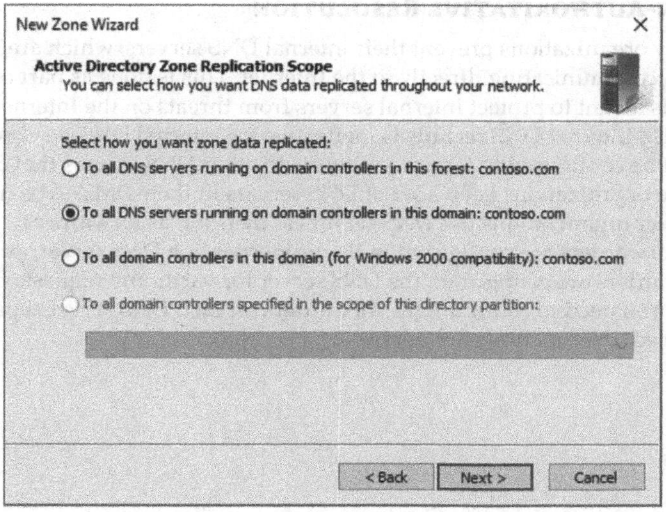

7. On the Zone Name page, in the Zone Name box, enter the name of the zone you are creating and click Next.

8. On the Dynamic Update page, select Allow Only Secure Dynamic Updates (Recommended For Active Directory), and click Next. Secure dynamic updates prevent unauthorized computers from overwriting existing DNS records.

9. On the Completing the New Zone Wizard page, click Finish.

After you create a new zone, verify that the new zone is visible in DNS Manager on the local server and any servers to which it is supposed to replicate. Within a single location, replication should happen within a few moments. Between physical locations, replication can take an extended period of time, depending on how AD DS replication is configured.

Name Resolution Processing

When a DNS server is authoritative for a domain, it means that it has a copy of the zone for that domain. When the DNS server receives a request for that domain, it can authoritatively respond with an answer, including an answer indicating that the record does not exist. Your DNS servers will be authoritative for your domains, but DNS resolution for your clients is not limited to just your internal DNS. Clients also need to resolve DNS names for services on the Internet and partner organizations. You can configure multiple methods to resolve DNS requests for which your DNS servers are not authoritative.

Root hints are used to identify DNS servers that are responsible for a domain. When you install a DNS server in Windows Server 2016, it is automatically configured with root hints, as shown in Figure 5.9. These root hints may be updated by Windows Updates, but you do not need to manually update the root hints. Notice that these servers are on the Internet and your DNS server must have access to the Internet to use the root servers.

NON-AUTHORITATIVE RESOLUTION

Many organizations prevent their internal DNS servers, which are typically domain controllers, from communicating directly to the Internet. This is done as part of a general security policy and is meant to protect internal servers from threats on the Internet. So, using roots hints to resolve Internet DNS records is ineffective for internal DNS servers. Instead, the DNS servers must be configured to forward requests to other DNS servers that do have access to the Internet. Some organizations keep a set of DNS servers in their DMZ to be used as forwarders. Some smaller organizations use DNS servers at their ISP as forwarders.

Forwarders are configured in the properties of a DNS server, as shown in Figure 5.10. When forwarders are configured, the DNS server forwards any requests for which it is not authoritative. You need to configure the forwarders on each DNS server separately. When forwarders are enabled, the root hints are not used.

FIGURE 5.9
Root hints

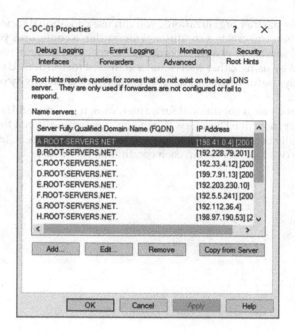

FIGURE 5.10
DNS forwarders

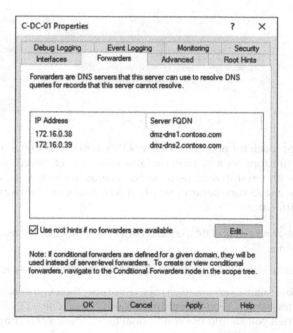

If you have partner organizations, you can use conditional forwarders for specific DNS domains. When you create a conditional forwarder, it configures your DNS server to use the partner DNS servers to resolve records for the specified domain only. Other DNS records are still resolved by using either root hints or standard forwarders. Using conditional forwarders is particularly useful when you have direct network connectivity or a VPN with the partner's organization.

When you create a conditional forwarder, shown in Figure 5.11, you have the option to store the forwarder in Active Directory. When you store a conditional forwarder in Active Directory, it automatically becomes available to the DNS servers you select. Ideally, to be fault tolerant, you should have two DNS servers in each conditional forwarder.

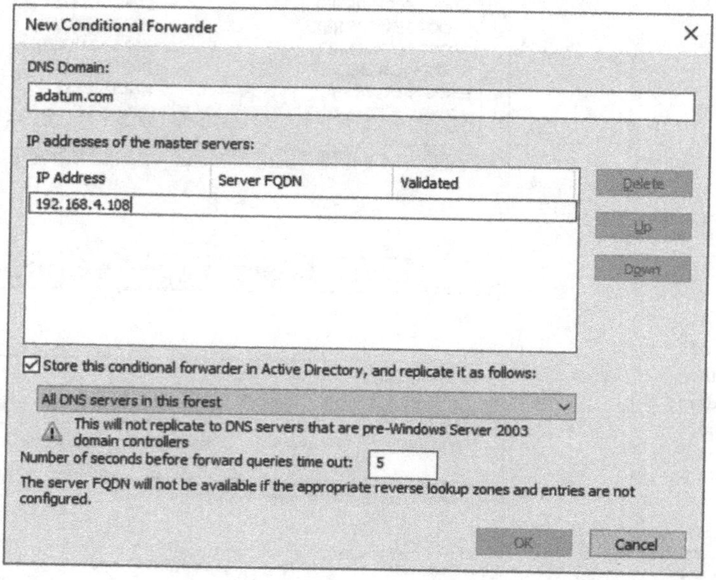

FIGURE 5.11
New conditional forwarder

A final approach for non-authoritative DNS domains is to use a stub zone for a specific domain. A stub zone for a domain contains name server records for a domain. The DNS server configured with the stub zone uses the NS records to identify the DNS servers for the domain. Functionally, a stub zone behaves similarly to a conditional forwarder. However, there are the following differences:

◆ A stub zone can update the NS records automatically to adjust to DNS servers changing over time.

◆ A stub zone is configured with a master server that it uses to query its list of name servers.

If you expect name servers to change over time, then you should use a stub zone instead of a conditional forwarder. If you need direct control over which DNS servers the requests are forwarded to, then you should use conditional forwarders. For example, firewalls may only allow access to a subset of DNS servers for the partner domain.

CACHING

To minimize the number of DNS lookups on a network, the results from DNS requests are cached. Caching can occur on DNS clients and non-authoritative DNS servers. For example, if a client requests the IP address for www.contoso.com and the internal DNS server also uses a forwarding DNS server in a DMZ, the results are cached on the client, the internal DNS server, and the DNS server in the DMZ.

Cached DNS lookups are retained based on the time to live (TTL) configured on the authoritative DNS server. A default TTL is set for each forward lookup zone, but that can be overridden by setting a TTL on specific DNS records. It was once common for DNS records on the Internet to have a TTL of 24 or 48 hours, but it is now more common to see 30 or 60 minutes for a TTL. When you are troubleshooting DNS resolution, it can be useful to view the DNS cache or clear it.

To view the DNS client cache on a Windows computer, you can use ipconfig /displaydns or Get-DnsClientCache. To avoid waiting for cache entries to time out, you can use ipconfig /flushdns or Clear-DnsClientCache.

For a Windows Server 2016 server running DNS, there is a separate cache in the DNS server that you can view and clear. With Windows PowerShell, you can use Show-DnsServerCache and Clear-DnsServerCache. You can also use DNS Manager to view and clear the cache.

To view cached DNS lookups in DNS Manager:

1. In DNS Manager, in the Navigation pane, click DNS or click the DNS server.

2. Click the View menu and click Advanced. This makes the Cached Lookups node visible in DNS Manager.

3. Select the Cached Lookups node and browse through the lookups.

To clear all cached DNS lookups in DNS Manager, right-click Cached Lookups or the DNS server, and click Clear Cache. You can also browse through the list of cached DNS lookups and delete individual entries. Restarting the DNS services also clears the cache.

ADVANCED NAME RESOLUTION SETTINGS

A few settings related to name resolution are on the Advanced tab for a DNS server, as shown in Figure 5.12. In most cases, you don't need to modify these settings, but it's useful to be aware of them just in case.

The advanced settings for name resolution include:

◆ Disable Recursion. When you enable this option, the DNS server responds only to requests for which it is authoritative. No root hints or forwarders are used. This option is disabled by default.

◆ Enable Round Robin. When this option is enabled, a single host name can resolve to multiple IP addresses. The DNS server will provide all the available IP addresses for a host to the requesting client. DNS Round Robin is used to implement a simple type of load balancing to provided high availability in case of server failure. Most large organizations use a hardware-based load balancer, with more advanced features, rather than DNS Round Robin. DNS Round Robin is enabled by default.

◆ Enable Netmask Ordering. When this option is enabled, the results provided when using DNS round robin are sorted based on the IP address of the DNS client. The IP address that most closely matches the IP address of the client is returned at the top of the list. In theory, this allows clients to contact the closest host if it is available. When this option is not enabled, the list is in a random order. This option is enabled by default.

FIGURE 5.12
Advanced DNS
settings

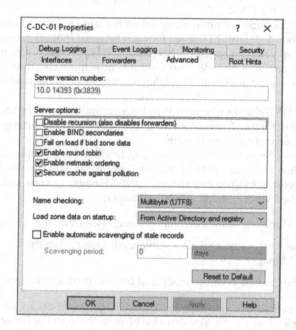

DNS POLICIES

DNS policies are a new feature in Windows Server 2016 that allow the DNS server to provide different responses to DNS queries based on characteristics of the request. The characteristics based upon which you can create policies include:

◆ Client subnet

◆ Server interface IP address

◆ Name being queried

◆ Query type

◆ Time of day

Being able to use the client subnet as a characteristic enables you to create location-aware DNS. Without DNS policies, to create location-aware DNS, you might have created multiple DNS servers and configured DNS clients to use the correct DNS server. Now you can have a single DNS server that provides different responses based on client location. For example, you could have a record wsus.contoso.com that is used by clients to download updates. That record can be configured to resolve to the closest Windows Server Update Server (WSUS) for each location.

By default, one zone scope is used to resolve DNS requests. To provide alternative responses, you need to do the following:

- Create additional zone scopes.
- Create policies that reference the zone scopes.
- Create DNS records that are assigned to the zone scopes.

DNS policy management is not available in DNS Manager. You need to use PowerShell cmdlets such as Add-DnsServerClientSubnet, Add-DnsServerZoneScope, Add-DnsServerResourceRecord, and Add-DnsServerQueryResolutionPolicy.

For more detailed information about implementing DNS polices, see "DNS Policy Scenario Guide" at https://docs.microsoft.com/en-us/windows-server/networking/dns/deploy/dns-policy-scenario-guide.

Removing Stale DNS Records

Over time, computers will be removed from your network as they are retired. The dynamic DNS names registered for these computers are not removed from DNS by default. You need to enable scavenging to remove old dynamic DNS records that are no longer required. By default, static DNS records that were created manually are not removed automatically by the scavenging process. You can enable scavenging for a static DNS record by selecting the Delete This Record When It Becomes Stale option.

To enable scavenging, you need to enable it on the primary DNS server and the DNS zone. If you are using Active Directory–integrated zones, you only need to enable scavenging on one DNS server and the DNS zone. The changes made by that one server will replicate to other DNS servers through AD DS. You can enable scavenging on multiple DNS servers to provide fault tolerance for scavenging, but this is not critical.

The timing for the scavenging process is not intuitive. There are three relevant time periods as listed in Table 5.4.

TABLE 5.4:   Scavenging Time Periods

TIME PERIOD	DESCRIPTION
No-refresh interval	After a dynamic DNS record has been created the no-refresh interval defines a time period during which the time stamp on the record will not be updated. This avoids unnecessary changes in AD DS. The default value is seven days.
Refresh interval	After the no-refresh interval has expired, the refresh interval is a time period when the time stamp on the record can be updated. If the DNS client performs a dynamic DNS update during this time, the time stamp is updated and the no-refresh interval begins again. If the refresh interval expires without an update, the record can be scavenged. The default value for the refresh interval is seven days.
Scavenging period	The scavenging period defines how often the DNS server reviews DNS records to find those available for scavenging. When records available for scavenging are found, those records are deleted. The default scavenging period is seven days.

You can modify the settings for aging and scavenging by using DNS Manager. You can also use Set-DnsServerScavenging and Set-DnsServerZoneAging.

Securing DNS

The most basic level of security you should implement is secure dynamic updates for Active Directory–integrated DNS zones. Turning on this option ensures that only the original client that registered a host name can update the IP address for that host name.

If you use secondary zones as part of your DNS configuration, you should configure the security for zone transfers on the properties of the primary zone. By default, zone transfers are not allowed. When you enable zone transfers, you should restrict them to legitimate DNS servers that you allow. You can limit zone transfers to specific IP addresses or servers listed as name servers for the domain.

To prevent DNS spoofing, where an unauthorized DNS server intercepts and responds to DNS requests, you can implement Domain Name System Security Extensions (DNSSEC). When you implement DNSSEC, responses from an authoritative DNS server are digitally signed to prove their authenticity. The digital signature for a DNS record is stored in a corresponding resource record signature (RRSIG) records.

Unlike some other encryption methods where you need to obtain a certificate from a certificate authority, the encryption keys you require for DNSSEC are generated by the DNS server in Windows Server 2016. For each zone, one DNS server is designated as the Key Master responsible for managing the signing keys.

The Key Master generates at least one key signing key (KSK) and a zone signing key (ZSK) for each zone. The ZSK is used to generate RRSIG for records in the zone. The KSK is used to digitally sign the ZSK. Figure 5.13 shows the options available when a ZSK is created for the DNS server in Windows Server 2016.

FIGURE 5.13
ZSK options

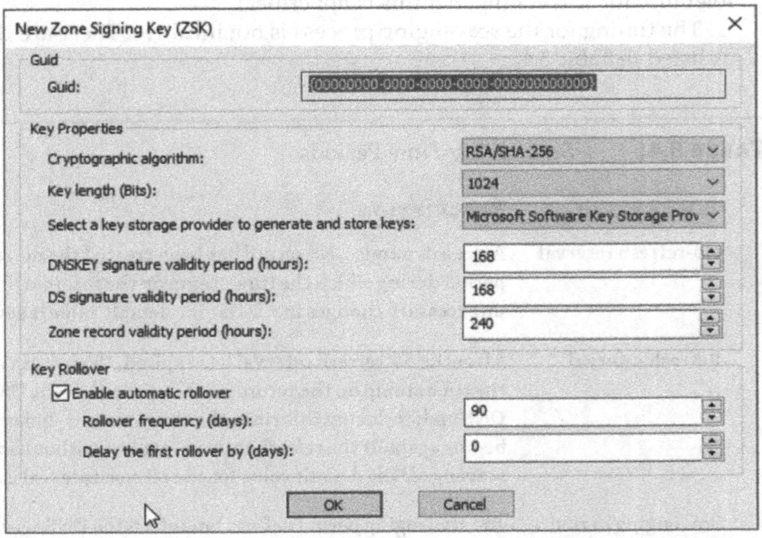

Clients and non-authoritative DNS servers that need to verify the validity of digital signatures use two additional DNS record types. DNSKEY records contain public keys for the KSK and ZSK. These DNSKEY records are added as trust points to indicate that they are valid and should be trusted. This is similar to designating that a self-signed certificate should be trusted. The steps to sign a zone for internal use are as follows:

1. Open DNS Manager.

2. In DNS Manager, if necessary, expand the server and expand Forward Lookup Zones.

3. Right-click the zone you want to sign, point to DNSSEC, and click Sign The Zone.

4. In the Zone Signing Wizard, click Next.

5. On the Signing Options page, click Use Default Settings To Sign The Zone and click Next.

6. Review the configuration and click Next.

7. When zone signing is complete, click Finish.

8. In DNS Manager, notice that the zone you signed now has a lock icon.

9. Right-click the zone you signed, point to DNSSEC, and click Properties.

10. In the DNSSEC properties for your zone dialog box, click the Trust Anchor tab, select Enable The Distribution Of Trust Anchors For This Zone check box, and click OK.

11. In the Warning dialog box, click Yes.

12. In the Updating Your Zone dialog box, click OK.

13. In the Trust Points folder, verify that your zone now appears with two DNSKEY records. You may need to press F5 to refresh the data.

14. Close DNS Manager.

For a detailed description of DNSSEC and its implementation in Windows server 2016, see "DNSSEC in Windows Server 2012" at https://technet.microsoft.com/en-us/library/dn593694(v=ws.11).aspx. This functionality has not been updated in Windows Server 2016.

Monitoring and Troubleshooting DNS

Most of the issues you will have related to DNS won't be functionality problems in the DNS server. It is much more likely that you will end up tracking down a configuration error when a host name does not resolve as expected.

To verify the basic functionality of a DNS server, you can use the monitoring tool built into the DNS server. When you view the properties of the server in DNS Manager, on the Monitoring tab, you have the option to perform a simple query and a recursive query. The simple query verifies that the DNS server responds to a request for a zone for which it is authoritative. The recursive query confirms that the DNS server can resolve DNS records for which it isn't authoritative. The simple and recursive queries can be done on demand or as scheduled, but typically are done only on demand.

You can also monitor DNS server performance counters by using Performance Monitor. This allows you to see detailed performance statistics for items such as zone transfers, dynamic update requests, and recursive queries. These performance counters are typically used only when you're trying to resolve a specific performance problem.

By default, the DNS server in Windows Server 2016 is configured to log errors, warnings, and other events to the DNS Server event log. You can view the contents of this log by using Event Viewer and browsing to the Applications and Services Logs. You can also limit the events logged to only errors or errors and warnings. However, it is a best practice to leave logging on for all events.

The event logging for the DNS server does not include information about the queries that are performed on the server. If you need to track individual queries against a DNS server for troubleshooting, then you need to enable Debug Logging in the properties of the DNS server, as shown in Figure 5.14. You can select to record detailed information about actions that the DNS server is performing.

FIGURE 5.14
DNS Debug
Logging

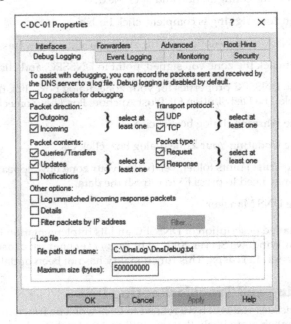

Debug logging can generate a very large amount of data. The default log file size of 500 MB is large and is often necessary if you want to review DNS queries over time. Ensure that you select a file size big enough to capture the data you want. Because such a large amount of data is generated, debug logging is usually enabled only when you are trying to resolve a specific problem.

QUICK DNS TROUBLESHOOTING TOOLS

If you need to test DNS name resolution, the easiest way to verify that a name resolves properly is to use the Ping utility. When you ping a host by name, the name is resolved as the first part of the process. Even if there is no response to the ping request, you will still be able to see that the name resolves.

To quickly test reverse DNS lookups, you can use the Ping utility with the -a option. When you run ping -a for an IP address, the Ping utility performs a reverse DNS lookup to find the name of the host. If the name of the host is not displayed, you know that the reverse DNS lookup failed.

The most commonly used tool for DNS troubleshooting is Nslookup. You can use Nslookup to query various record types for any domain you want. Another key benefit to using Nslookup is the ability to select the DNS server that you want to query. Figure 5.15 shows Nslookup being used to query the DNS server 8.8.8.8 on the Internet to resolve www.microsoft.com.

FIGURE 5.15
Nslookup

Dig is a tool similar to Nslookup for querying DNS information. Dig is commonly used in Linux environments, and some administrators prefer to use it for Windows. However, Dig is not included as part of Windows Server 2016, and you need to download it from the Internet.

DCDiag is a tool that tests many configuration aspects of a domain controller. One of the things it can do is verify that the correct records are created in DNS to locate domain controllers. To specifically test the DNS functionality, run `dcdiag /test:dns`.

Finally, for detailed troubleshooting, you might want to use a packet sniffer. A *packet sniffer* is software that monitors the packets sent over the network and decodes them into a readable format. Unlike debug logging, which allows you to view activity only at the server level, you can use a packet sniffer to see activity from the perspective of an individual client. Microsoft has an older packet sniffer named Network Monitor that is still quite popular and an updated packet sniffer named Microsoft Message Analyzer. There is also a popular open source packet sniffer named Wire Shark. All three packet sniffers can be downloaded at no cost.

DHCP

Dynamic Host Configuration Protocol (DHCP) is used to dynamically provide IP address configuration to clients. Although it is possible to configure servers by using DHCP, it is more commonly used for client computers.

When a computer is configured to use a dynamic IP address, the following process is performed at startup:

1. The client sends a DHCPDiscover packet. This is a broadcast to which all available DHCP servers can respond.

2. All DHCP servers send a DHCPOffer packet. This packet contains IP addressing information that can be used by the client.

3. The client sends a DHCPRequest indicating that it accepts the DHCPOffer. The first DHCPOffer received is the one that is accepted. All DHCP servers identify which offer was accepted, so that they don't reserve addresses for too long.

4. The DHCP server responds with a DHCPAck. This identifies that the DHCP knows that the offer was accepted and that the client can begin using the IP address information that was in the offer.

Because routers almost always block broadcast packets from passing between networks, DHCP Discover packets are not normally able to cross from one network to another through routers. To allow a single DHCP server to service multiple subnets, you need to implement a DHCP relay. A DHCP relay listens on a subnet and forwards DHCP packets to a subnet with a DHCP server. The DHCP server uses the IP address of the DHCP relay to identify the subnet that the request is coming from and provide an offer on that subnet.

IMPLEMENTING A DHCP RELAY

Windows Server 2016 includes DHCP Relay Agent as part of Routing and Remote Access. You place the server on the subnet you want to service and provide DHCP Relay Agent with the IP address of the DHCP server. In a large organization, you might have many subnets that need to be serviced by DHCP, and it's not practical to put a Windows server on each subnet to act as a DHCP relay.

Most routers also have DHCP relay functionality. Most organizations use their routers for DHCP relay because the routers are already connected to all subnets. This feature is often named IP helper in router configuration instead of DHCP relay.

To install the DHCP server role in Windows Server 2016, complete the following steps:

1. In Server Manager, click Manage and click Add Roles And Features.

2. In the Add Roles and Features Wizard, click Next.

3. On the Select Installation Type page, click Role-Based Or Feature-Based Installation and click Next.

4. On the Select Destination Server page, select the server on which you want to install the DHCP Server role and click Next.

5. On the Select Server Roles page, select the DHCP Server check box, click Add Features, and click Next.

6. On the Select Features page, click Next.

7. On the DHCP Server page, read the information and then click Next.

8. On the Confirm Installation Selections page, click Install.

9. On the Installation Progress Page, wait for the installation to complete and then click Close.

After a DHCP server has been installed, it needs to be authorized before it can begin servicing requests. Authorization is a setting in AD DS that the DHCP server reads. This is done to prevent a DHCP server from accidentally servicing requests and providing incorrect configuration information to clients.

ROGUE DHCP SERVERS

When an unauthorized DHCP server is connected to a network, it can hand out incorrect configuration information to clients. Windows-based DHCP servers can be controlled through authorization, but non-Microsoft DHCP servers have no mechanism for authorization.

Most of the time, a rogue DHCP server is identified when one or more clients are configured with incorrect DHCP addresses. It's pretty rare for someone to set up a Linux-based DHCP server on your network—unless it's done accidentally by IT staff who are doing something like building a test lab. A more common scenario would be when network users add an unauthorized network device, such as a wireless access point (AP) that has DHCP functionality.

Tracking down a rogue DHCP server is difficult because you need to do it based on the MAC address of the DHCP server. However, by using the MAC address, and reviewing the MAC addresses in the routing tables of switches, you should be able to identify a specific switch port to which the rogue DHCP is attached.

A DHCP server can be used to provide IP addressing information for both IPv4 and IPv6. However, it is relatively rare to use IPv6 internally, and this section focuses on using IPv4. If you choose to implement DHCPv6, there are two modes:

♦ **Stateless.** In this mode, the DHCP client generates its own IPv6 on the network based on router advertisements from the local router. DHCP options such as DNS server are still obtained from the DHCP server.

♦ **Stateful.** In this mode, the DHCP client is configured with an IPv6 address from the DHCP server. This is similar to how DHCPv4 operates.

DHCP Scopes

To configure the DHCP server to begin handing out addresses to clients, you need to create a scope. The scope defines the IP address range as well as options such as subnet mask and default gateway.

To create an IPv4 scope, follow these steps:

1. In the DHCP management console, if necessary, expand the server and click IPv4.

2. Right-click IPv4 and click New Scope.

3. In the New Scope Wizard, click Next.

4. On the Scope Name page, in the Name box, enter a name for the scope and click Next. This name should be meaningful, so that you can easily understand where it is used.

5. On the IP Address Range page, shown in Figure 5.16, enter the correct Start IP address, End IP address, and Subnet mask, and then click Next.

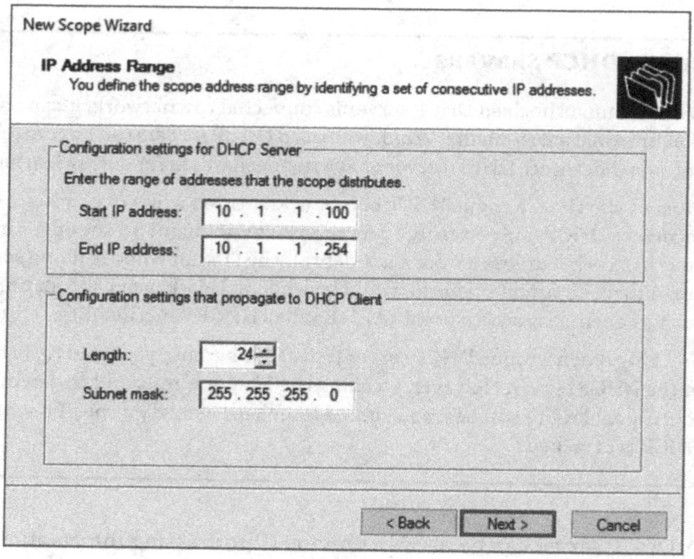

FIGURE 5.16
New Scope
Wizard - IP
Address Range

6. On the Add Exclusions and Delay page, enter any IP address in the range that should not be given to clients. For example, you might have an IP address range that is reserved for printers.

7. In the Subnet Delay In Millisecond box, you can enter the number of milliseconds that this scope should wait before responding and then click Next. The delay is used in some high-availability scenarios, but is not typically used.

8. On the Lease Duration page, enter how long you want clients to be able to use an IP address and click Next.

9. On the Configure DHCP Options page, click No, I Will Configure These Options Later and click Next.

10. On the Completing the New Scope Wizard page, click Finish.

11. In the DHCP management console, right-click the scope and click Activate. Just as DHCP servers need to be activated, so do scopes.

When you create a scope, the default lease length is eight days. Clients will attempt to renew that lease with the original DHCP server at 50 percent of lease length (four days) and if not successful, again at 87.5 percent complete (seven days). If the lease cannot be renewed by the time the lease expires, then the client loses its IP address configuration and might obtain a lease from another DHCP server or begin using an APIPA address.

While eight days ensures that clients can use the IP address for an extended period, it can also make it difficult to make network changes. For example, if you wanted to change the subnet mask for a scope, the earliest it could possibly take effect would be four days, because clients won't get updated information until they renew. To facilitate making network changes, you should use a shorter lease time. Many organizations use a lease time of one day. On networks with a very high level of change, such as guest wireless networks, you might keep the lease time as short as an hour.

After a scope is created, you have the option to create reservations. A *reservation* is an IP address in the scope that is given to a specific DHCP client. The DHCP server identifies the client based on the client's MAC address. So, you need to identify the MAC address of the client before you make a reservation. Alternatively, you can select an existing lease and convert it to a reservation. The IP address for a reservation must be within the IP address pool configured in the scope.

Reservations can be used in any situation where a consistent IP address is required for a client. Some organizations use reservations for printers that are on the same subnets with client computers. Reservations can also be configured for computers that require specific firewall rules to access secure resources.

It is easier to change the IP address of a computer or device when they use a reservation rather than a static IP address. Static IP addresses typically need to be changed by visiting each device. DHCP reservations can be changed centrally in the DHCP management console.

Two special scope types that are rarely used are listed here:

◆   Superscope. A super scope combines two existing scopes into a single logical scope. This is used when a second subnet is added to an existing network. For example, a network might originally have only the 192.168.2.0/24 network, but the 192.168.3.0/24 is added to the same segment due to a shortage of IP addresses.

◆ Multicast scope. Some applications use multicast addresses to deliver network packets to multiple computers at the same time. For example, deploying operating system images to new computers. If the application can use DHCP, you can configure a multicast scope to provide the multicast address to the application.

DHCP Options

The most basic configuration of a DHCP scope provides only an IP address and subnet mask to clients. However, to be functional, most clients also need at least a default gateway and DNS server. DHCP can include additional information as part of a lease by configuring DHCP options.

The most common DHCP options are listed here:

◆ 003 Router

◆ 006 DNS Servers

◆ 015 DNS Domain Name

You can configure DHCP options for the server, scope, or reservation. Settings at a more specific level have high priority. For example, options configured for a reservation would override options configured for a scope.

DNS servers and the DNS domain name are usually consistent for the entire site that a DHCP server services. So, these options are commonly configured at the server level.

The default gateway for computers in each subnet is unique. So, the router configuration option is configured for each scope, as shown in Figure 5.17.

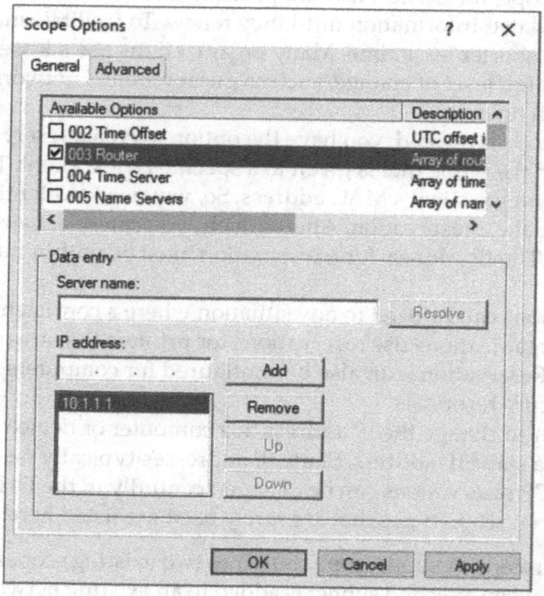

FIGURE 5.17
Scope Options
dialog box

DHCP Policies and Filters

You can also use DHCP filters and policies to control how settings are delivered to DHCP clients. Filters are configured separately for each server. Policies can be configured at the server or scope level.

Filters define only whether clients are allowed or denied. You can't use filters to define options for clients. There are separate Allow and Deny lists, which are disabled by default. Each list identifies clients by MAC addresses. The filtering behavior varies, depending on which filtering list is enabled:

♦ When only the Allow list is enabled, then all clients are denied unless they are on the Allow list.

♦ When only the Deny list is enabled, then all clients are allowed unless they are on the Deny list.

♦ When the Allow and Deny lists are both enabled, then all clients are blocked unless they are on the Allow list. However, if a client is on the Allow list and the Deny list, then the client is blocked.

WILDCARDS FOR FILTERS

Using individual MAC addresses for filters works well when only a few clients need to be controlled, but it can be tedious if you have large groups of clients to exclude. For example, if you want to ensure that IP phones never get IP information from your DHCP server, you need to enter the MAC address of each IP phone.

To simplify filter configuration, you can use wildcards. Because hardware vendors have specifically assigned ranges of MAC addresses, you can use wildcards to block clients from a specific vendor. For example, if your IP phone vendor has MAC addresses that all begin with AA-AA-AA, you can use AA-AA-AA-* in the Deny filter to block all of the IP phones.

Policies contain a set of conditions and DHCP options. The conditions define the clients to which the policy applies. Clients that match the conditions are given the DHCP options defined in the policy. This can be used to give clients that are running unique software the additional options required for that software.

The criteria that can be used to build the conditions are listed here:

♦ Vendor Class

♦ User Class

♦ MAC Address

♦ Client Identifier

♦ Fully Qualified Domain Name

♦ Relay Agent Information

High Availability

The DHCP protocol does not include any functionality for high availability. In part, this is because there is a limited impact when DHCP is unavailable for brief periods of time. Sometimes, a DHCP server can be restarted and no clients will be affected at all because they already have a lease.

Some environments used two DHCP servers to provide high availability. However, because the DHCP servers did not coordinate, each DHCP server needed to be configured with a separate range of IP addresses in the scope. When clients requested a lease, both DHCP servers responded. Adding a delay to the scope on one DHCP server effectively designated that DHCP server as secondary for the scope because clients selected the first lease that was offered. The scope was typically split 80/20 with the primary DHCP server configured to hand out 80 percent of the IP addresses.

While this older method for high availability worked as a stopgap, it wasn't very efficient because 20 percent of the addresses were held in reserve. It also didn't replicate configuration information like options or DHCP reservations. To address these concerns, true high availability was added to the DHCP server role in Windows Server 2012, and it continues to be part of the DHCP role in Windows Server 2016. High availability for DHCP can be configured in hot standby mode or load-balanced mode.

In hot standby mode, one DHCP server is primary for a scope and a second DHCP server is the standby node. If the primary node fails, the standby node begins servicing requests. This configuration is useful when there is a local DHCP server in a site and another DHCP server at a different site. The local DHCP server is configured as the primary DHCP server. DHCP relay is configured between the two sites.

In load-balanced mode, both DHCP servers respond to client requests for a lease. However, the two DHCP servers coordinate to prevent duplicate DHCP offers. For example, if the scope is split 50/50, each DHCP server responds to 50 percent of the lease requests. If one of the DHCP servers fails, the remaining DHCP server will take over and issue leases for the entire scope. This mode is best suited to scenarios where both DHCP servers are in the same site, such as a large office.

To configure high availability of DHCP, you need to create a DHCP failover relationship. Each DHCP server can have up to 31 failover relationships. A single failover relationship can be used for multiple DHCP scopes.

Although the term "failover relationship" sounds similar to the Failover Clustering feature in Windows Server, the *failover relationships in DHCP* are a completely separate technology. It is also possible to configure a DHCP server in a failover cluster for high availability, but doing so is not recommended because it is more complex than using the failover relationships in DHCP.

To create a failover relationship, follow these steps:

1. In the DHCP console, right-click the IPv4 node or a scope, and click Configure Failover.

2. In the Configure Failover Wizard, on the Introduction to DHCP Failover page, select the scopes you want to make highly available and click Next. By default, all scopes are selected.

3. On the Specify the Partner Server to Use for Failover page, click Add Server.

4. In the Add Server dialog box, in the This Server box, enter the name of the partner server and then click OK. Alternatively, you can browse for a specific server.

5. On the Specify the Partner Server to Use for Failover page, click Next.

6. On the Create a New Failover Relationship page, shown in Figure 5.18, configure the appropriate settings and click Next.

FIGURE 5.18
Creating a
new failover
relationship

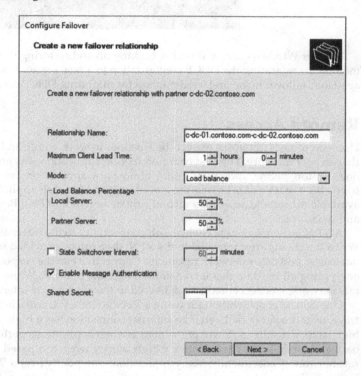

7. On the Summary page, click Finish.

8. In the Configure Failover dialog box, read the task status and click Close.

9. Verify that the configured scopes now exist on both servers.

DHCP Database

The configuration information for a Windows DHCP server is stored in a database. Other than making backups, you don't need to manage or maintain this database. By default, the DHCP database is in C:\Windows\System32\dhcp.

Backing up the DHCP database is useful in case you ever make a mistake when modifying a DHCP scope or reservation. By default, the DHCP configuration is automatically backed up every 60 minutes. You can view the configuration of the DHCP database by using the Get-DhcpServerDatabase cmdlet, as shown in Figure 5.19.

```
PS C:\Users\administrator.CONTOSO> Get-DhcpServerDatabase

FileName               : C:\windows\system32\dhcp\dhcp.mdb
BackupPath             : C:\windows\system32\dhcp\backup
BackupInterval(m)      : 60
CleanupInterval(m)     : 60
LoggingEnabled         : True
RestoreFromBackup      : False
```

In older Windows Server versions, backing up and restoring the DHCP database was the best method for migrating the DHCP configuration to a new server. However, now that failover is available, failover is the preferred method for migrating DHCP configuration to a new server.

Remote Access

Users on today's networks expect the freedom to work where and when needed. That is to say, they expect mobility. The first common mobile application was email, and it's now on everyone's laptop, phone, and tablet. Today almost any application can be made available to mobile users. It's a matter of selecting the correct method for each application. In general, the options available for remote access are virtual private network (VPN), Remote Desktop Services (RDS), and web apps.

A VPN provides remote clients with connectivity to the internal network over the Internet. When the clients are connected to the VPN, they can be provided with access to file servers, databases, and other network resources. Connectivity to the corporate network is secured by encrypting all the data that is transmitted over the Internet. When the data arrives at the corporate network, it is decrypted and delivered to the appropriate internal servers.

One critical consideration for using a VPN is latency. *Latency* is the time it takes for data to travel over the network. Even if an Internet connection has a high maximum speed (bandwidth), high latency results in slower performance when applications perform a lot of communication back and forth. VPNs have relatively high latency when compared to a computer on the corporate network. Consequently, many applications run poorly over a VPN connection. VPNs are best suited to simple communication scenarios such as opening a document rather than running an application that communicates with a database.

To run desktop applications remotely, RDS provides good performance. RDS allows you to run the application on an RDS server or a virtual desktop and only the screen drawing commands are sent back to the remote client. Because the application runs in the same data center where the data is stored, latency is not an issue for the application.

To natively support remote users, many applications are now being created as web-based applications. Web-based applications run the application code on a web server and send screen information back to clients as web pages. In this way, web-based applications avoid latency issues. Older web-based applications had very limited user interfaces, but modern web-based applications have very rich functionality. For example, Outlook on the web for Exchange Server email has almost the same functionality as using the desktop Outlook client. Also, as part of Office 365, Microsoft provides web-based versions of Word, Excel, and PowerPoint.

The Remote Access server role in Windows Server 2016 includes the following role services:

◆ DirectAccess and VPN (RAS). This role service allows the server to be used as a VPN server. DirectAccess is a specialized VPN server.

◆ Routing. This role service allows the server to be configured as a router. While not commonly used for local area networks (LANs), this can be useful for virtual machines in test environments.

◆ Web Application Proxy (WAP). This role is used to protect web-based applications by isolating them from the Internet. WAP is a reverse proxy that controls communication between Internet clients and web-based applications.

VPN

Windows Server 2016 can be used to provide VPN connectivity to clients. Most firewalls can also be configured to provide VPN connectivity to clients. Most large organizations use a dedicated VPN appliance or functionality in their firewall. When you don't use Windows Server 2016 as your VPN server, you may need to install vendor-specific VPN client software.

In addition to providing client-to-server VPN connectivity, you can also provide site-to-site VPN connectivity. Site-to-site VPNs are often used to connect to branch locations over the Internet. Although it is possible to use Windows Server 2016 for a site-to-site VPN, it is rarely done. Firewalls are more commonly used to configure site-to-site VPNs.

VPN PROTOCOLS

Windows Server 2016 supports several different VPN protocols. A VPN protocol defines how authentication is performed and how data is encrypted. There is still support for older protocols, but newer protocols are more secure. Table 5.5 describes the available VPN protocols. All of these protocols are enabled by default when you enable Windows Server 2016 as a VPN server.

TABLE 5.5:   VPN Protocols

VPN PROTOCOL	DESCRIPTION
Point-to-Point Tunneling Protocol (PPTP)	PPTP is an older protocol (1990s) that is no longer considered secure. You should not use PPTP because it is too easy to capture the username and password used for authentication. Some organizations continue to use PPTP because it is easy to implement and widely supported by firewalls. To allow PPTP through a firewall, you need to allow TCP port 1723 and GRE packets. GRE packets are IP protocol type 47.

TABLE 5.5: VPN Protocols *(CONTINUED)*

VPN PROTOCOL	DESCRIPTION
Layer 2 Tunneling Protocol (L2TP)	An L2TP VPN is actually a combination of L2TP for tunneling and IPsec for encryption. This VPN protocol is more secure than PPTP, but it is also more difficult to configure because both L2TP and IPsec need to be authenticated.
	L2TP is authenticated by using a username and password. However, IPsec has three authentication options:
	◆ A pre-shared key (password) can be configured on client computers and the VPN server. However, because all client computers share the same key, this is relatively insecure.
	◆ A trusted certificate can be configured on client computers and the VPN server. A properly maintained public key infrastructure (PKI) for certificates is very secure, but distributing certificates to non-domain-joined clients can be cumbersome.
	◆ Kerberos authentication can be used when computers are part of the same domain as the VPN server. Computers on a domain already use Kerberos authentication when they join the domain.
	To allow L2TP VPN connectivity through a firewall, you need to allow UDP port 5000, UDP port 4500, and IP protocol type 50. IP protocol type 50 is the ESP (Encapsulating Security Payload) type used by IPsec for encryption.
Secure Socket Tunneling Protocol (SSTP)	SSTP is preferred over PPTP and L2TP because of its security and simple configuration. SSTP uses the same Transport Layer Security (TLS) protocol for encryption that is used by web servers. Authentication is based on username and password.
	To allow an SSTP VPN through a firewall, you need to allow TCP port 443. This is the same port used by secure websites. Consequently, this protocol works from almost any location. Whereas on public networks, such as a hotel, other VPN protocols may be blocked.
	This protocol is available in Windows Vista SP1 and later.
Internet Key Exchange v2 Tunneling Protocol (IKEv2)	IKEv2 uses IPsec for data encryption; but unlike L2TP, it does not require IPsec authentication to be configured separately. Authentication can be performed with only a username and password.
	The main benefit of IKEv2 over SSTP is the VPN reconnect feature. When IKEv2 is used on unstable network connections, it can reconnect automatically. For other VPNs, you need to reconnect manually when the VPN is interrupted.
	Because IKEv2 is based on IPsec, you need to allow the same ports and protocol types as an L2TP VPN. You need to allow UDP port 5000, UDP port 4500, and IP protocol type 50.
	This protocol is available in Windows 7 and newer clients.

CONFIGURING A VPN SERVER

The first step to configuring a VPN server is to install the DirectAccess and VPN (RAS) role service from the Remote Access server role. To configure a VPN server, follow these steps:

1. In Server Manager, click Tools and click Remote Access Management.

2. In the Remote Access management console, in the Navigation pane, click DirectAccess And VPN and click Run The Getting Started Wizard.

3. In the Configure Remote Access Wizard, click Deploy VPN Only.

4. In the Routing and Remote Access windows, right-click your server and click Configure And Enable Routing And Remote Access.

5. In the Routing and Remote Access Server Setup Wizard, click Next.

6. On the Configuration page, click Remote Access (Dial-Up Or VPN) and click Next.

7. On the Remote Access page, select the VPN check box and click Next.

8. On the VPN Connection page, shown in Figure 5.20, select the network interface that is connected to the Internet and then click Next. In many cases, this adapter is in a DMZ rather than directly on the Internet.

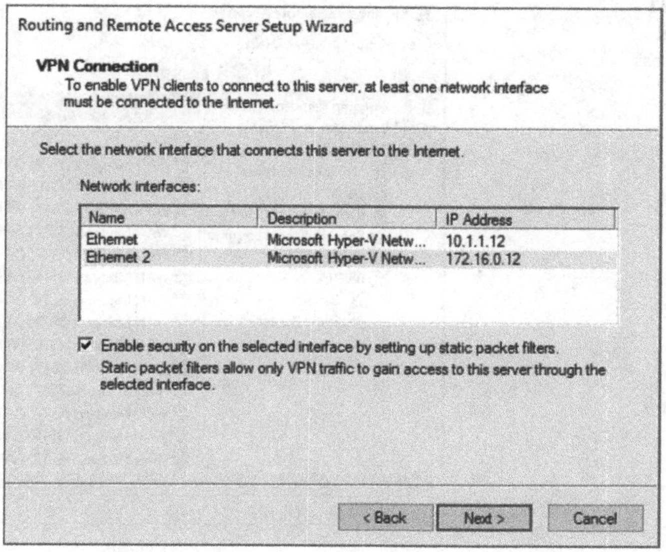

FIGURE 5.20
Selecting the
Internet adapter

Routing and Remote Access Server Setup Wizard

VPN Connection
 To enable VPN clients to connect to this server, at least one network interface must be connected to the Internet.

Select the network interface that connects this server to the Internet.

Network interfaces:

Name	Description	IP Address
Ethernet	Microsoft Hyper-V Netw...	10.1.1.12
Ethernet 2	Microsoft Hyper-V Netw...	172.16.0.12

☑ Enable security on the selected interface by setting up static packet filters.
 Static packet filters allow only VPN traffic to gain access to this server through the selected interface.

< Back   Next >   Cancel

9. On the IP Address Assignment page, select how you want IP addresses to be assigned to clients and then click Next. You can select Automatically to have the VPN server lease IP addresses from a DHCP server and distribute them to clients. Or, you can configure a specific range of IP addresses on the VPN server that will be distributed to clients.

10. On the Managing Multiple Remote Access Servers page, select whether the VPN server will perform authentication itself, or whether a RADIUS server will be used for authentication, and then click Next. A RADIUS server allows you to centralize authentication requests for multiple VPN servers.

11. On the summary page, click Finish.

12. In the Routing and Remote Access dialog box, click Yes to acknowledge that you need to configure the DHCP Relay Agent with the IP address of your DHCP Server to service VPN client requests. This dialog box appears only if you selected to use a DHCP server for distribution of IP addresses.

After the VPN server has been configured, management is performed by using the Routing and Remote Access tool, shown in Figure 5.21, which is accessible from Server Manager. The Remote Access Management console, which is also accessible in Server Manager, has a limited amount of monitoring information for the VPN role.

FIGURE 5.21
Routing and
Remote Access
dialog box

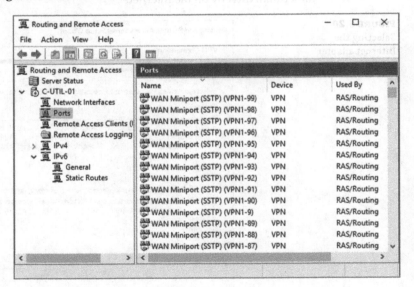

When a VPN server is configured, no users have access by default. You can enable access for individual users or by configuring network policies. To allow a single user to sign in to the VPN, you configure the Dial-in properties of the user account, as shown in Figure 5.22. Even though the name indicates dial-in, it also applies to VPN access. The default network access permission is Control Access Through NPS Network Policy. To allow VPN access, select Allow Access.

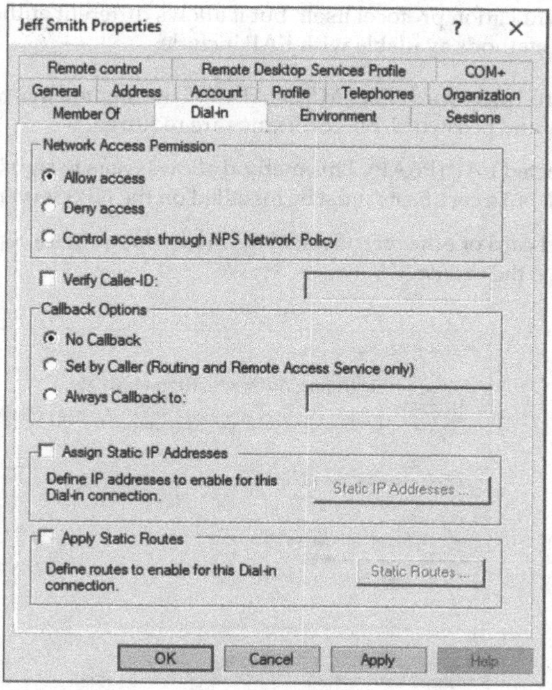

FIGURE 5.22
Network Access
Permission

NETWORK POLICY SERVER

In smaller organizations, enabling VPN access for each user individually is not too much work. However, in a larger organization, you need to have a more manageable way to control VPN access. Larger organizations use network policies in Network Policy Server (NPS). NPS is installed when you configure the VPN server.

Remote Access Dial-In User Service (RADIUS) is a protocol that is used to forward authentication requests from a service to a RADIUS server that performs the authentication. This protocol was originally used by dial-in servers, but it is also used by VPN servers, wireless access points, and for 802.1x authentication on switches. NPS in Windows Server 2016 provides RADIUS server functionality.

Network policies in NPS are rules that define which users can connect to the network. The default network policies block all connections, so you need to create additional network policies to allow access. You can allow access based on various characteristics such as IP address or day and time restrictions. However, the most commonly used characteristic is membership in a group.

As part of a network policy, you also need to select acceptable authentication methods. Some older, less secure authentication methods are enabled by default, as shown in Figure 5.23. We strongly recommend using Extensible Authentication Protocol (EAP) methods instead. EAP is not an authentication protocol itself, but it allows different authentication methods to be integrated. The methods available with EAP include:

- Secured password (EAP-MSCHAPv2). This method allows users to sign in with a username and password. No certificates are required.

- Protected EAP (PEAP). This method allows users to sign in with a username and password, but a certificate must be installed on the NPS server to secure the communication.

- Smart card or other certificate. This method requires a certificate for user authentication and on the server.

FIGURE 5.23
Network policy
authentication
methods

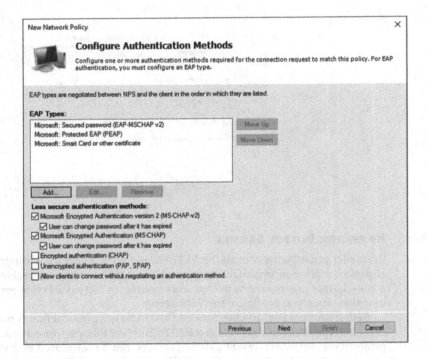

You can also configure constraints on each network policy. They enforce limits such as time outs or day and time restrictions. If you configure multiple constraints, then all constraints must be matched or the connection request will be denied.

Finally, you can configure settings that are applied to a connection in a network policy. Some settings include IP filters, encryption, and RADIUS attributes.

Rather than maintaining separate sets of network policies on each VPN server, you can centralize the policies on one NPS server. To do this, you need to modify the properties of the VPN server to act as a RADIUS client. The default configuration for authentication and accounting is to perform it locally. In Figure 5.24, this is shown for the accounting provider (logging) as Windows Accounting. The authentication provider is configured to forward authentication requests to a RADIUS server.

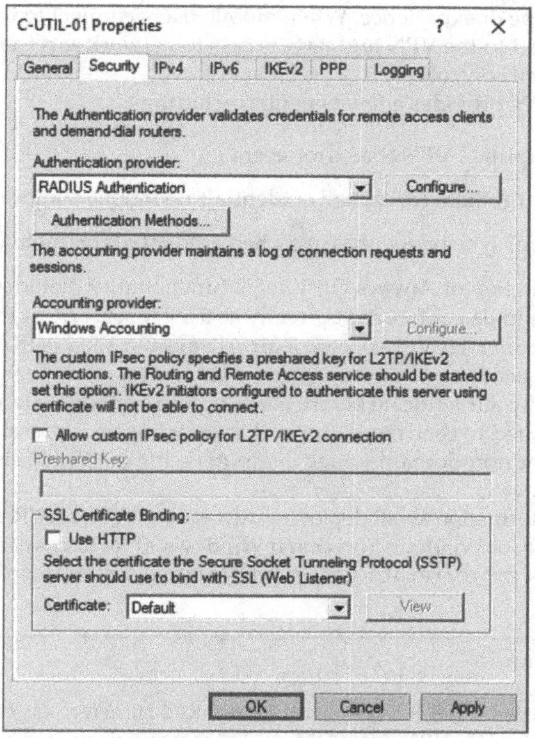

FIGURE 5.24
Configuring a
VPN server to use
RADIUS

C-UTIL-01 Properties   ? ☓

General | Security | IPv4 | IPv6 | IKEv2 | PPP | Logging

The Authentication provider validates credentials for remote access clients
and demand-dial routers.

Authentication provider:

| RADIUS Authentication ▾ | Configure... |

| Authentication Methods... |

The accounting provider maintains a log of connection requests and
sessions.

Accounting provider:

| Windows Accounting ▾ | Configure... |

The custom IPsec policy specifies a preshared key for L2TP/IKEv2
connections. The Routing and Remote Access service should be started to
set this option. IKEv2 initiators configured to authenticate this server using
certificate will not be able to connect.

☐ Allow custom IPsec policy for L2TP/IKEv2 connection

Preshared Key:

┌─ SSL Certificate Binding: ──────────────────────────┐
│ ☐ Use HTTP   │
│ Select the certificate the Secure Socket Tunneling Protocol (SSTP) │
│ server should use to bind with SSL (Web Listener)   │
│   │
│ Certificate: | Default ▾ | View   │
└──┘

   OK   Cancel   Apply

RADIUS PROXY

In most cases, configuring your VPN server (RADIUS client) to use a specific RADIUS server (NPS server) is sufficient. However, if you have a more complex environment with multiple Active Directory forests or domains, then you might want to implement a RADIUS proxy to route authentication requests to the correct RADIUS server.

NPS can act as a RADIUS proxy by using connection request policies. The default connection request policies authenticate all requests locally. You can create additional connection request policies that send authentication requests for some domains to a RADIUS server in another domain. For example, you could route requests based on the domain in the user UPN of an authentication request.

ALWAYS ON VPN

The best-case scenario for mobile users is to move seamlessly between the internal network and roaming. If your clients are using Windows 10 (build 1607 or later), you can use Always On VPN to provide this type of experience. When mobile users connect to the Internet, they are automatically authenticated to the VPN and have access to network services, including authentication services on domain controllers.

Always On VPN provides a few benefits, including:

◆ Allows simplified VPN access for users

◆ Avoids requirement for cached credentials on mobile computers

◆ Avoids out of sync passwords in cached credentials on mobile computers

The implementation of Always On VPN is functionality included in Windows 10. Windows Server 2016 needs to be configured correctly as a VPN server, but the client is responsible for connecting. The preferred VPN protocol for Always On VPN is IKEv2, but if IKEv2 fails to connect then SSTP is used.

To automatically authenticate before users sign in, authentication is based on computers. A certificate is issued to each computer and this certificate is presented to the VPN server for authentication. For non-domain-joined computers, the certificate can be distributed by using Microsoft Intune.

For detailed information about deploying Always On VPN, see "Remote Access Always On VPN Deployment Guide for Windows Server and Windows 10" at https://docs.microsoft.com/en-us/windows-server/remote/remote-access/vpn/always-on-vpn/deploy/always-on-vpn-deploy.

DIRECTACCESS

In Windows Server 2008 R2, Microsoft introduced DirectAccess to provide benefits like those provided by Always On VPN. After DirectAccess was implemented, clients could seamlessly roam from the internal network to mobile locations. In the future, Microsoft will be focused on Always On VPN for these benefits. However, if you already have DirectAccess in place, it will be supported for many years and can be used to support older clients.

DirectAccess was much more complex to configure than Always On VPN. Also, only Enterprise editions of Windows clients could be used as DirectAccess clients. Always On VPN is supported by Windows 10 Pro, which is used by many smaller organizations.

WAP

To provide remote access to web-based applications, you can use WAP. WAP is a reverse proxy that resides between Internet clients and the web-based application, as shown in Figure 5.25. Internet clients never communicate directly with the web-based application. Instead, WAP isolates the web application to protect it from exploits.

FIGURE 5.25
WAP server
placement

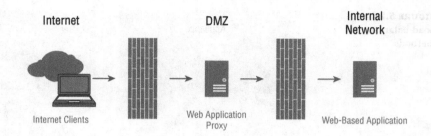

For increased security, WAP can be configured to pre-authenticate users before connectivity to the web-based application is allowed. Requiring authentication before a request can be sent to the login screen of an application will prevent almost all attacks from the Internet.

WAP is dependent on Active Directory Federation Services (AD FS). For more information about WAP, see Chapter 11.

Network Load Balancing

Load balancing is a system that allows the processing load for an application to be spread over multiple servers. For example, you could have a website application installed on two servers and load balancing would direct client requests to both servers. This provides high availability because if one of the servers fails, the remaining server can still respond to client requests (you can also remove a node temporarily for maintenance). Load balancing also provides scalability because you can add more servers.

A key consideration for load balancing is that each node in the load-balancing cluster needs to have the same information. Otherwise, clients get inconsistent information that depends on the node with which they are communicating. For a simple website, this means that you need to copy the same website to all the servers. For something more complex like a web-based application, it means that all the front-end web servers for the application need to use a single, shared data source, such as a SQL Server database.

Some applications need to maintain session state in memory. For example, a website with a shopping cart may keep the contents of the shopping cart in memory until you pay for the items. The client needs to keep communicating with the node containing the shopping cart for the entire session. Applications that require authentication also require connectivity to a consistent node. Connecting clients to a consistent node is referred to as *affinity*.

You can use the Windows Network Load Balancing (NLB) feature in Windows Server 2016 to perform load balancing. However, this load-balancing feature operates differently from most load-balancing solutions. Most load-balancing solutions are implemented as an appliance and all client requests are directed to the appliance. The appliance then sends the request to a node for servicing. NLB operates as a distributed service where all nodes see all requests, but only the correct node responds to the request. All nodes use an algorithm to calculate which node responds to the request. Figure 5.26 shows the difference in how each type of load-balancing responds.

FIGURE 5.26
Load-balancing
methods

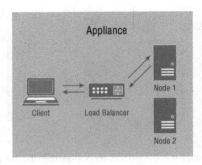

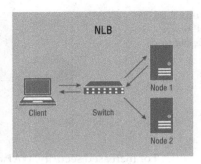

When you configure an NLB cluster, you can set the affinity for clients. If the application does not keep any session state information, you can use no affinity at all. If affinity is required, it can be based on a source IP address or an entire source subnet. In most cases, using the source IP address for affinity is preferred because it provides a more even distribution of load across the nodes.

Although NLB is a valid solution for smaller environments, most organizations that require load balancing use a specialized appliance. This is because NLB has the following drawbacks:

◆ Limited scalability. NLB works fine for a few nodes, but it does not work well for a large number of nodes that are required in larger environments. Load-balancing appliances are more scalable.

◆ Incompatible with Failover Clustering feature. The NLB feature cannot be installed on a node that is already using the Failover Clustering feature. This is a problem for Exchange Server deployments that use database availability groups (DAGs) for high availability. Load-balancing appliances avoid this problem by removing the required functionality from the servers.

◆ Not application-aware. NLB stops distributing requests to a node that doesn't respond to heartbeats, but it does not monitor application health. If the application is in a failed state, but the operating system is still healthy, NLB still sends requests to the failed server resulting in errors for users. Load-balancing appliances can be configured to monitor applications and take a node out of service if the application fails.

For detailed information about configuring NLB, see "Network Load Balancing" at https://docs.microsoft.com/en-us/windows-server/networking/technologies/network-load-balancing.

Software Defined Networking

A Software Defined Network (SDN) virtualizes network configuration to provide greater flexibility. SDN brings cloud-like network configuration to your environment running Hyper-V. Many of the features in SDN for Windows Server 2016, such as the software load balancer, originally appeared in Windows Azure.

When you implement SDN, the network configuration is abstracted from the physical network and Hyper-V hosts. You can create a new network and connect virtual machines to that network without regard for which Hyper-V hosts the virtual machines are running on. You do not need to manually create separate Hyper-V networks across the Hyper-V hosts to support network isolation.

This chapter provides an overview of SDN. To get detailed information about SDN and how to deploy it, see "Software Defined Networking (SDN)" at https://docs.microsoft.com/en-us/windows-server/networking/sdn/software-defined-networking.

To see a demonstration of SDN, see "An Introduction to Software Defined Networking with Windows Server 2016" at https://youtu.be/f501zUUcXD0.

Network Controller

The Network Controller is the component responsible for configuring network devices. When you make configuration changes, the changes are given to the Network Controller. The Network Controller then makes the configuration changes that are necessary on Hyper-V hosts.

When you communicate with the Network Controller to make configuration changes and monitor the existing configuration, it is through the Northbound application programmer interface (API). The communication path used by the Network Controller to configure and monitor network devices is referred to as the Southbound API. It is important to understand the terms Northbound API and Southbound API only because some Microsoft documentation refers to them.

You can make configuration changes on the Network Controller by using Windows PowerShell. However, doing so is relatively complex. It is far simpler to work with SDN by using System Center Virtual Machine Manager (VMM). VMM is part of the System Center suite of applications that is designed for managing a Hyper-V environment. It can deploy and manage virtual machines, Hyper-V hosts, and SDN.

Network Controller is a critical component in SDN, and you should make it highly available by creating a Network Controller cluster. Microsoft recommends three virtual machines with the Network Controller role installed.

Hyper-V Network Virtualization

Hyper-V Network Virtualization is the technology operating in the background that allows SDN to dynamically create and manage networks in the private cloud. The network packets that move been virtual machines on different Hyper-V hosts are encapsulated so that the physical network does not need to be configured to route the IP addresses for the virtual machines.

Within the private cloud, you can create isolated networks with no connectivity. This allows you to create multiple environments with no risk of IP address conflicts. A development environment for an application can use exactly the same configuration as the production environment (including IP addresses) with no risk of network conflicts.

From a virtual machine management perspective, Hyper-V Network Virtualization enables live migration of virtual machines across subnets. Without Hyper-V Network Virtualization, a virtual machine can be live-migrated only between Hyper-V hosts on the same subnet.

RAS Gateway

RAS Gateway is a router for SDN. It routes traffic between the physical network and virtual machines. Due to network virtualization applied throughout the private cloud, RAS Gateway can perform routing for traffic from any virtual machine regardless of the Hyper-V host on which it is hosted.

To simplify routing updates with the physical network and between tenants, RAS Gateway uses border gateway protocol (BGP). BGP is a routing protocol that can advertise and accept routing information. This avoids the need for manual routing table updates because RAS Gateway can accept and provide routing table updates from other routers.

Other features of RAS Gateway include:

◆ Site-to-site VPN. A site-to-site VPN connects two locations into a single private network over public infrastructure such as the Internet. You can use this feature to connect multiple data centers or connect a data center with a Microsoft Azure tenant for a hybrid environment.

◆ Point-to-site VPN. A point-to-site VPN allows individual clients to connect to the private network. You can use this to allow administrators and staff to connect to the private cloud and access resources.

◆ GRE Tunneling. Generic Routing Encapsulation (GRE) is a lightweight tunneling protocol that can be used to move data packets between tenants in the private cloud or between virtual networks within a tenant.

To provide high availability for RAS Gateway functionality, you can create gateway pools. In Windows Server 2012 R2, you were limited to a single gateway pool. In Windows Server 2016, you can have multiple gateway pools. This provides additional flexibility to dedicate pools to a single purpose such as VPN access or a single tenant.

Datacenter Firewall

You can use Datacenter Firewall for SDN to apply firewall policies to individual virtual machines or entire networks. You can implement firewall rules to protect hosts that are Internet facing or are on the internal network. In a multi-tenant environment, tenant administrators can create rules within their own tenant. Rules in the firewall policies can be based on:

◆ Protocol

◆ Source and destination IP address

◆ Source and destination port number

Software Load Balancing

Software Load Balancing (SLB) for SDN is a Windows Server 2016 feature that is used to provide load balancing. The functionality of SLB is similar to a load-balancing appliance rather than the NLB feature in Windows Server 2016. This means that SLB is flexible for deployment and highly scalable. SLB also has health monitoring based on TCP port or an HTTP probe to a specific URL. For high availability of SLB, you can have multiple virtual machines running SLB. Table 5.6 list some of the terms you should be familiar with in order to understand SLB.

TABLE 5.6: SLB Terminology

TERM	DESCRIPTION
Virtual IP address (VIP)	An IP address that clients use to access the load-balanced resource.
Dynamic IP address (DIP)	An IP address of a virtual machine in the private cloud that is hosting the load-balanced resource. If there are three virtual machines hosting the resource, then there are three DIPs.
SLB Multiplexer (MUX)	A logical collection of one or more virtual machines running SLB. A MUX is configured by using load-balancing polices that define VIPs and DIPs for specific workloads. Client requests are sent to the MUX, and the MUX forwards the requests to a DIP.

Because the entire SDN functions as a single unit, SLB can be more efficient than traditional load-balancing appliances. Inbound requests from outside the SDN are handled by the MUX, but responses are not. The virtual switch on the Hyper-V host performs the necessary network address translation (NAT) for the virtual machine to respond directly to the client. When the client is located within the SDN, after the initial connection is made, even client requests bypass the MUX and are sent directly to the DIP.

The NAT functionality in SLB can be used without implementing load balancing. You can use this to allow virtual machines on the SDN to access external resources without assigning them an externally accessible IP address. You can also use this functionality to allow external clients to access a virtual machine on the SDN. You can configure NAT rules to allow only specific TCP or UDP ports to be accessed.

For a video about SLB functionality, see "Software-Defined Networking Load Balancer in Windows Server 2016" at https://channel9.msdn.com/Blogs/windowsserver/Software-defined-Networking-Load-Balancer-in-Windows-Server-2016.

Switch Embedded Teaming

Switch Embedded Teaming (SET) in Windows Server 2016 is an alternative to using network adapter teaming on a Hyper-V host. Without SDN, you can combine multiple physical network adapters into a team and create a virtual network that uses the team. This makes the virtual network highly available, but it is manageable only at the Hyper-V host level.

When you use SDN, you should use SET instead of network adapter teaming. SET enables management through the SDN Network Controller. SET also supports Remote Direct Memory Access (RDMA), which allows for higher speed data connectivity.

Some considerations for using SET include:

◆ All network adapters must be identical.

◆ You cannot use 802.1x authentication because EAP packets are dropped.

◆ Receive Side Scaling (RSS) is not supported because virtual machine queues (VMQ) and virtual machine multi-queue (VMMQ) are used instead.

◆ Virtual Machine Quality of Service (VM-QoS) causes unpredictable results when enabled.

Internal DNS Service

Internal DNS Service (iDNS) for SDN allows you to centralize DNS for all tenants. The iDNS server is accessible to all tenants and avoids the need for your tenants to host their own DNS server. Each tenant can use iDNS to resolve DNS records on the Internet or within their own tenant.

The iDNS server is not directly available from tenant networks. Instead, each virtual machine runs an iDNS proxy service that allows communication with the iDNS server for name resolution and registration. To configure a virtual machine to use iDNS, it must be configured to obtain an IP address and DNS servers from DHCP. The Network Controller provides the virtual machine with the correct configuration for the IP address and the iDNS proxy.

The Bottom Line

Configure networking in Windows Server 2016. Windows Firewall is a host-based firewall included in Windows Server 2016. To avoid the configuration problems that occurred when Windows Firewall was first introduced, the majority of modern applications automatically configure Windows Firewall as part of the installation process. You should disable Windows Firewall only when testing connectivity where you think Windows Firewall might be the problem.

Master It You have an application server that has been running properly for several months. You know that Windows Firewall was properly configured when the application was installed. However, after a recent power outage where the uninterruptible power supply (UPS) failed, the application server refused network requests from clients. When you disable Windows Firewall, the application works properly. What caused the misconfiguration of Windows Firewall?

Solution Windows Firewall has different sets of rules for the domain, work, and public profiles. Windows Server 2016 normally uses the domain profile, which is identified because the server can communicate with a domain controller. During an outage, it is likely that the application server was unable to communicate with a domain controller during startup and is not using the domain profile for the network connection. Because the wrong profile is in use, the wrong set of firewall rules is being used. Now that the network has recovered from the outage, restarting the server should allow it to properly detect the network profile.

Make DNS highly available. DNS is a critical resource in Windows-based networks. If DNS is unavailable, all network services will be unavailable. DNS is required for clients to sign in to Active Directory. DNS is also required for users to access the Internet.

Master It Your organization has a branch office with 500 users. You have decided that this branch office is now large enough to host some of its own resources. You want to place a domain controller and a file server in this site. How should you configure DNS for this site?

Solution When a domain controller is located in a remote site, it will get a copy of Active Directory–enabled DNS zones automatically when you install the DNS server role. No additional configuration should be necessary. If connectivity between the main office and the branch office is down, clients in the branch office can continue using the local DNS server without interruption. The DNS server in the branch office will need to be configured to perform Internet DNS resolution without requiring access to the main office.

Configure DHCP for a new subnet.   Most client computers and many network devices such as printers are configured to obtain an IP address from DHCP. Using DHCP simplifies network configuration for these devices and avoids IP conflicts when deploying new devices. In addition to handing out IP addresses, DHCP also hands out options such as default gateway and DNS servers.

Master It   Your organization has expanded in your building to include another floor. The network on this new floor was configured by the network team as a new subnet of 10.100.38.0/24. Windows Server 2016 is already configured to provide highly available DHCP for other floors. What configuration changes do you need to make for the new floor and subnet?

Solution   You need to create a new scope for the new subnet. In this scope, you will need to configure the Router option to provide clients with the correct default gateway on the subnet. You should also verify that the DNS server options have been properly configured at the server level. Finally, you will need to confirm with the network team that they configured the local router interface on the new subnet to act as a DHCP relay (IP helper).

Configure a VPN server.   You can use the Remote Access server role to configure Windows Server 2016 as a VPN server. A VPN server allows mobile clients to access internal resources such as file shares, but it is not well suited to running database applications.

Master It   Your organization decided to add two VPN servers running Windows Server 2016 to make VPN access highly available. Your colleague configured the NPS rules on both servers to be the same. This seems like it will be error prone when updating; is there a better way to configure the new VPNs?

Solution   You can centralize VPN authentication by configuring the VPN servers to use a RADIUS server. The NPS server role in Windows Server 2016 can perform as a RADIUS server. However, the NPS server will become a single point of failure.

To resolve NPS as a single point of failure, you need to load balance access to the two NPS servers (Windows NLB cannot be used). Also to sync the configuration between the two NPS servers, you will need to export the configuration by using Windows PowerShell and then import on the other NPS server. Ideally, you will script the synchronization process.

Identify a load-balancing solution.   Load balancing can be used to make applications and services highly available and scalable. Windows Server 2016 includes NLB and SLB for load balancing. You can also obtain third-party load-balancing appliances.

Master It   Your organization needs a load-balancing solution for a web-based application. If the web-based application fails on one of the servers, the load-balancing solution needs to stop directing client requests to the failed instance. Your virtualization infrastructure uses Hyper-V. What is the best solution for implementing load balancing?

Solution   Because you require application-level monitoring, you can't use NLB for load balancing. However, you can use SLB for load balancing if you implement SDN. You must implement SDN, including a Network Controller, to use SLB. If you don't want to implement SDN for your virtualization infrastructure, you will need to use a third-party load-balancing appliance.

Chapter 6

File Services

File Services provide users working on computers from various locations with the ability to access corporate files needed for their everyday work and to access different types of documents. Over the years and different Windows Server versions, File Services have evolved in order to provide better performance, productivity, and availability for organizations. In Windows Server 2016, File Services are included in all editions, including GUI, Server Core, and Nano Server. Depending on the Windows Server edition, File Services can be installed by using the Server Manager console or Windows PowerShell.

IN THIS CHAPTER, YOU WILL LEARN TO:

- ◆ Install and configure File Services
- ◆ Provide different convenient solutions for your organization's different file access and printing scenarios
- ◆ Always start with the organization's business requirements
- ◆ Save the network bandwidth with BranchCache
- ◆ Use File Server Resource Manager to allow the automation processes to work for you

File Services Overview

In Windows Server 2016, File Services include multiple components that will help organizations, from simple small businesses to large, geographically dispersed enterprises, to effectively access documents. File Services in Windows Server 2016 are categorized under File and Storage Services.

The most straightforward way to see what components are included in File and Storage Services in Windows Server 2016 is by using the Server Manager. From the Start menu, choose Server Manager and then start the Add Roles and Features Wizard. Figure 6.1 displays both locations where server roles in Server Manager are located by selecting the appropriate check box.

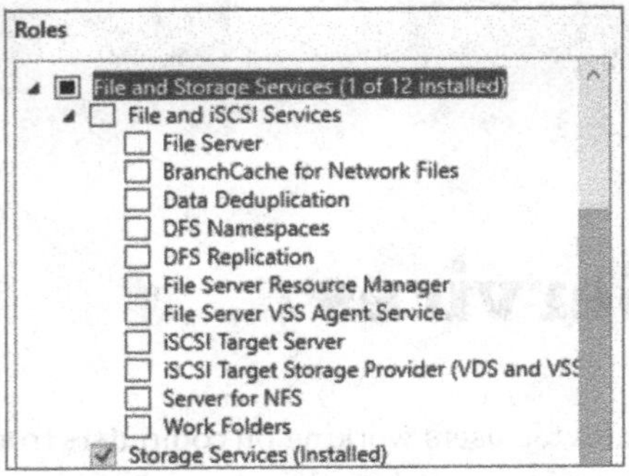

FIGURE 6.1
The File and iSCSI services subcomponents in Server Manager

Under File and Storage Services, there are two components. The first component is named File and iSCSI Services and is used to configure your server as a file server, as well as a storage server by using iSCSI technology. The second component is Storage Services, and it provides storage management functionality. It is installed by default and cannot be removed.

Let's take a quick look on the File and iSCSI Services subcomponents under the File and Storage Services role:

♦ File Server enables creating, managing, and securing shared folders and provides access for users.

♦ BranchCache for Network Files is a WAN network optimization technology used for caching files on computers located in local branch offices.

♦ Data Deduplication is a technology that optimizes free space on a volume by storing only one copy of duplicated portions of a volume.

♦ DFS Namespaces is a technology that creates a file-server logical structure with folders physically stored on many different servers.

♦ DFS Replication is a technology that replicates multiple physical folders that are part of the DFS Namespaces infrastructure.

♦ File Server Resource Manager provides various automated file management tasks, such as creating storage reports, configuring quotas, screening files and folders, and classifying.

♦ File Server VSS Agent Service provides volume shadow copies of the data to be created.

♦ iSCSI Target Server enables a server to act as a storage solution by using iSCSI technology.

♦ iSCSI Target Storage Provider (VDS and VSS hardware providers) enables applications that connect to iSCSI Target Server to perform volume shadow copies.

♦ Server for NFS provides file sharing for clients that use NFS protocol, such as UNIX-based operating systems.

♦ Work Folders is a technology that provides access to folders on a server from any type of work or personal device, over the local network or over the Internet.

Storage Services were discussed in Chapter 4, but covering all the service roles would take considerably more pages than this book has. Therefore, we will not cover all of the file services.

File Server

File server components are installed on servers that need to provide access to files from different locations in your organization. File sharing has been around for all previous Windows Server versions. Many advanced technologies (including SharePoint and Public Folders in Exchange, and One Drive for Business) have been developed through the years to replace file server functionality, but the file server still exists and is still used in many organizations.

As with any other IT solution, you should work on the design of the File Services solution before you deploy the file server. Design concepts include the following:

Number of Users   How many users will connect to the File Services? This is important for scaling. In a test environment, 10 users might connect well; however, a thousand or more users in a working environment might experience slow responses. Therefore, you need to estimate the impact the actual number of clients connected to the file server will have on performance. Scaling might include adding more memory, adding faster disk drives, and adding more servers. For you to make a scaling estimate, you will need additional information, including how often users will connect to the file server and how big the files located on the file server will be.

High Availability   If an OS or driver update is installed, it will probably request a server reboot. This will result in users being disconnected during the downtime. No matter how fast the server reboots, there will always be some unhappy users who needed access to documents during that downtime. Furthermore, some server component, such as a power supply or memory chip, might eventually stop working, resulting in server unavailability until the failing component is replaced. Therefore, deploying high availability for file servers is recommended in every organization. High availability for file servers can be achieved by deploying failover clustering or Distributed File System (DFS), which is described later in this chapter.

Server Placement   In a distributed-organization scenario, you should carefully plan where to locate the servers; an increased number of server requests might saturate the wide area network (WAN) links between data centers and branch offices. In this chapter, you will read about BranchCache and DFS technologies, which will provide you with information on how to optimize your infrastructure's server placement.

Disaster Recovery   Nobody wants to think that something bad can happen to their IT infrastructure. However, having a proper disaster-recovery plan will help you bring your servers and data back from disaster as soon as possible. Therefore, you should plan carefully the backup and restore procedures for your file servers. Furthermore, you should design a plan to bring your critical file servers online at an alternative location if the primary location will be unavailable for an extended length of time.

Security   Sharing file servers doesn't mean that everyone should be able to access, change, or delete any document. Security is one of the greatest concerns for every organization, and IT teams are responsible for making sure that no data is accessed without authorization. Furthermore, data must be protected from any internal or external attacks, malware, or, even worse, ransomware. You can read more about Windows Server 2016 security features in Chapter 8.

Installing the File Server

Installing the File Server component in Server Manager is straightforward. Just select the File Server check box and complete the wizard. An even easier method is to just share a folder on a server you want users to access, and the File Server component will be installed automatically. If you prefer to use Windows PowerShell, type the following cmdlet:

```
Install-WindowsFeature File-Services
```

After the File Server component is installed, a new item will be added on the Server Manager navigation menu. Under File and Storage Services, you will notice the Shares item, as shown in Figure 6.2.

FIGURE 6.2
Shares item in
Server Manager

Creating a File Share

From the Shares dashboard, you can select Tasks to create a new share. The New Share Wizard will guide you through the steps to create a new file share (see Figure 6.3).

FIGURE 6.3
Selecting the pro-
file for a share

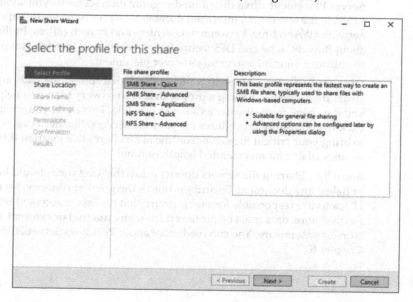

1. Select the profile for this share:

- SMB Share—Quick is used for common file sharing, where customization may be configured later by opening the Properties window of the folder.

- SMB Share—Advanced is used for configuring advanced features, such as the folder owners for access-denied assistance, data classification, access policies, and quotas. This profile needs the File Server Resource Manager component to be previously installed. This is the typical choice for small businesses to provide the most flexibility.

- SMB Share—Applications is used for server applications such as Hyper-V.

- NFS Share—Quick is used for common file-sharing scenarios for clients that run UNIX operating systems.

- NFS Share—Advanced is used for configuring advanced sharing features for clients running UNIX operating systems, as discussed previously for advanced SMB sharing. This profile needs the Server for NFS and File Server Resource Manager components to be previously installed.

2. Choose the server and path name for the shared folder location.

3. Edit or confirm the chosen values for the share name and location.

4. You will be prompted to choose from additional settings such as the following:

    - Whether to enable access-based enumeration, which is a process that hides files and folders that users do not have permissions to access.

    - Enable caching of share and BranchCache.

    - Enable share encryption.

5. Once you configure the additional settings, you will need to edit or confirm the default security settings. This step is important to protect the documents from unauthorized access from the network.

6. You will be able to edit the shared folder settings after it is created. However, this is a good time to verify that everything is configured according to the shared folder requirements.

7. If you are sure that you are finished with the configuring settings, click Create as the final step to create the file share.

Assigning Permissions

You can add more folders to be shared and configure the appropriate permissions. However, in many organizations we have seen different misconceptions about shared folders permissions. Because disk drives are formatted with NTFS, all files and folders have NTFS permissions configured. Additionally, shared folders have their own permissions. Now, which permissions apply and in which order?

Here is how it works:

◆ If you are signed in locally to a file server, only NTFS permissions apply to you. (Of course, the situation where a non-admin user is signed in locally to a file server should not be allowed.)

◆ If you are signed in on your client computer and you try to access a folder over a file share, both shared permissions and NTFS permissions are combined so that the most restrictive permissions apply. For example, if a user has NTFS permission Full Control but shared permission Read Only, when accessing through the network, the user will have Read Only permission because that permission is more restrictive.

From the information, you can plan your permissions this way:

◆ Assign permission to groups, not to users. If you work for a company with thousands of users, you might never be able to configure permissions for each employee individually. By assigning permissions to groups, you can just configure group membership, and users will receive permission according to their group membership. If users are members of multiple groups, then the less restrictive permission for that resource applies.

◆ Assign shared folder permissions to Everyone: Full Control. (Before you think this suggestion is unreasonable, wait! We're not finished; read the next bullet.)

◆ Assign restrictive NTFS permissions on the shared folder from the previous bullet, and let's check once again:

    ◆ If the user connects locally, then restrictive permissions apply. (Again, this is unlikely but used for discussion.)

    ◆ If the user connects over the network, the shared and NTFS permissions combine and the more restrictive permissions are in effect.

◆ Be careful with the Deny permission. Deny has the highest priority. Even if you are a member of multiple groups that have Full Control over some resource, Deny permission will not allow you to access the resource.

You can read more about security best practices in Chapter 8.

BranchCache for Network Files

BranchCache is a technology that optimizes network traffic for users who access files across a WAN. It was introduced in the Windows 7 and Windows Server 2008 R2 operating systems. The primary benefit of BranchCache is saving network bandwidth, because the content that is initially accessed through the network is cached in the branch office—hence, every subsequent request for content is accessed locally.

🌐 Real World Scenario

BRANCHCACHE DEPLOYMENT IN THE REAL WORLD

A mobile gaming company in Los Angeles grew rapidly and decided to open an office in Phoenix. Phoenix users used all the infrastructure in Los Angeles. Later, the company opened locations in New York and Miami. Soon, remote employees reported slow performance getting data from Los Angeles. However, adding more servers and creating new data centers in each location would have been a very expensive investment. Therefore, the company deployed BranchCache in all of its offices, so that many of the files that needed to be accessed over the network were cached and accessed locally.

BranchCache Modes of Operation

BranchCache (illustrated in Figure 6.4) has two configuration options for where content can be stored locally: on the client computer itself or on the server located in the branch office. When content is stored on the client computers, the BranchCache is working in *distributed cache mode*. When content is stored on a server in a branch office, the BranchCache is working in *hosted cache mode*.

FIGURE 6.4
BranchCache modes of operation

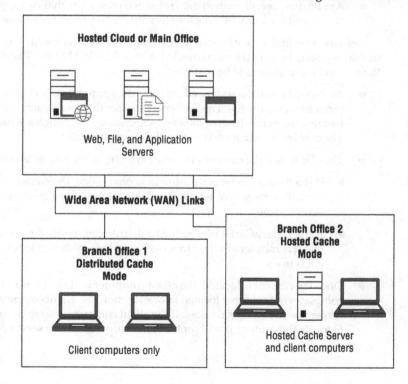

You can use different modes for different branch offices, depending on the business scenario and IT infrastructure topology.

Note that distributed cache mode is limited to the same subnet where client computers are located. For example, a client computer from a subnet in London caches the content from the headquarters' server in New York. In distributed cache mode, client computers from subnet Paris are unable to discover and retrieve the cached content from subnet London. The London client computer will need to retrieve the content directly from the headquarters' server in New York. From the other side, hosted cache mode is not limited by subnet; if the hosted cache server is located in London, then the Paris client computers will be able to retrieve the cached content from the London server.

What type of data can be cached? Windows Server 2016 is configured for BranchCache technology and can offer different types of data that can be cached:

◆ File Server content data that is located on servers that run the File Services server role and the BranchCache for Network Files role. Cached data includes folders that are shared with appropriate permissions for users who need to access the data across the network. Content is accessed with the SMB protocol.

◆ Web Server content data is located on servers that run the Web server role and the BranchCache for Network Files. Content is accessed with the HTTPS protocol.

◆ Application Server content data is located on servers that run applications such as WSUS server and the BranchCache for Network Files. Content is accessed with the BITS protocol.

Let's assume that a user located in the branch office needs a file located on a file server in the corporate headquarters, connected with a slow WAN link. The file server needs the BranchCache component to be installed.

◆ At the first place the user needs to have the appropriate NTFS and share permissions in order to access the file. The file server verifies the permissions and then generates the content information—hash of data and segment secret, which are used to encrypt the content. The content information is sent to the client computer.

◆ The client uses the content information to locate the requested content:

   ◆ If the BranchCache is running in hosted mode, the content will be searched on a hosted cache server, where the client computer is configured with the hosted cache server name.

   ◆ If the BranchCache is running in distributed mode, the content will be searched on client computers in the branch office, where Web Services Dynamic Discovery protocol is used.

◆ Once the content is located, the client computer will start retrieving the content. If the complete content is not located in one location, the client computer will try to collect the content from multiple sources. If the client computer fails to complete the content or fails to locate the content, it will contact the headquarters' file server directly.

◆ When the content is finally downloaded to the client computer, depending on the BranchCache mode, the following actions will be performed:

   ◆ In distributed cache mode, the content will be cached to the client computer.

   ◆ In hosted cache mode, the content will be cached both to the hosted cache server and to the client computer. The client computer will update the hosted cache server content by using the Hosted Cache Protocol.

In a network environment, multiple shared documents are accessed and edited by multiple users. You might ask yourself, now that content is cached, will I always access the most updated version of the file? The answer is yes; BranchCache technology updates all edits made by the users to the cached copies of the files. For example, if a user modifies a document that was previously cached, the edits are directly written to the headquarters' server. If another client computer requests the same file, the segments of the file that have been edited will be downloaded from the headquarters' server and added to the cached content on the hosted cache server or the client computer that hosts the cached content.

You can install the BranchCache component of the File Server role by using Server Manager or Windows PowerShell. BranchCache deployment consists of following steps:

1. Configure the BranchCache content server. On a file server that is intended to be BranchCache content server located at the corporate headquarters, install the BranchCache for Network Files component from the File Server role, as shown in Figure 6.5. If the BranchCache is used for a web server or application server, you should also install the BranchCache feature, as shown in Figure 6.6.

FIGURE 6.5
Installing
BranchCache for
Network Files in
Server Manager

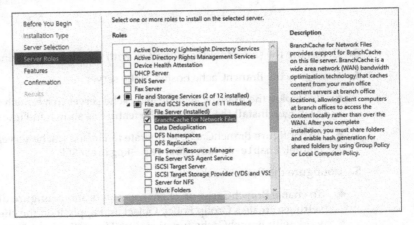

2. Create a Group Policy Object that will apply on the BranchCache content server. Select the Enable radio button under Hash Publication for BranchCache, as shown in Figure 6.7. This setting is located under `Computer Configuration/Policies/Administrative Templates/Network/Lanman Server/Hash Publication for BranchCache`.

FIGURE 6.6
Installing the
BranchCache
feature in Server
Manager

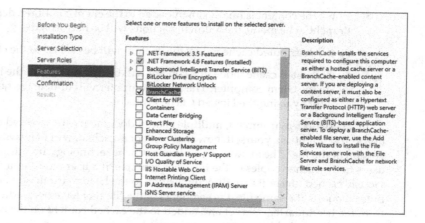

FIGURE 6.6
Installing the
BranchCache
feature in Server
Manager

FIGURE 6.7
The Group Policy
Object setting
to enable Hash
Publication for
BranchCache

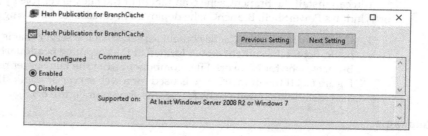

3. Configure the shared folder properties with Caching setting Enable BranchCache.

4. Configure the BranchCache hosted cache server:

♦ To deploy the BranchCache hosted cache server in a branch office, from Server Manager, install the BranchCache feature as shown in Figure 6.6.

♦ To configure BranchCache to operate in Hosted Cache server mode, run the following cmdlet: `Enable-BCHostedServer –RegisterSCP`.

5. Configure the BranchCache client:

♦ To enable BranchCache on client computers and configure different BranchCache settings, create a Group Policy Object and apply it on the client computers that will work with BranchCache functionality. The settings are located under `Computer Configuration\Policies\Administrative Templates\Network\BranchCache`. The various settings include: turning on BranchCache, specifying the hosted cache servers, and specifying the percentage of disk space used for cached content, as shown in Figure 6.8.

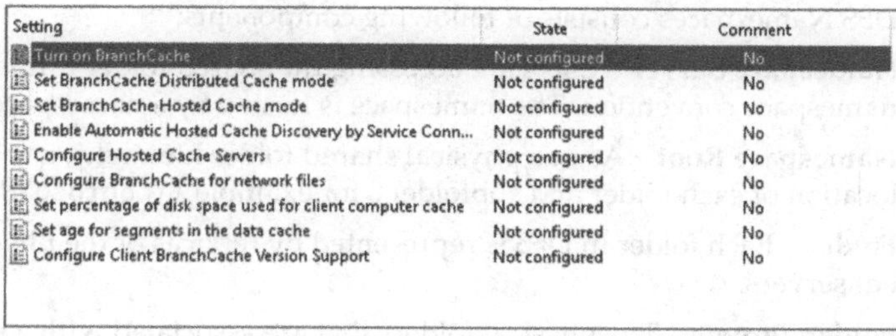

FIGURE 6.8
Group Policy
Object setting
to configure
BranchCache set-
tings on a client
computer

Setting	State	Comment
Turn on BranchCache	Not configured	No
Set BranchCache Distributed Cache mode	Not configured	No
Set BranchCache Hosted Cache mode	Not configured	No
Enable Automatic Hosted Cache Discovery by Service Conn...	Not configured	No
Configure Hosted Cache Servers	Not configured	No
Configure BranchCache for network files	Not configured	No
Set percentage of disk space used for client computer cache	Not configured	No
Set age for segments in the data cache	Not configured	No
Configure Client BranchCache Version Support	Not configured	No

DFS Namespaces and DFS Replication

Many organizations are distributed throughout multiple different locations. Some of them are contained within a city, and some of them have many branch offices throughout the country or even worldwide. In such scenarios, providing consistent access to documents is challenging because the number of file servers can go up to the hundreds, and the number of shared folders can go up to hundreds of thousands and even more.

Distributed File System (DFS) was introduced in Windows Server 2000 and has continued to be improved to help organizations effectively manage their shared folders in distributed orga-nization scenarios. DFS provides users with access to folders and files in the closest server loca-tion, and at the same time it provides high availability by having replicas on servers located in different locations. Furthermore, users will not need to remember dozens or even hundreds of file server names.

DFS Namespaces is a component of File and Storage Services. It provides users with access to shared folders that are distributed to different servers, where physical location is not visible to end users. Instead, users see the shared folders logical infrastructure with a convenient, user-friendly naming convention. When accessing the folder, DFS automatically connects users to their closest physical server. Furthermore, DFS can be configured to replicate shared folder con-tent, so that if the closest file server is not available for any reason, the request will be redirected to a folder replica on another file server. One example of DFS architecture is shown in Figure 6.9.

FIGURE 6.9
DFS architecture

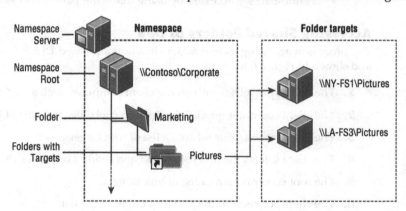

DFS Namespaces consists of following components:

Namespace Server   Users are accessing the shared folder infrastructure by using the namespace convention. The namespace is hosted by a namespace server.

Namespace Root   As in a physical shared folder hierarchy, a root represents the starting location of each folder and subfolders, for example \\Contoso\HR\.

Folder   Each folder in DFS is represented by replicas of the physical folder located on different servers.

Folder Targets   The physical folders that are associated with a folder in DFS represents folder target. For example, folder \\Contoso\HR might match the folder target \\NY-FS07\Shares\Departments\HR.

You can choose from two types of DFS Namespaces:

◆   Domain-Based Namespaces, which has the following features:

　　◆   The organization is using Active Directory Domain Services.

　　◆   Namespace information is stored in Active Directory.

　　◆   Multiple namespace servers are used for high availability.

　　◆   Namespaces are accessed by using the following path: \\NetBIOSDomainName\RootName.

◆   Stand-Alone Namespaces has the following features:

　　◆   The organization does not use Active Directory Domain Services.

　　◆   The Namespace information is stored in the Registry and in a memory cache.

　　◆   Failover clustering is used for namespace high availability.

　　◆   If Active Directory Domain Services are not used, DFS replication cannot be used for replication.

　　◆   Namespaces is accessed by using following path: \\ServerName\RootName.

Accessing Shared Folders in DFS

The process of accessing shared folders in a domain-based DFS infrastructure is described here and shown in Figure 6.10.

1. The user types a DFS path on the client computer, such as \\Contoso.com\HR.

2. The client computer queries the domain controller for a list of DFS root targets.

3. The domain controller returns a list of root targets.

4. The client selects the first root target and sends a query for the requested DFS path.

5. The root server returns a list of link targets.

6. The client connects to the first link target in the list.

FIGURE 6.10
The process of accessing shared folders in DFS

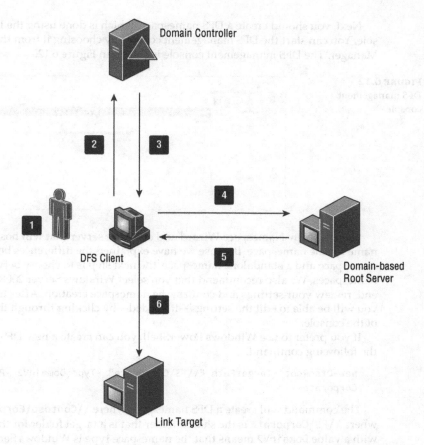

DFS Namespaces can be installed with either GUI or Windows PowerShell. For a GUI installation, open the Server Manager and start the Add Roles and Features Wizard. Navigate through File and Storage Services, select DFS Namespaces, and complete the wizard, as shown in Figure 6.11.

FIGURE 6.11
Installing DFS Namespaces in Server Manager

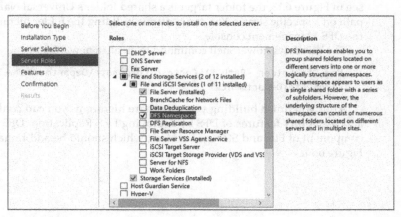

Next, you should create a DFS namespace, which is done using the DFS management console. You can start the DFS management console by choosing it from the Tools menu in Server Manager. The DFS management console is shown in Figure 6.12.

FIGURE 6.12
DFS management
console

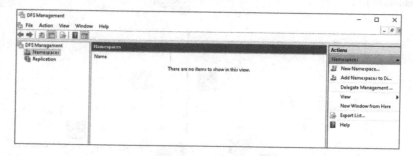

Start the New Namespace Wizard and enter the server that will host the namespace and a name for the namespace. Because we have explained the differences between a domain-based namespace and a standalone namespace, the next step is to choose between these two types of namespaces. We also recommend that you select Windows Server 2008 namespace mode. At the end, review your settings and confirm the namespace creation. After the namespace is created, you will be able to edit the settings—if needed—by clicking through the tabs in the Details pane of the console.

If you prefer to use Windows PowerShell, you can create a new DFS namespace by running the following command:

```
New-DfsnRoot -TargetPath "\\FS\Corporate" -Type DomainV2 -Path \\Contoso\
Corporate
```

The command will create a DFS namespace where \\Contoso\Corporate is a root at the path where \\FS\Corporate is the shared folder that is a target folder for the root path. The switch with a value DomainV2 means that the namespace type is Windows Server 2008 mode.

Once the namespace is created, it is time to create the shared folder hierarchy. You can create folder and folder target by right-clicking the namespace and choosing New Folder. You may notice that the namespace preview will look as \\DomainName\Namespace\FolderName, while the folder target will contain the actual server name \\ServerName\FolderName\. As you can see in Figure 6.13, the folder target is a shared folder's Universal Naming Convention (UNC) path on a specific server. You can continue building the folder hierarchy by using this wizard in the DFS Management console.

The Windows PowerShell command to create a new folder is

```
New-DfsnFolder -Path "\\Contoso\Corporate\Departments" -TargetPath "\\FS\
Corporate\Departments"
```

After you finish building your file share hierarchy, you can configure the high availability and scalability features of DFS by deploying DFS Replication. DFS Replication is also a component of File and Storage Services, which should be additionally installed, as shown in Figure 6.14.

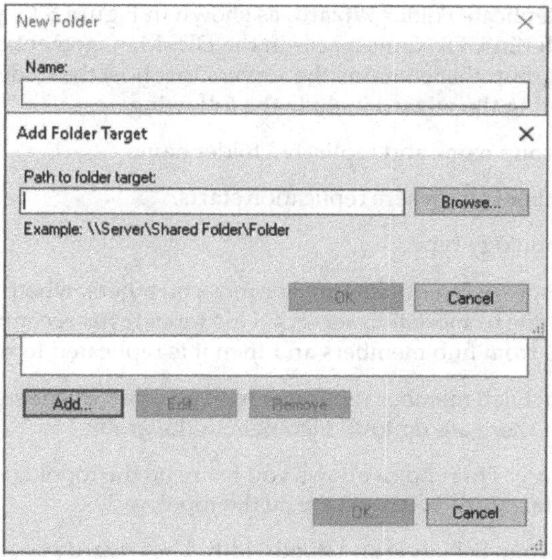

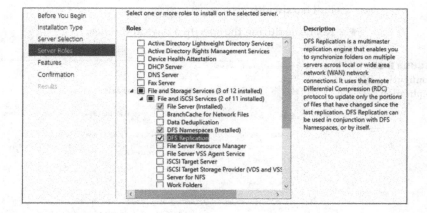

FIGURE 6.13
Creating a folder
name and the
path to the folder
target

FIGURE 6.14
Installing DFS
Replication in
Server Manager

Configuring DFS Replication

DFS Replication allows you to create multiple folder targets and configure replication to ensure that the content is the same between the targets. Folder targets can be configured with the ordering method for referral, which means that when a client computer attempts to connect to a shared folder, it receives a list of targets from the namespace server. The client attempts to access the first target in the list. If the target is not available, the client tries with the next target. In order to optimize bandwidth utilization, you should configure Active Directory sites because, by default, targets in the client's site are always listed first in the referral. You can also customize the order of the targets located in other sites.

By running the Replicate Folder Wizard, as shown in Figure 6.15, you can configure DFS Replication on a folder in DFS Namespaces in the DFS Management console. The wizard will create a replication group that contains the servers that host the folder targets. Parameters that should be entered using the wizard include the following:

◆ Replication group name and replicated folder name.

◆ Primary member from where replication starts.

◆ Replication topology type.

   ◆ Hub and spoke: It requires three or more members, where spoke members are connected to one or more hub servers. This topology is recommended when content originates from hub members and then it is replicated to spoke members.

   ◆ Full Mesh: Each member replicates with all other members. This topology is recommended if there are up to 10 members in the group.

   ◆ No topology: This choice allows you to create the topology later, where replication will not start until you don't create the topology.

◆ Replication Group Schedule and Bandwidth. The wizard provides two options:

   ◆ Replicate continuously and select appropriate bandwidth, in a range from 16Kbps to Full bandwidth.

   ◆ Replicate during the specified days and times.

FIGURE 6.15
Configuring DFS
Replication

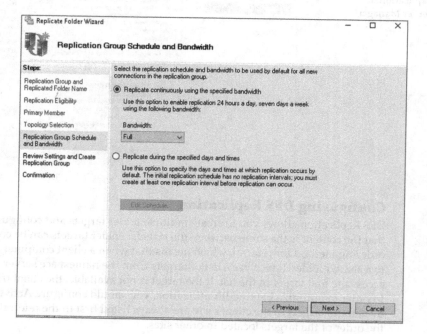

After the wizard is completed, a confirmation page will be displayed with the tasks status information. You can edit the replication group at any time—for example, you can add more members to the group. Edits can be made by using the DFS Management console or Windows PowerShell. By default, all DFS Management tasks can be performed by members of the Domain Admin group. However, you may customize the permissions by right-clicking the namespace and choosing the Delegate Management Permissions option.

To configure folder replication with Windows PowerShell, run the following command:

```
New-DfsReplicatedFolder -GroupName "Departments" -FolderName "HR"
```

You can also create a replication group by starting a New Replication Group Wizard, which will offer you two types of replication groups:

- Multipurpose replication group. Used to configure replication between two or more servers for publication and content sharing.

- Replication group for data collection. Configures a two-way replication between two servers, such as a branch office server and a hub server. This group type is used to collect data at the hub server and back up the hub server data.

To edit the Namespace properties, right-click the namespace and then select Properties. Clients will cache the namespace referrals by default for 300 seconds. The ordering method for targets located outside the client's site can be configured as follows:

Lower Cost
Random Order
Exclude Targets Outside of the Client's Site!

During their operation, namespace servers poll a domain controller to obtain current namespace metadata. You can choose between two types of polling: Optimized for Consistency and Optimized for Scalability. When Optimized for Consistency polling is selected, the namespace servers poll the domain controller with the PDC emulator role every time the namespace changes. When Optimized for Scalability is selected, each namespace server polls its closest domain controller at regular intervals. You can also configure access-based enumeration for the namespace, which is a process that hides files and folders that users do not have permissions to access.

Folder properties can be further edited after they are configured by right-clicking the folder and selecting Properties. Clients cache the folder referrals by default for 1800 seconds. The referrals settings are inherited from the root, and in a failover and failback scenario, clients can be configured to fail back to preferred targets.

Due to a business's requirements, someday you might need to reorganize the folders in the DFS folder hierarchy. If that happens, you can rename or move a folder in a DFS namespace. Be sure to inform the users about all the changes in the folder namespace, so they can access the folders correctly.

DFS Monitoring and Troubleshooting

As with any other technology deployed in your organization, you should monitor and if necessary troubleshoot DFS for any potential issues. The DFS Management console provides you with the tools needed to monitor and troubleshoot DFS. Those tools include:

- The Diagnostic Reports Wizard allows you to run the following reports and tests:

- The Health Report generates an HTML report for replication health and efficiency that includes information about errors, warnings, servers that are not available for reporting, and server details regarding errors, warnings, and informational messages.

- The Propagation Test tests for replication progress by generating a test file in a replicated folder. At the end, the test displays the status of the test and information about errors if any.

- The Propagation Report generates an HTML report that includes information from each replication member about tracking the replication progress, a list of tests completed, a list of incomplete or tests with errors, a graph of replication time, and a list of replication member servers included in the test.

- The Verify Topology tool displays the topology status information about the specific replication group.

- Some of the Windows PowerShell commands you can use for monitoring and troubleshooting DFS issues include:

  - `Get-DfsnServerConfiguration` displays the DFS namespace settings for a DFS namespace root server.

  - `Get-DfsnRoot` displays the settings for DFS Namespaces.

  - `Get-DfsnRootTarget` displays the settings for root targets of a DFS namespace.

  - `Get-DfsnFolder` displays the settings for a DFS namespace folder.

  - `Get-DfsnFolderTarget` displays the settings for targets of a DFS namespace folder.

  - `Get-DfsnAccess` displays the permissions for a DFS namespace folder.

NOTE During the initial DFS replication deployment, replication between branch offices might be time-consuming. To speed things up, you might choose to clone the database for the initial replication. You can use following command to export a DFS database and create a clone of the database:

```
Export-DfsrClone -Volume C: -Path "C:\DFSClone"
```

The command will create a DFS database clone and store it on `C:\DFSClone` folder. Next, you can copy the cloned database on a DFS server in a branch office in a folder named `C:\DFSClone` and use the following command to import the cloned database:

```
Import-DfsrClone -Volume C: -Path "C:\DFSClone"
```

Administrators who work with the DFS deployment should share a network port list with the networking team, so that the appropriate ports are open and DFS will function properly. Table 6.1 shows all the ports used by the DFS as well as the computers involved in the DFS communication.

TABLE 6.1:   DFS Network Port List

SERVICE NAME	COMPUTERS	UDP	TCP
NetBIOS Name Service	Domain controllers; root servers that are not domain controllers; servers acting as link targets; client computers acting as link targets	137	137
NetBIOS Datagram Service	Domain controllers; root servers that are not domain controllers; servers acting as link targets; client computers acting as link targets	138	
NetBIOS Session Service	Domain controllers; root servers that are not domain controllers; servers acting as link targets; client computers acting as link targets		139
LDAP Server	Domain controllers	389	389
Remote Procedure Call (RPC) Endpoint Mapper	Domain controllers		135
Server Message Block (SMB)	Domain controllers; root servers that are not domain controllers; servers acting as link targets; client computers acting as link targets	445	445

File Server Resource Manager

Another component in File and Storage Services of Windows Server 2016 is File Server Resource Manager (FSRM). It was introduced in Windows Server 2008 R2 as a role service that enables users to classify and manage data stored on file servers. FSRM addresses multiple scenarios in modern file-server data management, such as controlling disk quota provided to users, controlling what type of data is allowed to be saved on the file servers, classifying data for data protection and security purposes, and automating different types of notification services regarding the file server processes.

FSRM includes the following features:

File Classification Infrastructure   File Classification Infrastructure provides you with an automation of processes that perform data classification. Classification can be performed based on different criteria. Each file that meets the criteria defined by the administrator will be assigned with a specific classification.

File Management Tasks   File Management Tasks provides you with automated file-management capabilities that are performed on files based on the classification. Once the data is classified, you can create policies that will perform a specific action based on the file classification. For example, you can apply a policy that restricts access only for users working in the finance department, for files that have classification of being financial data.

Quota Management Quota Management is extremely useful for controlling how much disk space is used by the users, as well as for preserving disk space on file servers. Everyday file uploading by users, together with the trends of continuously increasing file size, might quickly fill the hard disks of the file servers. Administrators can create quota templates for different scenarios that will be applied to folders or volumes.

Storage Reports Storage Reports help administrators monitor the disk usage and identify any potential situation where a disk might run out of free space. If your organization has users who work intensively with a lot of data, you can define monitoring for those users, as most of the files on file servers are uploaded by these users.

File Screening Management There are a lot of examples where administrators find file servers with almost no free disk space. Upon examination, administrators frequently discover that most of the disk space is taken by personal, nonbusiness data, especially files with music and video content. File screens will detect any types of files that users are not allowed to store on the file servers.

You can install the FSRM component by selecting it in the Server Manager under File and Storage Services, as shown in Figure 6.16. You can also install it by running the following command in Windows PowerShell:

```
Install-WindowsFeature -Name FS-Resource-Manager -IncludeManagementTools
```

FIGURE 6.16
Installing File
Server Resource
Manager in
Server Manager

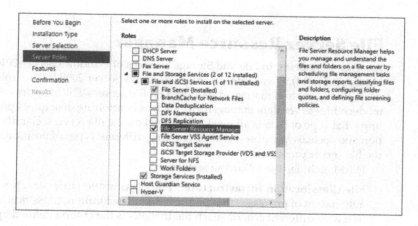

Note that FSRM is supported only on volumes formatted with NTFS.

FSRM Features Deployment

FSRM contains multiple features, but the deployment type of each of these features will depend on an organization's business requirements. After installing the FSRM component, you can start configuring the FSRM features by running the File Server Resource Manager console from the Tools menu in Server Manager, as shown in Figure 6.17.

FIGURE 6.17
File Server
Resource Manager
console

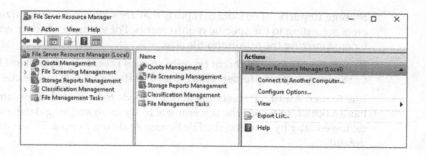

Configuring General FSRM Options

Before configuring each of the FSRM options, you might want to configure the general options by selecting Configure Options from the Actions pane in the FSRM console, as shown in Figure 6.18.

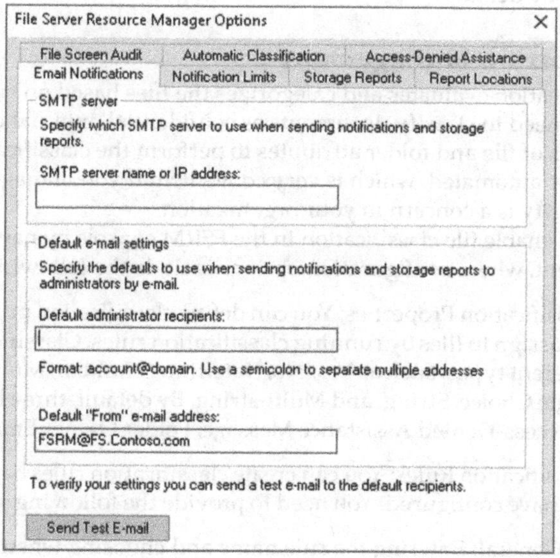

FIGURE 6.18
File Server
Resource Manager
Options

The FSRM options include:

Email Notifications   You can configure the SMTP server name or IP address that will be used to send notifications and storage reports, configure sender and recipients, and verify settings by sending a test email.

Notification Limits   You might want to prevent the FSRM from creating a huge number of events, so you can apply limits to the notifications that will create events on a specific interval (default is 60 minutes).

Storage Reports   The storage reports that are sent can be customized with different parameters according to the specific requirements. For example, you can edit the Large Files report by customizing the minimum file size.

Report Locations   Different types of storage reports by default are located under the `C:\StorageReports` folder. This folder and its subfolders can be customized.

File Screen Audit   If screening activity needs to be recorded for later examination, FSRM has an option to record the screening activity in an auditing database. Activity can be reviewed later by running the File Screen Auditing Report. This option is not enabled by default.

Automatic Classification   This tab contains settings about schedules and when File Classification runs. Furthermore, you can configure time limits, generate log files, and configure log file types.

Access-Denied Assistance   If users are denied access to files, they can request assistance from the support team in their organization. The information about the assistance, such as general support and share permissions support, is configured in this tab. This option is not enabled by default.

Classification Management

File classification evaluates and categorizes the files based on customized criteria. For example, you might need to classify documents as confidential, internal only, or public. You can use different types of file and folder attributes to perform the classification. Furthermore, classification tasks can be automated, which is very convenient if you manage a large number of file servers and if security is a concern in your organization.

You can enable file classification in the FSRM console by navigating to Classification Management, where configuration options include the following two components:

◆ Classification Properties: You can define classification properties and values, which you can assign to files by running classification rules. Classification properties can include different types, such as Yes/No, Date-time, Number, Multiple Choice List, Ordered List, Single Choice, String, and Multi-string. By default, three local properties are included, such as Access-Denied Assistance Message, Folder Owner Email, and Folder Usage.

◆ Classification Rules: You can create classification rules based on classification properties you have configured. You need to provide the following settings for the classification rule:

  ◆ General: Entering the rule name and choosing whether the rule should be enabled.

  ◆ Scope: It will include specific types of data, such as application files, backup and archival files, group files, and user files. You can also include specific folders in the scope.

  ◆ Classification: You can choose the classification method, such as content classifier, folder classifier, or classifier created with a Windows PowerShell script. Furthermore, you should configure the property that is assigned to the files and any additional parameters needed by the classification method.

  ◆ Evaluation Type: Configure whether you want the existing classification properties to be reevaluated, since by default they are ignored if they are set in the past.

File Management Tasks

File management tasks perform specific actions on the files that meet the file classification criteria. Management tasks are automated and include multiple processing actions on a scheduled basis. They can be created in the FSRM console by navigating to File Management Tasks and selecting Create File Management Task Action.

To create the file management tasks, you will need to configure the following options:

General   Here you enter the task name and choose whether the task should be enabled.

Scope   As with classification management, the scope will include specific types of data, such as application files, backup and archival files, group files and user files, and specific folders.

Action   The type of action that will be performed includes:

File Expiration   Configure the expiration directory to where files will be moved. After expired files are moved, the administrator might back up the files and delete them from the expiration directory. To avoid creating an iterative loop, the expiration directory should not be within the scope of the management task.

Custom   Run an executable command and choose whether the command is run as Local Service, Network Service, or Local System.

Rights Management Services (RMS) Encryption   Choose an RMS template or manually configure the users that will have Read, Change, or Full Control permissions. You can read more about the Active Directory Rights Management Services (AD RMS) in Chapter 8.

Notification   In this tab, you can create a notification channel for the action that was performed on the file. You can choose between the following types of notifications:

E-mail Message   If you choose email as a notification channel, you should specify the email address of the administrators where email will be sent. Furthermore, you should specify the email subject and body for the users with affected files. For example, the email message might contain the number of days until the message will expire and the message body should have more details explaining the upcoming action. There is also an option where the message attaches the list of files on which the action will be performed.

Event Log   If you choose this option, a warning message will be written to the event log. You can customize the content of the message with your own text and add variables such as Admin Email and Days Before File Action. A complete list of the variables is available in the drop-down list of the variables.

Command   You can choose to run a command or a script that will generate a specific notification to the users. You can configure a command, arguments used by the command, and the command security (i.e., under which security account the command will run: Local Service, Network Service, or Local System).

Report   This tab allows you to record information in the Log file, Error log file, and the Audit log file. You can also generate a report in different formats, including DHTML, HTML, XML, CSV, and Text. Furthermore, the report can be sent to the email address of the selected administrators.

Condition This tab configures conditions that need to be met in the order that tasks run. The configuration settings include:

Property Conditions You can select a property condition, an operator (Equal, Not equal, Exist, Not exist) and a value (Yes/No).

Days since file was created, last modified and last accessed. The task will be applied only to files that have not been created, modified, or accessed for more than the specified number of days.

Effective Starting Here you can set a start date for the file management task.

Schedule You can modify the default schedule for file management tasks and configure file management tasks to run daily, weekly, monthly, or continuously.

Quota Management

Quota Management in FSRM is an efficient way of controlling how much disk space can be used on a volume or folder. FSRM provides automation in Quota Management so you don't have to worry about manually trying to find out why some volumes fill up very quickly compared to others or why some file servers always lack free disk space compared to others.

Quotas in FSRM can be managed by navigating to Quota Management in the FSRM console. The configuration options for Quota Management include two components:

- **Quotas:** When creating quotas, you should enter the quota path. Next, you should choose between the following options:
  - Creating a quota on path
  - Automatically applying template and creating quotas on existing and new subfolders

You should also choose between deriving properties from a quota template and defining custom quota properties.

- **Quota Templates:** By default, multiple quota templates are included in the FSRM console. You can choose to create a quota from this template, you can edit an existing template, or you can create your own custom template. Quota templates include the following settings:
  - Template Name
  - Space Limit
  - Hard Quota: Users will not be allowed to exceed the limit.
  - Soft Quota: Users will be allowed to exceed the limit, but administrators will be notified about quota limits being exceeded.
  - Notification Thresholds: Three default notification thresholds send warnings when disk space reaches 85, 95, and 100 percent of its capacity. You can edit these thresholds or add more customized thresholds. You can also configure different notification channels such as email, event log, command, or a report if the quota is exceeded.

Templates for Monitoring Disk Usage

Because you have multiple file servers in your organization, it would be very convenient if you had a tool that could generate reports on a regular basis about the storage usage on the file servers in your organization. The FSRM console manages storage reports by enabling administrators to create a storage report task. The storage report can be scheduled to run on specific days, or it can be run manually if a report is needed immediately.

When creating a storage report task, you can configure the following properties located in four different tabs:

Settings In this tab, you should enter a report name and select which type of predefined report to generate. There are ten predefined reports, including Duplicate Files, File Screening Audit, Quota Usage, and others. Each predefined report may be edited to meet your organization's business requirements. For example, a Duplicate Files report can be edited so you can configure the maximum number of files in a duplicate group per report. Reports can be generated in different file formats, such as DHTML, HTML, XML, CSV, and Text.

Scope You can choose which types of data should be included in the report, such as application files, backup and archival files, group files, and user files.

Delivery You can have reports sent to the email addresses of the administrators. By default, reports are saved in C:\StorageReports\Scheduled.

Schedule You can schedule when the report will run and limit the hours. If you want to run a report outside the schedule, choose the report in the Details pane of the FSRM console and click Run Report Task Now in the Actions pane.

File Screening Management

Employees often save their favorite personal document, audio, and video files on corporate file servers. Such habits can cause disk drives to fill very quickly, leaving no more space for corporate documents. File-screening management provides administrators with the necessary tools to block users from saving specific file types on a file server volume or in a folder hierarchy. To configure file screening, you should navigate to File Screening Management in the FSRM console.

File Screening Management has three components: File Screens, File Screen Templates, and File Groups. Let's examine each of these components and see how they are used.

File Screens This component allows you to create file screens and file screen exceptions. When creating a file screen, you should provide a file screen path, use file-screening properties for a template, or define custom file-screen properties. Available templates include: Block Audio and Video Files, Block Executable Files, Block Image Files, Block E-mail Files, and Monitor Executable and System Files.

File Screen Templates You can create or edit a file screen template with the following settings:

Choose between active screening (users are not allowed to save unauthorized files) and passive screening (users are allowed to save unauthorized files but they are monitored).

Choose between different predefined file groups, such as audio and video files, executable files, email files, and others.

You can specify notification channels such as email, event log, command, and report. You can configure an email to be sent to administrators as well to users affected by the file screening tasks. Email content can be customized with your own text and predefined variables. The predefined location where reports are stored is `C:\StorageReports\Incident`.

File Groups This component displays predefined types of files. For example, the Audio and Video Files file group includes files with extensions `.aac`, `.aif`, `.mp3`, and many more. You can edit the file group by adding more types of file extensions. Furthermore, you can create a new file group with custom files or file extensions. The new file group may contain files to include as well as files to exclude.

Work Folders

Work Folders is a technology that supports BYOD (Bring Your Own Device) technology, where people can safely and securely perform their work in corporate environments and at the same time use their own computers and devices without compromising corporate security. Work Folders allow users to connect to the file servers from any device and any place and securely work on their corporate documents. This technology was introduced in Windows Server 2012 R2, and improved features were introduced in Windows Server 2016.

Some of the major benefits of deploying Work Folders include:

◆ Secure access to corporate documents located on the file servers in the corporate network from any device and any location.

◆ Documents can be accessed online and offline. All the document changes that are made offline are synced once the device establishes local network or Internet connectivity.

◆ Support for current File Services technologies, such as FSRM, Offline Files, folder redirection, and home folders.

Before deploying Work Folders, you should prepare your infrastructure first. Components and requirements needed for Work Folders deployment include:

◆ Servers that will host the Work Folders must have disks formatted with NTFS file system.

◆ Work Folders need a certificate because communications between clients and the servers are encrypted. The certificate can be issued from an internal CA server; however, we recommend that you purchase a certificate from a public trusted CA.

◆ We also recommend that Active Directory Domain Services run in Windows Server 2012 R2 forest and domain functional level. You may optionally update the Active Directory schema with the Windows Server 2012 R2 schema update. This update will allow you to configure the `msDS-SyncServerURL` attribute on each user object in Active Directory so that users are automatically directed to the appropriate sync server.

◆ If users need to access Work Folders from the Internet, your network team needs to configure your reverse proxy servers or firewalls to allow access from the Internet to servers where Work Folders are deployed. Furthermore, you need to create an A (Host) DNS record that will resolve your Work Folders servers' Internet name to public IP addresses.

♦ Optionally, you may deploy Active Directory Federation Services (ADFS) in your organization if you plan to use ADFS authentication for Work Folders. In order that you sync work folders when connected from the Internet, you can use a reverse proxy, including Web Application Proxy or Azure Application AD Proxy. Web Application Proxy acts as a reverse proxy and is included in Windows Server 2016, where ADFS performs pre-authentication of users who connect from the Internet. You can read more information about ADFS and Azure AD Application Proxy in Chapter 11. Details about how to configure Work Folders with ADFS can be found at the following link: https://docs.microsoft.com/en-us/windows-server/storage/work-folders/deploy-work-folders-adfs-overview.

♦ Optionally, you may deploy Work Folders on servers that run as virtual machines in Microsoft Azure.

When deploying Work Folders, you can choose between three main topologies:

Single-Site Deployment In this topology, Work Folders are deployed on the file servers in the headquarters data center, where branch offices do not host any Work Folder servers. Single-Site Deployment assumes that an organization has fast and reliable WAN connections between the headquarters data center and the branch offices.

Multiple-Site Deployment In this topology, file servers with Work Folders deployment are hosted in multiples in both the headquarters' data center and the branch offices. This scenario assumes that an organization needs to optimize WAN links that do not have high-speed connections.

Hosted Deployment This topology uses Work Folders file servers that are virtual machines located in a cloud solution, such as Microsoft Azure. The scenario assumes high availability and fast Internet links.

Once you have determined the Work Folders topology design and once the infrastructure preparation is completed, you can go on and deploy the Work Folders in your organization. You may deploy Work Folders on the file server by using Server Manager, as shown in Figure 6.19, or by using Windows PowerShell and running the following command:

```
Add-WindowsFeature FS-SyncShareService
```

FIGURE 6.19
Installing Work
Folders in Server
Manager

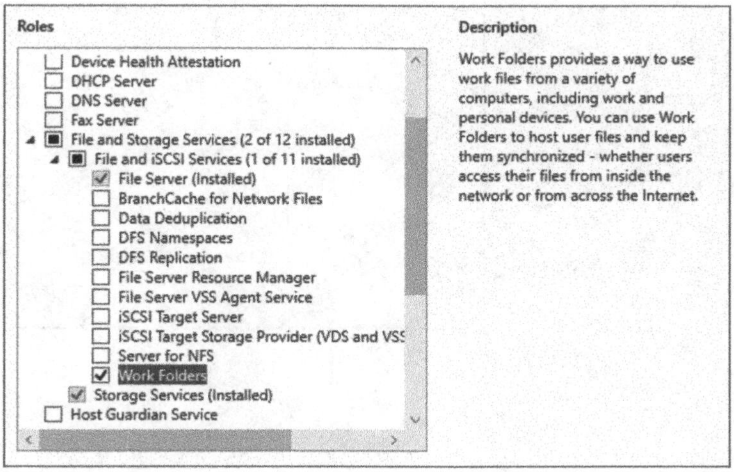

Roles	Description

☐ Device Health Attestation
☐ DHCP Server
☐ DNS Server
☐ Fax Server
▲ ■ File and Storage Services (2 of 12 installed)
  ▲ ■ File and iSCSI Services (1 of 11 installed)
    ☑ File Server (Installed)
    ☐ BranchCache for Network Files
    ☐ Data Deduplication
    ☐ DFS Namespaces
    ☐ DFS Replication
    ☐ File Server Resource Manager
    ☐ File Server VSS Agent Service
    ☐ iSCSI Target Server
    ☐ iSCSI Target Storage Provider (VDS and VSS
    ☐ Server for NFS
    ☑ Work Folders
  ☑ Storage Services (Installed)
☐ Host Guardian Service
	Work Folders provides a way to use work files from a variety of computers, including work and personal devices. You can use Work Folders to host user files and keep them synchronized - whether users access their files from inside the network or from across the Internet.

Work Folders use HTTPS protocol for communication between client computers and the Work Folder servers. Therefore, you need to obtain certificates that will be imported on Work Folder servers. Depending on the number of Work Folder servers deployed, you might choose between single certificate (if one server is deployed) and SAN or wildcard certificate (if multiple servers are deployed). Certificates issues by a trusted public CA will ensure that all devices will trust the certificate so that potential communication issues are avoided.

When connecting from the Internet, client computers will use the URL format convention —for example, `https://workfolderserver.contoso.com`. Therefore, an A (Host) record should be created in an Internet-accessible DNS zone that will resolve the hostname `workfolderserver.conotos.com` to a public IP address that will be assigned to the Work Folders server. If multiple servers will be deployed, then you can choose between creating multiple A records or one A record that resolves to multiple IP addresses (DNS round robin) or one IP address assigned to a network load-balancing solution.

Each organization has its own business scenarios that will define the permissions for accessing shared folders. Therefore, Work Folders will also utilize permissions in order to provide the users with secure access to data. During your design process, you should define security groups as well as the level of access to different Work Folders. Security groups will be created in the Active Directory Users and Computers console or in Windows PowerShell. You will need one security group per sync share.

Once you have finished creating security groups and configuring group membership, the next step is to create sync shares for the user data. If you use Server Manager, you should navigate to File and Storage Services and then to Work Folders. From the Tasks menu, choose New Sync Share and then follow the New Sync Share Wizard, as shown in Figure 6.20.

FIGURE 6.20
Creating a New Sync Share by using a New Sync Share Wizard in Server Manager

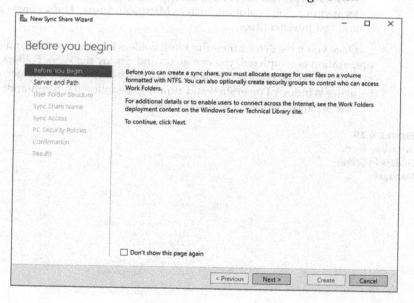

You will be given the following options:

- Select the server and path: In this step, you will need to provide the file share or local path.

- Specify the structure for user folders: In this step, you will need to choose a folder naming format. There are two options:

    - User alias: This format does not contain the domain name. It maintains compatibility with existing user folders that use only aliases for their names.

    - User alias@domain: This format does contain the domain name, and it eliminates conflicts between identical user aliases located in different domains.

- Sync only the following subfolder: This option is used if you want to share only a specific subfolder.

- Enter the sync share name: In this step, you will need to enter the name of the sync share and optionally a description.

- Grant sync access to groups: Here you should add the security group that you have created earlier for this specific sync share. By default, the Disable Inherited Permissions option is selected that will grant users exclusive access to their files.

- Specify security policies for PCs: In this step, you can choose to Encrypt Work Folders (option not enabled by default) and automatically lock the screen and require a password (option enabled by default).

- Confirmation: The last step is to review your settings and select the Create button.

- View results: Displays the progress and the status of the Sync Share creation. If successful, the status should display Completed.

NOTE Be careful not to confuse *file share* with the *sync shares*. Sync shares are not by default available through the file share access. If you want sync shares to be available through the file share access, you should share the folders using the steps explained at the beginning of this chapter.

After completing the wizard for all the sync shares you want to deploy, you can configure additional settings in Server Manager by navigating in `File and Storage Services/Servers` and then right-clicking the Work Folder server and choosing Work Folder settings. The options available in Work Folders Settings include:

- Authentication: You can choose between Windows authentication and ADFS. If you choose ADFS, you should also provide a path to the Federation Service URL.

- Support Email: You can provide an email address for the support team that will be provided to the users if they choose the Tech Support link on their device.

- Suspended Groups: You can configure which groups should be temporarily suspended from the ability to sync their Work Folders.

Organizations that have deployed multiple sync servers might optionally choose to configure automatic discovery of servers. This process requires updating an attribute of the user accounts in Active Directory. The attribute name is msDS-SyncServerURL, and it is a multivalue property that has URL format.

For an efficient domain-joined client configuration, you can use Group Policy Object, as shown in Figure 6.21, by navigating to the following paths:

◆ For a user configuration: User Configuration\Policies\Administrative Templates\ Windows Components\WorkFolders

◆ For a computer configuration: Computer Configuration\Policies\Administrative Templates\Windows Components\WorkFolders

FIGURE 6.21
Configuring a GPO for Work Folders user settings

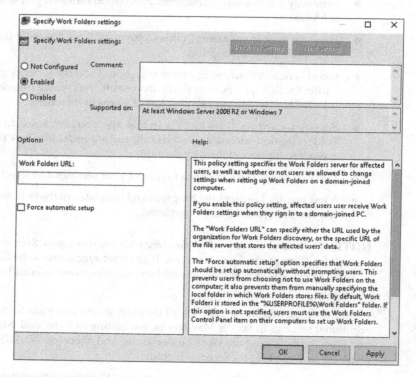

If you have been upgrading your organization infrastructure, the improved capabilities of Work Folders in Windows 10 and Windows Server 2016 will include following improvements:

◆ Faster change replication. Any edit in the documents in the Work Folders in Windows Server 2016 initiates an immediate notification to all devices that synchronize with those Work Folders. In earlier versions, the devices could wait up to 10 minutes for the change.

◆ Enterprise Data Protection (EDP) policy integration. If EDP is deployed, Work Folders will encrypt the data on the PC.

◆ Microsoft Office integration. Work Folders can be added to the list of locations in Microsoft Office applications recently opened or to saved files.

The Bottom Line

Always start with the organization business requirements. In this chapter, you learned about many different file and storage services technologies. Not all of them are applicable to every organization, and not all File Services should be deployed in the same organization. Once you decide which service you need, check the deployment guide carefully and look at possible unsupported scenarios, such as deploying Data Deduplication on Exchange Server.

Once you go through the deployment guide, give your best effort to estimating system performance for your solution. Sometimes a deployment that performed well in a test environment will fail to provide reasonable performance in a production environment.

For each solution, check the high availability recommendations. Even the best designed services in terms of scalability and performance can sometimes experience downtime, no matter if it is planned (reboot because of installing an update) or unplanned (failure of some hardware or software component). In each of these scenarios, high availability will provide users with continuous access to services and data.

Master It When designing a file and storage services solution for your organization, what is the primary goal and what is your approach to the design process? Do you have a long-term plan regarding solution support, scalability, and high availability?

Solution File server design includes the following components:

◆ Number of Users: Because you should estimate the right performance for your File Services.

◆ High Availability: Because you need to provide continuous access to File Services and documents for your organization.

◆ Server Placement: Because you need to optimize WAN links between data centers and branch offices.

◆ Disaster Recovery: Because you need a recovery plan that brings your servers and data back online as soon as possible if any unexpected server downtime occurs.

◆ Security: Because IT teams are responsible for making sure that no data is accessed without authorization and that data is protected from any internal or external attacks.

Save the network bandwidth with BranchCache. You often hear statements such as "We have fast WAN links." However, WAN links are not used just for file sharing between branch offices. Think of all the applications in your organizations that use WAN bandwidth, such as Active Directory replication, Exchange Server, SharePoint, Skype for Business, and many more. Because WAN bandwidth is so widely used, why don't you try to optimize the network bandwidth that will provide much more efficiency and better network and application response?

Master It You need to design a BranchCache solution for your organization. What parameters will you consider when choosing the most appropriate topology for your organization?

Solution BranchCache technology can offer different types of data that can be cached:

♦ File Server content data that is located on servers that run File Services server role and the BranchCache for Network Files role.

♦ Web Server content data is located on servers that run Web server role and the BranchCache for Network Files.

♦ Application Server content data is located on servers that run applications such as WSUS server and the BranchCache for Network Files.

BranchCache can be configured to work in the following modes:

♦ When content is stored on the client computers, the BranchCache is working in distributed cache mode.

♦ When content is stored on a server in a branch office, the BranchCache is working in hosted cache mode.

Use FSRM to let the automation processes work for you.   Even though you have read the FSRM part of this chapter, you may still be wondering if your organization needs it. Of course, it does! No matter if you have just a couple of file servers or a farm of servers distributed all over the world, automation processes will work for you. They will bring you storage reports, classify your data, screen the files that are not needed for a corporate environment, and protect critical information.

Master It   You need to evaluate FSRM components for your organization. How will you introduce FSRM components in order to automate the file server management processes?

Solution   Start with a single business scenario that will be addressed by FSRM. Try it in an isolated test environment. Then deploy it in production and monitor how it works. Customize it if necessary. Once you complete that business scenario, check for any other business scenarios your organization needs. Do not deploy multiple components at the same time. Troubleshooting potential problems will be much easier if the components are deployed one at a time.

Chapter 7

Windows Server Containers

Containers are a new form of virtualization introduced in Windows Server 2016. They are not a replacement for virtual machines and Hyper-V, but they can be a complement. The key to using containers is to understand the proper use cases so you use them only when appropriate. For server-side applications, containers can provide greater flexibility than virtual machines.

IN THIS CHAPTER, YOU WILL LEARN TO:

- ◆ Identify container features
- ◆ Create container images
- ◆ Configure containers
- ◆ Evaluate application suitability for containers

Containers Overview

Containers are a type of operating-system virtualization that allows applications to operate in an isolated environment. From the perspective of the applications, each application is the only application installed in an operating-system instance. You can also configure the operating system differently in each container. For example, Internet Information Services (IIS) can be installed in one container but not another. However, all containers on a host share a single operating-system kernel.

KERNEL VERSIONS

One key consideration for containers is that you need to maintain the operating-system kernel for the container host and the containers at the same level. This is required because they all share the same kernel.

After you deploy a container host running Windows Server with kernel version 1709, the containers on that host also need to be built using an operating-system image using kernel version 1709. This means you need to create an integrated update process that includes container hosts and not just containers.

One of the driving forces for using containers instead of virtual machines is their more efficient use of hardware. Because containers are virtualized at a higher level, you can have more containers than virtual machines on a given set of hardware. By deploying containers at a higher density than virtual machines, you need to purchase fewer pieces of hardware and thereby reduce operating costs. Some specific benefits of using containers over virtual machines are listed in Table 7.1.

TABLE 7.1: Benefits of Using Containers over Virtual Machines

BENEFIT	DESCRIPTION
More efficient memory utilization	Each virtual machine has a completely independent operating system that needs to be loaded into memory. Each container has its own set of processes running in memory, but because a single kernel is being used, memory sharing is implemented among containers. So, while a process may be running independently in multiple containers, the executable can be loaded into memory just once.
More efficient storage utilization	Containers share the same operating-system base image. So, the core operating-system files are stored only once for all the containers. Depending on how you configure your containers, other files may also be shared among containers. This is similar to how you can have base and differential images for virtual hard disks in Hyper-V. Most virtual machine deployments have a completely independent instance of the operating system for each virtual machine.
Faster startup	When you start a virtual machine, the virtual machine needs to load all operating-system components, including the kernel. Because containers share the kernel with the host operating system, the kernel for a container is already running, which reduces start-up time. In some cases, a container can start and be functional in less than one second.

Figure 7.1 shows how the architecture for containers and virtual machines differ. For virtual machines, a hypervisor runs on the hardware and virtualizes access to the hardware. For containers, a container engine runs in the host operating system and virtualizes access to the operating-system kernel.

FIGURE 7.1
Virtual machine and container architecture

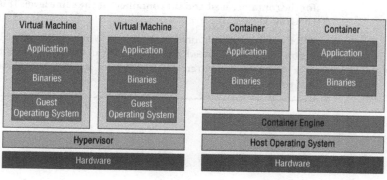

Container Limitations

It's important to note that containers are not a direct replacement for virtual machines. Containers do not allow access to a graphical user interface (GUI). Microsoft provides container images for Server Core and Nano Server only. So, any application that requires a GUI is not suitable for containers. For example, containers can't be used for Remote Desktop Session Hosts (RD Session Hosts) or Virtual Desktop Infrastructure (VDI).

When a container is deployed, it has a randomly generated computer name and is a stand-alone server. Containers are not designed to be domain members. A container can be configured to authenticate to a domain to access data, but that's not the same thing as being a domain member. Therefore, containers are not suitable for domain controllers, DNS servers, or DHCP servers. Additionally, Group Policy Objects cannot be applied to containers.

Containers are designed for fast and flexible deployment. As such, configuration needs to be automated. So, they are not suitable for scenarios with specific hardware or drivers that may need to be updated. For example, print servers are not good workloads for containers.

To support easier deployment and updating, containers should not contain application data. For example, a SQL server running in a container should not contain the database files. Instead, the database files should be stored external to the container on a file share or on the container host. This will allow a new updated container to be deployed without losing the data.

Container Terminology

Containers have been used in Linux for some time and have only become available on Windows starting with Windows Server 2016 and Windows 10. Fortunately, when you work with documentation for Windows containers or Linux containers, the same terminology is used. Table 7.2 lists commonly used terms.

TABLE 7.2: Container Terms

TERM	DESCRIPTION
Container host	This is the operating system with the Containers feature installed and has containers running in it. A container host can be a physical server or a virtual machine.
Container image	This is one or more files that contain the data for a container. The container image is analogous to the virtual hard drives in virtual machines. When you deploy a container on a container host, the container image is copied to the container host. If multiple containers are created using the same container image, all the containers share one copy of the container image on the host.
Sandbox	Each container has a sandbox that contains file and Registry changes that have occurred since the container was started. When a container is stopped, you can discard the sandbox contents or create a new container image that includes the sandbox contents.
	The sandbox operates in much the same way as a virtual machine snapshot. Discarding the sandbox contents is like reverting to a virtual machine snapshot. The sandbox is like the AVHD file that captures changes after a virtual machine snapshot is taken.

TABLE 7.2: Container Terms *(CONTINUED)*

TERM	DESCRIPTION
Container operating-system image	This is the base operating-system image you use to create a container image. It is possible to create your own operating-system images, but we recommend downloading the images that Microsoft makes available for Server Core and Nano Server.
Container repository	Each container host has a local container repository. The local container repository is a file-system location that stores container images deployed on the container host.
Layers	Changes made to a container and then incorporated into a new image are called a *layer*. For example, the initial operating-system image is the first layer and then installing IIS creates a second layer. When you deploy a container, you select an image containing the layers you want. You do not select multiple layers and merge them together.
Namespace isolation	Containers provide namespace isolation to applications. The namespaces are the local file system and Registry in the container.
Microservices	Microservices are created when applications are divided into their smallest logical parts. Each microservice is deployed in its own container to provide the best control for updates and scalability.

Hyper-V Containers

Hyper-V containers combine the elevated level of isolation in Hyper-V virtual machines with the ability to deploy containers. This extra level of isolation is useful in multitenant environments where extra security is required. To allow each container to run in its own Hyper-V environment, each Hyper-V container runs its own kernel that is independent of the container host. Figure 7.2 shows how the architecture for Hyper-V containers differs from that of standard Windows containers.

FIGURE 7.2
Hyper-V container and Windows container architecture

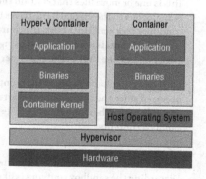

By running Hyper-V containers, you lose some of the efficiency that containers normally provide. For example, having each container run its own kernel increases the memory required for each container. Also, the start-up time for each container is increased because the kernel also needs to start. However, you still retain storage efficiency by storing a container image only once.

An independent kernel in each Hyper-V container provides additional deployment flexibility. When you use Hyper-V containers, the kernel in the container does not need to match the kernel in the container host's operating system. This means you can deploy updates to the containers and the host independently of each other.

Real World Scenario

LINUX CONTAINERS

Many organizations have a mix of server applications that run on Windows Server and Linux. In the past, running containers for these applications would have required Linux and Windows Server container hosts. This requires separate procedures for managing each type of container host. To simplify management, you can run Windows and Linux containers on Windows Server.

Starting with Windows Server 2016 version 1709, Hyper-V containers also enable Linux containers on Windows. At the time of this writing, this feature was in preview rather than fully developed. For more information about Linux containers and the new developments, see Linux containers at https://docs.microsoft.com/en-us/virtualization/windowscontainers/deploy-containers/linux-containers.

Creating and Maintaining Containers

Windows Server 2016 provides the operating-system functionality to host containers, but it does not include a management interface for containers. The container engine for creating and managing containers is provided by Docker. Docker is both a company and the software you use to create and manage containers. Microsoft has partnered with Docker to implement containers on Windows Server 2016. However, Docker is not included as part of Windows Server 2016. Instead, you need to download and deploy Docker on your container hosts.

Docker on Windows Server 2016 uses the same commands as Docker on Linux. This simplifies the deployment of containers on Windows for anyone who is already familiar with Docker on Linux. However, the features do vary between the two operating systems. For example, Hyper-V containers are not available on Linux.

Hardware and Software Requirements

Before you attempt to implement Windows containers, you should ensure that your container host meets the hardware and software requirements. The container host can be either a physical computer or a virtual machine.

If you plan to use Hyper-V containers, you need to install the Hyper-V server and meet the requirements for Hyper-V. You can run Hyper-V containers in a virtual machine if you enable nested virtualization in the virtual machine. To enable nested virtualization, the processor in the Windows Server 2016 container host needs to have Intel VT-x extensions enabled.

A container host needs to have at least two processor cores. All modern physical processors have multiple cores. However, many virtual environments default to allocating a single processor core when a new virtual machine is created. If you are using a virtual container host, you should verify that two or more virtual cores have been allocated.

There is no specific minimum memory requirement for enabling the Containers feature in Windows Server 2016. Instead, memory needs to be allocated based on the expected load generated by the containers on the container host. You need to consider the memory required by the operating system and the application. Table 7.3 shows the approximate operating-system memory utilization in containers.

TABLE 7.3: Container Memory Utilization

OPERATING SYSTEM	WINDOWS CONTAINER	HYPER-V CONTAINER
Nano Server	30 MB	110 MB
Server Core	45 MB	360 MB

You can use Windows Server 2016 Standard or Datacenter on the container host. Both the full desktop experience and Server Core can be used. At its initial release, Nano Server could be used to host containers; however, beginning in Windows Server version 1709, Nano Server is supported only for running inside containers and not as a container host. To minimize resource utilization, you should use Server Core.

 Real World Scenario

CONTAINER LICENSING

When you begin deploying containers, you need to consider whether your existing Windows Server licensing is appropriate for containers. If you will be using only Windows containers, you will not require any additional licensing. A license for Windows Server 2016 allows you to run an unlimited number of Windows containers.

If you need Hyper-V containers, you will need to identify whether the container host licenses are Standard edition or Datacenter edition. Like the virtualization licensing for Hyper-V, if you are using Windows Server 2016 Standard for the container-host operating system, you can run two Hyper-V containers. If you are using Windows Server 2016 Datacenter, you are licensed for an unlimited number of Hyper-V containers.

Installing Docker

To install Docker in Windows Server 2016, you use the package management functionality in Windows PowerShell. First, you download a provider and then use that provider to download the Docker package. Both Microsoft and Docker have providers for this purpose, and both are available in the PowerShell Gallery. The provider from Microsoft is DockerMsftProvider. The provider from Docker is DockerProvider.

To download a provider, use the following Windows PowerShell command:

```
Install-Module DockerMsftProvider
```

To install Docker, use the following Windows PowerShell command:

```
Install-Package Docker -ProviderName DockerMsftProvider
```

When you install the Docker package, the Containers feature on your server is automatically installed if you have not already enabled it. The package installation also downloads the current release of Docker Enterprise Edition Basic and installs it as a service. After installation, you may be prompted to restart.

To update an already running instance of Docker, use the following Windows PowerShell command:

```
Install-Package Docker -ProviderName DockerMsftProvider -Update
```

 Real World Scenario

CONTAINER HOSTS WITHOUT INTERNET CONNECTIVITY

Most organizations do not allow their servers to access the Internet because doing so creates a security risk. This lack of access means you'll need to manually copy the Docker package to your container hosts. To download the Docker package, use the following command from a computer running Windows 10 that does have Internet access to save the Docker package to the Temp folder:

```
Install-Module DockerMsftProvider
Save-Package Docker -ProviderName DockerMsftProvider -Path C:\temp
```

The zip filename will vary depending on the version of the package. So, after you save the package, you will need to verify the filename.

Perform the following steps on each container host:

1. Copy the contents of the package zip file to C:\Program Files\Docker.

2. Set the environmental variables.
   ```
   # Add path to this PowerShell session immediately
   $env:path += ";$env:ProgramFiles\Docker"

   # For persistent use after a reboot
   $existingMachinePath = [Environment]::GetEnvironmentVariable("Path",[System.EnvironmentVariableTarget]::Machine)
   [Environment]::SetEnvironmentVariable("Path", $existingMachinePath + ";$env:ProgramFiles\Docker", [EnvironmentVariableTarget]::Machine)
   ```

3. Register Docker as a Windows service.
   ```
   dockerd --register-service
   ```

4. Start the Docker service.
   ```
   Start-Service Docker
   ```

You should check regularly for updated installation instructions from Microsoft. Instructions for this process are maintained at https://docs.microsoft.com/en-us/virtualization/windowscontainers/manage-docker/configure-docker-daemon.

Retrieving Container Images from Docker Hub

Docker Hub is a cloud service provided by Docker for repositories of container images. To simplify the deployment of their products, many software vendors maintain official container images there. Microsoft makes container images for Server Core and Nano Server available there. You don't need to invest your time into learning how to create an operating-system container image. Instead, you can download the image built by Microsoft and customize it to meet your needs. Microsoft updates the container images as new operating-system updates are released.

You can also have your own public or private repository in Docker Hub. A private repository can be used as a central distribution point to multiple data centers. A public repository can be used to collaborate with partner organizations. It is also possible to configure your own internal repository to manage container images.

You can browse container images available from Microsoft in Docker Hub at https://hub .docker.com/r/microsoft/. To access Docker Hub and browse the images, you will need to create an account and sign in.

Some of the container images available in the Microsoft official repository include:

◆ microsoft/windowservercore

◆ microsoft/nanoserver

◆ microsoft/iis

◆ microsoft/dotnet

◆ microsoft/powershell

To copy an image from Docker Hub to the local container host, use the command docker pull <*imagename*>, where *imagename* is the name of the container image listed in Docker Hub. Figure 7.3 shows the command to download the microsoft/servercore image.

FIGURE 7.3
Pulling an image from Docker Hub

```
PS C:\Users\administrator.CONTOSO> docker pull microsoft/windowsservercore
Using default tag: latest
latest: Pulling from microsoft/windowsservercore
3889bb8d808b: Pull complete
ead9f4ead3c5: Pull complete
Digest: sha256:c2ab4a537f6f312fe147e259011025561f8a1c4ee3bcc2c62f688b528ea57b28
Status: Downloaded newer image for microsoft/windowsservercore:latest
PS C:\Users\administrator.CONTOSO> _
```

Notice that the pull command in Figure 7.3 shows that two layers have been downloaded. Each layer is identified by a 12-digit identifier and has a status of Pull complete. One layer is the latest iteration of Server Core, and the other layer is the cumulative update that has been applied. Other images available from Docker Hub can have more layers, depending on how they were created.

When you retrieve an image from Docker Hub, only the required layers are downloaded. For example, the microsoft/iis image is based on the microsoft/windowsservercore image. If you have already retrieved the microsoft/windowsservercore image, only the additional layers are downloaded. You can see this in Figure 7.4 where the two layers in the microsoft/windowsservercore image are shown with a status of Already exists.

FIGURE 7.4
Pulling a second
image

```
PS C:\Users\administrator.CONTOSO> docker pull microsoft/iis
Using default tag: latest
latest: Pulling from microsoft/iis
3889bb8d808b: Already exists
ead9f4ead3c5: Already exists
1a9fc5e44b61: Pull complete
bc6b84b5fe4d: Pull complete
7c7fde321573: Pull complete
94e2c059f9d1: Pull complete
Digest: sha256:1242bf545abc4043c7f8a232e3ebe803668b48a201aaeebd9dfb125cc8e18faa
Status: Downloaded newer image for microsoft/iis:latest
PS C:\Users\administrator.CONTOSO> _
```

Creating and Running a Container

Once you have obtained a base image, you can create a container. To view the images that you have pulled to the container host, you can use the docker images command shown in Figure 7.5. Note that the Created column lists when the image was created and not when you pulled it from the repository.

FIGURE 7.5
Listing images

```
PS C:\Users\administrator.CONTOSO> docker images
REPOSITORY                        TAG       IMAGE ID       CREATED      SIZE
microsoft/iis                     latest    a9659b02e767   3 weeks ago  10.7GB
microsoft/windowsservercore       latest    1fbef5019583   3 weeks ago  10.4GB
PS C:\Users\administrator.CONTOSO> _
```

You need to think about creating and running containers in a fundamentally different way than you think of virtual machines. When you start a virtual machine, it remains running and waits for you to interact with it. When you create and run a container, you need to specify a process to run in that container. That process is referred to as the *entrypoint*. When that entrypoint process stops, the container exits because the task is complete.

The docker run command is used to create start containers. It has the following syntax:

```
Docker run [options] image [command]
```

The command is the name of the executable to start in the container. For example, if you specify app.exe, the container will be created and app.exe will be running in it. When app.exe ends, the container closes.

Real World Scenario

ENTRYPOINT FOR IIS

Many applications running in containers are web-based. For some web servers, such as Apache, you can run the web server executable when the container starts to specify the process as the entry-point for the container. However, if you use IIS as the web server, the World Wide Web Publishing Service is already started and is not a specific executable. The World Wide Web Publishing Service is started by svchost.exe, as are several other services.

To work around this for web-based applications in IIS, you need an alternative entrypoint. Fortunately, Microsoft has created an IIS ServiceMonitor GitHub project that is hosted at https://github.com/Microsoft/IIS.ServiceMonitor. You can use ServiceMonitor as an IIS entry-point in containers. Unfortunately, you need to download the source code and compile it yourself.

When you use ServiceMonitor as an entrypoint, it monitors the World Wide Web Publishing Service and exits when the status changes to anything other than running. You need to copy ServiceMonitor.exe into your image to use it. Microsoft already includes ServiceMonitor .exe in the IIS, ASP.NET, and WCF images on Docker Hub. To use ServiceMonitor as an entrypoint when you are starting a container, use the following syntax:

```
docker run <image> C:\\ServiceMonitor.exe w3svc
```

You can use many options to configure a container when you create it by using docker run. You can view all of the available 1ptions by using the docker run --help command. These options all require two dashes before the option name.

One of the commonly used options is --detach. The detach option allows you to start a container and allow it to run in the background independently of the prompt you used to start the container. If you don't use the detach option, the prompt you used to start the container will wait until the container is stopped before you can control it again. Use the detach option any time you don't need to interact directly with the container by using the prompt. When a container is detached, you can still interact with it over the network.

Another commonly used option is --name. The name option lets you give your containers a name that you can refer to when running Docker commands. It's generally easier to use names when referring to your containers rather than the container ID. If you don't specify a name, Docker will create one automatically. The automatic names are composed of two randomly selected words separated by an underscore. For example, an automatically generated name could be optimistic_galileo.

You can use a command prompt to review the default configuration of a container, as shown in Figure 7.6, by using the following steps:

1. Open a Windows PowerShell or a command prompt running as Administrator.

2. If necessary, use Docker to download the microsoft/windowsservercore container image.

3. Type **docker run --interactive microsoft/windowsservercore cmd.exe** and press Enter. The interactive option keeps the local prompt connected to the command prompt that you are running in the container.

4. At the command prompt, type **hostname** and press Enter. You will see a randomly generated name that is 12 characters long.

5. At the command prompt, type **ipconfig** and press Enter. The IP address is on the virtual network that was created automatically when Docker was installed.

6. Type **exit** and press Enter. This stops the container.

FIGURE 7.6
Reviewing the
default container
configuration

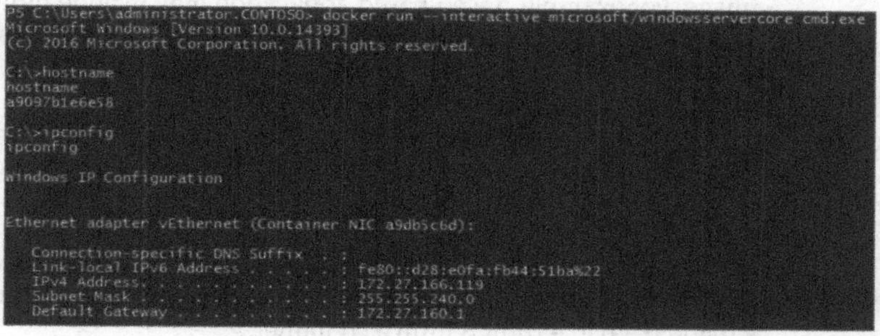

A few additional Docker commands can be useful when you're working with containers. They are listed in Table 7.4.

TABLE 7.4:   Additional Docker Commands

DOCKER COMMAND	DESCRIPTION
attach	Attach the current prompt to a running container.
ps	Lists all running containers. When used with --all, it lists stopped and running containers.
create	Used to create a container without running it. This command has the same options as run.
start	Starts a stopped container. For example, after creating a container, you can start it.
stop	Stops a running container.
pause	Temporarily stops all processes in a container.
unpause	Restarts paused processes in a container.
exec	Runs a command inside of a running container
rm	Removes a container after it is stopped. This frees up the disk space used by the scratchpad for the container.

Manually Customizing an Image

To deploy an application by using containers, you need to customize the containers. Whenever possible, you should try to use one of the official containers that include the components you need. For example, instead of using microsoft/windowsservercore and adding IIS, download the microsoft/iis image that includes both. However, you will still need to customize the configuration as required by your application.

Many times, you will need to copy additional files for your application while customizing an image. For example, a web-based application may include multiple HTM or ASP files and a web .config file. The HTM files are static web pages. The ASP files are web pages with dynamic content. Finally, the web.config file has website configuration information such as how authentication should be performed.

You can use the Docker cp command to copy files from the container host to the container or vice versa. Use the following syntax to copy files to a container:

```
docker cp <src_path> <container>:<dest_path>
```

You can also customize the image by using a command prompt or by using Windows PowerShell. For example, to enable additional features, you can use dism.exe or Enable-WindowsFeature from within a container.

The following example provides the steps to create a simple website by using the microsoft/iis image:

1. Open a Windows PowerShell or command prompt running as Administrator.

2. If necessary, use Docker to download the microsoft/iis container image.

3. Create a C:\newweb folder on the container host for the files to be copied to the container.

4. Type **"<p>Simple Web Page</p>" | Out-File C:\newweb\mypage.htm** and press Enter.

5. Type **docker run --name newweb --detach microsoft/iis** and press Enter. This starts a new container for you to customize. The container is detached so that it will run in the background.

6. Type **docker cp C:\newweb\mypage.htm newweb:C:\inetpub\wwwroot\mypage.htm** and press Enter. This command copies the mypage.htm file into the container.

7. Type **docker exec --interactive newweb powershell.exe** and press Enter. This command creates an interactive Windows PowerShell prompt in the Newweb container. This is done without changing the entrypoint of the container. Notice that the prompt is now using C:\ as the current folder.

8. Type **dir C:\inetpub\wwwroot** and press Enter. Use this output to verify that the file was copied.

9. Type **ipconfig** and press Enter to view the IP address of the container. Take note of this IP address for accessing your web page.

10. On the container host, open Internet Explorer and browse to http://newwebIPaddress/mypage.htm. This displays the web page you created and copied to the container.

11. At the Windows PowerShell prompt, type **exit** and press Enter. This closes the Windows PowerShell prompt in the container, but the container remains running.

12. Type **docker stop newweb** and press Enter. This stops the container.

13. Type **docker commit newweb webappimage** and press Enter. This incorporates the changes you made and creates a new image named webappimage. The configuration changes you made are added as a new layer that is dependent on the microsoft/iis image.

14. Type **docker images** and press Enter. This displays all of the images on your container host and now includes webappimage.

15. Type **docker history webappimage** and press Enter. This displays all of the layers in your image, as shown in Figure 7.7. In Figure 7.7, only the most recent layer was created from the changes in this process. The bottom two layers are from the microsoft/windowsserver image. The remaining layers are part of the microsoft/iis image.

FIGURE 7.7
History for an image

Automating Image Creation

You should automate the deployment process for applications in containers whenever you can. This is critical to simplifying the update process. Unlike virtual machines where you apply updates to existing virtual machines, with containers you create new images when there are operating-system updates. For example, let's say that you've used the microsoft/iis image to create a web application image. When a windows cumulative update is released, the microsoft/iis image is updated in Docker Hub, but you can't apply that updated microsoft/iis image to your existing web application image. Instead, you need to rebuild your web application image by using the new microsoft/iis image.

If you have automated the build process for your images, the work involved in updating your images to incorporate an updated base operating system is minimal. Automating the build process also makes it more reliable. You can automate the build process by using a dockerfile and the docker build command.

A *dockerfile* is a text file with a list of commands in it. The commands in a dockerfile can perform any action that you can perform while connected to a container. For example, a dockerfile can copy files and configure Windows roles and features. Some of the common commands in a dockerfile are listed in Table 7.5.

TABLE 7.5:   Dockerfile Commands

DOCKERFILE COMMAND	DESCRIPTION
`#`	The # at the beginning of any line signifies a comment. Comments are used for documentation and description in the dockerfile and do not change the image.
`FROM <image>`	Defines the starting image that is used to create the new image
`RUN ["<executable>", "<param1>","<param2>"]`	Runs a command that creates changes that are added to the new image.
`COPY ["<source>","<destination>"]`	Copies files from the container host to the new image. The source path is relative to the dockerfile. It is not possible to specify an absolute path. Therefore, it is best to keep the dockerfile and all necessary source files in a single folder with subfolders if necessary. Also, all slashes in paths must be forward slashes (/) rather than the backslashes (\) typically used for paths in Windows. The square brackets, quotes, and commas can be omitted if there are no spaces in the paths.
`ADD ["<source>","<destination>"]`	Copies files from the container host or a URL to the new image. Like the COPY command, the source path for a file path is relative to the dockerfile. Also, slashes in paths and URLs need to be forward slashes. The square brackets, quotes, and commas can be omitted if there are no spaces in the paths.
`CMD ["<executable>","<param>"]`	This command embeds a command that you might use when using `docker run` to create a container. This defines the entrypoint. When you are creating a container, specifying a command in the `docker run` command overrides the value specified in the image.
`ENTRYPOINT ["<executable>","<param>"]`	This command has similar functionality to CMD, but it overrides the CMD command. This makes it useful to prevent users who are creating containers from overriding the default entrypoint in the image. When you are creating a container, using the `--entrypoint` option overrides the entrypoint specified in the image.

For detailed information about the options you can use in a dockerfile, see "Dockerfile Reference" at https://docs.docker.com/engine/reference/builder/.

To create an image by using a dockerfile, use the following steps:

1. Create a folder in which to store the files used during the build process. You should have a consistent and easy-to-follow naming convention for these folders so that everyone involved in the build process understands it. For example, you could use C:\builds\ webappimage2.

2. Copy the necessary files to the folder you created. Files that will be copied to the image should be placed in this folder or a subfolder.

3. Create a dockerfile with the commands for your build process. This file must be named dockerfile with no file extension. Figure 7.8 shows an example of dockerfile.

FIGURE 7.8
Dockerfile example

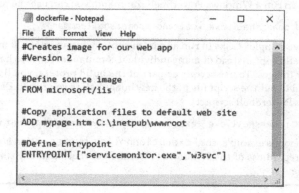

4. Run the docker build command as shown in Figure 7.9. The --tag option defines the new name for the image. You also need to specify the path for the dockerfile. In Figure 7.9, the path is .\ (period backslash), which refers to the current directory. Notice that a new layer is created for each command in the dockerfile.

FIGURE 7.9
Building an image

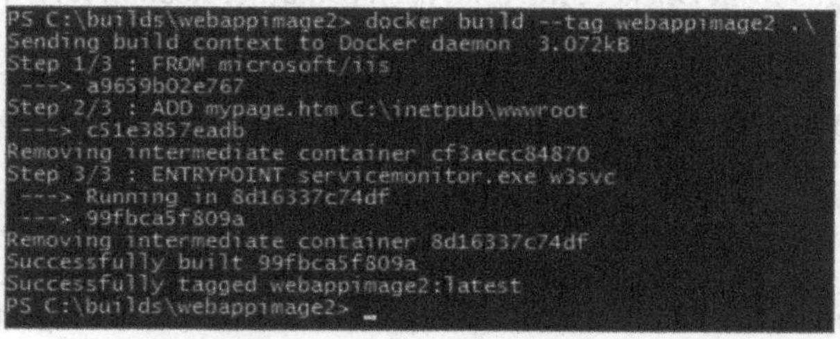

Real World Scenario

USING WINDOWS POWERSHELL IN DOCKERFILES

Windows PowerShell has become the most common scripting language for Windows Server administration and configuration. You can use Windows PowerShell to configure almost any aspect of Windows Server. It makes sense that you would want to leverage your skills in Windows PowerShell for use with dockerfiles.

Dockerfiles don't have any specific Windows PowerShell support, but you can run both Windows PowerShell commands and scripts. Commands can be complex commands with piping and multiple cmdlets. To run a Windows PowerShell command, you can use the following syntax:

```
RUN powershell.exe -command <powershellcommand>
```

If you have complex tasks to run as part of configuring an image, it makes sense to use a Windows PowerShell script instead of many individual commands. You also have the option to reuse scripts for other images. To use scripts as part of the build process, you'll need to use the COPY or ADD command to put the script file in the new image before you run it. Use the following syntax to run Windows PowerShell scripts:

```
RUN powershell.exe -executionpolicy bypass <scriptpath>
```

In the previous example, the -executionpolicy bypass option is used to ensure that the script can run regardless of the Windows PowerShell execution policy that is configured for scripts in the image.

Managing Container Images

When you download container images from Docker Hub, they are stored on the local container host. In most cases, you will have multiple container hosts, so it will not be efficient to download the images from Docker Hub onto each container host. In fact, many container hosts probably won't be given access to the Internet.

The other consideration is storage of your customized images. It is possible to use Docker Hub to privately store your customized images. However, some organizations want to keep as much data as possible on-premises to minimize the risk of data leakage.

You can create your own on-premises Registry as an alternative to using Docker Hub for image storage and retrieval. After creating your own Registry, you can use docker pull and docker push commands to retrieve and store images. Unfortunately, the Registry container provided in Docker Hub uses a Linux kernel. Docker provides instructions on how to build a Windows container for a Registry at https://github.com/docker/labs/tree/master/windows/registry.

Real World Scenario

WORKING WITH A SMALL C: DRIVE

On a container host, the default storage location for images and containers is C:\ProgramData\ docker. Depending on the number of images and containers you have, this can grow to be a large amount of data.

Many organizations deploy servers with a relatively small C: drive that is intended only to host the operating system and not application data. If the C: drive is too small, you can specify an alternative path to store images and containers by using the following process:

1. Create a file named daemon.json in C:\ProgramData\docker\config.
2. Edit daemon.json and add the line {"graph": "e:\\docker"}.
3. Restart the Docker service.
4. Use the docker info command to verify that the Docker Root Dir property has been updated.

When you specify a new location to store Docker data, the path you specify needs to use \\ to separate folder names. Also, be aware that the directory for configuration files does not change—only the data location changes. Finally, note that existing containers and images are not moved to the new storage location. You will need to retrieve the images again after modifying the storage location.

If you are using Hyper-V containers, the graph setting in the daemon.json does not control the location of the container. Instead, you need to modify the default folder to store virtual disks in Hyper-V.

Configuring Containers

Because containers are dynamic and not meant for persistent configuration, configuring containers presents unique management challenges. When you deploy new virtual machines, you expect the configuration to be persistent for an extended period of time. So, a few manual configuration changes after deployment, such as configuring an IP address, are expected. For containers, we need a better way to do this because containers are built and destroyed often over time.

Storage

Containers are not designed for long-term storage of data. A container should contain the files for an application, but not the data. If there is any persistent data, such as a database, it needs to be stored outside of the container. Fortunately, containers provide several ways to storage data externally.

If possible, configure your application to use data on a file share instead of the local file system. For example, you can configure a container with a database engine to store the database on a file share. Then when you update or redeploy that container, it will automatically reconnect the file share and have access to the database files.

Docker allows containers to use file storage on the container host for persistent data storage. Docker uses the term *volume* to refer to the allocated storage on the container host, but this is different from creating a volume inside of Windows. Instead, Docker creates a mount point in the container that is linked to a folder on the container host in C:\ProgramData\docker\volumes. You define the path in the container that acts as the mount point. For example, you could make the mount point C:\SQLData.

You can create volumes by using a VOLUME command in the dockerfile for an image. This command links an empty or nonexistent folder in the container to a subfolder in C:\ProgramData\docker\volumes. The syntax for this command is

```
Volume <MountPointPath>
```

For individual containers, you can create volumes when you use the docker run command. This method allows you to specify the path on the container host instead of only using C:\ProgramData\docker\volumes. The syntax for defining a volume when starting a container is

```
Docker run --volume <hostpath>:<containerpath> <imagename>
```

 Real World Scenario

PRIVATE DATA IN CONTAINERS

If you make any of your images publicly available on Docker Hub, you need to be very conscious of any private data that is stored in those images. One of the most common types of private data accidently included in images is a certificate that includes private keys. Many web applications require the secure HTTPS protocol, which uses a certificate to perform encryption. That certificate includes a private key that should not be available to the public. Never upload an image that contains a certificate and make it publicly available.

To enable access to different storage types from within a container, Docker can be configured to use volume plug-ins. Volume plug-ins are provided by vendors of different storage types and can be used to connect to cloud storage or storage area networks. If this feature is important for you, you should verify that a plug-in is available when new storage systems are purchased. The vendors provide instructions on how to use their plug-ins.

Networking

The networking available for containers is similar to the networking functionality for Hyper-V. Multiple types of networks are available that you can select depending on your needs. By default, a network named nat is created when you install Docker.

The default nat network provides network address translation (NAT) for containers. This allows containers to communicate with hosts and services on the local area network (LAN) and possibly the Internet if firewall rules allow it. All communication from the container uses the IP address of the container host as the source IP address.

To allow the container host to communicate on the nat network, a new virtual network interface is created. This virtual network interface is named vEthernet (HNS Internal NIC).

Containers connected to the default nat network are provided with an IP address on the 172.16.0.0/16 network. The containers are also configured with a default gateway and DNS servers. The default gateway is the IP address of the container host on this network because the container host acts as the router to the LAN. The DNS servers include the IP address of the container host and the DNS servers the container host is configured to use. The automatic configuration of IP address information on the nat network is similar to dynamic host configuration protocol (DHCP), but the configuration process does not use DHCP. Static IP address configuration is assigned to the container by the container host.

Using the default nat network works well if all the containers for an application are running on the same container host. All of the containers can communicate on the nat network and limited connectivity is provided for clients to the front-end services on a few specific ports that you define.

There are other network types that you can create:

◆ Transparent. This type of network behaves as though the container is on the LAN. Containers on this network type can be assigned an IP address from DHCP on the LAN or they can be statically assigned. To use DHCP reservations, use this type of network because a DHCP reservation is based on the MAC address of the container.

◆ L2bridge. This type of network requires containers to be on the same subnet as the container host. Outgoing packets from the containers retain their own IP address, but share a MAC address with the container host. Due to the shared MAC address, you can't use DHCP for containers on this network type

◆ Overlay. This type of network is used for containers in swarm mode that are managed across multiple container hosts. An overlay network allows containers on different container hosts to behave as if they are on the same network.

To create a new network, use the following syntax:

```
docker network create -d <networktype> -o <option> <networkname>
```

For example, to create a new transparent network attached to the Ethernet interface:

```
docker network create -d transparent -o com.docker.network.windowsshim.
interface="Ethernet" TransparentNet
```

To view the networks available on a container host, you can run docker network ls, as shown in Figure 7.10.

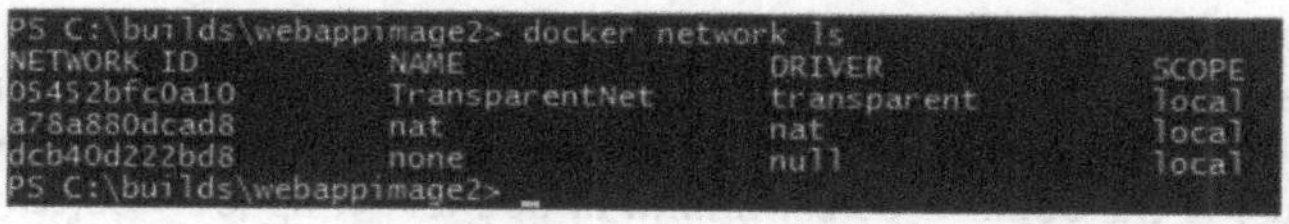

FIGURE 7.10
Listing networks

```
PS C:\builds\webappimage2> docker network ls
NETWORK ID          NAME                DRIVER              SCOPE
05452bfc0a10        TransparentNet      transparent         local
a78a880dcad8        nat                 nat                 local
dcb40d222bd8        none                null                local
PS C:\builds\webappimage2> _
```

Because containers are designed to be deployed rapidly, the IP configuration information should not be embedded in the container image. Instead, you can configure the container to obtain an address from DHCP or define a static IP address. Defining a static IP configuration can be done as part of the docker run command. Table 7.6 lists some of the options you can use to configure networking for a container.

TABLE 7.6:   Docker Run Options for Network Configuration

OPTION	DESCRIPTION
`--ip="<ipv4address>"`	Sets the IPv4 address used by the container.
`--dns=<dnsserver,dnsserver>`	Sets one or more DNS servers for the container. If this setting is not defined, the DNS servers are copied from the host.
`--network=<networkname>`	Specifies the network to which the container will be connected.
`--mac-address="<macaddress>"`	Specifies a specific MAC address for the container. If this setting is not defined, a MAC address is generated automatically based on the IP address. This setting is useful for static DHCP reservations.

To support the assignment of static IP addresses for containers, a network needs to have both a subnet and a gateway assigned to it. To allow for this, you should assign a subnet and gateway to all transparent and L2bridge networks when you create them. The subnet and gateway should match the LAN that the transparent network is connected to. Use the following syntax:

```
docker network create -d transparent --subnet=10.1.1.0/24 --gateway=10.1.1.1
```

To make services within containers available to users and application components running in other containers, you need to explicitly configure the networking in those containers. Exposing a network port in a container allows connectivity to that network port. The easy way to understand this is to think of each container as being completely firewalled and no external connectivity to the container is allowed. When you expose a port in the container, it is like opening a port in the firewall. As an example, to allow connectivity to a web server running on port 80 in a container, you need to expose port 80 of the container.

To expose a port on a container, you can use either the EXPOSE command in a dockerfile or the `--expose` command with docker run. The `--expose` option used with docker run is additive to the EXPOSE command in the image. For example, if the EXPOSE command in the image is for port 80 and docker run `--expose` is used for port 443, both ports 80 and 443 will be exposed.

If a container is attached to a transparent network where it has its own IP address on the LAN, then exposing a port is sufficient for clients to access it. If the container is attached to a nat network, you need to publish the port on the host. After publishing a port from a container, that port is accessible through the IP address of the host.

If you use docker run with the -P option, all exposed ports in a container are automatically published on the host with random port numbers. For example, the microsoft/iis image has port 80 exposed. If you run the microsoft/iis image with -P, a random port number such as 48056 on the host is mapped to port 80 of that container. You can view the external port that was selected by using the docker ps command or docker inspect <container>.

Randomized ports can be difficult to work with because they are unpredictable. If you want precise control over the ports published on the host, you can use the -p option with docker run. Use the following syntax:

```
Docker run -p <hostport>:<containerport> <image>
```

CONTAINER NETWORKING GOTCHAS

There are a few considerations for container networking that are not obvious but are nonetheless important:

◆ IPv6 must be enabled on container hosts.

◆ If the container host is a virtual machine and you create a transparent network, you need to enable MAC address spoofing on the network adapter in the virtual machine settings.

◆ Each network adapter in the container host can be assigned only to one transparent or L2bridge network.

◆ You can create multiple NAT networks only if they are subnets of the first NAT network. For example, if the first NAT network is 172.16.0.0/16, you can create an additional NAT network 172.16.1.0/24. This allows you to segment the larger NAT network.

◆ Some networking options for docker run, such as --ip6, are not available for Windows containers.

To view the latest documentation for Windows Container networking, see "Windows Container Networking" at https://docs.microsoft.com/en-us/virtualization/windowscontainers/manage-containers/container-networking.

Resource Constraints

By default, there are no limits on the resources that any individual container can use on the container host. To prevent a single container from affecting the performance of other containers, you might want to use resource constraints. Constraints can be configured for memory, CPU, and storage. There is no functionality in Docker to restrict network utilization. Some of the constraints available for use with docker run are listed in Table 7.7.

TABLE 7.7: Resource Constraint Options

OPTION	DESCRIPTION
--memory	Specifies the maximum memory allocated to the container.
--memory-reservation	Specifies the minimum memory allocated for the container.
--cpu-shares	Defines a relative weight for CPU allocation. The default value is 1024. Specifying a value larger than 1024 gives a container more CPU time when the processing capacity is at 100 percent.
--cpus	Specifies the maximum number of CPU cores that can be allocated to the container. Effectively, this is a percentage of CPU resources. For example, if the container host has four CPUs, you could assign two CPUs for an effective maximum of 50 percent overall CPU. You can assign partial CPUs by using decimals.

TABLE 7.7: Resource Constraint Options *(CONTINUED)*

OPTION	DESCRIPTION
--cpu-percent	Specifies the maximum percentage of CPU that the container can use. This is simpler to use than --cpus because you don't need to know the number of CPUs in the container host.
--blkio-weight	Defines a relative weight for disk activity. The default value is 500. Specifying a value greater than 500 gives a container higher priority access to storage than other containers.
--io-maxbandwidth	Specifies the maximum communication rate with disk storage based on data throughput.
--io-maxiops	Specifies the maximum communication with disk storage based on IOPS.

A very large number of resource constraints are available. For a complete list, see the "Runtime Constraints on Resources" section in "Docker Run Reference" at https://docs .docker.com/engine/reference/run/#runtime-constraints-on-resources.

Authentication to AD

Having the appropriate access to resources is one of the challenges that need to be addressed with Windows Server containers. In a traditional Windows environment, application servers are joined to an Active Directory (AD) domain and AD provides authentication services for collaboration between servers. This is what allows a service running on one server to access resources on another server.

Windows containers are never joined to AD. This creates an authentication problem when a service runs in a container and needs to access network resources like a file share.

The solution for accessing network resources and AD authentication for containers is using a group managed service account (gMSA) in AD. Use the following steps:

1. Create a gMSA in AD.

2. Install the ActiveDirectory PowerShell module on the container host:

   ```
   Add-WindowsFeature RSAT-AD-PowerShell
   ```

3. Install the CredentialSpec module available from https://github.com/MicrosoftDocs/ Virtualization-Documentation/tree/live/windows-server-container-tools/ ServiceAccounts.

4. Use New-CredentialSpec to create the CredentialSpec and store it as a JSON file.

   ```
   New-CredentialSpec -Name <nameoffile> -AccountName <gMSA>
   ```

5. Run the container using the credential:

   ```
   Docker run --security-op "credentialspec=file://<nameoffile>.json" <image>
   ```

After you assign the gMSA to the container, all services that run as LocalSystem or NetworkService in the container use the gMSA when accessing resources over the network.

In a traditional Windows environment, those services would access resources over the network by using the computer account.

Depending on the application type, additional steps may be required for authentication using the gMSA for a container. For example, IIS requires you to configure service principal names for a container. See more detailed information about configuring IIS and containers at https://blogs.msdn.microsoft.com/containerstuff/2017/07/31/ getting-iis-win-auth-to-work-in-a-container/. For an example using SQL server and containers, see https://github.com/artisticcheese/artisticcheesecontainer/wiki/ Using-Group-Managed-Service-Account-(GMSA)-to-connect-to-AD-resources.

Application Development and Deployment

While you may be able to simply move some existing small applications to containers, that is not where the true benefit of containers comes into play. The full benefit of containers is realized when you start to develop your applications for containers. When done properly, containers can easily move from your development environment to testing and then on to production. The fact that containers don't contain persistent data makes this possible.

When you create an image in development, it does not have any of the application data inside it. Instead, that application data will be stored outside the image in a centrally accessible location such as a file share. The image also does not have an IP address defined internally. The network configuration is defined when the container is created by using docker run. After the image is completed in development, you can easily deploy it in your test environment and create new containers from it. You just need to make sure that the proper data storage location is available and that you set the IP address appropriately for the test environment. When testing is complete, the same image is moved to production where new containers are created.

Keeping configuration data outside of the container image also enables easy scalability. For example, if you have a web-based application that stores data in an SQL database, you can scale out by creating additional containers using the image for the web-based application. As you create new containers, you can give each a new IP address. Load balancing will also have to be in place for clients communicating with the web servers so that clients are isolated from the actual web servers.

Finally, the lack of persistent data in containers simplifies updates. Let's take the example of an image with an SQL database and the database is stored on a file share. After you create a new image that includes operating-system updates or SQL engine updates, you can create a new container that uses the same IP address. The new image will automatically access the data on the file share, and clients will continue communicating with the SQL engine at the same IP address.

As you can see, containers are not meant to be a static configuration. They are designed to allow continuous updating, and automated build processes facilitate that. However, it is easier to maintain the containers for an application if an application is divided into microservices—that is, divided into the smallest possible logical components. As long as the communication between application parts is well defined, it allows developers to constantly update each microservice and their associated containers without breaking the overall application. This allows for continuous improvement of the application.

DevOps is a relatively new application development and maintenance process that focuses on continuous improvement of applications and automating software deployment. Windows containers support that process.

Deployment automation goes beyond just using a dockerfile to build an image. Automation can be used to deploy containers across multiple container hosts. This is referred to as *container orchestration*.

The two container orchestration tools most widely used for Windows containers are

◆ Docker Swarm

◆ Kubernetes

Using a container orchestration tool changes your set of container hosts from separate, isolated hosting environments into a single integrated environment. In some ways, this creates your own private set of cloud resources in your organization.

Here are some tasks that an orchestration tool can help you perform:

◆ Ensure that instances of an application are spread across multiple container hosts to provide fault tolerance.

◆ Automatically start additional containers to service high loads.

◆ Automatically configure load balancing for microservices as new containers are created and removed.

For more detailed information about Docker Swarm, see "Getting Started with Swarm Mode" at https://docs.microsoft.com/en-us/virtualization/windowscontainers/manage-containers/swarm-mode.

For more detailed information about Kubernetes, see "Kubernetes on Windows" at https://docs.microsoft.com/en-us/virtualization/windowscontainers/kubernetes/getting-started-kubernetes-windows.

The Bottom Line

Identify the features of a container. Containers provide a new type of virtualization for applications. Instead of virtualizing hardware for an operating system as a virtual machine does, a container virtualizes the operating system for an application.

Master It Your organization is evaluating the use of containers to support new application development. A colleague is worried about being locked into running on a single Windows kernel version on all containers. What feature for containers on Windows Server mitigates this problem?

Solution If you implement Hyper-V containers, then each container is isolated and runs its own kernel. This avoids the need to synchronize operating-system updates on the container host with the containers running on it. You can even use Linux containers with Hyper-V containers.

Create the container images. You typically create container images by downloading images from Docker Hub and then modifying them to suit your needs. Microsoft makes images for commonly used configurations, such as Nano Server, Server Core, and IIS, available there. Microsoft also updates those container images when new operating-system updates are available.

Master It Your organization is using containers for only a few applications as you learn how to best work with them. You are starting to be overwhelmed by the number of updates that are necessary due to operating-system and application updates. How can you reduce your workload?

Solution The key to managing container updates is to automate the deployment process as much as possible. At minimum, you should be using a dockerfile to create your images after a container update. Using that dockerfile, you can install Windows features, copy files into the image, and run configuration scripts.

Configure the containers. You can configure many aspects of containers when you create the container using the docker run command. You can configure access to storage, networking, resource constraints, and authentication to AD. Keeping this configuration something to be configured at runtime makes it easier to update the container images.

Master It After installing Docker and configuring Windows Server 2016 as a container host, you noticed that only the default NAT network is available. You created a container running a website on port 443 that is attached to that network. However, clients are unable to connect to the website. How do you resolve this?

Solution It is likely that you forgot to publish the container port. For a container on a NAT network to receive connections from the LAN, the port on the container needs to be published. Publishing links the service port on the container with a port on the container host. After a port is published, clients on the LAN can access it through the IP address of the container host.

If you use the microsoft/iis image, port 80 is automatically exposed. However, port 443 is not automatically exposed. No ports are published automatically when containers are connected to a NAT network.

Evaluate an application's suitability for containers. Not all applications are well suited to run in containers. At minimum, you need to ensure that the application runs on Nano Server or Server Core. However, the application architecture is also a consideration. Applications need to be designed to support DevOps where the applications are frequently updated.

Master It You have an in-house custom application that you are testing in a container. The application has multiple services, and it seems that each day you need to update the container. How can the update process be simplified?

Solution Along with DevOps came the term *microservices*, where an application is split into its smallest logical parts. The best configuration for containers is to split each service into its own container. This makes updates to containers simpler and easier to automate.

Chapter 8

Security Mechanisms

Since the early days of computer technology, security has been a vital issue for both IT professionals and developers. How do we secure our computers, operating systems, software, networks, and communications? These were the questions that computer professionals were asked all the time—and many projects in every organization were performed to configure security settings at the maximum possible level. Well, so many years after those first computers, the questions remain the same. Technology is evolving. Unfortunately, computer attacks have also evolved.

IN THIS CHAPTER, YOU WILL LEARN TO:

◆ Identify the security risks for your organization data and services

◆ Deploy and configure multiple technologies that will provide security for your organization's IT resources

◆ Protect accounts from attacks

◆ Protect organization data

◆ Utilize best practices to monitor and protect your network for any potential security threat

Security Overview

Beginning with Windows Server 2003, Microsoft introduced a new strategy for operating systems—secure by default and secure by design. This means that many security settings are enabled by default. For example, Windows Firewall with Advanced Security is enabled by default and Windows Updates are enabled by default. From that version until now, many new technologies have been introduced and included in the Windows Server operating system that organizations can use to increase their security to the maximum level. Furthermore, operating system features have been developed with security design in mind. However, providing security for your organization's IT resources has never been nor will it ever be something that you can "set it and forget it." Every organization must be aware of the latest security threats and act appropriately to protect their IT resources.

Where to Begin?

Even if you have never worked with security solutions, there are a couple of things that you can do before you bring the experts into your organization or before you start your own security technologies and techniques training. We have identified several important components of operating system security that are great starting points for protecting your organization from malicious behavior and attacks.

Windows Firewall   You should always run Windows Firewall and open only the ports that are needed for network communication of the specific server. Best practice is to work closely with your colleagues from the other departments (such as network admins and AD admins) so they can tell you what ports are being used by your infrastructure servers (such as domain controllers and DNS servers) and application and database servers (such as intranet applications, Exchange Server, SQL Server, Skype for Business, and SharePoint).

Windows Updates   Most of the viral Internet attacks in the past spread over the Internet so quickly because computers had not been updated with the latest operating system updates. Furthermore, the updates that would have prevented those attacks weren't newly released updates; they were released long before an actual attack was executed. Remember, because you are working with servers running different kinds of software, best practice is to test new Windows updates in a nonproduction environment first, before you deploy them to production servers.

Anti-Malware Software   Depending on the type of a server, anti-malware protection must be enabled and updated with latest malware definitions. Best practice is to be aware of application restrictions on anti-malware software, such as for Exchange Server, where you need to configure exclusions so that certain folders or file types are not scanned. Furthermore, ensure that all other clients and devices in your network have anti-malware installed and updated.

User Permissions   Users (including administrators) must have sufficient permissions to perform their job-related activities and nothing more; this is also known as the "principle of least privilege."

Admin Permissions   Even admins should work as standard users and only run administrative tasks with elevated permissions, because any type of malware that tries to use user permissions will be restricted to user-level permissions.

User Credentials   Security best practices for user credentials are explained in other chapters in this book, where you will read that passwords need to meet complexity requirements in order to be more secure. Furthermore, password lockout policies must be in place to protect against *brute force attacks,* where an attacker tries multiple combinations of words in order to guess user passwords.

Be regularly informed about the latest security threats and read the recommendations and best practices from the software and hardware vendors of the equipment and solutions you are using in your organization.

Now that you have a foundation on which to learn, let's get into the detailed planning for security in Windows Server.

What Are the Risks?

In every organization, identifying the critical resources that each individual business depends on is extremely important. These resources will be first on your list for protection against malware, attacks, and unauthorized access. No less important, however, is identifying the dependencies for those business-critical resources. For example, if email is business critical and attackers successfully bring down your DNS services, Exchange Server will not be able to resolve different types of records, which means it will not be able to send and receive email.

After identifying your critical resources and dependencies, you should know what types of threats can harm your organization's critical resources.

Thinking Like an Attacker

You have probably heard this statement: "In order to protect from attackers, you should think like the attacker." Attackers use so-called *attack vectors,* the activities that lead the path to unauthorized access to an organization's resources. From the other side, an organization's resources need to minimize the *attack surface area,* the resources that can potentially be attacked. Shutting down unneeded services will minimize the attack surface area. Furthermore, technologies such as the Server Core installation of Windows Server and Nano Server reduce the attack surface area even more. However, some services have to be running and available for business processes, so they need to be protected.

Attackers use a lot of different methods to breach an organization's security. An attack vector might contain multiple components, including:

♦ Attacks against network components, firewalls, routers, and VPN gateways. Your networking department should already know how to protect the equipment with regular software updates released by networking equipment vendors.

♦ Attacks against operating systems. These attacks include finding and exploiting vulnerabilities in server or client operating systems.

♦ Attacks against software products and custom applications. These attacks include exploiting vulnerabilities in applications.

♦ Attacks against virtualization infrastructure. If an attacker compromises the virtualization host, then all virtual machines could be compromised.

♦ Malware or malicious software. Malicious software can be differentiated into several types, including:

    ♦ Viruses. Self-replicating malware that infects computers.

    ♦ Trojans. Malware that gives the attacker remote access to the infected system.

    ♦ Ransomware. A new and increasingly more advanced type of malware that encrypts important data. Decryption keys are sold to organizations that pay the ransom fee to the malware authors.

♦ Phishing. An attack where an individual unintentionally infects their computer with malware by visiting a specially created website or by opening a specially created email. Phishing is an email that attempts to convince a large number of recipients to perform an action (such as opening an email or visiting a website) that triggers an infection.

♦ Social engineering. Maybe one of the most underestimated but yet one of the most dangerous threats. The goal of this type of attack is to deceive people inside an organization and trick them into revealing security information (such as usernames, passwords, and IP addresses) that would help attackers access corporate data and services. As an example, someone could contact the support department and pretend to be a general manager requesting a password change immediately.

Ethical Hacking

Finding security breaches requires knowledge of operating systems, applications, networking, and security technologies. Many organizations hire IT security professionals as full-time employees or external consultants responsible for securing infrastructure, data, and services. Security professionals regularly perform *ethical hacking*, which includes running applications and performing procedures in order to try to compromise the security systems of the organization, but with the desired outcome of fixing potential security issues found during the testing. Ethical hacking procedures might include *penetration testing*, where security professionals try to attack and enter the internal IT infrastructure from the Internet. Some procedures include just scanning to determine which ports are unnecessarily open as a potential surface attack area.

 Real World Scenario

PHISHING ATTACK SIMULATION

A financial institution realized that numerous phishing attacks were being executed worldwide. These attacks on financial institutions typically included email with a logo very similar to an institution's original logo. The email asked recipients to click on a link and enter their username and password due to the update of an internal application. The security department's plan was to simulate a phishing attack by sending an email with phishing content to all company employees. So that they could check their users' security awareness, they planned to count the number of users who clicked on the link over the course of several days. However, on the very same day the phishing email was planned to be sent, the IT department was working on optimizing the email server infrastructure with an external messaging consultant. Once the "phishing email" was sent, the messaging team and consultant detected the phishing email and warned everyone not to open it, which ruined the plan to test employee security awareness. The lessons learned from this real situation were two-fold. Number one, the business users weren't given a chance to react, so the next time they planned to conduct a test, the IT department needed to be informed about the phishing simulations of the security department so they wouldn't warn users about the simulation. Number two, the IT department demonstrated a high level of readiness and a fast reaction to prevent phishing attacks from being distributed across the organization.

Protecting Accounts

User accounts are some of the most attractive objects of attack. Why? Because correctly entered user account information provides the necessary permission to access all the resources that user can access. Therefore, attackers have developed many types of techniques to steal user credentials and obtain access to data and services.

In the following sections, you will learn about the different technologies that will help you maximize the security and protection of your user accounts.

Privileged Access

For a long time now, one of the best principles for securing a Windows Server infrastructure is to grant users and administrators the lowest level of privilege needed so they can perform their everyday activities. That way if an account is compromised, the attackers gain access only to the minimal set of privileges assigned to that account.

For this reason, administrators and developers need to have separate accounts for day-to-day activities such as reading email and browsing content on the Internet, and they should use privileged accounts only when they are performing tasks that require those specific privileges.

You may wonder how do to achieve this. It is much more convenient if you assign rights to groups rather than to users; once a group's security permissions are defined, an administrator can just add or remove users from those groups, where group membership will automatically define the user permission over resources and admin tools.

Furthermore, you can use Group Policy to assign user accounts rights in the Group Policy Editor, which is located under `Computer Configuration\Policies\Local Policies\User Rights Assignment`. The settings are described in Table 8.1.

TABLE 8.1: User Account Rights in Group Policy Editor

USER RIGHTS ASSIGNMENT POLICY	FUNCTION
Access Credential Manager as a trusted caller	Used by Credential Manager during backup and restore.
Access this computer from the network	Defines which users and groups can connect to the computer from the network.
Act as part of the operating system	Allows a process to impersonate a user without authentication.
Add workstations to domain	Enables you to join workstations to the domain.
Adjust memory quotas for a process	Defines which security principals can adjust the maximum amount of memory assigned to a process.
Allow log on locally	Defines which users can sign in locally to a computer.
Allow log on through Remote Desktop Services	Defines which users and groups can sign in remotely by using Remote Desktop.
Back up files and directories	Gives permission to backup files, directories, and Registry.
Bypass traverse checking	Enables the user with this right with the ability to traverse directories on which they don't have permission.
Change the system time	Enables the user with this right to alter the system time.

TABLE 8.1: User Account Rights in Group Policy Editor *(CONTINUED)*

USER RIGHTS ASSIGNMENT POLICY	FUNCTION
Change the time zone	Enables the user with this right to alter the time zone.
Create a pagefile	Enables the user with this right with the ability to create and modify the page file.
Create a token object	Defines which user accounts can be used by processes to create tokens that allow access to local resources.
Create global objects	Defines which user accounts can create global objects that are available to all sessions.
Create permanent shared objects	Defines which user accounts can create directory objects by using the object manager.
Create symbolic links	Defines which user accounts can create symbolic links from the computer to which they are signed in.
Debug programs	Defines which user accounts can attach a debugger to processes within the operating system kernel.
Deny access to this computer from the network	Blocks specified users and groups from accessing the computer from the network.
Deny log on as a batch job	Blocks specified users and groups from signing in as a batch job.
Deny log on as a service	Blocks service accounts from registering a process as a service.
Deny log on locally	Blocks accounts from signing on locally.
Deny log on through Remote Desktop Services	Blocks accounts from signing in by using Remote Desktop Services.
Enable computer and user accounts to be trusted for delegation	Defines whether you can configure the Trusted For Delegation setting on a user or a computer object.
Force shutdown from a remote system	Users assigned this right can shut down computers from remote network locations.
Generate security audits	Defines which accounts can be used by processes that will generate security security logs.
Impersonate a client after authentication	Allows apps that are running on behalf of a user to impersonate a client.
Increase a process working set	Accounts assigned this right can increase or decrease the number of memory pages visible to the process in memory.

TABLE 8.1:   User Account Rights in Group Policy Editor   *(CONTINUED)*

User Rights Assignment Policy	Function
Increase scheduling priority	Accounts can change the scheduling priority of a process.
Load and unload device drivers	Accounts can dynamically load and unload device drivers into kernel mode.
Lock pages in memory	Accounts can use a process to keep data stored in physical memory, blocking that data from paging to virtual memory.
Log on as a batch job	Users can sign in to a computer through a batch-queue facility. This right is applicable only to versions older than Windows 10 and Windows Server 2016.
Log on as a service	Allows a security principal to sign in as a service.
Manage auditing and security log	Users can configure object-access auditing options for resources such as files, folders, and AD DS objects; they can also view events in the security log and clear the security log.
Modify an object label	Users can modify the integrity level of objects, including files, Registry keys, or processes.
Modify firmware environment values	Defines which users can modify firmware environment variables.
Obtain an impersonation token for another user in the same session	When this privilege is assigned to a user, all programs that run on behalf of that user can obtain an impersonation token of other users who interactively logged on within the same session.
Perform volume maintenance tasks	Defines which user accounts can perform maintenance tasks on a volume. Assigning this right is a security risk, because users who have this permission might access data stored on the volume.
Profile single process	Defines which user accounts can leverage performance-monitoring tools to monitor nonsystem processes.
Profile system performance	Defines which user accounts can leverage performance-monitoring tools to monitor system processes.
Remove computer from docking station	When assigned, user account can undock a portable computer from a docking station without signing in.
Replace a process level token	When assigned, user account can call the `CreateProcessAsUser` application programming interface (API) so that one service can trigger another.

TABLE 8.1:   User Account Rights in Group Policy Editor   *(CONTINUED)*

USER RIGHTS ASSIGNMENT POLICY	FUNCTION
Restore files and directories	Allows users to bypass permissions on files, directories, and the Registry so that they can overwrite these objects with restored data.
Shut down the system	Assigns the ability for a locally signed-in user to shut down the operating system.
Synchronize directory service data	Assigns the ability to synchronize AD DS data.
Take ownership of files or other objects	When assigned, user account can take ownership of any securable object, including AD DS objects, files, folders, Registry keys, processes, and threads.

Securing User Accounts

User accounts in organizations are one of the most sensitive objects that attackers want to obtain. You can configure the security of a user account by opening the properties window of the user account in Active Directory Users and Computers and selecting the Account tab, as shown in Figure 8.1.

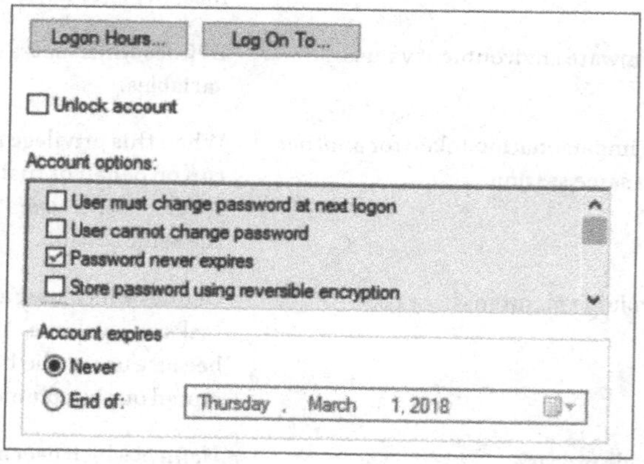

FIGURE 8.1
Configuring User Account settings in Active Directory Users and Computers

The following security options can be configured for an account:

◆ Logon Hours. The Logon Hours setting can be used to configure when users can use an account. For example, the account can be configured so that users can only use it from 7:00 AM to 8:00 PM Monday to Friday. By default, users can always sign in.

◆ Log On To. The Log On To settings can be used to limit the computers to which an account can sign in. By default, users can use an account to sign in to any computer in the domain.

- Unlock Account. Used to unlock accounts that are locked because an incorrect password was entered multiple times and the Account Lockout Policy threshold was reached.

- User Must Change Password At Next Logon. This setting is used when an administrator creates a new account or resets a password, so that users can choose their own password that is not known to anyone else.

- User Cannot Change Password. This option is not recommended to be configured because changing the password on regular intervals increases the security.

- Password Never Expires. This option is not recommended to be configured because it makes the accounts easier to compromise.

- Store Password Using Reversible Encryption. Unless there is some legacy application requirement that uses protocol for password authentication, this option is not recommended because it enables passwords to be decrypted,

- Account Is Disabled. Used for disabling or enabling the user account.

- Smart Card Is Required For Interactive Logon. When this option is enabled, it ensures that a smart card must be present for the account sign-in to occur.

- Account Is Sensitive And Cannot Be Delegated. When this option is enabled, it ensures that trusted applications cannot forward an account's credentials to other services or computers on the network.

- Use Only Kerberos DES Encryption Types For This Account. This option configures an account to use only Data Encryption Standard (DES) encryption.

- This Account Supports Kerberos AES 128-bit Encryption. This option allows Kerberos AES 128-bit encryption to occur.

- This Account Supports Kerberos AES 256-bit Encryption. This option turns on Kerberos AES 256-bit encryption.

- Do Not Require Kerberos Preauthentication. Enabling this option is not recommended because it will lower the security of the logon process.

- Account Expires. This option configures expiration dates where accounts do not remain in AD DS after they are no longer needed.

Configuring Account Policy Settings

Account policies are divided into password policies and account-lockout policies. The domain password and account-lockout policies apply at the domain level. They can be configured via the default domain Group Policy Object (GPO) by using the Group Policy Management Editor located under `Computer Configuration\Policies\Security Settings\Account Policies`.

The Domain Password policy can be overridden by configuring a fine-grained password policy that applies to the members of security groups or individual user accounts. Fine-grained password policies are configured by using the Active Directory Administrative Center console.

The password policy defines:

◆ How many previous passwords are remembered. The default value is 24 passwords remembered. This means that when changing a password, users cannot use any of their previous 24 passwords.

◆ Maximum password age. This is the maximum amount of time that can elapse, in days, before a user must change their password. The default value is 42 days.

◆ Minimum password age. The minimum length of time that a user must retain a password before changing it. This setting ensures that users do not continually change their password, exhaust the password history, and return to using the same password. The default is one day.

◆ Minimum password length. The minimum number of characters that a password must include. The default is seven characters.

◆ Whether password must meet complexity requirements. Passwords must include three of the following four elements: uppercase letters, lowercase letters, numbers, and symbols. This is enabled by default.

The Domain-Account Lockout policy defines:

◆ How long an account is locked when a user types a specified number of incorrect passwords. The default is no lockout.

◆ How many incorrect passwords the user may type, in succession, during a specific time period before Windows locks the account.

◆ How much time must pass before the account lockout counter is reset.

Protected Users, Authentication Policies, and Authentication Policy Silos

Some of the attacks that are happening frequently are *pass-the-hash*, where an attacker authenticates by using the NTLM hash of the user's password. Since Windows Server 2012 R2 and later, there are new features that prevent these types of attack. By limiting the use of the account with less-secure security and authentication options, Protected Users groups are used to help protect highly privileged user accounts against compromise. A Protected Users group differs from other users because Windows does not cache their credentials locally. User accounts that are members of this group cannot use:

◆ Default credential delegation

◆ Windows Digest

◆ NTLM

◆ Kerberos long-term keys

◆ Sign-on offline

If the domain functional level is Windows Server 2012 R2 or higher, user accounts that are members of the Protected Users group cannot:

- Use NT LAN Manager (NTLM) for authentication
- Use DES for Kerberos preauthentication
- Use RC4 cipher suites for Kerberos preauthentication
- Be delegated using constrained delegation
- Be delegated using unconstrained delegation
- Renew user ticket-granting tickets (TGTs) beyond the first 240-minute lifetime

Only user accounts should be added to the Protected Users group. Computer and service accounts should not be added to the Protected Users group.

Using an authentication policy will allow you to configure settings, such as TGT lifetime and access-control conditions, that specify conditions a user must meet before logging in to a computer. For example, you might configure an authentication policy that specifies a TGT lifetime of 180 minutes and limit a user account so that users can use it only with specific devices. Authentication policies require that you set the domain functional level to Windows Server 2012 R2 or newer.

Authentication policy silos allow administrators to define a relationship between the user, computer, and managed service accounts, and they certify that the accounts belong to a single authentication policy silo only. You associate accounts in an authentication policy silo with a silo claim, and you then can use this silo claim to control access to claims-aware resources. For example, you must associate accounts that can access particularly sensitive servers with a specific silo claim.

Delegating Privileges

When you are planning the security permission assignment in an organization, you, as the administrator, might want to choose from the default built-in groups that have a specific set of privileges. For example, a member of the Domain Admins group can perform one specific set of administrative tasks, and a member of the Schema Admins group can perform another set of administrative tasks.

However, in many scenarios, the default security groups won't fit your organization's security requirements. Therefore, you can create new security groups and delegate to them specific and custom security permissions. You can do this by delegating specific rights using the Delegation of Control Wizard. The Delegation of Control Wizard allows you to delegate the following rights:

- Create, delete, and manage user accounts
- Reset user passwords and force password change at next logon
- Read all user information
- Create, delete, and manage groups

- ◆ Change group membership

- ◆ Manage Group Policy links

- ◆ Generate Resultant Set of Policy (Planning)

- ◆ Generate Resultant Set of Policy (Logging)

- ◆ Create, delete, and manage inetOrgPerson accounts

- ◆ Reset inetOrgPerson passwords and force password change at next logon

- ◆ Read all inetOrgPerson information

The wizard can also be used to create a custom task that can be delegated. When this is done, the objects are specified within the organizational unit (OU) or folder over which you want to delegate control and the permissions over those objects for which you want to delegate control.

Credential Guard

Credential Guard protects organizations from *pass-the-ticket* and pass-the-hash attacks by using virtualization-based security that isolates cached credentials, so that only specially privileged system software can access them. Credential Guard can restrict access to the special processes and memory that manage and store authorization and authentication-related data.

Credential Guard includes the following features and solutions:

- ◆ Credential Guard takes advantage of hardware security including secure boot and virtualization, where all credentials are isolated from the operating system.

- ◆ Credential Guard is managed by using Group Policy, Windows Management Instrumentation (WMI), or Windows PowerShell.

Credential Guard can be deployed only on computers that fulfill certain hardware requirements, such as 64-bit CPU, CPU virtualization extensions plus extended page tables, and Windows hypervisor. If a protected operating system runs on a virtual machine, the Hyper-V host must run Windows Server 2016 or minimum Windows 10 version 1607. The virtual machine must be Generation 2. Enabling Credential Guard on domain controllers is not supported.

To enable Credential Guard, you can use the Group Policy Management Editor's Computer Configuration\Administrative Templates\System\Device Guard node, and enable "Turn On Virtualization Based Security" setting, as shown in Figure 8.2.

FIGURE 8.2
Configuring
Credential
Guard in the
Group Policy
Management
Editor

When you're configuring this policy, it first must be set to Enabled, and then the platform security level is set to Secure Boot or Secure Boot and DMA Protection. After that, the

Credential Guard Configuration option must be set to Enabled With UEFI lock or Enabled Without lock.

Protecting Data at Rest

Data at rest represents all data that is stored on client computers, servers, databases, or backup media. Data at rest is also a popular target for attackers because, if successfully accessed, it can be copied, transferred, and then used for different types of illegal activities. Numerous examples of stolen personal user information and credit card numbers from different parts of the world have been reported by the news media. All these examples show that protection of the data at rest should be taken very seriously. We will explain some technologies that will help you to protect your data stored on multiple locations in your organization.

Encrypting File System

Encrypting File System (EFS) has been around in Windows operating systems for many years. The only prerequisite for deploying EFS is that the disk needs to be formatted with NTFS file system. It encrypts files and folders, allows only authorized users to decrypt data, and prevents unauthorized users from viewing its content, no matter of the type of permissions users have to a file. The process of encryption and decryption is transparent to the user and applications. When encrypting a file or folder, users just need to select a check box to encrypt the contents to secure data, as shown in Figure 8.3.

FIGURE 8.3
Configuring EFS
on a folder editor

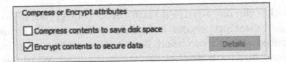

When users access the encrypted files or encrypted folders, they open them the same way they would open a nonencrypted file. When unauthorized users attempt to open the file, they will receive a message stating that access is denied.

The EFS encryption and decryption processes include the following steps, as shown on Figure 8.4:

FIGURE 8.4
The process of
encryption and
decryption in EFS

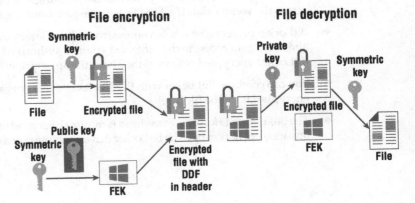

1. When a user wants to encrypt a file, EFS first generates a random symmetric file encryption key (FEK) for each file that has to be encrypted. EFS then encrypts the file with the generated FEK and encrypts the FEK with the user's public key. EFS stores the encrypted FEK with the user's public key, in the Data Decryption Field (DDF). This ensures that only the user who has the matching private key can decrypt the FEK and then decrypt the file with the FEK.

2. If you define a recovery agent, EFS creates a Data Recovery Field (DRF). A DRF contains the FEK that is encrypted by the data recovery agent's public key. EFS obtains the recovery agent's public key automatically from the recovery agent's file recovery certificate, which is stored in Group Policy.

3. Users can decrypt a file if they have at least Read access permissions to the file. Only users who have a matching private key to the public key that is stored in the DDF or DRF can decrypt the file. To decrypt a file, EFS uses the user's private key to decrypt the FEK. If EFS decrypts the FEK successfully, EFS uses it to decrypt the file content.

BitLocker

While EFS protects files and folders, BitLocker is a volume-encryption technology that encrypts the whole volume to protect data from unauthorized access. BitLocker was introduced for the first time on the Windows Vista operating system; it has the following features:

◆ BitLocker can encrypt an entire volume or only the used parts of a volume.

◆ BitLocker can use a Trusted Platform Module (TPM) to protect the integrity of the Windows startup process. BitLocker verifies that the required boot files have not been tampered with nor modified. If the verification process finds files that were modified—for example, by a rootkit or boot sector virus—then Windows does not start.

◆ BitLocker can require multifactor authentication, such as a PIN or a USB startup key.

◆ You can configure Network Unlock at Startup for BitLocker. With Network Unlock, the BitLocker-protected device will start automatically when it is connected to a trusted company network; otherwise, you will need to provide a startup PIN.

◆ BitLocker provides a recovery mechanism, a 48-digit recovery key, or a recovery agent to access the volume data if a TPM fails or the password is lost.

◆ BitLocker protects the whole volume from offline attacks. After the Windows device starts and users gain access to the protected volume, authorized users can access data on the BitLocker-encrypted volume if they have the appropriate file permissions.

◆ You can combine BitLocker with EFS. BitLocker encrypts at the volume level, whereas EFS encrypts data at the file level.

◆ The BitLocker performance overhead is minimal. For most installations, the performance impact is not noticeable. The BitLocker drive encryption architecture is described in Figure 8.5.

FIGURE 8.5 The architecture of BitLocker drive encryption

Encrypted volume
Sealed VMK
TPM
TPM key
Unseal VMK
Decrypt FVEK
Decrypt data using FVEK
Clear text data

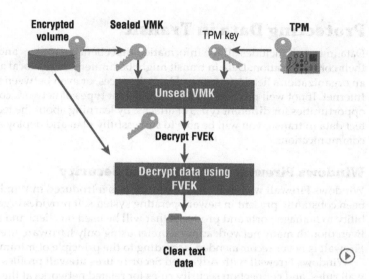

Sectors are encrypted by the full-volume encryption key (FVEK). The FVEK is further encrypted with the volume master key (VMK). The FVEK must be stored securely, because it has the capability to decrypt the volume. The FVEK (encrypted with the VMK) is stored on the disk as part of the volume metadata. The VMK is also encrypted (or protected) by one or more key protectors. The default key protector is the TPM, but you can configure additional protectors, such as a PIN and a USB startup key. If the device does not have a TPM, you can configure BitLocker to store a key protector on a USB drive.

For more information on BitLocker, visit the following link: `https://docs.microsoft.com/en-us/windows/device-security/bitlocker/bitlocker-overview`.

BitLocker uses the AES algorithm with 128-bit keys encryption by default. You can modify this setting with Group Policy—for example, to configure the use of 256-bit keys. BitLocker encrypts each volume sector individually, and part of the encryption key is derived from the sector number. Therefore, each two sectors have different encrypted data, even if the two sectors have the same unencrypted data. The settings in the Group Policy Management Editor are illustrated in Figure 8.6.

FIGURE 8.6 The process of drive encryption configured in the Group Policy Management Editor

BitLocker Drive Encryption 9 setting(s)
Setting
Fixed Data Drives
Operating System Drives
Removable Data Drives
Store BitLocker recovery information in Active Directory Domain Services (Windows Server 2008 and Windows Vista)
Choose default folder for recovery password
Choose how users can recover BitLocker-protected drives (Windows Server 2008 and Windows Vista)
Choose drive encryption method and cipher strength (Windows 8, Windows Server 2012, Windows 8.1, Windows Server 2012 R2, Windows 10 [Versi
Choose drive encryption method and cipher strength (Windows 10 [Version 1511] and later)
Choose drive encryption method and cipher strength (Windows Vista, Windows Server 2008, Windows 7, Windows Server 2008 R2)
Provide the unique identifiers for your organization
Prevent memory overwrite on restart
Validate smart card certificate usage rule compliance

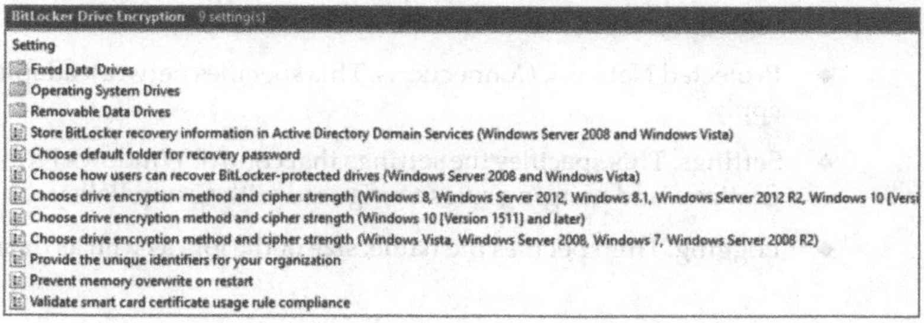

Protecting Data in Transit

Data in transit includes all the information that client computers and servers transfer during their communication. Data in transit might be limited only in local area networks, between an organization's headquarters and branch offices, or even between an organization and the Internet. If not well protected, all these different types of network communications provide opportunities for different types of attacks. By learning about the technologies available to protect data in transit, you will be able to successfully plan and deploy security for your network communications.

Windows Firewall with Advanced Security

Windows Firewall with Advanced Security was introduced in Windows Server 2008, and it has been constantly present in newer operating systems. It provides organizations with the capability to manage ports and protocols that will be used on client and server operating systems. Even though many network admins prefer using only hardware firewalls, turning off Windows Firewall is never recommended, according to the principle of minimizing attack surface area.

Windows Firewall with Advanced Security uses firewall profiles that consist of settings, firewall rules, and connection security rules for related networks at the same security level. Three network profiles are available in the Windows Firewall management console:

◆ Domain Networks. Represent networks at a workplace that are attached to a domain, which means they communicate with a domain controller.

◆ Private Networks. Represent nondomain but trusted networks, such as network connections configured with business partner that collaborates with your company.

◆ Guest or Public Networks. Represent networks in public places and are less secure than the previous two.

Each network location has the following information:

◆ Windows Firewall State. This refers to whether Windows Firewall is turned on or off.

◆ Inbound Connections. This provides the status of what will be performed on the incoming connections, such as Allow or Block connections.

◆ Outbound Connections. This provides the status of what will be performed on the outgoing connections, such as Allow or Block connections.

◆ Protected Network Connections. This specifies network adapter where the settings will apply.

◆ Settings. This specifies the settings that control Windows Firewall behaviors, such as notifications, and merging rules configured with Group Policy.

◆ Logging. This specifies the name, size of the log, as well as data to be logged.

Windows Server 2016 allows multiple firewall profiles to be simultaneously active on a server. For example, a server with two network adapters that is connected to both the internal network and the perimeter network can apply the Domain firewall profile to the internal network and Public firewall profile to the perimeter network.

The Windows Firewall with Advanced Security properties window is displayed on Figure 8.7.

FIGURE 8.7
Windows Firewall with Advanced Security properties window

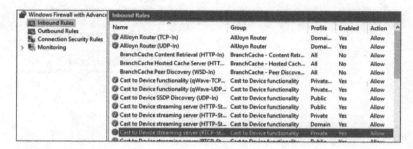

The navigation pane (left pane) provides for more-granular control of firewall rules, connection security rules, and monitoring. When the Windows Firewall with Advanced Security On Local Computer object is selected in the navigation pane, the results pane shows an overview of the firewall configuration with links to the various configuration panes and dialog boxes. Finally, the Actions pane (right pane) provides the following options:

◆ Import Policy. Allows you to overwrite the current settings with a previously exported policy.

◆ Export Policy. Allows you to save the current configuration.

◆ Restore Default Policy. Resets any changes that have been made to the Windows Firewall settings.

◆ Diagnose/Repair. Starts the Network and Internet Troubleshooting Wizard.

The final tab in this Properties dialog box is the IPsec Settings tab. This tab lets you configure the customized values for IPsec configuration.

As in other network firewall technologies, Windows Firewall with Advanced Security includes Rules as a collection of criteria that define which IP address, port, and protocol you will allow, block, or secure with the firewall, as shown on Figure 8.8.

◆ Inbound and outbound rules explicitly allow or block traffic that matches the criteria in the rules. For example, you can configure a rule to allow HTTP traffic from the internal network through the firewall but block the same traffic if it is coming from the Internet.

◆ For Windows Server roles and features, you do not have to create the rules. For example, enabling Microsoft Internet Information Services (IIS) automatically adjusts Windows Firewall to allow the appropriate traffic. You can change the default action to allow or to block all connections regardless of any rules.

FIGURE 8.8
Configuring
rules in Windows
Firewall with
Advanced
Security

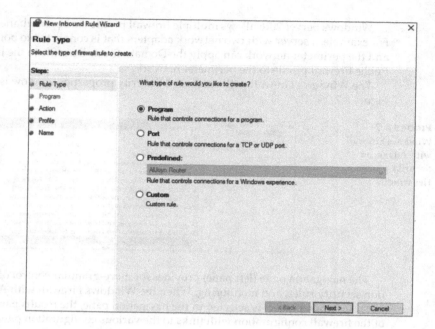

INBOUND AND OUTBOUND RULE TYPES

Following kinds of inbound and outbound rules exist:

- Program rules. These rules can control connections for a program regardless of the port numbers it uses. Use this kind of firewall rule to allow a connection based on the program that is trying to connect. These rules are useful when you are not sure of the port or other required settings because you specify only the path of the program executable file (.exe file).

- Port rules. These rules can control connections for a TCP or UDP port regardless of the application. Use this kind of firewall rule to allow a connection based on the TCP or UDP port number over which the computer is trying to connect. You specify the protocol and individual or multiple local ports.

- Predefined rules. These rules can control connections for a Windows component—for example, File or Print Sharing or Active Directory Domain Services. Use this kind of firewall rule to allow a connection by selecting one of the services from the list. These kinds of Windows components typically add their own entries to this list automatically during setup or configuration. You can enable and disable a rule or rules as a group.

- Custom rules. These rules can be combinations of the other rule types, such as port rules and program rules.

- Connection security rules help to secure traffic by using IPsec while the traffic crosses the network. Use connection security rules to specify that connections between two computers must be authenticated or encrypted. In Figure 8.9, you can see how connection security rules are configured.

◆ Windows Firewall uses the Monitoring interface to display information about current firewall rules, connection security rules, and security associations (SAs).

FIGURE 8.9
Configuring connection security rules in Windows Firewall with Advanced Security

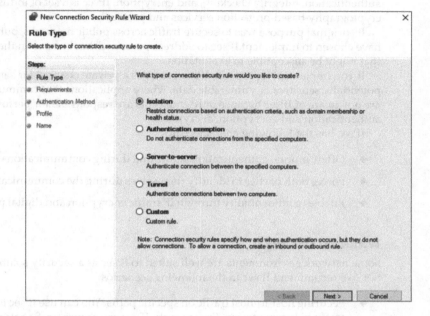

ADDITIONAL CONFIGURATION OPTIONS

You can configure settings for Windows Firewall either individually on each computer or by accessing the following location from the Group Policy management console:

```
Computer Configuration\Policies\Windows Settings\Security Settings\Windows
   Firewall with Advanced Security
```

You can enable and configure Windows Firewall by using Windows PowerShell cmdlets from the NetSecurity module. Table 8.2 describes these cmdlets.

TABLE 8.2:   Windows PowerShell Cmdlets

WINDOWS POWERSHELL CMDLET	DESCRIPTION
New-NetFirewallRule	Creates a new inbound or outbound firewall rule and adds the rule to the destination computer.
Enable-NetFirewallRule	Enables a network firewall rule that was previously disabled.
Show-NetFirewallRule	Displays all of the existing firewall rules in the policy store along with the associated objects.
Get-Help *Net*	Lists all the cmdlets that have "Net" in their names. This returns all of the Windows Firewall cmdlets.

IPsec

IPsec is a suite of protocols that can help protect data in transit through a network by providing authentication, integrity checking, and encryption. IPsec is a set of industry-standard, cryptography-based protection services and protocols.

Its original purpose was to secure traffic across public networks, but many organizations have chosen to implement IPsec to address perceived weaknesses in their own private networks that might be susceptible to exploitation.

If you implement it properly, IPsec provides a private channel for sending and exchanging potentially sensitive or vulnerable data, where applications that communicate over the network are not aware of IPsec because only endpoints are responsible for performing the processes of authentication and encryption/decryption.

IPsec has the following characteristics:

◆ Offers mutual authentication before and during communications

◆ Forces both parties to identify themselves during the communication process

◆ Enables confidentiality through IP traffic encryption and digital packet authentication

WHEN TO USE IPSEC

Some network environments are well suited to IPsec as a security solution, whereas others are not. We recommend IPsec in the following scenarios:

◆ Securing host-to-host traffic on specific paths. You can use IPsec to provide protection for traffic between servers. For example, IPsec can secure traffic between computers in a network that requires maximum security.

◆ Securing traffic to servers. You can require IPsec protection for all client computers that access a server. Additionally, you can set the restrictions on which computers can connect to a server that is running Windows Server 2016.

◆ Using L2TP/IPsec for VPN connections. You can use the combination of Layer Two Tunneling Protocol (L2TP) and IPsec (L2TP/IPsec) for all VPN scenarios.

◆ Site-to-site (gateway-to-gateway) tunneling. You can use IPsec in tunnel mode for site-to-site (gateway-to-gateway) tunnels when you need interoperability with third-party routers (i.e., gateways). In this scenario, computers within each site are not aware of IPsec because gateways perform authentication, encryption, and decryption of the data.

◆ Enforcing logical networks (server/domain isolation). You can logically isolate server and domain resources in a Windows-based network, which limits access to authenticated and authorized computers.

◆ IPsec depends on IP addresses for establishing secure connections, so you cannot specify dynamic IP addresses.

IPsec Modes

You can configure IPsec in one of two modes, as shown in Figure 8.10:

◆ Transport mode. Use transport mode when you enable end-to-end communications between two hosts. In this mode, which is the default mode, the data payload is encrypted, but the header data remains unchanged.

◆ Tunnel mode. In this mode, the entire original packet is encrypted and becomes the payload of a new packet, which then is transmitted between IPsec-aware routers. Tunnel mode enables IPsec-aware routers to encapsulate and encrypt network traffic from hosts that are not IPsec aware, transmit that traffic over an unsecured network, and then decrypt it for use on the destination network by other hosts that are not IPsec aware.

FIGURE 8.10
Transport and tunnel mode in IPsec

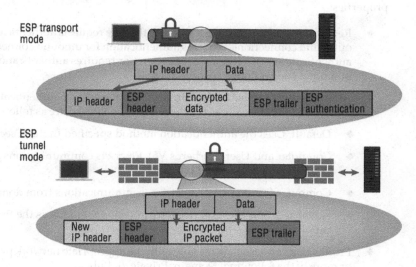

Settings for Connection Security Rules

You can use connection security rules to configure IPsec in Windows Firewall with Advanced Security. With these connection security rules, you can associate IPsec rules with Windows Firewall network profiles. The advantage of combining IPsec and Windows Firewall is that you can avoid overlapping rules and policies that might conflict, and you can streamline the process of securing your computer against unauthorized access.

The configurable connection security rules include:

◆ Isolation. An isolation rule isolates a computer by restricting its connections based on credentials such as domain membership or health status

◆ Authentication exemption. You can use an authentication exemption to designate connections that do not require authentication. You can designate computers by a specific IP address, an IP address range, a subnet, or a predefined group such as a gateway.

◆ **Server to Server.** A server-to-server rule helps to protect connections between specific computers.

◆ **Tunnel.** A tunnel rule helps to protect connections between gateway computers. You typically use a tunnel rule when you connect across the Internet between two security gateways. You must specify the IP addresses that will be the tunnel endpoints and then specify the authentication method to use.

◆ **Custom.** Use a custom rule to authenticate connections between two endpoints when you cannot set up the necessary authentication rules by using the other rules available in the New Connection Security Rule Wizard.

When you enable and configure a connection security rule, you must define the following properties:

◆ **Requirements.** You can select whether the rule requests authentication for inbound and outbound connections, requires authentication for inbound connections and requests authentication for outbound connections, or requires authentication for both inbound and outbound connections.

◆ **Authentication methods.** You can select among several authentication methods. The options in the New Connection Security Rule Wizard are as follows:

   ◆ **Default.** Uses the authentication method specified in the IPsec settings.

   ◆ **Computer and User (Kerberos V5).** Restricts communications to connections from domain-joined users and computers.

   ◆ **Computer (Kerberos V5).** Restricts communications from domain-joined computers.

   ◆ **Advanced.** Specifies custom authentication methods as the first and second authentication methods.

◆ **Profile.** You can associate the rule with the appropriate network profile. You can select one or more of the following: Domain, Private, or Public.

◆ **Exempt computers.** For authentication exemption rules, you can define the exempt computers by specifying their IP addresses, the IP address range, or the IP subnet.

◆ **Endpoints.** For server-to-server rules, you can define the IP addresses affected by the rule.

◆ **Tunnel endpoints.** For tunnel rules only, you can define the tunnel endpoints affected by the rule.

As you advance through the New Connection Security Rule Wizard to create a new connection security rule, you will configure the rule's main options on the Requirements and Authentication Method pages.

Requirements Page

On the Requirements page, you can configure when authentication will occur by using the following options:

◆ **Request Authentication For Inbound And Outbound Connections.** Choosing this option means that computers will authenticate whenever possible, but the authentication is not required.

- Require Authentication For Inbound Connections And Request Authentication For Outbound Connections. Choosing this option forces any clients that are trying to connect to the computer to authenticate, but it allows the computer to connect without authentication.
- Require Authentication For Inbound And Outbound Connections. This is the most secure option, because all connections must authenticate.

Authentication method

Computer Certificate   The Computer Certificate method requests or requires a valid computer certificate to authenticate; you must have at least one certification authority (CA) to do this. Use this method if the computers are not part of the same AD DS domain.

Accept Only Health Certificates   The Accept Only Health Certificates method requests or requires a valid health certificate to authenticate. Health certificates declare that a computer has met system health requirements, such as when all software and other updates that network access requirements have been met.

Advanced Option   If you choose the Advanced option, you can configure any available method and specify the methods for both the first authentication and the second authentication. The following sections detail the available authentication methods.

Computers always use the first authentication method when establishing an IPsec connection. You can specify more than one authentication method, and the computers will try the authentication methods in the order that you specify until the authentication succeeds. The options available for the first authentication method are listed here:

- Computer (Kerberos V5). This authentication method requests or requires the computer to authenticate by using the Kerberos V5 authentication protocol. You can use the Kerberos V5 authentication protocol only if both computers are domain members.

- Computer (NTLMv2). This authentication method uses the Microsoft challenge/response authentication protocol. Both computers must be domain members.

- Computer Certificate From The Certification Authority (CA). This is the same Computer Certificate method that the preceding "Computer Certificate Method" section describes, with one addition. If you use this method, you can select the Enable Certificate To Account Mapping check box. This retrieves an access token from AD DS for the computer. This includes the list of user rights assigned to the computer, which allows you to control access by using Group Policy security settings and by assigning the Access This Computer From The Network user right or the Deny Access To This Computer From The Network user right to individual or multiple computers, as necessary.

- Preshared Key. This method allows you to specify a plaintext key. Each computer must have the same key configured. If you use the Preshared Key method, you cannot configure a second authentication method.

Second Authentication Method   You can use the second authentication method to authenticate a user. You can also choose Computer Health Certificate From The Certification Authority (CA) for the second authentication method. You cannot use any second authentication method if Preshared Key is chosen for the first authentication method. You cannot choose Preshared Key for the second authentication method, regardless of the first authentication method. The options available for the second authentication method are listed here:

◆ User (Kerberos V5). This authentication method requests or requires the user to authenticate by using the Kerberos V5 authentication protocol. You can use the Kerberos V5 authentication protocol only if the user is a domain member.

◆ User (NTLMv2). This authentication method uses the Microsoft challenge/response authentication protocol. You can use this authentication protocol only if the user is a domain member.

◆ User Certificate From The Certification Authority (CA). This authentication method requests or requires a valid user certificate to authenticate, and you must have at least one CA to do this. This method supports the Enable Certificate To Account Mapping option, which generates an access token for the user based on the mapped account.

◆ Computer Health Certificate From The Certification Authority (CA). This authentication method uses the computer health certificate, and it supports the Enable Certificate To Account Mapping option.

There are multiple ways to configure IPsec, depending on your environment and goals. Ultimately, you will configure and deploy IPsec as a policy. Computers that are domain members can have IPsec configured through a GPO. You can configure both IPsec policies and Windows Firewall with Advanced Security connection security rules by using a GPO. Domain and nondomain members can have IPsec configured locally by using the Windows Firewall with Advanced Security management console. Additionally, you can use Windows PowerShell to script the creation of IPsec rules.

The IPsec default settings are on the IPsec Settings tab of the Windows Firewall with Advanced Security on Local Computer Properties dialog box. Click Customize to configure the methods that you want IPsec to use for:

◆ Key Exchange (Main Mode). This sets up the session.

◆ Data Protections (Quick Mode). This encrypts network traffic.

◆ Authentication Method. This validates the computer identity.

CONFIGURING IPSEC

There are multiple ways of configuring IPSec. You can use GPO, Firewall Rules, or Windows PowerShell.

Using a GPO

When configuring IPsec policies by using a GPO, you define the IPsec settings in the Computer Configuration\Policies\Windows Settings\Security Settings\IP Security Policies on Active Directory (Domain) node. Although you can use GPOs to assign different policies to different computer groups, there is a single repository for all IPsec policies. There are three predefined IPsec policies, but none of them are assigned. All GPOs display all of the defined

IPsec rules, and within the GPO, you assign the IPsec rule that you want the GPO to apply. Each GPO can assign IPsec policies independently of other GPOs. However, you can assign only one IPsec policy within a single GPO. Furthermore, clients can have only one IPsec policy applied to them at a time. The three predefined policies are listed here:

- **Client (Respond Only).** This policy configures computers to negotiate security and authentication methods when requested. Within the policy, you can define the allowable security and authentication methods.

- **Server (Request Security).** This policy configures a computer to always request security by using the Kerberos V5 authentication protocol for all IP traffic, and it allows unsecured communications.

- **Secure Server (Require Security).** This policy configures a computer to always require a secure connection for all IP traffic and to block untrusted computers. This rule uses only the Kerberos V5 authentication protocol by default.

You can create your own IPsec policies. Some of the options that you can use when creating your own IPsec policies are listed here:

- **IP Filter Lists.** Allow you to define the following:
  - **IP Traffic Source.** Options include Any IP Address, My IP Address, A specific DNS name, A specific IP Address or Subnet, and more.
  - **IP Traffic Destination.** Options include Any IP Address, My IP Address, A specific DNS name, A specific IP Address or Subnet, and more.
  - **IP Protocol Type.** Options include Any, ICMP, TCP, UDP, Other, and more.
  - **IP Protocol Port.** If you are defining the IP protocol type as TCP or UDP, you can specify the source and destination ports.
- **Filter Actions.** Allows you to define the:
  - **Filter Action General Options.** Allows you to specify the filter to Permit, Block, or Negotiate security.
  - **Communicating With Computers That Do Not Support IPsec.** This option is available only if the action is Negotiate Security. You can use this option to define what happens when attempting communication with a computer that does not support secure connections.

Using Firewall Rules

Using firewall rules to define IPsec is a more granular experience than using GPOs. First, you must create a connection security rule to define the authentication method. After you configure the connection security rules, you can configure the inbound rules and outbound rules to enable the Allow The Connection If It Is Secure option. Some rules, such as the ICMPv4 rule, do not support this option. If you choose to require security on an inbound or outbound rule, the following policies are available:

◆ Allow the connection if it is authenticated and integrity-protected. This policy does not require encryption.

◆ Require the connections to be encrypted. This policy requires encryption for all connections. If you select the Allow The Computer To Dynamically Negotiate Encryption check box, unencrypted traffic can be used during the security negotiation.

◆ Allow the connection to use null encapsulation. This policy allows you to require authentication but does not provide integrity or privacy protection.

◆ Override Block Rules. This check box allows you to specify computers that can connect without authentication or encryption—for example, servers that run remote administration tools.

When you use firewall rules to configure IPsec encryption, negotiation between both systems is always in use to find the most secure encryption method that both systems support.

Using Windows PowerShell to Administer Windows Firewall

You can use the following commands to administer Windows Firewall.

To enable the firewall, at the Windows PowerShell command prompt, type the following command and then press Enter.

```
Set-NetFirewallProfile -Profile Domain,Public,Private -Enabled True
```

To create a firewall rule, at the Windows PowerShell command prompt, type the following command and then press Enter.

```
New-NetFirewallRule -DisplayName "Allow Inbound Telnet" -Direction Inbound
-Program %SystemRoot%\System32\tlntsvr.exe -RemoteAddress LocalSubnet -Action
Allow
```

To modify an existing rule, at the Windows PowerShell command prompt, type the following command and then press Enter.

```
Set-NetFirewallRule -DisplayName "Allow Web 80" -RemoteAddress 192.168.0.2
```

To delete an existing rule, at the Windows PowerShell command prompt, type the following command and then press Enter.

```
Remove-NetFirewallRule -DisplayName "Allow Web 80"
```

Isolation zones logically separate your network into computers that can authenticate with one another and those that cannot authenticate. IPsec is the basis for these network isolation zones, which you implement by using Windows Firewall with Advanced Security connection security rules.

To create an isolated network, you must separate the various types of computers in your organization's network according to the access you want those computers to have.

The following factors apply to isolated networks:

◆ Computers in an isolated network can initiate communication with any computer, regardless of whether they are isolated.

♦   Computers that are not in the isolated network:

- ♦   Can initiate communication with other computers that are not in the isolated network
- ♦   Cannot initiate communication with computers in the isolated network

It is important to remember that computers in your isolated network ignore all requests to initiate communication from computers that are not in the isolated network. Windows Server 2016 supports two types of isolation: domain isolation and server isolation.

You can monitor IPsec through the IP Security Monitor snap-in or through the Monitoring node in the Windows Firewall with Advanced Security management console. The IP Security Monitor shows additional details that relate to the IPsec policy applied either locally or through a GPO. The Monitoring node in the Windows Firewall with Advanced Security management console does not show policy-related information.

When monitoring IPsec that you configure by using the Windows Firewall with Advanced Security management console, the two top-level nodes that you can view are the Connection Security Rules and Security Associations nodes. In the Security Associations node, there are nodes for Main Mode monitoring and Quick Mode monitoring. Each of these nodes shows details about their associated configuration item.

Monitoring IPSec

To ensure that IPSec is working properly, you should monitor how IPSec is functioning. Therefore, you can use IP Security Monitor snap-in, where you can use two views, Main Mode and Quick Mode.

Main Mode

Main Mode—or Phase 1 Internet Key Exchange (IKE) negotiation—establishes a secure channel known as the Internet Security Association and Key Management Protocol (ISAKMP) SA between two systems. The ISAKMP SA protects the key exchanges between peer computers that establish the Quick Mode connection. When establishing the secure channel, the Main Mode negotiation determines a common set of cryptographic suites that both systems use, establishes the shared secret key that the systems will use, and authenticates the computer identities.

Monitoring Main Mode SAs provide information about peers that are currently connected to the computer, including:

- ♦   **Local Address.** This is the IP address of the computer you are monitoring.
- ♦   **Remote Address.** This is the IP address of the remote computer.
- ♦   **First Authentication Method.** This is the authentication method that the systems use to establish their identities.
- ♦   **Second Authentication Method.** This displays the second method that the systems will use, if you configure a secondary method.
- ♦   **Encryption.** This shows the cipher algorithm that the systems use to encrypt the session.
- ♦   **Integrity.** This shows the hash function that the systems use to help ensure that no tampering occurred with the session.
- ♦   **Key Exchange.** This shows the method that the systems use to exchange security keys.

Quick Mode

Quick Mode IKE negotiation establishes a secure channel between two systems that will help protect data during transmission. The SAs that the Quick Mode IKE negotiates in this phase are IPsec SAs for the IPsec service. Quick Mode can use the existing keying material or generate new keys as necessary. During this negotiation, the Quick Mode IKE selects a common protection suite for use with the IP traffic to which this rule applies.

Monitoring Quick Mode SAs can provide information about which peers are currently connected to the computer, and the information they show includes:

- Local Address. The IP address of the computer being monitored.

- Remote Address. The IP address of the remote computer.

- Local Port. The local port that traffic in this session can use.

- Remote Port. The remote port that traffic in this session can use.

- Protocol. The protocol that can be in this session.

- AH Integrity. The AH protocol-specific data integrity method that peer communications use.

- ESP Integrity. The ESP protocol-specific data integrity method that peer communications use.

- ESP Encryption. The ESP protocol-specific encryption method that peer communications use.

Protecting Administrative Access

In many attack scenarios, administrators are some of the most wanted targets because they have access to the Enterprise Admins and Domain Admins accounts. Attackers might try to obtain access to an administrator's username, password, or even workstation or laptop. Therefore, administrators must be acutely aware that they have one of the most important roles in an organization's security. By learning about and executing some of the following technologies, they can strengthen even more the security of their credentials.

Privileged Access Workstations

One way to mitigate the risk of an attack on an administrator's credentials is to use a Privileged Access Workstation (PAW)—or secure administrative host—that represents a computer that is used only for performing administrative tasks.

PAWs are configured with following options:

- Only authorized users can sign in to the PAW.

- Device Guard and AppLocker policies should be configured to allow only authorized applications to run on PAW.

- Credential Guard should be configured to protect the credentials.

◆ BitLocker should be configured to protect the boot environment and the hard disk data.

◆ Configure PAW to control access by using a firewall.

You can also configure a PAW as a jump server that represents a PAW that can be accessed remotely by using Remote Desktop protocol. If not configured securely, jump servers can be compromised if they are accessed by a compromised computer.

SECURING DOMAIN CONTROLLERS

Domain controllers are also favorite targets for attacks. If an attacker gains access to domain controllers, the attacker will have access to all of the domain objects. The steps to secure your domain controllers include the following:

◆ Regularly update domain controllers with the most recent operating system updates.

◆ Deploy domain controllers on a Server Core installation in order to reduce the domain controller's attack surface area.

◆ Configure Windows Firewall with Advanced Security to protect the ports on domain controllers from unauthorized access.

◆ To minimize the chance that unauthorized executable files and scripts can run on the computer, control the execution of executables and scripts on the domain controller with AppLocker and Device Guard.

◆ Deploy domain controllers on hardware that includes a Trusted Platform Module (TPM) chip, and configure all volumes with BitLocker Drive Encryption.

◆ Consider configuring domain controllers in branch offices as read-only domain controllers (RODC). Be aware that some applications, such as Exchange Server, do not support RODC.

◆ The virtualized domain controllers should run either on separate virtualization hosts or as a shielded virtual machine on a guarded fabric.

◆ Configure Remote Desktop Protocol (RDP) through a Group Policy assigned to the domain controller's OU to limit RDP connections so that they can occur only on PAWs.

Local Administrator

Each computer has a Local Administrator account. The Local Administrator account allows IT operations personnel to sign in to the computer if they cannot establish connectivity to the domain, or if the computer is not a domain member. Managing passwords for the Local Administrator account for every computer in the organization can be challenging, especially if the number of computers is very large.

Local Administrator Password Solutions (LAPS) provides organizations with a central repository for Local Administrator passwords for domain-member machines with the following functionalities:

◆ Unique Local Administrator passwords are on each computer managed with LAPS.

◆ It randomizes and changes Local Administrator passwords regularly.

◆ It stores Local Administrator passwords and secrets securely within AD DS.

◆ It configures permissions control access to passwords and secrets.

◆ LAPS retrieves and transmits encrypted passwords to the client.

LAPS is downloaded from Microsoft Download Center and is configured through a Group Policy client-side extension. LAPS requires an update to the Active Directory schema performed by running the `Update-AdmPwdADSchema` cmdlet, which is included in a Windows PowerShell module that becomes available when you install LAPS on a computer. Security permission for update the schema require membership of Schema Admins group and this cmdlet should be executed on a computer that is in the same Active Directory site as the computer that holds the Schema Master role for the forest. LAPS requirements also include .NET Framework 4.0 and Windows PowerShell 2.0 or newer to be installed.

The LAPS process runs every time Group Policy refreshes, and it includes the following steps:

1. LAPS determines if the password of the Local Administrator account has expired.

2. If the password has expired, LAPS performs the following steps:

   a. Changes the Local Administrator password to a new random value based on the configured parameters for Local Administrator passwords.

   b. Transmits the new password to AD DS, which stores it in a special confidential attribute associated with the computer account of the computer that has had its Local Administrator Account password updated.

   c. Transmits the new password-expiration date to AD DS, where it is stored in a special confidential attribute associated with the computer account of the computer that has had its Local Administrator Account password updated.

Authorized users can read passwords from AD DS, and an authorized user can initiate a Local Administrator password change on a specific computer.

Several steps need to be taken to configure and manage passwords by using LAPS. The first set of steps involves configuring AD DS. It starts by moving the computer accounts of computers that want to use LAPS to manage passwords to an OU. After the computer accounts are moved into an OU, the `Set-AdmPwdComputerSelfPermission` cmdlet is used to assign computers in an OU the ability to update the password of their Local Administrator account when it expires.

For example, to allow computers in the London OU to update their passwords by using LAPS when they expire, the following command should be used:

```
Set-AdmPwdComputerSelfPermission -Identity "London"
```

By default, accounts that are members of the Domain Admins and Enterprise Admins groups can access and view stored passwords. You can use the `Set-AdmPwdReadPasswordPermission` cmdlet to allow customized groups to access to Local Administrator password.

For example, to assign the LondonAdmins group the ability to view the Local Administrator password on computers in the London OU, the following command should be used:

```
Set-AdmPwdReadPasswordPermission -Identity "London" -AllowedPrincipals
"LondonAdmins"
```

The next step is to install the GPO templates into AD DS. After the templates are installed, the following policies can be configured:

◆ Enable Local Admin Password Management. This policy will enable LAPS and will allow you to manage the Local Administrator Account password centrally.

◆ Password Settings. This policy allows configuration of the complexity, length, and maximum age of the Local Administrator password. The default is to utilize uppercase and lowercase letters, numbers, and special characters. The default password length is 14 characters, and the default password maximum age is 30 days.

◆ Do Not Allow Password Expiration Time Longer Than Required. When enabled, the password updates according to the Domain Password Expiration policy.

◆ Name of Administrator Account to Manage. Use this policy to identify custom Local Administrator accounts.

You can view the passwords assigned to a computer by using one of the following methods:

◆ View the properties of the computer account with Advanced Features enabled in Active Directory Users and Computers by examining the ms-Mcs-AdmPwd attribute.

◆ Use the LAPS user interface (UI) app.

◆ Use the Get-AdmPwdPassword Windows PowerShell cmdlet, which is available through the AdmPwd.PS module when you install LAPS.

Just Enough Administration

In previous sections, we mentioned that one of the best practices for users is to have enough security permissions to perform the job and nothing more. Just Enough Administration (JEA) is a technology that helps administrators achieve this security best practice by granularly defining what actions are allowed on specific resources by running Windows PowerShell commands. Once JEA is configured, an authorized user can connect to a specially defined endpoint and use a specific set of Windows PowerShell cmdlets, parameters, and parameter values. For example, a JEA endpoint can be configured to allow an authorized user to restart a specific service, such as the IIS, but not have permissions to restart any other service or perform other administrative actions.

JEA performs tasks by using a virtual account rather than the user's account. The benefits of this method include:

◆ The user's credentials are not saved on the remote system, so the user's credentials cannot be compromised.

◆ The user account that is used to connect to the endpoint does not need to be with administrative permissions. It only needs permission to be allowed remote connections.

◆ The virtual account is limited to the system on which it is hosted. The virtual account cannot be used to connect to remote systems. Attackers cannot use a compromised virtual account to access other protected servers.

◆ The virtual account has Local Administrator privileges but is limited to performing only the activities defined by JEA. The virtual account can be configured with membership of a group other than the Local Administrators group to further reduce privileges.

JEA is supported on Windows Server 2016 and Windows 10 version 1511 or later operating systems. If Windows Management Framework 5.0 is installed, then JEA functions on minimum Windows 7 and Windows Server 2008 R2 operating systems. JEA also needs PowerShell, which is enabled on each computer running minimum Windows Server 2012. Optionally, you might enable PowerShell module and script blocking as we described earlier in this chapter.

Role-Capability Files

JEA needs role-capability files that enable specifying actions that can be performed in a Windows PowerShell session. Only actions that are listed in this file will be allowed.

You can create a role-capability file by using the New-RoleCapabilityFile cmdlet, which creates a file with a .psrc extension. Once created, the role-capability file can be edited as needed.

Role-capability files support the components shown in Table 8.3.

TABLE 8.3: Role Capabilities

CAPABILITY	DESCRIPTION
ModulesToImport	Allows custom modules to import
VisibleAliases	Lists aliases that will be available in the JEA session
VisibleCmdlets	Lists Windows PowerShell cmdlets that will be available in the session
VisibleFunctions	Lists which Windows PowerShell functions will be available in the session
VisibleExternalCommands	Allows users connected to the session to run external commands
VisibleProviders	Lists Windows PowerShell providers that are visible to the session
ScriptsToProcess	Configures Windows PowerShell scripts to run automatically when the session is started
AliasDefinitions	Defines Windows PowerShell aliases for the JEA session
FunctionDefinitions	Defines Windows PowerShell functions for the JEA session
VariableDefinitions	Defines Windows PowerShell variables for the JEA session
EnvironmentVariables	Specifies environment variables for the JEA session
TypesToProcess	Configures Windows PowerShell–type files to load for the JEA session
FormatsToProcess	Configures Windows PowerShell formats to load for the JEA session
AssembliesToLoad	Specifies which assemblies to load for the JEA session

Let's see some examples. For example, to allow the Restart-Service cmdlet to be used only for DNS service, we should provide the following entry in the role-capability file:

```
VisibleCmdlets = @{ Name = 'Restart-Service'; Parameters = @{ Name='Name';
ValidateSet = 'DNS'}}
```

Session-Configuration Files

When deploying JEA, you should register and configure an endpoint. When configuring an endpoint, you should define who will have access to the JEA endpoint, which roles will be assigned to the object accessing the endpoint, and the name of the endpoint.

To create a new session-configuration file, you should use the New-PSSession-ConfigurationFile cmdlet, which will create a file with the .pssc file extension.

Session configuration files have the components shown in Table 8.4.

TABLE 8.4:   Session Configuration Files Components

FIELD	EXPLANATION
SessionType	Configuration of the session's default settings. If the setting is to RestrictedRemoteServer, it can use the Get-Command, Get-FormatData, Select-Object, Get-Help, Measure-Object, Exit-PSSession, Clear-Host, and Out-Default cmdlets. The Session-Execution policy will be set to RemoteSigned. Example: SessionType = 'RestrictedRemoteServer'
RoleDefinitions	Assigns role capabilities to specific security groups. Example: RoleDefinitions =@{'CONTOSO\DNSOps' = @{RoleCapabilities='DNSOps'}}
RunAsVirtualAccount	Configures JEA to use a privileged virtual account created just for the JEA session. This virtual account has local administrator's privileges on member servers and is a member of the Domain Admins group on a domain controller.
TranscriptDirectory	Specifies the location where JEA activity transcripts are stored.
RunAsVirtualAccountGroups	If you do not want the virtual account to be a member of the Local Administrators group or Domain Admins group, you can use this field instead to specify the groups in which the virtual account is a member.

One server can have multiple JEA endpoints, and each JEA endpoint can be used for a different administrative task. For example, you can use one endpoint to perform IIS administrative tasks and a different endpoint to perform DNS administrative tasks. Users do not have to have administrative permissions to connect to an endpoint. Once connected, users are assigned administrative permissions assigned to the virtual account configured in the session-configuration file.

JEA endpoints are created by using the `Register-PSSessionConfiguration` cmdlet. When using this cmdlet, you specify an endpoint name and a session-configuration file hosted on the local machine.

For example, to create the endpoint named IISManagement by using the IISManagement `.pssc` session-configuration file, run the following command:

```
Register-PSSessionConfiguration -Name 'IISManagement' -Path IISManagement.pssc
```

Connecting to a JEA endpoint is done by using the `Enter-PSsession` cmdlet from a Windows PowerShell session. For example, in order to connect to JEA endpoint named IISManagement on computer NY-DC1, using credentials from user Paul in the Contoso domain, run the following command:

```
Enter-PSSession -ComputerName NY-DC1 -ConfigurationName IISManagement -Credential
Contoso\Paul
```

After completing the administrative tasks, you can use `Exit-PSSession` cmdlet to end the interactive session.

The first step of deploying JEA is to test the configuration. If the test is successful, the configuration can be deployed to other computers by copying the role-capability files and session-configuration files to the target computer, and creating JEA endpoints on that computer. You can use JEA Desired State Configuration (DSC) that allows central deployment of JEA to computers within the organization that have their configuration maintained by DSC. Furthermore, by using DSC, users and role mapping can be centrally managed.

Protecting Active Directory Infrastructure

Active Directory is a foundation of every Windows-based server infrastructure. It stores user accounts, computer accounts, and groups. Many applications (such as Exchange, SharePoint, Skype for Business, and SQL Server) use Active Directory for storing information and for authentication and authorization purposes. An attack on Active Directory is an attack against all the applications that depend on Active Directory. Protecting Active Directory is one of the most important tasks for security administrators.

Enhanced Security Administrative Environment

Enhanced Security Administrative Environment (ESAE) forests represent a specific architectural approach to designing Active Directory infrastructure. In ESAE, a dedicated administrative Active Directory forest hosts privileged access workstations, security groups, and accounts with administrative permissions, while resources and non-admin user accounts are located in a separate production forest. The ESAE forest is configured with a one-way trust relationship from the production forest to the administrative forest, which means that administrative forest accounts will have permissions to access the production forest resources.

The ESAE forest should be a single-domain Active Directory forest in order to avoid complexity. Furthermore, ESAE forest hosts only a small number of accounts to which strict security policies must be applied. No applications are deployed in the ESAE forest, because it is used only for hosting admin accounts.

The ESAE forest servers need to be configured in the following ways:

◆ Installation media should be validated.

◆ Servers should run the most recent version of the Windows Server operating system.

◆ Servers should be updated automatically with security updates.

◆ Security compliance manager baselines should be used as the starting point for server configuration.

◆ Servers should be configured with secure boot, BitLocker volume encryption, Credential Guard, and Device Guide.

◆ Servers should be configured to block USB storage.

◆ Servers should be on isolated networks. Inbound and outbound Internet connections should be blocked.

ESAE forests have the following benefits:

Locked-Down Accounts   Standard nonprivileged user accounts in the ESAE forest can be configured as highly privileged in the production forest. For example, a standard user account in the ESAE forest is made a member of the Domain Admins group in a domain in the production forest. It is possible to lock down the standard user account hosted in the ESAE forest so that it cannot sign on to hosts in the ESAE forest and can only be used to sign on to hosts in the production forest. This design is more secure if an account is compromised while it is used in the production forest, because the attacker cannot use that account to perform administrative tasks in the ESAE forest.

Selective Authentication   ESAE forest design allows organizations to leverage the trust relationship's selective authentication feature. For example, sign-ins from the ESAE forest will be restricted to specific hosts in the production forest. This is another method that helps limit credential exposure. For example, you can limit credential exposure when you configure selective authentication so that privileged accounts in the production forest can be used only on privileged access workstations or jump servers.

Privileged Access Management

Privileged Access Management (PAM) is a technology that grants administrative permission to admin users for a limited amount of time instead of permanently. It uses temporary membership of a security group that has been delegated privileges, instead of permanent membership of a security group. PAM increases security because rights are assigned temporarily instead of permanently, and PAM can be configured so that privileges are assigned when requested or assigned only after approval has been requested and granted.

When implemented, PAM can provide the following security improvements:

◆ All accounts that need admin privileges are standard user accounts. Privileges are granted only after being requested and approved. If a user account used by an admin team becomes compromised, the attacker gains no additional rights beyond those assigned to a standard user account.

◆ All requests for privileges are logged.

◆ Privileges are temporary. This makes it much more difficult for members of the IT Operations team to carry out unauthorized activities.

Once privileges are granted, a user must establish a new session by opening a new Windows PowerShell session or by signing out and signing in again to leverage the new group memberships configured for their account.

In order to deploy a PAM solution, you will also need to deploy Microsoft Identity Manager (MIM) 2016. MIM functionality includes managing users, credentials, policies, and access within an organization, including hybrid and cross forests scenarios.

The architecture of deploying PAM in an organization is shown on Figure 8.11.

FIGURE 8.11
Privileged Access
Management
(PAM)
architecture

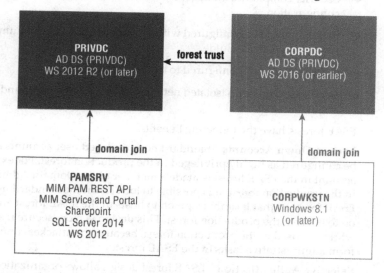

A PAM deployment consists of the following components:

♦ **Administrative Forest.** An administrative, or bastion, forest is configured as an ESAE management forest.

♦ **Microsoft Identity Manager (MIM) 2016.** A product that is used to manage accounts and group membership from so called bastion forest. A bastion forest is a separate forest contains the accounts that administer the production forest.

♦ **Production Forest.** This is the forest that hosts the organization resources.

♦ **PAM Client.** A client software that interacts with the MIM PAM functionality and is used to request access to a PAM role.

♦ **PAM Component Service.** Manages the life cycle of the privileged accounts.

♦ **PAM Monitoring Service.** Monitors the production forest and duplicates changes to the administrative forest or the MIM service.

♦ **PAM REST API.** Can be used to enable a custom client to interact with PAM.

- ◆ MIM Service. The MIM server manages the privileged account management process.

- ◆ MIM Portal. The MIM Portal is a SharePoint site. It provides management and configuration functionality.

- ◆ MIM Service Database. The MIM service database can be hosted on SQL Server 2012 or SQL Server 2014. It holds configuration and identity data that the MIM Service uses.

PAM uses shadow accounts and shadow groups that represent a copy of the account and groups that exists in the production forest. When a user is added to a PAM role, MIM adds the user's shadow account in the administrative forest to the shadow group in the administrative forest. When the user logs in by using this account, their Kerberos token will then include a security identifier that matches the security identifier of the original group from the production forest.

A shadow user is created by using the New-PAMUser cmdlet, where a trust relationship must exist between the production forest and bastion forest. You must also specify the source domain and source account name. For example, to create a new shadow user based on the George account in the Contoso.com domain, you should use the following command:

```
New-PAMUser -SourceDomain Contoso.com -SourceAccountName George
```

You can configure the following PAM role settings by using the MIM portal web interface:

Display Name   The name of the PAM role.

PAM Privileges   A list of security groups to which a user that is granted access to the role is temporarily added.

PAM Role TTL(sec)   This is the maximum amount of time that the member can be granted this role. The default is 3,600 seconds (1 hour).

MFA Enabled   MIM's PAM functionality can be integrated with Azure Multi-Factor Authentication. MFA requires two forms of authentication. This second form of authentication can include a text message or a telephone call.

Approval Required   You can configure PAM role membership to be granted only if a PAM administrator approves the request.

Availability Window Enabled   When configured, the PAM role can be used only during certain hours.

Description   Provides a description of the PAM role.

Finally, by combining PAM with JEA, you maximize the level of security by limiting who can perform administrative tasks, you granularly control what tasks are allowed to be performed, you secure privileged user accounts by isolating them in the separate forest, and you limit the time duration where administrative privileges are assigned. However, this infrastructure adds complexity for managing and maintaining such a solution. Therefore, you should carefully analyze your organization's business requirements and decide what security scenario and solution you will deploy.

Malware Protection

Malicious software, or *malware,* has been around since personal computers came into existence. Unfortunately, malware keeps being developed, and attackers keep finding new ways to harm operating systems. Every now and then we hear about new viruses spreading across the Internet and ransomware attacks that encrypt users' and organizations' data.

Windows Server 2016 includes Windows Defender that helps protect a user's computer from various types of malware. Windows Defender uses anti-malware definitions to determine if software that it detects is malicious, and it alerts the user about potential risks. Since there are new threats on the Internet every day, Windows Defender automatically checks for new definitions and installs them as they are released. When Windows Defender detects potential malware activity, it raises a different level of alert, depending on the type of the threat. Windows Defender also sends an alert if any software attempts to change important Windows operating system settings. To help prevent malware and other unwanted software from running on a computer, turn on Windows Defender real-time protection.

Windows Defender has three scanning options, which are listed in Table 8.5.

TABLE 8.5:   Windows Defender Scan Options

SCAN OPTION	DESCRIPTION
Quick	Checks the areas such as system folders and Registry, where malware will most probably attack
Full	Checks all files on your hard disk and all running programs
Custom	Enables users to scan specific drives and folders

When Windows Defender detects a potentially harmful file, it moves the file to a quarantine area; it does not allow it to run nor allow other processes to access it. Users can examine the quarantined files and decide if they should be removed or restored by using the Remove or Restore Quarantined Items option. Additionally, the user can choose to allow items by maintaining the Allowed list.

VERIFYING MICROSOFT SUPPORT AND DISABLING WINDOWS DEFENDER

Before enabling Windows Defender on a Windows Server 2016 operating system, check whether the scenario is supported by Microsoft. For example, if you run Exchange Server, Windows Defender is not Exchange-aware so it will scan Exchange databases as regular files. Because Windows Defender is not aware of the database structure, there is a potential risk of corrupting the database files. Therefore, we recommend disabling Windows Defender on a machine running Exchange Server—or at least configuring Windows Defender not to scan files and folders used by Exchange Server. As a best practice, before enabling Windows Defender you should always check the supportability statement from Microsoft, which varies for the different products running on Windows Server (such as Skype for Business, SQL Server, Domain Controller, and other types of server roles).

Software Restriction Policies

Software Restriction Policies (SRPs) were introduced in the Windows Server 2003 operating system, and they provide administrators with the capability to specify which applications can run on client computers. An SRP contains rules and security levels and is configured through Group Policy.

Rules govern how SRP answers to an application that is being run or installed and are based on one of the following criteria:

◆ Hash. A cryptographic fingerprint of the file.

◆ Certificate. A software publisher certificate that signs a file digitally.

◆ Path. The local or Universal Naming Convention (UNC) path to where the file is stored.

◆ Zone. The Internet zone.

Each applied SRP can be configured with a security level that determines how an operating system responds to different types of applications. The three available security levels are listed here:

◆ Disallowed. The software that the rule identifies will not run, regardless of the user's access rights.

◆ Basic User. The software that the rule identifies as a standard user is allowed to run.

◆ Unrestricted. The software that the rule identifies is allowed to run unrestricted by the SRP.

SRPs can be configured at the following location in the Group Policy Management Editor: `Computer Configuration\Policies\Windows Settings\Security Settings\Software Restriction Policies`, as shown in Figure 8.12.

FIGURE 8.12
Configuring Software Restriction Policies in the Group Policy Management Editor

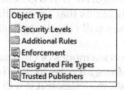

AppLocker

AppLocker was introduced with the Windows Server 2008 R2 operating system, and it controls which applications users can run. AppLocker is applied through Group Policy to computer objects within an organizational unit (OU). Individual AppLocker rules can be applied to individual Active Directory Domain Services (AD DS) users or groups. AppLocker can be used to monitor or audit the application of rules. By using the AppLocker technology, administrators can control how users can access and use files such as .exe files, scripts, Windows Installer files (.msi and .msp files), dynamic-link libraries (DLLs), and packaged applications, such as Windows Store apps.

AppLocker can be used to restrict software that is not allowed in a company, is not supported or used in the company anymore, or is limited for usage only in specific departments.

AppLocker settings are configured at the following location in the Group Policy Management Editor: `Computer Configuration\Policies\Windows Settings\Security Settings\ Application Control Policies`, as shown in Figure 8.13.

FIGURE 8.13
Configuring
AppLocker in
the Group Policy
Management
Editor

AppLocker uses the Application Identity service to verify a file's attributes. You should configure this service to start automatically on each computer on which you are applying AppLocker

Rules in AppLocker are defined based on the file attributes that it derives from the file's digital signature. File attributes in the digital signature include the following:

◆ Publisher name

◆ Product name

◆ File name

◆ File version

Allow and Deny are rule actions that permit or forbid the execution of applications based on an application list that is configured. If you choose Allow Action, your organization's computers will run only those applications that are specifically allowed. If you choose Deny Action, your organization's computers will run all applications except those that are on a list of denied applications.

An AppLocker policy has two modes of enforcement: Enforce and Audit Only. If you choose Enforce, AppLocker will enforce all rules and audit all events. If you choose Audit Only, AppLocker will only evaluate the rules and it will write events to the AppLocker Log. You can use the Audit Only option to help you evaluate what could happen if AppLocker is configured with the Enforce option, so you can test scenarios before actually enforcing them.

Device Guard

Device Guard is a new feature, introduced in Windows Server 2016, and it is a combination of hardware and software components ensuring that only trusted and authorized applications are allowed to run on a computer. Device Guard uses virtualization-based security to isolate the code integrity service and run it alongside the Windows kernel in a hypervisor-protected container. Administrators can configure what applications can run on the computer where Device Guard is implemented. This is done using a Code Integrity policy to protect the environment. The location of the Code Integrity policy is in the file: `C:\Windows\System32\CodeIntegrity\ sipolicy.p7b`.

Device Guard includes the following technologies:

Virtual Secure Mode   Virtual Secure Mode is a virtual shell that isolates the Local Security Subsystem Service LSASS.exe process from the operating system. In Windows 10 and Windows Server 2016, the hypervisor is on top of the hardware, and it interacts directly with the hardware to allow sharing of the hardware with virtual guests.

Configurable Code Integrity (CCI)   CCI verifies the code that the Windows operating system is executing. It doesn't allow nonauthorized applications to be started.

Virtual Secure Mode Protected Code Integrity   Configurable Code Integrity policies have two components: user mode code integrity (UMCI) and kernel mode code integrity (KMCI). The KMCI offers memory management improvements over the previous Windows versions, and it allows organizations to set their own KMCI and UMCI settings. Configurable Code Integrity should be running along with other security solutions, such as antivirus software or AppLocker.

Platform and Unified Extensible Firmware Interface (UEFI) Secure Boot   Secure Boot was introduced in Windows 8 and ensures that boot loader code and firmware are protected from tampering by malicious code. This feature requires UEFI booting and Secure Boot option enabled in the UEFI.

Configuring Device Guard

To enable Virtual Secure Mode in Windows 10 or Windows Server 2016, the following steps must be performed:

1. Enable Secure Boot and UEFI in BIOS.

2. Enable Trusted Platform Module (TPM).

3. Install Microsoft Hyper-V hypervisor. The Hyper-V services and management tools are not needed.

4. Enable Isolated User Mode.

5. Enable the Virtual Secure Mode policy named Enabled Credential Guard. You can locate this setting in the Computer Configuration\Administrative Templates\System\ Device Guard\Turn on Virtualization Based Security policy.

6. Configure the Boot Configuration Data (BCD) to start Virtual Secure Mode by running the following command as an administrator and then restarting the machine:

   ```
   bcdedit /set vsmlaunchtype auto
   ```

7. Verify that the Virtual Secure Mode is running in System logs in the Event Viewer, and verify that Secure System process is running in Task Manager.

To ensure that only trusted publisher-signed software is on the server, the code-integrity file should be created on a server with a preconfigured setting that runs only software that is needed. You can create the code integrity file by running the New-CIPolicy cmdlet as shown here:

```
New-CIPolicy -Level Publisher -FilePath C:\CI\audit-publisher.xml -UserPEs -audit
```

The command scans through user mode and kernel mode files, and then finds all the signers and puts them into the Code Integrity policy XML file that is created using the `New-CIPolicy` cmdlet. Once the XML file is created, it needs to be converted into a binary file by running the following command:

```
ConvertFrom-CIPolicy .\software.xml .\software.bin
```

Once the `.bin` file is created, it needs to be copied to the CodeIntegrity folder under Windows System32 by using the graphical interface or by running following command and then restarting the computer:

```
Copy-Item .\software.bin C:\Windows\System32\CodeIntegrity\sipolicy.p7b
```

After Device Guard is enabled, it will start working in audit mode. Once the administrator reviews the audit log and is confident that the Code Integrity policy is correct, Device Guard can be switched from audit mode to enforcement mode on computers with Windows 10 and Windows Server 2016 operating systems. The `New-CIPolicy` cmdlet allows you to build policies based on your audit log by using the `-Audit` parameter. Furthermore, you can capture policies from several servers and merge them by using the `Merge-CIPolicy` cmdlet. For example, you can merge the policy that you created from your audit logs and with your initial policy. The `ConvertFrom-CIPolicy` cmdlet converts the policy in XML into a binary format. After the policy is in a binary format, you can copy it to the CodeIntegrity folder, as shown in the following example and then restart the computer:

```
ConvertFrom-CIPolicy C:\CI\MergedPolicy.xml c:\CI\software.bin
cp  C:\CI\software.bin c:\Windows\System32\CodeIntegrity\SIPolicy.p7b
```

The Configurable Code Integrity policy includes different rule options. To examine the various Rule Options for Device Guard, you can use the following command:

```
Set-Ruleoption - Help
```

The previous command will display following options:

- 0 Enabled: UMCI
- 1 Enabled: Boot Menu Protection
- 2 Required: WHQL
- 3 Enabled: Audit Mode
- 4 Disabled: Flight Signing
- 5 Enabled: Inherit Default Policy
- 6 Enabled: Unsigned System Integrity Policy
- 7 Allowed: Debug Policy Augmented
- 8 Required: EV Signers
- 9 Enabled: Advanced Boot Options Menu
- 10 Enabled: Boot Audit On Failure
- 11 Disabled: Script Enforcement

To change the Device Guard from audit mode to enforcement mode, you can use the Set-RuleOption cmdlet and choose the appropriate option from the previous list, as shown in following example:

```
Set-RuleOption -Option 5 -FilePath [file location] -Delete
```

A complete scenario would look like this:

```
Set-RuleOption -FilePath C:\ci\newci.xml -Option 3 -Delete
ConvertFrom-CIPolicy .\newci.xml .\newci.bin
Copy-Item .\ newci.bin C:\Windows\System32\CodeIntegrity\sipolicy.p7b.
```

After you restart the machine, the Code Integrity policy will be in enforcement mode. If you attempt to execute a file that is not allowed by Device Guard, you will see the message, "The system cannot execute the specified program."

Device Guard supports working with different types of applications, including signed and those that do not have any digital signatures. Two types of digital signatures are supported, as follows:

Embedded Signature The binary and signing information are self-contained, and these signatures are required for boot-start drivers or a run-time check.

Catalog Signing A catalog signature is a signed file that identifies one or more binaries. These catalogs are located in the [System32]\CatRoot folder. They are required for driver packages or an install-time check. You can manage and deploy catalog signing independently of the package binaries, and they preserve any existing signatures.

Hardening Operating Systems Security with Additional Microsoft Products

In our everyday experience, we usually meet tools that have additional features compared to standard operating system technologies. Some of those tools are also developed by Microsoft and some are developed by third-party vendors. In this section, we will learn about Advanced Threat Analytics, a security tool developed by Microsoft that can help administrators monitor their infrastructure for potential security threats.

Advanced Threat Analytics

Advanced Threat Analytics (ATA) is a separate product by Microsoft that you can install on Windows Server, and it has an intrusion detection system (IDS) functionality. IDS systems detect attacks and alert security admins. Different vendors provide security products known as intrusion prevention systems (IPS), which not only detect but also prevent attacks.

ATA is a network-based intrusion-detection system (NIDS) that uses both signature-based and anomaly-based detection. ATA helps identify known malicious attacks and techniques, security issues, and risks by using a signature-based method. In addition, the anomaly-based detection analyzes, learns, and identifies normal and abnormal entity (user, devices, and resources) behaviors. ATA is an on-premises solution that monitors Active Directory activity. It examines Active Directory Domain Services (AD DS) traffic to understand authentication patterns. ATA is a behavior analytics tool, which means that a malicious hacker can no longer hide behind a valid user account. Attackers do not know the normal user behavior of the account that is captured in the baseline, so even if they try to make some changes slowly, ATA would detect a change in the pattern for that user.

After ATA is installed, the system is in the analyze phase; this is a simple, nonintrusive port-mirroring configuration that copies all Active Directory–related traffic, while remaining unseen for attackers. It studies all AD DS traffic and collects relevant events from SIEM and other sources.

After the analysis phase comes the learning phase. In this phase, ATA automatically starts learning and outlining object behavior. It identifies normal behavior for objects and learns non-stop to update the activities of users, devices, and resources.

The third phase is the detection phase; it arises automatically with no user involvement. It looks for abnormal behavior and identifies suspicious activities. It raises red flags only if abnormal activities are contextually aggregated.

The last phase is the alert phase. In this phase, ATA reports all suspicious activities on a simple, functional, and actionable timeline. It identifies who, what, when, and how. For each suspicious activity, ATA provides recommendations for investigation and remediation.

Deploying ATA is nonintrusive and does not affect production systems. ATA listens and gives reports based on the traffic it monitors, so there is no effect on the network.

For more information on Advanced Threat Analytics, visit the following link: `https://docs.microsoft.com/en-us/advanced-threat-analytics/what-is-ata`.

Evidence of the Attack

Breach detection consists of finding evidence on a system that attackers have compromised it. In most cases, attackers leave evidence on a compromised computer. You need to be educated and skilled in depth about how operating systems, applications, and network infrastructures work; and you need to use different security products, such as Intrusion Detection Systems (IDS). For example, Microsoft Advanced Threat Analytics has automatic processes that look for this evidence. Nevertheless, if you know where to look, you might find proof of breaches when they take place. Typically, you suspect that a breach has occurred when you notice something wrong with a system. For example, you might notice that a server is uploading large amounts of data outside of office hours, or that an abnormal amount of processor resources or memory is being used.

Event logs are used to record activities that occur on a computer. When auditing is configured properly, it records nearly all events that have any security significance. This makes event logs your first checking point when it comes to determining if a computer was the target of a security breach. IDS also uses event logs to identify malicious activities. Event logs should be moved off a computer on regular basis, because a sophisticated attacker will clear the event logs in order to hide an attack. Windows Server has an option to forward the event log; this is a built-in technology that enables you to configure automatic forwarding and storing event logs at another location. Moreover, administrators should create archives of event logs so that if they identify an attack, investigators can look at the event logs prior to the attack's detection to find out how long attackers have been compromising the system. Administrators also should certify that event logs are configured in a fashion that events are not overwritten when the log becomes full.

Attackers frequently compromise user, computer, and service accounts in the privilege escalation phase of an attack. In some cases, you can discover security breaches by identifying changes in accounts or changes in membership of privileged groups, such as the Domain Admins group.

Your organization might have suffered a security breach if you find proof that new accounts have suddenly appeared. They can be local accounts or accounts existing in Active Directory. Your organization should have a process that controls when an account was created, by whom, and for what reason. New accounts that are created by an attacker are unlikely to have names, which is an indication that the accounts are suspicious. Then again, a well-prepared attacker might use account names in correlation with organizational names that they have learned through social engineering, such as generating an account with the name of a former employee who no longer works for the organization.

An increase in privilege often indicates that an attacker added rights to an account they have already compromised. This usually happens with standard user accounts, as well as service accounts and computer accounts when an attacker is in the privilege escalation phase of an attack. For example, you would be suspicious if you found that a user account associated with the accounting department was a member of the Domain Admins group. Some evidences of security attack might include:

- Changes in membership of privileged groups. Attackers target groups such as the Domain Admins group and the Local Administrators group as these offer simple paths to privilege escalation.

- Creation of new groups. Well-prepared and sophisticated attackers who have compromised an organization's Active Directory environment create groups with special privileges that have similar privileges to built-in privileged groups, such as the Domain Admins and Local Administrators groups.

In order to detect such changes, you should ensure that regular audits of account management activity take place.

Auditing

The Windows Server operating system includes tools for analyzing logs that contain security audit information. Those tools provide auditing functionality that you can use to detect any unusual activity or attempts for unauthorized access.

An audit policy monitors different security-related activities and stores the results of that monitoring in audit logs. Audit policies are managed on a domain level by using the Group Policy Editor under the Computer Configuration node. In Computer Configuration, expand `Policies\Windows Settings\Security Settings\Local Policies` and then click Audit Policy, as shown in Figure 8.14.

FIGURE 8.14
Audit Policy settings in the Group Policy Management Editor

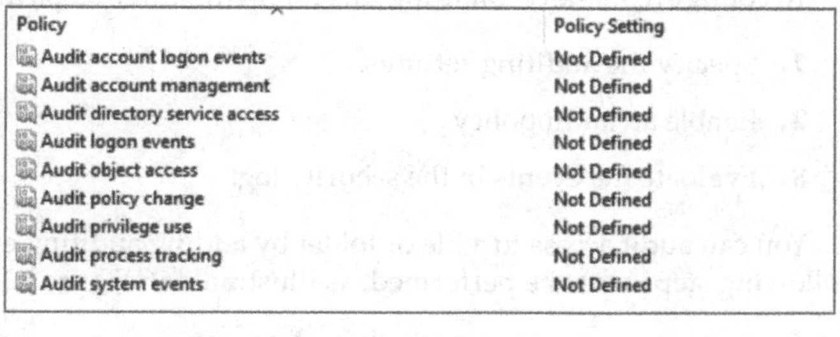

Policy	Policy Setting
Audit account logon events	Not Defined
Audit account management	Not Defined
Audit directory service access	Not Defined
Audit logon events	Not Defined
Audit object access	Not Defined
Audit policy change	Not Defined
Audit privilege use	Not Defined
Audit process tracking	Not Defined
Audit system events	Not Defined

Table 8.6 defines each audit policy on a Windows Server 2016 domain controller.

TABLE 8.6:   Audit Policy Settings

AUDIT POLICY SETTING	DESCRIPTION
Audit Account Logon Events	Generates an event when a user or computer logs on by using a Windows Server Active Directory account to authenticate.
Audit Account Management	Audits events, including the creation, deletion, or modification of user, group, or computer accounts and the resetting of user passwords.
Audit Directory Service Access	Audits events when user attempts to access Active Directory objects that are specified in the system access control list (SACL), which can be seen in an Active Directory object's Properties Advanced Security Settings dialog box.
Audit Logon Events	Generates an event when a user logs on interactively (locally) to a computer or over the network (remotely).
Audit Object Access	Audits access to objects such as files, folders, Registry keys, and printers that have their own SACLs. In addition to enabling this audit policy, you must configure the auditing entries in the objects' SACLs.
Audit Policy Change	Audits changes to user-rights assignment policies, audit policies, or trust policies.
Audit Privilege Use	Audits the use of a permission or user right. See the explanatory text for this policy in the Group Policy Management Editor.
Audit Process Tracking	Audits events such as program activations and process exits. See the explanatory text for this policy in the Group Policy Management Editor.
Audit System Events	Audits system restarts, shutdowns, or changes that affect the system or security logs.

Of course, every organization should customize their auditing policy according to their own security and compliance regulations. Besides auditing logon events, organizations might choose to audit different levels of access on file servers, such as successful or unsuccessful attempts to access specific folders and their content.

To configure file-level auditing, the following three steps must be completed:

1. Specify the auditing settings.

2. Enable an audit policy.

3. Evaluate the events in the security log.

You can audit access to a file or folder by adding auditing entries to its SACL. To do this, the following steps must be performed, as illustrated in Figure 8.15.

1. Open the Properties dialog box of the file or folder, and then click the Security tab.

2. On the Security tab, click Advanced.

3. Click Auditing.

4. To add an entry, click Edit. The Auditing tab will open in Edit mode.

5. Click Add, and then select the user, group, or computer to audit.

6. In the Auditing Entry dialog box, select the type of access to audit.

FIGURE 8.15
Auditing the security settings on a folder

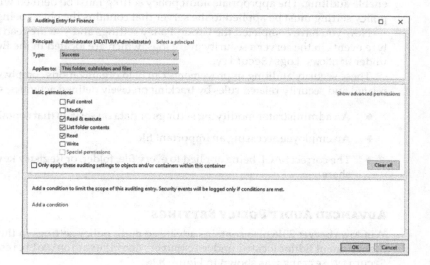

Real World Scenario

AUDITING FOR SUCCESS AND FAILURE

A software development company working on a brand-new product wanted to securely store their project data on different file servers. In order to audit the access to security-sensitive documents, they configured Auditing for Success and Failure attempts on all the data folders on their file servers. However, after some time they realized that they had thousands of entries in the security log files that were very difficult to analyze because they had selected to audit all file server folders instead of only the folders with critical data that contained their new project.

By using one or more of the access levels, you can audit for successes, failures, or both as the specified user, group, or computer attempts to access the resource.

You can audit successes for the following purposes:

◆ Audit successful accesses to verify security permissions so that you do not allow some users more permissions than they need for specific folders.

◆ Audit successful accesses to identify access from users who shouldn't have been allowed, which might indicate an unauthorized privilege.

♦ Audit failed accesses to monitor attempts to access a resource by unauthorized users.

♦ Audit failed accesses to identify failed attempts to access a file or folder to which a user does require access. This indicates that the permissions are not sufficient to meet a business requirement.

Once you have completed setup in the security descriptor of a file or folder, you should then enable auditing. The appropriate audit policy setting must be defined within Group Policy. The policy setting must be applied to the server that contains the object being audited.

Now you have completed the Group Policy settings and you are ready to monitor and analyze events in the server's security event logs, which are located in the Event Viewer console, under `Windows Logs\Security`.

These security auditing improvements can help organizations comply with important business-related and security-related rules by tracking precisely defined activities, such as:

♦ An administrator modifying settings or data on servers that contain sensitive information

♦ An employee accessing an important file

♦ The correct SACL being applied to every file, folder, or Registry key on a computer or file share

ADVANCED AUDIT POLICY SETTINGS

Windows Server 2016 also contains advanced audit policy settings in the Group Policy Management Editor located under `Computer Configuration\Policies\Windows Settings\Security Settings`, as shown in Figure 8.16.

FIGURE 8.16
Advanced Audit Policies settings in the Group Policy Management Editor

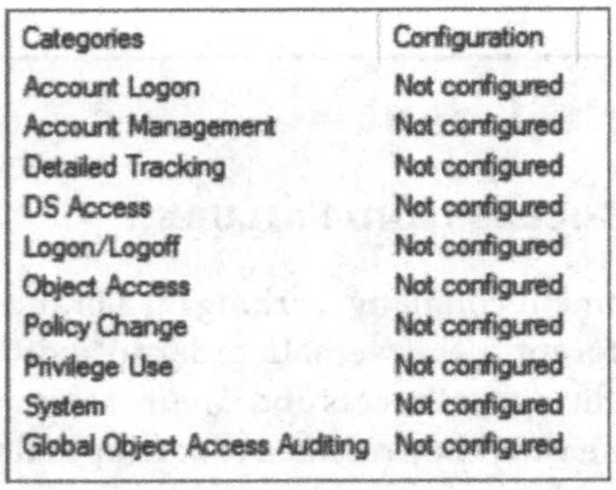

Categories	Configuration
Account Logon	Not configured
Account Management	Not configured
Detailed Tracking	Not configured
DS Access	Not configured
Logon/Logoff	Not configured
Object Access	Not configured
Policy Change	Not configured
Privilege Use	Not configured
System	Not configured
Global Object Access Auditing	Not configured

These are the settings:

Account Logon   These settings enable auditing of the validation of credentials and other Kerberos-specific authentication and ticket operation events. The validation of credentials in a domain environment occurs on domain controllers, which means that the auditing entries are logged on domain controllers.

Account Management   You can enable auditing for events that are related to the modification of user accounts, computer accounts, and groups with these settings. This group of auditing settings also logs password change events.

Detailed Tracking   These settings control the auditing of encryption events, Windows process creation and termination events, and remote procedure call (RPC) events.

DS Access   These audit settings involve access to AD DS, including general access, changes, and replication.

Logon/Logoff   This group of settings audits standard logon and logoff events. They also audit other account-specific activity, such as Internet Protocol security (IPsec), Network Policy Server, and other uncategorized logon and logoff events.

Object Access   These settings enable auditing for any access to AD DS, the Registry, applications, and file storage

Policy Change   When you configure these settings, internal changes to audit policy settings are audited.

Privilege Use   When you configure these settings, Windows Server audits attempts at privilege use within the Windows environment.

System   These settings are used for auditing changes to the state of the security subsystem.

Global Object Access Auditing   These settings are for controlling the SACL settings for all objects on one or more computers. When settings in this group are configured and applied with Group Policy, the configuration of the policy setting determines SACL membership, and the SACLs are configured directly on the server itself.

Organizations that have deployed Dynamic Access Control can leverage Expression-based auditing that will bring them additional auditing capabilities, such as auditing files and folders based on their specific classification, user, or action. For example, based on a folder classification, it will be audited automatically for security access.

AUDITPOL

AuditPol (Auditpol.exe) is a command-line tool can be used to manage advanced audit policy settings with the following functionalities:

◆   Configuring auditing on individual computers. For example, you can use AuditPol to manage auditing settings on individual computers that are not joined to an Active Directory domain.

◆   Getting the current auditing settings. By running the auditpol /get /category:* command, you can verify the current auditing settings across all of the advanced auditing categories.

◆   Backing up and restoring audit settings. You can use AuditPol to back up auditing settings from one computer and restore them on another computer.

EVENT LOG FORWARDING

Analyzing security logs on many different servers can be a challenge to perform. Therefore, you can use event forwarding in Windows Server where a remote computer forwards the events. There are two types of event forwarding: source-initiated and collector-initiated. In order to collect security events from computers, you must verify that `winrm` service is running as an administrator. Use the following command in Windows PowerShell:

```
winrm qc
```

After the event source computer is configured, you, as an administrator, should run the following command in Windows PowerShell at an elevated command prompt on the collector computer.

```
wecutil qc
```

You must then add the computer account of the collector computer to the Event Log Readers group on each of the source computers, by using `Add-ADGroupMember` cmdlet to add a computer to the Event Log Readers Active Directory group.

```
Add-ADGroupMember -identity 'Event Log Readers' -members AuditSRV$
```

After the configuration is complete, you will be ready to create a new subscription to specify the events you want the event sources to forward to the event collector. To create a new subscription, perform the following steps:

1. Run Event Viewer as an administrator.

2. In the console tree, click Subscriptions.

3. On the Actions menu, click Create Subscription and complete the requested information as shown in Figure 8.17.

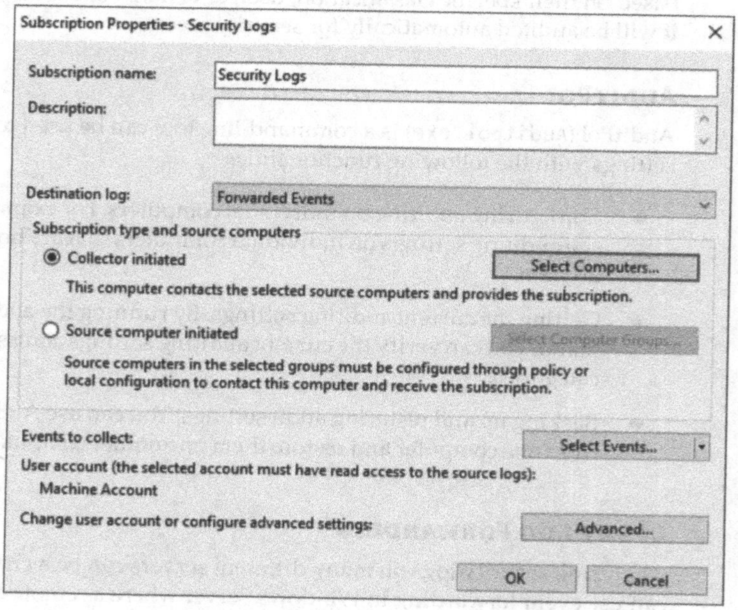

FIGURE 8.17
Configuring subscriptions in the Event Viewer

4. In the Subscription Name box, type the name you want for the subscription.

5. In the Description box, type an optional description.

6. In the Destination Log box, select the log file where the collected events will be stored.

7. Click Add, and then select the computers from which events will be collected. Click Select Events to display the Query Filter dialog box. Use the controls in the Query Filter dialog box to specify the criteria that events must meet to be collected.

8. In the Subscription Properties dialog box, click OK. The subscription will be added to the Subscriptions pane, and if the operation was successful, the status of the subscription will be Active.

Nowadays IT departments rely on Windows PowerShell to automate administrative tasks. Therefore, you can use Windows PowerShell, which provides cmdlets for security auditing and analyzing audit logs, as described in Table 8.7.

TABLE 8.7: Windows PowerShell Cmdlets for Managing Auditing Logs

WINDOWS POWERSHELL CMDLET	DESCRIPTION
Clear-EventLog	Deletes all entries from specified event logs on a local or remote computer
Get-Event	Gets the events in the event queue
New-Event	Creates a new event
New-EventLog	Creates a new event log and a new event source on a local or remote computer
Remove-Event	Deletes events from the event queue
Remove-EventLog	Deletes an event log or unregisters an event source
Show-EventLog	Displays the event logs of the local or remote computer in the Event Viewer
Write-EventLog	Writes an event to an event log
Limit-EventLog	Sets the event log properties that limit the size of the event log and the age of its entries

Windows PowerShell allows you to retrieve specific events based on certain criteria. For instance, if you want to retrieve the newest 50 security events, you can run following command:

```
Get-EventLog -Newest 50 -LogName "Security"
```

If your security department requests that all administrative commands be logged in a separate log, you can enable logging by using the `LogPipelineExecutionDetails` property of the PowerShell module and setting it to value `$true`. You can also enable logging by configuring Group Policy in `Administrative Template/Windows Components/Windows PowerShell`, as shown in Figure 8.18.

FIGURE 8.18
Windows
PowerShell
logging settings in
the Group Policy
Management
Editor

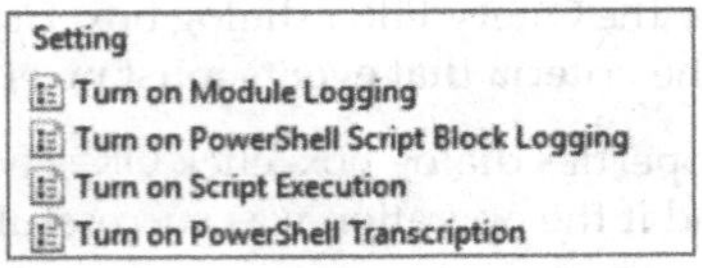

Setting
🔲 Turn on Module Logging
🔲 Turn on PowerShell Script Block Logging
🔲 Turn on Script Execution
🔲 Turn on PowerShell Transcription

The Bottom Line

Always start with the organization's business requirements. Security is one of the greatest concerns for any organization. However, different types of organizations require different levels of protection and security strategies. You may notice a huge difference if, for example, you compare the security procedures of a company that sells newspapers to those of a banking institution. In this chapter, you have learned about many different security technologies.

Master It Do you have a security strategy for your organization? Do you have security procedures in your IT department? Are they documented? What security technologies listed in this chapter will best fit your organization's requirements?

Solution The security technology you choose will depend on your organization's business requirements. One of the most important things to understand is that security is not proportional with cost and with user-friendly solutions. For example, the more secure the password is, the less user friendly the password is. This is because complex passwords are more difficult for an attacker to guess; however, they are also more difficult to remember. Inability to remember can lead to situations where users write down their passwords on some notes located at their work stations. And speaking about cost, the more sophisticated the security product is that you deploy, the more expensive it is. Organizations must choose the compromise in the middle of complexity, cost, and best security.

Perform regular security evaluations. Many administrators rely just on the brand name of their security equipment and do not pay attention to how that equipment is installed and configured. They don't update their operating systems or malware software definitions. They can also be quite surprised when a security breach occurs in their organization.

Master It How do you guard against a security breach?

Solution We always recommend that you perform regular security evaluations of your security solutions—even utilizing ethical hacking experts to simulate different attacks and generate reports about the level of your organization's infrastructure security vulnerability.

Automate the processes as much as possible. IT departments are growing every day, and the lack of automation tools, such as Windows PowerShell and Group Policy, can be very challenging for an administrator who must manage and monitor different security solutions deployed in the company.

Master It How do you get to know automation tools?

Solution Create a library of useful Windows PowerShell scripts that will help you easily go through the necessary commands. Learn how Windows PowerShell and Group Policy work so you can, for example, configure firewall settings on 100 computers at once. Manually configuring a system in today's world is impractical, if not impossible. By using automation tools, you can shut down multiple attack surface areas or run malware scans simultaneously on different clients and servers whenever some security issue is reported.

Chapter 9

Active Directory Domain Services

Active Directory Domain Services (AD DS) was first introduced with Windows 2000 Server (it existed in Windows NT but was known just as a Windows NT domain). Active Directory is an LDAP-compliant directory service. Directory services go way back, before the introduction of the Windows operating system. In this chapter, we will discuss Active Directory as it exists today in Windows Server 2016. Because Active Directory is a huge topic, we'll skip any introductory material and cover the topics that admins deal with regularly. This means that some topics, even new features, will not be covered in detail in this chapter.

IN THIS CHAPTER, YOU WILL LEARN TO:

- ◆ Design Active Directory forests and domains
- ◆ Design an organizational unit structure
- ◆ Implement and troubleshoot Group Policy

Overview of Features

Each new version of Windows Server introduces new functionality for Active Directory. You should be familiar with the features, especially if they help you solve challenges in your environment. Although the lists in this section aren't exhaustive, they do cover the primary new features.

What Changed in AD DS for Windows Server 2016

With Windows Server 2016, the following new features and changes were introduced:

Privileged Access Management (PAM)   PAM isolates your privileged user accounts from the rest of your Active Directory environment. It does this by introducing a new Active Directory forest and domain, Microsoft Identity Manager (MIM), and new functionality such as workflows and on-demand privilege escalation.

Windows Server 2003 at "End of Life"   In other words, Windows Server 2003 isn't supported. Therefore, you need to move away from it if you still have it running in your environment. The Windows Server 2003 forest functional level and domain functional level are officially deprecated now. That means they are supported but will have a limited amount of time before they become unsupported.

Features from Windows Server 2012 R2

If you haven't had a chance to look at the new functionality introduced with Windows Server 2012 R2, the following features were new or improved then and continue to be available in Windows Server 2016:

Workplace Join   This feature enables users to associate their personal devices with your Active Directory domain. This ties into authentication because you can use it for conditional access. For example, imagine that you have an employee web application. You only want to grant access to users who have company-owned devices or personal devices associated with your domain. With Workplace Join, you can do that!

Conditional Access   This feature is tied closely to Active Directory Federation Services (AD FS), to which Chapter 11 is dedicated. With conditional access, you can decide whether a user is granted access based on the access control list (ACL) and other factors such as the source network and the user's device type.

Multifactor Authentication   This feature also relies on AD FS. We are listing it here because it is an enhancement to authentication, which is ultimately handled by Active Directory.

Features from Windows Server 2012

If you haven't had a chance to look at new functionality introduced with Windows Server 2012, the following features were new or improved then and continue to be available in Windows Server 2016:

Virtualization Enhancements   Starting with Windows Server 2012, you can use *checkpoints* (snapshots) for domain controllers. You can also clone a domain controller. Both enhancements enable organizations to embrace virtualization for domain controllers.

Dynamic Access Control (DAC)   Imagine being able to calculate permissions to a resource on-the-fly. With DAC, you can do just that! For example, a user can access a shared folder if they are in the HR department and they are using a company-owned device.

Active Directory Recycle Bin   You are familiar with the Windows Recycle Bin. The Active Directory Recycle Bin is effectively the same feature but for directory objects such as user objects, group objects, and computer objects.

Fine-Grained Password Policies   Should administrators have stronger passwords than regular end users? Often, the answer is yes. But before Windows Server 2012, Active Directory didn't offer a way to do that without third-party software. Since Windows Server 2012, you can have multiple passwords policies with each having unique settings.

Revisiting Privileged Access Management

Although we covered PAM in Chapter 8, we are covering it again here from a slightly different angle. As you know, Privileged Access Management (PAM) helps secure a network from attacks, especially credential attacks.

PAM is a concept made up of several technologies to provide better security for IT administration. The key components of PAM include:

◆   A new Active Directory domain in a new forest.

◆   A one-way trust from the existing forest to the new forest.

◆ A Microsoft Identity Manager (MIM) implementation.

◆ Just in Time administration (JIT). JIT is a time-restricted functionality that enables an administrator to temporarily elevate their access rights to perform specific tasks. Instead of always having access rights, you get them for short periods of time (when you need them).

◆ Just Enough Administration (JEA). JEA is a toolkit, based on PowerShell, that enables you to define acceptable administrative commands and computers that administrators can use as part of their work.

Figure 9.1 shows a high-level PAM implementation with the key components.

FIGURE 9.1
Privileged Access
Management

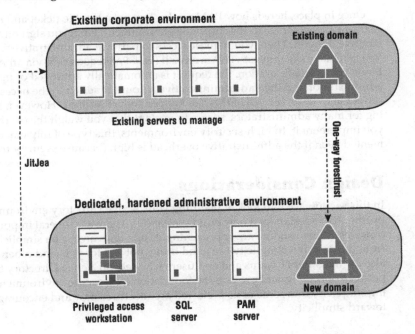

In Figure 9.1, the existing environment is shown at the top. There is an existing Active Directory environment and a server environment. At the bottom is a new environment. It is dedicated to administrative functions (IT people doing administrative work) and hardened with enhanced security (whether configurations or additional software). In the new environment, you build out all new servers and services:

Deploy new servers. Do not use media, updates, scripts, patches, or deployment services from the existing environment. This follows the "assume breach" mindset, which dictates that you presume that the existing environment has been exposed long enough to have been secretly compromised. By deploying without any reliance on the existing environment, you can minimize the chances of the new environment being compromised during the deployment.

Deploy a new single-domain forest. This forest will house administrative IT accounts but not general user accounts.

Implement a one-way trust with the existing domain trusting the new domain. The trust can be a forest trust or a domain trust.

Deploy a Microsoft Identity Manager (MIM) environment in the new domain. In many environments, this is likely to consist of multiple servers. You need the MIM server, a server for the MIM portal (based on SharePoint), and a database server (SQL Server).

Deploy privileged access workstations (PAWs) in the new domain. Administrators will use these workstations to perform administrative tasks. As with the deployment of servers, do not use a deployment method with reliance on any technology or service in the existing domain.

Once in place, here is how PAM works. You get a trouble ticket and need to troubleshoot an issue on a DNS server in the corporate environment. First, you sign into your PAW in the administrative domain. Then, you request access to perform administrative work on the DNS server. You can make the request via PowerShell (New-PAMRequest) or via an API or REST endpoint. Based on the configuration, the request is automatically approved or manually approved by an administrator and then an administrative account is added to the necessary group to troubleshoot the DNS server. All of this can happen in just seconds. However, it is a new way of working for many administrators, so it is important that you weigh the overhead that it brings before you implement it. In high-security environments, this type of implementation is often implemented even if the administrative overhead is high (because security trumps everything else).

Design Considerations

In this section, we will look at planning your Active Directory environment, whether it is for an overhaul, a redesign, or a new build (*greenfield*). There are several important design elements to consider. Many vendors are approaching design with an eye on simplicity, which is a change from the past. But simplicity is a good thing, not just for you (and other administrators), but also for the other IT teams and end users who rely on Active Directory to always be available, perform optimally, and provide the foundation for a secure environment. Microsoft is building simplicity into some of its preferred architectures now and encouraging designs that lean toward simplicity.

Forests and Domains

A forest is the topmost container in an Active Directory environment. Beneath it are domains (at a minimum, at least one domain). Beneath those domains are the *objects* such as users, computers, and groups. A forest has two dedicated naming contexts: the schema naming context and the configuration naming context. Naming contexts are just portions of the overall directory that are replicated independently. A third naming context—the domain naming context—is part of each domain.

A *forest* is the security boundary. This is a change from Windows Server 2000 when a domain was considered the security boundary. If you hear someone say *security boundary*, they mean independent forests that are totally segmented. You can have one set of administrators in one forest and another set of administrators in another forest and feel confident that they can manage only their own forest. With multiple domains in a single forest, administrators in one domain can gain unauthorized access to another domain. Therefore, use forests for high-security environments where boundaries are required.

A *domain* is the topmost container under a forest. A domain is a logical boundary that separates domain-specific objects from other domains in the forest. For example, you might have one domain for users in Europe and another domain for users in North America. You must have at least one domain in a forest. Optionally, you can have many more. Domains underneath other domains are referred to as *child domains*. Domains above child domains are referred to as *parent domains*. The topmost domain is known as the *forest root domain*. Figure 9.2 shows a domain named contoso.com with multiple child domains.

FIGURE 9.2
Forests and domains

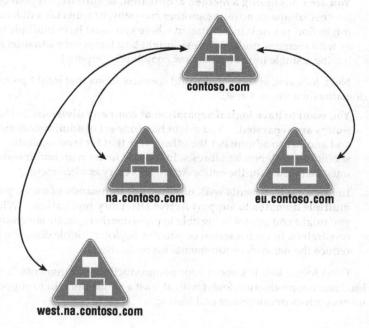

Now that you have an idea of what a forest and domain are, how do you go about figuring out how many forests and domains you need? Let's walk through the process.

First, let's start with a proclamation: always start with a single forest and a single domain. Until you find a good reason to have additional forests or domains. In many cases, after you review the requirements and "nice-to-haves," you'll find that you can usually meet or exceed them with a single forest and a single domain. If you can, then you will be lucky to be able to maintain a simple environment. Let's review some real-world considerations that might drive you to consider multiple forests.

You need to separate the administration of portions of Active Directory due to legal, compliance, or security concerns. In this case, multiple forests might be the only viable option. Because the forest is the security boundary, you might need to have more than one to meet your organization's requirements. Microsoft advocates the use of a secure and dedicated forest for credential portioning. This is referred to as an Enhanced Security Admin Environment (ESAE) and sometimes is called a *red forest* design. In such an environment, all administrative work is performed from the secure forest via dedicated administrative client computers.

You need to run independent instances of an application or service with each requiring its own forest.   For example, Microsoft Exchange Server can have a single Exchange organization in a forest. If you have a separate Exchange organization for two divisions of your company, you need to have a forest for each. This scenario is common when applications modify the schema and you need to deploy independent instances of the application.

You are undergoing a merger, acquisition, or spinoff.   If your company merges with another company, acquires another company, or spins off a division as a separate entity, you might find yourself in a situation where you must have multiple forests. In some cases, such as with mergers, multiple forests might be a temporary situation (with the eventual goal of having a single forest for the new combined company).

Next, let's look at some real-world considerations that might prompt you to consider multiple domains (in a single forest).

You want to have logical separation of company divisions so that users, groups, and computers are separated.   You might have one set of administrators to administer one domain and another to administer the other. Note that for true separation for security concerns, you should use independent forests. In a single forest with multiple domains, all administrators must be trusted for the entire Active Directory environment.

In large environments with hundreds of thousands of users, you might need to have multiple domains to support Active Directory replication.   Without multiple domains, you might end up not being able to consistently replicate successfully due to bandwidth constraints. In such a scenario, you can deploy multiple domains to control replication and reduce the network requirements for replication.

Don't forget to think about your nonproduction requirements. It is a good idea to have at least one nonproduction forest with at least a single domain to support nonproduction requirements such as development and testing.

Active Directory Trusts

An Active Directory *trust* is a relationship between two forests or two domains that enables users to seamlessly authenticate between them or across them. In a simple environment, such as one with a single forest and a single domain, you don't need a trust. Trusts come into play only when you have multiple domains or when you have multiple forests. Let's look at the most common reasons that you need trusts.

You need accounts from one forest to access resources in a different forest.   Although you can do this without trusts, the user experience is degraded. Without a trust, users must provide their credentials when they access resources in the other forest. With trusts, users can seamlessly authenticate to resources in the other forest, as though the resources are in the same forest as their user accounts.

You need administrators from each forest to be able to manage objects and resources in both forests.   This is common in merger scenarios. Imagine that two companies are merging. Each company has administrators who will support the entire environment (with the future intention of all administrators being on the same team in a single combined company). While there are two forests, the trust enables seamless cross-forest authentication.

You have a single forest with multiple domains. The tree structure has multiple child domains, and you need to maximize the performance when users from one of the child domains need to authenticate with a child domain in one of the other trees. See Figure 9.3 for an example of a shortcut trust.

FIGURE 9.3
Trusts

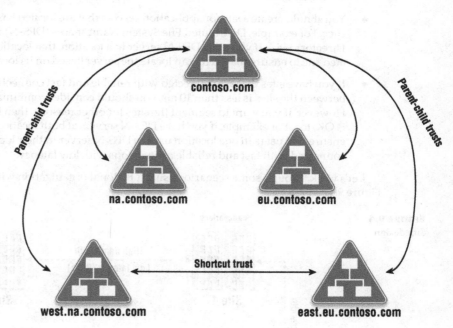

In Figure 9.3, there is a single forest with multiple domains. Imagine that a user in west .na.contoso.com needs to authenticate to east.eu.contoso.com. In such a scenario, without a shortcut trust, the user must traverse up the domain tree (west.na.contoso.com, na.contoso .com, contoso.com) and then down the other domain tree (contoso.com, eu.contoso.com, east.eu.contoso.com) to authenticate. With a shortcut trust, authentication goes directly between west.na.contoso.com and east.eu.contoso.com. This greatly enhances authentication performance.

Active Directory Sites

After your forest and domain are designed, you need to turn to the site design. Sites and site link connections are the foundation for Active Directory replication. In Active Directory, a site is a logical designation for a physical location (such as an office or a data center) or a group of well-connected (reliable and fast connectivity) locations (offices, data centers). Sites are used to facilitate Active Directory replication and to enable clients to locate the closest domain controller or other site-aware service. When you properly design a site topology, you ensure that replication is efficient and you optimize the use of WAN bandwidth. For example, when a user in Boston needs to authenticate, that user can authenticate in Boston instead of going over the WAN to a location a couple of thousand miles away.

Let's look at the considerations for your site design.

◆ You should create an Active Directory site for any location that will house at least one domain controller. This enables clients in the same location to use the local domain controller(s).

◆ You should create a site for application servers that are located based on Active Directory sites. For example, Distributed File System Namespaces (DFS-N) is found by using Active Directory sites. If you put a DFS-N server in a location, that location should have an associated site to ensure that users can locate the server based on its location.

◆ If you have sites that are connected with reliable and fast connections, and the latency between the sites is less than 10 ms, you should consider combining them into a single site. However, if you want to segment the sites for other reasons, then having separate sites is OK, too. For example, if you have DFS-N servers at both locations, you might want to ensure that users in one location use the DFS-N server in their location, even if the sites are connected with fast and reliable connections with low latency.

Let's walk through some scenarios using a fictional organization with four sites. First, review Figure 9.4.

FIGURE 9.4
Site design

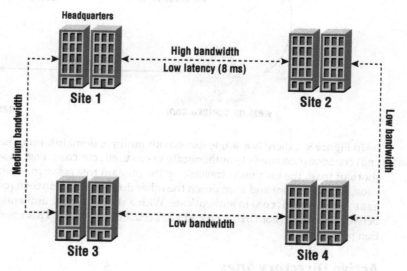

In Figure 9.4, the organization has four sites: Site 1 (headquarters), Site 2, Site 3, and Site 4. We are designing the Active Directory sites based on these physical locations.

Site 1   This is the headquarters site. It is where most of the workers are housed. It is also the site of the primary data center. We need an Active Directory site for Site 1 and at least two domain controllers.

Site 2 This is a branch office site. It is connected directly to Site 1 with a high bandwidth, low latency connection. Site 2 will not have any servers. Therefore, we should consider not having an associated Active Directory site. Instead, we can associate the Site 2 subnets with the Site 1 site. Therefore, users in Site 2 will go to Site 1 for authentication and services.

Site 3 This is a branch office that is connected directory to Site 1 with medium bandwidth. You should create an associated Active Directory site for Site 3 if Site 3 will have servers or if Site 3 has more than 100 users. If the site has a small number of users, such as 25, then you can opt not to have an associated site or any domain controllers. Instead, you can associate the site's subnets with Site 1. However, the key metric will be the latency. If the latency is high, then we recommend deploying domain controllers to the site.

Site 4 This is a sales office but without direct connectivity to Site 1. Site 4 has direct connectivity to Site 2 and Site 3 but low bandwidth for both connections. In this scenario, you should have an Active Directory site and two domain controllers. This enables Site 4 users to work locally, without having to rely on the low bandwidth (and the double hop connectivity to headquarters). There is a high likelihood that users will also have to get to resources in Site 1 but if you can keep authentication and some services locally, that would help improve the user experience. If Site 4 has direct Internet connectivity (and especially if that connectivity is better than the connectivity between offices), then using cloud-based domain controllers is feasible for Site 4. You deploy two domain controllers to the public cloud and have connectivity to those domain controllers over a persistent VPN or similar.

SITE LINK DESIGN

After you design your site layout, you need to turn your attention to the site link design. Site links connect Active Directory sites together to enable replication. Every site should be associated with a site link. Let's walk through our previous diagram, modified with site link information, with a focus on the site links and costs this time. Figure 9.5 shows the site link information.

FIGURE 9.5
Site link design

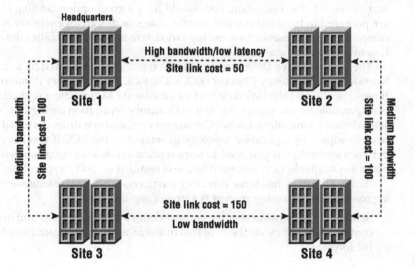

In Figure 9.5, we have four sites and we've opted to have an Active Directory site associated with each one. Now, we must figure out the site links and site link costs. Let's walk through each site and discuss the details.

Site 1   This is the headquarters site. It physically connects to Site 2 and Site 3. But remember, site links are not meant to be logical representations of the physical network connectivity. Although sometimes that is the case, on this network there are two paths to Site 4: going through Site 2 or going through Site 3. Because of the low bandwidth between Site 3 and Site 4, you should opt to replicate through Site 2. By default, site links are bridged. That means they are transitive. Although the diagram doesn't show a site link between Site 1 and Site 4, replication is still possible (by adding up the costs of the available paths).

Site 2   What about replication between Site 2 and Site 3? There are two paths. With equal cost site links (or site link costs that favor Site 2 to Site 4 to Site 3), replication traffic will go over the low bandwidth connection. That isn't ideal. Instead, ensure that your site link costs favor Site 2 to Site 1 to Site 3 (which is the case in Figure 9.4).

Site 3   Site 3 is like Site 2, but with less bandwidth and higher latency to Site 1. In this scenario, we want to ensure that replication to other sites does not go over the low bandwidth connection to Site 4.

Site 4   Because Site 4 has a low bandwidth connection to Site 3, we configure the site link cost higher to ensure that replication isn't preferred for that route. The site link costs are also used when users try to locate a DFS-N server nearby. If DFS-N servers are in Site 4, you want to minimize the chances of users in the other sites using those servers (if other DFS-N servers are available in other sites).

Active Directory Replication

While Active Directory often does an excellent job of building out the replication infrastructure and managing the replication, you should have a good understanding of how it works so you are prepared to troubleshoot and resolve issues or design an environment that meets a specific company's requirements. In some scenarios, you might have to alter the replication configuration to achieve optimal results.

The default Active Directory replication topology is generated by a component named Knowledge Consistency Checker (KCC). The KCC runs on every domain controller in a forest. It uses the site and site link data that you configure to generate a replication topology. The KCC is responsible for managing the Active Directory replication configuration and data such as the sites, domain controllers, Global Catalog servers, and site links. As an administrator, you might need to adjust the replication topology generated by the KCC if you have limited connectivity between some sites, if you need to force replication down a certain network path when multiple paths are available, or if you need to use scheduled or SMTP replication.

Active Directory has three directory partitions. These partitions are often referred to as *naming contexts*. Each naming context is a unit of replication.

Schema   The Schema naming context defines classes, objects, and attributes. This naming context is shared by all the domains in the forest. It is replicated to all domain controllers in the forest.

Configuration The Configuration naming context handles the forest topology, forest settings, and domain settings. For example, it contains a list of all domains, domain controllers, and Global Catalog servers. The DN for the Configuration naming context in a domain named contoso.com is CN=Configuration,DC=contoso,DC=com. This naming context is forest-wide and is replicated to all domain controllers in the forest.

Domain The Domain naming context contains the users, groups, computers, and other objects for a single domain. For example, user and computer objects are stored in the Domain partition. The Domain naming context contains a full replica of the domain but not a replica of other domains in the forest. A Global Catalog server contains the full replica of the domain and a partial replica of all other domain in the forest.

Two types of replication are available:

RPC over IP This type of replication is the default mechanism for replication within a site (*intrasite*) and replication between sites (*intersite*). It is preferred because it is a high-speed protocol. By default, Kerberos is used, which provides authentication and data encryption of the replication data.

SMTP This type of replication can be used for replication between sites (intersite) but not within a site. It will handle replication only between different domains. You should use SMTP only when you have to due to connectivity issues.

HIGH-LEVEL REPLICATION STEP-BY-STEP

Let's look at how replication works. In this walkthrough, we'll show the high-level replication steps that occur when a domain controller named DC01 has a user object named Bob updated and the change replicates to DC02, which is in the same site.

1. The user object is updated on DC01.

2. DC01 checks replication configuration to find its current replication partners.

3. DC01 sends a change notification to its replication partners to tell them that it has updates.

4. The replication partners, in this case just DC02, ask DC01 for all needed changes.

5. DC01 sends the updates to DC02.

6. DC02 updates its copy of the Active Directory database (NTDS.DIT).

Note that, by default, change notification is not enabled for intersite replication. However, you can enable that feature, and it is quite common to use it in medium- and large-sized organizations. By default, domain controllers poll each other on a schedule to find updates. By default, this occurs every 180 minutes for intersite replication. This default setting is often much higher than companies want, so it is uncommon to see the default setting. Many organizations choose to set the default replication interval to 15 minutes, the lowest allowed by the Active Directory Sites and Services tool. You can further reduce the replication interval by editing the Registry, although in most environments you shouldn't do this.

USING POWERSHELL TO MANAGE REPLICATION

You can use PowerShell to review and configure your replication. The following cmdlets are available for looking at your configuration:

- ◆ Get-ADReplicationAttributeMetadata
- ◆ Get-ADReplicationConnection
- ◆ Get-ADReplicationFailure
- ◆ Get-ADReplicationPartnerMetadata
- ◆ Get-ADReplicationQueueOperation
- ◆ Get-ADReplicationSite
- ◆ Get-ADReplicationSiteLink
- ◆ Get-ADReplicationSiteLinkBridge
- ◆ Get-ADReplicationSubnet
- ◆ Get-ADReplicationUpToDatenessVectorTable
- ◆ New-ADReplicationSite
- ◆ New-ADReplicationSiteLink
- ◆ New-ADReplicationSiteLinkBridge
- ◆ New-ADReplicationSubnet
- ◆ Remove-ADDomainControllerPasswordReplicationPolicy

The following commands are available for configuring replication:

- ◆ Set-ADReplicationConnection
- ◆ Set-ADReplicationSite
- ◆ Set-ADReplicationSiteLink
- ◆ Set-ADReplicationSiteLinkBridge
- ◆ Set-ADReplicationSubnet

Flexible Single Master Operation Roles

Active Directory is a multimaster database that enables updates by any domain controller in your environment. A multimaster system provides many benefits, such as more resiliency and higher performance. However, a multimaster system can occasionally have conflicts where two domain controllers try to make different changes to the same object around the same time. For routine updates, such as to user objects, there is a built-in conflict-resolution process that works well. For more complex situations, Microsoft opted to try to avoid conflicts. To do this, they came up with special Active Directory roles. They are called Flexible Single Master Operation roles (FSMO roles). For the specific tasks that each role handles, updates are handled in a single-master fashion. Whichever domain controller is the master handles the updates. The five FSMO roles are listed here:

Schema Master   The schema master role holder is the domain controller that handles updates to the Active Directory schema. For example, if you are updating the schema for Exchange 2016, the updates go through the schema master and then replicate to all other domain controllers. The schema master role is forest-wide, so there is only one per forest.

Domain Naming Master   The domain naming master role holder is responsible for adding and removing domains from the forest and object movement between domains. It is a forest-wide role, so only one role holder exists per forest.

RID Master   Each time a domain controller creates a new object, it combines the domain security identifier (SID) and a relative ID (RID). The RID master role holder allocates pools of RIDs to other domain controllers. Because the RID master role holder is responsible for its domain, you will have one RID master role holder for every domain.

PDC Emulator   The primary job of the PDC emulator role holder is to manage time for the domain. The role holder also handles password changes, authentication failures due to bad passwords, and account lockouts. In a multidomain forest, the PDC emulator role holder at the root domain is responsible for forest-wide time.

Infrastructure Master   The infrastructure master role holder cross references objects in different domains. In a single-domain forest, there is nothing for the infrastructure master role holder to do!

By default, the first domain controller that you deploy will hold all five roles. As part of an implementation, you should plan to separate the roles to improve performance and availability of the roles. It is common to combine the forest roles on one domain controller and the domain roles on another.

Designing the Organizational Unit Structure

An organizational unit (OU) is a logical object in Active Directory that is used to house Active Directory objects such as users, computers, and groups. There are other objects, too, but those aren't important right now. By default, Active Directory has a very limited OU structure and a few default containers. In virtually all environments, you will need to create OUs to meet your requirements.

There are two primary reasons to create OUs:

◆   To facilitate the delegation of administration. For example, if you have a desktop support team that manages all your client computers, you can create an OU named Client Computers. You can store the computer objects for client computers in the Client Computers OU and then delegate that OU to the desktop support team. This enables that team to reset computer objects, delete old objects, and even create new computer objects in that OU. But they can't manage objects in other OUs or containers.

◆   To facilitate the application of Group Policy. Group Policy automates the application of computer and user settings for computers. We will discuss it in detail later in this chapter. For now, understand that each Group Policy Object (GPO) needs to be linked to an OU. The GPO applies to objects in the OU. If you have an OU structure that is friendly to Group Policy, it simplifies your environment. This in turn means less administrative overhead for you, easier troubleshooting, and a higher likelihood for stability.

Real World Scenario

REAL-WORLD OU LAYOUT

Let's look an OU layout for a fictional organization and discuss some of the design decisions. Figure 9.6 shows the OU layout.

FIGURE 9.6
Sample OU layout

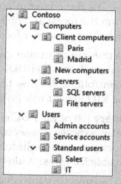

This is a partial OU structure. In this example, the top-level OU named Contoso is at the root of the OU layout, along with the default containers and OUs. In this design, every OU that you need to create should be created under the Contoso structure. Let's walk through some key attributes of this layout:

◆ All computers, whether servers or client computers, are stored in the Computers OU (either under the OU for client computers or the OU for servers). This enables you to target a GPO to all computers (for example, security-related GPOs that target all computers can be linked to the Contoso/Computers OU).

◆ All client computers are stored in the OU named "Client computers." This enables you to delegate client computer administrator to the team that manages the client computers, without having to give them access to other computers (that they don't manage). Further, location-based OUs are used to further segment client computers by location. If you have a desktop support team in Paris, you can delegate administration of the client computers in Paris only. If you have a GPO to enable specific settings for the Paris computers, you can link it to the Contoso/Client computers/Paris OU.

◆ All servers are stored in the Servers OU or in a child OU under the Servers OU. This enables you to facilitate the linking of server GPOs and use the principle of least privilege for delegation. Servers are further segmented by function. With this structure, you can delegate administration of just the SQL servers to the database team. You can link functional GPOs to the functional OUs—or for server-wide GPOs, you can link them to the Servers OU. In some cases, you might choose to break out servers by location instead (or in addition to function). You would do so if it is required for your organizational structure (for example, if you have site-specific admins or you need to apply different GPOs to SQL servers based on their locations).

◆ User accounts are separated by function: regular user accounts in one OU, service accounts in another OU, and administrative accounts in a separate OU. This enables you to target GPOs to users based on function. You might also segment users by location, especially if you have site-specific user support. This enables you to delegate user functions such as password resets to site-specific user administrators.

While we show you a sample layout and walk through some of the benefits of the design decisions, there are many other functional OU layouts that are supported and functional, too. When you design (or redesign) your OU layout, keep the following points in mind:

Don't use OUs as folders.   Some administrators use OUs as folders. They organize Active Directory objects just as they organize data on a file server. This can lead to OU sprawl where you have so many OUs that they become difficult to manage, and troubleshooting is time-consuming.

Before you create an OU, ask yourself if the OU will be used for linking GPOs or for delegating administrative rights.   If neither, you probably don't need the OU. Exceptions do apply, as usual.

Use meaningful names for your OUs.   If another administrator browses through the OU structure, he or she should be able to understand which objects are stored in it based on the name.

Add a description to each OU (use the Description attribute).   When you first create your OU design, you might think that a description isn't beneficial. At that time, you have the entire structure memorized, you've been working on the design, and you are comfortable with it. But fast forward a few years. You might be working at another company and the new administrators don't have the OU design information. That's when the descriptions become especially useful.

Protect your OUs from accidental deletion.   Protection from accidental deletion is a feature of some Active Directory objects, such as OUs. You can set the `ProtectedFromAccidentalDeletion` attribute to $true to protect an OU from accidental deletion. For example, to protect the Madrid OU in our sample structure, run the `Set-ADOrganizationalUnit -Identity 'OU=Madrid,OU=Client computers,OU=computers, DC=Contoso,DC=com' -ProtectedFromAccidentalDeletion $true` PowerShell command. This optional setting is helpful and can protect you if a script or an administrator attempts to delete an OU unknowingly or mistakenly. The protection often makes an administrator think twice. Although they can remove the protection and delete the OU, they will often reach out to the rest of the team to find out if they can delete it before proceeding.

Domain Controllers

The final design element that we'll look at focuses on domain controllers. There are some key design decisions to make prior to implementing your design. Let's walk through the process of figuring out how many domain controllers you need, knowing where to place them, choosing the operating system, choosing the operating system installation type, and configuring the hardware and software components.

Domain Controller Counts and Placement

This section will walk through key considerations to think about when you are figuring out how many domain controllers you'll need for your environment and where to place them. This topic goes together with the hardware sizing that we'll go through a bit later in this chapter.

Here are some important points:

◆ Always place at least two domain controllers at every site that requires a domain controller. If you do, you'll have redundancy at your sites.

◆ If a site doesn't have a secure server room or data center, do not place read-write domain controllers at the site. Instead, use read-only domain controllers that do not store a copy of the Active Directory database locally on the computer.

◆ If a site will have servers, it is usually a good idea to place domain controllers at the site. This is especially important with application servers that depend on Active Directory such as Microsoft Exchange Server.

◆ If a site has 100 users or more, you should consider placing domain controllers at the site. This is a general rule of thumb so there are exceptions (such as if you have 50 users but also have six or eight member servers).

Regarding placement, there are other factors to consider, too.

Where do you put the forest root domain controllers?   Whether you have a single-domain forest or a multidomain forest, you should place the forest root domain controllers in your primary data center. The primary data center is usually the data center with the critical infra-structure and highly available components such as network and storage, and it is often clos-est to the rest of the servers.

Where do you put Global Catalog servers?   A Global Catalog server is a domain controller that has a full copy of its domain information and a read-only partial copy of objects from other domains in the forest. In many environments, all domain controllers are configured as Global Catalog servers. You should consider placing a Global Catalog server in every site that has a domain controller. In your primary data center and key locations, you should have at least two Global Catalog servers. For sites with Microsoft Exchange or other applications that rely heavily on Active Directory and/or Global Catalog services, you might need additional Global Catalog servers.

Besides your own data centers and office locations, you should also consider the public cloud—for example, Amazon Web Services and Microsoft Azure. You can deploy domain con-trollers into Infrastructure as a Service (IaaS) environments in the public cloud. This enables you to deploy domain controllers without needing to worry about the infrastructure, site secu-rity, or server hardware. Using the public cloud is especially compelling when the public cloud provider's data centers are close to your users because that optimizes the end-user experience.

Choosing the Operating System

In a perfect world, you would use only the latest operating system. Today, that is Windows Server 2016. In the real world, it is common to be behind the latest version by one or two versions. Many environments have a mix of different operating systems for their domain controllers. This book is written around Windows Server 2016. As you might imagine, that is the operating system we recommend for your domain controllers—all of them. Let's look at why you might opt to go with Windows Server 2016 over the previous version, Windows Server 2012 R2.

◆ Windows PowerShell 5.0 is built-in. Windows PowerShell 5.0 enhances the security and usability of PowerShell, making it much easier to use for overall management of your environment.

◆ Windows Server 2016 introduces Just Enough Administration (JEA). JEA enables you to secure administration by authorizing specific commands for specific administrators, logging PowerShell transactions, and providing granular role-based access to any resource that can be managed with PowerShell.

◆ Windows Server 2016 introduces Credential Guard. When administrators connect to servers via Remote Desktop Protocol (RDP), their credentials are not stored on the destination server. This protects against Pass-the-Hash (PtH) attacks.

◆ Shielded Virtual Machines are available for Hyper-V running on Windows Server 2016. Shielded VMs protect your virtualized domain controllers (and other VMs) against a compromised virtualization infrastructure.

◆ Networking enhancements are introduced in Windows Server 2016. There are TCP performance improvements to speed up some communications and a new feature named Software-Defined Networking, which enables you to segment workloads.

◆ Windows Server 2016 introduces enhancements to Active Directory Certificate Services (AD CS) and to Active Directory Federation Services (AD FS). We won't cover those enhancements here but instead will cover them in the dedicated chapters for AD CS and AD FS.

Although the list of enhancements with Windows Server 2016 isn't meant to be an exhaustive list of everything new, it does provide a compelling list of enhancements to consider. For a complete list of changes to Windows Server 2016, see "What's New in Windows Server 2016" at https://technet.microsoft.com/en-us/windows-server-docs/get-started/what-s-new-in-windows-server-2016.

CHOOSING THE INSTALLATION TYPE

With Windows Server 2016, you have two choices for the installation type:

◆ Windows Server 2016 full installation (GUI)

◆ Windows Server 2016 Server Core (no GUI)

The default installation type for Windows Server 2016 is the Server Core installation (this default started in Windows Server 2012). Optionally, you can opt for the full installation with a GUI. In the real world, we mostly see the full installation. However, in large enterprises or high-security environments, we see a preference for the Server Core installation type. The target audience for this book should already know about the full installation type. In this section, we are going to look at the Server Core installation type and examine how it is different and why you should consider it for your domain controllers.

◆ Server Core does not have a browser and does not support a graphical browser. This enhances security because your domain controllers are not susceptible to web-based malware. Additionally, the vulnerabilities that are routinely discovered in browsers do not impact Server Core.

◆ Because Server Core is browserless, you don't have to worry about browser add-ons such as Java and Adobe (Flash and Shockwave). Browser add-ons are notorious for having security vulnerabilities and administrators routinely spend a big chunk of time managing hotfixes and versions.

◆ Server Core does not have a graphical user interface. This reduces the attack surface of the domain controller. It also reduces the number of hotfixes that you need to deploy.

◆ Server Core requires less CPU, less RAM, and less disk space. While these components are no longer cost prohibitive, you can eke out a little bit more performance with Server Core than you can with the full installation on the same hardware/virtual hardware.

◆ Server Core encourages remote administration whereby administrators perform all their administration from a remote computer, and not from the domain controller. This enhances security, especially if you choose to use dedicated and secure administrative computers. It also enhances performance by removing the remote RDP sessions and locally running management tools from domain controllers.

Although this isn't an exhaustive list of all the benefits, it paints a compelling picture of why you should consider the Server Core installation type for your domain controllers. But let's talk about the real-world ramifications. We've deployed the Server Core installation to many organizations, used it since its inception, and hear from the community about it regularly. Here are a couple of the downsides to the Server Core installation type:

Some administrative tasks are more difficult to perform. Often, some tasks take longer to perform. This is because some admin tasks are well-suited for the GUI. For example, working with certificates is quick and easy using the Certificates MMC. But without a GUI, it becomes a bit harder. Working with DCOM permissions in the GUI is straightforward. Without a GUI, not so much. You can get used to some of this stuff, but the result is still the same—some administrative work will be a little degraded when you use Server Core.

Some third-party agents and clients might not work. Most of you probably have antivirus agents, monitoring agents, management agents, and security agents running on your domain controllers. Some might not work with Server Core. The good news is that the majority work by default. In some cases, you might lose the GUI of the agent on the domain controller (while maintaining full functionality otherwise). Most of the largest vendors have support for Server Core. But this is an area that you should investigate before you decide on the installation type for your environment.

A final thought about this topic on installation types. Security isn't about simplifying administration or making our jobs easier. The reality is, most of the security technologies available to us make administration more complex and make our jobs harder. But that's part of running a secure environment. It is a trade-off. Each organization must decide how secure they want to be, and the decision is usually based on their industry, the importance and sensitivity of their data, and their agreements with their customers and partners. Our job is to ensure that our environment security meets or exceeds our organization's requirements. Server Core might be one way to get you closer.

SIZING YOUR DOMAIN CONTROLLERS

Here's the good news. You might not have to spend much time sizing your domain controllers. That's because, for most environments, a modern server (something built within the last two years) running on a modern operating system (Windows Server 2012 R2 or later) can easily handle running Active Directory Domain Services, even for a medium-sized organization. As an example, at the time of this writing, we reviewed a major server vendor's server offerings. The default rack server comes with two 6-core Intel Xeon processors and 16 GB of RAM. You can customize it to go with 22-core processors and up to 3 TB of RAM. Of course, you should think about other applications and services besides Active Directory. Some applications (for example, Microsoft Exchange) can put a large workload on Active Directory. Be sure to account for all the workloads during your planning!

If your organization has struggled with the performance of domain controllers, or if you work in a large organization, you should spend some time planning the domain controller size. At a high-level, you should perform the following tasks:

◆ Review the existing environment. Is the current size acceptable? Does it underperform? Are there any existing performance problems? If you aren't sure, you should gather performance statistics. That will be your starting point. Then, move onto the next task, which is assessing the direction of your company.

◆ Is your company on the verge of making a major acquisition? Is growth at 20 percent? Is the company about to split into two independent companies? These are areas to consider because they might impact your sizing (whether you need to size up or size down from what you currently have). You'll use the information you gained from the first two steps to move onto the last step—sizing the domain controllers.

◆ Size your domain controllers (CPU, memory, storage).

Now that we've introduced sizing, let's look at the individual components: CPU, memory, and storage.

CPU

Processors today are incredibly powerful and can handle many workloads with ease. But this is only applicable if you are working with modern hardware or a modern virtualization infrastructure. If your default physical server comes with four 22-core Intel Xeon processors, you are probably not going to have to worry about the processor sizing. However, if your new domain controllers will be virtualized and the virtualization team allocates a single virtual CPU (vCPU) for each new VM, you are going to need to be prepared to explain why you are asking for more. You can use the information you gather in the existing environment review to help you. You need to show what is currently being used, what the projected use is, and how much processing power you need to support that use. You should also know that other applications, such as Microsoft Exchange Server, often have their own domain controller sizing requirements. For example, Microsoft Exchange requires that for every eight Microsoft Exchange Server CPU cores, there must be at least one domain controller CPU core available. If you deploy multiple Exchange servers (and powerful servers) into a single data center, it might impact your domain controller sizing. Beyond Microsoft Exchange, there are a myriad of applications that rely on your domain controllers. Sometimes, these applications don't "behave well." That might mean that the applications query Active Directory inefficiently—maybe too often or maybe searching the entire directory instead of specifying a search base lower in the tree. You also need to be wary of many applications pointing to a single domain controller instead of spreading the load around. These things can put pressure on your domain controller's processor(s).

Memory

With domain controllers, memory plays a critical role in your environment. If you have enough memory, then the entire Active Directory database can fit into that memory, which relieves your storage environment. If your database doesn't fit into memory, then your storage performance becomes much more important. To figure out how much memory your domain controllers need, you need to add up the memory required for the operating system, the total size of your Active Directory database (NTDS.DIT), the size of your SYSVOL, and memory that is required for third-party application agents (antivirus, antimalware, monitoring, management, backup, etc.). Let's walk through an example that represents a typical environment with Windows Server 2016. Table 9.1 represents the memory requirements of all the components in this example.

TABLE 9.1: Domain Controller Memory Sizing Example

COMPONENT	MEMORY REQUIRED
Operating system (Desktop Experience)	2 GB
SYSVOL	200 MB
Active Directory database	2 GB
Management agent	125 MB
Antivirus agent	300 MB
Monitoring agent	100 MB
Antimalware agent	175 MB
Backup agent	124 MB
Minimum RAM required	5 GB

In Table 9.1, you see a layout of the minimum memory required for various components of a domain controller. In some environments, you will have more agents. But note that this is the minimum amount of memory required. When sizing your environment, you need to account for spikes, for growth, for administrative work, and for unknowns. Therefore, for this example domain controller, a good minimum target would be 8 GB. A more conservative approach would be 12 GB. When sizing your domain controllers, you need to rely on the data you gathered while looking at your existing environment. You should perform the following tasks to help:

◆ Review your existing domain controllers to find out how much RAM they are using during various times of the day (especially during peak periods).

◆ Use Performance Monitor to gather data and verify assumptions.

◆ Add in your estimated growth and company changes (mergers or similar things).

◆ Go up to the next amount of RAM for sizing. In other words, if you calculate that you need 9 GB of RAM for your domain controllers, go with 12 GB of RAM. This is mostly applicable to physical servers where adding RAM isn't quick and easy. In a virtualized environment, you can safely go closer to the actual RAM that you need, presuming changes can be made relatively quickly (if needed).

There is one last key consideration about memory for domain controllers. If you are using a virtualized environment, it is a good practice to avoid overcommitting memory on the virtualization hosts. If you do, there is a chance that your domain controllers will be relying on virtualized disks instead of memory when the memory is exhausted. This can have a negative impact on the performance of your domain controllers.

Storage

Storage considerations for domain controllers are mostly limited to storage performance and redundancy, not storage space. That's because the total amount of data for a domain controller is quite limited, often just several gigabytes or less (plus the operating system and program files). Therefore, for this section, we will focus on performance. The end goal with storage performance is to ensure that your domain controllers have adequate performance to service your environment. That might seem generic—and it is. But the idea is to figure out the I/O operations per second (iOPS) required and design the storage to meet or exceed the requirements. We are going to walk through a storage layout based on physical domain controllers with direct attached storage (DAS). Some of this information has limited relevance in a large storage area network or in some virtualized environments, but it represents a good starting point for all deployments. With physical domain controllers, by separating reading, writing, and operating system storage, you can maximize the overall performance of your domain controllers. In Table 9.2, a storage layout is shown that maximizes overall performance. While this layout isn't always feasible in every organization due to budget, time, or manpower, you should strive to get as close as you can in your physical environment.

TABLE 9.2:   Domain Controller Storage Layout

RAID LEVEL	VOLUME
RAID 1	System volume
RAID 0, 5, or 10	Database volume + SYSVOL
RAID 1	Log volume

Let's look at the details of the database volume first. Most activity to the database volume will be read operations. It is estimated that 90 percent of the input/output (I/O) for Active Directory is related to reading data. For most environments, the performance of the reads will be adequate on RAID 0, RAID 5, or RAID 10. What we typically recommend to customers if they can't make precise RAID-level selections per volume is to strive for the volume separation first and then specific RAID levels second. Besides the database, the database volume should also house the SYSVOL data. By default, SYSVOL data will be stored on the operating system volume, and you run the risk of issues if the volume runs out of space.

Now, let's discuss the *log volume*. The log volume is where the database transaction logs are stored. There is heavy write activity. Therefore, you need to choose a storage layout and RAID level that maximizes write performance. Writing across many disks (*spindles*) often increases performance. Writing a single transaction multiple times across multiple disks (spindles) decreases performance. Some RAID levels, such as RAID 5, have parity information that must be written to disk. This adds overhead, especially to write-heavy volumes. For log volumes, RAID 1 or RAID 10 provides good performance while still providing redundancy. If performance were the only consideration, then RAID 0 would be the best choice. Because RAID 0 doesn't have any overhead, it provides the best overall performance. RAID 0 is best suited for specific scenarios where the loss of a server is negligible (such as a large web server farm). For domain controllers, we generally recommend against RAID 0 because it increases the chance of data loss and an outage.

CONFIGURING AUDITING AND LOGGING

Capturing auditing information and logging operational information is important across your entire environment. However, for your domain controllers, it is critical. Because the domain controllers handle authentication and authorization, they are often key targets of malicious users. You need to ensure that your domain controllers are configured to capture data relevant to your organization's security.

Two types of auditing are available in Windows Server 2016:

Basic Security Auditing   Basic security auditing offers nine categories of auditing. This type of auditing has been around for several versions of Windows Server. It can suffice for small environments that demand a simple configuration. But it isn't granular enough to routinely satisfy high security organizations.

Advanced Security Auditing   Advanced security auditing offers 61 auditing settings. It was originally introduced in Windows Server 2008 but not incorporated into Group Policy until Windows Server 2008 R2. Advanced security auditing offers granularity. This enables you to capture what you need without having to capture vast amounts of data.

Note that basic and advanced auditing capture exactly the same data if they are both configured to capture everything. The benefit of advanced auditing is tied to the reduction of data captured, simplifying the management of the data, and reducing storage requirements. If you configure both types of auditing, the advanced audit policy settings take precedence. That's because they are applied last and the existing auditing settings are cleared out before application of advanced audit policy settings.

There are nine categories of basic auditing. Each represents a high-level category, as shown in the Figure 9.7.

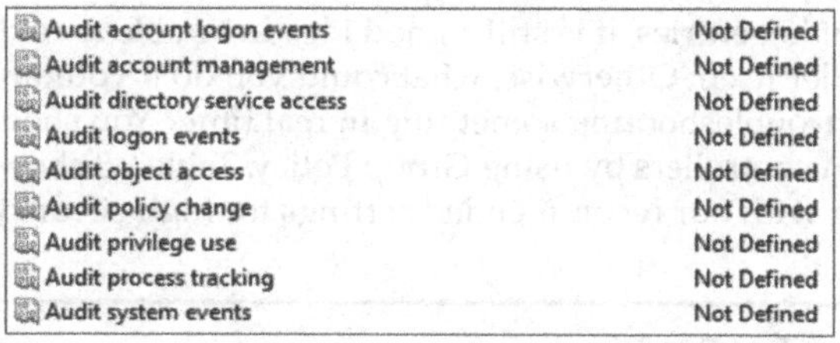

FIGURE 9.7
Basic auditing settings

Audit account logon events	Not Defined
Audit account management	Not Defined
Audit directory service access	Not Defined
Audit logon events	Not Defined
Audit object access	Not Defined
Audit policy change	Not Defined
Audit privilege use	Not Defined
Audit process tracking	Not Defined
Audit system events	Not Defined

For basic security auditing in a high-security environment, you should enable success and failure auditing across all the audit categories. However, that will generate a large amount of auditing data, and managing that data requires administrative overhead. You must figure out where to put it, how to archive it, and how to easily search through it. You might have to use a third-party product to help you. In most environments, you should look at the audit data that you capture and figure out which (if any) categories of auditing your organization doesn't need to capture. Then, adjust the audit settings accordingly. In a perfect world, you would configure auditing to capture just what you need and nothing more.

There are 61 advanced audit policy settings. There are 10 high-level categories that each contain specific advanced audit policy settings, as shown in Figure 9.8.

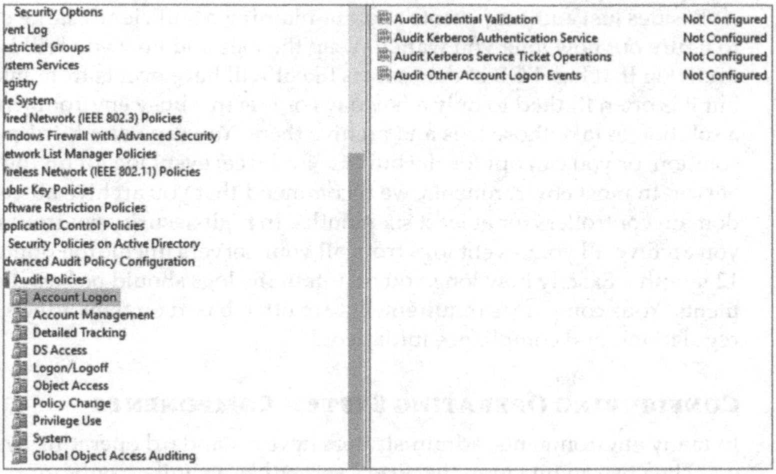

FIGURE 9.8
Advanced audit policy settings

Security Options
Event Log
Restricted Groups
System Services
Registry
File System
Wired Network (IEEE 802.3) Policies
Windows Firewall with Advanced Security
Network List Manager Policies
Wireless Network (IEEE 802.11) Policies
Public Key Policies
Software Restriction Policies
Application Control Policies
Security Policies on Active Directory
Advanced Audit Policy Configuration
Audit Policies
  Account Logon
  Account Management
  Detailed Tracking
  DS Access
  Logon/Logoff
  Object Access
  Policy Change
  Privilege Use
  System
  Global Object Access Auditing

Audit Credential Validation	Not Configured
Audit Kerberos Authentication Service	Not Configured
Audit Kerberos Service Ticket Operations	Not Configured
Audit Other Account Logon Events	Not Configured

In a high-security environment, you should enable success and failure across all audit categories. But, as mentioned previously, you will need to figure out a way to work with all the data. Consider using advanced audit policy settings to enable you to capture everything you need without having to capture information you don't need. That is the biggest selling point for advanced auditing—capture only what you need.

Besides auditing data, you also want to capture data in your Windows event logs. If you use the default settings, your Security event log will not be large enough to hold more than an hour or two of data (on a domain controller in a medium to large production environment). While that might be sufficient if you are archiving all event data to a database and using a third-party tool to review event log entries, it is still a good idea to be able to review a day or two of data on the domain controller itself. Otherwise, what could you do if your archiving system isn't available? Or if you are troubleshooting something in real time? You should control your event log settings for domain controllers by using Group Policy. Table 9.3 shows the applicable settings in Group Policy along with our recommended settings for high-security environments.

TABLE 9.3: Event Log Settings

POLICY SETTING	RECOMMENDED SETTING VALUE
Maximum application log size	262,144
Maximum security log size	4,194,240
Maximum system log size	262,144

Be careful with event log size settings. In earlier versions of Windows, such as Windows Server 2003, the operating system did not support having large event logs and such a setting could cause instability or missed events.

Besides just auditing events and maintaining a sufficiently large event log size, you also need to figure out how long you want to keep the logs and how you will keep the logs. A Security event log that has 4 GB of data seems like it will have events from multiple weeks of activity, but it is often limited to only a few days or less in a busy environment. As logs fill up, you need a solution to take those logs and archive them. You can use a third-party event log archiving solution, or you can opt for the built-in (and free) event log archiving feature built into Windows Server. In most environments, we recommend that you archive all your event logs from all your domain controllers for at least six months. In high-security environments, we recommend that you archive all your event logs from all your servers (including domain controllers) for at least 12 months. Exactly how long you maintain the logs should be based on your company's requirements. Your company's requirements are often based on their adherence to various laws, rules, regulations, and compliance initiatives.

CONFIGURING OPERATING SYSTEM COMPONENTS

In many environments, administrators have a standard operating system deployment for servers. They use an image so that every server has a similar configuration (at least when initially deployed). You should do something similar for your domain controllers. There are many operating system components and settings that can enhance the security, performance, or stability of domain controllers. Once you have standardized on the settings, you should add them to your server image and use Group Policy to enforce settings thereafter. Let's look at some of the key components that we recommend configuring on domain controllers.

Windows Firewall   Unless you use another host-based firewall, you should use the built-in Windows firewall on your domain controllers. It adds some administrative overhead to the initial deployment and to ongoing administration and troubleshooting, but it adds another security layer to a critical part of your infrastructure.

Remote Management   While enabled by default, you should keep it enabled. With domain controllers, virtually all administration should be performed remotely. Only when you cannot perform administration remotely (such as during a troubleshooting situation when remote administration isn't functional), should you perform local administration on a domain controller.

Remote Desktop   The best setting for Remote Desktop isn't as clear-cut as some of the others. By disabling it, you highly encourage remote administration (which is good). However, in a troubleshooting situation, you might have to enable Remote Desktop remotely or from the console (or virtual console). We recommend keeping it on, but there are environments where keeping it off makes sense, too (mostly high-security environments where security trumps uptime and administrative overhead).

Windows Defender   This is on by default. Unless you use another anti-malware product on your domain controllers, you should keep it on. Like the Windows firewall, it offers you another security layer to protect your environment.

User Account Control (UAC)   This is on by default, set to notify you when apps try to make changes to the computer. Administrators often prefer that UAC be set to never notify. However, for domain controllers, we recommend going the other direction and configuring it to always notify. This means that whenever you make any changes to the computer settings, apps are installed, or apps try to make changes, UAC will notify you.

Computer, User, and Group Management

Once you have your Active Directory designed and deployed (or for most of you that are working in an existing environment), your day-to-day administrative tasks shift to object management. The primary objects you will manage are computers, users, and groups. In this part of the chapter, we will focus a section for computer management, user management, and group management. We'll provide some initial information for each section, but the primary focus will be on the operational tasks of managing objects.

Computer Management

Computer objects in Active Directory are like user objects. They share a common set of attributes, although computer objects have a few attributes that user objects don't. Unbeknownst to some administrators, computer objects have passwords! Computers can be granted access to resources, too. Some of the concepts we'll walk through in this section are applicable to computers and users, because of their similarities. But you'll notice that the PowerShell cmdlets change slightly depending on the object type with which you are working.

In the Active Directory schema, a computer is one of the classes. A class is a description of a unique object stored in the directory. There are three types of classes. Computer objects are one of the structural classes. A computer is a subclass of the User class. This is interesting background info, but let's look at some of the information you'll deal with day-to-day.

By default, when you create a new computer object and don't specify the location (such as when joining a computer to a domain), the object will be stored in the default Computers container. Because Computers is a container, you can't link GPOs to it. Therefore, it is a good practice to use an OU for the default location for new computer objects. This enables you to target GPOs to the OU so that new computers get some of your GPOs upon joining the domain. This is important from a security perspective. First, create a new OU for new computer objects. This will be a temporary location for newly joined computers. The permanent location will be based on its location and role (and the OU structure you created). For our upcoming example, we will use the Contoso/Computers/New computers OU from our OU sample layout in Figure 9.6. Then, we'll use the Redircmp command (this command is added to Windows when you add the Active Directory management tools) to update the default location, as shown in the following command:

```
Redircmp 'OU=New computers,OU=Computers,OU=Contoso,DC=Contoso,DC=com'
```

Once you have a new OU for new computers, you should link your security-related GPOs to that OU. This enables new computers, before they are relocated to their final OU, to receive the security-related settings.

 Real World Scenario

MANAGING COMPUTER OBJECTS MANUALLY

In many organizations, most computers objects are created when you join computers to the domain. You join computers to the domain locally after installing the operating system. Or, you might have an automated operating system deployment solution that installs the operating system and joins the computer to the domain (along with other customizations). There are times, though, when you also need to create computer objects manually.

You have non-Windows computing devices or appliances that are going to join the domain. In this scenario, another team manages the devices or appliances. They will walk through the domain join process. But those administrators don't have rights to join computers to the domain. In this scenario, you (as an Active Directory administrator) can create a computer object for the device or appliance ahead of time. During that creation, you typically specify the team or administrator that will join the device or appliance to the domain. That gives them rights to join that one device or appliance to the domain. The creation of the computer object is often referred to as *prestaging* a computer account.

An administrator without administrative rights in Active Directory is deploying a new failover cluster. In this scenario, the Failover Cluster Wizard will automatically create the necessary computer object, but only if the administrator running it has rights in Active Directory. In this scenario, the administrator doesn't have that right. You, as the Active Directory administrator, can pre-create a computer object in Active Directory, and the other administrator can reference that during the failover-cluster-creation process.

To create a new computer named Corp-FS-01, run the `New-ADComputer -Name Corp-FS-01` command.

The computer object will be created in the default location (the Computers container if you didn't update the default location; otherwise, the OU that you've configured as the default location). It will have a sAMAccountName that matches the name (in this case, CORP-FS-01). The computer account password will be assigned automatically, and the computer will be enabled and ready for use.

Beyond creating computer objects, you will also need to occasionally delete computer objects, reset computer account passwords, and move computer objects. Most of these tasks are straightforward using Active Directory Users and Computers or Active Directory Administrative Center. Right-click a computer object, and you can click Reset Account, Move, or Delete.

You can also use PowerShell. Use the following command to reset the local computer account password (on the server that you are signed into and running the command from):

```
Test-ComputerSecureChannel -Repair
```

Use the following command to move a computer object named Server1 in the Computers container to an OU named Servers:

```
Move-ADObject -Identity 'CN=Server1,OU=Containers,DC=Contoso,DC=com' -TargetPath
'OU=Servers,DC=Contoso,DC=com'
```

Use the following command to delete a computer object named Server1:

```
Remove-ADObject 'CN=Server1,OU=Containers,DC=Contoso,DC=com'
```

For computer management, there is another administrative task with which you should be familiar: dealing with "stale" computer accounts. Stale computer accounts are computer accounts in the domain that are no longer in use. In other words, the computer objects are still in the directory but the computer itself was retired, decommissioned, or otherwise taken offline permanently. In a perfect world, every time a computer was retired or taken out of service, the process would include removing the associated computer account from Active Directory—but this doesn't happen often. Eventually, you end up with many stale computer objects in Active Directory. As an administrator, you need to know how to find these computer objects and what to do them with thereafter. Here is our recommended high-level process for dealing with stale computer accounts:

1. Define what a stale computer object is in your organization. Is it a computer that hasn't had any activity in 180 days? Ninety days? Forty-five days? Ninety days is a pretty typical number used in the real world, but you might have reasons to make that number smaller or larger.

2. Run a PowerShell query to find all the stale computer objects. Output the query results to a .csv file. Send the results to key people in the IT department notifying them that the stale computer objects are set for deletion. Give them the date of the planned deletion and give them about two weeks to review the computers.

3. Disable all the stale computer objects and move them to a dedicated OU. Typically, an OU is used for objects pending permanent deletion. Move the stale computer objects to that OU and wait a few days. This is the last safety net before the computer objects are permanently deleted. Because computer objects are disabled as part of this step, this will

be a common time to hear about issues related to the computer objects (because once the computer is disabled, it can't be used and will often uncover uses of computer objects that nobody thought of or remembered).

4. Wait for a week—or two weeks. We recommend waiting at least a few days, at a minimum. After the waiting period, permanently delete the stale computer objects.

5. Repeat this process twice a year.

There are some commands to help you find stale computer objects and move them. Use the following command to find computer accounts that have not signed in for 90 days:

```
Search-ADAccount -ComputersOnly -AccountInactive -TimeSpan '90'
```

Note the use of the single quotes around the time span. While quotes are often optional, they are mandatory with the use of the -TimeSpan parameter.

Use the following command to find computer accounts that have not signed in for 90 days and then move them to the "New computers" OU:

```
Search-ADAccount -ComputersOnly -AccountInactive -TimeSpan '90' | Move-ADObject
-TargetPath 'OU=Stale computers,OU=Contoso,DC=Contoso,DC=com'
```

User Management

In the Active Directory schema, one of the key structural classes is User. A user object represents the User class. In most organizations, a single user object is associated with a single employee, contractor, or any other entity that requires authentication and authorization on your network. For example, when a new employee starts working at your company, you will create new user objects for them. You will populate the object attributes with their identifying information such as their work address, their work phone number, and their manager's name. In your day-to-day administrative work, you will routinely work with user objects. Whether creating new user objects, resetting passwords, or deleting user objects, you'll need to be very familiar with these common tasks.

As with computer objects, there is a default location for newly created user accounts. The default location is the Users container in the root of the tree. Because the Users container is a container, you can't link GPOs to it. Therefore, from a security perspective, you should try not to store user objects there (even newly created user objects). Because user objects in the Users container will not have any GPOs applied to them, you can use the Redirusr command to change the default location of newly created user objects—and you should. To change the default location of user objects to the "New users" under the Contoso OU in the root of the tree, run the Redirusr 'OU=New users,OU=Contoso,DC=Contoso,DC=com' command.

Like other objects in Active Directory, the schema defines the rules about user objects. For example, user objects have a specific set of attributes that are mandatory. In other words, when a user object is created, the attributes must be populated based on the schema rules for user objects. Otherwise, you can't create a new user object. In addition to the mandatory attributes, there are many optional attributes. Optional attributes enable you to populate additional information about the user account, such as contact information, job title, and if the account expires. Figure 9.9 shows the list of mandatory attributes for user objects. Note that this listing is a snippet from the Active Directory Schema management console.

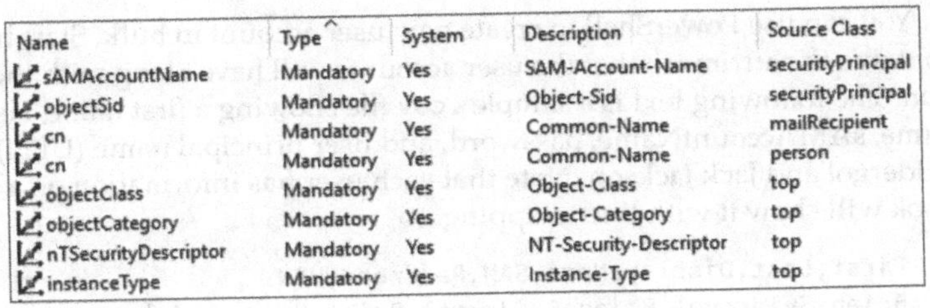

FIGURE 9.9
Mandatory
attributes

Name	Type	System	Description	Source Class
sAMAccountName	Mandatory	Yes	SAM-Account-Name	securityPrincipal
objectSid	Mandatory	Yes	Object-Sid	securityPrincipal
cn	Mandatory	Yes	Common-Name	mailRecipient
cn	Mandatory	Yes	Common-Name	person
objectClass	Mandatory	Yes	Object-Class	top
objectCategory	Mandatory	Yes	Object-Category	top
nTSecurityDescriptor	Mandatory	Yes	NT-Security-Descriptor	top
instanceType	Mandatory	Yes	Instance-Type	top

Mandatory attributes are just that—mandatory. The good news is that the management tools often take care of some of them for you. For example, when you go through the new-user creation process with the wizard in the GUI tools, the tools populate the objectClass, object-Category, nTSecurityDescriptor, objectSid, and InstanceType attributes. In Table 9.4, we look at some of the automatically populated attributes.

TABLE 9.4: Automatically Populated Attributes

ATTRIBUTE	DEFAULT VALUE	DESCRIPTION
objectSid	<Unique, per domain>	Domain prefix + Relative Identifier (RID), unique within domain.
objectClass	User	Calculated based on management tool or command.
objectCategory	CN=Person,CN=Schema,CN=Configuration,DC=Contoso,DC=com	Where in the schema the object category is defined.
nTSecurityDescriptor	Schema + Inherited	Merges inheritable permissions with default permissions from schema for user objects.
instanceType	4	Object is writable in the directory.
sAMAccountName	<none>	The string used to sign in. For example, "Brian."

That covers some of the informational aspects of user objects in the directory. Now, let's walk through some of the management tasks associated with user accounts, such as user creation and user management.

You can use PowerShell to create a new user account and populate a few of the attributes:

```
New-ADUser -Name 'Brian Svidergol' -GivenName 'Brian' -Surname 'Svidergol'
-SamAccountName 'bsvidergol' -UserPrincipalName 'bsvidergol@contoso.com'
-AccountPassword (ConvertTo-SecureString 'Df7838&^3duyreieWWX' -AsPlainText
-Force) -Enabled $true
```

If you don't specify an account password, the account can't be enabled.

You can use PowerShell to create new user account in bulk. Start by creating a `.csv` file that contains the attributes that the user accounts will have along with the user account information. The following text is a sample `.csv` file showing a first name, last name, display name, name, sAMAccountName, password, and user principal name (UPN). It has two users—Brian Svidergol and Jack Jackson. Note that each user has information on a single line, although the book will show it with line wrapping.

```
First,Last,Display,Name,SAM,Password,UPN
Brian,Svidergol,Brian Svidergol,Brian Svidergol,bsvidergol,Df7838&^3duyreieWWX,bs
vidergol@contoso.com
Jack,Jackson,Jack Jackson,Jack Jackson,jjackson,fIEU873#$feiACOVieu8,jjackson@
contoso.com
```

Once you have a `.csv` file, run the following command to create new user accounts from the input file:

```
Import-Csv .\import.csv | foreach {New-ADUser -GivenName $_.First -Surname $_.
Last -DisplayName $_.Display -Name $_.Name -SamAccountName $_.SAM -
AccountPassword (ConvertTo-SecureString $_.Password -AsPlainText -Force)
-UserPrincipalName $_.UPN -Enabled $True}
```

You can get more complex with bulk user creation, too. You can take existing spreadsheets with employee information and map those to Active Directory attributes and then use that for an initial bulk user creation. In medium- and large-sized organizations, it is common to have a human resources software solution that is used to track employees and contractors. The human resources software solution is often the authoritative source for employee identity information (legal name, title, department, employee ID, and similar). The human resources software is typically synced with Active Directory. When the human resources department creates a new employee record in the human resources software, a new Active Directory user account is created during the next sync. This automates provisioning. Some organizations also automate deprovisioning, which works similarly when employees leave an organization.

Beyond user creation, you need to modify user objects on a routine basis. While you can easily use the GUI tools, find a user, and update information in the text fields, it is inefficient if you need to modify many users. Let's walk through a couple of such scenarios.

For the first scenario, use PowerShell to change all user accounts with a department of Inside Sales, Outside Sales, or Sales Department to have a department named Sales & Marketing:

```
Get-ADUser -Filter {Department -like '*Sales*' -or Department -like 'Marketing'}
 | Set-ADUser -Department 'Sales & Marketing'
```

Note that we can filter the retrieval of users in the first portion of the pipeline (during the `Get-ADUser` command) or after retrieving users (prior to using the `Set-ADUser` command). By filtering early in the pipeline, the command runs more efficiently. Instead of having to retrieve every single user and then find users that have departments we are looking for, we can retrieve only the users with those departments (what we do in the example, which is more efficient).

CREATING USER ACCOUNT REPORTS WITH POWERSHELL

One of the common requests you'll get from various parts of your organization is a request for a list of all Active Directory users. Various departments use the information. For example, sometimes software is licensed per user account. Sometimes, the information security team will want to ensure that all the users are authorized and valid. Other times, another IT person might want to use the accounts to automate the granting of entitlements in other applications. Whatever the use, you'll need to know how to generate useful reports. The easiest way to do it is by using PowerShell. In the following command, all user accounts are exported to a .csv file with the specified information.

```
Get-ADUser -Filter * -Properties
DisplayName,Department,Title,Office,City,SamAccountName,EmployeeID | Select
DisplayName,Department,Title,Office,City,SamAccountName,EmployeeID | Export-Csv
-NoTypeInformation users.csv
```

The downside to this report is that it exports a list of all user objects even if they are disabled or in an OU dedicated to service accounts. Often, you should use a filter to reduce which user objects are exported or to just export specific user objects. In the following command, all user accounts that are enabled and not in the Service Accounts OU are exported.

```
Get-ADUser -Filter {Enabled -eq 'True'} -Properties
DisplayName,Department,Title,Office,City,SamAccountName,EmployeeID | Where
DistinguishedName -NotLike '*Service Accounts*' | select
DisplayName,Department,Title,Office,City,SamAccountName,EmployeeID | Export-Csv
-NoTypeInformation users.csv
```

In this command, we use a filter to retrieve only user accounts that are enabled. Thereafter, we use the Where-Object (Where is the alias) to ensure that the exported user accounts are not in the Service Accounts OU. Because we are filtering for the location after we've retrieved all the objects, the query performance is diminished. Filtering with Where-Object is required sometimes.

MANAGING STALE USER ACCOUNTS WITH POWERSHELL

Ever since the Search-ADAccount cmdlet was introduced in Windows Server 2008 R2, finding stale user accounts is greatly simplified. Like computer objects, which we discussed earlier in this chapter, user objects can also become stale. A stale user is one that hasn't signed in lately. "Lately" is a bit vague, but it generally means 60 days, 90 days, or 180 days. You choose. Stale user objects represent a risk to your environment. They are out there, enabled, and ready for use. The user accounts likely have access to company data. It is a good idea to run stale user account queries quarterly so you can remediate the accounts. In the following command, we get all user accounts that haven't signed in for 90 days.

```
Search-ADAccount -UsersOnly -AccountInactive -TimeSpan '90' | where LastLogonDate
-ne $NULL | select Name,LastLogonDate
```

Notice that you use a filter to weed out accounts that have never signed in. That is optional. You might want to look for accounts that have never logged in, although we typically do that separately from the stale user report. Now that you have a list of stale user accounts, what should you do with them? Here is what we recommend:

1. Disable the stale accounts.

2. Move the stale accounts to a dedicated OU such as "Pending Deletion" or a similarly named OU.

3. Send a notification with the stale account names to a subset of the IT department so they can review the accounts. Sometimes, there is a need for a stale user account so this notification is important.

4. Wait seven days.

5. Delete the stale accounts.

RESTORING DELETED ACCOUNTS WITH POWERSHELL

You can restore deleted user accounts by using PowerShell, but that's only if you have enabled the Active Directory Recycle Bin (and prior to the deletion of user accounts that you want to restore). Without the Recycle Bin, a deleted user object is marked as a tombstone and moved to the Deleted Objects container. Most of the populated attributes are cleared (for example, the group memberships). Therefore, restoring objects from the Deleted Objects container isn't very helpful. However, when the Recycle Bin is enabled, a deleted user object is not marked as a tombstone. Instead, it is logically deleted. The attribute data is maintained so that you can restore the user objects to the same state they were in at the time of deletion.

With the following command, you can look at the complete list of deleted objects in the Deleted Objects container.

```
Get-ADObject -SearchBase 'CN=Deleted Objects,DC=contoso,DC=com'
-IncludeDeletedObjects
```

Note the use of the `-IncludeDeletedObjects` parameter. Without that, you won't get any deleted objects! The output of the command includes users and computers. In a large and active environment, you might want to use a filter to reduce the output.

Once you verify that the object you want to restore is there, you can use `Restore-ADObject` to restore it. In the following example, we use PowerShell to restore a user account named Mary.

```
Get-ADObject -SearchBase 'CN=Deleted Objects,DC=contoso,DC=com' -Filter {Name
-Like 'Mary*'} -IncludeDeletedObjects | Restore-ADObject
```

Remember, this works only when the Recycle Bin is enabled. It isn't enabled by default. To enable it for the `contoso.com` domain, you can run the `Enable-ADOptionalFeature -Identity 'CN=Recycle Bin Feature,CN=Optional Features,CN=Directory Service,CN=Windows NT,CN=Services,CN=Configuration,DC=contoso,DC=com' -Scope ForestOrConfigurationSet -Target 'contoso.com'` command.

Group Management

Active Directory is used for authentication and authorization. The authorization part grants users access to resources. As a good practice, when you configure authorization, you should use groups. For example, instead of individually granting a user read access to a shared folder, you should create a group and grant access to the group. Then, in the future, you can add users to the group when they need access to the shared folder. As an administrator, you will routinely work with groups. Before we look at working with groups, let's review some key concepts about Active Directory groups.

GROUP TYPES

Two types of groups are available in Active Directory—security groups and distribution groups. Security groups are used for granting or denying access. Distribution groups are used for email (often, in combination with Microsoft Exchange). In this chapter, we are going to focus on security groups.

GROUP SCOPES

There are three group scopes. Each scope aligns with a few different use cases and scenarios. However, there is also some overlap. In Table 9.5, the scopes are defined.

TABLE 9.5: Group Scopes

GROUP SCOPE	CAN HAVE MEMBERS FROM	CAN BE GRANTED PERMISSIONS IN	NOTES
Domain local	Any domain in the forest (except if a domain local group which must be in same domain)	The same domain	Useful for environments with trusts so you can add Global groups from a trusted domain as members
Global	The same domain	Any domain in the forest	Often used as a role group and then nested into domain local groups
Universal	Any domain in the forest	Any domain or forest	

Many administrators opt to use role-based access control (RBAC) to grant access to users and other administrators. With RBAC, you have groups for roles. Roles are often tied to job functions. For example, you might have a role named "Email administrator," and you might have a group named Email Administrators that is used for that role. The Email Administrators group might be granted access to connect to the email servers by using Remote Desktop. In such a case, it is common to use a domain local group for the permission granting. In this scenario, you might create a domain local group named "RDP-Email" and assign permissions. Then, you would add the Email Administrators role group to the RDP-Email group. Most roles have many permissions combined, and many administrators will have multiple roles. By understanding the group scopes and knowing the limitations of each scope, you will be prepared to implement and support RBAC in your environment.

GROUPS AND TOKEN SIZES

When users sign into a computer, the Local Security Authority (LSA) generates an access token. That token, which is used to gain access to resources, contains the security identifiers (SIDs) for every group that the user is a member of (including nested groups). This works quite well, and most users (and even many administrators) are unfamiliar with the access token creation process. That's because there isn't much need for it. However, things quickly change if the access token gets too big. The access token can hold a maximum 1,024 SIDs. However, nine of the SIDs are used by default. That leaves 1,015 SIDs. This number can vary in the documentation and sometimes is shown as 1,010 SIDs. If a user's access token exceeds the max number of SIDs, the LSA might be unable to create an access token. That results in the user being unable to sign in! This problem is known as *token bloat*. In large enterprise environments (or complex environments), token bloat is often a never-ending battle.

So far, we've described a scenario where a user can't sign in because he is a member of too many groups (and the access token couldn't be generated). However, there are some other issues that can crop up before you get to a point where the access token can't be generated. Let's look at those two scenarios:

◆ A user is a member of a few hundred groups. He can sign in, but he can't gain access to some websites hosted in IIS. This is because IIS, by default prior to Windows Server 2012, allocates 12,000 bytes for the authentication buffer. Windows 7 and Windows Server 2008 R2 also have a default buffer of 12,000 bytes. The good news is that Windows 8 and later, along with Windows Server 2012 and later, have a default buffer size of 48,000 bytes.

◆ A user is a member of a few hundred groups. He can sign in, but he is having sporadic issues with gaining access to some resources that rely on RPC. In this situation, RPC relies on the same sized authentication buffer as IIS. The biggest impacts are when you are running client operating systems prior to Windows 8 or server operating systems prior to Windows Server 2012.

For operating systems prior to Windows 8 and Windows Server 2012, you can set a Registry setting to increase the default buffer size. The setting that controls the buffer size is `HKEY_LOCAL_MACHINE\SYSTEM\CurrentControlSet\Control\Lsa\Kerberos\Parameters\MaxTokenSize`. In many environments, you need to add the `MaxTokenSize` DWORD (32-bit) Value (REG_DWORD). Set the value to 48,000 (decimal).

For IIS, you can create two new values - `MaxFieldLength` and `MaxRequestBytes`. You create these in `HKEY_LOCAL_MACHINE\System\CurrentControlSet\Services\HTTP\Parameters`. Set `MaxFieldLength` to 32768 (note that it goes to 65,534 as a maximum value). Set `MaxRequestBytes` to 32,768 to match the `MaxFieldLength` value. After creating the Registry entries, reboot the server.

For most environments, you should use Group Policy to set the Registry settings. This will help reduce the administrative overhead and ensure that all computers have the same settings.

CREATING NEW GROUPS

Creating new groups in ADUC or ADAC is straightforward. You can right-click the OU where you want to create a group and then use the context menu to start the New Group Wizard. You input the name and choose the type of group and you are finished. In this section, we'll focus on using PowerShell to create groups.

In the following command, we create a new global security group named Finance Department.

```
New-ADGroup -Name 'Finance Department' -GroupCategory Security -GroupScope Global
-Description 'All members of the Finance department'
```

When we create one group at a time, we'll usually use ADUC or ADAC because they are quick and easy. But when we want to create a bunch of groups at one time, we use PowerShell. Imagine that you have a list of 50 groups that you want to create. Put the group names into a text (.txt) file with one group name per line. Save it as Groups.txt. Then, run the following commands to create the 50 groups:

```
$Groups = Get-Content .\Groups.txt
foreach ($Group in $Groups) {
New-ADGroup -Name $Group -GroupCategory Security -GroupScope Global }
```

You can add more complexity to suit your needs. For example, you can use a .csv file as input and have a list of groups with different scopes and different OU locations.

Adding Members to Groups

After you create groups, you usually need to add some members to the groups. Adding a single member is very straightforward. In ADUC, you get the properties for the group, go to the Member tab, and then add the member! In PowerShell, to add a user named Brian to a group named Server Administrators, you can run the following command:

```
Add-ADGroupMember -Identity 'Server Administrators' -Members Brian
```

What if you have a list of 50 users that you want to add to the Server Administrators group? That is also straightforward. Add the users, one per line, to a text file named Users.txt, and then run the following commands:

```
Get-Content .\Users.txt | foreach ($User in $Users) {Add-ADGroupMember -Identity
Group2 -Members $User}
```

Notice the slight change in the method we use here compared to creating new groups. This is a *one-liner*. The previous method used a few lines. In PowerShell, there are often multiple ways to accomplish the same thing. Some are more efficient, while some are easier to understand or remember. Let's look at one more scenario for adding members to groups. Let's say you have a list of 50 users, and those 50 users need to each be added to 50 groups. Add the groups, one per line, to a file named Groups.txt. Add the users, one per line, to a file named Users.txt. Then, run the following commands:

```
$Groups = Get-Content .\Groups.txt
foreach ($Group in $Groups) {
Add-ADGroupMember -Identity $Group -Members (Get-Content .\Users.txt)}
```

Note that this example doesn't have any checks to see if a user is already a member of a group. However, if you are going to routinely do this type of bulk update, you should add checks and error handling to make the script fully featured.

Group Policy

So far, we've looked at designing an Active Directory environment, domain controllers, and object management, but we have barely touched on a key technology in Active Directory: Group Policy. Most of you already know what Group Policy is and probably work with it routinely. We'll skip over the introduction.

Group Policy plays a critical role in most Active Directory environments. That's because Group Policy is often one of the configuration management technologies used to secure servers and client computers. If Group Policy isn't configured correctly, your computers might not be as secure as you need them to be—and that can lead to infiltration or worse.

Before we look at some of the operational aspects of Group Policy, let's work through some of the detailed architecture. A Group Policy Object (GPO) is defined in a set of files and in the Active Directory database. Group Policy template files have the core configuration, such as the GPO settings. A file named `GPT.INI` has the version number of the GPO (each time a GPO is updated, the version number increments). The files are stored in the `SYSVOL\<yourdomain>\Policies` directory on each domain controller. Each GPO has a separate directory in the `Policies` directory. The directory name is the GUID of the GPO, as you can see in Figure 9.10.

FIGURE 9.10
Group Policy template files

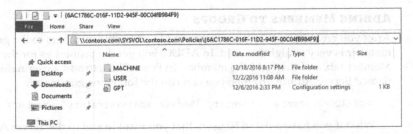

In the diagram, notice the path to the files. You can see that we are in the main directory for a GPO based on the directory being named after a GUID. A subdirectory named `MACHINE` contains any configured computer settings for the GPO. A subdirectory named `USER` contains any configured user settings for the GPO.

In the Active Directory database, there is a Group Policy container that stores other information about a GPO, such as the file path to the GPT files and the display name of the GPO. But where else is Group Policy information stored? Group Policy links are stored as attribute values on objects such as OUs. For example, if you have a GPO linked to an OU, then the OU's gPLink attribute value would be the LDAP (Lightweight Directory Access Protocol) path to the GPO. For example:

```
[LDAP://CN={6AC1786C-016F-11D2-945F-00C04fB984F9},CN=Policies,CN=System,DC=contoso,DC=
com;0]
```

Interestingly, Group Policy is replicated with two different mechanisms. One mechanism, Distributed File Service Replication (DFS-R) replicates the Group Policy template files. In legacy versions of Windows Server (and occasionally in newer version of Windows Server when you've updated or upgraded your domain), File Replication Service (FRS) is used. However, DFS-R is much preferred due to better performance and stability. The second part of Group Policy replication is handled through the regular Active Directory replication (RPC over IP in most cases, although RPC over SMTP is optional but degraded).

Group Policy Inheritance and Enforcement

For some of you, this information might be a quick refresher. If you are very familiar with linking, inheritance, and enforcement, just skip ahead to the next section.

Group Policy linking is the process of taking a GPO and associating it with one or more locations in Active Directory. A GPO can be linked to the domain, to a site, or to an OU. We'll show you how to link GPOs with PowerShell later in this section.

Group Policy inheritance works like NTFS inheritance. Policies linked to parent OUs (or higher level OUs) are inherited by child OUs (and OUs further down). Imagine you have an OU named Servers. Underneath the Servers OU, you have an OU named SQL Servers. If you link a GPO to the Servers OU, it is automatically inherited by the SQL Servers OU. This is typically desired because it reduces administrative overhead (imagine having to link a GPO explicitly to every OU that you need it linked to!), but occasionally inheritance creates problems. Let's look at one such scenario in a diagram, Figure 9.11. Then, we will talk through it.

FIGURE 9.11
Group Policy
inheritance

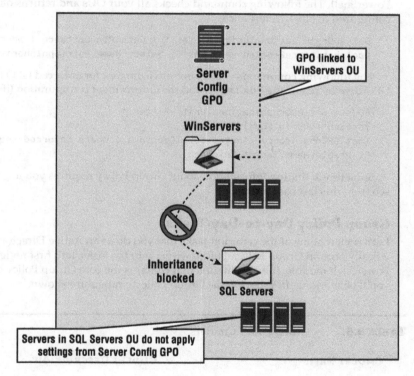

In Figure 9.11, we have a GPO named Server Config. The GPO sets Event log settings for Windows servers. Due to inheritance, the GPO also applies settings to SQL Server computers in the SQL Servers child OU. Sometime later, the database team reports that the event log sizes are not large enough to accommodate the massive amount of event log entries on their database servers. What should you do? You can use Group Policy inheritance blocking! Inheritance blocking is configured at the OU level. In this example, you can configure inheritance blocking on the SQL Servers OU. Then the Server Config GPO won't apply to the computers in the SQL Servers OU. However, be aware that this adds complexity to your environment and complicates troubleshooting. We recommend using inheritance blocking only if you must (for example, you can't change the OU layout or use a WMI filter). There are a couple of other points to discuss about using inheritance blocking:

♦ When you use inheritance blocking, you don't get to choose which GPOs are not inherited. Instead, all GPOs linked at the parent level or higher are blocked.

♦ A GPO link can be enforced. When a link is enforced, it overrides inheritance blocking. That means that an enforced GPO applies even if inheritance blocking is enabled.

If you are like us, you probably want to see if your environment has ample use of inheritance blocking or GPO enforcement in use. Let's see how you can quickly find out by using PowerShell. The following command checks all your OUs and returns only the OUs that are configured to block inheritance:

```
Get-ADOrganizationalUnit -Filter * | Get-GPInheritance | where
GpoInheritanceBlocked -eq 'Yes' | Select Name,Path,GpoInheritanceBlocked
```

The following commands check your environment for enforced GPO links, returning the GPO display name, the link target, and the enforcement configuration (if True):

```
$OUs = Get-ADOrganizationalUnit -Filter *
foreach ($OU in $OUs) {
(Get-GPInheritance -Target $OU).GpoLinks | where Enforced -eq 'True' |
FL DisplayName,Target,Enforced}
```

Sometimes, finding information about Group Policy requires you to get creative, as you can see from this last command.

Group Policy Day-to-Day Tasks

Let's review some of the common tasks that you do as an Active Directory administrator, specifically around Group Policy. Before we get into the tasks, let's first review the GroupPolicy PowerShell module. It is the module that contains the core Group Policy cmdlets with which you'll be working. In Table 9.6, the Group Policy cmdlets are shown.

TABLE 9.6:   Group Policy Cmdlets

CMDLET NAME	CMDLET DESCRIPTION
Backup-GPO	Backs up one GPO or all GPOs in a single command
Copy-GPO	Copies a GPO and its settings to a new GPO within the domain or in another domain in the forest
Get-GPInheritance	Retrieves the inheritance configuration for a domain or OU
Get-GPO	Retrieves the properties of a GPO
Get-GPOReport	Outputs a report in HTML or XML for GPO(s)

TABLE 9.6:   Group Policy Cmdlets   *(CONTINUED)*

CMDLET NAME	CMDLET DESCRIPTION
Get-GPPermission	Retrieves the current Group Policy permissions for a GPO
Get-GPPrefRegistryValue	Retrieves Registry-based preference setting(s)
Get-GPRegistryValue	Retrieves Registry-based policy setting(s)
Get-GPResultantSetOfPolicy	Retrieves RSoP information for a user or computer
Get-GPStarterGPO	Retrieves the properties of a starter GPO
Import-GPO	Imports settings from a backed-up GPO
Invoke-GPUpdate	Refreshes Group Policy on a computer
New-GPLink	Creates a new link for a GPO
New-GPO	Creates a new GPO
New-GPStarterGPO	Creates a new starter GPO
Remove-GPLink	Deletes an existing link for a GPO (but leaves the GPO in place)
Remove-GPO	Deletes an existing GPO
Remove-GPPrefRegistryValue	Removes Registry preference item(s) from a GPO
Remove-GPRegistryValue	Removes Registry policy item(s) from a GPO
Rename-GPO	Renames a GPO
Restore-GPO	Restores GPO(s)
Set-GPInheritance	Configures inheritance blocking or removes inheritance blocking
Set-GPLink	Changes the configuration of a GPO link
Set-GPPermission	Changes the permissions for a GPO
Set-GPPrefRegistryValue	Configures a Registry preference item

FIND EXISTING GPOs

You can use the Get-GPO to get the properties of a GPO. To get all the GPOs, you can run the Get-GPO -All command. Notice that it returns only some information such as the display name, owner, GPO status, and version information. Some things are missing, including the links. To get the links, you need to look at the objects you can link to: OUs, sites, and domains. For example, run the following command to get any GPOs links to an OU named Servers in the Contoso domain:

```
Get-ADOrganizationalUnit -Identity 'OU=Servers,DC=contoso,DC=com' -Properties * |
FL Name,gPLink
```

The output displays the name of the OU and any GPOs that are linked. For example, here is one linked GPO for the Servers OU:

```
[LDAP://cn={788624D2-11E0-40A6-9024-03EACD67D460},cn=policies,cn=system,DC=contos
o,DC=com;0][LDAP://cn={1307DA17-1787-42BA-BF65-F61134FDAA7A},cn=policies,cn=syste
m,DC=contoso,DC=com;0]
```

You might be asking yourself, where is the name of the GPO? The command doesn't retrieve that. Instead, it just retrieves the GPO's GUID. To get the name, you can use the GUID to get the GPO details such as the display name:

```
Get-GPO -Guid '{788624D2-11E0-40A6-9024-03EACD67D460}' | Select DisplayName
```

You might be wondering if there is a better way. There is! You can use the Get-GPInheritance cmdlet. For example, if you want to find out which GPOs are linked to the Servers OU in the contoso.com domain, run the following command:

```
Get-GPInheritance -Target 'ou=Servers,dc=contoso,dc=com'
```

The nice thing about this command is that it reports the display name of the linked GPOs. Additionally, it shows the inherited GPOs that are linked at a higher level but are still applicable to the Servers OU (for example, the Default Domain Policy). The output is shown here:

```
Name                  : Servers
ContainerType         : OU
Path                  : ou=Servers,dc=contoso,dc=com
GpoInheritanceBlocked : No
GpoLinks              : {Server-Config, Windows Firewall}
InheritedGpoLinks     : {Server-Config, Windows Firewall, Default Domain Policy}
```

RUN REPORTS ON EXISTING GPO SETTINGS

If you want to figure out which settings a GPO configures, you should run a GPO report. You can do this in the Group Policy management console or by using PowerShell. To run a report using PowerShell, for a GPO named Server-Config, run the following command:

```
Get-GPOReport -Name Server-Config -ReportType HTML -Path C:\Users\Brian-admin\
Desktop\Server-Config-report.htm
```

The output is quite nice and enables you to browse through the settings quickly and easily. In Figure 9.12, a snippet of the HTML output is shown.

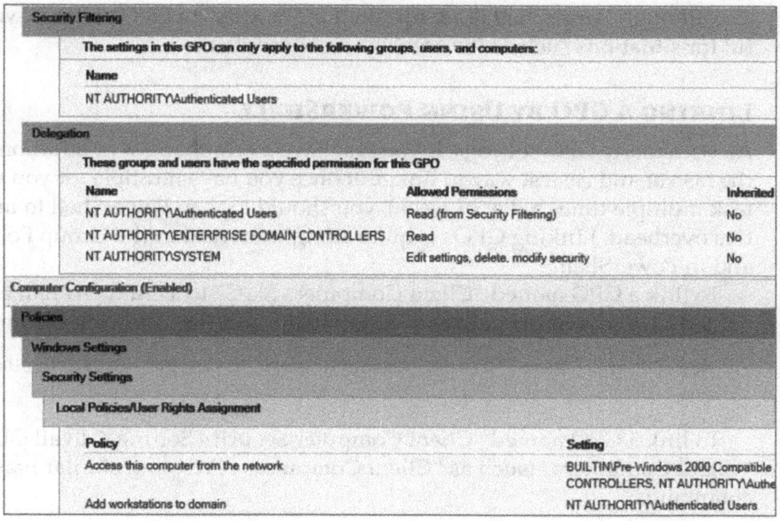

FIGURE 9.12
Group Policy tem-
plate files

FIGURE 9.12
Group Policy template files

You can also export settings to an XML file, which is helpful if you want to reuse the settings for a script.

MODIFY SOME SETTINGS OF A GPO WITH POWERSHELL

Most administrators modify GPO settings by using the Group Policy Management Editor. That's because the GUI tool has been the only way to efficiently modify most of the settings in a GPO (beyond third-party tools). With the introduction of the `Set-GPRegistryValue` cmdlet, we can now modify Registry-based settings in a GPO by using PowerShell. It isn't efficient because you must call out the entire path to the value, know value names, value types, and value settings to create a command. But just imagine that you have 35 GPOs for client computers (one GPO for each branch office), and you have a couple of Registry settings for Internet Explorer that you want to put into all 35 GPOs. That's when the `Set-GPRegistryValue` and PowerShell can be used to make the process much simpler (and faster). Let's walk through how you can do that. First, enter the display names of the 35 GPOs into a text file named GPOs.txt (one GPO display name per line). If your 35 GPOs start with "Client Computer" (such as "Client Computer Dallas" and "Client Computer NYC"), you can run the `Get-GPO -All | where DisplayName -Like 'Client Computer*' | select DisplayName -ExpandProperty DisplayName | Out-File GPOs.txt` command to create the input file. Next, run the following command to add a Registry entry for disabling Adobe Flash in Internet Explorer (this is just an example of one Registry entry). The commands presume that you are running them from the directory where the GPOs .txt file is located. If not, specify the full path to the GPOs.txt file in the first command.

```
$GPOs = Get-Content .\GPOs.txt
foreach ($GPO in $GPOs) {
Set-GPRegistryValue -Name $GPO -Key 'HKLM\Software\Policies\Microsoft\Internet
Explorer' -ValueName 'DisableFlashinIE' -Type String -Value '1'}
```

Although PowerShell is a bit limited for modifying GPO settings, you might still find it useful for situations such as the scenario just described.

LINKING A GPO BY USING POWERSHELL

As with many GPO settings, if you just have a few changes or additions, the GUI tools might be the fastest and easiest way to link. But once you have multiple (or you need to perform the same task multiple times a day or week), you should look to PowerShell to minimize the administrative overhead. Linking GPOs is quite straightforward in the Group Policy management console and in PowerShell.

To link a GPO named "Client Computers NYC" to a child OU named NYC (in a parent OU named Contoso) in the contoso.com domain, run the following command:

```
New-GPLink -Name 'Client Computers NYC' -Target 'OU=NYC,OU=Contoso,DC=contoso,DC=
com'
```

To link a GPO named "Client Computer Security Settings" to all OUs that start with "Client Computers" (such as "Client Computers NYC" and similar names), run the following commands:

```
$OUs = Get-ADOrganizationalUnit -Filter {Name -like 'Client Computers*'}
foreach ($OU in $OUs) {
New-GPLink -Name 'Client Computer Security Settings' -Target $OU}
```

With PowerShell, you can do a lot more. For example, if you wanted to build a .csv file that had the names of your GPOs in Column1 and the OU DNs to link to in Column2, you could use PowerShell to implement the links.

WORKING WITH GPO LINKS BY USING POWERSHELL

Earlier in this chapter, we talked about GPO links, inheritance, and enforcement. In this section, we'll walk through a couple of examples of how to work with GPO by using PowerShell.

To enforce a GPO link for a GPO named Server-Config for the link to an OU named Servers, run the following command:

```
Set-GPLink -Name Server-Config -Target 'OU=Servers,OU=Contoso,DC=contoso,dc=com'
-Enforced Yes
```

Sometimes, you might need to disable a GPO link. For example, if you link a GPO to an OU and the outcome isn't what you expected, you might want to disable that link until you can figure out the problem. To disable a GPO link for a GPO named Server-Config for the link to an OU named Servers, run the following command:

```
Set-GPLink -Name Server-Config -Target 'OU=Servers,OU=Contoso,DC=contoso,dc=com'
-LinkEnabled No
```

To enable the link again, you can change the value of the LinkEnabled parameter to Yes.

TROUBLESHOOTING GROUP POLICY

Group Policy is a complex topic. In some environments, the implementation of Group Policy is also complex. When a GPO isn't applying, or the wrong GPO settings are applying to some computers, you need to be able to troubleshoot the problem and figure out a solution. In this section, we'll look at some common reasons why Group Policy isn't doing what you think it should be doing.

First, let's review a little background. Group Policy relies on Active Directory replication. For the Group Policy templates (the files in SYSVOL), replication is handled by DFS-R (or FRS in legacy environments or environments that are not configured for DFS-R). For the Group Policy container configuration, replication is handled by standard Active Directory replication. As such, you can use built-in tools such as Repadmin.exe to troubleshoot replication issues. For example, you can run the Repadmin /ShowRepl command to view the replication status.

Next, let's look at when Group Policy is processed. By default, member servers and client computers apply Group Policy on startup, when a user signs in, or when policy is refreshed by a command (such as GPUpdate). Group Policy is refreshed on member servers and client computers every 90 minutes (although there is a random offset of up to 30 minutes). Therefore, refreshes can happen up to 120 minutes from the last refresh. Domain controllers are a bit different. While they also apply GPOs in the same situations as member servers and client computers, they refresh GPOs every 5 minutes (without a random offset).

Now, let's look at some of the most common reasons why a GPO named GPO1 isn't doing what it seems like it should be doing:

GPO settings are disabled. Every GPO has two sets of settings: user-based settings and computer-based settings. By default, all settings are enabled (and, therefore, applicable). But you can disable user-based settings or computer-based settings (or all settings). When settings are disabled, they are not applied. When you're troubleshooting, check to see if settings are disabled.

Another GPO has settings that take precedence over the settings in GPO1. The settings in the last GPO that is applied take precedence over the same settings in GPOs applied previously. Therefore, the last GPO to be applied "wins" when multiple GPOs are applying the same settings. There are two contributing factors for when a GPO is applied. One is the processing order. Local GPOs are applied first, GPOs linked to the site level second, GPOs linked to the domain level third, GPOs linked to OUs fourth, and GPOs linked to child OUs last. An easy way to remember this is that the lower the link, the later in the processing order it is. An acronym covers most of it—LSDOU (local, site, domain, OU). This acronym doesn't account for child OUs, but it is a good memory aid. The second factor is the link order. When you have multiple GPOs linked to the same OU, the link order is used to figure out the order of GPO application. The lowest link order applies last and, therefore, wins. For example, a GPO with a link order of 1 is applied after a GPO with a link order of 2.

The security filtering doesn't include the intended users or computers. By default, the security filter for a GPO has the Authenticated Users group. This covers all users and all computers. However, often administrators remove the Authenticated Users group and use other groups to narrow the focus of a GPO. When troubleshooting, check the security filtering and compare that with the user or computer group membership to figure out if the security filtering is configured correctly.

There are some built-in tools to help you track down Group Policy problems. The first place you should start is the Group Policy Operational event log. It has a detailed log of the local computer's Group Policy activities down to a very detailed level. Figure 9.13 shows an entry from the log. Notice the number of events captured at the same time. That should give you an idea of the level of detail captured during Group Policy processing.

FIGURE 9.13
Group Policy
Operational log

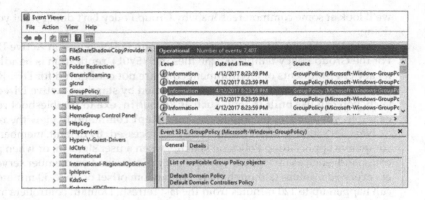

In the Group Policy management console, you can use the Group Policy Results Wizard to evaluate which settings a user or computer will get based on the current Group Policy configuration. You can run it for the local user or computer or a remote user or computer. It displays the settings and details of the GPO.

Also available in the Group Policy management console is a tool named the Group Policy Modeling Wizard. It enables you to simulate a GPO deployment without having to deploy a GPO. This tool will display which settings a user or computer will get if the GPO were to be deployed in the environment. It evaluates slow link processing, loopback processing, group memberships, and WMI filters.

From the command line, you can use GPResult.exe to display the resultant set of policy (RSoP) information for a user or computer (whether local or remote). For example, you can run the GPResult /r /z command to look at detailed RSoP information for the signed-in user on the local computer. To facilitate searching through the information, you can pipe the output to a text file (for example, GPResult /r /z >output.txt). Once you have the output in a text file, you can search through it for keywords such as "fail," "error," "denied," or similar terms.

Finally, let's look at the high-level troubleshooting steps when you are looking at Group Policy issues:

◆ Find out if the GPO applied. You can use the event log to find out, or you can use the GPResult tool.

◆ Find out if the GPO settings applied. You can get the RSoP information to see if the settings applied. Use the GPResult tool or the Group Policy Results functionality in the GPMC to check for applied settings.

◆ If the GPO wasn't applied (and, therefore, no settings applied), find out if a configuration issue is preventing the application. Check the security filter and WMI filter, look for disabled settings or an empty GPO, and make sure the GPO is linked to the right location).

◆ If the GPO wasn't applied but the GPO configuration looks correct, look at the backend. Is Active Directory replication healthy? Did a recent GPO change finish replicating? Is the target computer able to communicate with a domain controller? Try to force a Group Policy refresh by using GPUpdate /Force or Invoke-GPUpdate.

The Bottom Line

Design Active Directory forests and domains.   In many organizations, administrators move to the implementation phase of a project too fast. Often, they implement before they design with the idea of adjusting along the way (or "sometime later"). Often, the adjustments never happen, and the organization is left with the implementation. It might not meet the business requirements or needs, or it might not perform adequately.

Your Active Directory design should reflect your organization's requirements. For example, if branch office performance is high on your organization's list, you should consider placing domain controllers at the branch offices. If your organization requires high availability in a site, you should place multiple domain controllers in each site.

Master It   Your company recently acquired another company. Each company has their own Active Directory environment. The long-term plan is to migrate to a single Active Directory forest and domain. But temporarily, the management team asks you to make the environments work together as seamlessly as possible. Which Active Directory feature should you consider for this scenario?

Solution   In a merger or acquisition scenario, you should consider an Active Directory trust to connect the forests and/or domains. Often, the trust will be a temporary solution until the companies finalize the long-term strategy for the IT infrastructure. In this scenario, a two-way forest trust provides an optimum solution.

Design an organizational unit structure.   You inherited the Active Directory implementation at your company. You find that there are thousands of OUs. Many are empty and seemingly unused. Multiple naming conventions and several OU substructures for housing objects appear to be in use. Remember the following good practices regarding OU management:

◆   Use a single naming convention for OUs to simplify administration.

◆   Add a description to each OU with text indicating the use of the GPO.

◆   Protect OUs from accidental deletion.

Master It   You decide to redesign the OU structure at your company. For each OU, you need to decide whether you should keep it or delete it. Which two factors will you use to figure out whether you should keep an OU or delete it?

Solution   Many factors go into an OU design. Some factors are company-specific. Others are based around good practices identified by IT administrators. In this scenario, you should consider the following factors when deciding whether to keep or delete an OU:

◆   Is the OU empty? If so, that makes it a likely candidate for deletion.

◆   Does the OU have a limited number of objects? For example, is there a single computer object or are there three group objects? If so, then the OU is a good candidate for deletion. Just move the objects elsewhere first!

◆ Are GPOs linked to the OU? If so, then additional investigation is required before you proceed with a deletion. Instead, consider putting OUs with GPO links on the long-term list for further investigation.

◆ Are applications referencing the OU by DN? If so, you will need to perform additional investigation and might need to schedule a deletion or an OU move.

Implement and troubleshoot Group Policy. Group Policy is a big and complex technology. However, an implementation doesn't have to be. You should strive to configure a simple Group Policy environment that meets your company's requirements. Use the following good practices with regard to Group Policy:

◆ Use a naming convention to enable other administrators to understand the primary use of a GPO.

◆ Add a description to GPOs to describe the detailed use of a GPO.

◆ Minimize the use of WMI filters when possible.

◆ Use security filtering to limit the scope of a GPO.

◆ Minimize the use of inheritance blocking and GPO enforcement.

Master It You are troubleshooting a GPO issue. Your existing OU structure has a Contoso-Users OU. Underneath that, there are five child OUs. One of the child OUs is named Sales. A GPO named User Configuration configures user settings and is linked to the Contoso-Users OU. However, the sales users report that the GPO breaks key functionality because they are routinely disconnected from the corporate network. You need to ensure that the GPO doesn't apply to the Sales OU. What are two ways to achieve this?

Solution

In this scenario, you have two primary options:

◆ Block inheritance at the Sales OU. If you block inheritance at the Sales OU, the User Configuration GPO will not be inherited by the Sales OU. While this fixes the issue, it might create other issues. For example, if other GPOs are linked at the Contoso-Users OU, then those GPOs will also be blocked.

◆ You can use security filtering on the GPO. By default, all GPOs have security filtering for Authenticated Users, which enables all users and computers to read and apply GPO settings. In this scenario, you can create a new security group named All Contoso Except Sales. Add all users except sales users to the group. Then configure the GPO security filtering for the All Contoso Except Sales group. This ensures that the sales users won't be impacted by the GPO. This fixes the issue but also introduces some administrative overhead to your environment. For example, how do you maintain the group membership going forward? You can do it manually or use automation, but both will add additional administrative overhead.

Chapter 10

Active Directory Certificate Services

AD CS is a public key infrastructure (PKI) solution for managing certificates in a network. Microsoft has enhanced and expanded AD CS through many of the major versions of Windows Server. The last major updates occurred in Windows Server 2012 R2, while only minor enhancements were made in Windows Server 2016. In this chapter, we are going to discuss Active Directory Certificate Services as it exists today in Windows Server 2016. Like Active Directory Domain Services, Active Directory Certificate Services is a huge topic. It can easily fill an entire book (and has). We'll focus on the most relevant material that most admins must deal with when planning and implementing AD CS. This means that some topics will not be covered in detail in this chapter so that we can focus on the most important.

IN THIS CHAPTER, YOU WILL LEARN TO:

- ◆ Understand What's New in AD CS Windows Server 2016
- ◆ Understand Public Key Infrastructure and AD CS
- ◆ Plan Your Design
- ◆ Implement a Two-Tier Hierarchy
- ◆ Work with Certificate Templates
- ◆ Understand the Benefits of Auto-Enrollment

What's New in AD CS Windows Server 2016

Most new versions of Windows Server introduce new functionality for AD CS. You should be familiar with the features, especially if they help you solve challenges in your environment. Although the following lists aren't exhaustive, they do cover the primary changes for AD CS in Windows Server 2012, Windows Server 2012 R2, and Windows Server 2016. With Windows

Server 2016, AD CS has been incrementally improved with bug fixes and a couple of minor enhancements. The following new features and changes are introduced:

Network Device Enrollment Service Support for Key Attestation Enrollment Enforcement Network devices can take advantage of this feature, whereas in the past, only a Certificate Authority (CA) could take advantage of it.

Key Attestation Improvements Windows Server 2016 allows clients to generate a key pair in a Trusted Platform Module (TPM), which was already supported, or use a smart card key storage provider. This provides a bit more flexibility, especially for organizations with no TPMs deployed or in use.

Windows Server 2012 R2

The following AD CS features are new since Windows Server 2012 R2 and Windows Server 2012 and continue to be available in Windows Server 2016:

Verification That a Certificate's Private Key Is Protected by a Hardware-Based TPM This feature verifies that a private key is protected by a TPM and ensures that the TPM is trusted by the Certification Authority (CA).

Ability to Back Up and Restore a CA Database with PowerShell This feature introduces two new PowerShell cmdlets. Backup-CARoleService backs up the CA database. Restore-CARoleService restores the CA database.

Enhanced Support for Over-the-Air Enrollment AD CS adds support for third-party policy modules for bring-your-own-device (BYOD) scenarios. In such scenarios, a personally owned device can request a certificate from AD CS, even if the device is not domain joined. You can support over-the-air enrollment on the Internet by deploying a Network Device Enrollment Service (NDES) server in the perimeter network.

Windows Server 2012

The following AD CS features are new since Windows Server 2012 and continue to be available in Windows Server 2016:

Enhanced PowerShell Support Managing AD CS with PowerShell prior to Windows Server 2012 was challenging because there were no PowerShell modules for AD CS. With Windows Server 2012, Microsoft introduced deployment and management cmdlets for AD CS.

Support for Version 4 Certificate Templates Version 4 templates are valid for Windows 8 and later Windows client operating systems, as well as Windows Server 2012 and later Windows server operating systems. With Version 4 templates, you can specify a minimum supported operating system (such as Windows Server 2012 R2), and you can require a certificate renewal to use the same key. There is support for cryptographic service providers and key service providers, too.

AD DS Site Awareness Although this new feature isn't enabled by default, it can be enabled so that clients query Active Directory for the nearest site with a CA, which can improve performance such as template-based certificate enrollment.

Protect PFX Files with Group Protection Prior to Windows Server 2012, Windows Server offered only password protection for PFX files. With Windows Server 2012, you can opt to specify an Active Directory group (or even a user) instead of a password. This ensures that only members of the group (or a directly specified user) can work with the PFX file.

Introduction to a Public Key Infrastructure and AD CS

If this is your first time deploying or managing a public key infrastructure (PKI), you should begin your journey by reviewing cryptography, the foundation of a PKI. By understanding cryptography, even at just a high level, you will be better positioned to implement and maintain a well-functioning PKI.

Before we look at some of components of a PKI, we want to review the primary reasons you would deploy a PKI in the first place. Here are some of the most common reasons (note that this list is far from exhaustive):

Protect Internal Websites with HTTPS (Management Sites, Intranet Sites)   To protect websites, you need to issue certificates to the web servers.

Provide Secure Communication (LDAPs) to Your Active Directory Domain Controllers By default, Lightweight Directory Access Protocol (LDAP) traffic is unencrypted on port 389. By issuing certificates to your domain controllers, you can have applications communicate with your domain controllers over an encrypted connection on port 636.

Issue Certificates to Users   Users can use certificates to encrypt email (such as S/MIME), protect data with Encrypting File System (EFS), or use as an authentication factor (sometimes as a second authentication factor for multifactor authentication).

Active Directory Certificate Services is Microsoft's PKI solution. It is a full-featured solution that is in alignment with industry-standard PKI methodologies first described in various Request for Comments (RFC) documents. Figure 10.1 shows the primary components of an AD CS environment.

FIGURE 10.1
AD CS primary components

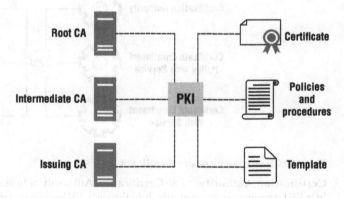

The main components are as follows:

Root CA   A root CA is the top-most CA in a PKI. It is the foundation of a PKI as it issues certificates to the other CAs in the PKI. The root CA's certificate is self-issued. In a small environment, a single CA performs all the CA roles, although such a design doesn't adhere to good PKI practices. In a high-security environment, the root CA is often an offline CA and is brought online only for maintenance. This enhances the security of your PKI.

Intermediate CA An intermediate CA, sometimes referred to as a subordinate CA, is a CA that is subordinate to another CA (often the root CA). Its job is to issue certificates to other CAs (typically, the issuing CAs). An intermediate CA is an optional CA. Some organizations choose to have a root CA and issuing CAs, without an intermediate CA.

Issuing CA An issuing CA is a CA that issues certificates. An issuing CA is often subordinate to an intermediate CA or a root CA, depending on whether the PKI is a two-tier or three-tier hierarchy.

Certificate A certificate is a digitally signed file that contains identifying information about users, computers, or devices along with information about the issuing PKI.

Policies and Procedures As part of your PKI, you define policies and procedures in a few documents: a *security policy* that defines the security standards of your organization, a *certification policy* that outlines how your organization will validate a certificate's subject and a certificate's usage, and a *certification practice statement*, which is a public document that outlines how your PKI is managed and operated.

Template A certificate template is used to predefine certificate configuration items (e.g., validity period, minimum key size, and key usage). Then, when a request comes in for a new certificate using the template, the predefined information does not have to be specified by the requestor. A template helps you maintain security standards, enforce specific certificate configurations, and simplifies the process of requesting a certificate.

Beyond the primary components, you need to be familiar with the six role services that are part of the Active Directory Certificate Services role, as shown in Figure 10.2.

FIGURE 10.2
AD CS role services

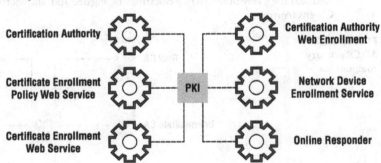

The AD CS role services are as follows:

Certification Authority The Certification Authority role service is the primary role service in a PKI. In some environments, it is the only PKI role service. Your root CAs and intermediate CAs run this role service and issue certificate to users and devices.

Certificate Enrollment Policy Web Service The Certificate Enrollment Policy Web Service provides certificate enrollment policy information to users and computers. It is often combined with the Certificate Enrollment Web Service to enable users and computers to obtain certificates through a web browser.

Certificate Enrollment Web Service   The Certificate Enrollment Web Service enables users and computers to obtain certificates through a web browser. This is useful when a computer is not part of the Active Directory domain. By combining this role service with the Certificate Enrollment Policy Web Service, you can enable automatic certificate enrollment for users and computers.

Certification Authority Web Enrollment   The Certification Authority Web Enrollment role service provides a web-based method for users to request certificates. Without it, users can use the Certificates MMC or command-line tools to request certificates.

Network Device Enrollment Service   The Network Device Enrollment Service (NDES) enables routers, switches, and other network devices to obtain certificates, even without having an associated user account.

Online Responder   The Online Responder role service is responsible for providing certificate revocation information to requestors (typically, computers).

Planning and Design Considerations

Before you start installing and configuring any technology, it is a good idea to work through the pre-implementation tasks. For example, you want to gather requirements from the business. You should gather technical requirements to ensure the implementation meets security and architecture requirements. You should understand the organization's business continuity and disaster recovery requirements and capabilities. While we don't have room to dive into these topics in this chapter, we are going to pick out a few topics that are directly relevant to implement AD CS. That doesn't mean you should avoid the other topics; we just won't cover them here. Let's look at the following questions and see how to go about answering them.

◆ Do you need documentation outlining the security and configuration of your PKI?

◆ Do you need certificate policies and a certificate practice statement (CPS)?

◆ How many tiers do you need?

◆ Who is going to manage the environment?

◆ Which technologies are you using to integrate with certificates?

◆ How many servers do you need?

◆ Where should you place the PKI servers?

DO YOU NEED DOCUMENTATION OUTLINING THE SECURITY AND CONFIGURATION OF YOUR PKI?

Yes, you do! Although the answer might seem obvious, many organizations opt out of documentation, which is unfortunate. In medium- and large-sized organizations, it is common to have existing security policies in place. So, when it comes time to deploy a PKI, you can often use those policies as a starting point for your documentation. Sometimes, the policies might need to be amended to cover a PKI. Small organizations might not have existing security policies, and you might not have the time or personnel to create them. At a minimum, consider drafting up a basic security policy that outlines the goals of the PKI, such as:

◆ Why you are implementing the PKI

◆ Which technologies you plan to protect with the PKI

◆ How you plan to, at a high-level, secure the PKI

◆ How you plan to handle private keys (whether for backup/archival or enabling exportation)

Although many technologies can be documented after deployment (in a worst-case scenario), you should try to avoid doing that with your PKI. The PKI is one of your key security technologies that protects, in many scenarios, your entire computing environment. So, planning, testing, documentation, and implementation are critical to the security of your network.

Do You Need Certificate Policies and a Certificate Practice Statement (CSP)?

Certificate policies and CSPs aren't common in small organizations, but you should consider them even if you work in a small environment. In medium- and large-sized environments, consider certificate policies and CSPs mandatory to effectively meet your organization's requirements (and in some scenarios, your customers' requirements) and maximize security. Let's define these concepts:

Certificate Policy A certificate policy dictates how your organization handles key aspects of certificate allocation, such as the identity of the requestor, the uses of the certificate, and private key storage. In many environments, a certificate policy covers more than just those few areas. The goal is to provide customers (whether internal or external) with enough information for them to figure out whether to use your PKI and its issued certificate, or not.

Certificate Practice Statement (CSP) A CSP documents the security configuration of your PKI. For example, it usually outlines what your organization's practices are regarding certificate revocation and how your organization handles auditing of the PKI. RFC 2527, titled "Internet X.509 Public Key Infrastructure Certificate Policy and Certification Practices Framework," has detailed information about how to craft a CSP and certificate policy. See https://www.ietf.org/rfc/rfc2527.txt for more detail. Your CSP is often publicly available so other organizations can determine if your PKI meets their security requirements (keep this in mind to avoid sensitive information from making it into the document). In large organizations, other divisions or departments can review the CSP to ensure it meets their individual requirements, too. For organizations that are in the business of selling certificates to the public, CSPs are extremely important and very detailed. For example, look at Thawte's CPS at https://www.thawte.com/cps/.

In general, certificate policies are shorter and less detailed. A CSP is often a very long and precise document that gets into the details of an organization's operations around certificate distribution and security.

How Many Tiers Do You Need?

As part of your planning and design, you need to figure out how many tiers you need in your PKI. A *tier* represents one level of your PKI. For example, in Figure 10.3, there are three tiers: one tier with the root CA, one tier with the intermediate (subordinate) CAs, and one tier with the issuing CAs.

FIGURE 10.3
PKI tiers

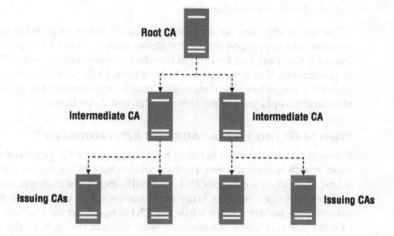

Let's walk through the available tiers and how they are often used in PKI deployments:

Single-Tier Hierarchy A single-tier hierarchy is typically found in small organizations. For example, imagine a law office with 50 attorneys and 150 support staff. In such an environment, there might be a single IT person—and that person must deploy and manage everything! That person requires an easy-to-deploy and an easy-to-maintain PKI. A single-tier hierarchy is likely the best choice. It would consist of a single enterprise CA that issues certificates. Although it is a single point of failure, that might be acceptable in a small organization.

Two-Tier Hierarchy A two-tier hierarchy is a common deployment found in many medium-sized and large-sized organizations. It represents the smallest and simplest PKI hierarchy that provides some additional layers of security and availability that many organizations require but without the complexity and overhead of a three-tier or four-tier hierarchy. A two-tier hierarchy typically includes an offline root CA and one or more issuing CAs. Later in this chapter, we will walk through a step-by-step deployment of a two-tier hierarchy. A two-tier hierarchy enables you to provide a highly available PKI to your organization. This, along with the added security of the offline root CA, is what separates a two-tier hierarchy from a single-tier hierarchy.

Three-Tier Hierarchy A three-tier hierarchy provides what a two-tier hierarchy does, and it provides additional security and flexibility. Instead of issuing CAs being the second tier, policy CAs are the second tier. This enables you to define different policies and different CSPs. For example, you might have one policy and CPS for North America and a different policy and CPS for Europe. In a three-tier hierarchy, it is common to have an offline root and offline policy CAs. This further protects your PKI from network-based attacks.

Four-Tier Hierarchy   A four-tier hierarchy is the least common PKI hierarchy. That's because each time you add a tier, you add complexity and overhead, and many organizations prefer to minimize complexity and overhead. In a four-tier hierarchy, the third and fourth tiers are used for issuing CAs. By having multiple tiers of issuing CAs, you have greater control over which CAs issue certificates to groups of users or computers. This might be required in highly secure and complex organizations, such as a branch of the government or a multinational conglomerate.

So how many tiers do you need? You need as few as possible to meet your organization's security and operations requirements (as well as your PKI requirements). We recommend starting with two tiers and looking at the characteristics to see if it will meet your organization's requirements. If not, then go with three tiers. Only go to four tiers with much scrutiny, and only go with a single-tier if you manage a small environment that accepts the risk of a CA compromise and accepts the potential for unplanned downtime.

Who Is Going to Manage the Environment?

When you consider who is going to manage your PKI, you need to think about two things. First, which team will own it—information security, a server administration team, or another team? Second, in a complex PKI, you will often have multiple teams managing it (and often, different portions of it). In large organizations, it is common to have the PKI owned by the information security team while the PKI is operated by a server administration team. As part of your initial documentation, you need to walk through all the management scenarios to capture who owns what.

Which Technologies Are You Using to Integrate with Certificates?

The idea of deploying a PKI often starts when an application team (or another team in IT) needs a certificate for their application or service. Maybe your organization has been using third-party certificates for everything. For example, you buy a third-party certificate for management servers on your local area network. That can get expensive, and obtaining third-party certificates is sometimes a slow process. However, many third-party certificate providers have enterprise-level services to enable organizations to immediately request and receive third-party certificates. Frequently, deploying a PKI internally comes down to costs and/or security. Some of the most common technologies that integrate with your PKI include:

Email Services   Sending secure email requires a certificate. Enabling secure communication between email servers requires a certificate. Securing the communication from clients checking their email with a browser requires a certificate. So, email services are a common technology that will use your PKI.

Web Services   Whether you have an intranet site or an application management website, you need to use certificates to secure the sites. Today, many large or security-minded organizations use HTTPS across all web services. Your PKI can provide certificates to your web servers more cost effectively than using third-party certificates.

Encryption   Many encryption technologies require the use of certificates. For example, Encrypting File System (EFS) uses client certificates for encryption. An internal PKI is almost always the best choice for this scenario because of the large number of certificates required (costs go up exponentially when using third-party certificates).

As part of your initial PKI design work, you need to collaborate with the IT teams to ascertain their current usage and their future needs. This will help to ensure that you design a PKI that will meet or exceed all the organization's requirements.

How Many Servers Do You Need?

Once you've figured out how many tiers you will have in your PKI, you can figure out how many servers you will need. For the root CA, you need a single server. For the issuing CAs, you should deploy two or more to provide redundancy and high availability. In a three-tier hierarchy, you might have two policy CAs and four issuing CAs (for a total of seven servers with one being the offline root CA). A four-tier hierarchy typically has a minimum of eight servers. It isn't uncommon to see environments with many more servers, especially if there are limited virtualization options in the environment. However, with a strong virtualization environment, you can reduce the total number of servers and rely on the virtualization's high availability and site resilience.

Where Should You Place the CAs?

Placement is often decided per organization. For example, if your organization has two data centers, then you deploy CAs to both data centers. If you have a single data center, then you deploy server(s) to that data center. For large organizations, you won't deploy CAs to every available data center. For example, imagine a company that has 15 data centers across the world. The company might need CAs in only two or three data centers. By maintaining the simplest design that meets your requirements, you can minimize cost and overhead. Fewer data centers often mean a simpler design.

Implementing a Two-Tier Hierarchy

In this section of the chapter, we will show you how to implement a two-tier hierarchy from the beginning. You just need an existing Active Directory domain, one member server running Windows Server 2016, and one standalone server running Windows Server 2016. For this walkthrough, we'll use the following setup:

- An existing Active Directory domain named contoso.com

- A computer named C-OFFLINE-ROOT to be our standalone server, which will serve as our offline root CA

- A computer named C-PKI-01 to be our enterprise subordinate CA

- A computer named C-UTIL-01 to be our utility server, which will host the CRL Distribution Point (CDP) and the Authority Information Access (AIA) information

You should use a lab environment to follow along. Consider using your existing domain (if you have one) and adapt the steps accordingly. If you don't have an existing domain, consider using contoso.com and the exact configuration we walk through in this chapter.

INSTALLING A CA OFFLINE ROOT ON C-OFFLINE-ROOT

In this section, we are going to walk through the installation of an offline root CA. In a two-tier hierarchy, an offline root CA represents one of the tiers (the first tier). It is a good and common practice to use a standalone server (not joined to a domain) for the offline root CA. This is because the server will mostly be powered down and is at risk of losing its domain membership due to lack of connectivity. We recommend that you power up offline root CAs monthly for maintenance tasks, such as the installation of security updates, the installation of antivirus and anti-malware updates, and for the collection of logs. In this section, we will use a server named C-OFFLINE-ROOT. It is a standalone computer not joined to a domain. We manually created a DNS entry in the contoso.com zone so that we can reference the server with the C-OFFLINE-ROOT.contoso.com fully qualified domain name.

1. Log on to C-OFFLINE-ROOT as the local Administrator.

2. Click Start and then click Server Manager.

3. Click Manage and, in the drop-down menu, click Add Roles and Features.

4. If the Before You Begin page appears, select the Skip This Page By Default check box and then click Next.

5. On the Select Installation Type page, ensure that the Role-Based or Feature-Based installation option is selected and click Next.

6. On the Select Destination Server page, ensure that C-OFFLINE-ROOT is selected and click Next. Generally, you would use a management server instead of performing this task directly on the target server, and you would select the name of the server from the list here.

7. On the Select Server Roles page, select the Active Directory Certificate Services check box. When prompted to add features that are required for Active Directory Certificate Services, click Add Features and then click Next. This will ensure that all the required dependencies are installed with the role.

8. On the Select Features page, click Next.

9. On the Active Directory Certificate Services page, click Next.

10. On the Select Role Services page, ensure that the Certification Authority check box is selected and then click Next. Because we're creating an offline root server, we won't need any of the other services, such as online responder or the web services. These services are used to communicate with clients for enrollment or revocation details.

11. On the Confirm Installation Selections page, select the Restart The Destination Server Automatically If Required check box and click Install. Wait for the installation to complete.

12. Once the installation completes, on the Installation Progress page, click Configure Active Directory Certificate Services on the destination server.

13. On the Credentials page, ensure that the credential listed is a member of the local Administrators group and a member of the domain's Enterprise Admins group. Then click Next.

14. On the Role Services page, select the Certification Authority check box and then click Next.

15. On the Setup Type page, click Standalone CA and then click Next. A standalone CA is used when the server will be mostly offline, not connected to a network, or not connected to Active Directory. An Enterprise CA is used for integration with Active Directory.

16. On the CA Type page, ensure that Root CA is selected and then click Next. A Root CA is used as the base for a PKI hierarchy. This contrasts with a subordinate CA, which can be used only under a root CA.

17. On the Private Key page, ensure that the Create A New Private Key option is selected and then click Next. We'll use this option because it is the first CA in the organization. If we already had a CA, we could use an existing key.

18. On the Cryptography for CA page, set the hash algorithm to SHA512, set the key length to 4096, and then click Next. The hash algorithm and key length recommendations change every couple of years. We recommend SHA512 and a key length of 4096 to future-proof your offline root CA (at least for a few years).

19. On the CA Name page, accept the default value of the Common name for this CA, set Distinguished Name Suffix to DC=contoso,DC=com, and then click Next. Note that if this server were joined to a domain, it would populate the distinguished name suffix of the domain automatically.

20. On the Validity Period page, accept the default validity period of 5 years and click Next.

21. On the CA Database page, accept the default location of the certificate database and its log, and click Next. In a production environment, it is a good practice to use a non-system volume for the storage of the database and database log (although not from a performance perspective, such as with SQL Server or Microsoft Exchange Server).

22. On the Confirmation page, make sure the settings are what you need and then click Configure (see Figure 10.4).

FIGURE 10.4
AD CS configuration

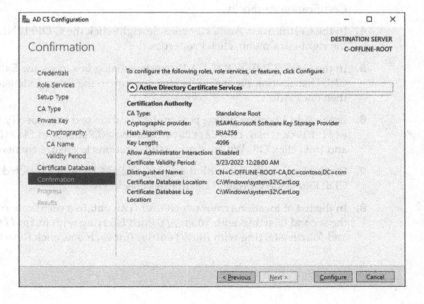

23. On the Results page, wait until the configuration completes and then click Close.

24. On the Installation Progress page, click Close.

At this point, you have installed a root CA. However, before you are ready to move forward with the second tier, you need to perform some post-installation tasks to prepare the root CA for production.

POST-INSTALLATION CONFIGURATION OF CA OFFLINE *ROOT* C-OFFLINE-ROOT

In this section, we are going to configure the offline root CA. This prepares the CA to begin servicing our planned subordinate CA.

1. On C-OFFLINE-ROOT, right-click Start and then click Command Prompt (Admin).

2. From the Administrator: Command Prompt window, configure the CA registry entries under the HKLM\SYSTEM\CurrentControlSet\services\CertSvc\Configuration\C-OFFLINE-ROOT-CA\ registry key and restart the Active Directory Certificate Services service. In the commands, we set the validity period and all of the auditing options. To proceed, run the following commands:

```
certutil.exe -setreg ca\DSConfigDN CN=Configuration,DC=contoso,DC=com
certutil.exe -setreg ca\DSDomainDN "DC=contoso,DC=com"
certutil.exe -setreg ca\ValidityPeriodUnits 5
certutil -setreg CA\CRLPeriodUnits 2
certutil -setreg CA\CRLPeriod "Years"
certutil -setreg CA\AuditFilter 127
net stop certsvc
net start certsvc
```

3. From the Start menu, expand the Windows Administration Tools folder and double-click Certification Authority.

4. In the Certification Authority console, right-click the C-OFFLINE-ROOT-CA node and, in the right-click menu, click Properties.

5. In the C-OFFLINE-ROOT-CA Properties dialog box, click the Extensions tab, ensure that CRL Distribution Point (CDP) entry appears in the Select Extension drop-down list, and then click Add.

6. In the Add Location dialog box, in the Location text box, specify the following http://c-util-01.contoso.com/CertData/<CaName><CRLNameSuffix><DeltaCRLAllowed>.crl and then click OK. We must add valid locations to ensure clients can reach them.

7. On the Extensions tab, with the newly added CDP entry selected, click the Include In The CDP Extension Of Issued Certificates check box.

8. In the list of locations from which users can obtain a certificate revocation list, remove the second (starting with ldap://), third (starting with http://<ServerDNSName >), and fourth (starting with file://) entries (for each one, click Remove, and click Yes when prompted to confirm). Once completed the list should contain only two entries—the first one referencing the local file system (starting with `C:\Windows\system32\CertSrv\CertEnroll`) and the second one using HTTP (starting with `http://c-util-01.contoso.com/CertData`), as shown in Figure 10.5.

FIGURE 10.5
CDP extensions

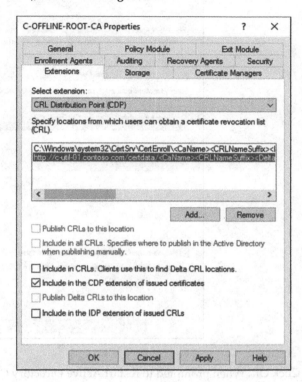

9. In the Select Extension drop-down list, click the Authority Information Access (AIA) entry and click Add.

10. In the Add Location dialog box, in the Location text box, specify `http://c-util-01.contoso.com/CertData/<ServerDNSName><CaName><CertificateName>.crt` and then click OK.

11. On the Extensions tab, with the newly added AIA entry selected, click the Include In The AIA Extension Of Issued Certificates check box.

12. In the list of locations from which users can obtain the certificate for this CA, remove the second (starting with `ldap://`), third (starting with `http://<ServerDNSName >`), and fourth (starting with `file://`) entries (for each one, click Remove, and click Yes when prompted to confirm). Once completed, the list should contain only two entries—the first one referencing the local file system (starting with `C:\Windows\system32\CertSrv\`

CertEnroll) and the second one referencing HTTP (starting with `http://c-util-01`
`.contoso.com/CertData`), as shown in Figure 10.6.

FIGURE 10.6
AIA extensions

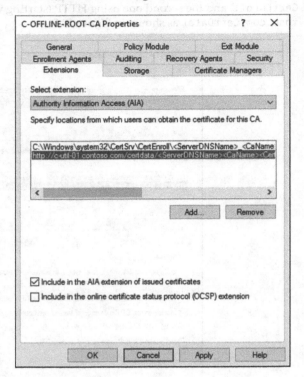

13. Click OK. When prompted to restart Active Directory Certificate Services, click Yes.

14. In the Certification Authority console, expand the C-OFFLINE-ROOT-CA node, right-click Revoked Certificates folder, click All Tasks, and click Publish. Now, we'll publish the CRL to the newly added locations.

15. In the Publish CRL dialog box, click OK to publish a new CRL.

16. From the command prompt, copy the `*.crl` and `*.crt` files from `C:\Windows\`
`System32\certsrv\CertEnroll` to the root of the C: drive by running the `Robocopy C:\`
`Windows\System32\certsrv\CertEnroll C:\ *.cr?` command.

17. From the command prompt, launch the Certificates – Local Computer console by running the `certlm.msc` command.

18. In the Certificates – Local Computer console, expand the Personal folder and its Certificates subfolder, right-click on C-OFFLINE-ROOT-CA certificate, click All Tasks, and then click Export.

19. In the Certificate Export Wizard window, on the Welcome to the Certificate Export Wizard page, click Next.

20. On the Export Private Key page, ensure that the No, Do Not Export The Private Key option is selected and then click Next.

21. On the Export File Format page, ensure that the DER Encoded Binary X.509 (.CER) option is selected and then click Next.

22. On the File to Export page, in the File Name text box, type C:\C-OFFLINE-ROOT.cer and then click Next.

23. On the Completing the Certificate Export Wizard page, click Finish and click OK in the dialog box notifying you that the export was successful.

This completes the post-configuration tasks for the offline root CA. Next, we'll move on to configuring a server to host the CDP. Then, we'll deploy and configure an enterprise subordinate CA.

CONFIGURING A SERVER TO HOST THE CDP

To configure a server to host the CDP, perform the following steps:

1. Log on to C-UTIL-01 as a member of the Domain Admins group.

2. On C-UTIL-01, launch an administrative Windows PowerShell console.

3. From the PowerShell console, create a file share named CertData and grant Read and Change Permissions share-level permissions and Full Control file-system permissions on the folder to the CA-PKI-01 computer account by running the following commands:

```
New-Item -Path C:\CertData -ItemType Directory
New-SMBShare -Name CertData -Path 'C:\CertData' -ChangeAccess 'CONTOSO\C-PKI-01$'
Grant-SmbShareAccess -Name CertData -AccessRight Change -AccountName
'Administrators' -Force
$acl = Get-Acl C:\CertData
$car = New-Object System.Security.AccessControl.FileSystemAccessRule(
"CONTOSO\C-PKI-01$", "FullControl", "Allow")
$acl.SetAccessRule($car)
Set-Acl C:\CertData $acl
```

4. Click Start and then click Server Manager.

5. Click Manage. In the drop-down menu, click Add Roles And Features.

6. If the Before You Begin page appears, select the Skip This Page By Default check box and then click Next.

7. On the Select Installation Type page, ensure that the Role-Based or Feature-Based installation option is selected and then click Next.

8. On the Select Destination Server page, ensure that C-UTIL-01 is selected and click Next.

9. On the Select Server Roles page, select the Web Server (IIS) check box. When prompted to add features that are required for Web Server (IIS), click Add Features and then click Next.

10. On the Select Features page, click Next.

11. On the Web Server Role (IIS) page, click Next.

12. On the Select Role Services page, accept the default settings and click Next.

13. On the Confirm Installation Selections page, select The Restart The Destination Server Automatically If Required check box; when prompted to confirm, click Yes and then click Install.

14. On the Installation Progress page, click Close After The Installation Succeeds.

15. In Server Manager, click Tools and then click Internet Information Services (IIS) Manager.

16. In the Internet Information Services (IIS) Manager console, expand the Sites folder, right-click Default Web Site, and then click Add Virtual Directory.

17. In the Add Virtual Directory dialog box, set Alias to CertData and Physical Path to C:\CertData and click OK.

INSTALLING AN ENTERPRISE SUBORDINATE CA C-PKI-01

Now that an offline root CA is configured and running, we'll walk through the initial installation of the enterprise subordinate CA on a computer named C-PKI-01. This CA will be subordinate to the offline root CA that we just deployed and configured.

1. Sign in to C-PKI-01 as a member of the Enterprise Admins group.

2. Click Start and then click Server Manager.

3. Click Manage and, in the drop-down menu, click Add Roles and Features.

4. If the Before You Begin page appears, click the Skip This Page By Default check box, and then click Next.

5. On the Select Installation Type page, ensure that the Role-Based or Feature-Based installation option is selected and click Next.

6. On the Select Destination Server page, ensure that C-PKI-01 is selected and click Next.

7. On the Select Server Roles page, click the Active Directory Certificate Services check box. When prompted whether to add features that are required for Active Directory Certificate Services, click Add Features and then click Next.

8. On the Select features page, click Next.

9. On the Active Directory Certificate Services page, click Next.

10. On the Select Role Services page, ensure that the Certification Authority check box is selected and click Certification Authority Web Enrollment. When prompted to add features that are required for Certification Authority Web Enrollment, click Add Features and then click Next.

11. On the Select Role Services page, click Next. Notice that this time different options are selected to indicate the role services that are being installed on the server.

12. On the Web Server Role (IIS) page, click Next.

13. On the Select Role Services page, click Next. The necessary IIS role services are already added that will support the AD CS deployment on this server.

14. On the Confirm Installation Selections page, click the Restart The Destination Server Automatically If Required check box. When prompted to confirm, click Yes and then click Install.

15. Once the installation completes, on the Installation Progress page, click Configure Active Directory Certificate Services On The Destination Server.

16. On the Credentials page, ensure that the listed credential is a member of the Local Administrators group and the domain's Enterprise Admins group and then click Next.

17. On the Role Services page, click the Certification Authority and Certification Authority Web Enrollment check boxes and then click Next.

18. On the Setup Type page, click Enterprise CA and then click Next.

19. On the CA Type page, click the Subordinate CA option and then click Next.

20. On the Private Key page, ensure that the Create A New Private Key option is selected and then click Next.

21. On the Cryptography For CA page, set the hash algorithm to SHA512, set the key length to 4096, and then click Next. Note that these options match the root CA.

22. On the CA Name page, accept the default value of the Common Name for this CA, ensure that the distinguished name suffix is set to DC=contoso,DC=com, and then click Next.

23. On the Certificate Request page, click the Save A Certificate Request To File On The Target Machine option, accept the default file `C:\C-PKI-01.contoso.com_contoso-C-PKI-01-CA.req` and then click Next.

24. On the CA Database page, accept the default location of the certificate database and its log and then click Next. As mentioned during the deployment of the root CA, you should use a non-system volume in a production environment.

25. On the Confirmation page, click Configure, as shown in Figure 10.7.

FIGURE 10.7
AD CS
configuration

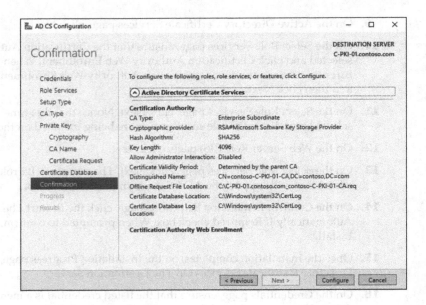

26. Wait until the configuration completes, note the warning regarding installation of Active Directory Certificate Services, and click Close. The warning notice indicates that the subordinate CA needs a certificate from the parent CA, as shown in Figure 10.8. We'll walk through the process to get the certificate from the root CA in the next section.

27. On the Results page, click Close.

FIGURE 10.8
AD CS configuration results

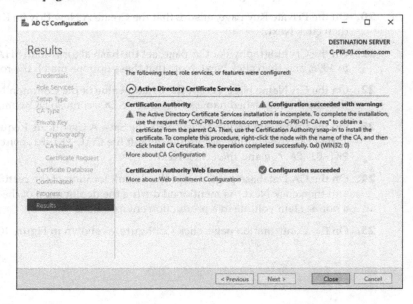

POST-INSTALLATION CONFIGURATION OF ENTERPRISE SUBORDINATE CA C-PKI-01

In this section, we'll perform the post configuration steps for the enterprise subordinate CA, such as configuring the CDP and AIA information and installing the CA certificate.

1. On C-PKI-01, right-click Start and then click Command Prompt (Admin).

2. From the command prompt, create a drive mapping to the C: drive on C-OFFLINE-ROOT (provide the password for the local Administrator account if prompted) by running the `net use Z: \\C-OFFLINE-ROOT.contoso.com\C$ /u:C-OFFLINE-ROOT\Administrator` command.

3. From the command prompt, copy the `C-OFFLINE-ROOT.cer` file from the C: drive on C-OFFLINE-ROOT to the root of the local C: drive by running the `Robocopy Z:\ C:\ C-OFFLINE-ROOT.cer` command. Note that the Robocopy command has a syntax of `<source>` then `<destination>` then `<filename>` (with the filename being optional).

4. Start File Explorer, browse to the root of the C: drive, right-click the `C-OFFLINE-ROOT.cer` file, and in the right-click menu, click Install Certificate.

5. On the Welcome to the Certificate Import Wizard page, select the Local Machine option and click Next.

6. On the Certificate Store page, select the Place All Certificates In The Following Store option, use the Browse command button to set the Certificate Store to Trusted Root Certification Authorities, and click Next. This step ensures that the root CA is trusted.

7. On the Completing the Certificate Import Wizard page, click Finish. Click OK in the confirmation window indicating that the import was successful.

8. From the command prompt, copy the CRL and AIA files you generated from the C: drive on C-OFFLINE-ROOT to the CertData share on C-UTIL-01 by running the `Robocopy Z:\ Windows\System32\certsrv\CertEnroll \\C-UTIL-01\CertData *.cr?` command.

9. At the command prompt, copy the request file you generated to C-OFFLINE-ROOT by running the `Robocopy C:\ Z:\ C-PKI-01.contoso.com_contoso-C-PKI-01-CA.req` command.

10. On C-OFFLINE-ROOT, in the Certification Authority console, right-click the C-OFFLINE-ROOT-CA node; in the right-click menu, click All Tasks and then click Submit New Request.

11. In the Open Request File dialog box, browse to the `C:\C-PKI-01.contoso.com_contoso-C-PKI-01-CA.req` file and click Open.

12. In the Certification Authority console, click the Pending Requests folder and right-click on the request entry; in the right-click menu, click All Tasks and then click Issue.

13. In the Certification Authority console, click the Issued Certificates folder and then double-click the newly issued certificate.

14. In the Certificate window, click the Details tab and then click Copy To File.

15. In the Certificate Export Wizard window, on the Welcome to the Certificate Export Wizard page, click Next.

16. On the Export File Format page, click the Cryptographic Message Syntax Standard – PKCS #7 Certificates (.P7B) option, click the Include All Certificates In The Certification Path If Possible check box, and then click Next.

17. On the File to Export page, in the File Name text box, type **C:\C-PKI-01.p7b** and click Next.

18. On the Completing the Certificate Export Wizard page, click Finish and click OK in the dialog box notifying you that the export was successful.

19. On C-PKI-01, from the command prompt window, copy the ***.P7B** file to the C: drive by running the Robocopy **Z:\ C:\ *.P7B** command.

20. On C-PKI-01, from Server Manager, click Tools and then click Certification Authority.

21. On C-PKI-01, in the Certification Authority console, right-click the contoso-C-PKI-01-CA node, click All Tasks, and then click Install CA Certificate.

22. In the Select File To Complete CA Installation window, browse to the **C:\C-PKI-01.P7B** file and then click Open.

23. In the Certification Authority console, right-click the contoso-C-PKI-01-CA node, click All Tasks, and then click Start Service.

24. In the Certification Authority console, right-click the contoso-C-PKI-01-CA node, and in the right-click menu, click Properties.

25. In the Properties dialog box, switch to the Extensions tab, ensure that the CRL Distribution Point (CDP) entry appears in the Select Extension drop-down list, and then click Add.

26. In the Add Location dialog box, in the Location text box, type **http://c-util-01 .contoso.com/CertData/<CaName><CRLNameSuffix><DeltaCRLAllowed>.crl** and click OK.

27. With the newly added CDP entry selected, click the Include In The CDP Extension Of Issued Certificates and Include In CRLs checkboxes. Clients use this to find Delta CRL locations options.

28. Click Add to add another location.

29. In the Add Location dialog box, in the Location text box, specify the following **file://c-util-01.contoso.com/CertData/<CaName><CRLNameSuffix><DeltaCRLAllowed>.crl** path and then click OK.

30. With the newly added CDP entry selected, click the Publish CRLs To This Location and Publish Delta CRLs To This Location options.

31. In the list of locations, remove the entry starting with "`http://<ServerDNSName>`" and remove the entry starting with "`file://<ServerDNSName>`". Once completed, the list should contain four entries, the first one referencing the local file system (starting with "`C:\Windows\system32\CertSrv\CertEnroll`"), the second one starting with "`ldap://`", the third one starting with "`http://c-util-01.contoso.com/CertData`", and the fourth one starting with "`file://c-util-01.contoso.com/CertData`".

32. In the Select Extension drop-down list, click the Authority Information Access (AIA) entry and click Add.

33. In the Add Location dialog box, in the Location text box, specify `http://c-util-01` `.contoso.com/CertData/<ServerDNSName><CaName><CertificateName>.crt` and then click OK.

34. With the newly added CDP entry selected, click the Include In The AIA Extension Of Issued Certificates option.

35. In the list of locations, remove the entry starting with `http://<ServerDNSName>` and remove the entry starting with `file://<ServerDNSName>`. Once completed, the list should contain three entries, the first one referencing the local file system (starting with `C:\Windows\system32\CertSrv\CertEnroll`), the second one starting with `ldap://`, and the third one starting with `http://c-util-01.contoso.com/CertData`, as shown in Figure 10.9.

FIGURE 10.9
Extensions tab

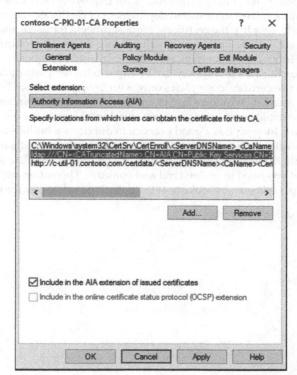

36. Click OK. When prompted to restart Active Directory Certificate Services, click Yes.

37. In the Certification Authority console, expand the contoso-C-PKI-01-CA node, right-click the Revoked Certificates folder, click All Tasks, and click Publish.

38. In the Publish CRL dialog box, ensure that the New CRL radio button is selected and then click OK.

39. As a final step for this section, delete all the copied certificate files and certificate request files on the file system of the servers.

You now have a functional two-tier PKI. At this point, you normally shut down the offline root CA until the next monthly maintenance period. In the remaining sections of the chapter, we'll look at some of the operational aspects of managing a PKI.

Beyond planning and designing a PKI and deploying a PKI, you will also need to know how to operate the PKI by performing common tasks related to a PKI. In the next section, we'll go through a couple of key areas for management including working with certificate templates and configuring automatic certificate enrollment. While these aren't the only two tasks you'll need to know how to do, they represent key starting points.

Working with Certificate Templates

Certificate templates simplify the process for deploying certificates. Not only do templates help administrators ensure a consistent deployment of certificates across their environment, but they also help simplify the certificate request process for users and other administrators. This is because a certificate template can greatly reduce the amount of information that requestors need to know or input during a certificate request. Instead of requestors choosing the key length or whether a certificate's private key can be exported, a template dictates that information.

You can use certificate templates only with Enterprise CAs. Therefore, you won't find templates on a root CA. Windows Server comes with many built-in templates. You could use the templates to deploy certificates, but you shouldn't because the default settings don't provide high security. Instead, it is a good practice to duplicate a built-in template, adjust the settings per your organization's requirements, and then use the duplicated template to deploy certificates. We will walk through the key properties of a certificate template and explain the important options that you need to understand and consider. Thereafter, we'll walk through the process step-by-step. Let's start by looking at the default templates, as shown in Figure 10.10.

FIGURE 10.10
Built-in templates

FIGURE 10.10
Built-in templates

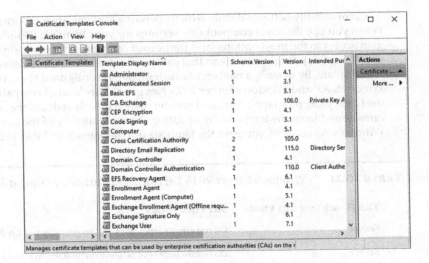

Figure 10.11 shows some of the built-in templates. To get started with your own templates, right-click the template you want to duplicate and then click Duplicate Template. A new window with several tabs will be displayed. From there, you can customize the settings in the tabs to meet your organization's requirements.

FIGURE 10.11
Compatibility tab

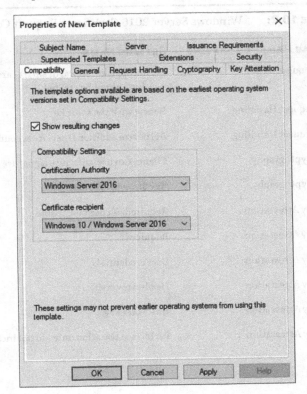

Compatibility settings dictate which operating systems are supported for the template. When you use the latest compatibility settings for your template (Windows Server 2016), you gain access to the most options (and the newest options). This is usually a good thing for security. However, it might also mean that earlier versions of Windows Server won't be able to use the template. By default, a new certificate template is configured to enable compatibility with Windows XP and Windows Server 2003. Not good! This level of compatibility also limits you to the Legacy Cryptographic Service Provider, which greatly reduces the security of your certificates issued from the template. By updating the compatibility of the Certification Authority to Windows Server 2016, you gain the template options shown in Table 10.1.

TABLE 10.1:   Windows Server 2016 Certification Authority Compatibility Settings

TAB NAME FOR SETTING	SETTING NAME
Server	Do not store certificates and requests in the CA database.
Server	Do not include revocation information in issued certificates.

By updating the certificate request compatibility to Windows 10/Windows Server 2016, you gain the template options shown in Table 10.2.

TABLE 10.2:   Windows Server 2016 Certificate Request Compatibility Settings

TAB NAME FOR SETTING	SETTING NAME
Request Handling	For automatic renewal of smart card certificates, use the existing key if a new key cannot be created.
Request Handling	Renew with the same key.
Request Handling	Authorize additional service accounts to access the private key.
Cryptography	Clients can use a discrete signature during certificate requests.
Cryptography	Key Storage Provider
Key Attestation	Required, if client is capable
Key Attestation	Required
Key Attestation	User credentials
Key Attestation	Hardware certificate
Key Attestation	Hardware key
Key Attestation	Perform attestation only (do not include issuance policies).

TABLE 10.2: Windows Server 2016 Certificate Request Compatibility Settings *(CONTINUED)*

TAB NAME FOR SETTING	SETTING NAME
Subject Name	Use subject information from existing certificates for auto-enrollment renewal requests.
Issuance Requirements	Allow key-based renewal.
Extensions	Basic Constraints
Extensions	Enable requestor specified issuance policies.

We recommend that you use the least compatible settings based on the operating system versions that will use the certificate template. In high security environments, you should create version-specific templates so that you take advantage of the security options available, even if just for a subset of your computers.

On the General tab (see Figure 10.12), you name your template, specify the validity period, specify the renewal period, and choose whether to publish the certificate in Active Directory:

Template Display Name   Use a descriptive name that is meaningful to administrators and users who will be requesting certificates.

Template Name   This is automatically populated based on the display name.

Validity Period   By default, it is one year. You can decrease or increase it, based on the certificate usage. In general, the shorter the validity period, the more secure the certificate is. However, like most areas of security, you need to balance security and usability. For example, you can set a validity period to just a few hours. But that means certificate renewals are going to be happening constantly and will likely impact performance and management. On the other hand, a validity period of several years is often not feasible because it exposes certificates to extended attacks. In addition, you can't take immediate advantage of security enhancements (such as key sizes) without swapping out the certificate.

Renewal Period   The renewal period, by default, is set to six weeks. This means that renewal will be attempted when there are six weeks left in the validity period. Note that this renewal period is only valid if reenrollment is enabled on the template.

Publish Certificate in Active Directory   This option, when enabled, publishes the certificate as an attribute on a user or computer object in Active Directory.

FIGURE 10.12
General tab

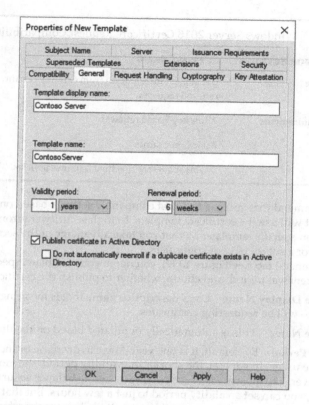

The Request Handling tab (see Figure 10.13) has several optional features. By default, all of them are disabled. While most of the options are self-explanatory, you should be aware of the security implications of enabling a private key to be exported on a template. When you enable the exportation of a private key, you decrease the security of the certificate. In most scenarios, you should avoid enabling that option. But there are some valid use cases, such as when a certificate is being shared across multiple computers and you want to be able to export and import easily. The following options are available on the Request Handling tab.

- Delete revoked or expired certificates (do not archive)

- Include symmetric algorithms allowed by the subject

- Archive subject's encryption private key

- Use advanced Symmetric algorithm to send the key to the CA

- Authorize additional service accounts to access the private key

- Allow private key to be exported

- Renew with the same key

- For automatic renewal of smart card certificates, use the existing key if a new key cannot be created

- Enroll subject without requiring any user input

- Prompt the user during enrollment

- Prompt the user during enrollment and require user input when the private key is used

FIGURE 10.13
Request Handling
tab

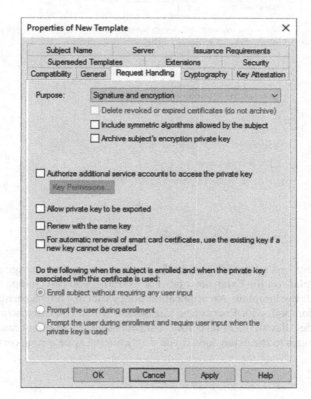

On the Cryptography tab (see Figure 10.14), you can choose the provider category, algorithm name, minimum key size, and whether requests must use a specific list of providers or any provider available on the subject's computer. You can set the request hash (MD2, MD4, MD5, SHA1, SHA256, SHA384, SHA512) and whether to use an alternative signature format. The provider category supports two options: the Legacy Cryptographic Service Provider and the Key Storage Provider. When you use the Legacy Cryptographic Service Provider, you lose the ability to choose the algorithm name or hash type. In most cases, you should opt to use the Key Storage Provider because it is newer and offers enhanced security (such as support for the latest enhanced key storage mechanisms, stronger key algorithms, and stronger signature algorithms). Besides specifying the provider category, you can also specify the minimum key size. At the time of this writing, the default (and most often used) minimum key size is 2,048 bits. However, we recommend that you opt for a minimum key size of 4,096 bits to enhance security.

FIGURE 10.14
Cryptography tab

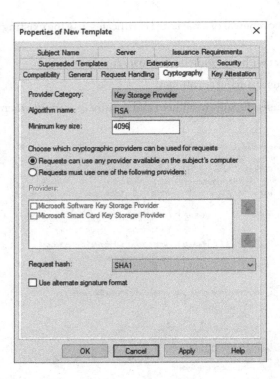

On the Extensions tab (see Figure 10.15), you can review and change some key details of a certificate template on the Extensions tab. For example, you can change the application policies associated with the template. An application policy dictates how a certificate can be used, such as an application policy for Encrypting File System (EFS). You can also add issuance policies. Issuance policies dictate the criteria for certificate issuance. In many cases, you won't have to make any changes to the extensions if you duplicate the appropriate certificate template.

FIGURE 10.15
Extensions tab

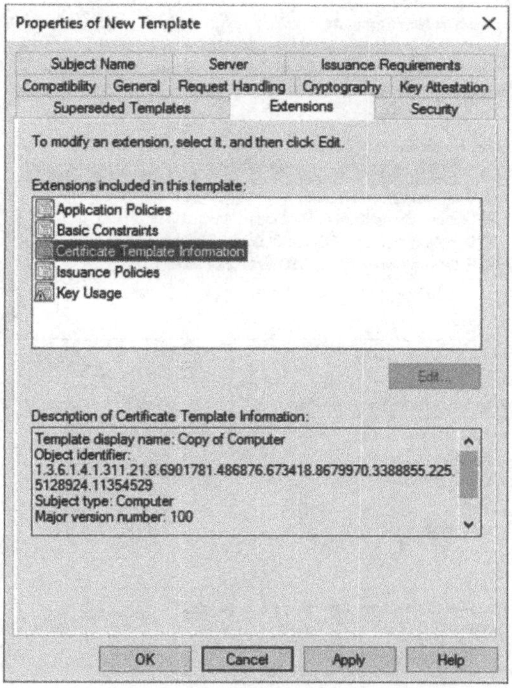

On the Security tab (see Figure 10.16), you configure which rights users and groups have—for example, whether members of the Sales department can request a certificate using the template. If you want to grant a user or group rights to request a certificate using a template, it is important to note that beyond Read permissions, you must grant Enroll permissions, too. There is a separate permission for automatic enrollment (see later in this chapter for a section on setting up auto-enrollment).

FIGURE 10.16
Security tab

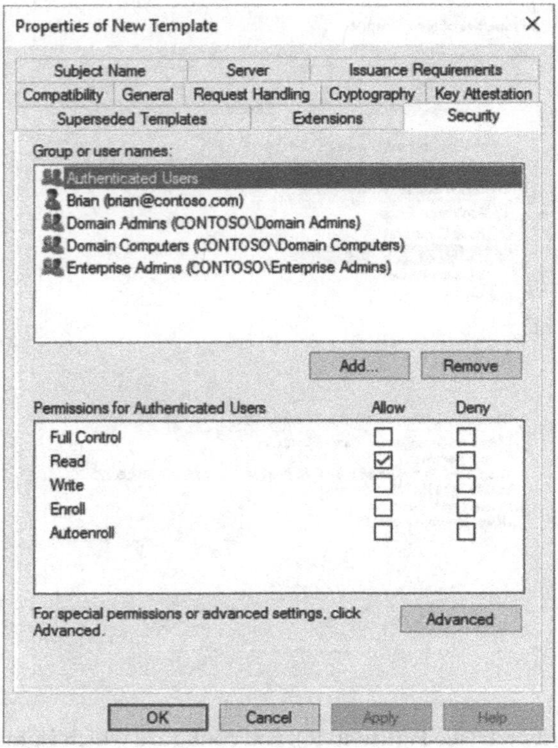

By default, certificate processing includes storing a record of each certificate request and issued certificate in the CA database. *Nonpersistent certificate processing* refers to processing certificate requests and issuing certificates without storing requests and certificates in the CA database. This configuration is intended to address the needs of high-volume certificate issuance scenarios including Network Access Protection (NAP) deployments with Internet Protocol security (IPsec) enforcement in which hundreds or thousands of certificates with short validity periods are issued every day. In scenarios that do not require certificate revocation, certificate validation times can be reduced by enabling the certificate template Do Not Include Revocation Information In Issued Certificates option. If no certificate revocation information is present in a certificate, revocation status is not checked during certificate validation. This option is recommended when the Do Not Store Certificates And Requests In The CA Database option is enabled. In Figure 10.17, the Server tab is shown. There are only two options. One dictates whether certificates and requests are stored in the CA database (enabled by default) and whether revocation information is included in issued certificates (included by default).

FIGURE 10.17
Server tab

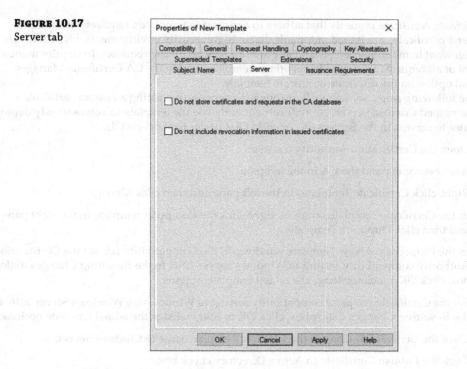

In Figure 10.18, the Issuance Requirements tab is shown.

FIGURE 10.18
Issuance
Requirements tab

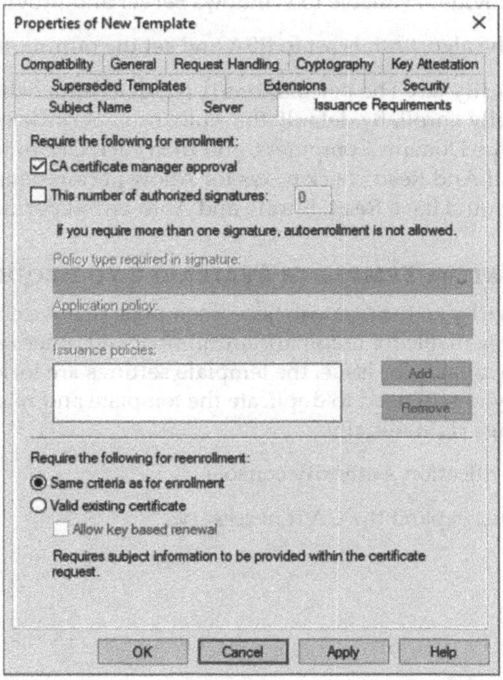

By default, certificate requests that adhere to a certificate template's requirements are processed and certificates are issued automatically. In high-security environments, PKI administrators often want to manually review and approve all new certificate requests. To require manual approval of all requests for a specific certificate template, enable the CA Certificate Manager Approval option on the duplicate certificate template.

In the following steps, we will walk through the process of creating a custom certificate template named Contoso Server. We will subsequently use the template to automatically deploy certificates to servers in the Servers OU or child OUs under the Servers OU.

1. Open the Certification Authority console.

2. If necessary, expand the CA in the left pane.

3. Right-click Certificate Templates in the left pane and then click Manage.

4. In the Certificate Templates console, right-click the Computer template in the right pane and then click Duplicate Template.

5. In the Properties of New Template window, on the Compatibility tab, set the Certification Authority compatibility setting to Windows Server 2016. In the Resulting Changes dialog box, click OK to acknowledge the added template options.

6. Set the Certificate recipient compatibility setting to Windows 10/Windows Server 2016. In the Resulting Changes dialog box, click OK to acknowledge the added template options.

7. Click the General tab. Change the template's display name to **Contoso Server**.

8. Click the Publish Certificate In Active Directory check box.

9. Click the Cryptography tab and set the Provider Category to Key Storage Provider. This is the newest provider available to Windows Server and provides the strongest algorithms.

10. Ensure that the algorithm is set to RSA and set the minimum key size to 4096.

11. Click the Security tab. The permissions listed determine which users or groups can enroll or automatically enroll. By default, the Autoenroll permission isn't granted to anybody. Click Add, type Domain Computers, and then click OK. In the permissions list, click the Autoenroll And Read check boxes for Allow permissions. When you finish, Domain Computers should have Read, Enroll, and Auto-enroll permissions.

MAKING THE CUSTOM TEMPLATE AVAILABLE TO REQUESTORS

In this section, we will take the Contoso Server template that we customized in the previous section and make it available for automatic enrollment and other requestors. Note that once you make the template available for issue, the template settings are locked in. If you need to make changes thereafter, you will need to duplicate the template and reissue it. Therefore, it is a good idea to get the settings right initially.

1. Open the Certification Authority console.

2. In the left pane, expand the CA if necessary.

3. In the left pane, right-click Certificate Templates, click New, and then click Certificate Template To Issue.

4. In the Enable Certificate Templates window, click the Contoso Server template and then click OK.

5. The certificate template will be available for requestors and the auto-enrollment GPO (which we'll create in the next section).

Auto-Enrollment

While you can manually request individual certificates for individual servers, there are scenarios in which you should automate the deployment of certificates to many servers. For example, imagine that you have 25 domain controllers and each one needs to have a certificate to enable secure communication. In such a scenario, you can create a single GPO linked to the Domain Controllers OU to automate the certificate deployment process. Such a configuration is known as auto-enrollment. Many organizations use it for their server environment. In some organizations, auto-enrollment is used for client computers (often in a scenario where client certificates are used for authentication, such as a secure wireless network).

In this section, we'll walk through the process of setting up a GPO to automatically deploy certificates to all servers. In this walkthrough, we will target all servers that are in the Contoso\ Servers OU or a child OU under the Servers OU. Before we begin, we already have a customized certificate to deploy. If you didn't follow along with the exercise in the previous section where we customized a certificate template, go back and do that now before moving forward.

1. Open the Group Policy management console.

2. If necessary, expand the Forest and Domains containers. Expand the Contoso OU.

3. Right-click `Contoso\Computers\Servers OU` and then click Create A GPO In This Domain, And Link It Here.

4. In the New GPO window, provide the name **Autoenrollment**, and then click OK (see Figure 10.19).

FIGURE 10.19
New GPO window

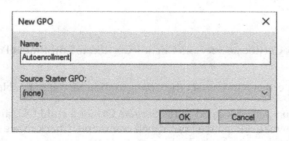

5. Right-click the Autoenrollment GPO, and then click Edit.

6. In the Policy Editor, browse to Computer Configuration ➤ Policies ➤ Windows Settings ➤ Security Settings ➤ Public Key Policies.

7. In the right pane, locate and double-click the policy named Certificate Services Client – Auto-Enrollment.

8. Set the Configuration Model to Enabled. Enable the "Renew expired certificates, update pending certificates, and remove revoked certificates" option and enable the "Update certificates that use certificate templates" option (see Figure 10.20).

FIGURE 10.20
Setting the configuration model

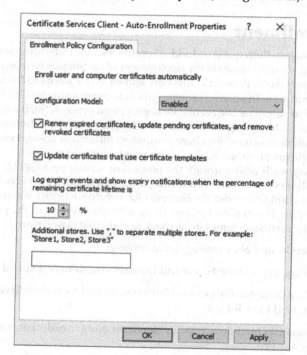

9. Click OK.

10. Right-click Certificate Services Client – Certificate Enrollment Policy and then click Properties.

11. In the Properties window, set the Configuration Model to Enabled and then click OK.

Next, sign in to a server located in the Servers OU (or a child OU) and refresh Group Policy by running the Invoke-GPUpdate PowerShell command. Check to see if the computer has a certificate from the deployment by looking at the local computer's certificate store. If you are running Windows Server 2012 or later, you can run the certlm.msc command to open the Certificates MMC targeted at the local computer store.

The Bottom Line

Understand what's new in AD CS Windows Server 2016   As a PKI administrator, you need to stay up-to-date on the latest enhancements to AD CS as new versions of Windows Server are released. Often, enhancements implement stronger security, reduced overhead, and higher performance.

Master It   Your company has AD CS running on Windows Server 2008 R2. The management team wants to determine three key benefits of moving to AD CS on Windows Server 2016. Which benefits should you report?

Solution   There are several benefits, many starting with AD CS running on Windows Server 2012. Three key improvements that you should report are enhanced PowerShell support (backup, restore, automation, and scripting), version 4 certificate templates (enhanced security and ability to specify a minimum supported operating system), and AD DS site awareness (clients query for nearest site with a CA for improved performance). In Windows Server 2016, AD CS offers enhanced key attestation functionality, which is a fourth benefit you should report.

Understand Public Key Infrastructure and AD CS   Having an internal PKI provides your organization with a fast and efficient way to issue certificates. There are many new concepts to learn. AD CS is Microsoft's implementation of PKI, and implementing it requires a good understanding of how a PKI works.

Master It   Your company is preparing to implement its first PKI by using AD CS. For some servers, the company wants to automatically deploy certificates. Which infrastructure component is required to offer automated certificate deployment?

Solution   For automatic certificate deployment, you need to use auto-enrollment. Auto-enrollment requires AD DS and Group Policy, with a GPO being the automatic certificate deployment method.

Plan your design   Because the PKI is a critical component of your environment's security, you should spend extra time planning and designing it. Consider the following tasks as part of your planning and design work:

◆   Meet with all the various teams and/or departments that will use and/or rely on the PKI. Understand their planned usage and existing requirements. Understand their major projects over the next couple of years.

◆   Meet independently with your information security team(s) to gather all your organization's security requirements. Work with the information security team to understand how the existing requirements map to PKI configurations. Gain approval for your proposed configuration and design prior to beginning the implementation.

◆   Deploy a PKI in a lab environment. Don't use your primary lab environment; use a temporary lab environment that you can tear down when you are finished. Ensure that your desired configuration functions. Make sure that it meets all the requirements. Tweak your design and/or configuration as needed. Use the lab deployment as the starting point to document your implementation plan. If possible, deploy your design more than once.

Then, when you are ready to proceed with your real deployment, deploy your final design in your nonproduction environment first.

◆ Have an independent security test of your PKI and supporting components (such as Active Directory). This could be a security test performed by your internal team early in the project (such as after the lab is environment up and running). Once in production, consider an independent security test of your production environment using an outside security company.

Master It You are a consultant. One of your customers has 1,500 employees, 300 servers, and an existing Active Directory environment. They are interested in deploying a PKI. Their security requirements are average; they don't require high security but want something more than a small business would want. Based on this limited information, how many tiers do you think are appropriate for this customer?

Solution In this scenario, you should deploy a two-tier hierarchy. With an offline root CA, you get enhanced security. Because it has only two tiers, you will not introduce unnecessary complexity for the customer. A single-tier hierarchy is best suited for a small business, while three or more tiers are best suited for large and complex organizations.

Implement a two-tier hierarchy You are preparing to deploy a new PKI for your company. The existing security policies don't specify hash algorithms or minimum key lengths. You want solid security but without impacting performance or usability. Remember the following good practices regarding cryptography options:

◆ Use the Key Storage Provider whenever possible. It provides access to the RSA algorithm. Otherwise, your only other choice is the legacy provider and you can't choose an algorithm at the template level.

◆ Consider a minimum key size of 4096. Although many Internet and vendor sites recommend a minimum key size of 2048, it is only a matter of time before they update their recommendations to 4096. By using 4096 today, you can help future-proof your implementation without much of an impact on performance.

◆ Read the extensive documentation available about the algorithms, key sizes, and providers available. This will help you make the right design choices.

Master It You duplicate a certificate template. You try to update the Cryptography tab to use the new Key Storage Provider, but the option is grayed out. What should you do to enable the template to use the Key Storage Provider?

Solution In this scenario, you need to update the compatibility settings in the duplicated template. That is usually the first step after you duplicate a template because it opens up most of the new features and enhanced security options. Once you update the compatibility settings to the latest version, you will be able to update the template to use the Key Storage Provider.

Work with certificate templates. To customize your environment and ensure it adheres to the company security policies, you will need to use certificate templates.

Master It   What are three benefits of using custom templates instead of the built-in templates?

Solution   There are many benefits to using custom templates. Three common benefits include changing the validity period, publishing certificates to Active Directory, and changing the cryptography options such as key length, provider, and algorithm.

Understand the benefits of auto-enrollment.   Auto-enrollment enables you to automate the process of deploying certificates. In many organizations, there is a mix of manual certificate deployment (such as for use with an internal web server) and automatic certificate deployment (such as for use with all domain controllers).

Master It   Your company is investigating auto-enrollment as a potential deployment method for certificates. What are three benefits of auto-enrollment?

Solution   Auto-enrollment reduces the administrative overhead of deploying certificates to users and computers, it improves the penetration rate of certificate deployments (the percentage of users and/or computers that successfully obtain a certificate), and it reduces human errors related to deployment.

Chapter 11

Active Directory Federation Services

Active Directory Federation Services (AD FS) was first introduced after Windows Server 2003 R2 as an additional download. Officially, that was AD FS 1.0. It was quite limited in features, and few organizations deployed it. However, it was the start of Microsoft offering a standards-based federation and claims-based identity service. Today, AD FS is widely deployed and very commonly used in large enterprise environments as well as for federation with Microsoft Azure and Office 365.

As with some of the other big topics in this book, we could write an entire book about AD FS. However, in this chapter we are going to focus on the most relevant aspects of designing and deploying an AD FS environment. For those of you who are interested, we will also include key links to external material that will enable you to dive deep into specific target areas. Don't discount the links. They are specifically included because of the high quality of the content and the additional resources they provide.

IN THIS CHAPTER, YOU WILL LEARN TO:

- ◆ Understand how AD FS works
- ◆ Understand AD FS terminology
- ◆ Plan and design AD FS
- ◆ Deploy an AD FS Environment

Overview of AD FS

Active Directory Federation Services (AD FS) is a Microsoft identity federation technology that enables organizations to securely share identity information with other organizations to provide a seamless user-authentication experience across disparate applications and services. AD FS works with existing Internet standards such as WS-Federation and Security Assertion Markup Language (SAML), which are used across a wide variety of platforms and applications. AD FS is sometimes referred to as a Security Token Service (STS). The idea is that AD FS generates security tokens that users use to access apps and services. The authentication is handled by Active Directory Domain Services.

AD FS was first introduced after Windows Server 2003 R2. Subsequently, AD FS 1.1 was released as a role with Windows Server 2008 and Windows Server 2008 R2. AD FS 2.0 was released as a downloadable installation for Windows Server 2008 and Windows Server 2008 R2. Then, AD FS 2.1 was released with Windows Server 2012. For Windows Server 2012 R2, AD FS 3.0 was introduced. Today, with Windows Server 2016, AD FS is version 4.0.

For those of you who haven't worked with AD FS or identity federation, let's review what it is and how it works. *Identity federation* is the concept of using a single identity (such as a username/password in an AD DS domain) to access apps and services (such as the online version of Microsoft Word) regardless of whether they are deployed on-premises, are deployed at another organization's facility, or are cloud-based. If you've spent a bit of time on the Internet, you've undoubtedly seen identity federation in practice. For example, you can use a Facebook or Google credential to sign into many unrelated websites. That's identity federation. From a corporate perspective, the same concept applies. You use your corporate credentials to access corporate resources (for example: corporate websites, corporate email accounts, cloud-based payroll systems, cloud-based ERP systems) even if third-parties provide the resources. Identity federation provides a good user experience because users don't need to maintain user accounts across a wide variety of systems.

Let's look at a couple of common use cases:

Microsoft Office 365 When a company subscribes to Office 365, they have a few choices as to how their users will be authenticated. Although we won't review all the options, let's look at a few. One option is to create a new Azure Active Directory user account for each user. When users authenticate to Office 365, they use their Azure Active Directory user account. A second option is to sync the on-premises users from Active Directory Domain Services (AD DS) to Azure Active Directory along with their passwords (not the actual password but simplified here on purpose). Users use the same username and password that they use for the company resources, which simplifies the user experience. A third option is to use AD FS. In this case, all authentication takes place on-premises with the company domain controllers authenticating users. Users use their corporate credentials. User objects are synced with Azure Active Directory, but the passwords do not need to sync (optionally, you can sync them for use if AD FS were to go down). Companies that put a focus on security often prefer the use of AD FS for authenticating to cloud-based resources because the companies control the authentication. That means they also maintain authentication logs and can use all their existing security software, policies, and procedures to manage identities. Note that we left off Azure Pass-Through Authentication and Single Sign-On purposely to keep our focus on AD FS. To understand more about identity options with Office 365 and see how AD FS fits in, see https://support.office.com/en-us/article/Understanding-Office-365-identity-and-Azure-Active-Directory-06a189e7-5ec6-4af2-94bf-a22ea225a7a9#bk_federated.

Salesforce Salesforce is a cloud-based software-as-a-service (SaaS) customer-relationship-management platform. As with Office 365, you have several options on how to authenticate users to Salesforce. For example, Salesforce supports SAML. Identity federation with single sign-on is often the choice, especially for larger organizations or organizations that have already deployed an identity federation solution. AD FS can be configured to enable single sign-on (SSO) to Salesforce so that users coming from corporate computers are automatically authenticated to Salesforce during sign-in. Compare this with having to manage a second set of credentials, and you can easily see how identity federation provides a valuable solution for companies.

What about using AD FS to provide access to shared folders, Microsoft Exchange, or SQL Server? You can't. With technology, there might be some fun way to glue things together to get some functional deployment. But natively, AD FS doesn't support the expected authentication methods of your typical on-premises technology. Often, the traditional on-premises technology expects integrated Windows authentication. Applications expect Kerberos or NT LAN Manager (NTLM). However, the public cloud isn't a good place for integrated Windows authentication because the target resources are often not part of the same domain, users are often using devices that aren't associated with any domain, and devices run a variety of non-Windows operating systems.

As you can imagine, there are options besides AD FS. Third-party companies provide competitive solutions with similar functionality. For example, Ping Identity offers PingOne, a cloud-based identity-as-a-service (IDaaS) solution. Another company, named Okta, offers a single sign-on solution that simplifies the application provisioning process and offers multifactor authentication. Meanwhile, Microsoft has greatly expanded and enhanced Azure Active Directory Premium to provide identity federation in the cloud. It offers much of the same functionality as AD FS but also provides a myriad of related identity functionality (such as self-service password reset, advanced security reports, multifactor authentication, and identity protection).

To discover what's new in AD FS for Windows Server 2016, watch "What's New in AD FS & AD DS in Server 2016" from Microsoft Ignite 2016 at `https://channel9.msdn.com/events/Ignite/2016/BRK3074?term=Active%20Directory%20Federation%20Services%202.0`.

AD FS Terminology

Many administrators have never heard of some of the AD FS terms, and the terminology has changed over the years. To really understand the technology, you need to have a good grasp of the terminology. Before we look at how AD FS works, we will define the key AD FS terms that you should know. Refer to this table during this chapter if you come across a term you don't understand.

Table 11.1 shows AD FS terms and definitions.

TABLE 11.1:   AD FS Terms and Definitions

TERM	DEFINITION
Account partner organization	The company with users who will access a claims-aware application. The user accounts are often user objects in Active Directory Domain Services. Account partner organization is interchangeable with "claims provider."
Claims	A specific statement about a user account made by a federation server. A claim can be an email address, name, or other identifying information. It can also be group memberships. Claims are the foundation of authentication and authorization requests.
Claims provider	The company with users who will access the claims-aware application. Interchangeable with "account partner organization."

TABLE 11.1: AD FS Terms and Definitions *(CONTINUED)*

TERM	DEFINITION
Relying party	The company that hosts the claims-based web application and relies on the account partner organization's claims. This term is interchangeable with "resource partner organization."
Relying party trust	A trust object in your AD FS configuration that contains information about the two companies that have a federated trust.
Resource partner organization	The company that hosts the claims-based web application ("the resource"). This term is interchangeable with "relying party."

To see a comprehensive list of terminology related to AD FS, go to `https://technet
.microsoft.com/en-us/library/cc754236(v=ws.11).aspx`.

How AD FS Works

AD FS is a claims-based authentication solution. It relies on claims about users. Claims are made up of user data such as name, department, city, and group memberships. When users authenticate, AD FS gathers information about the user (often from Active Directory Domain Services but can also be from Active Directory Lightweight Directory Services, a database, or an XML store). Then, AD FS, acting as the issuer, issues a token to the user. That token is sent on to claims-based applications (for example, a cloud-based service such as Salesforce). Let's look at how this might work in the real world. In the following example, we will walk you through a scenario where you visit a resort hotel and walk up to the front desk to begin the check-in process. Figure 11.1 shows the decision tree and how authentication and authorization work during the resort hotel visit.

The following are the steps of the hotel visit, beginning from the Start icon:

1. Upon entering the hotel, you go to the registration desk where a clerk asks if they can help you. You say that you want to check into the hotel. The registration desk attendant asks for identification. This begins the authentication process.

2. You present your identification card. The registration desk attendant performs several checks:

   Does the picture on the ID appear to be the person at the registration desk?

   Does the identification card appear to be genuine?

   Does the person's age meet the minimum requirements for staying at the hotel?

3. If the identification card passes the tests, authentication is complete (marked by the number 1 in Figure 11.1). Even though you've successfully authenticated, you can't get into a hotel room yet. If the identification card fails one or more of the checks, the authentication fails and the attendant might ask you to leave or call security.

FIGURE 11.1
Decision tree for a
hotel visit

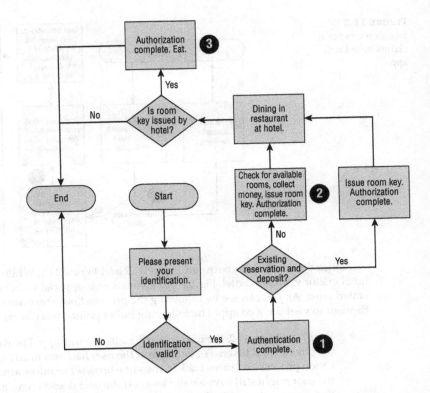

4. Next, the attendant checks to see if you have a reservation for a room and whether you have paid the required deposit. If you don't have a reservation, the attendant will check for available rooms, collect any necessary money, and then issue you a room key. If you already have a reservation and have paid a deposit, the attendant will issue you a room key. This represents successful authorization (signified by the number 2 in Figure 11.1).

5. Once you are authenticated and authorized, you can go to your room and enjoy the facilities. If you want to dine at one of the hotel restaurants, you have the option to use your existing hotel key (your authorization) to pay for the meal. The room key is like a set of claims in AD FS (in AD FS, instead of obtaining a key, you obtain a security token). The hotel issued the key to you. The restaurant trusts the issuer (in this example, the hotel) so they don't have to perform their own authentication or authorization (although, optionally, they can opt to authenticate and/or authorize you a second time if circumstances are suspicious). This second authorization is labeled with the number 3 in Figure 11.1.

Next, let's look at how this process flow looks with a claims-based web app and AD FS. In the following example, two companies have a federated trust with each company having an AD FS environment. Company1 (the claims provider or account partner organization) has users who will use a claims-based web app at Company2 (the relying party or resource partner organization). Figure 11.2 shows the process flow.

FIGURE 11.2
Decision tree for a
claims-based web
app

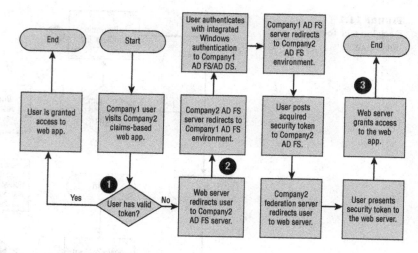

Notice the similarities between Figure 11.2 and Figure 11.1. While Figure 11.1 represented a hotel visitor visiting a hotel, Figure 11.2 shows a web-app visitor in an environment with a federated trust. As you can see by following the process flow, there are several redirects to enable the user to visit the web app. The following bullet points describe parts of the flow.

◆ For #1 in Figure 11.2, the user initially visits the web app. The web app checks to see if the user has a valid token. For example, if the user had previously gone through the authentication process and came back in the same browser window after visiting another website, the user might still have a valid token. If the user doesn't have a valid token, the redirection process starts. The first redirection sends the user to the AD FS federation server at Company2. When the AD FS federation server sees that the user is from Company1, it issues a redirect to have the user start the authentication process to the Company1 environment.

◆ For #2 in Figure 11.2, the redirection of the user back to the Company1 environment begins. The user ends up authenticating with integrated Windows authentication to the Company1 AD FS / AD DS environment. The user is issued a security token. Thereafter, the user is redirected back to the Company2 AD FS environment to present the security token.

◆ For #3 in Figure 11.2, the web server validates the security token and grants access to the user. Because of the federation trust, Company2 trusts security tokens issued by Company1. The user is now free to use the web app.

To learn more about AD FS concepts including the details of the claims processes, see "Understanding Key AD FS Concepts" at https://docs.microsoft.com/en-us/windows-server/identity/ad-fs/technical-reference/understanding-key-ad-fs-concepts.

Now that we've finished the overview for AD FS, we will look at some of the planning and design considerations you need to work through before you begin implementing AD FS in your environment.

Planning and Design Considerations

Before you deploy an AD FS environment, you need to go through the planning and design. At a high level, the planning and design work should include the following high-level tasks:

Getting Functional and Nonfunctional Requirements for the Implementation A functional requirement is a requirement that dictates a specific functionality that the technology should do. For example, a functional requirement might be "Facilitate user authentication to web applications for users on the Internet." A nonfunctional requirement is a requirement that describes how an implementation should perform. For example, a nonfunctional requirement for an AD FS deployment might be "Provide 99.99% uptime" or "Provide site resilience." Until you know the requirements for the project, you can't get very far planning and designing. The requirements will help you figure out whether you need high availability, site resiliency, or IT infrastructure changes.

Performing a Discovery During the discovery, you are looking at the existing environment. For an AD FS implementation, you need to find out if there is an existing AD FS implementation or if AD FS is replacing another product performing similar functionality. You also need to look at the technologies on which AD FS will depend or with which it will integrate. That means you need to look at the Active Directory Domain Services environment, DNS, the public key infrastructure, SQL Server, network connectivity, firewalls, and load balancers. You need to find out which versions they are running, the locations of the various services, and whether they are healthy or in a degraded state.

Planning and Designing Once you have the requirements and have performed a discovery, you are ready to begin the planning and design. The goal is to figure out which components you need, how many of them you need, and where you need to place them. But you must account for all the details, too. For example, which versions will you use? In what order will you deploy the technologies? Which prerequisites exist? How many people do you need to perform the implementation? When can you complete the work? Which changes to the environment are required to ensure that the implementation will function (network, firewall, load balancing, DNS, operating system changes, etc.)?

Specific to an AD FS implementation, there are some key decisions that you need to make prior to the deployment. We will walk through the key consideration points for some of these decisions now, focusing on the placement of services, database, certificates, and service accounts.

Where Should You Place the AD FS Components?

For an AD FS implementation, you need to pay close attention to the placement of the components. AD FS servers (specifically, the federation servers) are intended to be treated like other critical security servers on your local area network (such as domain controllers and certification authority servers). You should deploy federation servers to your local area network and ensure that they are not directly connected to the Internet (or directly accessible from the Internet). To maximize security of your environment, you should deploy Web Application Proxy (WAP) servers in the perimeter network. The WAP servers should handle all communication from the Internet and securely proxy valid communication to the federation servers. Figure 11.3 shows a typical AD FS deployment along with some of the supporting infrastructure.

FIGURE 11.3
AD FS infrastructure
diagram

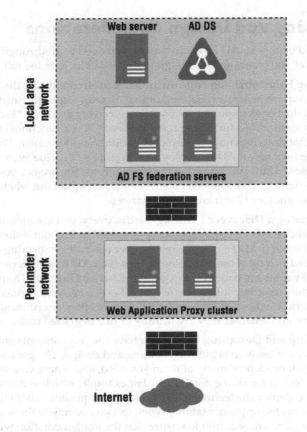

In Figure 11.3, several components are shown:

AD FS Federation Servers   Figure 11.3 shows two servers, which provide for high availability within the site. In a multisite environment, it is common to have at least two servers in another site to provide site resiliency. The number of servers you need is based on capacity requirements. Note the placement of the federation servers—in the local area network and separated from the perimeter network by a firewall.

AD DS   The AD DS domain is represented with the domain (triangle) icon and is represented only in the local area network. The AD FS federation servers are joined to the domain.

Web Server   The web server represents a server with a claims-based web application. Such applications are often on the local area network. However, such applications could also be in the perimeter network or in a public cloud network.

Web Application Proxy Cluster   The Web Application Proxy cluster is shown in the perimeter network. This is the most common placement. They are separated from the federation servers by a firewall. They are separated from the Internet by a firewall. In some organizations, the same firewall is used to separate the WAP servers from the federation servers and the Internet. In high-security environments, separate firewalls are often used. An optional layout is to place the WAP servers in the local area network and use a network-based security device in the perimeter network to be the initial contact point for Internet communications.

During your planning, you need to account for your project requirements and factor in the characteristics of your infrastructure. Not every implementation has to follow the model shown in Figure 11.3.

Should You Use SQL Server for the AD FS Database?

AD FS requires a database. You have two choices: use SQL Server or use the Windows Internal Database (WID). If the decision is based purely on a capacity perspective, it will be simple:

◆ If you have fewer than 30 AD FS servers in a farm and fewer than 100 relying-party trusts, then use the WID.

◆ If you have more than 30 AD FS servers in a farm or more than 100 relying-party trusts, then use SQL Server.

But as you might've imagined, it isn't that simple. Besides capacity, you must also consider capabilities:

◆ WID does not support SAML artifact resolution. This feature improves security by making it more difficult for a SAML assertion to be modified during communication.

◆ WID does not support SAML/WS-Federation token-replay detection. Token-replay detection is used in high-security environments to drop attempts at replaying token requests.

◆ WID does not support database replication such that some servers host read-only copies of a database and get updates from a read/write copy of the database.

◆ WID does not support high-availability such as failover clustering.

There are smaller implications that you must think about, too. For example, when you use the WID, each federation server has a little bit of extra work to do: manage and maintain replication changes for the AD FS database. With SQL Server, that is handled outside of the federation servers.

Beyond technical capacity and capabilities, there are also the "real world" things to consider. For example, many companies have standards around their IT technologies. For databases, there could be a company standard that all databases use the official database standard such as SQL Server. Some companies want the database team to manage all databases. By using SQL Server, such companies can use standard configurations, use database security and management software, and maximize efficiency. Instead of having app teams deploy and manage their own databases (and call the database team when a catastrophic failure occurs), companies deploy straight to SQL Server from the beginning. Often, companies with database standards have built highly available, site-resilient database environments with highly available enterprise storage and security. So even if your initial use of AD FS could function with WID, is that the appropriate choice in such companies? Probably not. Go with SQL Server.

What Are Your Certificate Options for Your AD FS Environment?

In your deployment, you will need a certificate for client communication, a token-signing certificate, a token-decryption certificate, and a service-communications certificate. There are many things to consider during your planning and design. The following bullet points outline the key considerations along with information to help guide you for your implementation.

◆ You can use certificates from your internal PKI environment or third-party certificates. When you use your internal PKI, the certificates are typically not trusted by external parties. Thus, there is extra work to enable that trust. In most environments, it is common to use third-party certificates. They are trusted by default, and companies are often more comfortable trusting the third-party certificates than certificates issued from private CAs. For AD FS implementations for Office 365, you must use a third-party certificate. There are other situations like that, too, so it is important to check with your vendors during your planning and design work.

◆ You can use a wildcard certificate. If you aren't familiar with a wildcard certificate, it is a certificate that is associated with any fully qualified domain names (FQDNs) for a specified domain. For example, for the contoso.com domain, a wildcard certificate would be valid for www.contoso.com, sts.contoso.com, and ftp.contoso.com. A standard certificate is valid for a single domain name (such as sts.contoso.com). A SAN certificate is valid for several domain names. The primary benefit of using a wildcard certificate is that you don't have to worry about the names for your certificate—all names work with the wildcard certificate. The drawback of using a wildcard certificate is that some providers will allow companies to have only a single wildcard certificate per domain. You might want to save that for another use instead of for AD FS. Wildcard certificates are also more expensive than standard and SAN certificates. Some companies have policies that forbid the use of wildcard certificates. Thus, for some environments, a SAN certificate is the best choice.

◆ You can use a single certificate across your federation servers and your Web Application Proxy servers (to cover all four certificate uses). This simplifies the deployment and ongoing maintenance. When possible, strive for a single certificate that includes all the names for your environment. High-security organizations might have a security policy that prohibits sharing certificates between servers on the local area network and servers in the perimeter network. In such cases, you can obtain one certificate for the internal servers and one certificate for the perimeter servers.

Should You Use a Group-Managed Service Account for Your AD FS Environment?

Every AD FS farm requires a service account. As part of your design and planning, you need to figure out whether you want to use a group-managed service account (gMSA) or a standard service account (one that you manually create in Active Directory). Before we look at the pros and cons of those options, be aware that you should not use the Network Service account. If you do, you will likely experience failures during Windows integrated authentication. The following bullet points outline the key considerations for your AD FS service account.

◆ If you use a standard service account, you must manage the password (store the password in a vault or similar and change the password prior to expiration). In some organizations, service accounts have non-expiring passwords. However, in high-security environments, it is common to have a security policy that limits or prohibits having non-expiring service account passwords.

◆ If you use a gMSA, you do not have to manage the password. It is managed by Active Directory. By default, the password is changed every 30 days. If desired, you can configure a different password-change frequency. The automation of the password changes is often enough justification to use a gMSA. Often, taking advantage of small improvements in efficiency add up to significant savings for IT administrators.

For most environments, it is a good idea to use a gMSA. However, be aware of the prerequisites before you finalize your design. You need your Active Directory forest functional level to be at Windows Server 2012 or later, servers that run Windows Server 2012 or later to use gMSAs, and a Key Distribution Services (KDS) root key in Active Directory (which is used to generate passwords for the gMSAs). If your environment doesn't meet the requirements, you should find out if updating the environment to support gMSAs can coincide or precede your AD FS implementation.

To explore more about AD FS, refer to the AD FS content map, which has links to a plethora of AD FS content for integrating AD FS in various environment with specific technologies. See `https://social.technet.microsoft.com/wiki/contents/articles/2735.ad-fs-content-map.aspx` for more information.

Deploying an AD FS Environment

This section will document the process of deploying AD FS. You should go through these steps in your lab environment (whether at home or at work) to become familiar with the process and understand the deployment options. As a prerequisite, you need to have Active Directory Domain Services and DNS name resolution. The deployment sections after this section will build on this section. The following bullet points represent the environment in the steps. Substitute your own domain name(s) and computer names or use the ones shown here for your lab.

◆ Existing Active Directory Domain Services domain named `contoso.com`.

◆ A VM named adfsVM running on Windows Server 2016.

◆ A certificate file in `.pfx` format for the `15360x8640.com` domain. This is a test domain and the domain that the sample application uses. In your environment, you can use a single domain or you can opt for two domains like we do here.

Installing the AD FS Server Role

Follow these steps to install the AD FS server role:

1. Log on to adfsVM as a member of the Domain Admins group.

2. On adfsVM, run Windows PowerShell.

3. From the PowerShell window, create the Key Distribution Services KDS Root Key by running the `Add-KdsRootKey -EffectiveTime (Get-Date).AddHours(-10)` command.

DON'T BYPASS THE KDS ROOT KEY WAITING PERIOD

Adding a root key takes up to 10 hours, by default. We do not recommend that you bypass the initial waiting period in a production environment, but doing so for this example will allow you to use a GMSA immediately when deploying AD FS. You should immediately force replication after adding the KDS root key.

---

4. Log on to adfsVM as a member of the Domain Admins group.

5. Click Start and then click Server Manager.

6. Click Manage and, in the drop-down menu, click Add Roles and Features.

7. If the Before You Begin page appears, select the Skip This Page By Default check box and then click Next.

8. On the Select Installation Type page, ensure that the Role-Based Or Feature-Based Installation option is selected and click Next.

9. On the Select Destination Server page, ensure that ADFSVM is selected and click Next.

10. On the Select Server Roles page (Figure 11.4), click the Active Directory Federation Services check box and then click Next.

FIGURE 11.4
Adding the AD
FS role

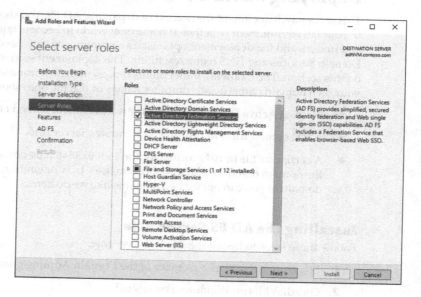

11. On the Select Features page, click Next.

12. On the Active Directory Federation Services (AD FS) page, click Next.

13. On the Confirm Installation Selections page, select the Restart The Destination Server Automatically If Required check box, click Yes when prompted for confirmation, and click Install. Wait for the installation to complete.

14. Once the installation completes, on the Installation Progress page, click Configure The Federation Service On This Server. This will start Active Directory Federation Services Configuration Wizard.

15. On the Welcome page (Figure 11.5), ensure that the Create The First Federation Server In A Federation Server Farm option is selected and click Next.

FIGURE 11.5
AD FS
Configuration
Wizard

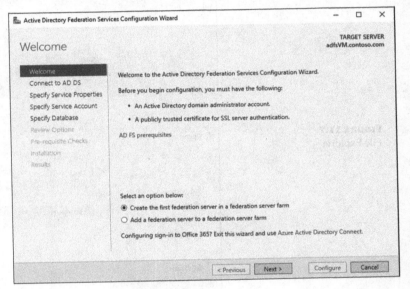

16. On the Connect To AD DS page, if the administrative credentials are shown and acceptable, accept the default settings and click Next. Otherwise, click Change, provide the administrative credentials, and then continue.

17. On the Specify Service Properties page (Figure 11.6), click Import.

18. Navigate to the location of the *.pfx file with the private key of the key pair of the certificate that will be used by your AD FS farm (Figure 11.7) and click Open.

FIGURE 11.6
Importing the
certificate

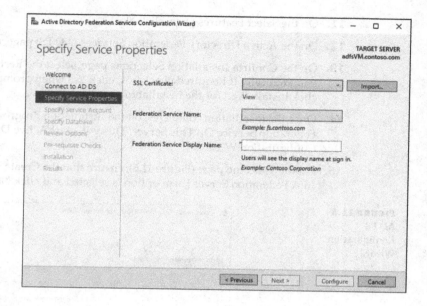

FIGURE 11.7
File Explorer

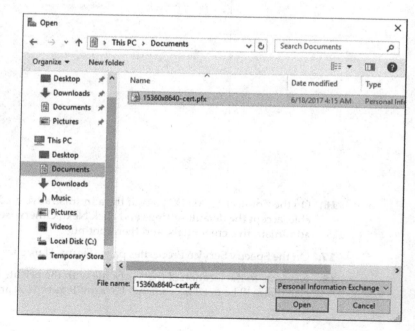

When prompted, provide the password protecting the private key and click OK. Note that you should securely delete the .pfx file once you are finished deploying the federation server.

19. Back on the Specify Service Properties page, specify the Federation Service Name and the Federation Service Display Name and then click Next. In our environment, we are using the name fs.15360x8640.com as the federation service name and Contoso Corporation as the display name (Figure 11.8).

FIGURE 11.8
AD FS federation
service name

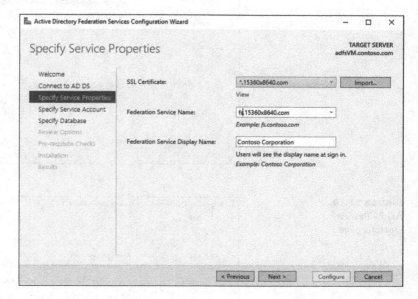

20. On the Specify Service Account page (Figure 11.9), click the Create a Group Managed Service Account option, specify the name of the group Managed Service Account to create, and then click Next. Optionally, you can create a new gMSA if you didn't create one ahead of time. While you could create and use a standard service account, it's a good practice to use a gMSA. It ensures that the account password is managed by Active Directory, which reduces administrative overhead.

21. On the Specify Configuration Database page, ensure that the Create A Database To Store The Active Directory Federation Services Configuration Data option is selected and then click Next. The internal database should be used only for development or small-scale installations. If you plan to use this in a large or highly available environment, you should use a SQL Server database to store the AD FS configuration data.

22. On the Review Options page (Figure 11.10), read the configuration information to ensure that it matches your requirements. Then, click Next.

FIGURE 11.9
AD FS service
account

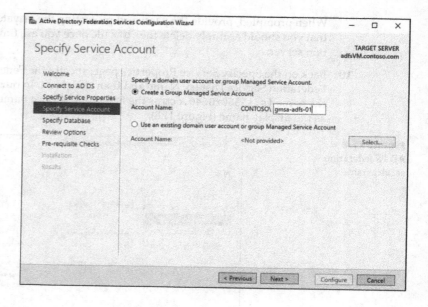

FIGURE 11.10
AD FS Review
Options page

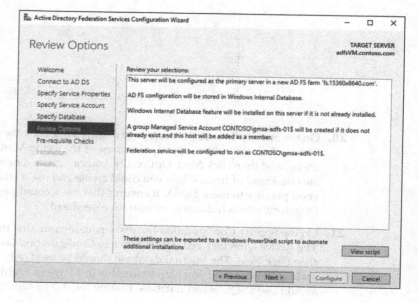

23. On the Pre-requisite Checks page (Figure 11.11), verify that all prerequisites have been satisfied and click Configure. You might see a warning about the KDS root key, but you can safely ignore that.

FIGURE 11.11
AD FS Pre-requisite
Checks page

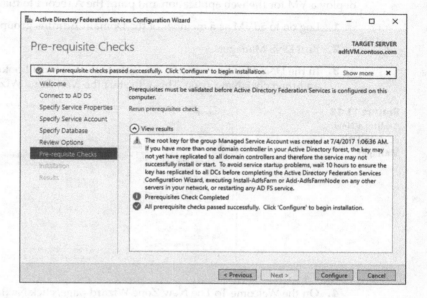

24. Wait until the configuration completes, review the results, and then click Close.

25. On the Installation Progress page, click Close.

26. Restart adfsVM to complete the installation.

Now that we have deployed the first federation server, we need to take care of some DNS resolution tasks. We'll do that next.

DEPLOYMENT CHECKLIST

To dive deeper into the deployment of a federation server farm, review the checklist and links on the "Deploying a Federation Server Farm" page at https://docs.microsoft.com/en-us/windows-server/identity/ad-fs/deployment/deploying-a-federation-server-farm.

Configuring Internal DNS Name Resolution

Next, we will create a dedicated DNS zone specifically for the web app. This might be irrelevant in your environment if you are hosting the web app in the same domain as your AD DS domain.

You can also follow the same general steps of creating the DNS records if you're hosting the DNS for your domain through a third-party. Note the reference to a new VM named appVM. That VM will host the web application. If you are following along in your environment, you can deploy a VM for the web application and point the A record to that server.

1. Log on to adVM as a member of the Domain Admins group.

2. Run DNS Manager.

3. In the DNS Manager console, navigate to the Forward Lookup Zones folder, right-click it, and then click New Zone. This will start the New Zone Wizard (Figure 11.12).

FIGURE 11.12
Adding a New
Zone in DNS
Manager

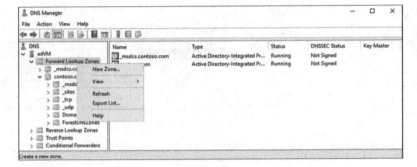

4. On the Welcome To The New Zone Wizard page, click Next.

5. On the Zone Type page, accept the default settings and click Next.

6. On the Active Directory Zone Replication Scope page, accept the default settings and click Next.

7. On the Zone Name page, type **15360x8640.com** and click Next.

8. On the Dynamic Update page, accept the default settings and click Next.

9. On the Completing the New Zone Wizard page, click Finish.

10. In the DNS Manager console, right-click the newly created zone and click New Host (A or AAAA).

11. In the New Host window (Figure 11.13), create a new record for fs with the internal IP address of adfsVM (in our environment, the IP address is 10.0.1.4).

12. Add another A record with the internal IP address of appVM (in our environment, the IP address is 10.0.2.4).

Now that we have name resolution, we will configure a sample claims-based application.

New Host   ✕

Name (uses parent domain name if blank):

fs

Fully qualified domain name (FQDN):

fs.15360x8640.com.

IP address:

10.0.1.4|

☐ Create associated pointer (PTR) record

☐ Allow any authenticated user to update DNS records with the
    same owner name

                              Add Host   Cancel

Configuring a Sample Federated Application

In this section, we are going to configure a simple .NET 4.5 sample federation application. This application is courtesy of Microsoft Consulting Services and is freely available for download and use for your testing. The prerequisite for this section is the federation server we deployed earlier in this chapter and the name resolution that we configured in the last section.

1. Log on to appVM as a member of the Domain Admins group.

2. On appVM, run Windows PowerShell ISE as administrator.

3. From the PowerShell ISE window, run the `Install-WindowsFeature -Name Web-Server, Web-App-Dev, Web-Net-Ext45, Web-Asp-Net45, Web-Mgmt-Tools, Web-Mgmt-Console,NET-Framework-45-Features,NET-Framework-45-Core,NET-Framework-45-ASPNET,RSAT-AD-PowerShell -Restart` command. This installs all role services and features required by the sample application and, if needed, restarts the server.

4. Wait for the installation to complete.

5. From the PowerShell ISE window, run the `New-ADUser -Name Svc_AppPool -AccountPassword (ConvertTo-SecureString -AsPlainText "Pa55w.rd1234" -Force) -Company Contoso -Description "App Pool Account" -DisplayName Svc_AppPool -Enabled $true -PasswordNeverExpires $true -SamAccountName Svc_AppPool -UserPrincipalName Svc_AppPool@contoso.com` command. This creates a new domain user that will be used to provide the security context for the AppPool in which our sample application will be running.

6. From the Administrator: Windows PowerShell ISE window, run the `Add-LocalGroupMember -Group IIS_IUSRS -Member CONTOSO\Svc_AppPool` command. This adds the newly created user to the local IIS_IUSRS group on the server.

7. Download the sample app from `https://msdnshared.blob.core.windows.net/media/TNBlogsFS/prod.evol.blogs.technet.com/telligent.evolution.components.attachments/01/8598/00/00/03/64/54/88/SampApp%20and%20Rules.zip`.

8. Extract SampleApp from the archive file and copy it to the `C:\inetpub\wwwroot` folder.

9. From the PowerShell window, run the `Invoke-Command -ComputerName adfsVM.contoso.com -ScriptBlock {Get-AdfsCertificate -CertificateType Token-Signing | Select-Object -ExpandProperty Thumbprint}` command to display the thumbprint of the AD FS token-signing certificate.

TOKEN-SIGNING CERTIFICATE

Note that this is different from the thumbprint of the wildcard certificate we're using in IIS. This certificate is strictly used for Token Signing from AD FS and has a separate thumbprint.

---

10. Copy the thumbprint to the Clipboard.

11. From the PowerShell window, run the `Notepad C:\inetpub\wwwroot\SampApp\Web.config` command.

12. Search for the word **thumbprint** in Notepad. There will be three matches. Replace the value within the double quotes immediately following `thumbprint=` with the content of the Clipboard. The key must match the token-signing certificate of the AD FS server.

13. Search for every occurrence of `app1.contoso.com` in Notepad and replace them with `appVM.15360x8640.com`. Just as with the thumbprints, you must replace every occurrence carefully or you'll receive an error message when navigating to the app URL.

14. Replace every occurrence of `sts.contoso.com` with `fs.15360x8640.com`.

15. Save the changes and close Notepad.

16. From the Administrator: Windows PowerShell window, run the `Notepad C:\inetpub\wwwroot\SampApp\FederationMetadata\2007-06\FederationMetadata.xml` command.

17. In Notepad, replace every occurrence of `app1.contoso.com` with `appVM.15360x8640.com`.

18. Save the changes and close Notepad.

19. Start Internet Information Services (IIS) Manager console.

20. In the console, click the Application Pools node. Then right-click DefaultAppPool and click Advanced Settings (Figure 11.14).

FIGURE 11.14
IIS Manager
Application Pools
settings

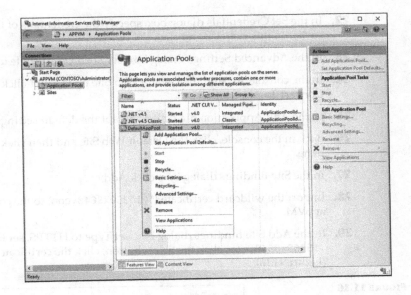

21. In the Advanced Settings dialog box, click Identity and then click the ellipses (…) to the right of the ApplicationPoolIdentity. In the ApplicationPoolIdentity dialog box, click Custom Account and then click Set (Figure 11.15).

FIGURE 11.15
IIS Manager
Application Pool
Identity page

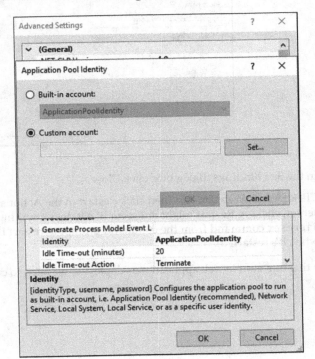

22. In the Set Credentials dialog box, specify the credentials of the domain user you created earlier in this exercise and click OK twice.

23. In the Advanced Settings dialog box, set Load User Profile to True and click OK.

24. In the console, expand the Default Web Site node, right-click SampApp, and then click Convert To Application.

25. In the Add Application dialog box, accept the default settings and then click OK.

26. Back in the console, click the Default Web Site and then click Bindings in the Actions pane.

27. In the Site Bindings dialog box, click Add.

28. Import the wildcard certificate (*.15360x8640.com) to the computer's Personal store on appVM.

29. In the Add Site Bindings dialog box, set Type to HTTPS, set Host Name to appVM .15360x8640.com, click the Select button, click the certificate to use, and then click OK (Figure 11.16).

FIGURE 11.16
IIS Manager Add
Site Binding dialog
box

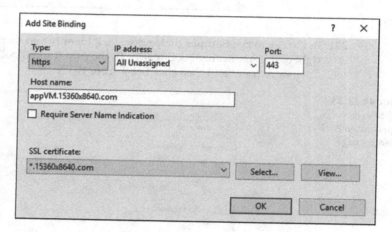

30. In the Site Bindings dialog box, click Close.

31. Click Default Web Site and then click Restart in the Actions pane. Depending on the server, clicking Restart might not seem like it does anything. You can also run the iisreset command from the command prompt to restart IIS (which gives a confirmation when it's restarted).

Now that our sample web application is deployed, we need to configure an AD FS relying party.

Configuring an AD FS Relying Party

In this section, we will configure an AD FS relying party. This enables the web application to accept claims from the claims provider.

1. Log on to adfsVM as a member of the Domain Admins group.

2. From adfsVM, , if needed, download the sample app from https://msdnshared.blob
.core.windows.net/media/TNBlogsFS/prod.evol.blogs.technet.com/telligent
.evolution.components.attachments/01/8598/00/00/03/64/54/88/SampApp%20
and%20Rules.zip.

3. Extract IssuanceAuthorizationRules.txt and IssuanceTransformRules.txt from the SampleApp and Rules subfolder in the .zip file and copy it to C:\.

4. On adfsVM, run Windows PowerShell ISE as administrator.

5. At the PowerShell ISE prompt, run the Add-AdfsRelyingPartyTrust -Name
"Sample Claims Aware Application" -IssuanceAuthorizationRulesFile
C:\IssuanceAuthorizationRules.txt -IssuanceTransformRulesFile C:\
IssuanceTransformRules.txt -MetadataUrl "https://appVM.15360x8640.com/
sampapp/federationmetadata/2007-06/federationmetadata.xml" command. This
creates a relying party representing the sample application.

6. Review the Relying Party Trusts folder in the AD FS console to verify that the relying party was created successfully.

Now that the relying party is configured, we are ready to test access to the web application.

Testing Application Access from an Internal Client

In this section, we will test the sample application from the local area network to ensure it functions correctly.

1. Start Internet Explorer on adfsVM.

2. In Internet Explorer, add https://*.15360x8640.com to the Local intranet zone (Figure 11.17).

3. Next, browse to https://appvm.15360x8640.com/SampApp/ and verify that the page displays the list of claims of the current user (Figure 11.18).

Up to this point, we have a functional web application available to users on the local area network. Next, we will deploy a Web Application Proxy server to facilitate users using the web application from the Internet (and it can be used for internal users, too).

FIGURE 11.17
Internet Explorer
Local intranet
zone

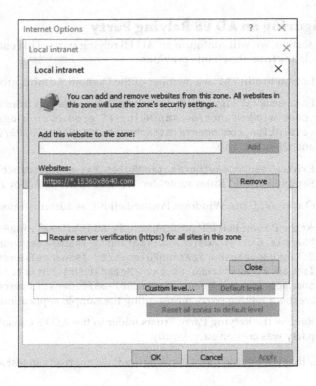

FIGURE 11.18
Sample app web
page

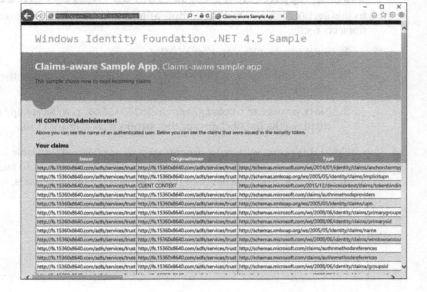

Installing Web Application Proxy Server Role Service

In this section, we will deploy the WAP server. This server is typically deployed in a perimeter network. For this section, you need a new VM named wapVM to host the WAP role.

1. Log on to wapVM as a local administrator.

2. Run Windows PowerShell ISE as administrator.

3. From the Administrator: Windows PowerShell ISE window, run the **certlm** command to open the Certificates – LocalComputer console.

4. In the console, right-click the Personal folder, click All Tasks, and then click Import. This will start the Certificate Import Wizard.

5. On the Welcome To The Certificate Import Wizard page, click Next.

6. On the File To Import page, click Browse.

7. In the Open dialog box, browse to the location of the ∗.pfx file, click it, and then click Open.

8. Back on the File To Import page, click Next.

9. On the Private Key Protection page, type the password protecting the private key and then click Next.

10. On the Certificate Store page, accept the default setting and click Next.

11. On the Completing The Certificate Import Wizard page, click Finish.

12. If the import was successful, a dialog box will notify you that it was successful. Click OK. Note that you should securely delete the .pfx file after the WAP server is deployed.

13. On wapVM, click Start and then click Server Manager.

14. Click Manage and then click Add Roles And Features.

15. If the Before You Begin page appears, click the Skip This Page By Default check box and then click Next.

16. On the Select Installation Type page, ensure that the Role-Based Or Feature-Based Installation option is selected and then click Next.

17. On the Server Destination Server page, ensure that wapVM is selected and then click Next.

18. On the Select Server Roles page, click the Remote Access check box and then click Next (Figure 11.19).

19. On the Select Features page, click Next.

20. On the Remote Access page, click Next.

21. On the Select Role Services page, click Web Application Proxy. This will display an additional dialog box prompting you to add features required for the Web Application Proxy role. Click Add Features and then click Next.

FIGURE 11.19
Add Roles and
Features Wizard

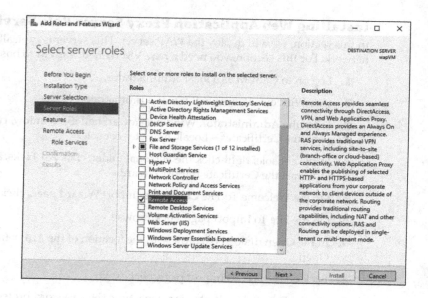

22. On the Confirm Installation Selections page, select the Restart The Destination Server Automatically If Required check box, click Yes when prompted for confirmation, and then click Install. Wait for the installation to complete.

23. Once the installation completes, on the Installation Progress page, click Open the Web Application Proxy Wizard. This will start Web Application Proxy Configuration Wizard (Figure 11.20).

FIGURE 11.20
WAP
Configuration
Wizard

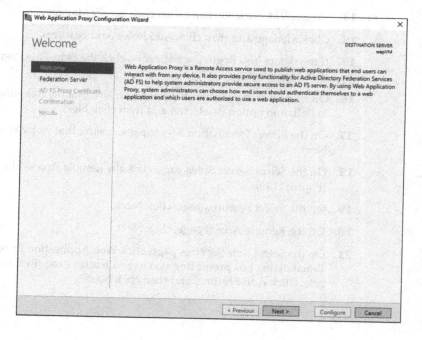

24. On the Welcome page, click Next.

25. On the Federation Server page (Figure 11.21), set the Federation Service Name to `fs
.15360x8640.com`, provide the credentials of the administrator account on the federation
servers, and then click Next.

FIGURE 11.21
Federation Server
page

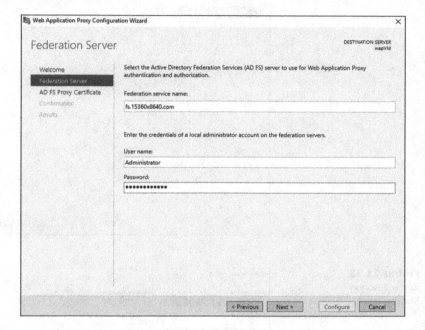

26. On the AD FS Proxy Certificate page (Figure 11.22), select the certificate you imported
earlier in this exercise and click Next.

27. On the Confirmation page, click Configure.

28. Wait until the configuration completes, review the detailed operation results, and
click Close. This will automatically open the Remote Access Management console
(Figure 11.23).

Now, we have a WAP server. Next, we need to publish our web application so it is accessible
through the WAP server.

Microsoft provides a checklist for setting up a WAP server. Take a look at `https://docs
.microsoft.com/en-us/windows-server/identity/ad-fs/deployment/checklist--
setting-up-a-federation-server-proxy` for the checklist and links to additional content
around this topic.

FIGURE 11.22
Selecting a
certificate

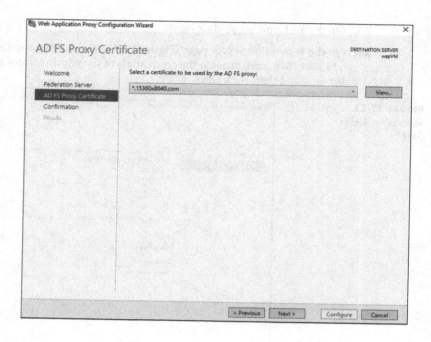

FIGURE 11.23
Remote Access
Management

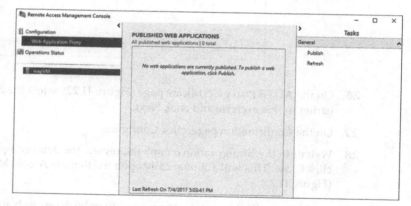

Publishing the Sample Federated Application

In this section, we will publish our web application.

1. On wapVM, in the Remote Access Management console, click Publish in the Tasks pane. This will start the Publish New Application Wizard. On the Welcome page, click Next.

2. On the Preauthentication page, accept the default option Active Directory Federation Services (AD FS) and click Next.

3. On the Supported Clients page, accept the default option Web and MSOFBA and click Next.

4. On the Relying Party page, select Sample Claims Aware Application and click Next (Figure 11.24).

FIGURE 11.24
Relying Party
page

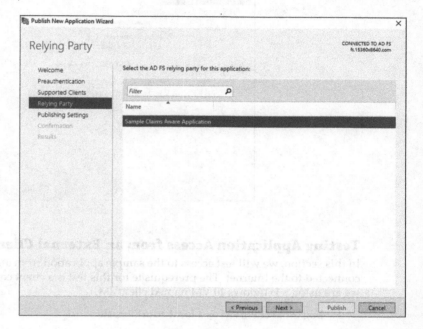

5. On the Publishing Settings page, set the name to Sample Claims Aware Application and set the External URL to https://appVM.15360x8640.com/SampApp/. For the External certificate, select the certificate you installed on appVM. Accept the default setting for the Backend Server URL (matching the External URL) and click Next (Figure 11.25).

6. On the Confirmation page, click Publish.

7. On the Results page, you should receive a message indicating that the application was published successfully. Click Close.

The sample web application is published. Next, we will test access to the web application from an external client.

FIGURE 11.25
Publishing
Settings page

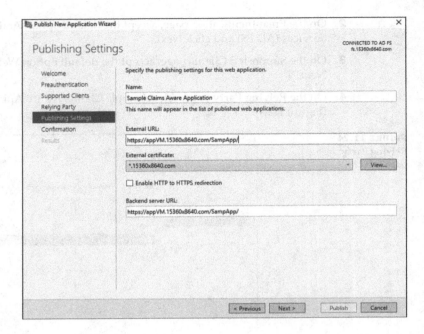

FIGURE 11.25
Publishing
Settings page

Testing Application Access from an External Client

In this section, we will test access to the sample application from an external client, such as one connected to the Internet. The prerequisite for this test is a client computer. In our environment, we are using a Windows 10 VM named clientVM.

1. Log on to clientVM as a local administrator.

2. On clientVM, right-click Start and click Windows PowerShell (Admin).

3. From the Administrator: Windows PowerShell window, run `Notepad c:\Windows\system32\drivers\etc\hosts` command.

4. In Notepad, add entries to the hosts file representing the external IP address of the wapVM and appVM:

   <public IP address>   `fs.15360x8640.com`

   <public IP address>   `appVM.15360x8640.com`

   Substitute the public IP addresses that you are using for *<public IP address>*. Note that, in a real-world environment, we would rely on the name resolution of a DNS server that clientVM is using. The DNS server would be able to resolve Internet-accessible names in the `15360x8640.com` namespace to their corresponding public IP addresses.

5. Save your changes and close Notepad.

6. Start Internet Explorer and browse to `https://appVM.15360x8640.com/SampApp/`. You should be redirected to an authentication page for Contoso Corporation, as shown in Figure 11.26.

FIGURE 11.26
Sample app authentication page

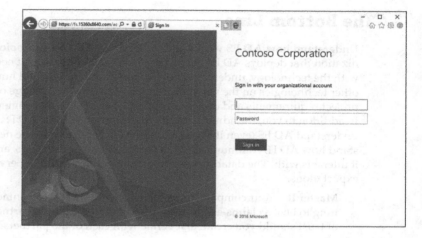

7. Specify the same credentials you used during the internal test and click Sign-in.

8. Verify that you have successfully authenticated (Figure 11.27).

FIGURE 11.27
Sample app page

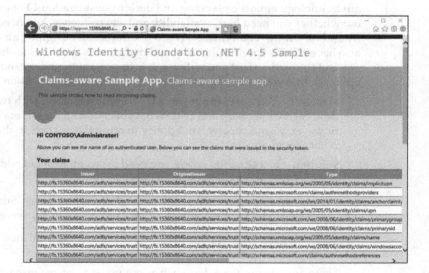

You can easily customize the AD FS sign-in page to align with your organization's standards. You can update the logo, the picture, and other areas of the sign-in page. See `https://docs` `.microsoft.com/en-us/windows-server/identity/ad-fs/operations/ad-fs-user-sign-` `in-customization` for more information on customizing the sign-in page.

The Bottom Line

Understand how AD FS works and understand AD FS terminology. When your organization first deploys AD FS, many people in the IT department need to become familiar with the technology, understand how it works, and understand how it integrates with the other technologies on the network. Having high-level knowledge of AD FS helps you gather project requirements and design an appropriate AD FS environment for your organization. In addition to you, the administrator who is responsible for AD FS, other teams also need to understand AD FS (even if at just a basic level). For example, the network team must understand how AD FS communicates, the protocols and ports it uses, and which other services it interacts with. The database team must understand the SQL Server requirements and expectations.

Master It Your company implements a new AD FS environment. The company is planning to host a claims-aware web application for multiple partner companies. Which type of trust should you create to federate with each of the partners?

Solution The company hosting the resource (in this case, the web application for partner companies) is the relying party (or resource partner organization). To federate with the partners, you need to create a relying party trust for each partner.

Plan and design AD FS. When you plan and design a technology for your network, there are technology-agnostic planning and design considerations. For example, you need to figure out whether you need high availability and site resilience. You need to figure out the capacity and hardware requirements. When planning and designing an AD FS environment, you also have AD FS–specific planning and design considerations such as the database you will use and the certificate(s) you will use. It is important to understand the pros and cons of each option so that you can make the best choices for your organization.

Master It You are planning an AD FS implementation with two federation servers in the local area network and two Web Application Proxy servers in the perimeter network. However, your company has a policy to minimize servers in the perimeter network. What should you do?

Solution In a situation where you need (or want) to avoid adding servers in your perimeter network, you have a couple of options:

◆ Use an existing reverse proxy in the perimeter network. Such a reverse proxy might be able to take the place of the Web Application Proxy server.

◆ Deploy the Web Application Proxy servers in the local area network and use an existing reverse proxy in the perimeter network.

There are other options, too, such as not using a reverse proxy as part of the solution. However, that reduces the security of your environment and is not advised.

Deploy an AD FS environment. If you understand AD FS and go through the planning and design phase, your AD FS deployment should be smooth and without issues. However, there are often deployments where you can't go through a learning phase and a planning and design phase (or, you must rush through one or more of those phases). This can put stress on the deployment, and you might end up with a deployment that doesn't meet the requirements or doesn't perform up to expectations. To mitigate this, always factor in enough time for your project so that you can perform your first deployment to a nonproduction environment. In the nonproduction environment, you can validate your design and create your deployment documentation. If a problem arises, you will have time to fix it because you are working in a nonproduction environment. By the time you do deploy to production, your knowledge will be greater, you will have created a deployment document, and you will have validated your design ahead of time. This often ensures success.

Master It You are deploying your first federation server in a new AD FS farm. The Installation Wizard prompts you for a certificate to use. Which type of certificate file should you specify?

Solution The primary requirement is that you have a certificate with the private key. So you need to use a `.pfx` file that contains the private key. As part of your pre-deployment work, you should obtain the certificate prior to your AD FS deployment. Then, copy the `.pfx` file to the federation server so it is ready during deployment. Once finished with the certificate, securely delete the `.pfx` file from the file system.

Chapter 12

Management with System Center

Like previous versions of the product, System Center 2016 plays a major service-management role in the information technology (IT) world. In this chapter, you will learn about the different high-level products in the suite. As IT professionals, we are not responsible for every task required to accomplish key business activities in our environments, so we will just cover the basics needed to support Windows Server. By providing key capabilities, called *services*, to enable businesses to achieve their goals, IT plays an important role in the server-management process. Although many activities fall under the IT department tag, we often see many of them separated into different departments rather than combined into one cohesive unit. Desktop support, application development, server support, storage administration, and so on are all aspects of IT, but they are not always as unified as they should be to deliver quality IT services. Often, the various roles are not clearly defined so responsibilities are not clear. To help you understand those ambiguities, we will define IT service management throughout the entire lifecycle of those services.

IN THIS CHAPTER, YOU WILL LEARN TO:

- ◆ Understand how all of the Microsoft System Center products map to service management
- ◆ Configure a SQL Server cluster
- ◆ Install System Center 2016
- ◆ Install Management Pack for Windows Server 2016

Overview of System Center 2016

Let's look at System Center 2016, explore the new features of the products, and examine how the products have developed into enterprise management tools that provide a total server-management solution for Windows clients.

Because most of you will be working on an upgrade path, we'll start with the upgrade sequence of System Center 2016. However, you may be working on a new install, so we'll cover the installation sequence next.

Understanding the Upgrade Sequence

Before you perform any new installation or upgrade process, you need to review the supported platform and system requirements of the software. Table 12.1 lists the various supported upgrade paths. You need to understand these upgrade paths if you are currently using System Center 2012 R2.

TABLE 12.1: Supported Upgrade Paths

COMPONENT	PREVIOUS VERSION
Data Protection Manager	System Center 2012 R2 with UR10 or later
Operations Manager	System Center 2012 R2 with UR9 or later
Orchestrator	System Center 2012 R2 with UR8 or later
Service Management Automation	System Center 2012 R2 with UR7 or later
Service Manager	System Center 2012 R2 with UR9 or later
Service Provider Foundation	
Virtual Machine Manager	System Center 2012 R2 with UR9 or later
System Center Configuration Manager	System Center 2012 R2 SP1 or later

You need to review and validate your existing environment before you can upgrade to System Center 2016. (System Center Configuration Manager will be covered later on this chapter.)

 Real World Scenario

SYSTEM CENTER UPGRADE SEQUENCE IN THE REAL WORLD

When we're working with customers, one of the most common questions we get is, What is the upgrade sequence? This is interesting because most of the customers we work with don't have all the products installed. However, it is still important to understand the upgrade sequence. It's recommended to upgrade in the following products in the order listed here:

1. Orchestrator
2. Service Manager
3. Data Protection Manager
4. Operations Manager
5. Virtual Machine Manager
6. System Center Configuration Manager

Before you move on and install System Center 2016, make sure you understand the different system requirements. You can review them at the following link: https://docs.microsoft.com/en-us/system-center/?view=sc-om-1711.

Understanding the Install Sequence

Installing a product or series of products can be a little bit of a challenge. Because we are focusing on Windows Server 2016 in this book, we are going to focus our install sequence on the hardware configurations of the products before we outline the steps to install the products and manage Windows Server with them.

RECOMMENDED HARDWARE

Before you build new servers for each of the products, it is important to know the recommended minimum CPU, memory, and disk space needed for each of the products, as shown in Table 12.2.

TABLE 12.2: Hardware Recommendations

SERVER	PROCESSOR	RAM	HARD DRIVE SPACE
DPM Server	2.33 GHz 8-core	16 GB	150 GB
OpsMgr Server	2.33 GHz 8-core	32 GB	125 GB
Orchestrator Server	2.1 GHz 4-core	8 GB	200 GB
ServiceMgr Server	2.66 GHz 8-core	32 GB	400 GB
Virtual Machine Manager Server	2.66 GHz 16-core	16 GB	200 GB
System Center Configuration Manager	2.66 GHz 16-core	96 GB	300 GB

Make sure your system meets the minimum hardware recommendations when you build each of the servers for System Center 2016. Otherwise, you could run into performance problems when the product is fully implemented.

SQL SERVER VERSION SUPPORT

SQL Server provides the foundation for the System Center 2016 products. Each product version has a database associated with it, also represents more than 80 percent of the process and information stored on each of the databases. Whether you should install SQL Server 2016 Standard or Enterprise Edition on a component will depend on the amount of data that it is going to hold. Take Configuration Manager for example; the Standard Edition can support a maximum number of 50,000 clients and the Enterprise Edition can support more than 50,000 clients.

DATABASE CLUSTER RECOMMENDATIONS

If you are going to install a one-for-all database cluster that will hold all instances to support System Center 2016, you can achieve this by having at least two nodes. For more information on how to create this cluster machine, review Chapter 3. However, you must keep in mind the amount of memory that is recommended for each instance as shown in Table 12.3.

TABLE 12.3: SQL Memory per SQL Instance

SQL INSTANCE	SQL MINIMUM MEMORY
Orchestrator	8 GB
Operations Manager	8 GB
Service Manager	8 GB
Virtual Machine Manager	8 GB
Data Protection Manager	8 GB
Configuration Manager	16 GB

Because each product will take ownership of the instance and perform changes in the SQL Security configuration as well on the system databases, each SQL instance should be a separate instance.

ALL-FOR-ONE DATABASE CLUSTER

As shown in Table 12.3, each SQL instance has been named to correspond to the name of the product. In SQL Server, you can choose the default instance or a named instance. We will select a named instance for our SQL Server Installation. The instance will require at least three cluster disks to store the information for the different databases.

DATABASES FILE TYPES

SQL creates three main databases file types:

◆ The first file type is usually a system database. The system databases will contain the master database and other files.

◆ The second file type is what we call the temp databases. We recommend storing this database on a separate drive and creating multiple database files to match the number of CPUs the server will have. Usually, the ratio is a 1:1. For every CPU, you will create a temp database file, except for those servers that have more than eight CPUs. In those cases, you will create a maximum of eight tempdb files.

◆ The last database type is the System Center database. You store this database on a separate drive as well.

Installing an Instance in a Cluster

To guide you through this process, we will create a SQL Server instance in a cluster. You can find more information at the following link:

https://docs.microsoft.com/en-us/sql/sql-server/failover-clusters/install/create-a-new-sql-server-failover-cluster-setup

For this scenario, you will have two nodes in a cluster. SQL01 will be Node 1, and SQL02 will be Node 2. Follow these steps:

1. Log in to Node 1, SQL01.

2. Insert the SQL Server Media or SQL Server 2016 installation media.

3. In the SQL Server Installation Center, as shown in Figure 12.1, click Installation.

FIGURE 12.1
SQL Server
Installation
Center

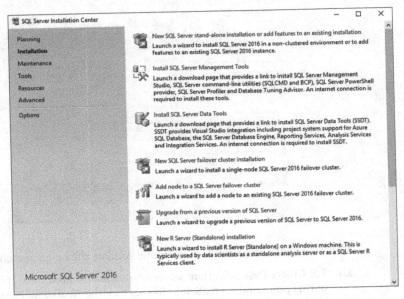

4. Select New SQL Server Failover Cluster Installation.

5. On the Install a SQL Server Failover Cluster screen, enter the product key or select a free edition. Once you have entered or selected the appropriate option, click Next.

6. Select I Accept The License Terms and then click Next.

7. Select Use Microsoft Update To Check For Updates (Recommended) and then click Next.

8. For Install Failover Cluster Rules, review each of the rules and address those that failed. Once you have addressed them, click Next.

9. For Feature Selection, you only need the database engine services for each instance. Click Next after you've made your selection.

10. For Feature Rules, review every rule that has passed. In the case of failure, address the specific failure and then rerun the rule. Once this step is completed, click Next.

11. For Instance Configuration, enter the details of the instance. For this scenario, you will use a named instance, as shown in Figure 12.2. You will add the name corresponding to the System Center Instance you will configure.

FIGURE 12.2
Installing a SQL
Server failover
cluster: Instance
Configuration

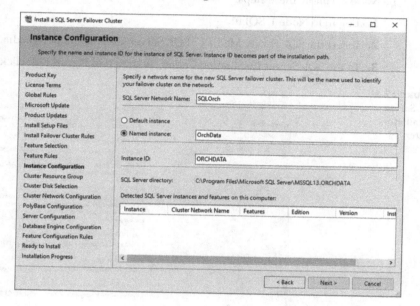

12. For Cluster Resource Group Name, validate the name and click Next.

13. For Custer Disk Selection, select an available shared disk. If none are available, create one at this point and then click Refresh. Once the Available Shared Disks list displays the drives as shown in Figure 12.3, select the best drive or drives for the cluster. Then click Next.

14. For Cluster Network Configuration, make sure to enter the static IP for the following SQL instance. Then click Next.

15. For Server Configuration, make sure the database engine is running using a Domain Service Account. Also make sure Collation is the one supported by the System Center product that is about to be installed. Once you have confirmed, click Next.

16. For Database Engine Configuration, click Add Current User. On the Server Configuration tab, add any security group that will be needed. Then click Data Directories and ensure

the data root and user database point to the correct cluster storage, as shown in Figure 12.4. Then click TempDB and add the same amount of CPU as number of files to avoid database contention, as shown in Figure 12.5. Once completed, click Next.

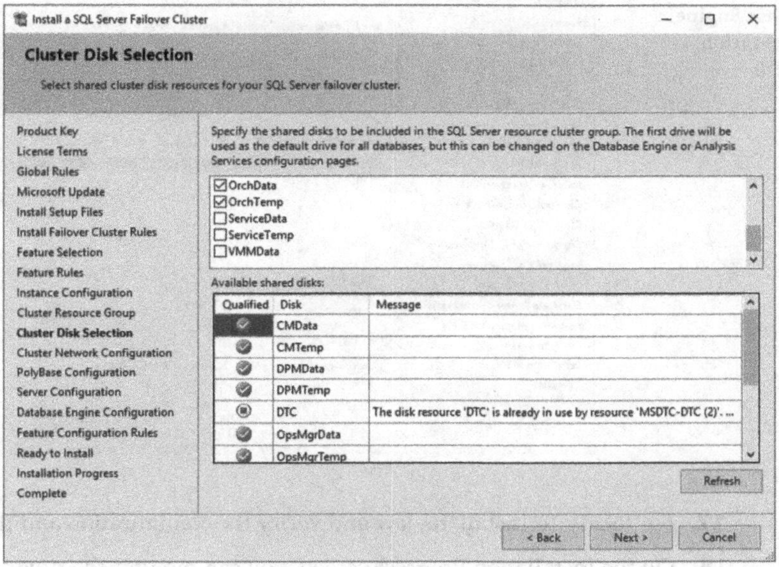

FIGURE 12.3
Installing a SQL Server failover cluster: Cluster Disk Selection

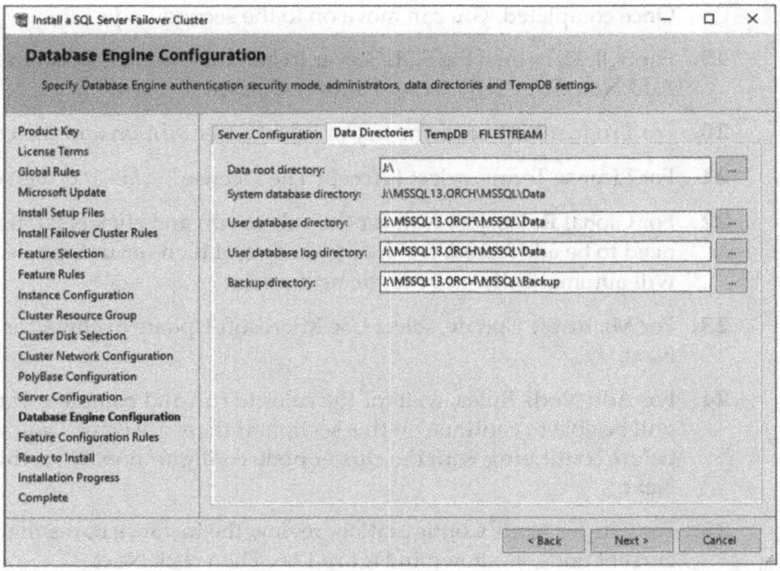

FIGURE 12.4
Installing a SQL Server failover cluster: Database Engine Configuration, Data Directories

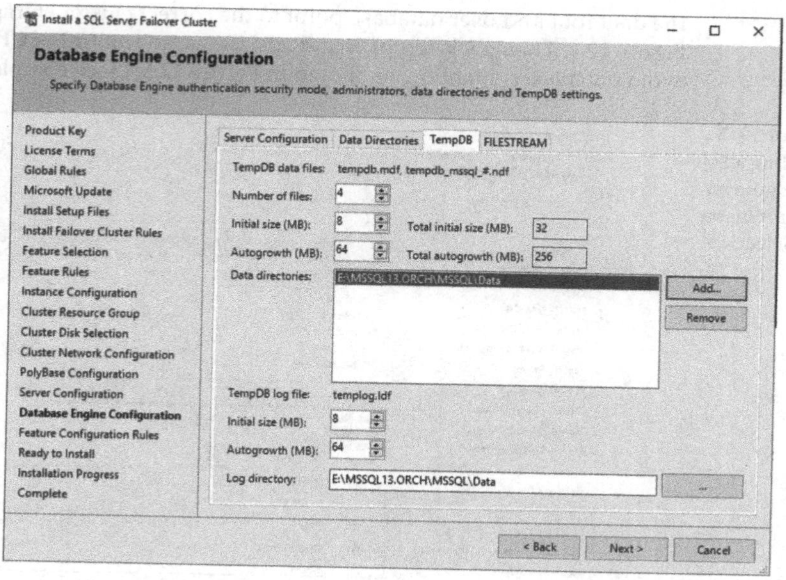

FIGURE 12.5
Installing a
SQL Server
failover cluster:
Database Engine
Configuration,
TempDB

17. For Ready To Install, review and verify the configuration and then click Install.

18. On the Installation Progress screen, you can monitor the progress. This will take several minutes to complete.

    Once completed, you can move on to the second node.

19. For SQL02, launch the SQL Server Installation Center, select Installation, and then click Add Note To A SQL Server Failover Cluster.

20. For Product Key, enter the key or select a free edition and then click Next.

21. For License Terms, select I Accept The License Terms and then click Next.

22. For Global Rules, just wait for the rule to run and click Next. If any items on this screen need to be addressed, feel free to do so and then rerun the rule. Otherwise, the system will automatically move to the next screen.

23. For Microsoft Update, select Use Microsoft Update to check for updates and then click Next.

24. For Add Node Rules, wait for the rules to run and complete. If there are no errors, you will be able to continue on this section. If there are errors, you will have to address them before continuing with the cluster node configuration. Once this step is completed, click Next.

25. For Cluster Node Configuration, review the instance name that you want to add to the current node, as shown in Figure 12.6. Then click Next.

FIGURE 12.6
Installing a
SQL Server
failover cluster:
Cluster Node
Configuration

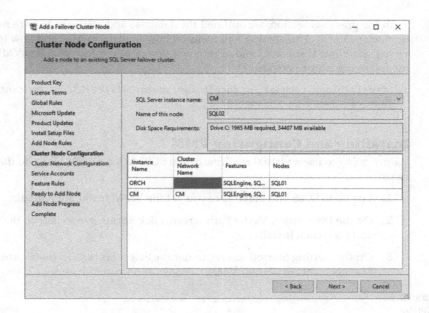

26. For Cluster Network Configuration, validate the network settings of the instance you are adding and then click Next.

27. For Service Account, select Grant Perform Volume Maintenance Task Privilege To SQL Server Database Engine and reenter the password for the service accounts; then click Next.

28. On the Read to Add Node screen, review the configuration and click Install.

For Add Node Progress, you will wait for a few minutes until this is completed.

Note that you will need to repeat this section for every SQL instance you want to add to the node.

Using System Center Virtual Machine Manager

In this section, we will focus on Virtual Machine Manager (VMM). The main goal of this product is to provision the fabric, deploy and manage virtual machines, and deploy multitier apps. With the 2016 version, the product supports new and enhanced Windows Server 2016 software-defined compute, storage, and networking technologies. You can create template-based deployments and ensure that the infrastructure is secure via shielded VMs and Host Guardian Service Support.

To read more about VMM, go to the following link:

```
https://technet.microsoft.com/en-us/system-center-docs/vmm/get-started/get-
started-overview
```

In the previous section, we outlined the database and software requirements needed to implement VMM. This section will focus on how to install VMM and how to deploy your first virtual machine. If you are looking for more demos and information on VMM, take a look at the following feature demos:

```
https://blogs.technet.microsoft.com/scvmm/2017/01/23/system-center-vmm-2016-
features-demos-on-channel-9/
```

Installing and Configuring VMM

We are going to use a virtual machine called SC05 to install VMM. To do that, just follow these steps:

1. Log on to SC05 and make sure you get the VMM installation media.

2. On the Installation Media Path screen, click Setup.exe to launch the installation media and then click Install.

3. On the Getting Started screen, under the Select Feature To Install area, select VMM Management Server and VMM Console, as shown in Figure 12.7, and then click Next.

FIGURE 12.7
The Getting Started screen in the VMM Setup Wizard

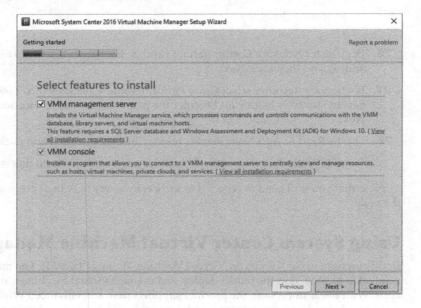

4. On the Product Registration Information screen, enter the product key. If no product key is entered, it will be in evaluation mode. Once you have completed the information, click Next.

5. On the Please Read This License Agreement screen, you need to accept it; if you don't, you won't to be able to continue. After you accept the terms, click Next.

6. On the Diagnostic And Usage Data screen, click Next.

7. On the Microsoft Update screen, select On (Recommended). This is the best approach to keep the system up-to-date. Then click Next.

8. On the Installation Location screen, select a path. We recommend using a drive other than C: so that more storage space will be assigned to the server. Once you have entered the correct path, click Next.

9. On the Prerequisite screen, make sure all the requirements are installed. If any of them are missing, just install them and click Check Prerequisites again. Then click Next.

DEPLOYING ADK TO MANAGE BOOT IMAGES

If the Windows Assessment and Deployment Kit checkmark is displayed, make sure to download ADK 10 from the following link: https://go.microsoft.com/fwlink/p/?LinkId=845542.

---

10. On the Database Configuration screen, as shown in Figure 12.8, select the Server Name or Cluster Name. Then enter the service account and password, and choose the instance name. In this case, it is VMM; however, it could be the default instance MSSQLServer in a nonclustered or shared SQL server. Then enter the new database name; by default it is VirtualManagerDB, but it can be renamed if needed. Once completed, click Next.

FIGURE 12.8
VMM Setup
Wizard: Database
Configuration

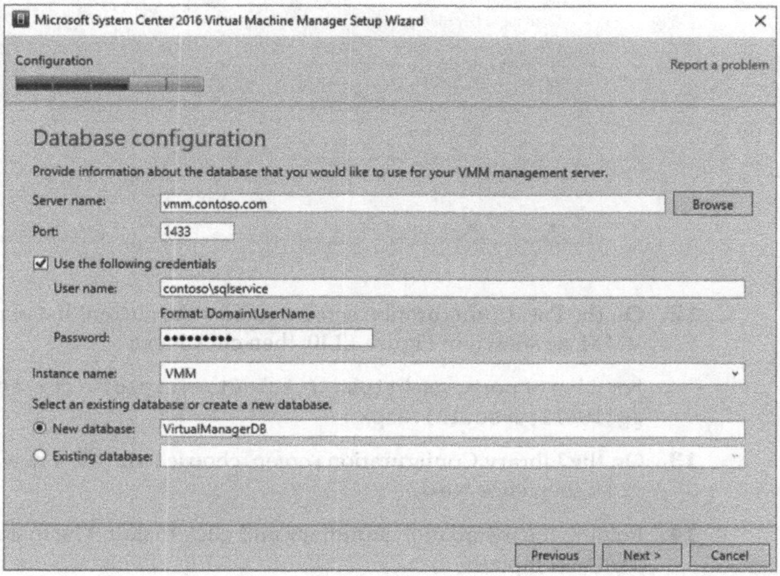

SQL SERVER SERVICE ACCOUNT

Make sure the service account has rights to the SQL Server. Usually, we give them sysadmin rights on the instance during installation to ensure that everything gets created. You can change it to dbreader and dbowner afterward. Also, you need to make sure to use port 1433 or any custom port. By default, the instance will use a dynamic port.

---

11. On the Configure Service Account and Distributed Key Management screen, enter the service account and the Distributed Key Management (DKM), as shown in Figure 12.9. Then click Next.

FIGURE 12.9
VMM Setup
Wizard: VMM
Service Account

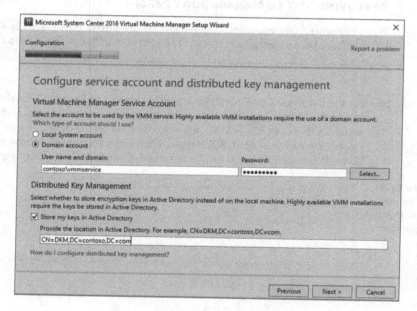

12. On the Port Configuration screen, review the current list of ports that are needed by VMM, as shown in Figure 12.10; then click Next.

For a list of ports, see `https://technet.microsoft.com/en-us/library/gg710871(v=sc.12).aspx`.

13. On the Library Configuration screen, choose to create a new library, as shown in Figure 12.11; then click Next.

14. Review the installation summary and click Install. The installation will take a few minutes to complete.

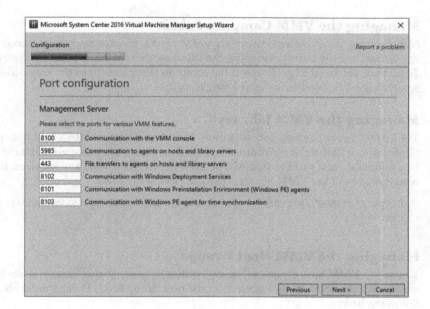

FIGURE 12.10
VMM Setup
Wizard: Port
Configuration

FIGURE 12.11
VMM Setup
Wizard: Library
Configuration

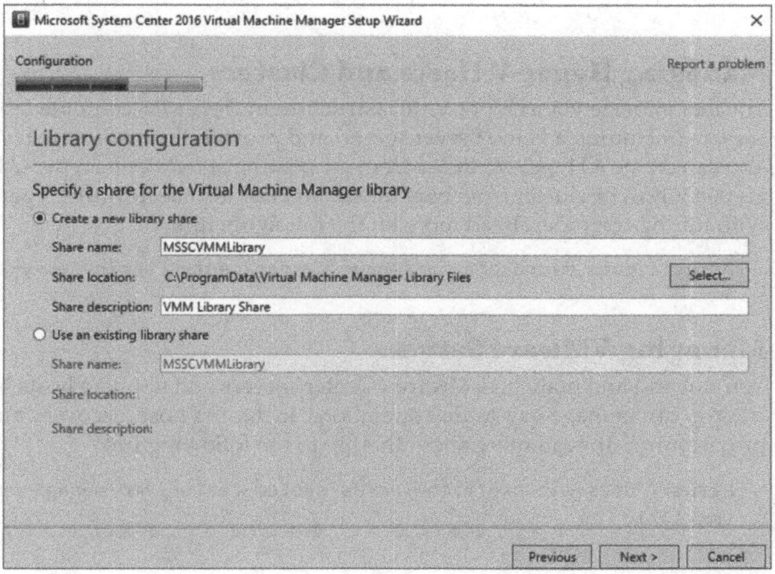

Managing the VMM Compute Fabric

Now that you have implemented your VMM server, you are ready to start our journey of building virtual machines and managing the Windows Server 2016 operating system in those VMs. To do that, you need to understand the compute fabric describes the way different parts of something work together to form a single entity.

Managing the VMM Library

The VMM library consists of one or more files shares that contain VMM resources. In the library, you will interact by adding file-based resources such as a virtual hard disk, configuration templates, and profiles that will be used to provision VMs and services. If you would like to read more about the VMM library, check the following link:

```
https://technet.microsoft.com/en-us/system-center-docs/vmm/manage/manage-library-
overview
```

Managing the VMM Host Groups

You set up VMM host groups as logical entities to group virtualization hosts together. You then assign and configure those resources at the host group level. To read more about this, check the following link:

```
https://docs.microsoft.com/en-us/system-center/vmm/host-groups?view=sc-vmm-1711
```

Managing Hyper-V Hosts and Clusters

You can manage your Hyper-V infrastructure in the VMM compute fabric. You can add existing servers (including a Nano Server server) and provide them with the Hyper-V role if required. You can create a Hyper-V cluster from an existing standalone Hyper-V host or provision a Hyper-V host or cluster from bare metal. You can also keep your Hyper-V clusters up-to-date with rolling upgrades. Read more on the following link:

```
https://docs.microsoft.com/en-us/system-center/vmm/hyper-v-hosts?view=sc-vmm-1711
```

Managing VMware Servers

You can add and manage VMware vCenter servers and vSphere hosts in the VMM compute fabric. You can manage day-to-day operations, including host discovery and management and VM provisioning. To read more about this, go to the following link:

```
https://docs.microsoft.com/en-us/system-center/vmm/manage-vmware-hosts?view=sc-
vmm-1711
```

Managing Infrastructure Servers

You can add infrastructure servers that are used by VMM for provisioning and networking. You can add Active Directory, Domain Name System (DNS), and Dynamic Host Configuration

Protocol (DHCP) servers so that you can manage and update all of these servers from the same location. To read more about this, review the following link:

https://docs.microsoft.com/en-us/system-center/vmm/infrastructure-server?view=sc-vmm-1711

Here's how to add a Windows Server 2016 ISO to the VMM library:

1. Open the Virtual Machine Manager console from Start ➤ Microsoft System Center 2016.

2. Go to the Library workspace and then expand Library Servers, as shown in Figure 12.12.

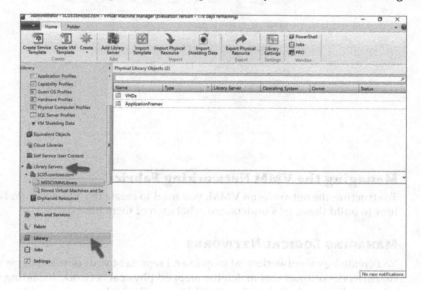

FIGURE 12.12
VMM Console:
Library Servers

3. Right-click MSSCVMMLibrary and click Explore.

4. You can copy the .iso to the root or create a folder and call it ISO Image, as shown in Figure 12.13. This is the approach we took when copying the Windows Server 2016 ISO.

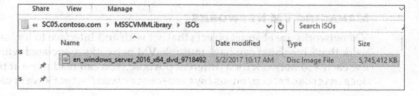

FIGURE 12.13
Folder Explorer:
MSSCVMMLibrary

5. Once you complete step 4, go to the Library Server node and right-click Refresh. The new ISO will show on the node, as shown in Figure 12.14.

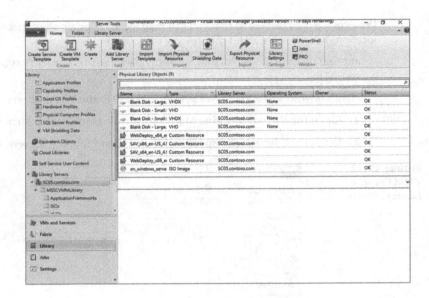

Managing the VMM Networking Fabric

To structure the networks on VMM, you need to create the VM network. Before we show you how to build these, let's understand what each of them mean.

MANAGING LOGICAL NETWORKS

You create *logical* networks that map to and represent your physical networks. You assign logical networks settings that match the mapped physical network, including the network type, the associated network sites, and static address pools if relevant. To read more, go to the following link:

```
https://docs.microsoft.com/en-us/system-center/vmm/network-logical?view=sc-
vmm-1711
```

MANAGING VM NETWORKS

VM networks are abstract objects that act with and interface to logical networks. A logical network that's insolated can have multiple VM networks associated with it, thereby allowing you to use each VM network for a different purpose. You can read more at the following link: `https://docs.microsoft.com/en-us/system-center/vmm/network-virtual?view=sc-vmm-1711`.

MANAGING NETWORK VIRTUALIZATION GATEWAYS

If you are using insolated VM networks, the VMs in that network can connect only to machines in the same subnet. If you want to connect further, you can set up network virtualization gateways. Read more at the following link:

https://docs.microsoft.com/en-us/system-center/vmm/network-gateway?view=sc-vmm-1711

Creating a Logical Network

Here's how to create a logical network:

1. Open the VMM console.

2. Then go to the Fabric workspace and click Networking, as shown in Figure 12.15.

FIGURE 12.15
VMM Console: Fabric Resources: Create Logical Network

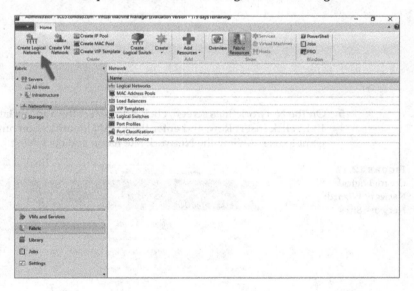

3. In the Create Logical Network Wizard, enter the name and description of your logical network and then click Next.

4. In the Specify Logical Network Settings screen, as shown in Figure 12.16, make the appropriate selections. When you are finished with the settings, click Next.

FIGURE 12.16
Create Logical
Network Wizard:
Specify Logical
Network Settings

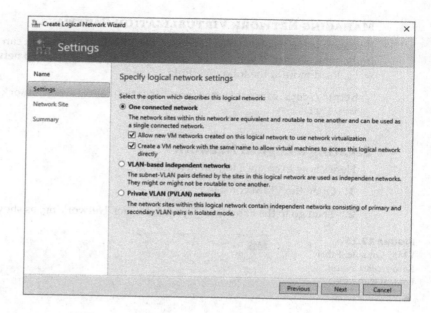

5. On the Network Sites screen, click Add, select the appropriate host, as shown in Figure 12.17, click Insert Row, and enter the VLAN identification number and IP subnet that you want to use. Review the Network Site name and click Next.

FIGURE 12.17
Create Logical
Network Wizard:
Network Sites

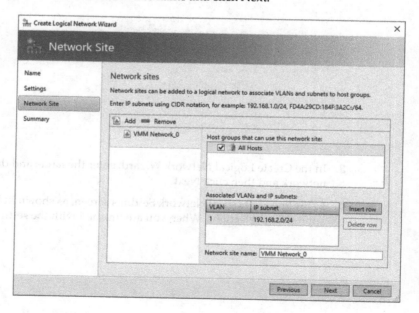

6. Review the summary and click Finish.

Creating a VM Network

Here's how to create a VM network:

1. Open the VMM console.

2. Go to the Fabric Workspace screen. Click Networking Node and then click Create VM Network, as shown in Figure 12.18.

FIGURE 12.18
VMM Console: VMs:
Create VM Network

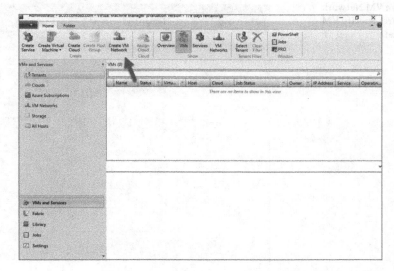

3. On the Specify a Name and Description for the VM Network screen, enter the name description and logical network, select the logical network, as shown in Figure 12.19, and then click Next.

FIGURE 12.19
The Create VM
Network Wizard

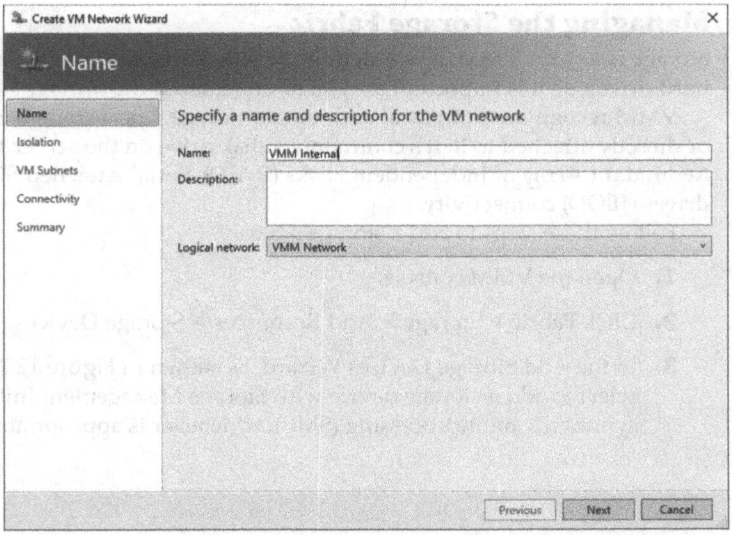

4. On the Select the Isolation for This VM Network screen, select Isolate Using Hyper-V Network Virtualization; leave the default and then click Next.

5. On the Specify VM Subnets screen, click Add; then enter the name and subnet as shown in Figure 12.20, and click Next.

FIGURE 12.20
Create VM Network Wizard: Specify VM subnets

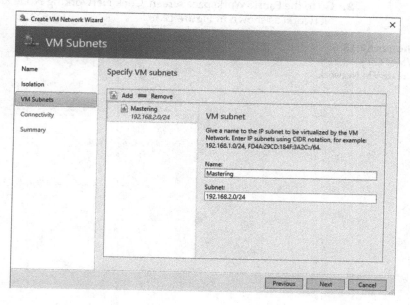

6. On the Connectivity screen, leave the settings set to the defaults and click Next.

7. On the Summary page, review all the settings and click Next.

Managing the Storage Fabric

Storage is key for VMM; it will determine where to store the virtual machines and their virtual hard drives, so it is important for you to understand the different storage options.

VMM recognizes both local and remote storage. Local storage is located on the VMM server or directly attached to it. It's commonly a disk drive on the server that's connected with built-in Redundant Array of Independent Disks (RAID), Serial Attached SCSI (SAS), or just a bunch of drives (JBOD) connectivity.

Follow these steps to add a storage device:

1. Open the VMM console.

2. Click Fabric ➢ Storage ➢ Add Resources ➢ Storage Devices.

3. In the Add Storage Devices Wizard, as shown in Figure 12.21, select the provider type, select to add a storage device with Storage Management Initiative Specification (SMI-S) or symmetric multiprocessing (SMP), whichever is appropriate for the device you are using.

FIGURE 12.21
Add Storage
Devices Wizard:
Select Storage
Provider Type

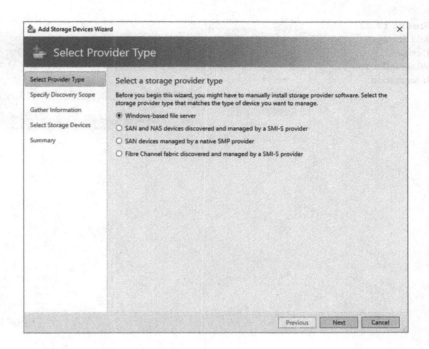

4. On the Specify Discovery Scope screen, if you are using SMI-S, specify whether the provider uses SMI-S CIMXML (Common Information Model Extensible Markup Language) or SMI-S WMI (Windows Management Instrumentation), add the IP address/FQDN, and add the port used to connect to the provider on the remote server. You can enable SSL if you are using CIMXML. Then specify an account to use to connect to the provider.

   If you are using SMP, select the provider from the list. If it is not in the list, click Import to refresh it.

5. On the Gather Information screen, as shown in Figure 12.22, VMM automatically tries to discover and import the storage device information. To retry, click Scan Provider.

6. If you select the option to use a Secure Sockets Layer (SSL) connection from an SMI-S Provider, note that during the discovery, the Import Certificate dialog box will appear. Check the settings and click Import. By default, the certificate common name (CN) will be verified. If there is no CN or it does not match, storage discovery might fail.

   If discovery fails due to the CN, disable CN verification in the Registry of the VMM server. In the Registry, go to HKEY_LOCAL_MACHINE/SOFTWARE/Microsoft/Storage Management/ and create a new DWORD value—DisableHttpsCommonNameCheck. Set the value to 1.

7. If the discovery process succeeds, the discovery storage arrays, storage pools, manufacturer, model, and capacity will be listed on the page when the process finishes. Click Next.

FIGURE 12.22
Add Storage
Devices
Wizard: Gather
Information

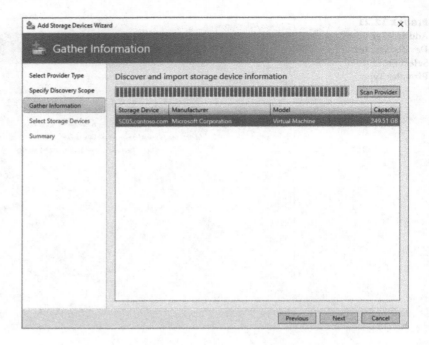

8. On the Select Storage Device screen, you can specify a classification for each storage pool. Storage pools with similar characteristics are grouped together into classifications so that you can assign a classification as storage for a host or cluster, rather than a specific storage device.

9. On the Summary page, confirm the settings and then click Finish. The Jobs dialog box will appear. When the status is Completed, you can verify the storage in Fabric ➤ Storage.

Creating Virtual Machines

Now that you have all the requirements for the VMM, it is time to create your first virtual machine for Windows Server 2016. To do that, you need to understand the process of *provisioning* VMs.

To create a virtual machine, follow these steps:

1. Open the VMM console.

2. Select VMs and Services ➤ Create Virtual Machine, as shown in Figure 12.23, and then click Create Virtual Machine.

3. Select Create Virtual Machine Wizard ➤ Select Source, click Create The New Virtual Machine With A Blank Virtual Hard Disk, as shown in Figure 12.24, and then click Next.

FIGURE 12.23
Create Virtual
Machine Wizard:
Create Virtual
Machine

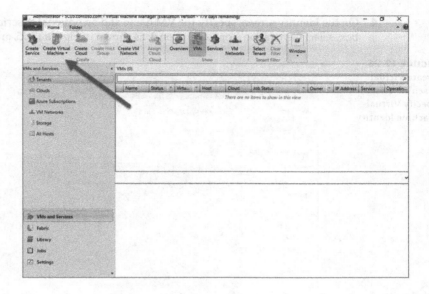

FIGURE 12.24
Create Virtual
Machine Wizard:
Create The New
Virtual Machine
With A Blank
Virtual Hard Disk

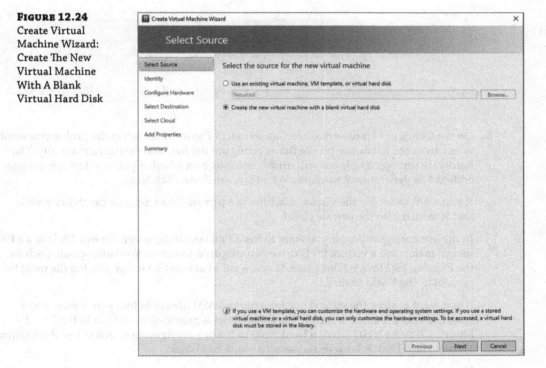

4. On the Identity screen, specify the VM name and an optional description. In the Generation box, select Generation 1 or Generation 2, as shown in Figure 12.25, and then click Next.

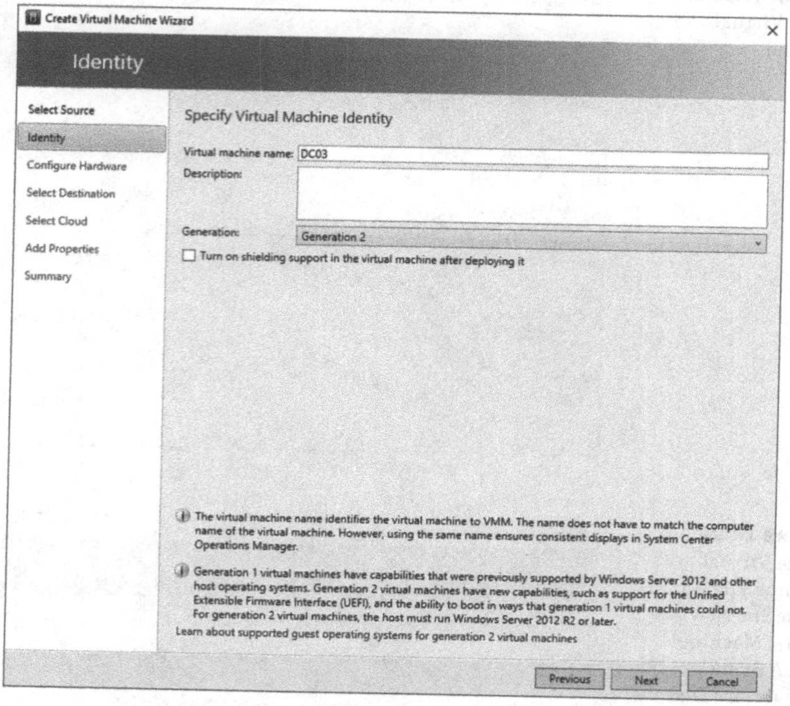

FIGURE 12.25
Create Virtual
Machine Wizard:
Specify Virtual
Machine Identity

5. On the Configure Hardware screen, as shown in Figure 12.26, select the profile you want to use from the hardware profile list or configure the hardware settings manually. The hardware settings displayed will differ depending on whether you are deploying a generation 1 or generation 2 machine. When you are done, click Next.

If you want to deploy the virtual machine to a private cloud, select a capability profile that is available to the private cloud.

In the bus configuration, if you want to install an operating system from a DVD or an ISO image, make sure a virtual DVD drive is configured to use an available option, such as the Existing ISO Image File option. If you want to use an ISO image file, the file must be present in the VMM library.

If you want to store the virtual machine in the VMM library before you deploy it to a host, use one of the blank virtual hard disks that is provided by default in the VMM library. Click the VHD (virtual hard disk) in the bus configuration. Select Use An Existing Virtual Hard Disk ➤ Browse and select a blank hard disk.

If the virtual machine is a generation 1 that boots from the network to install an operating system, use the legacy network adapter type.

6. On the Select Destination page, as shown in Figure 12.27, specify how the virtual machine should be deployed—in a private cloud, on a host, or stored in the library.

FIGURE 12.26
Create Virtual
Machine Wizard:
Configure
Hardware

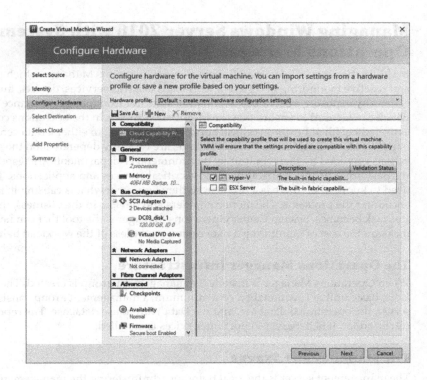

FIGURE 12.27
Create Virtual
Machine Wizard:
Select Destination

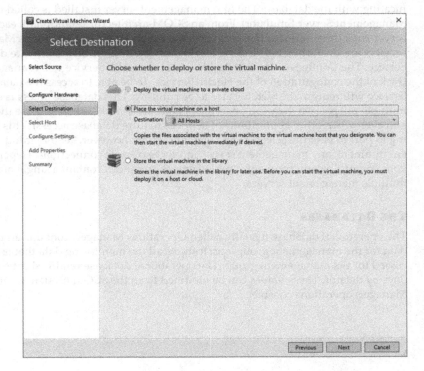

Managing Windows Server 2016 with System Center Operations Manager

In this section, we will focus on System Center Operations Manager, which provides proactive and reactive monitoring of different workloads (such as services, devices, and operations). This is done by exposing a set of key health indicators (for example, performance and availability), which can be used to ensure that the information shown in the operations console reflects the expected health of business-critical applications running in either a data center or in the private or public cloud. Businesses, small and large, are typically dependent on the services and applications provided by their computing environment. IT departments are responsible for ensuring the performance and availability of those critical services and applications. This means they need to know when there is a problem so they figure out what is causing it, ideally before users encounter the problems. The more computers and devices in the business, the more challenging this task becomes. System Center Operations Manager is the tool that can help organizations measure the cost of monitoring a data center, regardless of the workload being monitored.

The Operations Manager Infrastructure

When Operations Manager is installed, a management group is created. The management group is the basic unit of functionality. At a minimum, a management group consists of a management server, the operational database, and the Data Warehouse database. The reporting component can be added if SQL Server Reporting Services is installed.

THE MANAGEMENT SERVER

The management server is the focal point for administering the management group communicating with the database. The first management server installed is called the RMSE (Root Management Server Emulator). From an SCOM-architecture standpoint, each management server runs three services that form the core functionality of Operations Manager. These three services are the Config Service, the Health Service, and the SDK (software development kit) Service. The Config Service will decide what the Health Service will manage, as well as keep track of the configuration of the Health Service. To be able to access the database, the Config Service will require the SDK Service to be running. That database access is also requested for multiple purposes (when you open the operations console, when you use the operations shell, and even when other applications or services require database access). This is done by connecting to port 5724 of the selected management server; however, keep in mind that in a distributed environment, any management server can serve console connections. Depending on the size of your computing environment, a management group can contain a single management server or multiple management servers.

THE DATABASES

The operational database (usually called Operations Manager) contains all the configuration data for the management group, and it stores all the monitoring data that is collected and processed for the management group. The operational database retains short-term data for seven days by default. These values can be modified from the SCOM (System Center Operations Manager) operations console.

The Data Warehouse database is a SQL Server database that stores monitoring and alerting data for historical purposes. Data that is written to the Operations Manager database is also written to the Data Warehouse database, so the reports always contain current data. The Data Warehouse database retains long-term data, by default 400 days.

In both cases, the retention period depends on the type of data (Alert, State, Event, Aem, Perf). In the case of the Data Warehouse database, also the aggregation type (raw data, hourly aggregations, daily aggregations). These values can be modified by editing the StandardDatasetAggregation table (on the OperationsManagerDW database) and update the MaxDataAgeDays column for the selected dataset, that will update the corresponding retention period.

THE AGENTS

In System Center Operations Manager, an *agent* is a service that is installed on a Windows computer. The approach for any component is the same. If an object must be monitored, the machine on which that object resides needs to find a way to identify the data that will eventually be discovered and collected. Microsoft Monitoring Agent is the way to achieve this. (It was initially designed as a workflow agent; now it is used as a profiler by multiple applications—such as Operations Management Suite, Team Foundation Server, etc.) It basically captures information from the managed entity and then applies mechanisms to the data that is captured (such as rules and monitors) and finally performs actions (for example, generates an alert, populates a view, etc.). A management server receives and distributes configurations to agents on monitored computers.

Every agent reports to a management server in the management group. This management server is referred to as the agent's primary management server.

Agents watch data sources on the monitored computer and collect information according to the configuration that is sent to it from its management server. The agent also calculates the health state of the monitored computer and objects on the monitored computer, and reports back to the management server. When the health state of a monitored object changes or other criteria is met, an alert can be generated from the agent. This lets operators know that something requires attention. By providing health data about the monitored object to the management server, the agent provides an up-to-date picture of the health of the device and all the applications that it hosts.

THE SERVICES

In System Center Operations Manager, each component has an associated service with a specific purpose. This section will describe the interaction between all the services, first from a management server standpoint and later from an agent standpoint.

As stated earlier, the three services that provide the core functionality of the management server are the Microsoft Monitoring Agent, the Config Service, and the SDK Service. At this point, we'll discuss the functionality of those services:

◆ Every time the Config Service starts, the configuration state of the environment will be evaluated. After that, any updates will be pushed to the affected instances of Health Services accordingly. The following is identified by a cookie. That cookie will be compared and once a delta is identified, a new cookie will be compiled and the affected Health Services will be updated.

- The SDK Service will be in charge of transporting all the data that travels to and from the database and perform functions, such as provide access (via the console) to the database, write information (write event, state, performance data), and Import Management Packs.

- The Health Service will provide overall functionality, such as executing workflows and overall enabling the end-to-end monitoring. It was initially designed as a general execution environment, and nowadays that approach is taken a step further by adding profiling capabilities.

- On a monitored computer, the Operations Manager Agent is listed as the Microsoft Monitoring Agent Service. The Microsoft Monitoring Agent Service collects performance data, executes tasks, and so on. Even when the service is unable to communicate with the management server it reports to, it can still perform activities such as health detection, recovery tasks, and so on. The service continues to run and queues the collected data and events on the disk of the monitored computer. A few of the other capabilities of the Health Service include adding/removing management packs, updating workflows based on those management packs, managing credentials to be used by workflows, and handling the state of monitors.

THE MANAGEMENT PACKS

A *management pack* contains the definitions of the objects you model. It is a container of objects that can be used to logically define the components and key metrics of anything you need. Management packs are also used to move configurations between environments. There are two types of management packs: sealed (read-only, and usually provided by vendors) and unsealed, which are used to extend the functionality of the sealed management packs by changing its configuration. Any new management pack created from the SCOM console will be created as unsealed, and the sealed management packs will be read-only (either the ones installed with SCOM, or the ones that can be downloaded). Only SCOM administrators can see the list of imported management packs.

The workflows that management packs define the System Center management service runs. management packs define the information that the agent collects and returns to the management server for a specific application or technology. For example, the Windows Server 2016 management pack contains rules and monitors that collect and evaluate events and operations important to ensuring the health and efficiency of Windows Server 2016 roles and applications.

After Operations Manager installs an agent on a computer, it sends an initial configuration to the agent. The initial configuration includes object discoveries from management packs the management pack define the types of objects, such as applications and features, that will be monitored on computers that have been discovered Operations Manager. Agents send data to the management server that identifies the instances of objects discovered on the computer.

Installing the Prerequisites

As we mentioned earlier, understanding the different requirements needed to implement each of the System Center 2016 family of products is important—and Operations Manager is no exception. For the next steps, we will use one of the database instances created on our cluster and a reporting instance in the reporting server. We will also configure the prerequisites for the web console.

INSTALLING THE WEB CONSOLE PREREQUISITES

To install the web console prerequisites, follow these steps:

1. Open PowerShell and type the following:

```
Import-Module ServerManager
```

NOTE You need to hit enter after every command in powershell

2. Type the following, as shown in Figure 12.28:

```
Add-WindowsFeature Web-Server, Web-WebServer, Web-Common-Http, Web-Default-
Doc, Web-Dir-Browsing, Web-Http-Errors, Web-Static-Content, Web-Health,
Web-Http-Logging, Web-Log-Libraries, Web-Request-Monitor, Web-Performance,
Web-Stat-Compression, Web-Security, Web-Filtering, Web-Windows-Auth, Web-App-
Dev, Web-Net-Ext45, Web-Asp-Net45, Web-ISAPI-Ext, Web-ISAPI-Filter, Web-Mgmt-
Tools, Web-Mgmt-Console, Web-Mgmt-Compat, Web-Metabase, NET-Framework-45-
Features, NET-Framework-45-Core, NET-Framework-45-ASPNET, NET-WCF-Services45,
NET-WCF-HTTP-Activation45, NET-WCF-TCP-PortSharing45, WAS, WAS-Process-Model,
WAS-Config-APIs, web-asp-net -restart
```

FIGURE 12.28
Installing the
web console
prerequisites via
PowerShell

INSTALLING THE SQL CLR TYPES

To install the SQL CLR Types, follow these steps:

1. Go to https://www.microsoft.com/en-us/download/details.aspx?id=42295.

2. Click Download and select ENU\x64\SQLSysClrTypes.msi.

3. Double-click SQLSysClrTypes.msi and follow the default options on the wizard.

INSTALLING THE REPORT VIEWER

To install the Report Viewer, follow these steps:

1. Download the Report Viewer from https://www.microsoft.com/en-us/download/details.aspx?id=45496 .

2. Double-click the MSI package and click Run.

3. Complete the wizard, using the default options in the wizard.

INSTALLING THE SINGLE-SERVER MANAGEMENT GROUP CONFIGURATION

To install the single-server management group configuration, follow these steps:

1. Log on to the server by using an account that has local administrative rights. For this example, we will use a VM called SC04.

2. Navigate to the folder where the System Center 2016 Operations Manager installation media is located and run Setup.exe. Click Install, as shown in Figure 12.29.

FIGURE 12.29
The initial Installation screen

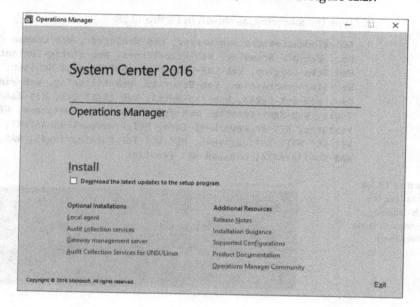

3. In the Select Features to Install window, select the features you want to install and click Next, as shown in Figure 12.30.

4. In the Select Installation Location window, select the folder to install. For this example, we will leave the default folder and click Next, as shown in Figure 12.31.

5. In the Proceed with Setup window, click Next as shown in Figure 12.32.

6. In the Specify an Installation Option window, make sure that the Create The First Management Server In A New Management Group option is enabled and click Next, as shown in Figure 12.33.

FIGURE 12.30
Selecting the
SCOM features to
be installed

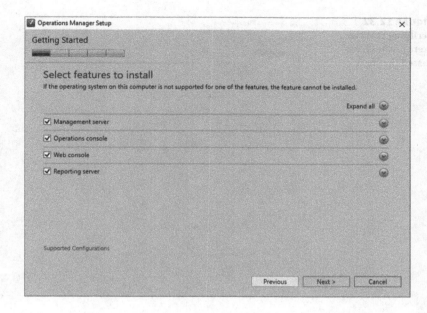

FIGURE 12.31
Selecting a
folder location
for Operations
Manager

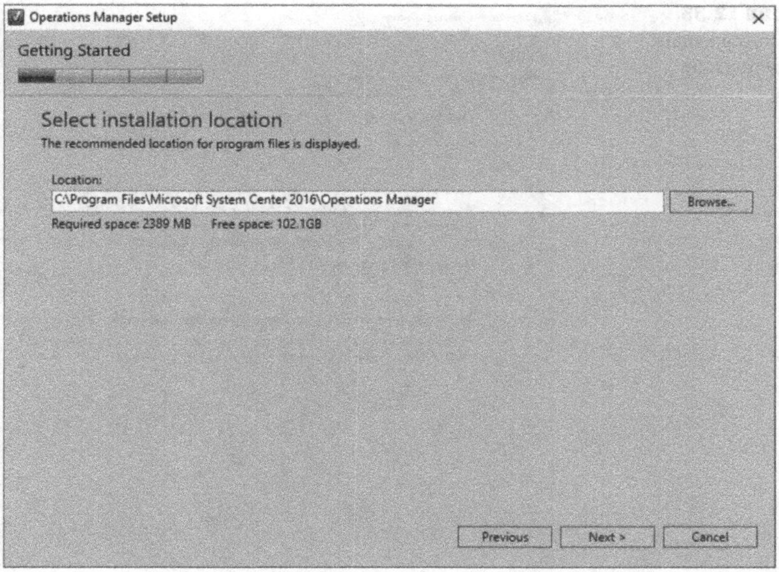

7. On the Please Read the License Terms, which is given on the screen, select the I Have Read, Understood, And Agree To These License Terms screen as shown in Figure 12.32.

FIGURE 12.32
Verifying that the prerequisites have passed the check

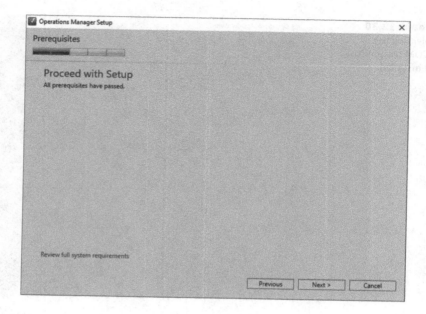

FIGURE 12.33
Specifying a management group name

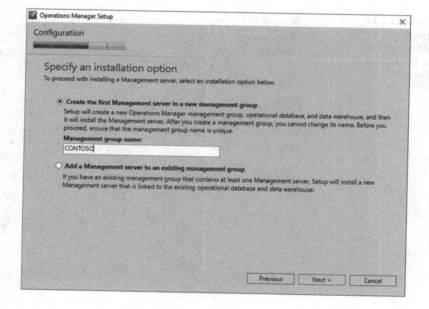

7. In the Please Read the License Terms window, review the contract and click I Have Read, Understood, And Agree To The License Terms, as shown in Figure 12.34.

FIGURE 12.34
Microsoft
Software License
Terms

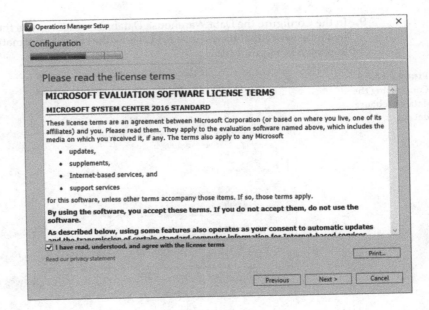

8. In the Configure the Operational Database window, type the name of the SQL server instance, verify that the various fields show the correct data, and then click Next, as shown in Figure 12.35.

FIGURE 12.35
Configuring
the operational
database

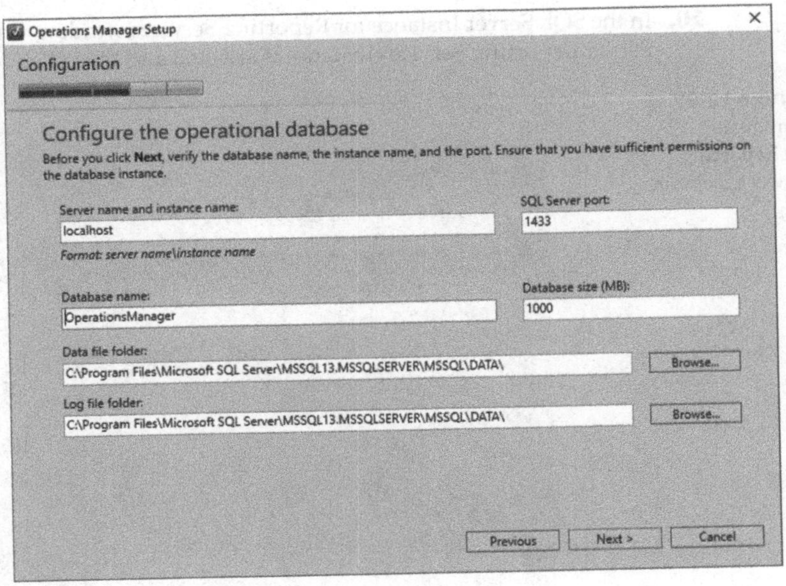

9. In the Configure the Data Warehouse Database window, type the name of the SQL server instance, verify that the various fields show the correct information, and then click Next, as shown in Figure 12.36.

FIGURE 12.36
Configuring the data warehouse database

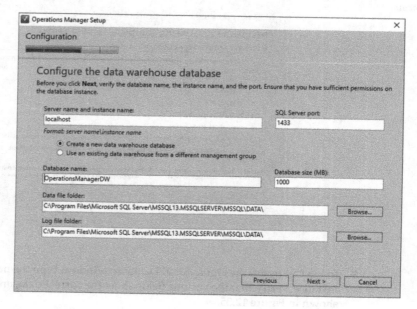

10. In the SQL Server Instance for Reporting Services window, verify that the correct SQL Server Reporting Services instance is selected and then click Next, as shown in Figure 12.37.

FIGURE 12.37
Configuring the Reporting Services instance

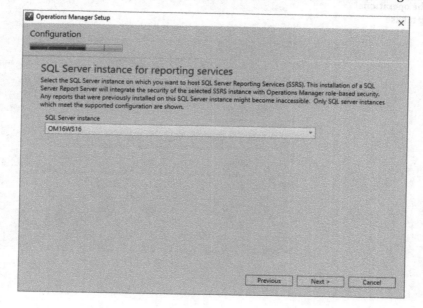

11. In the Specify a Web Site for Use with the Web Console window, review the information and click Next, as shown in Figure 12.38.

FIGURE 12.38
Specifying the website for the web console

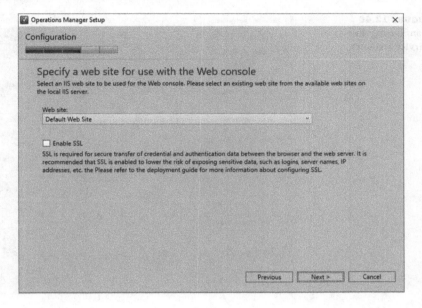

12. In the Select an Authentication Mode for Use with the Web Console window, leave the default value and click Next, as shown in Figure 12.39.

FIGURE 12.39
Selecting an authentication mode for the web console

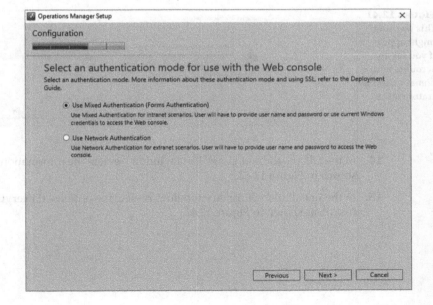

13. In the Configure Operations Manager Accounts window, type the login information for the accounts that were defined and click Next, as shown in Figure 12.40.

FIGURE 12.40
Configuring the
service accounts

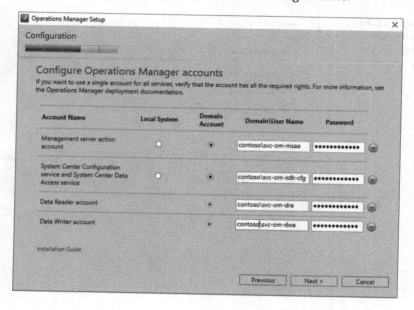

If you are using a domain administrator's account, you might get the warning shown in Figure 12.41. If you do, click OK to continue.

FIGURE 12.41
This warning
might appear
if you set up
accounts with
domain adminis-
trator rights.

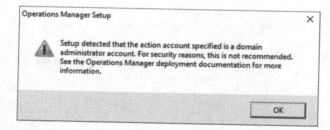

14. In the Diagnostic and Usage Data window, review the information and click Next, as shown in Figure 12.42.

15. In the Installation Summary window, review the options. If everything is OK, click Install, as shown in Figure 12.43.

FIGURE 12.42
A Diagnostic and
Usage Data for
System Center
Operations
Manager
disclaimer

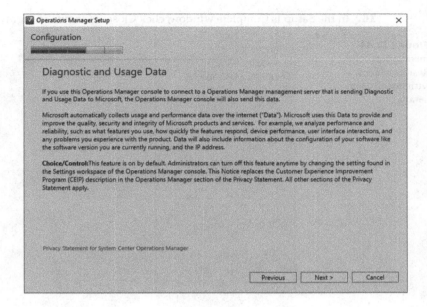

FIGURE 12.43
Installation
Summary page

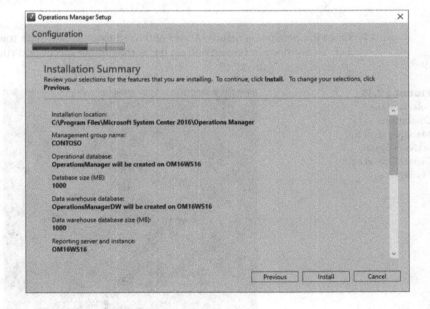

16. In the Setup Is Complete window, click Close, as shown in Figure 12.44.

FIGURE 12.44
Installation
Results window
with installation
details

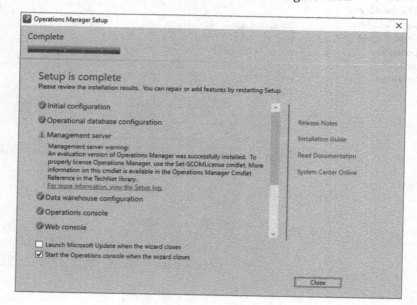

17. Once the product is installed, you will need to activate it with the provided serial number. To do so, open PowerShell on the management server and run it as an administrator, as shown in Figure 12.45.

FIGURE 12.45
Selecting the
Operations
Manager shell to
activate System
Center Operations
Manager

```
import-module operationsmanager
Get-SCOMManagementGroupConnection | Set-SCOMManagementGroupConnection
Set-SCOMLicense -ProductId xxxxx-xxxxx-xxxxx-xxxxx-xxxxx
```

Click Y to confirm.

Once the operation finishes, the System Center Data Access Service must be restarted on the Operations Manager management servers in your management group. (see Figure 12.46).

FIGURE 12.46
Activating System Center Operations Manager

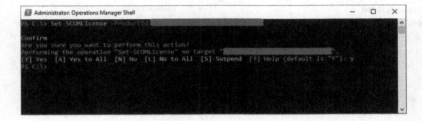

18. Once the server is restarted, open the console, click Help, and select About. You should see the System Center Operations Manager version (Retail), as shown in Figure 12.47.

FIGURE 12.47
Verifying that System Center Operations Manager is activated

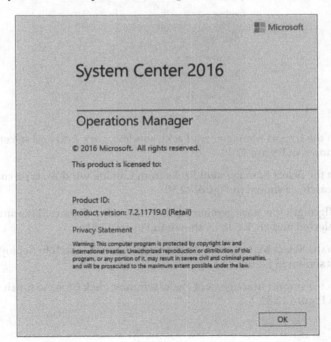

INSTALLING THE WINDOWS SERVER MANAGEMENT PACK

To install the Windows Server management pack, follow these steps:

1. Start the Operations Management console and navigate to the Administration section, as shown in Figure 12.48

FIGURE 12.48
Initiating the wizard to import management packs

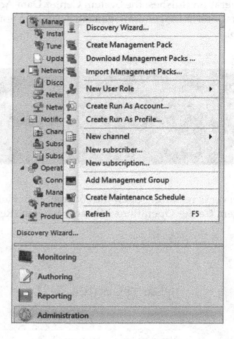

2. In the Import Management Packs window, click Add and select Add From Catalog, as shown in Figure 12.49.

3. In the Select Management Packs from Catalog window, type **core os 2016** and click Search, as shown in Figure 12.50.

4. Highlight the management packs you want to deploy. Make sure that no language pack is selected and click OK, as shown in Figure 12.51.

5. In the Select Management Packs window, click Install to deploy the management packs, as shown in Figure 12.52.

6. In the Import Management Packs window, click Close to finish the deployment, as shown in Figure 12.53.

FIGURE 12.49
Selecting a source for management packs

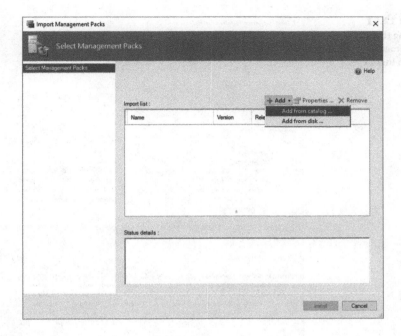

FIGURE 12.50
Finding management packs in the catalog

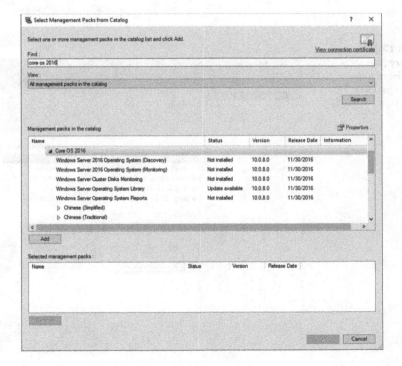

FIGURE 12.51
Selecting the
management
packs to install

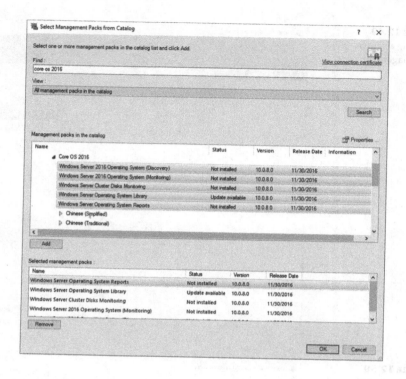

FIGURE 12.52
Summary page
with a list of man-
agement packs to
install

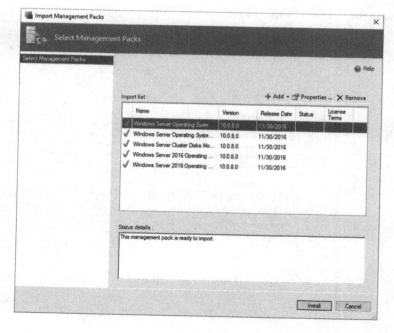

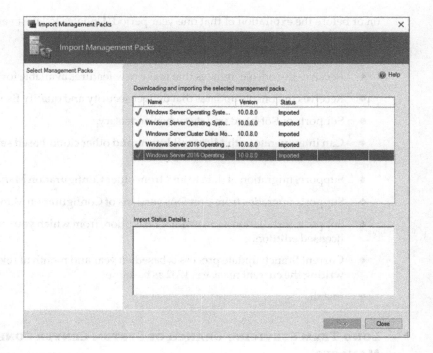

FIGURE 12.53
Viewing the status of the current Management Pack installation procedure

Managing Windows Server 2016 with System Center Configuration Manager

In this section, we will focus on System Center Configuration Manager. So just what is System Center Configuration Manager?

A product in the Microsoft System Center suite of management solutions, System Center Configuration Manager can help you manage devices and users both on-premises and in the cloud. On the next few pages, we will explain in more detail what it is and how can you use it to manage Windows Server 2016. System Center Configuration Manager, usually abbreviated as SCCM, is also known as ConfigMgr. It is focused on managing a large group of Windows, macOS, Linux, and Unix devices, as well as mobile devices such as Windows Phone, Android, and iOS.

Three Branches

Before we begin, you need to understand a few fundamental aspects of ConfigMgr. System Center Configuration Manager comes in three different branches; so which branch should you use?

CURRENT BRANCH

This version is updated several times a year with new features. Each update version is supported for one year after its release. You must update to a newer version of the current branch on or before the expiration of that one-year period. Updates to latest version are available as in-console updates.

The current branch has the following features:

- Receives in-console updates that make new features available for use.

- Receives in-console updates that deliver security and qualify fixes to exist features.

- Supports out-of-band updates when necessary.

- Can interoperate with Microsoft Intune and other cloud-based services and infrastructures.

- Supports migration of data to and from other Configuration Manager installations.

- Supports upgrades from previous versions of Configuration Manager.

- Supports installation as an evaluation edition, from which you can later upgrade to a fully licensed editition.

- Current Branch update process is based on year and month of release; at the time of this writing the current release is 1702 as baseline

- Install.

Long-Term Servicing Branch of System Center Configuration Manager

The Long-Term Servicing Branch (LTSB) is a licensed branch for use in production by Configuration Manager customers who are using the current branch but allowed their Configuration Manager Software Assurance (SA) or equivalent subscription rights to expire after October 1, 2016.

The LTSB is based on version 1606. This branch does not receive in-console updates that deliver new features nor does it update existing capabilities. However, critical security fixes are provided.

The LTSB has the following features:

- Receives in-console updates that deliver critical security fixes.

- Provides an installation option when your SA agreement or equivalent rights to ConfigMgr have expired.

- Supports upgrade (conversion) to the current branch when you have a current SA agreement or equivalent rights to ConfigMgr.

The LTSB is based on the current branch version 1606 and has the following limitations:

- Supported for 10 years of critical security updates after its general availability (October of 2016), after which support for this branch expires.

- Supports a limited set of server and client operating systems and related technologies, such as SQL Server versions.

- Does not receive updates for new features.

- Does not support adding a Microsoft Intune Subscription, which prevents the use of Intune in hybrid MDM configuration and on-premises MDM.

- Does not support the use of Windows 10 Servicing Dashboard, servicing plans, Windows 10 current branch or Current Branch for Business.

- Does not support feature releases of Windows 10 LTSB or Windows Server.

- Has no support for Asset Intelligence.

- Has no support for cloud-based distribution points.

- Has no support for Exchange Online as an Exchange connector.

- Does not support any prerelease features.

Technical Preview for System Center Configuration Manager

The technical preview is for use in a lab environment where you want to learn about and try the newest features being developed for ConfigMgr. The technical preview is not supported in a production environment and does not require you to have a Software Assurance License agreement.

The technical preview has the following features:

- Based on recent baseline versions of the current branch.

- Receives in-console updates that update your installation to the latest preview version.

- Includes new features that are being developed. (Microsoft developers would like to have your feedback regarding them.)

- Receives updates that apply only to the technical preview branch.

The technical preview has the following limitations:

- Support is limited, including only a single primary site and up to 10 clients.

- Cannot be upgraded to the current branch or LTSB.

- Does not support using migration to import or export data to another ConfigMgr installation.

- Does not support upgrades from a previous version of ConfigMgr.

- Does not support installation as an evaluation.

What You Should Know About Site Server Differences

If this is the first time you have installed ConfigMgr, you could easily be overwhelmed. To help prevent that, we will define what a site server is and what site server type you should install to support your Windows Server 2016.

Central Administration Site

The central administration site (CAS) is suitable for large-scale deployments, provides a central point of administration, and provides the flexibility to support devices that are distributed across a global network infrastructure. Once you install a central administration site, you will need to install one or more primary sites as child sites; we will learn more about primary sites in the next section. This configuration is necessary because a central administration site does not directly support device management, which is a function of a primary site. A central administration site supports multiple child primary sites. The child primary sites are used to manage devices directly and to control network bandwidth when your managed devices are in different geographical locations.

PRIMARY SITE SERVER

A standalone primary site is suitable for smaller deployments and can be used to manage devices without having to install additional sites. Although a standalone primary site can limit the size of your deployment, it will support a scenario to expand your hierarchy later by installing a new central administration site. With this site expansion scenario, your standalone primary site will become a child primary site. Then you can install additional child primary sites below your new central administration site. You can then expand your initial deployment for future growth of your enterprise.

SECONDARY SITE SERVER

A secondary site, this is the only site that is installed using the ConfigMgr Console, the other 2 sites are installed with the baseline media. This site can only be installed as child site below a primary site. This site type extends the reach of a primary site to manage devices in locations that have a slow network connection to the primary site. The site type extends the scope of a primary site to manage devices in a place that have a slow network connection to the primary site. Even thought a secondary site extends the primary site; the primary site manages all of the clients.

SITE SYSTEM SERVER AND SITE SYSTEM ROLES

Configuration Manager has different site system roles that help ConfigMgr extend its supported reach and device management ability.

Each ConfigMgr site installs system roles that support management operations. When you install a site, the following roles are installed by default:

◆ The Site server role is assigned to the computer where you install the site.

◆ The Site Database server role is assigned to the SQL server that hosts the site database.

◆ Other site system roles are optional and are used only when you want to utilize the functionality that is active in a site system role. Any computer that hosts a site system role is referred to a site system server.

Table 12.4 shows the available site system roles and their functionality.

TABLE 12.4: Site System Roles

ROLE NAME	DESCRIPTION
SMS provider	Supported application interface for the console and site database. Hosted on Windows Management Instrumentation (WMI).
Component server	Server hosting a Configuration Manager SMS_Executive service (typically, site server).

TABLE 12.4: Site System Roles *(CONTINUED)*

ROLE NAME	DESCRIPTION
Management point	Sends and receives communications to devices and clients.
Distribution point	Provides content to devices and clients.
Cloud-based distribution point	Provides content by using a Microsoft Azure cloud service.
Software update point	Uses Windows Server Updates Services (WSUS) to manage software updates.
Reporting Services point	Uses SQL Server Reporting Services (SSRS) to create and manage reports.
Services connection point	Manages mobile devices on-premises or with Microsoft Intune. Provides metadata to Microsoft and enables servicing ConfigMgr hierarchy.
Fallback status point	Gathers state messages from clients during installation and from existing clients with communication issues.
State Migration point	Stores user-state data while a computer is being migrated to a new operating system.
Application Catalog web service point	Provides software information to the Application Catalog website.
Application Catalog website point	Provides users with a list of available software from the Application Catalog.
Certificate registration point	Communicates with a server that runs the Network Device Enrollment Service to manage device certificate requests that use the Simple Certificate Enrollment Protocol (SCEP).
Endpoint protection point	Manages Microsoft Active Protection services to help protect devices from malware.
Enrollment point	Used to install clients on Mac computers and enroll devices you manage with on-premises mobile device management.
Enrollment proxy point	Manages enrollment requests from mobile devices and Mac computers.

ConfigMgr Prerequisites

Now that you understand the differences between a site server and a site system, you need to know the prerequisites for each of these roles.

SOFTWARE REQUIREMENTS

The list of requirements that are needed to install these roles successfully is extensive. You can review those requirements at the following link:

```
https://docs.microsoft.com/en-us/sccm/core/plan-design/configs/site-and-site-
system-prerequisites
```

You probably like to automate as many tasks as possible. To that end, we recommend using ConfigMgr Prerequisites Tool to install, configure, and validate each of the software requirements. This PowerShell tool was created by Nickolaj Andersen. (We discussed some aspects of PowerShell in Chapter 2.) You can download and access the tool at the following link:

```
https://gallery.technet.microsoft.com/ConfigMgr-2012-R2-e52919cd/
```

SUPPORTED CONFIGURATIONS

Server Core is not supported as a site server. To install a central administration site, primary site, or secondary site server, you will need to have Windows Server 2016 Full UI installed.

The server most be a domain member server; once installed you can't change the server name or its domain membership.

Each site system role has different supportability levels, and understanding them is important, as shown in Table 12.5.

TABLE 12.5:   Supportability Limits

SITE SERVER	SUPPORTABILITY LIMITS
Central Administration Site	1,025,000 total clients and devices.
	700,000 desktops running Windows, Linux, and Unix.
	25,000 devices running MAC and Windows CE 7.0.
Primary Site Server	100,000 on-premises devices or 300,000 cloud-based devices.
	25 child primary site servers.
	150,000 clients per child primary site.
	50,000+ if using SQL Enterprise Edition.
	175,000 total clients and devices.
	150,000 desktops running Windows, Linux, and Unix.
Secondary Sites	25,000 devices running MAC and Windows CE 7.0
	50,000 on-premise devices or 150,000 cloud-based devices.
	250 secondary sites.
	250 distribution points.
	2000 pull distribution points.
	5000 combined distribution points
	15 management points.
	15,000 desktops running Windows, Linux, and UNIX.
	250 secondary sites to a primary site.
	Single management point.

HARDWARE RECOMMENDATIONS

Understanding the hardware recommendations is very important. Our recommendations contain three elements: CPU cores, physical memory, and SQL memory. In this chapter, we also offer some additional recommendations about building an all-in-one cluster. The hardware recommendations in Table 12.6 use either a collocated SQL or Share SQL Server.

TABLE 12.6: Hardware Recommendations

SITE SERVER	CPU CORES	MEMORY GB	MEMORY % FOR SQL
Central Administration Site/Primary Site Server	16 Cores	96 GB	50–80 percent
Central Administration Site/Primary Site Server with Remote SQL	8 Cores	16 GB	
Site Database Server Role	16 Cores	64 GB	80–90 percent
Secondary Site	8 Cores	16 GB	80 percent

DISK SPACE RECOMMENDATIONS

When building and configuring a site server or site system, you need to know how to set up the disk drives and what to expect regarding sizing, as shown in Table 12.7.

TABLE 12.7: Disk Space Recommendations

DATA USAGE	MINIMUM DISK SPACE	50,000	100,000	150,000	700,000 (CAS)
ConfigMgr Application/Log Files	25 GB	50 GB	200 GB	300 GB	200 GB
Site Database MDF Files	75 GB	150 GB	300 GB	500 GB	2 TB
Site Database LDF Files	25 GB	50 GB	100 GB	150 GB	100 GB

Installing a Primary Site Server

Now that you understand the prerequisites, hardware recommendations, and disk space recommendations, it is time for us to dive deep into installing and configuring ConfigMgr to manage your Windows Server 2016. In this first part, we are going to install a primary site server and add the database to the all-in-one cluster; once you have installed the site server, we will configure it and give you specific recommendations to manage your Windows Server 2016.

INSTALLING AND CONFIGURING SCCM

Log on to the server that you want to configure. In this example, we will use SC06 to start the installation and configuration process.

1. Log on to SC06 and download the ConfigMgr Prerequisites Tool from the link provided earlier. Here it is again:

   ```
   https://gallery.technet.microsoft.com/ConfigMgr-2012-R2-e52919cd/
   ```

2. Once downloaded, extract the content and run ConfigMgrPrerequisitesTool.exe, as shown in Figure 12.54.

FIGURE 12.54
Windows Explorer:
Extracted Folder
ConfigMgrPrerequisitesTool

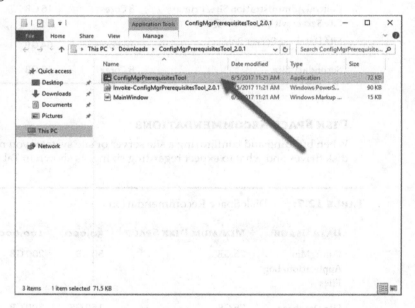

3. Once ConfigMgr Prerequisites Tool is up and running, click on Select A Site Type And Select A Primary Site. Then, on the Download Prerequisite files, select Browse and find Setupdl.exe, which is usually located under X:\SMSSETUP\BIN\X64. Once you have done this, click Install, as shown in Figure 12.55. The tool will configure the necessary roles for a Configuration Manager primary site and download the redistribution files.

FIGURE 12.55
ConfigMgr Prerequisites
Tool: Site Configuration

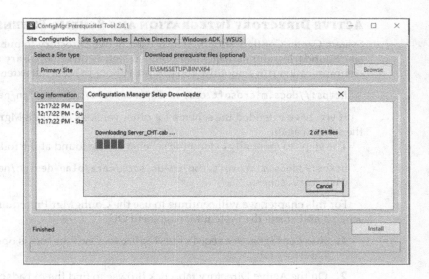

4. The process may take some time to install and configure the requirements. In this example, the system needed to configure 32 requirements, as shown in Figure 12.56.

FIGURE 12.56
ConfigMgr Prerequisites
Tool: Site Configuration:
Progress

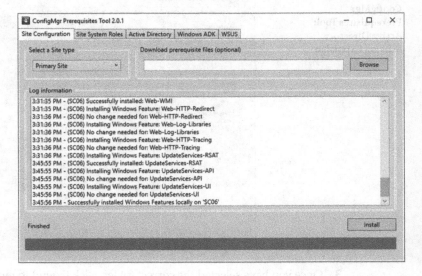

5. Once the process is complete, you will be ready to move on to the next steps.

ACTIVE DIRECTORY INTEGRATION AND SCHEMA EXTENSION

System Center Configuration Manager uses Active Directory to publish information about the site, boundaries, and management point, as well as other necessary attributes to make client communication run smoothly. You can read about the schema extensions at the following link:

https://docs.microsoft.com/en-us/sccm/core/plan-design/network/schema-extensions

If you have extended the schema for other versions of ConfigMgr, you do not need to extend the schema again.

The steps to manually extend the schema can be found at the following link:

https://docs.microsoft.com/en-us/sccm/core/plan-design/network/extend-the-active-directory-schema

For this chapter, we will continue to use the ConfigMgr Prerequisites Tool to extend the schema and create the System Management OU.

1. Run ConfigMgrPrerequisitesTool.exe. Once the tool is open, click the Active Directory tab.

2. On the Active Directory tab, click Browse to find the extadsch.exe tool, which can be found under SMSSETUP\bin\x64 as shown in Figure 12.57.

FIGURE 12.57
ConfigMgr
Prerequisites Tool:
Active Directory
Schema Extension

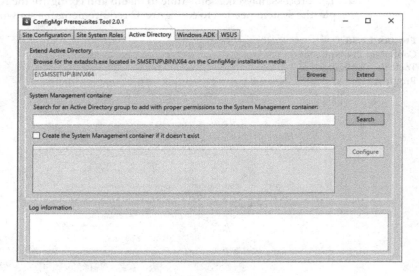

3. Once you have selected the correct folder, click Extend to monitor the progress on the Log Information section of the tool.

4. If you have rights to create the System Management OU, you can use the tool—or, in the section System Management Container, you can select a security group that contains the CM servers and then click Configure.

WSUS REQUIREMENTS

In order to use the software update point role in Configuration Manager, Windows Server Update Services (WSUS) is required. If you plan to support software updates in the product, you should install and configure the role on the ConfigMgr Primary Site server or a standalone server. You can read more about planning for this role at the following link:

https://docs.microsoft.com/en-us/sccm/sum/plan-design/plan-for-software-updates

We are going to use the ConfigMgr Prerequisites Tool to install and configure the WSUS server. To do that, follow these steps:

1. Make sure `ConfigMgrPrerequisitestool.exe` is running and open, and click the WSUS tab.

2. On the WSUS tab, select the SQL server and enter the FDQN of the SQL server and the SQL instance. Then enter the path of the WSUSContent and click Install, as shown in Figure 12.58.

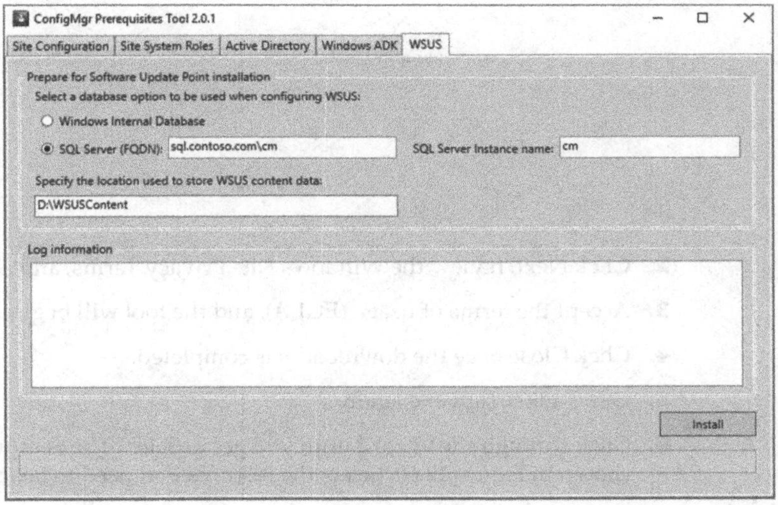

FIGURE 12.58
ConfigMgr
Prerequisites
Tool: WSUS tab

INSTALLING AND CONFIGURING ADK 1703

If you are planning to deploy an operating system, we recommend that you install ADK Windows 10 1703 on the server. It is also one of the main software requirements for the System Center Configuration Manager. You can download the tool from the following link:

https://blogs.technet.microsoft.com/ausoemteam/2017/04/06/download-windows-adk-for-windows-10-version-1703/

To install and configure ADK 1703, follow these steps:

1. Once adksetup.exe is downloaded, run the file and click Download The Windows Assessment And Deployment Kit, as shown in Figure 12.59.

FIGURE 12.59
ADK Window 10
1703 download

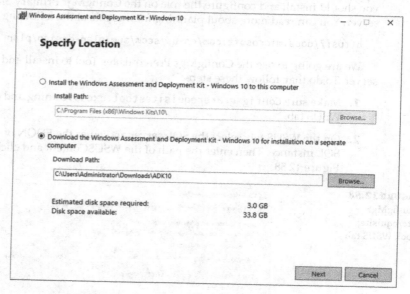

2. Click Next, review the Windows Kits Privacy Terms, and click Next.

3. Accept the terms of usage (EULA), and the tool will begin downloading the features.

4. Click Close once the download has completed.

5. Open adksetup.exe again.

6. Click through the wizard until you get to Select The Features You Want To Install, as shown in Figure 12.60. Select the features that need to be installed on the server.

7. Once you have selected all the features you need, click Install to install them on the server. The installation will take a few minutes.

8. Click Close when the installation is complete.

INSTALLING AND CONFIGURING THE PRIMARY SITE

Now that we have installed all the required software, we are ready to install the Configuration Manager primary site on the server; we will explain the installation steps and wizard information as we go through them on the server install.

1. Click splash.hta from the installation media.

2. In the splash.hta file, click Install.

3. On the Before You Begin screen, click Next.

4. On the Getting Started screen, select Install a Configuration Manager Primary Site in the Available Setup Options window, as shown in Figure 12.61. Then click Next.

FIGURE 12.60
ADK Windows
10 1703: Select
the Features You
Want to Install

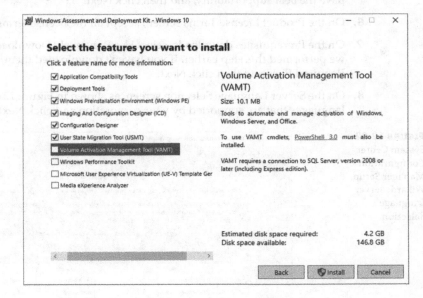

FIGURE 12.61
System Center
Configuration
Manager Setup
Wizard: Getting
Started: Available
Setup Options

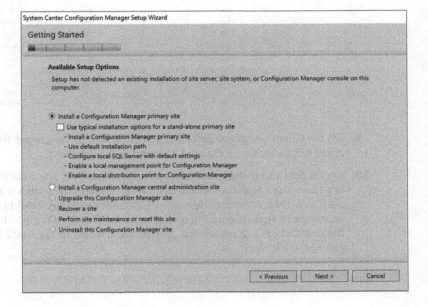

5. Enter the product key if it is available. If it isn't, you can select to install the site as an evaluation. (The evalutation period will last for about 180 days.) In order to support the current branch, select a Software Assurance date. Select a date a few years in the future to have the best supportability, and then click Next.

6. On the Product License Terms screen, accept all the license terms and then click Next.

7. On the Prerequisites downloads, select Use Previously Downloaded The File because we performed this step earlier. If you haven't downloaded them, click Download The Required Files and then click Next.

8. On the Server Language Selection screen, as shown in Figure 12.62, you need to select the languages that are supported by your corporation and click Next.

FIGURE 12.62
System Center
Configuration
Manager Setup
Wizard: Server
Language
Selection

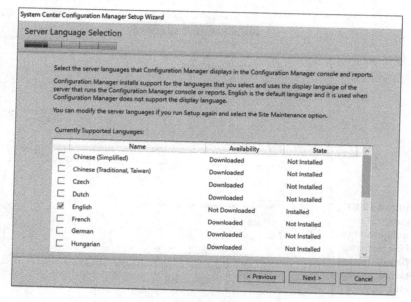

9. On the Client Language Selection screen, select the languages that are supported on the client OS, as shown in Figure 12.63, and then click Next.

10. On the Site and Installation Settings screen, enter the site code in the Site Code field. This is a three-digit alphanumerical field; it can contain the letters from A to Z and the numerals 0 to 9. Then enter the site name in its field; the name should be unique to the site. We recommend against entering a version or number for the site. Then enter a valid path for the installation and review the options we selected in Figure 12.64. After everything is entered, click Next.

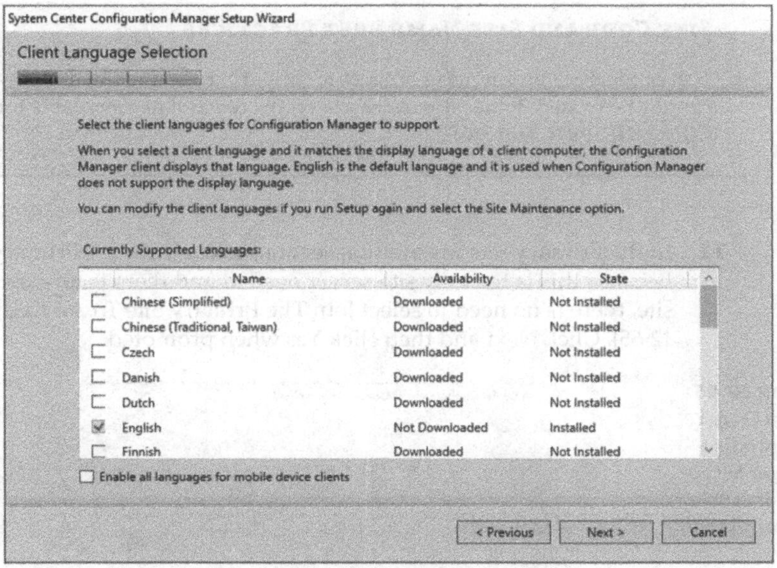

FIGURE 12.63
System Center
Configuration
Manager Setup
Wizard: Client
Language
Selection

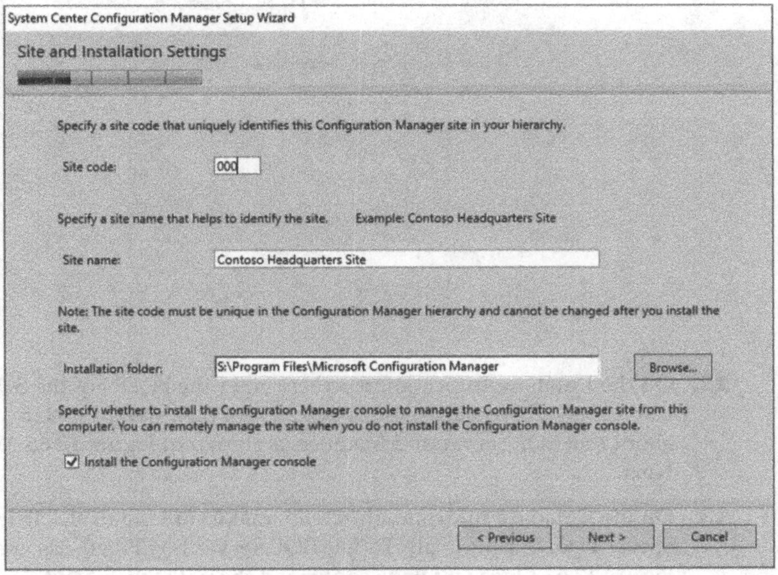

FIGURE 12.64
System Center
Configuration
Manager Setup
Wizard: Site
and Installation
Settings

SITE CODE AND SITE NAME BEST PRACTICES

A site code must be unique in order to identify that specific site in the system hierarchy. Site codes cannot be reused. Some site codes are restricted and not available for use—for example, AUX, CON, NUL, PRN, and SMS.

---

11. In the Primary Site Installation section, select Install A Primary Site As A Standalone Site. Because this is the only site server needed and there is no existing central administration site, there is no need to select Join The Primary Site To An Existing Hierarchy (see Figure 12.65). Click Next and then click Yes when prompted.

FIGURE 12.65
System Center
Configuration
Manager Setup
Wizard: Primary
Site Installation

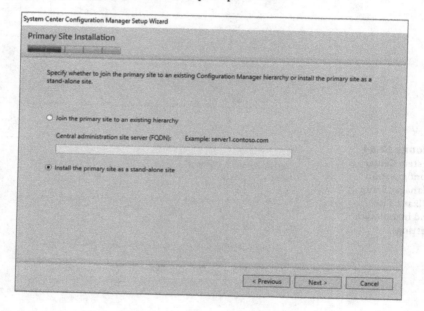

12. On the Database Information screen, enter the FQDN of the SQL server. If it is collocated, leave it as is. If you are using a SQL server on a shared instance, enter the information about that SQL server and instance as shown in Figure 12.66. When you are done, click Next.

13. On the Database Information screen, make sure the drives listed in the Path To The SQL Server Data File and Path To The SQL Server Log File fields are correct, as shown in Figure 12.67. Once you have confirmed the path, click Next.

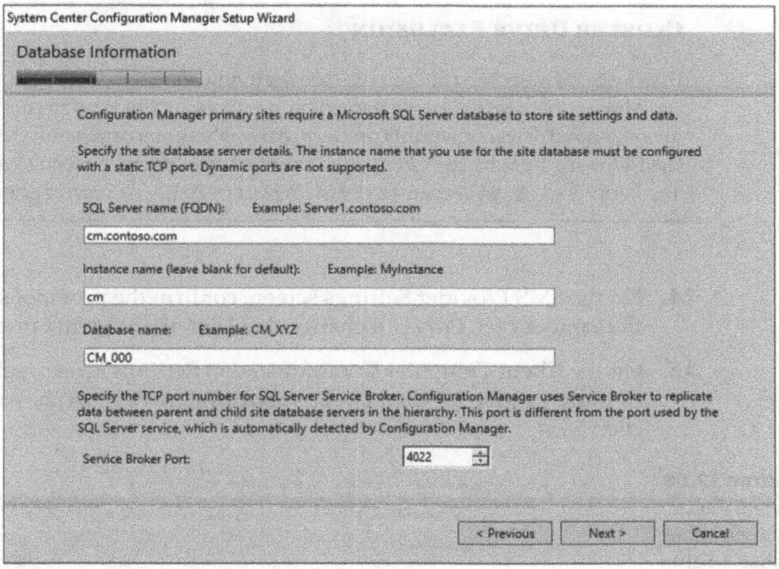

FIGURE 12.66
System Center
Configuration
Manager Setup
Wizard: Primary
Site Installation:
Database
Information

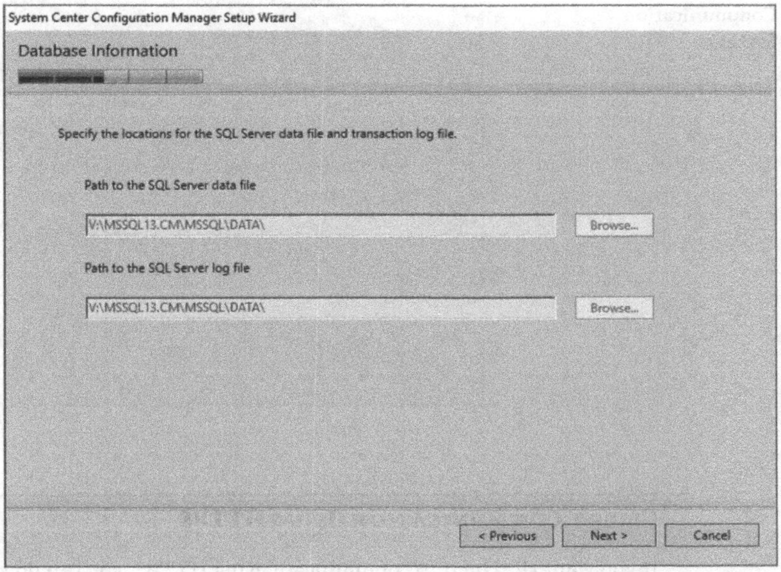

FIGURE 12.67
System Center
Configuration
Manager Setup
Wizard: Database
Information

CLUSTER DRIVE EXCLUSION

In a cluster SQL server, you cannot store the monitoring services in those drives that constitute a cluster. Make sure to include a file named `no_sms_on_drive.sms` so that you do not install the service on a clustered drive. Leave only one local drive where you can install the service. You can read more at the following link: `https://blogs.technet.microsoft.com/smartinez/2014/06/11/you-implemented-a-sql-cluster-for-sysctr-2012-r2-configmgr-and-you-forgot-what/`.

---

14. On the SMS Provider Settings screen, confirm the provider server name, which is usually the same server. (You can change this later after the first install.) Then click Next.

15. On the Client Computer Communication Settings screen, select Configure The Communication Method On Each Site System Role, as shown in Figure 12.68, and then click Next.

FIGURE 12.68
System Center Configuration Manager Setup Wizard: Client Computer Communication Settings

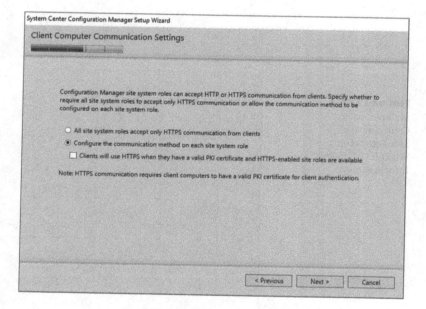

CLIENT COMMUNICATION USING HTTPS

If you want the client to communicate using HTTPS, you can do so after the install. For security purposes, you need to have PKI certificates already on the server and the clients before you select those roles.

---

16. On the site system role, leave default selections to install the management point and distribution point roles. Both of them will be using HTTP as the default client communication since we selected that in step 15. Review as shown in Figure 12.69, then click Next.

FIGURE 12.69
System Center Configuration Manager Setup Wizard: Site System Roles

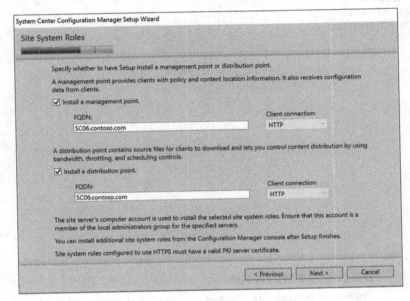

17. On the Diagnostic and Usage Data screen, click Next.

18. On the Service Connection Point Setup screen, leave the default settings to get connected. This role will be the one to notify the server about new updates and service. Click Next.

19. On the Setting Summary screen, review your settings, make sure they look good, and then click Next.

20. On the Prerequisite Check screen, review any warnings or errors that the prerequisite check found and address any of them before you click Begin Install.

21. On the Install - Overall Progress window, you can watch the progress indicator, as shown in Figure 12.70. The installation will take some time to complete, usually between 45 to 60 minutes.

Configuring System Center Configuration Manager

Once the Configuration Manager installation is complete, there are a series of configuration items that need to be present so that you can manage and maintain Windows Server 2016. We'll begin this discussion with the discovery methods that are available in Configuration Manager to find data from Active Directory and how we use each of the Active Directory discovery methods.

FIGURE 12.70
System Center
Configuration
Manager Setup
Wizard: Install:
Overall Progress

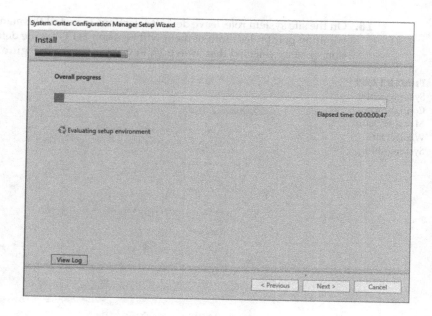

DISCOVERY METHODS

There are currently six discovery methods in Configuration Manager. ConfigMgr uses discovery to add new resources (users or computers) or information about existing resources (group or OU membership) to the ConfigMgr database. We also have a Delta Discovery for some of the Active Directory methods to speed up the process for new discovered records. For a more in-depth look at discovery methods, go to the following link:

```
https://docs.microsoft.com/en-us/sccm/core/servers/deploy/configure/about-
discovery-methods
```

Active Directory Forest Discovery

This discovery method does not discover resources or users. Instead, it will add boundary information that is found on site and services. This will help to ensure that the clients are correctly assigned to ConfigMgr sites.

Active Directory System Discovery

Active Directory System Discovery is a discovery method used to read computer objects from Active Directory Domain Services (AD DS) and add them to the Configuration Manager database. This discovery method is fully configurable to read resources either from an entire domain or a specific organizational unit (OU). Active Directory System Discovery is the main computer discovery method used in Configuration Manager. All domain-joined computers can be discovered by using this approach—and in most cases, using this method will avoid the need to use Network Discovery.

Active Directory System Discovery creates a DDR record for every Windows computer that exists in the domains or OUs that are configured to read; they have a name-resolution record in Domain Name System (DNS) or Windows Internet Name Service (WINS). This will ensure we can stablish communication with the clients, as configured in the site server's network configuration), regardless of site assignment.

Active Directory User Discovery

Software Deployments in Configuration Manager are far more user-centric than in the previous versions of the software. Therefore, getting all Active Directory user accounts into Configuration Manager is critical. Active Directory User Discovery is a discovery process used to add domain user account information to Configuration Manager. This discovery method should be enabled in most environments. After users are added, they can be used to target software distributions to specific users instead of computers.

By default, Active Directory User Discovery collects the following information:

◆ Username

◆ Unique username (includes domain name)

◆ Active Directory domain

◆ Active Directory container name

This type of discovery can be configured to discover user resources in an entire domain, a specific OU, or a group. A DDR record is created for every user account in the OU, group, or domain that is configured.

Active Directory Group Discovery

Active Directory Group Discovery searches AD DS for security group information that can be used to create collections and queries. It discovers local groups, global groups, and universal security groups. Active Directory Group Discovery also adds Active Directory group information about computer accounts to Configuration Manager.

Active Directory Group Discovery discovers the following information:

◆ Basic information about security groups. Adds the security group to Configuration Manager database.

◆ The OU and the Active Directory container of the security groups. Adds OU and domain information about security groups.

This discovery method discovers user/security group relationships. Security group information for user-based groups is contained in the user security identifier (SID). Simply adding the group to a collection will allow all the users in the group to get any software targeted at the group. Collections based on user security groups do not need to be updated because the user's SID indicates group memberships. The user needs to log out/log in when added to a group.

Active Directory Group Discovery discovers system/security group relationships. It discovers system group information that was formerly discovered by System Group Discovery. System group information is added to individual computer records. Collections created by using this information will add individual computers to a collection. These collections need to be updated to show the latest members.

Network Discovery

Network Discovery searches your network for IP-enabled resources by querying Dynamic Host Configuration Protocol (DHCP) servers, Address Resolution Protocol (ARP) caches in routers, and Simple Network Management Protocol (SNMP)-enabled devices. These resources can often be unreliable because SNMP devices are limited, and an ARP cache usually has a short Time to Live (TTL). Network Discovery can also search Active Directory domains and IP subnets.

To discover a resource, Network Discovery must be able to identify the subnet mask in addition to the IP address of the resource. Because you can have many different types of devices connected to the network, Network Discovery often finds resources that cannot support the Configuration Manager client software and, therefore, cannot be managed by Configuration Manager.

Network Discovery can provide an extensive list of attributes as part of the discovery record, including the following:

- NetBIOS name
- IP addresses
- Resource domain
- System roles
- SNMP community name
- Media Access Control (MAC) addresses

Heartbeat Discovery

Heartbeat Discovery is different from the other discovery methods in Configuration Manager because it is initiated by an installed client. The purpose of Heartbeat Discovery is to keep the client records up-to-date in Configuration Manager. Heartbeat Discovery is unique because it is the only discovery method that returns a client globally unique identifier (GUID) as part of the discovery record. It is also the only method to dictate whether clients are seen as installed in the Configuration Manager console.

Heartbeat Discovery is responsible for letting the site know that a client is still healthy and runs at the specified interval. The default interval is seven days, but it is often set at a shorter interval, such as daily. The Heartbeat Discovery data is used by the Delete Inactive Client Discovery Data and Clear Install Flag maintenance tasks to either delete records from the Configuration Manager database or change them to Client=No. Verify that these two maintenance tasks are set at an interval higher (recommended is 2.5 times the minimum) than the Heartbeat Discovery interval. When you're configuring these tasks, carefully consider what is a reasonable length of time for a client to be offline.

How Heartbeat Discovery Data Is Processed

When a scheduled Heartbeat Discovery cycle is initiated, the inventory agent thread on a client starts processing the heartbeat inventory. The inventory agent is responsible for hardware and software inventory and Heartbeat Discovery. The Heartbeat Discovery record is very small and is processed quickly.

After the inventory agent processes the record, it is copied to the outbound queues on the server and depending on the size, it is either copied to the CCM_Incoming directory or directly posted to the management point. The record is copied to the management point via Background Intelligent Transfer Service (BITS). The discovery and other inventory records are stored in the XML format in this folder as they are processed.

Delta Discovery

The information on Delta Discovery is also relevant for Active Directory User, Security Group, and System Group Discovery.

Active Directory Delta Discovery in Configuration Manager enhances discovery capabilities by discovering only new or changed resources in AD DS, instead of performing a full discovery cycle. The interval by which Delta Discovery searches for new resources can be configured to be a short interval because discovering only new resources does not affect the performance of the site server as much as discovering a full cycle. Delta Discovery can detect the following new resource types:

◆ New computers or users added to AD DS or a group

◆ Changes to basic computer and user information

◆ Computers or users that are removed from a group

◆ Changes to system group objects

Delta Discovery does not replace other Configuration Manager discovery methods. Because it finds only new or modified resources in AD DS, it must be used along with a discovery method that performs a full synchronization with AD DS.

Delta Discovery has the following limitations:

◆ Delta Discovery reads only Active Directory attribute changes that are replicated.

◆ Delta Discovery does not collect nonreplicated attributes that are changed, such as the member of attribute, unless a replicated attribute is changed at the same time.

Configuring Active Directory Methods

To configure the Active Directory methods, just follow these steps:

1. Open the ConfigMgr console and then go to the Administration workspace.

2. Expand Hierarchy Configuration and click the Discovery Methods node, as shown in Figure 12.71.

FIGURE 12.71
System Center
Configuration
Manager Console:
Hierarchy
Configuration:
Discovery
Methods

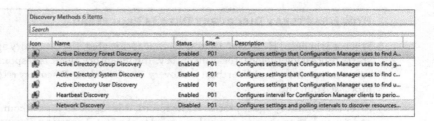

3. Right-click Active Directory Forest Discovery and select Properties.

4. As shown in Figure 12.72, select Enable Active Directory Forest Discovery, select Automatically Create Active Directory Site Boundaries When They Are Discovered, select Automatically Create IP Address Range Boundaries For IP Subnets When They Are Discovered, click Apply, and then click Yes. This will perform the discovery against site and services and will create the items under the boundaries.

FIGURE 12.72
Active Directory
Forest Discovery

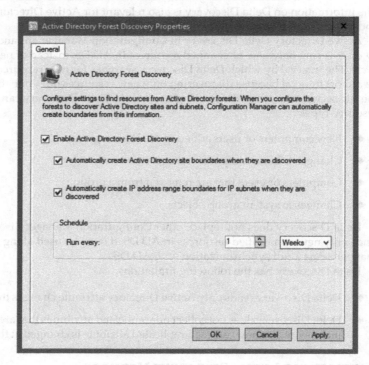

5. Click the boundaries, and you will be able to see the newly generated items by the Active Directory forest discovery, as shown in Figure 12.73.

FIGURE 12.73
Boundaries

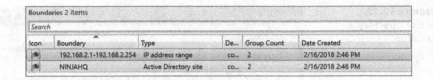

6. Go back to Discovery Methods and right-click Active Directory Forest Discovery and select Properties.

7. On the Active Directory Group Discovery Methods screen, select Enable Active Directory Group Discovery as shown in Figure 12.74. Then select Add ➤ Location on the Active Directory Location screen. Enter a name and select the LDAP location. To do this, just click Browse and find the OU or root to look for AD groups. Once you do that, click OK as shown in Figure 12.75.

FIGURE 12.74
Active Directory
Group Discovery
Properties

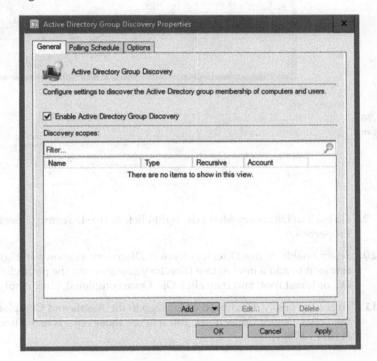

8. To see the newly discovered objects, click Assets And Compliance Workspace; then click the Users Collections node, and you will see the count of discovered objects on the All User Groups and the All Users and User Groups categories, as you can see in Figure 12.76.

FIGURE 12.75
Active Directory
Location

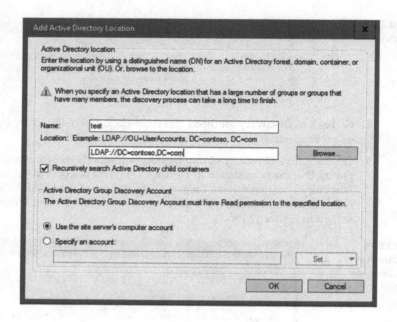

FIGURE 12.76
User Collections

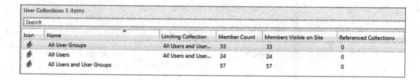

9. Go back to Discovery Methods, right-click Active Directory System Discovery, and select Properties.

10. Select Enable Active Directory System Discovery as shown in Figure 12.77. Then click the star icon to add a new Active Directory container on the path, click Browse to select an OU or forest root, and then click OK. Once completed, click Apply and then click Yes.

11. To see the newly discovered objects, go to the Assets and Compliance workspace and then click Device Collections. You will see those objects listed under All Systems (see Figure 12.78).

FIGURE 12.77
Active Directory
System Discovery

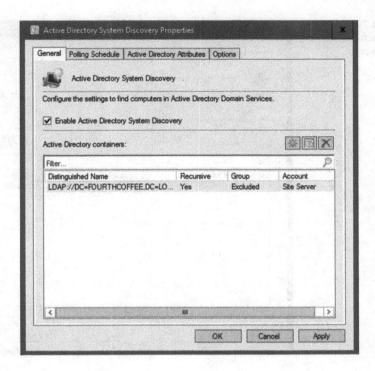

FIGURE 12.78
Device
Collections: All
Systems

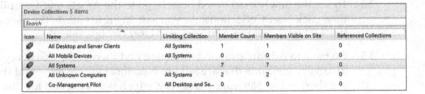

12. Go back to Discovery Methods on the Administration workspace, right-click Active Directory User Discovery, and select Properties.

13. On the Active Directory User Discovery Properties screen, as shown in Figure 12.79, select Enable Active Directory User Discovery and add an Active Directory container to the path. Click Browse and select an OU or forest root. Click OK and then Apply.

FIGURE 12.79
Active Directory
User Discovery

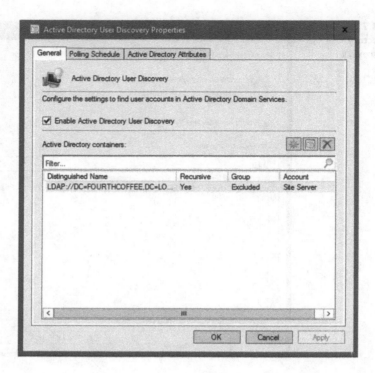

14. To see the newly discovered objects, go to the Assets and Compliance workspace and then click User Collections. As you saw in Figure 12.76, the user count will appear under the All Users and the All Users and User Groups selections.

15. Go back to Administration workspace and then to the discovery methods. The only two discovery methods that are left are Heartbeat Discovery—and there is nothing to configure there—and Network Discovery, which is not needed for this configuration.

NETWORK DISCOVERY NETWORK TRAFFIC

Network Discovery can cause heavy network traffic. We recommend using it only once or based only on a specific need. Otherwise, you should avoid using it for medium to enterprise businesses.

Boundaries and Boundary Groups

Each boundary represents a network location in Configuration Manager, and it's available from every site server in your hierarchy. A boundary does not enable you to manage clients at the network location. To manage a client, the boundary must be a member of a boundary group.

Use boundary groups to manage your network locations. You must assign boundaries to boundary groups before you can use the boundary group. Boundary groups have the following functions:

◆ They enable clients to find a primary site for client assignment (automatic site assignment).

◆ They can provide clients with a list of available site systems that have content after you associate the management point (optional), the distribution point, and the state migration point site system servers with the boundary group.

To support site assignment, you must configure the boundary group to specify an assigned site for clients to use during the automatic site assignment. To support content location, you must specify one or more site systems. You can specify site systems only with the distribution point or state-migration-point site system role. Both the site assignment and content location configurations are optional for boundary groups.

When you plan for boundary groups, consider creating one set of boundary groups for content location and the second set of boundary groups for automatic site assignment. This separation can help you avoid overlapping boundaries for site assignment. When you have overlapping boundaries and use automatic site assignment, the site to which a client is assigned might be nondeterministic.

CREATING A BOUNDARY

To create a boundary, follow these steps:

1. Open the ConfigMgr console; then go to the Administration workspace and select the Boundaries node.

2. Right-click Boundaries and select Create Boundary.

3. On the Create Boundary screen, as shown in Figure 12.80, you can select to create a boundary type of IP Subnet, Active Directory Site, IPv6, or IP address range.

4. Once you've determined the Boundary type you will create, enter the information required for the boundary and then click Apply.

CREATING BOUNDARY GROUPS

There are three type of boundary groups in Configuration Manager: one for site assignment, one for content location, and one for MP (Management Point) affinity.

To create a boundary, follow these steps:

1. Open the ConfigMgr console and click the Administration workspace.

2. Select the Boundary Group node, located under Hierarchy Configuration.

3. Right-click the boundary group and select Create Boundary Group.

4. Enter the boundary group name and description, as shown in Figure 12.81, and then click Add.

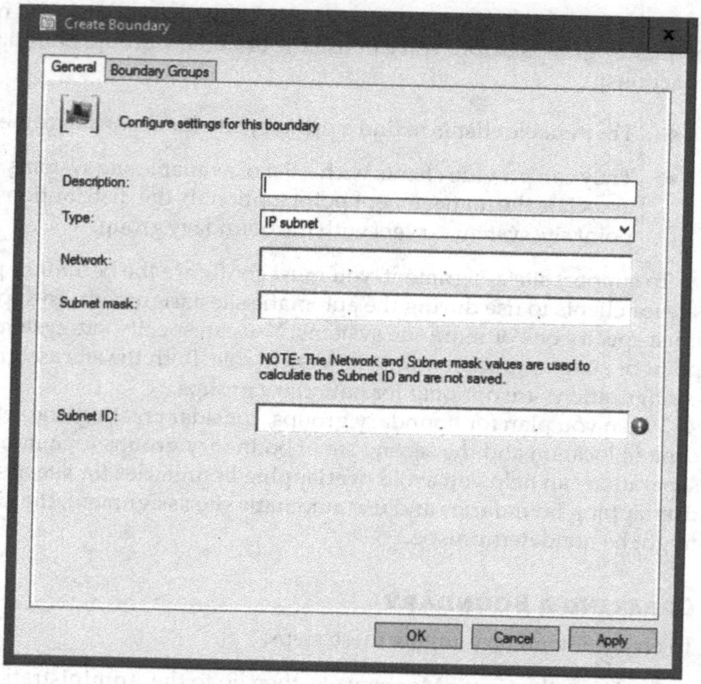

FIGURE 12.80
Create Boundary
screen

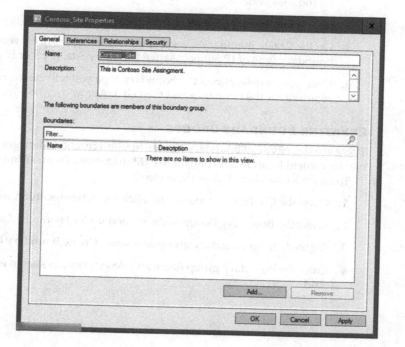

FIGURE 12.81
Create the bound-
ary group.

5. On the Add Boundaries screen, select all the listed boundaries. Because this is a site assignment boundary group and there is only one primary site, all of the clients will report to this primary site. Click OK.

6. Back on the Boundary Group Properties screen, click References and select Use This Boundary Group For Site Assignment, as shown in Figure 12.82. Click Apply.

FIGURE 12.82
Create Boundary
Group: References

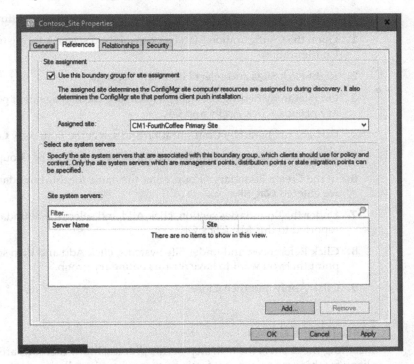

Note that we did not select any site systems in the boundary group for site assignment. This was to ensure that it was only for site assignment and not a mixed boundary.

Here's how to create a boundary group for content location.

1. Open the Configuration Manager console and select Administration Workspace ➤ Hierarchy Configuration.

2. Select the Boundary Groups node and right-click Create Boundary Group.

3. On the Create Boundary Group window, enter the name for the boundary group. For this example, we entered **CON_DP**.

4. Click Add and select the boundaries that will have access to this boundary group for content and location. When you have made your selection, click OK.

5. Click References. On the Select Site System Server screen, click Add and select the distribution point that is needed for this boundary group. When you have made your selection, click OK.

6. The boundary group for Content does not have a site assignment selected; it has only a site system. Click Apply and OK.

Here's how to create a boundary group for management point affinity:

1. Open the Configuration Manager console and select Administration Workspace ➤ Site Configuration.

2. Right-click Sites and select Hierarchy Settings.

3. On Hierarchy Settings, select Clients to use the management points specified in boundary groups. Click Apply and OK.

4. Go back to Hierarchy Configuration and select the Boundary Group node.

5. Right-click Boundary Groups and click Create Boundary Group.

6. In the Create Boundary Group, enter the name for this boundary group. For this example, we entered **CON_MP**.

7. Under the Boundaries section, click Add and select the boundaries that you want to be reported to this MP. Click OK.

8. Click References, and under Site Systems, click Add and then select the management point that you want to have for this boundary group.

9. Click Apply and then Close.

Installing Clients

Installing the client is the next step in this process. Many methods are available to install the client; for this section, we will focus on those client installation methods that work the best for Windows Server 2016.

INSTALLING CLIENT PUSH

Use the Client Push Installation method to automatically install the client to the assigned resources and to manually install the client to resources that are not assigned.

This method can be used to install the client to a single computer or a collection of computers using the Configuration Manager console.

It also can be used to automatically install the client on discovered computers. It can automatically use the client installation properties defined on the Client tab in the Client Push Installation properties.

Configuring Client Push

To configure Client Push, follow these steps:

1. Open the Configuration Manager console and select Administration Workspace ➤ Site Configuration ➤ Sites Node.

2. Right-click the primary site and select Client Installation Settings ➤ Client Push Installation.

3. In the Client Push Installation properties, select Enable Automatic Client Push Installation. In System Types, make sure that Servers are selected.

NOTE Specify whether to install configuration manager client on domain controllers when you use site-wide client push installation and the client push wizard. You can select Always Install the Configuration Manager Client On Domain Controllers. However, this is an optional step. You can decide not to do this and manually install the client on the domain controllers.

4. Click Accounts and make sure you have an account that will have access to install the client on the workstations and servers. Usually, this account has local administrator rights, once the account is added.

5. Click Installation Properties and review the current command-line properties. After you have reviewed it, click Apply and OK.

NOTE You should always perform the discovery methods before enabling automatic client push. If client push is enabled before you have clients in ConfigMgr, all of the discovered objects will install and create unexpected network traffic.

Excluding Servers from Client Push

You can exclude some servers from the client push if necessary. To do that, you will need to edit a multistring Registry key called ExcludeServers. You can find the Registry on the following path:

```
HKEY_LOCAL_MACHINE/SOFTWARE/Microsoft/SMS/Components/SMS_DISCOVERY_DATA_MANAGER.
```

Once you edit the key, you will be able to add one or many servers that you want to exclude from this process.

Installing the Client Manually

To install the client manually, you need to understand the client installation properties; you can read about the available properties at the following link: https://docs.microsoft.com/en-us/sccm/core/clients/deploy/about-client-installation-properties.

To install the client, you need to copy the ccmsetup.exe file and all the files that are located on %programfiles%\Microsoft Configuration Manager\Client. To do that, follow these steps:

1. Log on to the server that you want to obtain the client install.

2. Open the command prompt (Admin) with administrator rights.

3. Type **pushd \\NYCCAS\SMS_CAS\Client** and press Enter.

4. The client folder will map to the server at this point. Type **CCMSETUP.EXE SMSSITECODE=NYC** and press Enter.

5. Once the client is installed, you will see a new folder on c:\Windows\ccm. You should see a new icon on the Installed Programs Call Software Center. Another way to validate the client is to go to Control Panel ➤ Security.

Using Client Settings

Client settings can be used to configure specific items for the clients. You will be able to see the default client agent settings on the Configuration Manager console, Administration Workspace Client Settings node. When you change the default client settings, the settings are applied to all clients in the hierarchy or site server. You can create custom client settings, which override the default client settings when you assign them to a collection.

To learn more about client settings, read the information at the following link:

https://docs.microsoft.com/en-us/sccm/core/clients/deploy/about-client-settings

To create custom client settings for servers, follow these steps:

1. Open the Configuration Manager console and select Administration Workspace ➤ Client Settings.

2. Right-click the Client Settings node and select Create Custom Client Device Settings.

3. On the Create Custom Client Device Settings screen, enter a name and description.

4. Now that you have entered the name and description, you need to select a series of configurations for the Windows server.

5. On the left side of the settings screen, select Client Policy.

DEFAULT POLICY

The default policy is set to 60 minutes, for the servers I have recommended a 30-minute interval, and on the Enable User Policy On Clients = No since this is a server and not a workstation.

6. On the Create Custom Client Device screen, click General.

7. On the left side of the settings screen, select Computer Agent to select the agent.

COMPUTER AGENT

On the Computer Agent, we recommend using only the Organization Name setting. We do not recommend using the new Software Center because that is more focused on the workstation and users.

8. On the Create Custom Client Device screen, click General.

9. On the left side of the settings, select Hardware Inventory.

HARDWARE INVENTORY CYCLE

For the servers, we recommend an inventory cycle at least every five days. The servers are going to be online and usually their hardware will not change that often.

To add other classes, you will need to click Set Classes and enable the following classes for servers:

- Server Hardware Inventory Classes
- Logical Disk ➢ Enable Free Space (MB)
- Quick Fix Engineering
- Shares

10. On the Create Custom Client Device screen, click General.

11. On the left side of the settings screen, select Software Inventory.

SOFTWARE INVENTORY CYCLE

For software inventory, we recommend setting the inventory cycle to seven days. You'll need to set the file types and select a file extension. A file extension can be .exe or something similar. If you want to keep the server from scanning a drive, add an empty file and name it **skp-swi.dat**. If you want to read more about configuring software inventory, check the following link: https://docs.microsoft.com/en-us/sccm/core/clients/manage/inventory/configure-software-inventory.

12. On the Create Custom Client Device screen, click General.

13. On the left side of the settings screen, select Software Updates, as shown in Figure 12.83.

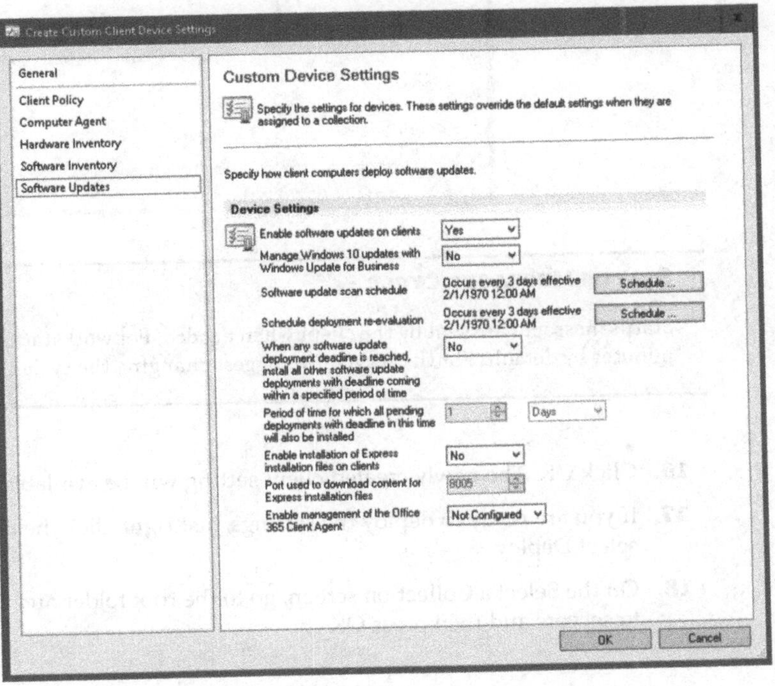

FIGURE 12.83
Create Custom Client Device Settings: Software Updates

> **CUSTOM CLIENT DEVICE SETTINGS**
>
> The most important part of the Software Update setting is the frequency. Avoid using the Workstation-related configuration.

14. On the Create Custom Client Device screen, click General. Now we are going to select State Messaging.

15. On the left side of the settings screen, select Software Updates as shown in Figure 12.84.

FIGURE 12.84
Create Custom
Client Device
Settings: State
Messaging

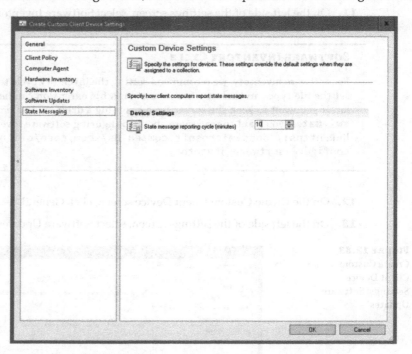

> **STATUS MESSAGES CYCLE**
>
> Status messages are sent by the client when needed. For workstations, messages are sent every 15 minutes by default. For the server, we suggest changing the cycle time to 10 minutes.

16. Click OK. The newly created client setting will be available in the Client Settings node.

17. If you are ready to deploy the settings, just right-click the newly created client setting and select Deploy.

18. On the Select a Collection screen, go to the root folder and find a collection that is related to servers and then press OK.

Using Collections

Collections help you organize resources into manageable units. You can create collections to match your client management needs and to perform operations on multiple resources simultaneously. You can read more about collections at the following link: `https://docs.microsoft.com/en-us/sccm/core/clients/manage/collections/introduction-to-collections`. Table 12.8 lists several ways collections can be utilized.

TABLE 12.8: Collection Use

OPERATION	EXAMPLE
Grouping Resources	You can create collections that group resources based on your organization's hierarchy.
Application Deployment	You can create a collection of computers that do not have Microsoft SQL Server Report Builder installed, and then deploy it to all computers in that collection.
Managing Client Settings	Although the default client settings in Configuration Manager apply to all devices and all users, you can create custom client settings that apply to a collection of devices or a collection of users. As you saw in the previous section, we can build Server Settings Client Settings.
Power Management	You can configure specific power settings per collection.
Role-Based Administration/Role Based Access Control (Reporting)	Use collections to control which groups of users have access to various functions in the Configuration Manager console.
Maintenance Windows	With maintenance windows, you can define a time-period when various Configuration Manager operations can be carried out on members of a device collection.
Software Updates	You can configure a set of collections just to validate the updates or to perform production deployments.
Operating System Deployments	By default, there are All Unknown Computers, which will be used for devices that are not already on the network. However, it is important to also define a set of collections for those that already exist.

There are two types of collections in Configuration Manager, the user collection and the device collection. For this section, we are going to focus on device collections.

To create an all-server collection, follow these steps:

1. Open the Configuration Manager console and select Asset and Compliance Workspace ➢ Device Collections, as shown in Figure 12.85.

FIGURE 12.85
Asset and
Compliance
Workspace:
Device Collections

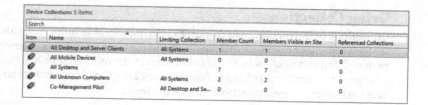

Icon	Name	Limiting Collection	Member Count	Members Visible on Site	Referenced Collections
	All Desktop and Server Clients	All Systems	1	1	0
	All Mobile Devices	All Systems	0	0	0
	All Systems		7	7	0
	All Unknown Computers	All Systems	2	2	0
	Co-Management Pilot	All Desktop and Se...	0	0	0

2. Right-click Device Collections, and select Create A Device Collection.

3. On the Create Device Collection Wizard, enter the name and description and then select Limiting Collection and click Next.

LIMITING COLLECTIONS

Limiting a collection provides the ability to control the number of resources that can be added as members to a collection. This is beneficial as protection and for role-based administration.

4. On the Membership Rules screen, click Add Rule and select Query Rule.

5. On the Query Rule Properties screen, enter the name for the rule and then click Edit Query Statement.

6. On the Query Statement Properties screen, select Criteria and then click Create New Criterion.

7. On the Criterion Properties screen, leave the Criterion Type as Simple Value and then on Where click Select.

8. On the Select Attribute, drill down to Attribute Class and select System Resource.

9. Leave alias as the default, and then click Attribute. Select Operating System Name and Version and then click OK.

10. On the Criterion Properties screen, change Operator to Is Like, and then on Value, enter **%Server%**.

11. The final results display all the available servers, if not go back to step 6.

12. Click OK three times, and you should be taken back to Membership Rules where the new rule is created.

13. Click Use Incremental Updates For This Collection, click Next two times, and then click Close.

As a best practice, the incremental updates for this collection can only be used in the first 200 collections. This configuration is associated to Delta Discovery that runs every 5 minutes and will bring new devices into the collection. To learn more about Best Practices for Collections, go to `https://docs.microsoft.com/en-us/sccm/core/clients/manage/collections/best-practices-for-collections`.

 Real World Scenario

DEPLOYING SERVER SETTINGS TO ALL SERVERS

Now that we have created an all-servers collection, it is time to deploy the server settings that were created in the previous section.

To have the recommended client agent setting deploy to the all-servers collection, you must go back to Client Settings on the Administration workspace and right-click the Server Settings and then select Deploy.

DEPLOY SOFTWARE UPDATES

Software Updates are an important part of administering Windows Server 2016 with Configuration Manager. Now that you have a good configuration, let's deploy some Windows Server 2016 Updates. However, before you can deploy them, you need to validate the product that is being synchronized with the Software Update Catalog.

To configure Windows Server 2016 for Software Updates, follow these steps:

1. Open the Configuration Manager console and select Administration Workspace ➤ Site Configuration ➤ Sites.
2. Right-click the primary site, select Configure Site Component, and then select Software Update Point.
3. On the Software Update Point Component Properties screen, select Products.
4. On the Products window, expand Windows and select Windows Server 2016.
5. Click OK.
6. Go to Software Library Workspace ➤ Software Updates ➤ All Software Updates.
7. Right-click All Software Updates ➤ Select Synchronize Software Updates and then click Yes.

You can monitor the Update's progress on the Monitoring Workspace ➤ Software Update Point Synchronization Status or `wsyncmgr.log`, which is located at `"Install Path"\Microsoft Configuration Manager\logs`.

8. On All Software Updates, click Add Criteria. From the drop-down, select Product, Date Released, Expired and Superseded and then click Add.
9. On the Search Criteria screen, select the configuration.
10. Select the Updates released, and right-click and select Create Software Update Group.
11. On the Create Software Update Group, enter the name and description of the update group and click Create.

continues

continued

12. Go to the Software Update Group node. You will be able to see the newly created software update group.

13. Right-click the new software update group and select Download.

14. On the Download Software Updates Wizard, select Create A New Deployment Package and enter the name, description, and package source.

15. Click Next.

16. On the Distribution Points screen, click Add, select Distribution Point, and then select the distribution point that is needed for the deployment. Click OK.

17. Click Next twice; on the Download Location screen, leave the default and click Next.

18. On the Language Selection screen, leave the default and click Next twice. Wait for the download.

The languages you choose should be the ones needed to support your organization. Also, note that the download may take some time to complete.

19. Once the download has finished, click Close.

20. Right-click the new software update group and select Deploy.

21. On the Deploy Software Update Wizard, click Browse and select the All Server Collection or a collection that focuses on Windows Server 2016. Click Next.

22. On the Deployment Settings screen, review the settings and click Next.

23. On the Scheduling screen, review when you want to deploy the updates and click Next.

24. On the User Experience screen, review whether or not you want to display messages. Click Next.

25. On the Alerts screen, you can generate alerts. You can review them on the Monitoring workspace.

26. On the Download Settings screen, review the settings and click Next.

27. On the Deployment Package screen, click Browse and select the Monthly Server Updates option.

28. On the Download Location screen, leave the default location and click Next.

29. On the Language Selection screen, leave the default and click Next.

30. On the Summary screen, click Next or click Save As Template if you are going to reuse the same settings.

31. Wait for the progress indicator to finish and click Close.

Software updates need to be coordinated and deployed on specific dates and times, depending on an organization's change-control process. You can also use rules to automatically deploy your software updates. To learn more, visit `https://docs.microsoft.com/en-us/sccm/sum/deploy-use/automatically-deploy-software-updates`.

The Bottom Line

Configure a SQL Server cluster. When you're installing and configuring a SQL cluster for System Center Configuration Manager, it is important to configure the proper disk drives—in other words, those that are local and those that are SAN attached.

Master It Reserve a local drive for the monitoring services as recommended in this book.

Solution Copy a `no_sms_on_drive.sms` file onto the SAN-attached drives to avoid the monitoring service installation of the specific drive. More information about this step can be found here:

`https://blogs.technet.microsoft.com/smartinez/2014/06/11/`
`you-implemented-a-sql-cluster-for-sysctr-2012-r2-configmgr-and-you-forgot-what/`.

Install System Center 2016. Installing System Center 2016 can be a little bit tricky; it is very important to understand what products to install first and how to integrate them all once they are installed.

Master It Products can be installed in any order. The best practice is to follow an upgrade process when it is time to upgrade the System Center Product; this avoids having conflicting product versions that are not able to interact against each other.

Solution The product installation sequence is similar to the upgrade sequence and should be as follows:

1. Orchestrator
2. Service Manager
3. Data Protection Manager
4. Operations Manager
5. Virtual Machine Manager
6. System Center Configuration Manager

Learn how to install Management Pack for Windows Server 2016. When we talk about the different integration components in the System Center Suite, we need to focus on the connectors that we have between System Center Service Manager and the other System Center components. In this case, we have the following set of components that are integrated:

- SCSM Connectors
  - Active Directory
  - System Center Operations Manager

- ◆ System Center Configuration Manager
- ◆ System Center Orchestrator
- ◆ System Center Virtual Machine Manager
- ◆ Deploy integration between SCOM and SCVMM.
- ◆ Deploy SCOM agents to all the System Center components.
- ◆ Import System Center Management Packs for SCOM and SCSM.
- ◆ Install integration packs in SC Orchestrator.

Master It   If we are talking about a clean System Center Suite install and those components are (initially) not integrated, there's no specific order in which they need to be deployed. In other words, the Suite is designed to be fully integrated to work well as isolated components. However, if the process is an upgrade, a specific sequence must be followed to ensure a successful upgrade. What is it?

Solution   The upgrade sequence for System Center components is the following:

1. Orchestrator—if you have the Operations Manager integration pack installed to support the runbook that performs automation against your Operations Manager management group. Upgrade resources are available here: `https://docs.microsoft.com/en-us/system-center/orchestrator/upgrade-to-orchestrator`.

2. Service Manager—if you configured the connectors to import alerts and the configuration data for any objects discovered and monitored from Operations Manager. Upgrade resources are available here: `https://docs.microsoft.com/en-us/system-center/scsm/upgrade-to-sm-2016`.

3. Data Protection Manager—if you have configured the central console to centrally manage your DPM environment. Upgrade resources are available here: `https://docs.microsoft.com/en-us/system-center/dpm/upgrade-to-dpm-2016`.

4. Operations Manager. Upgrade resources are available here: `https://docs.microsoft.com/en-us/system-center/scom/deploy-upgrade-overview`.

5. Virtual Machine Manager. If you have configured integration with Operations Manager to monitor the health of your VMM components, the virtual machines, and virtual machine hosts. Upgrade resources are available here: `https://docs.microsoft.com/en-us/system-center/vmm/upgrade`.

For more information, review the System Center documentation page at: `https://docs.microsoft.com/en-us/system-center/`.

Chapter 13

Management with OMS

This chapter will introduce you to Operations Management Suite (OMS), which is a management solution designed to manage and protect your on-premises and cloud infrastructures. Rather than deploying and managing on-premises resources, OMS components are entirely hosted in Azure. Configuration is minimum, and you can be up and running literally in a matter of minutes. In this chapter, we will cover the basics of OMS and how can you use it to monitor and get notifications from your Windows Server 2016 servers.

IN THIS CHAPTER, YOU WILL LEARN TO:

◆ Manage hybrid environments

◆ Expose security threats

◆ Maintain automated configuration updates

What Is Operations Management Suite?

Microsoft has long been providing products for managing enterprise environments. Multiple products were consolidated into the System Center suite of management products in 2007. This includes the family of products that were covered in Chapter 12.

With more computing resources moving to the cloud, System Center products gained more cloud features such as Operations Manager. However, those features were still fundamentally designed as on-premise solutions and required significant investment when being deployed and maintained in an on-premises management environment. To completely leverage the cloud and support future applications, a new approach to management was required.

Operations Management Suite is a set of components designed to deliver a unified IT management solution that brings together multiple IT operations and challenges with a suite of solutions that can resolve those challenges.

OMS is built on these four areas, as shown in Figure 13.1.

FIGURE 13.1
Types of solutions

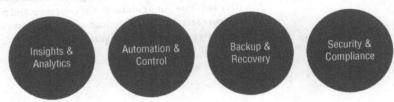

Insights & Analytics

Automation & Control

Backup & Recovery

Security & Compliance

A Brief History

Microsoft Operations Management Suite was released in January 2012 with System Center Advisor (formerly Microsoft codename Atlanta), and it enabled IT professionals to proactively avoid server configuration problems by assessing static, runtime, and operational data to identify potential issues that could cause outages or poor performance. Initially, Advisor provided support for Windows Server and SQL Server workloads and extended support to additional server products.

However, the Advisor product team realized that customers wanted more insight into their data. Their solution became what was called Azure Log Analytics. The program was then called Azure Operational Insights during a limited preview in 2014.

As a massive amount of machine data was captured by Ops Insights, customers wanted their problems remediated and sought solutions on top of the insights they had found. Those customer needs triggered the creation of Operations Management Suite. In May 2015, at Microsoft Ignite, it became generally available.

This service was built from the ground up to support hybrid cloud scenarios.

OMS Services

The core functionality of OMS is provided by a set of services that run in Azure. Each service provides a specific management function, as you can see in Table 13.1, and you can combine services to achieve different management scenarios.

TABLE 13.1:   OMS Services and Description

SERVICES	DESCRIPTION
Insight & Analytics	This platform helps you collect, correlate, search, and act on logs and data.
	It offers real-time operational insights using integrated search to readily analyze millions of records across all of your workloads and servers regardless of their physical location.
	Solutions can be easily added to Log Analytics that define data to be collected and specify the logic for its analysis.
Automation & Control	Azure Automation automates administrative processes with runbooks that are based on PowerShell and run in the Azure cloud. Runbooks can access any product or service that can be managed with PowerShell, including resources in other clouds such as Amazon Web Services (AWS). Runbooks can also be executed on a server in your local data center to manage local resources.
	Azure Automation provides configuration management with PowerShell DSC (Desired State Configuration). You can create and manage DSC resources hosted in Azure and apply them to cloud and on-premises systems to define and automatically enforce their configuration.

TABLE 13.1: OMS Services and Description *(CONTINUED)*

SERVICES	DESCRIPTION
Backup and Recovery	Azure Backup protects your application data and retains it for years with no capital investment and with minimal operating costs.
	Azure Site Recovery contributes to your business continuity and disaster recovery (BCDR) strategy by orchestrating replication, failover, and recovery of on-premises Hyper-V virtual machines, VMware virtual machines, and physical Windows/Linux servers.
Security & Compliance	Security & Compliance has solutions designed to expose security risks and act decisively to resolve those risks. The Security and Audit solution collects and analyzes security events on managed systems to identify suspicious activity.
	The Antimalware solution reports on the status of anti-malware protection on managed systems.
	The System Updates solution performs an analysis of the security updates and other updates on your managed systems so that you easily identify systems requiring patching.

Because of the complexity of the tools, the focus of this chapter will be on describing functionality for just the security and analytics features.

OMS Pricing

Operations Management Suite has a free trial with no expiration. It can be used as long as needed. The free trial comes with a 500 MB upload per day and keep data for 7 days, but it is and will be a free service. However, there are paid options. The different management solutions are part of the different services, which also include different pricing tiers.

These offers change at a very fast pace. To check the current pricing structure and identify the various solutions and services, go to the following link: https://docs.microsoft.com/en-us/azure/log-analytics/log-analytics-add-solutions#offers-and-pricing-tiers.

SLA Details

For paid tiers, Microsoft guarantees that at least 99.9 percent of the time, log data will be indexed within six hours of the data being queued for indexing by the Operations Management Suite Log Analytics Service. However, no service level agreement (SLA) is provided for the free tier of Operations Management Suite Log Analytics.

Monthly Uptime Percentage for the Operational Insights service is calculated as Total Queued Batches less Delayed Batches divided by Total Queued Batches in a billing month for a given Microsoft Azure subscription. Monthly Uptime Percentage is represented by the following formula:

Monthly Uptime Percentage = (Total Queued Batches – Delayed Batches) / Total Queued Batches

Table 13.2 lists the different SLAs for Operations Management Suite.

TABLE 13.2: Service Level Agreements for Operations Management Suite

MONTHLY UPTIME PERCENTAGE	SERVICE CREDIT
< 99.9%	10%
< 99%	25%

For more information, please visit `https://azure.microsoft.com/en-us/support/legal/sla/log-analytics/v1_1/`.

Operations Management Suite can enable multiple types of data. For example, the following can be used as data sources for OMS:

♦ Windows event logs

♦ Windows performance counters

♦ Linux performance counters

♦ IIS logs

♦ Custom fields

♦ Syslog

Data is aggregated approximately 60 minutes after data collection is initialized. However, keep in mind that Operations Management Suite is a log analytics tool by design, and it is not designed to provide real-time monitoring. Once data is inserted, the Service Level Agreement today is six hours. For reactive (almost) real-time monitoring, System Center Operations Manager can be the better fitting tool from a workload and alert management standpoint.

System Requirements

Table 13.3 lists the requirements for Operations Management Suite.

TABLE 13.3: Connected Sources and Data Sources

TYPE OF DATA	TYPE OF SOURCE	DESCRIPTION
Connected Sources	Windows agents	Windows Server 2008 SP1 or later, or Windows 7 SP1 or later.
	Linux agents	Amazon Linux 2012.09 to 2015.09; CentOS Linux 5, 6, and 7; Oracle Linux 5, 6, and 7; Red Hat Enterprise Linux Server 5, 6 and 7; Debian GNU/Linux 6, 7, and 8; Ubuntu 12.04 LTS, 14.04 LTS, 15.04, 15.10, 16.04 LTS; SUSE Linux Enterprise Server 11 and 12.
	Azure Virtual Machines	Enable the Log Analytics VM Extension.
	Azure resources	Collecting logs and metrics for Azure Services: Azure diagnostics direct to Log Analytics, Azure diagnostics to Azure storage to Log Analytics, Connectors for Azure services, Scripts to collect and then post data into Log Analytics.
	Diagnostic or log data from Azure storage	Log Analytics can read the logs for Service Fabric clusters, Virtual Machines, Web/Worker roles.
	Operations Manager	SCOM can extend capabilities with Log Analytics.
	Configuration Manager	SCCM can be connected to OMS to sync device collection data.
	OMS Gateway	Monitored computers can send data to the OMS service when they do not have Internet access.
Data Sources	Custom logs	Text files on Windows or Linux agents containing log information.
	Windows event logs	Events collected from the event log on Windows computers.
	Windows performance counters	Performance counters collected from Windows computers.
	Linux performance counters	Performance counters collected from Linux computers.
	IIS logs	Internet Information Services logs in W3C format.
	Syslog	Syslog events on Windows or Linux computers.

While the different features in Operations Management Suite will collect the data from the connected sources, the data sources will collect data from the connected sources as well. For example, a connected source running Red Hat Enterprise Linux Server will be collecting (if selected) the data sources for Linux performance counters.

You will also need an Azure subscription. For more information, see `https://docs.microsoft.com/en-us/azure/log-analytics/log-analytics-get-started`.

The following browsers are supported:

◆ Internet Explorer (10 and up)

◆ Chrome (latest)

◆ Firefox (Latest)

◆ Safari (7 and up)

Safari 6 and lower is not supported. If you're using macOS, you can use either Chrome or Firefox or you can upgrade to OS X Mavericks to get Safari 7.

The agent needs to use TCP port 443 for various resources. Table 13.4 lists the URLs needed to communicate.

TABLE 13.4: URL Access Needed for OMS

AGENT RESOURCE	PORTS	BYPASS HTTPS INSPECTION
`*.ods.opinsights.azure.com`	443	Yes
`*.oms.opinsights.azure.com`	443	Yes
`*.blob.core.windows.net`	443	Yes
`*.azure-automation.net`	443	Yes

Log Analytics

While the process required to deploy Operations Management Suite is simple, keep in mind that it can (eventually) be as complex as your organization requires. In anyway, the benefit is that this solution is designed in a way that data is collected in almost real time, which will help you perform ad hoc exploration, slice and dice, search and correlate through different sources, and ultimately get insight data that is unique to your organization, which will help achieve complete visibility of IT Operations.

The process of onboarding OMS into an organization is as follows:

1. Create an Azure account. (If you don't have an Azure account already, you must create an Azure Pass. It is a free account that you'll need to integrate into OMS. To get a free pass, navigate to `https://azure.microsoft.com/en-us/free`.)

2. You must create an Operations Management Suite workspace, so navigate to `https://portal.azure.com` and log in with the Live Account associated with the Azure account referenced in the previous step.

3. In the Azure portal, click More Services, and typing **log or analytics** will show Log Analytics, as shown in Figure 13.2.

FIGURE 13.2
The Azure portal

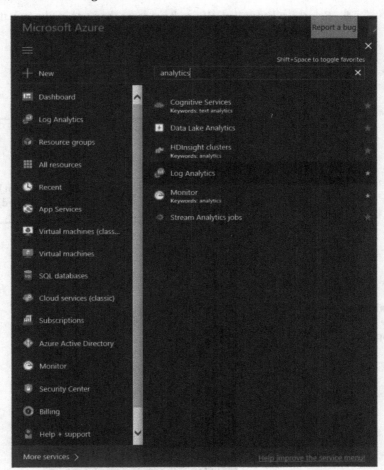

4. In the Log Analytics box, Click Add, as shown in Figure 13.3.

FIGURE 13.3
The Log Analytics
box in Azure

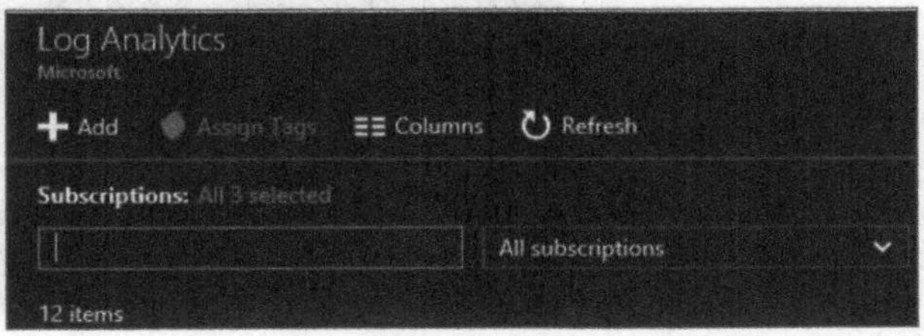

Log Analytics
Microsoft

+ Add   Assign Tags   ≡≡ Columns   ↻ Refresh

Subscriptions: All 3 selected

| | All subscriptions ⌄ |

12 items

5. Select a name for the OMS Workspace or enter a name for your workspace; it must be unique.

6. Select a subscription. (If you have more than one, make sure it is the one that was just created.)

7. Select (or create) a resource group.

8. Select a location.

 Real World Scenario

SELECTING A REGION

When you're on the job, you can select any region. However, the region East US is the one that usually gets the first updates to the suite. Other regions may have limited access to all the solutions.

9. Select a pricing tier.

10. Click OK, as shown in Figure 13.4.

FIGURE 13.4
Create a
workspace.

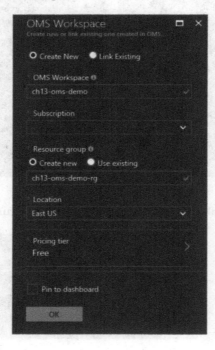

11. You should receive the message "Deployment succeeded," as shown in Figure 13.5.

FIGURE 13.5
Deployment
succeeded

12. Once the workspace is created, select it to see its details in the Azure portal.

13. Navigate to the Azure portal and verify that the portal is available, as shown in Figure 13.6.

FIGURE 13.6
Microsoft Azure
Log Analytics

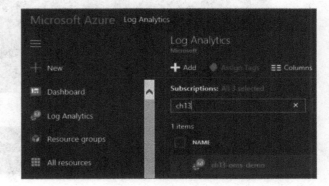

14. Click the Log Analytics workspace that was created.

15. Click the arrow to upgrade the Azure Log Analytics portal, as shown in Figure 13.7.

FIGURE 13.7
The OMS portal
with Azure Log
Analytics

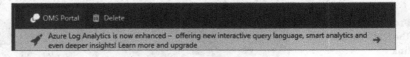

At the time of this writing, some regions are still running the legacy query language.

16. Click on the purple banner that says Learn More and Upgrade.

17. Review the information about the upgrade on the upgrade information page.

18. Click Upgrade Now, as shown in Figure 13.8.

19. Wait for the notification in the upper-right corner with the upgrade status, as shown in Figure 13.9.

FIGURE 13.8
Azure Log
Analytics is now
enhanced.

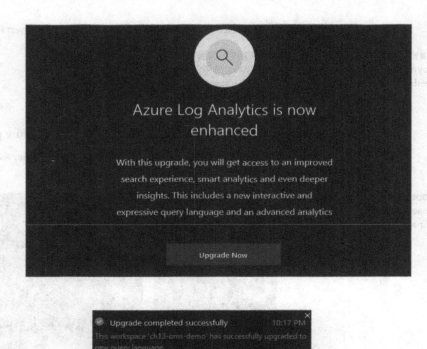

FIGURE 13.9
The work-
space upgrade
is completed
successfully.

Now you can deploy solutions to leverage efforts by Microsoft (to use the built-in dashboards instead of spending time creating queries).

1. In the Azure portal, click the OMS Portal link, as shown in Figure 13.10.

FIGURE 13.10
The OMS Portal
link

2. Click the gear icon, as shown in Figure 13.11.

FIGURE 13.11
The Data Based on
Last 1 Day box

3. Select Data ➤ Windows Performance Counters and click to Add the Selected Performance Counters, and then click the Save icon to complete, as shown in Figure 13.12.

FIGURE 13.12
Data Overview

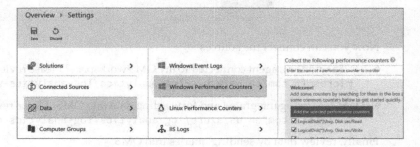

4. Add the Security and Audit solution.

5. Navigate to the OMS portal and click the Solutions Gallery, which is displayed as a shopping bag, as shown in Figure 13.13.

FIGURE 13.13
OMS Portal
Solutions Gallery

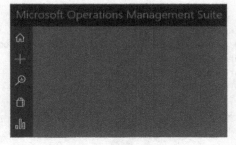

6. On the Solutions Gallery, click the Security and Audit Solution, as shown in Figure 13.14.

FIGURE 13.14
Security and
Audit Solution

7. Click the Add button, as shown in Figure 13.15.

FIGURE 13.15
Solutions Gallery
Add - Security and
Audit

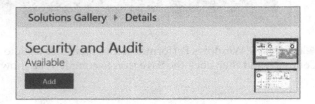

Now you can connect the sources.

◆ Is it a windows agent connected to my OMS workspace? Please review `https://docs`
`.microsoft.com/en-us/azure/log-analytics/log-analytics-windows-agents`.

◆ Is SCOM being integrated and forwarding data into OMS? Please review `https://docs`
`.microsoft.com/en-us/azure/log-analytics/log-analytics-om-agents`.

Finally, review data by sending queries into OMS.

Performance Queries

Here is a list of sample queries in OMS using the latest version of the OMS Query Language.

The following query will show the top processor-utilizations in the agents sending data to
the workspace; you can rename the y-axis as needed, as shown in Figure 13.16.

```
Perf
| where ObjectName == "Processor"
| summarize Average_CPU = avg(CounterValue) by Computer, CounterName
| where Average_CPU > 1
| render barchart
```

FIGURE 13.16
Azure Log Analytics
processor-
utilization query

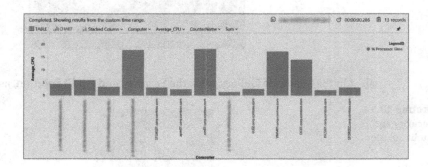

The following query will show the disk latency for the workspace, as shown in Figure 13.17.

```
Perf
| where CounterName == "Avg. Disk sec/Read"
| summarize Average_Latency = avg(CounterValue) by Computer, CounterName
| sort by Average_Latency desc
```

FIGURE 13.17
Azure Log
Analytics disk-
latency query

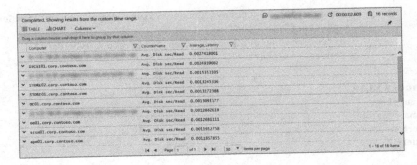

The following query will show the overall performance data for the environment, as shown
in Figure 13.18.

```
Perf
| where TimeGenerated >=ago (7d)
| where ObjectName == "Processor"
| where CounterName == "% Processor Time"
| summarize avg(CounterValue) by bin(TimeGenerated, 1h)
| render timechart
```

FIGURE 13.18
Azure Log
Analytics perfor-
mance query

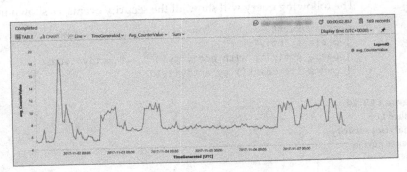

Once you find the one using most of the resources, you can drill down and expose data
quickly.

The following query will show the performance data for all the computers we have, as shown
in Figure 13.19.

```
let endTime=now();
let timerange =1d;
let startTime=now() - timerange;
let mInterval=4;
let mAvgParm= repeat(1, mInterval);
Perf
| where ObjectName == "Processor"
| where CounterName == "% Processor Time"
```

```
| make-series avgCpu=avg(CounterValue) default=0 on TimeGenerated in
range(startTime, endTime, 15m) by Computer
| extend moving_avgCpu = series_fir(avgCpu, mAvgParm)
| render timechart
```

FIGURE 13.19
Azure Log
Analytics total-
performance
query

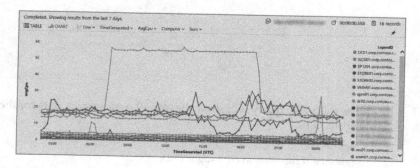

You could highlight the one you see using the most data.

Event Queries

The following query will show all the security events, as shown in Figure 13.20.

```
SecurityEvent
| project Activity
| parse Activity with activityID " - " activityDesc
| summarize count() by activityID
```

FIGURE 13.20
Azure Log
Analytics security-
events query

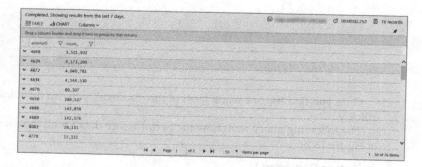

You can also query for the last time a specific computer was rebooted. In this case, the computer contains the clt keyword , as shown in Figure 13.21.

```
Event
| where Computer containscs "clt" and EventID == 6005 and EventLog == "System"
and Source == "EventLog"
| project Computer, TimeGenerated
| sort by Computer
```

FIGURE 13.21
Azure Log
Analytics query
for a specific
reboot

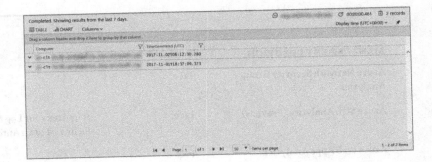

The Bottom Line

Manage hybrid environments. We are transitioning the current approach to IT, keeping workloads on-premises and in the cloud, and implementing hybrid environments. Managing these environments involves identifying new challenges and a collection of solutions from multiple vendors. That creates an integration challenge that could affect how troubleshooting and remediation actions are taken.

Master It The solutions included in Insight & Analytics help customers leverage a new cloud-based platform that is designed to help deliver assistance using a simplified experience unique to the environment, in order to gain full visibility into operations.

Solution Here is the list of solutions offered in Insight & Analytics. For the most updated version of this list, please visit `https://docs.microsoft.com/en-us/azure/log-analytics/log-analytics-add-solutions`.

MANAGEMENT SOLUTION	PRICING TIERS	NOTES
Activity Log Analytics	Free	Ninety days of data are available free of charge.
AD Assessment	Free	
AD Replication Status	Free	Not available to add from Azure portal/marketplace.
Agent Health	Free	Data is not subject to the Free tier cap.
Alert Management	Free	Not available to add from Azure portal/marketplace.
Application Insights Connector (Preview)	Free	
Azure Application Gateway Analytics	Free	

(CONTINUED)

MANAGEMENT SOLUTION	PRICING TIERS	NOTES
Azure Network Security Group Analytics	Free	
Azure SQL Analytics (Preview)	Free	Requires your Log Analytics workspace to be linked to an Automation account.
Azure Web Apps Analytics	Free	
Backup	Free	Requires a classic Backup vault.
Capacity and Performance (Preview)	Free	
Containers	Free	
IT Service Management Connector (Preview)	Free	
HDInsight HBase Monitoring	Free	
Key Vault Analytics	Free	
Logic Apps B2B	Free	Not available to add from Azure portal/marketplace.
Network Performance Monitor	Free	
Office 365 Analytics (Preview)	Free	
Service Fabric Analytics (Preview)	Free	
Service Map (Preview)	Free	Available in East US, West Europe, and West Central US.
Site Recovery	Free	Requires a classic Site Recovery vault.
SQL Assessment	Free	
Start/Stop VMs during off-hours	Free	Requires your Log Analytics workspace to be linked to an Automation account.
SurfaceHub	Free	Not available to add from Azure portal/marketplace.
System Center Operations Manager Assessment (Preview)	Free	

(CONTINUED)

MANAGEMENT SOLUTION	PRICING TIERS	NOTES
Update Compliance (Preview)	Free	No charge for data or nodes.
Upgrade Readiness	Free	No charge for data or nodes.
VMware Monitoring (Preview)	Free	
Wire Data 2.0 (Preview)	Free	Available in East US, West Europe, and West Central US.

Expose security threats.   Managing highly complex, hybrid-cloud, cross-platform infrastructure involves finding ways to quickly identify any security threat to the environment, in a cost and time-effective way.

Master It   The solutions included in Security & Compliance help customers evaluate the current security exposure in managed objects. Security & Compliance provides tools to quickly and easily identify possible threats. That is done by integrating the research done by Microsoft and partners in order to ensure a quick and efficient way to resolve possible security issues.

Solution   Here is the list of solutions offered in Security & Compliance. For the most updated version of this list, please visit `https://docs.microsoft.com/en-us/azure/log-analytics/log-analytics-add-solutions`.

MANAGEMENT SOLUTION	PRICING TIERS	NOTES
Malware Assessment	Free	If you add the Security and Compliance solutions after June 19, 2017, billing is per node, regardless of the workspace pricing tier. The first 60 days are free.
Security and Audit	Free	This solution is required to collect security event logs.

Maintain automated configuration updates.   From the ground up, Operations Management Suite is designed to manage workloads in a hybrid cloud, which includes AWS and Linux support.

Master It   The Automation & Control solutions let you automate and configure activities from a centralized platform. That is implemented by controlling and auditing timeframes for updates, by ensuring that configurations are automatically applied, and by leveraging solutions to ensure high availability of the infrastructure.

Solution   Here is the list of solutions offered in Automation & Control. For the most updated version of this list, please visit `https://docs.microsoft.com/en-us/azure/log-analytics/log-analytics-add-solutions`.

Management Solution	Pricing Tiers	Notes
Automation Hybrid Worker	Free	Requires your Log Analytics workspace to be linked to an Automation account.
Change Tracking	Free	Requires your Log Analytics workspace to be linked to an Automation account.
Update Management	Free	Requires your Log Analytics workspace to be linked to an Automation account.

Index

Symbol

> (redirection) operator, 65

A

About files, PowerShell, 55–56
activation, 10–11
    KMS (Key Management Service), 10–11
    MAK (Multiple Activation Key), 10
    OEM (Original Equipment Manufacturer)
        licensing, 10
Active Directory Users and Computers, 292–293
AD (Active Directory)
    auditing, 360–362
    authentication, containers, 280–281
    domain controllers
        auditing, 360–362
        counts, 354
        CPUs, 357–358
        forest root, 354
        Global Catalog servers, 354
        logging, 360–362
        memory, 358–359
        operating system, 354–355
        operating system components, 362–363
        placement, 354
        Remote Desktop, 363
        Remote Management, 363
        sizing, 357–360
        storage, 359–360
        UAC (User Account Control), 363
        Windows Defender, 363
        Windows Firewall, 363
    ESAE (Enhanced Security Administrative
        Environment), 318–319
    logging, 360–362
    OU (organization unit), creating, 351–353
    PAM (Privileged Access Management), 319–321
AD CS (Active Directory Certificate Services), 385
    CA (Certification Authority)
        certificate templates, 406–417
        database, 386
        enterprise subordinate installation, 400–406
        placement, 393
    configuration, 402
        results, 402

key attestation enrollment, 386
keys, TPM, 386
network devices, 386
new features, 385–386
over-the-air enrollment, 386
PFX files, 386–387
PKI (public key infrastructure)
    certificate policies, 390
    certificates, 387–388
    CSP (Certificate Practice Statement), 390
    documentation, 389–390
    email services and, 392
    encryption and, 392
    environment management, 392
    four-tier hierarchy, 392
    HTTPS and, 387
    intermediate CA, 388
    issuing CA, 388
    LDAPs and, 387
    policies and procedures, 388
    primary components, 387–388
    root CA, 387–388, 394–399
    servers, 393
    single-tier hierarchy, 391
    templates, 388
    three-tier hierarchy, 391
    tiers, 391–392
    two-tier hierarchy, 391, 393
    two-tier hierarchy implementation,
        393–406
    web services and, 392
PowerShell, 386
role services
    Certificate Authority, 388
    Certificate Authority Web Enrollment, 389
    Certificate Enrollment Policy Web
        Service, 388
    Certificate Enrollment Web Service, 389
    NDES (Network Device Enrollment
        Service), 389
    Online Responder, 389
servers, PKI (public key infrastructure), 393
site awareness, 386
Version 4 templates, 386
Windows Server 2012, 386–387
Windows Server 2012 R2, 386

AD DS (Active Directory Domain Services), 180
  Active Directory Recycle Bin, 370
  computer management, 363
    schema classes, 364
  computer objects, 364
  domains
    child domains, 343
    forest root domain, 343
    objects, 342
    parent domains, 343
  forests, 342
    domains, 342, 343
    multiple, 343–344
    security boundaries, 342
  FSMO (Flexible Single Master Operation)
  roles, 350
    domain naming master, 351
    infrastructure master, 351
    PDC emulator, 351
    RID master, 351
    schema master, 351
  GPO (Group Policy Object), 374
    links, PowerShell and, 380
    reports, 378–379
    searching for, 377–378
    settings, PowerShell and, 379–380
  Group Policy, 373, 374
    enforcement, 376
    inheritance, 375–376
    linking, 375
    tasks, 376–377
    troubleshooting, 380–382
  groups, 370
    adding members, 373
    creating, 372–373
    distribution, 371
    scopes, 371
    security, 371
    token sizes and, 371–372
  IPv4 configuration, 181
  LSA (Local Security Authority), 371–372
  objects, 342
  PAM (Privileged Access Management), 339
    JEA, 341
    JIT, 341
    MIM, 341
  replication
    configuration, 349
    domain, 349
    high-level, 349

    KCC (Knowledge Consistency
      Checker), 348
    PowerShell, 350
    RPC over IP, 349
    schema, 348
    SMTP, 349
  sites, 345–347
    link design, 347–348
  trusts, 344–345
  user management, 366–368
  Windows Server 2003 at End of Life, 339
  Windows Server 2012
    Active Directory Recycle Bin, 340
    DAC (Dynamic Access Control), 340
    Fine-Grained Password Policies, 340
    virtualization, 340
  Windows Server 2012 R2
    Conditional Access, 340
    Multifactor Authentication, 340
    Workplace Join, 340
  Work Folders and, 252
AD FS (Active Directory Federation Services)
  account partner organization, 425
  AD DS domain, 430
  application access
    external client, 452–454
    internal client testing, 445–446
  authentication, 423
  certificates, 432
  claims, 425
  claims provider, 425
  deployment, 433–454
  external client, application access, 452–454
  federation servers, 430
  gMSA (group-managed service
    account), 432–433
  identity federation, 424
  infrastructure, 430
  internal client, application access, 445–446
  internal DNS name resolution, 439–440
    DNS Manager host, 441
    DNS Manager zone, 440
  overview, 426–428
  planning and design, 429
    component placement, 429–431
  relying party, 426, 445
  relying party trust, 426
  resource partner organization, 426
  SAML (Security Assertion Markup
    Language), 423

sample federated Application
  appVM, 441
  IIS Manager, 442–443
  PowerShell ISE, 441–442
  token-signing certificate, 442
sample federated application, 441
  publishing, 450–452
server role installation
  adfsVM logon, 433–434
  certificate import, 436
  Configuration Wizard, 435
  File Explorer, 436
  Pre-requisite checks, 439
  Review Options, 438
  service account, 438
  service name, 437
SQL Server database, 431
STS (Security Token Service), 423
WAP servers, 429
  role service, 447–450
Web Application Proxy cluster, 430–431
web server, 430
WS-Federation and, 423
ADAC groups, creating, 372–373
Add Roles and Features Wizard, 21, 118, 227
ADFS (Active Directory Federation Services), 253
ADK (Assessment and Deployment Kit), 14
administrative access
  JEA (Just Enough Administration), 315–316
    role capability files, 316–317
  LAPS (Local Administrator Password
    Solutions), 313
    downloading, 314
  PAW (Privileged Access Workstation), 312–313
    domain controller security, 313
ADUC groups, creating, 372–373
Advisor, 542
AIA (Authority Information Access), 393
  extensions, 398
aliases, 56
Always On VPN, 217–218
AMD Virtualization (AMD-V), 118
Applications and System logs, 28–29
AppLocker, 323–324
architecture
  containers, 260
  Hyper-V, 117
  nested virtualization, 120
  stretch clusters, 149–150
  virtual machines, 260

[array] data type, 78
arrays, 61
  cmdlets and, 98
ATA (Advanced Threat Analytics), 327–328
attach command, 269
attack evidence, 328–329
  Audit Policy Settings, 330
    advanced, 332–333
  auditing, 329–332
    AuditPol, 333
    event log forwarding, 333–336
automated deployment, 11–12
  DISM (Deployment Image Servicing and
    Management), 13–14
  imaging, 12
    SID, 12
    Sysprep, 12–13
  MDT (Microsoft Deployment Toolkit), 19
  SIM (System Image Manager), 14–16
  virtualization and, 19–20
  WDS (Windows Deployment Services), 16–19
automatic variables, 83
Automation & Control (OMS), 541, 542
Azure Log Analytics, 542
Azure Operational Insights, 542

B

Backup & Recovery (OMS), 541, 543
BGP (border gateway protocol), 222
BIOS (Basic Input Output System), 4
BitLocker, 298–299
BitLocker Drive Encryption, 21
boot partitions, 8
BranchCache
  Application Server content, 234
  distributed cache mode, 233
  File Server content, 234
  Group Policy Object, 236
  hosted cache mode, 233
  installation, 235
  Web Server content, 234
[byte] data type, 78

C

CA (Certificate Authority)
  certificate auto-enrollment, 417–418
  certificate templates, 406–417
    built-in, 407
    compatibility, 407–409

cryptography, 411–412
issuance requirements, 415–416
properties, 410
publishing certificates, 409–410
request handling, 410–411
requestors, 416–417
security, 413–414
database, 386
enterprise subordinate installation, 400–406
placement, 393
CAL (Client Access License), 3
casting data types, 77
CAU (Cluster-Aware Updating), 148–149
CCI (Configurable Code Integrity), 325
CDP (CRL Distribution Point), 393
extensions, 397
server configuration, 399–400
Certificate Authority (AD CS), 388
Certificate Authority Web Enrollment (AD CS), 389
Certificate Enrollment Policy Web Service
(AD CS), 388
Certificate Enrollment Web Service (AD CS), 389
certificate templates, 406–407
built-in, 407
compatibility, 407–409
cryptography, 411–412
issuance requirements, 415–416
properties, 410
publishing certificates, 409–410
request handling, 410–411
requestors, 416–417
security, 413–414
certificates
AD FS, 432
policies, AD CS, 388
[char] data type, 77
checkpoints, virtual machines, 125
clearing variables, 84
CLI (command-line interface), 35
cloud, hybrid, 542
cluster upgrades, rolling, 117
clustering
categories
Active-Active, 137
Active-Passive, 137
multisite, 137
single-site, 137
failover, 134–136
application, 136, 138
categories, 137

clients, 136, 138
cluster storage, 138
components, 137–139
failback, 136
failover, 136
hardware, 139–140
high availability and, 135–136
management tasks, 144–145
migrating clusters, 141–142
network, 138
node management, 145–146
nodes, 136, 138
planned-*versus* unplanned, 146–147
properties, 145
quorum, 136, 138, 140–141, 147
resource, 138
roles, 143–144
scenarios, 139
service, 136, 138
shared storage, 136
terminology, 136
upgrading clusters, 141–142
Validation Wizard, 142–143
witness, 136, 138
guest clustering, 132–133
hardware, 139–140
host clustering, 132
networking, 147
SQL Server, instance installation, 461–465
stretch clusters, 137, 149–150
terminology, 136
types, 137
updates and, 148–149
cmdlets, 38
arrays and, 98
ConvertTo-Csv, 67
ConvertTo-Html, 68–69
ConvertTo-Xml, 69–71
Export-Clixml, 71–73
ExportTo-Csv, 67
Format-List, 95–96
Format-Table, 96
Format-Wide, 94–95
function naming, 86
Get-Credential, 71–73
Get-Eventlog, 49–51
Get-NetRoute, 182
Measure-Object, 62–63
Net-NetIPAddress, 182
New-NetRoute, 182

New-VHD PowerShell, 120
parameters, multiple values, 51–52
Remove-NetIPAddress, 182
Remove-NetRoute, 182
Select-Object, 63–65
Set-DnsClientServerAddress, 182
Set-NetIPAddress, 182
spaces in, 51
Test-Cluster, 143
collections, 61
command line functions, 98
comparison operators
-eq, 76
-ge, 76
-gt, 76
-le, 76
-lt, 76
-ne, 76
operands, 75
regular expressions, 75
strings, 75, 77
Computer Management, 24
Conditional Access, 340
configuration
computer name, 9
Desktop Enterprise, 9
IPv4 address, 9
Server Core and, 10
Server Manager and, 9
time zone, 9
workgroups, 9
-Confirm parameter, 54–55
containers
architecture, 260
configuration
AD authentication, 280–281
default, 268–269
networking, 276–279
resources, 279–280
storage, 275–276
creating, 267–269
Docker, 263
installation, 264–265
hardware requirements, 263–264
host, 261
Internet connectivity and, 265
Hyper-V, 262–263
IIS and, 259
images, 261
automated creation, 271–274

customizing, 270–271
Docker Hub, 266–267
storage, 274–275
kernels and, 259
layers, 262
licensing, 264
limitations, 261
Linux, 263
memory, 264
microservices, 262
namespace isolation, 262
Nano Server, 261
operating-system image, 262
RD Session Hosts, 261
repository, 262
running, 267–269
sandbox, 261
Server Core, 261
software requirements, 263–264
VDI (Virtual Desktop Infrastructure), 261
virtual machines comparison, 260
containment operators
-contains, 81
-notcontains, 81
-contains containment operator, 81
ConvertTo-Csv cmdlet, 66–67
ConvertTo-Html cmdlet, 68–69
ConvertTo-Xml cmdlet, 69–71
create command, 269
Create Virtual Switches page, 118
Credential Guard, 296–297
credentials
encrypting, 71–73
saving, to XML files, 73–74
cryptography, certificate templates, 411–412
CSP (Certificate Practice Statement), 390
CSVs (Cluster Shared Volumes), 152–155

D

Dashboard, Server Manager, 23–24
data, importing, to PowerShell, 74
data at rest
BitLocker, 298–299
EFS (Encrypting File System), 297–298
data deduplication
data optimization, 162–163
background operations, 164
reading data, 163–164

enabling, 164–165
excluding files, 165–166
minimum file size, 166
scheduling, 165
shared folders, 162
software installation data, 162
space-saving technologies, 161
virtualization files, 162
data in transit, Windows Firewall with Advanced
Security, 300–302
inbound rules, 302–303
outbound rules, 302–303
Data Protection Manager (System Center)
server, hardware requirements, 459
upgrade path, 458
data types
[array], 78
[byte], 78
casting, 77
[char], 77
[DateTime], 78
[decimal], 78
[double], 78
[hashtable], 78
[int], 78
-is operator, 79–80
[long], 78
[single], 78
[string], 77
[void], 78
[xml], 78
databases, System Center
cluster recommendations, 459–460
file types, 460
Datacenter Firewall, 222
[DateTime] data type, 78
DCDiag, 202
debugging, DNS and, 200–201
[decimal] data type, 78
DEP (Data Execution Prevention), 118
DES (Data Encryption Standard), 293
Desktop Enterprise
configuration, 9
installation, 7
Device Guard, 119, 324
CCI (Configurable Code Integrity), 325
configuration, 325–327
Platform and UEFI Secure Boot, 325
Virtual Secure Mode, 325
Virtual Secure Mode Protected Code
Integrity, 325

Device Manager, 24–25
devices, discrete, 124
DFS (Distributed File System), 229
DFS Management console
Diagnostic Reports Wizard, 243
Health Report, 244
Propagation report, 244
Propagation Test, 244
PowerShell commands, 244
Verify Topology tool, 244
DFS Namespaces, 237
DFS Replication, 242
Domain-Based Namespaces, 238
folders, 238
shared, 238–241
targets, 238
installation, 239–240
Namespace Root, 238
Namespace Server, 238
network ports, 245
PowerShell and, 240
Stand-Alone Namespaces, 238
DFS Replication
configuration, 241–243
installation, 241
DHCP (Dynamic Host Configuration
Protocol), 179
database, backups, 209–210
DHCPDiscover packet, 202
failover relationships, 208–209
filters, 207
high availability and, 208–209
IPv4 configuration, 181
policies, 207
Relay Agent, 202
reservations, 205
scopes, 204–205
multicast scope, 206
options, 206
superscope, 205
server role, installation, 203
servers, rogue, 203
Diagnostic Reports Wizard, 243
differencing disks, 121
DirectAccess, 218
VPN and, 211
discrete devices, 124
disk partitioning, planning, 5
DISM (Deployment Image Servicing
and Management), 13–14
DNS (Domain Name Service), 179

cashing, 195
DCDiag, 202
debug logging, 200–201
Dig, 201
domain controllers, 188
dynamic, 188
KSK (key signing key), 198
monitoring, 199–200
name resolution processing, 192
    advanced settings, 195–196
non-authoritative resolution, 192–194
Nslookup, 201
Performance Monitor and, 200–201
policies, 196–197
records
    AAAA (host), 189
    CNAME (alias), 189
    A (host), 189
    MX (mail exchanger), 189
    NS (name server), 189
    removing, 197–198
    scavenging, 197
    SRV (service location), 189
    TXT (text), 189
security, 198–199
SRV (Service Location), 188–189
troubleshooting, 201–202
zones, 189–192
    creating, 190–192
    ZSK (zone signing key), 198
Docker, 263
    commands
        attach, 269
        create, 269
        exec, 269
        pause, 269
        ps, 269
        rm, 269
        start, 269
        stop, 269
        unpause, 269
    DockerMsftProvider, 264
    DockerProvider, 264
    installation, 264–265
    provider download, 265
Docker Hub, container images, 266–267
dockerfiles, 271–272
    image creation, 273
    PowerShell, 274
domain controllers, 353
    auditing, 360–362

counts, 354
forest root, 354
Global Catalog servers, 354
installation, type, 355–357
logging, 360–362
operating system, 354–355
operating system components, 362–363
placement, 354
Remote Desktop, 363
Remote Management, 363
SRV records, 189
UAC (User Account Control), 363
Windows Defender, 363
Windows Firewall, 363
[double] data type, 78
dynamic IP addresses, DHCP and, 202
dynamic quorum, 140–141
dynamic witness, 141
dynamically expanding virtual hard disks, 120

E

EAP (Extensible Authentication Protocol), 215–216
EFI system partition, 8
EFS (Encrypting File System), 297–298
    certificate templates, 412–413
email, PKI (public key infrastructure) and, 392
encrypting
    credentials, 71–73
    FEK (file encryption key), 298
    VMK (volume master key), 299
encryption, PKI (public key infrastructure) and, 392
enterprise assurance licensing, 4
environment variables, 84–85
-eq comparison operator, 76
-eq operator, 75
ESAE (Enhanced Security Administrative Environment), 318
    locked-down accounts, 319
    selective authentication, 319
ethical hacking, 288
    penetration testing, 288
Event Viewer, 28–29
events, objects, 60
exec command, 269
Export-Clixml cmdlet, 71–73
exporting, credentials, 71–73
ExportTo-Csv cmdlet, 67
expressions, regular expressions, comparison operators, 75

F

Failover Clustering, 21
failover clustering, 134–136
    application, 136
    categories, 137
    clients, 136
    components
        application, 138
        clients, 138
        cluster storage, 138
        network, 138
        nodes, 138
        quorum, 138
        resource, 138
        service, 138
        witness, 138
    failback, 136
    failover, 136
    hardware, 139–140
    high availability and, 135–136
    Hyper-V, 151–152
        CSVs, 152–155
        implementing, 152–154
    Hyper-V Replica, 131
    management tasks
        cluster networks, 144
        cluster nodes, 144
        cluster permissions, 144
        configuration new services, 145
        migrating services, 145
        quorum settings, 145
        removing clusters, 145
    migrating clusters, 141–142
    nodes, 136
        managing, 145–146
    planned *versus* unplanned, 146–147
    properties, 145
    quorum, 136, 147
        dynamic, 140–141
        no majority, 140
        node and disk majority, 140
        node and file share majority, 140
        node majority, 140
    roles
        DFS Namespace Server, 143
        DHCP Server, 143
        DTC (Distributed Transaction
            Coordinator), 143
        file server, 144
        generic application, 144

        generic script, 144
        generic service, 144
        Hyper-V Replica Broker, 144
        iSCSI Target Server, 144
        iSNS Server, 144
        Message Queuing, 144
        Other Server, 144
        Virtual Machine, 144
        WINS Server, 144
    scenarios, 139
    service, 136
    shared storage, 136
    SQL Server, installation, 462–464
    terminology, 136
    upgrading clusters, 141–142
    Validation Wizard, 142–143
    witness, 136
Failover Clustering Management console, live
    migration, 128
failover relationships, DHCP and, 208–209
FEK (file encryption key), 298
File and iSCSI Services, 228
File and Storage Services, 227
    DFS Namespaces, 237
    File and iSCSI Services, 228
file server
    design concepts, 229
    permissions, assigning, 231–232
File Server component
    file shares, creating, 230–231
    installation, 229
File Services, 227
    disaster recovery, 229
    high availability, 229
    number of users, 229
    security, 229
    server placement, 229
file shares, 255
file systems
    NTFS (New Technology File System), 157
        change journal, 158
        ReFS comparison, 159–161
        reparse points, 158
        sparce file support, 158
    ReFS (Resilient File System), 157, 159
        block cloning, 159
        integrity streams, 149
        NTFS comparison, 159–161
files
    BranchCache, 232–233
        Application Server content, 234

distributed cache mode, 233
  File Server content, 234
  Group Policy Object, 236
  hosted cache mode, 233
  installation, 235
  Web Server content, 234
dockerfile, 271–272
  image creation, 273
filtering, 74–75
  DHCP filters, 207
  MAC addresses and, 207
  wildcards, 207
firewalls, 185–186
  Datacenter Firewall, 222
fixed-size virtual hard disks, virtual machines, 120
folders, shared, DFS Namespaces, 238–241
fonts, PowerShell, 37
for loop, 96–97
foreach loop, 97–99
Format-List cmdlet, 95–96
formats, objects, converting, 66
Format-Table cmdlet, 96
formatting, output
  Format-List cmdlet, 95–96
  Format-Table cmdlet, 96
  Format-Wide cmdlet, 94–95
Format-Wide cmdlet, 94–95
FSRM (File Server Resource Manager), 245
  Classification Management
    Classification Properties, 248
    Classification Rules, 248
  console, 247
  disk usage templates, 251
  features deployment, 246–247
  File Classification Infrastructure, 245
  File Management Tasks, 245–246
    Action option, 249
    Condition option, 250
    General option, 249
    Notification option, 249
    Report option, 249
    Schedule option, 250
    Scope option, 249
  File Screening Management, 246, 251–252
  installation, 246
  options
    Access-Denied Assistance, 248
    Automatic Classification, 248
    Email Notifications, 247
    File Screen Audit, 248
    Notification Limits, 247

    Report Locations, 248
    Storage Reports, 248
  Quota Management, 246
    quota templates, 250
    quotas, 250
  Storage Reports, 246
functions
  creating, command lines and, 98
  naming, cmdlets, 86
  PowerShell
    creating, 85, 86–88
    Get-Help About Functions, 85
    parameters, 88–93
    pipeline objects, 93
    pseudocode, 87
    splatting, 86
    viewing all, 94

G

gateway-to-gateway tunneling, IPsec and, 304
-ge comparison operator, 76
Generation 2 virtual machine, 123
Get-Credential cmdlet, 71–73
Get-Credential dialog box, 72
Get-Eventlog cmdlet, 49–51
GPO (Group Policy Object), 374
  account policies, 293–294
  Domain Password policy, 293–294
  Domain-Account Lockout policy, 294
  links, PowerShell and, 380
  reports, 378–379
  searching for, 377–378
  settings, PowerShell and, 379–380
GRE (Generic Routing Encapsulation), 222
Group Policy, 373, 374
  cmdlets
    Backup-GPO, 376
    Copy-GPO, 376
    Get-GPInheritance, 376
    Get-GPO, 376
    Get-GPOReport, 376
    Get-GPPermission, 377
    Get-GPPrefRegistryValue, 377
    Get-GPRegistryValue, 377
    Get-GPResultantSetOfPolicy, 377
    Get-GPStarterGPO, 377
    Import-GPO, 377
    Invoke-GPUpdate, 377
    New-GPLink, 377
    New-GPO, 377

New-GPStarterGPO, 377
Remove-GPLink, 377
Remove-GPO, 377
Remove-GPPrefRegistryValue, 377
Remove-GPRegistryValue, 377
Rename-GPO, 377
Restore-GPO, 377
Set-GPInheritance, 377
Set-GPLink, 377
Set-GPPermission, 377
Set-GPPrefRegistryValue, 377
enforcement, 376
tasks, 376–377
troubleshooting, 380–382
Group Policy Editor, user accounts, 289–292
Group Policy Management Editor, GPO
(Group Policy Object)
account policies, 293–294
Domain Password policy, 293–294
Domain-Account Lockout policy, 294
groups (Active Directory), 370
creating, 372–373
distribution, 371
members, adding, 373
scopes, 371
security, 371
token sizes, 371–372
-gt comparison operator, 76
guest operating systems, 116
GVLK (generic volume license key), 11

H

hacking
ethical, 288
penetration testing, 288
hard disks, virtual
differencing, 121
dynamically expanding, 120
fixed size, 120
pass-through, 121
recommendations, 121
hardening the system, 327–328
hardware
containers, 263–264
failover clustering, 139–140
[hashtable] data type, 78
high availability
DHCP and, 208–209
failover clustering and, 135–136
host resources, protection, 117

hybrid cloud, 542
Hyper-V, 2, 19–20, 115–116
AMD Virtualization (AMD-V), 118
architecture, 116
clustering
failover, 151–154
guest clustering, 132–133
host clustering, 132
configuration, 121–126
containers, 262–263
DEP (Data Execution Prevention), 118
failover clustering, 134–136
categories, 137
components, 137–139
hardware, 139–140
high availability and, 135–136
terminology, 136
high-availability option, 132
host computer, 115
host resource protection, 117
Hyper-V Manager functionalities, 117
installation, 118–119
PowerShell and, 119
prerequisites, 118
Intel VT (Virtualization Technology), 118
machine activation, 20
networking, 121–122
RDMA (Remote Direct Memory Access), 122
virtual switches, 121–122
VMQ (virtual machine queue), 122
new features, 116–117
virtual machines, 117–118
New-VHD PowerShell cmdlet, 120
NLB (Network Load Balancing), 133–134
partitioning, 120
PowerShell Direct, 116
PowerShell Direct and, 112
rolling cluster upgrade, 116
SLAT (second-level address translation), 118
start order priority, 117
storage, 120
storage QoS (Quality of Service), 117
virtual hard disks, 120–121
virtual machines
checkpoints, 125
configurations, 122–123
discrete devices, 124
exporting, 125–126
importing, 125–126
integration services, 124
live migration, 126

new features, 117–118
RDMA (Remote Direct Memory Access), 122
resource metering, 124
secure boot, 124
shielded, 117, 123–124
smart paging, 124
states, 124
VMQ (virtual machine queue), 122
virtualization, nested, 116, 119–120
VM Monitor Mode, extensions, 118
Hyper-V Containers, 2
Hyper-V Manager, 117
Hyper-V Network Virtualization, 221
Hyper-V Replica, 129–130
enabling, 131
failover, 131
planned failover, 131
test failover, 131
implementation, 130–131

I

identity federation, 424
Microsoft Office 365 and, 424
Salesforce and, 424
iDNS (internal DNS Service), 224
IDS (intrusion detection system), ATA, 327
if loop, 99–100
IIS (Internet Information Services), 259
entrypoint, 268
IKEv2 (Internet Key Exchange v2 Tunneling Protocol), 212
images
containers, 261
automated creation, 271–274
customizing, 270–271
Docker Hub, 266–267
storage, 274–275
deploying, 18–19
WDS (Windows Deployment Services), 16
importing, to PowerShell, 74
-in operator, 81–82
input operations, 65–66
Insights & Analytics (OMS), 541, 542
installation
automated deployment, 11–12
DISM, 13–14
imaging, 12–13
MDT, 19
SIM, 14–16
virtualization and, 19–20
WDS, 16–19

Desktop Enterprise, 7
drivers, 4
firmware
BIOS, 4
UEFI, 4
Hyper-V, 118–119
location, 8
Server Core, 7, 355–357
steps, 5–9
type, 7, 355–357
virtual machines, 5
[int] data type, 78
integration services, 124
Intel VT (Virtualization Technology), 118
IP (Internet Protocol), 179
configuration, 180–182
Ping utility and, 181
IPsec
configuration
firewall rules, 309–310
GPO and, 308–309
Windows Firewall administration, 310–311
connection security rules, 305–306
authentication exemption, 305
authentication method, 307–308
custom, 306
isolation, 305
Requirements page, 306–307
Server to Server, 306
tunnel, 306
modes, 305
transport mode, 305
tunnel mode, 305
monitoring
Main Mode, 311
Quick Mode, 312
uses, 304
IPv4, configuration, 180–182
IPv6, configuration, 181–182
-is operator, data type verification, 79–80

J

JEA (Just Enough Administration), 341
role-capabilities
AliasDefinitions, 316
AssembliesToLoad, 316
EnvironmentVariables, 316
FormatsToProcess, 316
FunctionDefinitions, 316
ModulesToImport, 316

ScriptsToProcess, 316
TypesToProcess, 316
VariableDefinitions, 316
VisibleAliases, 316
VisibleCmdlets, 316
VisibleExternalCommands, 316
VisibleFunctions, 316
VisibleProviders, 316
session-configuration files
RoleDefinitions, 317
RunAsVirtualAccount, 317
RunAsVirtualAccountGroups, 317
SessionType, 317
TranscriptDirectory, 317
JIT (Just In Time) administration, 341

K

Kerberos, long-term keys, 294–295
kernels, containers and, 259
KMCI (kernel mode code integrity), 325
KMS (Key Management Service), 10–11

L

L2TP (Layer 2 Tunneling Protocol), 212
LACP (Link Aggregation Control Protocol), NIC
Teaming and, 185
latency, VPNs and, 210
-le comparison operator, 76
licensing
CAL (Client Access License), 3
core-based, 3
enterprise agreement, 4
GVLK (generic volume license key), 11
OEM (Original Equipment Manufacturer), 3
software assurance, 4
virtualization, 3
volume, 3–4
-like operator, 76–77
Linux, containers, 263
live migration, 126
cleanup, 128
guest-memory transfer, 128
requirements, 128–129
setup, 128
shared-nothing live migration, 128
state transfer, 128
virtual machines, 127–128
load balancing, networks, 219–220

LOB (line-of-business) applications, 36
logs
Application and System logs, 28–29
debugging, DNS and, 200–201
[long] data type, 78
loops, PowerShell
for, 96–97
foreach, 97–99
if, 99–100
switch, 100–102
Where-Object method, 104–108
while, 102–104
LSA (Local Security Authority), 371–372
-lt comparison operator, 76

M

MAC address spoofing, virtual machines, 119
MAC addresses, filtering and, 207
MAK (Multiple Activation Key), 10
malware, 287
AppLocker and, 323–324
Device Guard, 324
CCI (Configurable Code Integrity),
325
configuration, 325–327
Platform and UEFI Secure Boot, 325
Virtual Secure Mode, 325
Virtual Secure Mode Protected Code
Integrity, 325
SRPs (Software Restriction Policies), 323
mandatory parameters, 90–91
MDT (Microsoft Deployment Toolkit), 19
Measure-Object cmdlet, 62–63
memory, containers, 264
methods, objects, 60
migration
clusters, 141–142
live migration, 126
cleanup, 128
guest-memory transfer, 128
requirements, 128–129
setup, 128
shared-nothing live migration, 128
state transfer, 128
virtual machines, 127–128
virtual machines, 126–127
Exporting and Importing Virtual
Machines, 127
Live Migration, 127

Quick Migration, 127
Virtual Machine and Storage Machine, 127
MIM (Microsoft Identity Manager), 341
monitoring
Event Viewer, 28–29
Performance Monitor, 32–33
Resource Monitor, 30–32
System Center Operations Manager, 27
Task Manager, 29–30
Multifactor Authentication, 340

N

named parameters, 88–90
NDES (Network Device Enrollment Service)
(AD CS), 389
-ne comparison operator, 76
nested virtualization, 117, 119–120
.NET Framework, 21
network adapter teaming, 182–183
NIC teaming, 183–184
LACP, 185
load-balancing modes, 185
Static Teaming mode, 185
Switch Independent mode, 185
virtualization hosts and, 183
Network Controllers, 221
NETWORK SERVICE account, 27
networks
cluster, 147
containers, 276–279
files, BranchCache, 232–237
load balancing, 219–220
New-VHD PowerShell cmdlet, 120
NIC teaming, 183
LACP, 185
load-balancing modes
Address Hash, 185
Dynamic, 185
Hyper-V Port, 185
new teams, 184
Static Teaming mode, 185
Switch Independent mode, 185
NLB (Network Load Balancing), 179, 219–220
-notcontains containment operator, 81
-notin operator, 81–82
NPS (Network Policy Server), 215–217
Nslookup, 201
NTFS (New Technology File System), 157
change journal, 158

ReFS comparison, 159–161
reparse points, 158
sparse file support, 158
NTLM (NT LAN Manager), 294–295

O

objects
arrays, 61
collections, 61
credential, encrypting, 71–73
events, 60
filtering, 74–75
comparison operators, 75–76
wildcards, 76–77
format conversion, 66
measuring, 62–63
members, 59–60
methods, 60
properties, 59–60
selecting, 63–65
sorting, 61–62
as table, 61–62
OEM (Original Equipment Manufacturer)
licensing, 3, 10
OMS (Operations Management Suite),
541
Automation & Control, 541, 542
Backup & Recovery, 541, 543
browsers supported, 546
history, 542
Insights & Analytics, 541, 542
Log Analytics, 546–552
onboarding, 546–550
portal link, 550
pricing, SLA, 543–544
Query Language
event queries, 554–555
performance queries, 552–554
Security & Compliance, 541, 543
Security and Audit Solution, 551
Solutions Gallery, 551
system requirements
connected sources, 545
data sources, 545
URL access, 546
one-liners, 373
Online Responder (AD CS), 389
OOBE (Out-of-Box Experience), 12
operands, 75

operating systems
    domain controllers, 354–355
    guest, 116
Operations Manager (System Center)
    activation, 495
    agents, 483
    databases, 482
        Data Warehouse database, 483
        retention period, 483
        StandardDatasetAggregation table, 483
    installation
        activation, 495
        administration rights, 492
        Diagnostic and Usage Data, 493
        initial screen, 486–487
        license terms, 488–489
        location, 487
        management group name, 488
        operational database configuration, 489–490
        Operations Manager shell, 494
        Reporting Services instance, 490–491
        results window, 494
        SCOM features, 487
        service accounts configuration, 492
        summary page, 493
        web console, 491
    management packs, 484
    management server
        Config Service, 482
        Health Service, 482
        RMSE (Root Management Server Emulator), 482
        SDK Service, 482
    prerequisites, 484
        passing, 488
        web console, 485
    Report Viewer, installation, 485
    server, hardware requirements, 459
    services
        Config Service, 483–484
        Health Service, 484
        Microsoft Monitoring Agent, 483, 484
        SDK Service, 483, 484
    SQL CLR Types, installation, 485
    upgrade path, 458
    web console, 485
    Windows Server management pack
        importing management packs, 496–498
        selecting for install, 498–499

operators
    > (redirection), 65
    comparison operators
        -eq, 76
        -ge, 76
        -gt, 76
        -le, 76
        -lt, 76
        -ne, 76
        regular expressions, 75
        strings, 75
    containment operators
        -contains, 81
        -notcontains, 81
    -eq, 75
    -in, 81–82
    -is, 79–80
    -like, 75
    -notin, 81–82
    operands, 75
    -replace, 82
Ops Insights, 542
Orchestrator (System Center), upgrade path, 458
OU (organizational unit), creating, 351–353
Out-File command, 65
output, formatting
    Format-List cmdlet, 95–96
    Format-Table cmdlet, 96
    Format-Wide cmdlet, 94–95
output operations, 65–66

P

packet sniffers, 202
PAM (Privileged Access Management), 319
    Administrative Forest, 320
    JEA (Just Enough Administration), 341
    JIT (Just In Time) administration, 341
    MIM (Microsoft Identity Manager), 320, 341
    MIM Portal, 321
    MIM Service, 321
    MIM Service Database, 321
    PAM Client, 320
    PAM Component Service, 320
    PAM Monitoring Service, 320
    PAM REST API, 320
    Production Forest, 320
parameters
    -Confirm, 54–55
    mandatory, 90–91

named, 88–90
positional, 91–92
switch, 92–93
values, passing multiple, 51–52
-WhatIf, 53–54
parenthetical commands, 52
partitioning
boot partitions, 8
EFI system partition, 8
recovery partition, 8
system partitions, 8
pass-the-hash, 294
pass-the-ticket attacks, 296–297
pass-through virtual hard disks, 121
pause command, 269
penetration testing, 288
Performance Monitor, DNS and, 200–201
permissions, assigning, 231–232
phishing, 287
simulation, 288
Ping utility, IP and, 181
pipelines, 59
objects, selecting subsets, 63–65
PKI (public key infrastructure)
certificate policies, 390
certificates, 388
issuing, 387
CSP (Certificate Practice Statement), 390
documentation, 389–390
email services and, 392
encryption and, 392
environment management, 392
HTTPS and, 387
intermediate CA, 388
issuing CA, 388
LDAPs and, 387
policies and procedures, 388
primary components, 387–388
root CA, 387–388
offline, 394–396
templates, 388
tiers
four-tier hierarchy, 392
single-tier hierarchy, 391
three-tier hierarchy, 391
two-tier hierarchy, 391
two-tier hierarchy implementation, 393–406
web services and, 392
point-to-site VPN, 222
positional parameters, 91–92

PowerShell, 35–36, 45
32-bit version, 36–37
64-bit version, 36–37
About files, 55–56
AD (Active Directory), replication and, 350
aliases, 44–46, 56
Begin statement, 93
CLI and, 35
CMD.EXE-like commands, 44–46
cmdlets, 38
auditing logs, 335
dialog boxes, 52–53
Get-Eventlog, 49–51
spaces in, 51
syntax, 49–51
Windows Firewall and Advanced
Security, 303
commands, 58–59
saving results, 65
shortened syntax, 56–58
console, customization, 37
ConvertTo-Csv cmdlet, 66–67
ConvertTo-Html cmdlet, 68–69
ConvertTo-Xml cmdlet, 69–71
credentials, encrypting, 71–73
cutting, 37–38
data types
[array], 78
[byte], 78
casting, 77
[char], 77
[DateTime], 78
[decimal], 78
[double], 78
[hashtable], 78
[int], 78
-is operator, 79–80
[long], 78
[single], 78
[string], 77
[void], 78
[xml], 78
DFS Namespaces, 240
Dir /S, 45
dockerfiles, 274
End statement, 93
execution policies, 43
Export-Clixml cmdlet, 71–73
ExportTo-Csv cmdlet, 67
fonts, 37

forward compatibility, 36
functions
    creating, 85, 86–88
    Get-Help About Functions, 85
    parameters, 88–93
    pipeline objects, 93
    pseudocode, 87
    splatting, 86
    viewing all, 94
GPO links, 380
GPO settings, 379–380
GUI and, 35
help
    Get-Help, 46–47
    Get-Help updates, 47–48
    online files, 48–49
Hyper-V installation, 119
importing to, 74
input operations, 65–66
-like operator, 76–77
LOB applications, 36
loops
    for, 96–97
    foreach, 97–99
    if, 99–100
    switch statement, 100–102
    Where-Object method, 104–108
    while, 102–104
Measure-Object cmdlet, 62–63
network, configuration, 182
objects
    arrays, 61
    collections, 61
    events, 60
    members, 59–60
    methods, 60
    properties, 59–60
    selecting, 63–65
    sorting, 61–62
    as table, 61–62
operators
    > (redirection), 65
    comparison, 75–76
    comparison operators, 75, 76
    containment operators, 81
    -eq, 75
    -in, 81–82
    -is, 79–80
    -like, 75
    -notin, 81–82

operands, 75
    -replace, 82
Out-File command, 65
output operations, 65–66
parameters
    -Confirm, 54–55
    multiple values, 51–52
    -WhatIf, 53–54
pasting, 37–38
pipelines, 59
Process statement, 93
remote systems
    commands, 110–111
    Enable-PSRemoting, 109
    persistent connections, 111–112
    PowerShell Direct, 112
    scripts, 111
    workgroup servers, 110
Run As Administrator, 37
selections, 38
Select-Object cmdlet, 63–65
Service object, properties, 60
sessions, recording, 44
Show-Command, 52–53
transcription operations, 44
user accounts
    deleted, restoring, 370
    reports, 368–369
    stale, 369–370
variables
    automatic, 83
    clearing, 84
    environment variables, 84–85
    preference, 83
    removing, 84
    user-created, 83
    Variable: drive, 84
wildcards, 76–77
PowerShell Direct, 112, 117
    virtual machines, 126
PowerShell ISE
    (Integrated Scripting Environment), 36, 38
    cmdlets, 38
    colors, 40
    Command add-on, 38
    Command pane, 38–39
    fonts, 40
    General Settings tab, 40, 41
    Intellisense, 40–41
    Options dialog box, 40

profiles, 41–42
    editing, 42–43
Script pane, 39
Tools, 39–40
PPTP (point-to-point tunneling protocol), 211
preference variables, 83
privileged access, Group Policy Editor, 289–292
privileges, delegating, 295–296
processes, finding all running, 104–108
processors, core-based licensing, 3
profiles, PowerShell ISE, 41–42
    editing, 42–43
properties
    objects, 59–60
    Service object
        CanShutdown, 60
        MachineName, 60
        StartType, 60
Protected Users groups, 294–295
protocols, VPNs
    IKEv2, 212
    L2TP, 212
    PPTP, 211
    SSTP, 212
ps command, 269
pseudocode, 87

Q

QoS (Quality of Service)
    storage, 157
        Hyper-V, 117
        Storage QoS, 176
quorums, dynamic, 140–141

R

RADIUS (Remote Access Dial-In Service), 215–217
ransomware, 287
RAS (Remote Access Server)
    DirectAccess, 211
    routing, 211
RAS Gateway, 221–222
RDMA (Remote Direct Memory Access), 122
    SET and, 223
RDS (Remote Desktop Services), 210
recovery partition, 8
recursive searches, 44
redirection (>) operator, 65
ReFS (Resilient File System), 157
    block cloning, 159

integrity streams, 159
    NTFS comparison, 159–161
regular expressions, comparison operators, 75
remote access, 210–211. *See also* RAS (Remote
  Access Server)
    NPS (Network Policy Server), 215–217
    RADIUS (Remote Access Dial-In
      Service), 215–217
    RDS (Remote Desktop Services), 210
    VPNs (virtual private network), 210
    WAP (Web Application Proxy), 211, 218–219
Remote Desktop, domain controllers and, 363
Remote Management, domain controllers and, 363
remote systems, PowerShell
    commands, 110–111
    Enable-PSRemoting, 109
    persistent connections, 111–112
    PowerShell Direct, 112
    scripts, 111
    workgroup servers, 110
removing variables, 84
-replace operator, 82
Replicate Folder Wizard, 242
replication, AD (Active Directory),
  PowerShell and, 350
resource metering, 124
Resource Monitor, 30–32
resources, containers, 279–280
reverse lookup zones, 189–190
rm command, 269
rolling cluster upgrades, 117
root CA, 387–388
    offline, 394–396
        configuration, 396–399
routing, RAS and, 211
Routing and Remote Access dialog box, 214
RSAT (Remote Server Administration Tools), 7

S

SAM (Security Accounts Management), 179
SAML (Security Assertion Markup Language), 423
SANs (storage area networks), 157
saving
    command results, 65
    credentials, to XML files, 71–73
scalar input, 80
SDN (Software Defined Network)
    iDNS (internal DNS Service), 224
    SET (Switch Embedded Teaming), 223

SLB (Software Load Balancing)
    DIP (Dynamic IP address), 223
    MUX (SLB Multiplexer), 223
    VIP (Virtual IP address), 223
SDN (Software Defined Networking), 179, 220–221
    Datacenter Firewall, 222
    Hyper-V Network Virtualization, 221
    Network Controller, 221
    RAS Gateway, 221–222
searches
    recursive searches, 44
    wildcards, 76–77
secure boot, 124
security, 285–286
    administrative access
        JEA (Just Enough Administration), 315–318
        LAPS (Local Administrator Password
          Solutions), 313, 314
        PAW (Privileged Access
          Workstation), 312–313
    anti-malware software, 286
    attack surface area, 287
    attack vectors, 287
    attacks, evidence, 328–336
    data at rest
        BitLocker, 298–299
        EFS, 297–298
    encryption, FEK, 298
    GPO (Group Policy Object)
        account policies, 293–294
        Domain Password policy, 293–294
        Domain-Account Lockout policy, 294
    Group Policy Management Editor, GPO
        (Group Policy Object), 293–294
    hacking, ethical, 288
    hardening system, ATA (Advanced Threat
        Analytics), 327–328
    IPsec
        configuration, 308–311
        connection security rules, 305–308
        modes, 305
        monitoring, 311, 312
        uses, 304
    malware, 287
        AppLocker and, 323–324
        Device Guard, 324–327
        protection, 322–327
        SRPs, 323
    pass-the-hash attacks, 294
    pass-the-ticket attacks, 296–297

    penetration testing, 288
    permissions
        admin, 286
        users, 286
    phishing, 287
    ransomware, 287
    risks, 286–287
    social engineering, 287
    Trojans, 287
    updates, 286
    user accounts, 288, 292–293
        Active Directory Users and
          Computers, 292–293
        Credential Guard, 296–297
        privileged access, 289–292
        Protected Users groups, 294–295
    user credentials, 286
    viruses, 287
    Windows Firewall, 286
Security & Compliance (OMS), 541, 543
security boundaries, 342
Select-Object cmdlet, 63–65
Server Core, 355–357
    configuration and, 10
    installation, 7
    PowerShell and, 7
Server Manager, 227
    configuration and, 9
    Dashboard view, 23–24
    features, 21–23
    File and Storage Services, 230
    monitoring, 23–24
    roles, 21–23
SERVICE account, 27
Service Management Automation (System Center),
    upgrade path, 458
Service Manager (System Center)
    server, hardware requirements, 459
    upgrade path, 458
Service object, properties
    CanShutdown, 60
    MachineName, 60
    StartType, 60
Service Provider Foundation (System Center),
    upgrade path, 458
SET (Switch Embedded Teaming), 223
shared-nothing live migration, 128
shielded virtual machines, 1, 123–124
shortened command syntax, 56–58
Show-Command (PowerShell), 52–53

sign-on offline, 294–295
SIM (System Image Manager), 14–16
    configuration passes, 15
[single] data type, 78
site system roles (System Center)
    Application Catalog web service point, 503
    Application Catalog website point, 503
    certificate registration point, 503
    cloud-based distribution point, 503
    component provider, 502
    configurations supported, 504
    distribution point, 503
    endpoint protection point, 503
    enrollment point, 503
    enrollment proxy point, 503
    fallback status point, 503
    management point, 503
    reporting services point, 503
    services connection point, 503
    SMS provider, 502
    software requirements, 503–504
    software update point, 503
    state migration point, 503
site-to-site tunneling, IPsec and, 304
site-to-site VPN, 222
SLAs (Service Level Agreements), OMS, 543–544
SLAT (second-level address translation), 118
SLB (Software Load Balancing), 222–223
    DIP (Dynamic IP address), 223
    MUX (SLB Multiplexer), 223
    VIP (Virtual IP address), 223
smart paging, 124
SMB (Server Message Block), 128
SMD Direct, 122
social engineering, 287
software assurance licensing, 4
Software Defined Networking, 2
splatting functions, 86
spoofing, MAC addresses, virtual machines, 119
SQL Server
    failover cluster, installation, 462–464
    Instance Configuration, 462–463
    instances, installation in cluster, 461–465
    System Center, file types, 460
SQL Server Installation Center, 461–462
SRPs (Software Restriction Policies), 323
SRV (Service Location), 188–189
    records, domain controller, 189
SSTP (Secure Socket Tunneling Protocol), 212
start command, 269

start order, priority, 117
Static Teaming mode, NIC Teaming, 185
stop command, 269
storage
    container images, 274–275
    containers, 275–276
    data deduplication, 157
        advanced settings, 165–166
        background and, 164
        enabling, 164–165
        optimization and, 162–163
        reading optimized data, 163–164
        shared folders, 162
        software installation data, 162
        space-saving technologies, 161–162
        virtualization files, 162
    domain controllers, 359–360
    file systems, 157
        NTFS (New Technology File
            System), 157–161
        ReFS (Resilient File System), 157,
            159–161
    storage QoS (Quality of Service), 157
    Storage Replica, 157
    Storage Spaces, 157
Storage QoS (Quality of Service), 157
    aggregated policy, 176–177
    dedicated policy, 176
Storage Replica, 2, 170–171
    AD DS and, 174
    asymmetric storage, 171
    asynchronous replication, 171, 173
    Datacenter Edition and, 174
    deployment, 174–176
    DFS (Distributed File System), 170
    network connectivity and, 174
    replication options, 172
    storage and, 174
    stretch clusters, 171
    symmetric storage, 171
    synchronous replication, 171
Storage Spaces, 166–167
    continuous availability, 168
    CSVs (Cluster Shared Volumes), 166
    resilience
        mirroring, 167
        parity, 167
        simple, 167
    storage tiering, 168
    write-back cache, 168

Storage Spaces Direct, 2, 168
    LAN (Local Area Network), 169
    local storage, 169
    servers, 169
    SMB, 169
stretch clusters, 137, 149–150
    Storage Replica, 171
[string] data type, 77
strings
    comparison operators, 75, 77
    -match operand, 80–81
STS (Security Token Service), 423
Switch Independent mode, NIC Teaming, 185
switch parameters, 92–93
switch statement, loops, 100–102
sync shares, 255
syntax, commands, shortened, 56–58
Sysprep, 12–13
    virtualization and, 12–13
SYSTEM account, 27
System Audit Mode, 13
System Center, 457
    Advisor, 542
    Configuration Manager
        boundaries, 526–527
        boundary groups, 526–530
        branches, 499–501
        Client Push Installation method, 530–531
        client settings, 532–534
        collections, 535–536
        Computer Agent, 532
        configuration, 517–526
        discovery methods, 518–521
        disk space recommendations, 505
        hardware inventory cycle, 532
        hardware recommendations, 505
        primary site servers, 506–517
        server hardware, 459
        site servers, 501–502, 505–517
        site system roles, 502–504
        software inventory cycle, 533
        upgrade path, 458
    Data Protection Manager
        server hardware, 459
        upgrade path, 458
    install sequence
        database clusters, 459–460
        database file types, 460
        hardware, 459
        SQL Server version, 459

Operations Manager
    activation, 495
    agents, 483
    databases, 482–483
    installation, 486–495
    management packs, 484
    management server, 482
    prerequisites, 484, 485, 488
    Report Viewer, 485
    server hardware, 459
    services, 483–484
    SQL CLR Types, 485
    upgrade path, 458
    web console, 485
    Windows Server management pack,
        496–499
Orchestrator
    server hardware, 459
    upgrade path, 458
Service Management Automation,
    upgrade path, 458
Service Manager
    server hardware, 459
    upgrade path, 458
Service Provider Foundation, upgrade path,
    458
SQL Server
    database clusters, 459–460
    database file types, 460
    instance installation in cluster, 461–465
upgrade sequence, 457–458
VMM (Virtual Machine Manager), 20,
    465–466, 470
    compute fabric, 470
    configuration, 466–469
    DHCP (Dynamic Host Configuration
        Protocol), 470–471
    DNS (Domain Name System), 470
    host groups, 470
    Hyper-V, 470
    infrastructure servers, 470–472
    installation, 466–469
    library, 470
    network fabric, 472–476
    server hardware, 459
    storage fabric, 476–477
    upgrade path, 458
    virtual machines, 478–481
    VMware vCenter servers, 470
    VMware vSphere host, 470

System Center Configuration Manager
(System Center)
    boundaries, 526–527
        creating, 527
    boundary groups, 526–527
        creating, 527–530
    branches
        current, 499–500
        LTSB (Long-Term Servicing Branch), 500–501
        technical preview, 501
    Client Push Installation method
        configuring, 530–531
        excluding servers, 531
        manual installation, 531
    client settings, 532–534
    collections, 535–536
        uses, 535
    Computer Agent, 532
    configuration, 517–518
        Active Directory methods, 521–526
        discovery methods, 518–521
    discovery methods
        Active Directory Forest Discovery, 518
        Active Directory Group Discovery, 519
        Active Directory System Discovery,
            518–519
        Active Directory User Discovery, 518–519
        Delta Discovery, 521
        Heartbeat Discovery, 520–521
        Network Discovery, 520
    disk space recommendations, 505
    hardware inventory cycle, 532
    hardware recommendations, 505
    primary site servers
        Active Directory and, 508
        ADK 1703, 509–510
        configuration, 510–517
        installation, 510–517
        SCCM, 506–507
        schema extension and, 508
        WSUS, 509
    server, hardware requirements, 459
    site servers
        CAS (central administration site), 501–502
        primary, 502
        installation, 505–517
        secondary, 502
    site system roles
        Application Catalog web service point, 503
        Application Catalog website point, 503
        certificate registration point, 503
        cloud-based distribution point, 503
        component provider, 502
        configurations supported, 504
        distribution point, 503
        endpoint protection point, 503
        enrollment point, 503
        enrollment proxy point, 503
        fallback status point, 503
        management point, 503
        reporting services point, 503
        services connection point, 503
        SMS provider, 502
        software requirements, 503–504
        software update point, 503
        state migration point, 503
    software inventory cycle, 533
    upgrade path, 458
System Center Operations Manager, 27
System Center VMM (Virtual Machine
    Manager), 221
system partitions, 8

T

tables, objects, 61–62
Task Manager, 29–30
Task Scheduler, 25–27
templates, certificate templates, 406–407
    built-in, 407
    compatibility, 407–409
    cryptography, 411–412
    issuance requirements, 415–416
    properties, 410
    publishing certificates, 409–410
    request handling, 410–411
    requestors, 416–417
    security, 413–414
Test-Cluster cmdlet, 143
tokens
    groups, 371–372
    token bloat, 372
Trojans, 287
troubleshooting, Application and System logs, 28–29

U

UAC (User Account Control), domain
    controllers and, 363
UEFI (Unified Extensible Firmware Interface), 4, 325

UMCI (user mode code integrity), 325
unpause command, 269
updates, cluster aware, 148–149
upgrades
    cluster, rolling, 117
    clusters, 141–142
user accounts
    Active Directory Users and Computers, 292–293
    Credential Guard, 296–297
    Group Policy, rights, 289–292
    PowerShell
        deleted, restoring, 370
        reports, 368–369
        stale, 369–370
    privileges, delegating, 295–296
    Protected Users groups, 294–295
    securing, 292–293
    security, 288
        privileged access, 289–292
user management, AD DS, 366–368
user-created variables, 83

V

Validation Wizard, 142–143
Variable: drive, 84
variables
    clearing, 84
    environment variables, 84–85
    PowerShell
        automatic, 83
        preference, 83
        user-created, 83
    removing, 84
VHDX format, 120
virtual hard disks
    differencing, 121
    dynamically expanding, 120
    fixed size, 120
    pass-through, 121
    recommendations, 121
Virtual Machine Connection window,
    checkpoints, 125
virtual machines, 2
    architecture, 260
    checkpoints, 125
    clustering
        guest clustering, 132–133
        host clustering, 132
    configurations, 122–123

    containers comparison, 260
    entrypoint, 267
    exporting, 125–126
    Generation 2, 123
    guest operating systems, 116
    high-availability option, 132
    Hyper-V
        discrete devices, 124
        integration services, 124
        new features, 117–118
        resource metering, 124
        secure boot, 124
        shielded, 123–124
        smart paging, 124
    Hyper-V Replica, 129–130
    importing, 125–126
    installation, 5
    live migration, 126, 127–128
    MAC address spoofing, 119
    migration, 126–127
        Exporting and Importing Virtual
            Machines, 127
        Live Migration, 127
        Quick Migration, 127
        Virtual Machine and Storage Machine,
            127
    PowerShell Direct, 126
    shielded, 117
    states, 124
    virtual switches, 121–122
Virtual Secure Mode, 325
Virtual Secure Mode Protected Code Integrity, 325
virtual switches, 121
    external, 122
    internal, 122
    private, 122
virtualization. See also Hyper-V
    deployment and, 19–20
    licensing, 1, 2
    nested, 117, 119–120
    network adapter teaming, 183
    Sysprep, 12–13
viruses, 287
VM Monitor Mode, extensions, 118
VMK (volume master key), 299
VMM (Virtual Machine Manager), System
    Center, 20, 221
    compute fabric, 470
    configuration, 466–469
        Database Configuration screen, 467–468

library configuration, 468
port configuration, 468–469
service account, 467–468
DHCP (Dynamic Host Configuration
Protocol), 470–471
DNS (Domain Name System), 470
host groups, 470
Hyper-V
clusters, 470
hosts, 470
infrastructure servers, 470–472
installation
Diagnostic and Usage Data, 467
Getting Started screen, 466
license agreement, 466
location, 467
prerequisites, 467
product registration, 466
library, 470
network fabric
logical, 472
creating, 473–474
virtualization gateways, 473
VM, 472
creating, 475–476
server, hardware requirements, 459
storage fabric
devices, 476–477
RAID, 476
SAS (Serial Attached SCSI), 476
upgrade path, 458
virtual machines
Create Virtual Machine Wizard, 479–480
destination, 480–481
hardware configuration, 480
provisioning, 478
VMware vCenter servers, 470
VMware vSphere hosts, 470
VMQ (virtual machine queue), 122
VMware, 2
[void] data type, 78
volume licensing, 3–4
VPN (virtual private network), 210
Always On VPN, 217–218
DirectAccess and, 211, 218
GRE (Generic Routing Encapsulation), 222
latency, 210
point-to-site, 222
protocols
IKEv2, 212

L2TP, 212
PPTP, 211
SSTP, 212
RADIUS, 217
server, configuration, 213–215
site-to-site, 222

W

WAP (Web Application Proxy), 211, 218–219
WDS (Windows Deployment Services)
image types, 16
installation, 16–19
web services, PKI (public key
infrastructure) and, 392
-WhatIf parameter, 53–54
while loop, 102–104
wildcards, 76–77
filters and, 207
Windows Defender
disabling, 322
domain controllers and, 363
scan options, 322
Windows Firewall, 179, 185
domain controllers and, 363
enabling, 186
profiles
Domain, 186
Private, 186
Public, 187
rules, inbound, 187
Windows Firewall with Advanced Security, 300–302
firewall profiles, 300
inbound rules, 302–303
outbound rules, 302–303
PowerShell, cmdlets, 303
Windows Server 2012
Active Directory Recycle Bin, 340
DAC (Dynamic Access Control), 340
Fine-Grained Password Policies, 340
virtualization, 340
Windows Server 2012 R2, AD DS
Conditional Access, 340
Multifactor Authentication, 340
Workplace Join, 340
Windows Server 2016
activation, 10–11
editions, 1–2
differences, 1–2
Hyper-V Containers, 2

Shielded Virtual Machines, 1
Software Defined Networking, 2
Storage Replica, 2
Storage Spaces Direct, 2
Virtualization Licensing, 1
Windows Server 2016 Datacenter, Standard
    comparison, 1–2
Windows Server 2016 Essentials, 4
Windows Server 2016 Standard
    Datacenter comparison, 1–2
    with Hyper-V, 2
Windows Server Backup, 21
Windows Storage Server 2016, 4
Work Folders
    deployment
        hosted, 253

multiple-site, 253
preparation, 252–253
single-site, 253
Server Manager installation, 253
workgroups, WORKGROUP, 179
Workplace Join, 340
WS-Federation, 423
WSUS (Windows Server Update Server),
    196–197

X

XenServer, 2
[xml] data type, 78
XML files, credentials, 71–73